# ESSENTIAL PSYCHOLOGY

Second edition

## G.C. Davenport

Collins Educational

*An Imprint of* HarperCollins*Publishers*

The author asserts the moral right to be
identified as the author of this work.

Published by
Collins Educational
An imprint of HarperCollins*Publishers*
77–85 Fulham Palace Road
Hammersmith
London W6 8JB

First published in 1992
Reprinted 1993, 1994
Second edition published 1996
Reprinted 1998

**British Library Cataloguing-in-Publication Data**

A catalogue record for this book is available from
the British Library

ISBN 0-00-3278573

Typeset by Harper Phototypesetters Ltd, Northampton
Printed in Great Britain by Scotprint, Musselburgh

# Contents

# Foreword

Every book in the Essential Series is designed carefully to put you in control of your own learning.

When you use this book, you will not only cover the core elements of your course, but you will also benefit from the author's use of modern teaching and learning techniques, with the result that you will make the best possible use of your time.

This book has:

- an introductory section at the beginning of each chapter, which focuses your attention on its contents and which tells you exactly what you should have learned by the end of the chapter. These are your 'learning objectives';

- periodic summaries which regularly remind you of the content you are covering and so reinforce your learning;

- notes in the margin of the text, where the author takes the role of a tutor: picking out key facts, highlighting and explaining difficult concepts, and guiding you to a better understanding of the main text;

- essay questions at the ends of chapters and other assignments in the margin of the text which will give you exam practice and help you to develop your skills in presenting written work;

- a further reading section at the end of the book, which will help you develop a broader understanding of your subject.

Learning is not easy: nobody learns without effort. However, if you use this book effectively you will not only succeed in your course and in your exam, but you will also enjoy the experience of learning.

# *Acknowledgements*

Thanks to my parents, Rosa and Dennis, for their love and support; to Alex, for her help and commitment; and to Brigitte Lee, for her diligence and patience in preparing this book. And to countless students who continue to inspire and frustrate!

The author and publisher would like to thank the following for permission to use material reproduced in this work:

The Hulton Deutsch Collection for the photographs appearing on pages 2, 99 and 328; Mary Evans Picture Library for the photographs appearing on pages 9 and 122; Range/Bettmann for the photographs appearing on pages 12 and 16; Albert Bandura, Stanford University, for the photograph appearing on page 15; Alexandra Milgram for the photograph appearing on page 56; Michael Nichols/Magnum Photos for the photograph appearing on page 140; and the Royal College of Physicians for the photograph appearing on page 311.

# 1 Introduction

## Introduction

Psychology is a vast subject and includes the study of the 'mind' and brain; of how people think and reason; of people's behaviour and the study of mental 'illness' and disturbed behaviour; and many more topics besides. Different psychologists have different views about each of these, and about what psychology is and should be about. The *Penguin Dictionary of Psychology* says: 'Psychology simply cannot be defined … it really isn't a thing at all, it is about a thing, or many things'.

For our purposes, though, we will say that 'psychology is that branch of knowledge concerned with studying human (and some other animal) behaviour, and human experiences'. It developed from the nineteenth-century philosophical view that it was appro-

■ (a) What is psychology about?
(b) What do you imagine most people think that psychology is about?

priate to apply the methods and principles of the natural sciences to the study of human beings, and from the advances made in sciences such as biology.

## WHAT DO PSYCHOLOGISTS DO?

▶ *Applied research* usually has some particular end which it is trying to achieve and which will have some direct benefit to someone else. *Basic research* may not have an immediate or obvious use, but may well provide ideas for further applied research.

Many psychologists are involved in *applied research*. They investigate things that some people face every day, such as finding ways of dealing with stress, or advising on the design of complicated equipment to make it as easy as possible for the operator to use. *Basic* (or *pure*) *research* seeks knowledge about things that may not have an immediate and obvious application. Much research into animal behaviour, such as the process by which younger members of a troupe of macaque monkeys learned to wash the sand off their sweet potatoes before eating them, doesn't seem to be of any direct benefit to humans.

As well as being involved in research, psychologists work in teaching and education, in social work and the probation service, in the police and prison service, in clinical and counselling areas, in hospitals, in personnel and marketing, in design and manufacture, and many other fields. While they all have some aspects of their training in common, each will have specialist knowledge of their own particular field, and will be applying that knowledge for the benefit of the organization for whom they work, or for its members.

Psychologists may be engaged in applying their knowledge in settings such as clinics, personnel departments, design and advertising agencies. They may be conducting further research, or pass on their knowledge through teaching.

## The development of psychology

Academic psychology is barely a century old and though we have had plenty of theories advanced to explain aspects of our behaviour and mental functioning, we are still a long way from understanding them completely. This section will review three of the more influential approaches. These are: *psychodynamic* theories of personality from Sigmund Freud; *behaviourist* theories of how we learn from Ivan Pavlov, B.F. Skinner and Albert Bandura; and *humanist* explanations of individual psychology from Abraham Maslow. We will be referring to these theories, and to others, in several of the following chapters.

## PSYCHODYNAMIC THEORIES OF PERSONALITY DEVELOPMENT

*Sigmund Freud*

*Psychodynamic* simply means 'mental change'. According to psychodynamic theories, our personalities are the product of two forces that have acted on us. First, biological forces within us have urged us to do, think and feel certain things. Second, our childhood experiences have shaped the kind of person we are. One of the founding fathers of psychodynamic theory was **Sigmund Freud**.

## Sigmund Freud's psychoanalytic theory

Sigmund Freud (1856–1939) was an Austrian doctor who spent most of his life, from the 1880s until his death, researching the part of the human *psyche* that he called the unconscious mind. Many of his patients behaved in strange, distorted ways for which Freud could find no physical cause. Some had severe headaches, rigidity of limbs, temporary blindness or deafness, and temporary amnesia. Many had been turned away from other doctors since there appeared to be nothing physically wrong with them. Freud described these symptoms as *hysteria*. Because the cause of their behaviour was not physical or conscious, Freud supposed that it had to be mental and unconscious.

As a doctor and researcher Freud believed that symptoms which are left untreated usually grow worse. Many illnesses and diseases result from some previous experience, such as being stung by an insect, eating something poisonous, or breathing in someone else's germs. Something similar, Freud reasoned, may be true of the 'illnesses' of his patients. Freud needed to know something of his patients' pasts.

### Techniques for studying the unconscious

Freud and his colleague **Josef Breuer** used *clinical interviews* (see Chapter 17) to find out about their patients' histories. Patients would relax and be encouraged to talk about their life and feelings. They would lie on a couch in Freud's consulting room, and he would sit behind their heads so that they couldn't see him. Occasionally Freud would need to prompt patients with a question, or by applying a little pressure to their temples with his hands. Patients were encouraged to remember events that had happened during their childhood and the feelings that were associated with them. This technique is called *free association*.

This free association technique seemed to help the patients, and Freud built up detailed case studies of their histories. When some early patients told Freud about their dreams he believed he had stumbled onto 'the royal road to the unconscious' (Freud 1976a). Freud believed that the unconscious mind contains many primitive desires, wishes, urges and memories which are too upsetting to be brought into consciousness. Some of these urges will have been in the unconscious since we were born. Others will have been *repressed* there, because they produced too much anxiety at the time. These primitive urges drive us to behave in all kinds of ways, including the symptoms Freud had described as hysteria.

All activity needs an energy source. According to Freud, the true unconscious mind is the isolated, primitive *id*, which is the source of all mental energy. Young babies who want to be fed or cleaned

► Personality is one of those annoying terms in psychology of which everyone knows the meaning, but which no one can really define. It is a shorthand way of describing what someone is generally like.

► The *psyche* is the Greek word for 'soul' or 'mind', from which the word psychology is derived.

► *Hysteria* comes from the Greek word meaning 'wandering uterus'!

► Freud believed the clinical situation had to be as unthreatening and undistracting as possible. He would listen to his patients, remembering all they said, and would make notes only after they had left.

► *Free association* is a means of allowing patients to think and talk about anything they want to, with the minimum of restrictions on them. In this way they could reveal their innermost thoughts and feelings.

► *Repression* means to hold back, to censor, to control some feeling that might otherwise produce anxiety, which could prevent healthy personality development. Repression is an unconscious process.

► The *id* is the first of three parts of personality to occur. It is the source of all psychic energy and demands immediate satisfaction.

► *Excitation* means physiological stimulation, i.e. activity in the nervous system.

► The *pleasure–pain principle* is the urge to seek comfort and satisfaction, and avoid unpleasantness or harm.

■ **Briefly explain what Freud meant by repression.**

■ **What is the id, and what is its function?**

► Remember, this idea about opposing, instinctive urges pushing us to behave in two different ways at the same time is only Freud's interpretation of what his patients appear to be telling him. There can be no biological evidence that such urges actually exist. On the other hand, many of us do seem capable of acts of great goodness and of great unkindness.

► *Libido*, or *Eros*, is the major life force which uses energy from the id to drive us towards achievement. The *death instincts*, or *Thanatos*, drive us towards our own destruction. Freud was fascinated by ancient Greek and Roman mythology, and used ideas and names from them to symbolize some of the concepts he described.

■ **Name and briefly define the two primary instinctive urges in traditional psychoanalytic theory. Give some examples of behaviour that Freud would claim was directed by (a) the libido and (b) the death instincts.**

► *Erogenous zones* are those parts of the body that produce sexual arousal when stimulated. Freud believed that the pleasure babies derive from feeding is in some sense sexual.

► The *reality principle* is the child's growing realization that its environment is real and will have to be dealt with appropriately.

will feel some kind of discomfort, tension or pressure. The id will demand that this *excitation* be removed, so the baby will try to attract the attention of an adult to satisfy its needs. The id operates on the *pleasure–pain principle*. Even quite young infants are said to try to achieve anything that gives them pleasure and avoid anything that does not or that causes pain.

### The two instinctive urges

From countless hours of studying patients, and from his researches in human physiology, Freud eventually concluded that we are born with two essential, instinctual, opposing urges. These are the *libido*, an unconscious force for life and sexuality, and the *death instincts*, which drive us towards danger and self-destruction. They both draw their energy from the id. Freud used the names of the Greek god *Eros* (the god of love) to describe the libido, and *Thanatos* (the god of death) to describe the death instincts. Throughout our lives the Eros and Thanatos urges will drive us to behave in different ways, until, at the moment of our death, Thanatos wins the struggle.

### Parts of personality and stages of development

The child's main source of pleasure (called an *erogenous zone*) during its first two years is its mouth (babies try to put many things into their mouths). Freud called this period the *oral stage*. If the child wants food, for example, the id will demand satisfaction to satisfy the need for food and avoid the pain of hunger (NB the pleasure–pain principle). Parents are mainly responsible for satisfying the id's demands by giving the child what it appears to want. The id is a primitive and irrational urge, and demands satisfaction immediately and at all costs. However, babies are not always fed or given things to play with on demand, and others may have too much oral stimulation. Either situation can create anxiety in a baby, who may not be able to deal with it. If it can't be dealt with it may be *repressed* into the unconscious, where it might remain until the individual is old enough to deal with it. Too much repression during the oral stage can create the *oral character* in the adult. Freud described the oral character as being either excessively optimistic, overgenerous and constantly excited (if the baby had experienced too much stimulation), or pessimistic, frequently depressed and aggressive (if the baby had experienced too little stimulation).

From around two years the id's demands no longer automatically receive satisfaction and children must learn strategies such as asking and saying 'thank you' in order to gain what they want. The second part of personality, the *ego*, is needed. The ego is supposed to be a more rational urge and tries to find more logical ways of satisfying the id. It operates on the *reality principle*. Some time around two years a second erogenous zone appears. Many patients could remember incidents concerning their potty training, and Freud concluded that the anus now became the source of the child's satisfaction, since it could control the release or retention of its faeces. This is the *anal stage*. Parents who are too strict, or not strict enough, in potty training their children could allow frustrations and anxieties to build up in the child which may be repressed into the unconscious, giving rise to the *anal character*. Overindulgent potty training leads to the *anal expulsive* character, which is untidy, over-generous, always gives in, and goes along with anyone else's ideas. Too strict training can create the *anal retentive* character, which is mean, obstinate, and obsessed by orderliness and hoarding.

From about three years children become able to follow instructions about what they should and shouldn't do. They will develop some limited sense of right and wrong from their parents, who reward and punish them. The id is still making demands which the ego is trying to satisfy. Some of the demands will contradict parental wishes. The child needs the third part of personality, the *superego*. The superego provides the basis for the child's sense of morality and ethical principles – the conscience. The superego operates on the *morality principle*.

Freud claimed that the opposite-sex parent becomes associated with pleasurable feelings in the young child. Unconsciously the child is drawn to its opposite-sex parent. It begins to feel jealous of its same-sex parent because he or she is favoured by the opposite-sex parent. In boys this is called the *Oedipus complex*, and the feelings associated with it are called *Oedipal conflict*. The equivalent in girls is the *Electra complex*. If these feelings become too great to bear, or if they are too strictly dealt with, then they, too, may become repressed into the unconscious, where they could cause disturbed behaviour in adulthood. Freud believed problems caused by inadequate resolution of Oedipal conflict were the major cause of adult neuroses in males. Freud called this third stage of personality development the *phallic stage*.

The ego provides a solution to Oedipal conflict. If the son was more like his father, then his mother could well want him instead of his father. So the child begins to *identify* with his father. *Identification* is a mental process. Children, probably unconsciously, take on aspects of other people's personalities and behaviour. A boy will begin to learn what it is like to be an adult by copying his father, helping him, repeating things he says and adopting his ideas and beliefs. He takes on his father's personality, as best he can. If the son is very much like his father, then his father surely will not hurt him because it would be like harming a part of himself.

Freud admitted that his views on girls' personality development and the Electra complex were rather speculative. They perform the same function as for boys, that of 'possessing' the opposite-sex parent and 'eliminating' the same-sex parent. Modern psychoanalytic theory pays little importance to some aspects of the Oedipus and Electra complexes.

By around five years the child should have sorted out many of its feelings about its parents, and should start channelling its energies into other relationships and activities. Games, sport, learning in school, and all kinds of adventures dominate personality development from about five until puberty. This is the *latency period*. It

■ **Outline the main features of personality development during the first two or three years, according to Freudian psychoanalytic theory.**

► The *superego* is the third part of personality to appear and provides the moral dimension to the id and ego.

► The *morality principle* modifies the reality principle as the child acquires a sense of right and wrong.

► Freud insisted that the id, ego and superego are not regarded as real biological structures. Rather, they are hypothetical concepts which describe the actions that are associated with early personality development.

► *Oedipus* was the son of the king of Thebes in ancient Greek mythology. He unwittingly fell in love with his own mother and killed his father. *Electra's* father was murdered by his wife's lover, and Electra urged her brother to kill their mother in revenge.

► A *neurosis* is (usually) a fairly minor psychological disturbance.

► The process of *identification* is very important, both in Freud's theories and other areas of psychology, in explaining how children (and older people) adopt characteristics that they think other people possess.

■ **How do the Oedipus and Electra complexes arise? How does the superego contribute?**

isn't a stage since major personality development has been temporarily suspended.

With puberty the major sex-linked hormones start to change body shape and body function, and the sex organs become biologically fertile. This is the *genital stage*, and lasts from puberty to old age. If the Oedipal or Electra conflicts have been resolved the young person's personality will start to become more sexually mature. They will have crushes on some familiar people, have their first serious boyfriend or girlfriend, and gradually emerge as sexually mature adults. If, on the other hand, some problems remain unresolved, the personality may become *fixated* or stuck on some person, such as the mother, or on an object, such as the mouth, from an earlier stage. This will frustrate making 'normal' relationships, and can contribute to various neuroses.

*Affective fixation* refers to the condition whereby the libido's energy has been so attached to one person or object that normal personality growth cannot proceed. While the person grows, their personality remains stuck in an earlier stage.

## Summary of the main stages in classical Freudian theory

| Stage of development | Erogenous zone | Part of personality involved | Based on | Main characteristics | Tasks to achieve |
|---|---|---|---|---|---|
| Oral | Mouth | Id | Pleasure principle | Pleasure from licking, biting, seeking immediate gratification | Weaning |
| Anal | Anus | Id and Ego | Reality principle | Controlling the bladder and bowels | Toilet training |
| Phallic | Phallus | Id, Ego and Superego | Morality principle | Pleasure from playing with genitals becoming associated with the opposite-sex parent | Successful resolution of Oedipal and Electra complexes by identifying with the same-sex parent |
| Latency | None | Id, Ego and Superego | Combination of all three | Energies directed into sport, schooling, etc. | None |
| Genital | Genitals | Id, Ego and Superego | Combination of all three | Increasing interest in sexual matters with members of both sexes | 'Normal', healthy relationships |

■ What happens to personality development during the genital stage?

■ Draw a diagram to show the relationship between the instinctive urges and other parts of the personality according to Freudian psychoanalytic theory.

### Summary – The main features of Freud's psychodynamic theory

Freud suggested that we have:
*two* instinctive urges: the libido and the death instincts;
*three* parts of personality: the id, ego and superego;
*four* stages of personality development: the oral, anal, phallic and genital stages.

### Conflict in the personality

There will be occasions when the id, ego and superego will come into conflict. Freud suggested three possible ways to resolve this conflict. Their aim is to work the conflict through in the unconscious. *Dreams* provide one way of achieving this. Dreams allow us to fulfil all those wishes and desires that we couldn't possibly fulfil in reality. Dreaming about being rich (by winning the lottery?) would take our mind off our immediate worries. (Freud regarded the *analysis of dreams* as one of the most useful tools therapists have. If they can interpret what someone dreams, they are well on the way towards understanding what is causing that person's anxieties and neuroses.)

▶ *Dreams* are one way in which conflicts between what people would like to do and what they know they can do are resolved.

Another way to stop the conflict from growing is for the ego to use one of its many *defence mechanisms*. Again, these are quite unconscious (and quite normal). They don't remove the conflict between id and superego, but they do distract us so that we don't notice it quite so much. It's rather like keeping busy when you are very upset. It doesn't make the cause of your unhappiness any less, but it does keep your mind off it. Perhaps the conflict between id and superego may disappear on its own, maybe you can convince someone that you're not to blame, or you weren't involved, or someone made you do it. The aim of defence mechanisms is to reduce the conflict.

▶ *Defence mechanisms* are unconsciously directed processes or behaviours intended to protect the self (or ego) from anxiety-producing situations.

Repression is the ultimate defence mechanism. If we can't deal with the anxiety in any other way it may become repressed into the unconscious. Clearly this should be avoided wherever possible so as to avoid fixation and potential neuroses later. *Identification* is a defence mechanism whereby we incorporate aspects of someone else's personality into our own so that we become like them. *Projection* is the opposite defence mechanism to identification. We project our own unpleasant feelings onto someone else and blame them for having the thoughts that we really have.

Other defence mechanisms include *rationalization*, which means making something up that justifies your own (or someone else's) unjustifiable behaviour. For example, a father might be annoyed by his son's behaviour, and hit the child harder than he might have intended. Feeling guilty he might say, 'It was in your own interests, it was entirely your fault, sometimes one has to be cruel to be kind'. Each of these statements represents rationalization. *Displacement* occurs when we take out our frustrations on some innocent object (like hitting or kicking the furniture, the cat, a toy, etc.). *Sublimation* is a special and acceptable kind of displacement. Excess energy is expended through sport, or frustrations are expressed through doing something creative, such as painting a picture or carving something in wood. Sublimation is the only defence mechanism that is usually successful in coping with anxiety without causing further problems.

■ **What are the functions of defence mechanisms in Freudian theory?**

There are dozens of defence mechanisms which are used unconsciously to protect the ego and provide some time for the frustrations that prompted them to be absorbed into our consciousness and dealt with in other ways. As such they are perfectly healthy, and to varying extents everyone uses them. However, danger could occur if they become overused, and a substitute for recognizing reality.

The third consequence of conflict between the parts of personality is the emergence of some neurotic symptoms during adulthood. Freud suggested that there are four main types of neuroses in adulthood, although he added others later. These are: *anxiety neuroses*, where the adult is particularly sensitive to some things that would upset him or her. There are *phobic neuroses*, such as fear of snakes, spiders, the dark, cinemas, and so on. There are *obsessive compulsive neuroses*, where the adult can't seem to stop thinking about something, e.g. the need for cleanliness, or can't stop behaving in some way, such as washing his or her hands. Finally, there are *hysterical neuroses*, where odd behaviour is a symptom of earlier repression.

▶ There are many forms of neurosis. These which Freud identified are still widely recognized by psychiatrists today.

### Summary – Freudian psychoanalytic theory

Freud's studies of many neurotic and other patients suggested to him that humans have an unconscious mind which contains irrational and primitive urges that find expression, as we grow, through bodily pleasure from the erogenous zones. The id is the source of all psychic energy, and demands immediate satisfaction. The ego seeks logical, realistic means of achieving the id's demands, and the superego provides the moral censor of the id and ego. Pre-genital 'phallic' pleasure results in identification with the same-sex parent to resolve Oedipal or Electra conflicts, thus creating the child's superego. Stressful external influences can become fixated and repressed into the unconscious, where they will remain until they seek expression through some maladapted, neurotic behaviour later. Freudian psychoanalysis aimed to seek out the causes of these anxieties, and so relieve them (see Chapter 10).

### Evaluation of Freudian theory

Freud's theories became widely known (although not always understood or appreciated) throughout Europe and America during the first half of the twentieth century. Psychoanalytic theory has had a powerful influence both on clinical practice (called psychoanalysis), with disturbed people, and on how childhood is viewed. Many other researchers have been influenced by psychoanalytic theory, which has become both a model for the acquisition of personality and a system of applied therapies. The theory has strengths and weaknesses.

*Strengths*
Psychoanalytic theory provided the first detailed explanation for the development of personality.

Some of Freud's explanations appear quite plausible at first sight.

Freud claimed to have identified the major stages of personality development, and the most sensitive erogenous zones.

The theory emphasized the importance of the child's relationship with its caregivers.

Freud offers a number of useful concepts, such as the id, libido, identification, and defence mechanisms.

The theory offers explanations for several features of human society, such as aggression, the development of sex roles and moral development.

Freudian psychoanalytic theory has stimulated a considerable amount of other research.

*Weaknesses*
Subsequent explanations may be improvements on Freud's original proposals.

Some explanations such as the Oedipus complex seem impossible to believe.

There is no evidence that personality development occurs in stages, or that erogenous zones are particularly important to personality growth.

Psychoanalytic theory views the role of the child as being rather passive, merely responding to external forces.

None of the concepts that Freud claimed to have identified can be shown to exist, so the whole theory lacks any scientific basis.

No independent research has supported any of Freud's major claims.

Yet despite these criticisms many people still find Freud's theories and explanations a source of inspiration, and at least in part, temptingly believable. Freud's contribution to psychology is becoming more that of a cultural phenomenon, a pioneer into the human mind, a dedicated and insistent researcher who was convinced of the truth of his own findings.

Another aspect of human functioning that was also being investigated during the first half of the twentieth century was *behaviour*. Whilst personality is about what we feel, behaviour is about what we do. Researchers interested in behaviour and learning are called *behaviourists*. Behaviourists aren't interested in imagined genetic urges but in learning and behaviour that can be observed and measured.

## BEHAVIOURISM AND LEARNING

### What is learning?

Learning has been defined as 'a relatively permanent change in behaviour that occurs as a result of previous experience'. The first

*Ivan Pavlov*

▶ Around the turn of the twentieth century, when Pavlov was conducting his research, psychology was very fragmented. Pavlov was not remotely interested in it, and threatened to dismiss any of his assistants if they used any psychological terms to describe his work.

▶ This is sometimes known as Stimulus–Response (S–R) psychology. A *stimulus* is anything that elicits (triggers) a response. A *response* is any behaviour that is elicited by a stimulus. The stimulus of intense heat triggers the response of moving away.

▶ After just a few trials the animals did start to salivate to the sound of the buzzer when it was presented with food. By the tenth trial the animals had been classically conditioned to salivate to the sound of a buzzer. So the CS elicited the CR.

■ How would you condition a dog to salivate at the sight of a blue circle painted on a white card? Identify the various stimuli and responses.

systematic attempts to study the acquisition of associations (the simplest form of learning) were conducted by a Russian Nobel-prize-winning physiologist, **Ivan Pavlov** (1849–1936). He was investigating the digestive system, using dogs as his subjects, and he developed the principles of what became known as *classical conditioning*.

### Classical (S–R) conditioning

Pavlov noticed that some of his older laboratory dogs were starting to salivate when his laboratory assistants were approaching with the dogs' food. They appeared to have learned that the sight or sound of the assistants meant that they were about to be fed. The stimulus of food should trigger the response of salivation. That was perfectly normal. But here the assistants were the stimulus that elicited the response. Pavlov decided to investigate.

The stimulus that naturally elicits a response Pavlov called an *unconditional stimulus* (US), and the response it triggers is an *unconditional response* (UR). So the US (food) elicits the UR (salivation). Pavlov paired the sound of a buzzer with the presentation of the food every time the animals were to be fed. Each time such a pairing is made is called a *trial*. The buzzer is a *conditional stimulus* (CS), i.e. any salivation response to it will occur only on condition that the animal has learned an association between it and food. So the US and the CS together elicit the UR. The salivation response to the food stimulus was now being given to the sound stimulus. It was becoming classically conditioned, and Pavlov termed it a *conditioned response* (CR).

---

### Classical conditioning

Stage 1    US » UR   (food » salivation)
Stage 2    CS + US » UR   (buzzer and food » salivation)
until
Stage 3    CS » CR   (buzzer » salivation)
Note: The response stays the same – salivation. What elicits it is determined by whether or not it has been learned by association.

---

Pavlov conditioned a number of dogs to salivate at the sound of buzzers, bells and metronomes. On average the response was fully conditioned in ten trials. He altered the original stimulus in a number of ways and measured the response. From these experiments he derived several principles of learning.

*Pavlov's principles of learning*

1 **Higher-order conditioning**. If an animal is fully conditioned to salivate to one CS (e.g. a bell tuned to the musical note, middle C), then if another CS (e.g. a buzzer) is associated with it, the animal will learn to salivate to some extent when it hears the buzzer. The animal might salivate to a stimulus which is of a higher order than the original CS.

2 **Stimulus generalization.** If the CS is a bell tuned to the musical note C, then presenting a similar response stimulus (a bell tuned to B) will elicit a small response (perhaps just a few drops of saliva). The stimulus (the bell) can be generalized to some extent.

3 **Stimulus discrimination.** Since the bell tuned to B wasn't followed by food, the animals soon learned not to salivate to it. They learned to discriminate between those stimuli that preceded food and those that did not.

4 **Response extinction.** Pavlov conditioned an animal to salivate to a particular CS. He then stopped presenting the food afterwards. The animal soon learned that the particular CS no longer meant the arrival of food, so the salivation response was extinguished.

5 **Spontaneous recovery.** Even after a CR had been extinguished, an animal would occasionally salivate after hearing the old CS. The response would immediately extinguish again. Presumably this spontaneous recovery occurs because the response wasn't completely extinguished. Rather it was inhibited.

---

### *Little Albert*

Classical conditioning has been used on humans, too, even quite young ones. In their 1919 experiment, **John B. Watson** and **Rosalie Rayner** found that a nine-month-old infant (called 'Little Albert') did not show a fear response to white furry animals such as monkeys, rats and rabbits, masks with and without hair, cotton wool, etc. However, he did show fear when a steel bar was hit by a hammer just behind his head! The noise was the US, and the fear was the UR. When Albert was just over 11 months old a white furry rat (CS) was paired with the hammer striking the bar (US). There were seven pairings, and by the last one the sight of the furry animal was enough to elicit the fear response. The fear response was also generalized to a fur coat, Santa Claus masks, and even Watson's hair. The response persisted (possibly for the rest of Albert's life, since the child was removed from the hospital before any deconditioning began!).

▶ Watson and Rayner's research may have been revolutionary at the time, but certainly wouldn't be allowed now.

---

### *Summary – Classical conditioning*

Classical conditioning shows how a reflexive response can be triggered by a stimulus which has become associated with it in the organism's mind. The response can be generalized and discriminated, and may extinguish if the stimulus is not followed by some benefit. Classical conditioning has been used with humans, too (see Chapter 10).

### *Evaluation of classical conditioning*

Classical conditioning does explain how some human (and other animal) reflexive behaviours are acquired. It does not explain the majority of human learning which is not reflexive. Only a few reflex responses can be conditioned, and generalizations can only be

*B.F. Skinner*

made to other reflexive responses. Several therapies have been developed to deal with such reflexive behaviours as phobias, increased blood pressure and sexual deviations, as we will see in Chapter 10. An attempt to explain other learning has been called *operant conditioning*. Operant behaviour is any behaviour that has an effect on the environment of the organism emitting it.

### Operant or instrumental conditioning

Operant conditioning developed from the pioneering work of Ivan Pavlov and **J.B. Watson** (1878–1958). It is more concerned with how voluntary behaviour is acquired. It started as instrumental conditioning, where an animal has to use some part of the experimental apparatus in order to gain some reward. Operant conditioning includes this, but also refers to any freely chosen behaviours in 'real life'.

Over the last half a century **Burrhus Frederic Skinner** (1904–90) investigated, refined and generalized the principles and applications of operant conditioning. He used strict scientific principles to test animal behaviour and learning, and applied some of his conclusions to humans. (Operant conditioning has been called behaviourism, Skinnerian psychology and learning theory.) Skinner was less concerned with explaining *why* we behave than in predicting and controlling *how* we will behave. This has led to much criticism of him and his theories.

#### ABC learning

Skinner insisted that learning could be explained in terms of antecedents, behaviour and consequences (ABC). *Antecedents* are situations or conditions in which something is likely to happen. A classroom may be an antecedent for learning, or displaying some work. In this case the antecedent is a place. It might be a process, e.g. going to bed is an antecedent to going to sleep. *Behaviour* is anything that is likely to happen in any given antecedent. *Consequences* are the results of the behaviour. If the consequences of any behaviour are beneficial then the behaviour becomes *reinforced*. 'Reinforcement' and 'reinforcers' can be precisely defined and measured. A *reinforcer* is anything that increases or maintains the likelihood of some behaviour recurring. Skinner isn't concerned with why or how it works, only that it does. If you ask some people why they go to work (antecedent to working behaviour), most will say something like, 'Because I need the money' (consequence of working behaviour). Money is a reinforcer. It maintains our 'going to work behaviour'. We do not need to know what someone does with their money, what they spend it on, how much they save, etc., to know that money is a reinforcer. Reinforcement is simply the process or consequence of being reinforced, e.g. getting paid, spending the money, and so on.

Skinner believed that the principles of learning are much the same for all animal species, including human beings. He tested many animals in cages known as *Skinner boxes*. The animals had to perform some behaviour in order to obtain a reinforcer. Food was

► *Reinforcement* increases the likelihood that a given response will be repeated when relevant or possible, in the future, in order to gain a similar beneficial or desirable response. Punishment increases the likelihood that some response will not be repeated. Punishment therefore is not a reinforcer.

the usual reinforcer for hungry animals. Skinner helped rats to learn to press levers, pigeons to turn full circle on their perches, various birds to peck at differently coloured disks, and even some pigeons to play a version of ping pong!

*Types of reinforcement*

A number of different types of reinforcer were identified by Skinner. There are *positive* and *negative reinforcers*. Positive reinforcement can be primary or secondary. *Primary reinforcers* satisfy some physiological need, something we may find it difficult to live without, e.g. food, water, rest, warmth, shelter or sexual expression. *Secondary reinforcers* have to be learned, by association with primary reinforcers. Often secondary reinforcers can be exchanged for primary reinforcers, for example money can be exchanged for food. Negative reinforcers are unpleasant, and we learn to avoid or escape from them. If we find the taste of avocado pear to be unpleasant, then we will try to avoid eating it. This is *avoidance learning*. If we are given an avocado pear at a party we may have to find a way to escape from eating it, perhaps by hiding it in our handkerchief! This is *escape learning*.

Skinner experimented with how and when he gave reinforcers, since it isn't necessary to reinforce after every correct response. He identified five other schedules of reinforcement, which are outlined in the summary box. If learning is being maintained by continuous or fixed schedules, it will also extinguish quite quickly when the reinforcement stops. When learning occurs as a result of variable schedules, it will be slow to extinguish.

**Skinner's schedules of reinforcement**

| Schedule of reinforcement | When the reinforcer is given | Resistance to extinction |
| --- | --- | --- |
| Continuous | After every correct response | Low |
| Fixed ratio | After a given number of correct responses | Low to medium |
| Variable ratio | The number of correct responses required varies | High |
| Fixed interval | After a fixed period so long as at least one correct response had been emitted | Low to medium |
| Variable interval | After variable periods so long as at least one correct response had been emitted | High |

Reinforcement can be used to 'shape' quite complex behaviour in both animals and humans. Skinner taught two pigeons to play ping pong using the technique called *behaviour shaping by successive approximations* (see Chapter 10). The complex task of hitting a ball in a particular direction has to be broken down into its smallest parts. Each part is reinforced until finally the animal can perform the whole task.

▶ Most early behaviourist research was conducted on animals since they were convenient subjects to use. Behaviourists assume that the principles of learning that describe the way lower-order animals learn will also describe the way humans learn.

■ What are the main kinds of reinforcers? Give an example of each one.

■ Why does the kind of schedule used affect the ease or difficulty with which the learning will extinguish?

**An example of behaviour shaping**

A pigeon is to be taught to play a simple version of table tennis. The animal must learn to approach a bouncing ball, then to hit the ball, to hit it hard enough to make it travel some distance, and to hit it in the right direction.

■ Draw up a plan to teach a child with some learning difficulties to put his or her own jumper on.

► In classical conditioning an organism learns that two stimuli go together. In Pavlov's experiments, for example, dogs learned to associate the ringing of a bell or buzzer (one stimulus) with the presentation of food (another stimulus). In operant conditioning an organism learns to associate some behaviour of its own with some result of that behaviour.

| Task | Reinforcement |
|------|---------------|
| 1. The pigeon is to allow itself to be struck by a table tennis ball. | The pigeon is reinforced every time it is struck by the ball. |

When this task is fully conditioned the reinforcement stops.

| | |
|------|---------------|
| 2. The pigeon is to seek a bouncing ball, and hit it with any part of its body. | A reinforcer is applied whenever the pigeon seeks and strikes a bouncing ball. |

When this task is fully conditioned the reinforcement stops.

| | |
|------|---------------|
| 3. Now the pigeon must hit the ball only with its upper body. | Only strikes with the head and upper body are reinforced. |

When this task is fully conditioned the reinforcement stops.

| | |
|------|---------------|
| 4. The pigeon must hit the ball with its beak. | Only strikes with the beak are reinforced. |

When this task is fully conditioned the reinforcement stops.

| | |
|------|---------------|
| 5. The ball must be hit by the beak in a given direction. | Only strikes towards the position of the other pigeon are reinforced. |

When this task is fully conditioned the reinforcement stops.

| | |
|------|---------------|
| 6. The beak must strike the ball hard enough in the required direction to make it travel to the other side of the 'court'. | Reinforcement is given to the pigeon only for those strikes which send the ball hard enough in the right direction. |

Repeat this procedure with another pigeon, and watch them play!

### Summary – Operant conditioning

Skinner argued that most behaviour, whether 'good', 'normal', 'bad' or 'disturbed', is learned by reinforcement. Reinforcement increases the chances that some particular behaviour is more likely to occur with a given stimulus than any other behaviour. Reinforcement can be positive or negative, and quite complex behaviours can be shaped by systematically and selectively applying reinforcers.

### Evaluation of operant conditioning

Operant conditioning techniques work well enough with animals, and some of the principles might apply to some human situations. For example, autistic (emotionally withdrawn) children have been taught to dress themselves, to use a knife and fork, and other life skills in this way. Mentally or behaviourally disturbed adults have also been 'trained' to behave more normally (as we shall see in Chapter 10.) But not all human learning is the result of previously reinforced responses. Some is totally novel (new), and nothing similar has ever been reinforced before. Some learning is accidental, some is spontaneous, and some occurs for no apparent reason at all.

Skinner is accused of taking a *mechanistic* and *reductionist* view of human beings. This means that he seemed to believe that all human functioning can be ultimately explained in simple, mechanical terms, just as the functioning of a motor car engine can, and can be reduced to the basic principles of physics and physiology. Various religious groups, philosophers and psychologists, among others, have claimed that people have free will, that is, the ability to make up our own minds about what we believe to be right and wrong, and how to behave accordingly. Skinner's view is also criticized for being *deterministic,* i.e. that everything has a cause or reason, and that it is possible to discover the cause or reason. Many psychologists disagree about whether we could ever know the cause of all human behaviour, or that we should want to!

### Social learning theory

Since the 1950s, interest in Freudian psychoanalytic theory has declined, partly because it can't be validated, partly because its applications do not always work, and partly because Freud's insistence that childhood experiences have effects in adulthood isn't entirely supported by studies of children (see Chapter 14). Skinner's behaviourism and his application of scientific techniques to the mechanisms of learning was popular around the middle decades of the twentieth century. People do learn by being reinforced, and sometimes bad behaviour can be learned by being accidentally associated with something pleasant. Social learning theorists have tried to combine aspects of behaviourism with psychoanalytic theory by applying laboratory techniques to the study of identification. Although social learning theory can be traced to a group of eminent researchers contributing to a Yale University conference in 1936, one of the most notable theorists is **Albert Bandura** (who has been developing social learning theory since the 1950s). Social learning theorists do not deny the value of reinforcement, but they do not believe that reinforcement alone can explain all learning. Certain cognitive (mental events to do with 'knowing') factors are involved between stimulus and response.

Children, and adults too, often learn by simply observing and then imitating someone whom they consider to be a powerful or attractive or important person. Observation and imitation lead to modelling. For children the most important models are parents. Parents need not deliberately try to influence the child or apply a reinforcer for observational learning to occur.

> ► Social learning theorists have tried to combine the psychoanalytic type of identification with the behaviourists' laboratory approach to learning.

*Albert Bandura*

> ► *Modelling* is one of the fundamental processes in socialization. Models are seen as very influential people, whom children may feel they need to imitate.

> ► Albert Bandura uses the term *observational learning* to describe learning that does not rely on reinforcement or shaping, but merely on some behaviour being observed.

> ■ What is meant by observational learning in social learning theory?

---

### The major features in observational learning

1 Paying attention to those parts of the model's behaviour that are important to the observer, and not misinterpreting or becoming distracted by other environmental events.
2 Accurately remembering what has been observed. Older children can model events from some time ago; younger children do not have such skills.
3 Accurately reproducing the observed behaviour. Younger children may need several observations and trials before successfully modelling some observed behaviour.
4 Motivation, being the desire to imitate one model rather than another.

■ How does Albert Bandura's social learning theory compare with the behaviourist approach of B.F. Skinner?

**Summary – Social learning theory**
Social learning theory combines aspects of previous theories and adds the importance of observation in learning. Where constantly needing reinforcement would make learning take too long, observing and imitating come naturally to humans, starting in early childhood. Modelling and identification serve to strengthen our understanding of who we are.

## Alternatives to behaviourist approaches

Behaviourism declined in credibility and popularity during the 1960s. One reason was that not all animal behaviour can be explained by 'ABC'. For example, some higher primates such as apes have been observed appearing to consider a task, then suddenly attempting a solution. This is called *insight learning* and was first investigated by **Köhler** in 1916 when Sultan, an ape, fitted two rods together to make one long one to reach some bananas outside his cage. Different species of animals are instinctively driven to behave in certain ways. Many birds fly, most fish swim, the majority of primates play. Any learning that involves these behaviours will be easier, and therefore more likely to be successful. These biological constraints on animals' behaviour have been investigated by Seligman and Hager (1972) and by Hinde and Stevenson-Hinde (1973). They found that if an animal has a natural response to something, such as taking flight or running away when danger approaches, it cannot learn to press levers or peck at symbols instead.

Other conditioning may begin to be performed less successfully with the passage of time. Breland and Breland (1961) trained pigs, chickens and racoons to perform a series of tricks. After a few weeks the way the animals performed them reflected their instinctive behaviours (the pigs took longer, spending time rooting, and the racoons played with the objects in their trick). This is an example of *instinctual drift*. Clearly, not all learning can be explained by operant conditioning.

### HUMANISM, THE 'THIRD FORCE' IN PSYCHOLOGY

**Abraham Maslow** (1908–70) was a revolutionary psychologist who, over 40 years ago, rejected psychology's preoccupation with psychoanalytic treatments for neuroses, and simplistic behaviourist explanations for behaviour and its mechanistic view of humanity. Instead, he proposed that psychology should be about maximizing each individual person's full human potential. Psychology should be about showing everyone how they can fully achieve the highest motives, the greatest knowledge, the fullest understanding, and the finest control and appreciation of the emotions of which they were

*Abraham Maslow*

capable. (Maslow himself was an intensely shy person who possibly might have benefited from the goal he set for psychology.) The result of this ultimate self-knowledge Maslow called *self-actualization*.

Humanist psychologists do not believe that psychology can deal with generalizations but must apply itself to each unique individual. It cannot be scientific, since it is concerned with individuals and doesn't seek similarities between people that can be generalized. Rather, it is involved with helping each person to maximize his or her individual talents.

> **Summary – Humanism**
> Maslow attempted to provide an alternative approach whereby psychologists aim to help individuals achieve a sense of fulfilment through the self-actualization process.

### Evaluation of the humanist approach

Humanism rejects grand theories in favour of individuals. Instead of seeking similarities between people so that predictions about them can be made, it emphasizes their individual uniqueness. Humanism provides an intuitive, qualitative approach which was a refreshing change from the science of behaviourism and pseudo-science of psychoanalytic theory.

### Chapter summary

Early psychological theories, such as Freud's psychoanalytic theory, were dominated by ideas about 'the mind'. They were most influential during the first few decades of the twentieth century. Behaviourists reject such ideas since they did not believe that 'the mind' could be investigated using scientific methods. This view was widely held after the 1940s. Humanism does accept the relevance of 'the mind' as a topic in psychology. It is in 'the mind' that we attend, perceive, reason, remember, form ideas, plan, dream, hope, think and 'know'. Such mental activities are called cognition, and interest in cognitive psychology has grown dramatically since the 1950s.

Cognitive psychology doesn't, as yet, have a single, unifying theory. Nor does it have one particular spokesperson. It isn't thought of as a major force in the way that the others are. Nevertheless, cognitive psychologists have made great contributions to our understanding of the way humans think, as we shall see in Chapters 11, 12 and 13.

### Exam questions – 60 minutes each

1 Describe and evaluate Freud's explanation of the growth of personality. (*25 marks*)

2 How do children learn? (*25 marks*)

▶ *Self-actualization* is both a process and a final state of human consciousness when one can think independently, resist outside temptations and pressures, and generally 'know' oneself.

■ **How do you think humanists might gather their data?**

# Part 1
## *Social psychology*

# 2 Social relationships

## Introduction

Sometime after puberty, during what Freud called the 'genital stage' of development, various bodily changes steer most humans towards taking an interest in the opposite sex. Teenagers begin to take more interest in and concern over their appearance, and often feel social pressure to appear attractive. As Cooley, Mead and others have shown (see Chapter 16), we receive feedback about what we are like from the way that other people react to us, and this includes our appearance. This pressure exists throughout our lives in some cultures, although different people perceive and respond to the pressures to varying extents. Physical attraction is important to us – why else do we spend so much money and effort in presenting ourselves as attractively as we can? We like to be attractive and to associate with attractive people. Equally, we try to avoid people we find unattractive.

Interpersonal attraction covers that area of social psychology concerned with how we are attracted to other people enough to want to become friends with them. The depth and duration of that friendship will inevitably depend on psychological factors, such as whether the characteristics that first attracted us to the others continue to be there, and whether we continue to value those characteristics. Also, is the relationship worth the effort it takes to maintain it? **Wiseman** (1986) says that friendships involve 'binds as well as bonds'. Social factors such as whether we maintain contact with them will also be important. 'Absence may not necessarily

► ... ...  ... is a tricky concept to define since what people find attractive varies so much. Loosely it covers physical and personal factors that draw some people to those who have them. The factors vary with time and place, and between individuals.

► Cultivating and maintaining friendship bonds means making some compromises, even some sacrifices. These are *binds*. If the binds exceed the bonds, the relationship may well fail, particularly if any other challenge occurs such as absence or alternative, more rewarding friendship opportunities.

make the heart grow fonder', since 'while the cat's away the mice might well play'! **Michael Argyle** (1993) said that 'close relationships are good for health and survival and are perhaps the greatest source of happiness'.

How are psychologists to gather their data about the role of attraction in the formation, maintenance and breakdown of relationships? In the early days (1960s and 1970s), some experiments were conducted by putting people together to see if they made friends, but it would be quite impossible to see if we could make two people fall in love. Instead, social psychologists relied on asking people to make judgements about what they think someone would be like based on fictitious accounts of children and adults. They have asked people who have been in relationships what sort of factors keep them together, or what led to their breakup. Asking people can be a useful source of information on which to base ideas and suggestions, but we can't always be sure that the answers we receive are unbiased and accurate.

## DETERMINANTS OF INTERPERSONAL ATTRACTION

If we asked a large number of people what characteristics they find most attractive in others, the following would probably dominate the list: sincerity, honesty, understanding, loyalty and truthfulness. However, we do not choose our friends only from people with these characteristics, otherwise such people would have everyone wanting to be their friend, while other people would have no one. Most of us try to be sincere and honest most of the time. Most of us try to be understanding towards other people's needs. No doubt we usually try to be loyal and tell the truth. But there are bound to be occasions when we fall short of these targets, so while these characteristics might be amongst the most likeable, it would be rare to find someone who embodied them all the time. Some of the main factors that will determine whether two people will like each other, become friends, or even lovers, are described below.

### *Familiarity*

Friendships include sharing knowledge, time and intimacy. Sharing details about ourselves that we wouldn't want everyone to know requires trust, and we're only likely to trust someone we know well since we can be pretty sure what their reaction is likely to be. This makes us feel more secure. We are likely to get to know better people we see most often. **Zajonc** and **Markus** (1974) suggest that we are more likely to like people we see most often because we have a more complete idea of 'what they are like'. They conducted numerous studies in which people were asked to express their feelings about all kinds of things, from photographs of strangers to groups of nonsense syllables. In each case people were more likely to say they liked the items they saw more than once. Whether this

▶ Inevitably, any list of factors involved in forming relationships will depend on what kind of relationship we are forming – friendships with the same or opposite sex – and the context in which the relationships occur – work or play. They also vary with age, sex and culture. This list is illustrative, not exhaustive.

■ Why should familiarity play a part in interpersonal attraction?

sort of evidence ought to be generalized to explaining interpersonal attraction is open to question.

## Similarity

Generally we like people who are similar to us, and maybe even think the same way that we do. **Don Byrne** (1961) suggests that the closer someone's attitudes, values, beliefs and so on are to our own, the more likely we are to say that we will like that person, find them more intelligent and attractive, etc. A similar social class background, place of origin, status and occupational background, educational experiences and so on are also influential. Similarities of personality seem rather less important. If someone else shares our attitudes, beliefs, values, norms and behaviour it tends to reinforce our belief that we are right. That person could become a trusted friend. That person could also be someone we could share activities with, such as visiting the cinema, sharing records, attending football matches. We don't always have to agree with our friends, but when we disagree more than we agree, the friendship will suffer.

Newcomb (1961) randomly allocated some male students to share rooms in a boarding house whilst studying at Michigan University. At the end of the year those whose attitudes were closest had become firm friends. In another study he tested 17 of one year's intake of male college students to discover their attitudes, likes and dislikes. He then assigned them to their study bedrooms. He matched some of them so that their room-mate had similar attitudes to themselves, and of these, 58 per cent developed close friendships. Some others were given room-mates who had quite different ideas and attitudes to themselves. Surprisingly, 25 per cent of them still managed to become good friends; 75 per cent did not! It seems that being forced to live very closely to someone else is enough to form friendships for some, even where attitudes are quite different.

It isn't only people who are similar to each other who can attract each other, however. Opposites can also attract. A dominant male may have a lasting relationship with a passive female. If both were similar, that is, if both were dominant, then the relationship would be very stormy indeed! This shows a *complementarity* of relationships.

## Reciprocal liking

*Reciprocity* means equality, give and take, co-operation among a group who are mutually benefiting. If someone who is similar to us likes us, we may feel we want to like them. The consequence is that people tend to like people who like them. Further, if we know our friend likes someone whom we have never met, we are prepared to like that person too. When we do meet the person we may, of course, find that we don't like them! Equally, we are prepared to

► Familiarity could be subdivided into *exposure* and *proximity*.

► Although we are most likely to become friends with people who are like us, it is still possible to become friends with people who have quite different ideas.

► Note that *similarity* and *familiarity* overlap. We are taking a complex social interaction and dissecting it for the purpose of illustration. In the real world all these factors overlap.

■ **Why should similarity affect our feelings towards someone?**

► One process of establishing reciprocal liking: A smiles at B, B nods, A says something uncontroversial ('nice weather'), B agrees, B says something uncontroversial ('cold yesterday'), A agrees and moves a bit closer to B. A asks what B does, B mentions her job and asks A 'what about you?', and so on. If both continue to like what they hear, they may establish a relationship. If one doesn't the relationship can be terminated.

► One reflexive NVC cue that scientists have noted is that when someone is physically attracted to another the pupils of their eyes dilate as they draw close. I hope you find this information of interest.

► Quite a few social psychology experiments in the 1960s and 1970s involved tricking people into believing something was true and seeing what they would do. It was justified as being the only way we could know what people would do under particular circumstances.

■ How are reciprocal liking and similarity linked in interpersonal attraction?

dislike someone whom we know our friends dislike, and this, too, could change after meeting them.

Thus if we know that someone likes us, we will be more likely to like them (after all, they must have excellent taste). If their *non-verbal communication* (NVC) and other signals confirm that they like us, then we may be more closely drawn to them. They may know some of our ideas or attitudes, and agree with them. They may have similar ideas or abilities to us, and want to pool resources and get together. When we find out more about them and become friends, we may learn from them, and we may moderate some of our opinions in line with theirs. After all, imitation is said to be the sincerest form of flattery.

**Elliot Aronson** and **Darwyn Linder** (1965) demonstrated the reciprocity principle in an experiment to show the effects on people of hearing other people's opinion of them. There were to be seven conversations between two females, one of whom was actually working with the researchers (that is, she was a *confederate*), and her responses were pre-arranged. After each conversation the confederate went into another room, where she would evaluate the genuine (called a naive participant) contribution, including saying how much she liked the naive participant. The naive participant was to 'overhear' these evaluations. Four groups of naive participants were used (i.e., there were four *experimental conditions*), each hearing a different evaluation of their performance. After the conversations the naive participant was asked to describe her feelings about her partner.

One group heard the confederate participant evaluate her positively. When her turn came she was quite complimentary about her partner too. In the second condition the confederate started by being fairly uncomplimentary, but as the conversations progressed she made more and more complimentary comments about the naive participant. Aronson and Linder called this the *gain condition*. The naive participants then rated the confederate even more highly than the naive participants in the *positive condition*. In the *negative condition* the naive participants consistently heard uncomplimentary things said about them, and they were uncomplimentary about the confederate in return. Finally, in the *loss condition*, naive participants heard the confederate saying complimentary things about them to begin with, but as the conversations went on her opinion worsened. The confederate was then evaluated even more harshly than when in the negative condition (see figure 2.1 for a summary of Aronson and Linder's results).

In the gain condition the naive participants heard fewer good things said about them than in the positive condition, yet they liked their partners more than those in the positive condition. It seems that if someone starts off by not liking us, and then improves their opinion until they do like us, this is even more a cause for liking them than if they simply liked us all along. So we expect people we like and who like us (our friends) to say good things about us. People in the loss condition heard fewer uncomplimentary state-

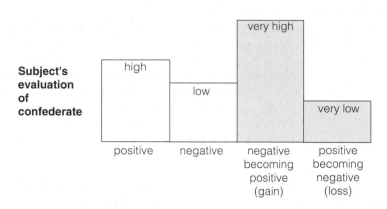

*Figure 2.1 Aronson and Linder's gain–loss theory of attraction*

ments than those in the negative condition, yet were disliked more. Losing someone's favour if they liked us to begin with seems worse than never being in someone's favour in the first place. If a stranger says uncomplimentary things it doesn't bother us too much because they don't know us. The other implication of this is that an insult from a friend will be very wounding and a compliment from a stranger will be much appreciated.

## Physical proximity

We are most likely to like people we are most familiar with, and we are most likely to become familiar with people we see most often. And we see most often the people who are physically closest to us. However, we do not automatically like those people we are physically closest to most of the time. We could quite dislike someone we are forced to be close to, for example, in the armed services, in prison or at boarding school. For two people to be drawn to each other, they usually need to be of similar status. A duchess is less likely to be attracted to a butler than she is to a duke. People we like are often members of the same organization such as a club, college course or workplace, and they are usually pursuing similar goals.

In a classic study **Festinger**, **Schacter** and **Back** (1950) studied the friendship patterns amongst retired, married servicemen and their wives living in two, quite different, halls of residence whilst studying at Massachusetts Institute of Technology. Two findings soon became apparent. First, that people became friendly with those who were in neighbouring rooms, and those friendships were deepest. Second, people living in the more central positions, nearest communal rooms, stair wells and so on, had a wider circle of friends compared to those living furthest down the hall.

**Byrne** and **Buehler** (1965) had their students sit in class in alphabetical order for the first term of their course. At the outset fewer than 10 per cent of the students knew each others' names. By the

■ What implications can be drawn from research on gain and loss of esteem for interpersonal attraction?

► Physical proximity isn't essential for attraction – many (sad?) men drool over Madonna or female *Baywatch* stars, although they're unlikely to meet their idols. Proximity is a factor in forming and maintaining friendship, though.

end of the term over 20 per cent knew all the others' names, but nearly 75 per cent knew the names of the people they sat near to. Numerous neighbourhood studies have shown that people know, and often like, the people living nearest to them. The further away people lived the less likely they were to know one another. For example, people living nearest the stairs or lifts in apartment blocks have been found to know more of their neighbours compared to those living in the middle of a hallway, who knew only those living next door.

## *Physical attraction*

The perception of beauty does lie in the eye of the beholder. Members of different cultures have surprisingly different conceptions of physical attraction. Japanese beauties have tiny feet, Samoans like people that we would regard as fat, whilst we in the West appreciate slimness and a 'healthy' look. In an early review of *anthropological* studies **Ford** and **Beach** (1951) found that societies differed in how they regarded such different parts of the body as the shape of the eyes, ears, the waist and pelvis, as well as overall height and weight.

Levels of physical attractiveness have implications for how people from quite a young age will be regarded. For example, **Dion** (1972) showed 243 people a (fictitious) child's record card with a black and white photograph attached. Each child was said to have behaved either badly or very badly, towards another child, or an animal. The participants filled in questionnaires, asking such things as whether they thought the child's behaviour was serious or not, how severely it should be punished, whether they thought it would have behaved similarly previously, and would they think it would behave as badly in the future. The less physically attractive children were more likely to be described negatively in answer to the questions than the attractive children.

If we asked all our friends how important good looks are to their choice of partner, compared to personality, sincerity, honesty and so on, most would probably say 'not very'. However, this is not what most research suggests. **Dion**, **Berscheid** and **Walster** (1972) asked a sample of people to give their impressions of others who were rated as being unattractive, fairly attractive or very attractive. They found that good-looking people were more likely to be expected to have characters that were kinder, stronger, more outgoing, nurturant and sensitive. Socially they were described as being interesting, poised, competent and sociable. Sexually they would be warm and responsive. They'd be more exciting to go on a date with and they'd make happier marriages. Professionally they'd enjoy higher prestige and achieve more success, too!

In the mid-1960s **Elaine Walster** and **Ellen Berscheid** arranged a 'computer-dating dance' for 18-year-olds at the beginning of a term at the University of Minnesota. The first 376 boys and girls who applied for tickets were told that their partners would be chosen for

■ How is physical proximity involved in interpersonal attraction?

▶ *Anthropology* is the study of the way people in different societies live.

▶ There does seem to be evidence that people make an *attribution error* here. That is, they imagine that attractive children or adults are also more successful in other areas of their lives. It seems it pays to be attractive.

▶ We are more likely to be drawn to attractive people as a friend in the first place. This also works the other way round. If I describe someone very positively, suggesting that they have all kinds of qualities, then when we meet them we may see them as being more attractive than we might otherwise have done.

them by computer on the basis of their interests, which they would declare on a questionnaire. They provided information about what they, and other people, thought about themselves, their expectations from their date, their interests, and so on. While doing this, experimenters rated each of them as 'attractive', 'average' and 'ugly'!

The participants were then randomly allocated a partner, the only stipulation being that no female was assigned a male who was shorter than she. Height is thought to be a factor in the likelihood of a female finding a male attractive. Two and a half hours into the dance, during an intermission, the participants were asked to fill out an 'anonymous' questionnaire asking such things as how they felt about their date, how attractive they found their date, how they thought their date felt about them, how similar their attitudes and beliefs were, and whether they were likely to have another date. Of course the questionnaire wasn't anonymous at all. The researchers knew which person filled in which questionnaire.

Generally, the more physically attractive the date was, the more highly their partner rated them, and the more they wanted to have another date. Attractiveness was seen as more important than personality, intelligence, social skills, and so on. About half of the 'ugly' males said they would date their partner again; the more attractive their dates were, the more they wanted another date. 'Average' males preferred the 'attractive' partners, but most of those who had 'average' partners were reasonably happy to date them again. Most 'average' participants with 'ugly' partners did not rate their partners highly, and did not want another date. 'Attractive' participants with 'attractive' partners were most likely to have another date.

This experiment concludes that physical attractiveness is of considerable importance in deciding who 18-year-old American college students wanted to 'go out with', and that the more attractive they were the more they would be sought after. Equally, the uglier they were the less would attractive people want to date them. However, the participants were asked to make judgements after two and a half hours at a dance, which may not have been long enough for them to make an informed decision, so that all they had to go on was their partner's looks. On the other hand, after two and a half hours, they would probably have formed a pretty good impression of their partner.

People who are of similar levels of attractiveness tend to go together. Walster and others have found a slight sex difference in that physical attractiveness plays a greater part for men than for women. Women tend to include men's personality, intelligence and social skills as well as their looks in their choice of partner.

**Sigall** and **Ostrove** (1975) found some evidence to suggest that attractive criminals, especially females, are less likely to be convicted or sent to prison than unattractive ones, unless they used their good looks to further the crime. They asked 120 participants to make recommendations for sentencing based on information pre-

▶ Naive participants were invited to provide personal information about themselves expecting to be matched to their ideal partner, when they were actually being used as part of a psychological experiment involving being rated as ugly, average or attractive. How would you have felt about this, if you had been one of those students and found out what was happening?

▶ Participants in this experiment genuinely thought they were being matched on the basis of their interests and had every reason to think they could get on with their assigned partner. Some would have been disappointed. Do you think it is fair to treat people like this?

■ **Describe one piece of evidence that suggests that physical appearance is important to interpersonal attraction.**

sented on a record card, similar to the procedure used by Dion (1972). Just how reliable such a method is should be questioned. Making judgements that do not actually affect anyone's real life in a psychology experiment may not generalize to a real life school or courtroom experience.

## Social competence

We usually prefer people who are socially competent and who are familiar with the usual norms and values of the particular culture, that is, people who are not excessively timid or inexperienced. However, we can excuse the occasional gaff from someone who has achieved some success in life. It reminds us that they are human and makes it possible for us to identify with that person. Aronson et al. (1966) asked participants to rate tape-recordings of two groups of people answering difficult quiz questions. One group were superior and answered over 90 per cent correctly. The average group answered only 30 per cent correctly. Some members of each group spilled some coffee. Although the superior group generally were more liked by the participants, those who spilled their coffee were liked best. Mistakes from unsuccessful people may not make them appear attractive to us.

We like people to live up to our expectations of them, since this maintains our *cognitive balance* and reassures us that we are good judges. Cognitive balance contributes to making us feel more secure, and we tend to like people who make us feel secure.

Clumsiness can be annoying and embarrassing, and it's hard to imagine many circumstances when we could actually like someone for their clumsiness. If someone we expect to be clumsy drops something, knocks something over, or walks into something, their behaviour confirms our expectations. If a rather superior person, and someone we do not expect to be clumsy, does something similar, this can increase their attractiveness. The clumsy person is frequently clumsy for a number of reasons, such as lack of attention or lack of thought. The superior person is usually competent at paying attention and thinking ahead. Their mistake merely shows that they are human, like the rest of us.

▶ Stupidity can be a source of attraction. A stupid person can be respected, pitied or appear appealing. But a clumsy person usually creates problems that other people have to clear up, and thus increases their work. This is not a source of attraction!

■ Why is social competence important in forming relationships?

**Summary – Determinants of interpersonal attraction**

Psychologists have identified several factors that are involved in attraction. These are the degree of familiarity, how similar the individuals are, the extent to which the individuals appear to like one another, how physically close they are likely to be, how physically attractive they regard one another, and whether they regard the others as being competent in social situations. These factors are not all equally involved in the likelihood of people becoming involved in a relationship, but some are more influential with some people than others.

## THEORIES OF INTERPERSONAL ATTRACTION

Psychologists have suggested several possible explanations for why some people are attracted to others, although those peculiar features of human cognitive processing that we call liking and love are so complex it is unlikely that any simple theory will explain all such human emotions. Even so, **Ellen Berscheid** (1985) argues that *evaluation* is the central issue. All the factors involved in attraction (familiarity, proximity, similarity, competence etc.) enable us to make an evaluation of someone. If we evaluate them positively we are more likely to like them than if we evaluate them negatively.

There are essentially three approaches to explaining attraction. These are *learning theories*, which emphasize reward; *trading theories*, which take an economic, profit and loss view; and *cognitive theories*, which emphasize cognitive similarity as a factor in attractiveness. These theories also contribute to explaining the formation and maintenance of relationships. When the factors that they suggest contribute to maintaining a relationship are absent, the relationship will fail.

## Learning theories

Pavlov's classical conditioning (see Chapter 1) says that learning comes about by an action being associated with something rewarding, satisfying, or in any other way beneficial. **Clore** and **Byrne** (1970) extend this to include learning about people or objects. If we are feeling really good, because we've just won a prize or just passed our exams, then anyone present at the time will be associated with that good feeling, and will become more highly liked or valued. Game show contestants who win big prizes often hug or kiss the show's presenter. It also works the other way round. If we are feeling depressed or rejected, then we might dislike anyone associated with those negative feelings. The person or object which is present has become a *secondary reinforcer*.

▶ You may remember from Chapter 1 that a *secondary reinforcer* is anything that has become associated with a primary one. So a primary reinforcer is sleep, and your bed is a secondary reinforcer. Another primary reinforcer is food, and the smell from the chip shop is a secondary reinforcer.

Operant conditioning emphasizes the role of reinforcement. A reinforcer is said to be anything that causes us to behave in a similar way in the future. So if we are complimented on our smile, our hair, our clothes, our wit and intelligence, our appearance generally, then we are more likely to like the person who is giving us the reward, and want to smile, style our hair, wear those clothes and so on again. This in turn might draw the person to compliment us further, since our response would reward them. **Lott** and **Lott** (1968) found that schoolchildren who are rewarded with praise and so on by their teacher were more likely to like their teacher, and one another. Children who were ignored or punished by their teacher were more negative towards one another.

▶ The ethics of Lott and Lott's study, which involved treating children in ways that they did not deserve, for the sake of psychological research, would ensure that it certainly could not, and should not, be repeated today.

### Evaluation of learning theories

There is a mass of evidence that people who have similar attitudes are drawn together, although this isn't necessarily explained by

■ How do conditioning and observational learning theories explain relationship formation, and how adequate are their claims?

reinforcement in its strict sense (see Chapter 1), but rather by 'plea-sure', 'boost to self-concept' (if someone is like me they must be brilliant!), 'reward' and so on. Other research has found that simi-larity is important in males and females, of all ages, in several cultures. No one doubts that we like people who are similar to us, but this doesn't mean that we find their similarity reinforcing. Anyway, we can't know exactly what someone finds reinforcing. Some people find others who agree with them attractive, others argue and fight, but their relationship thrives. The concept of rein-forcement isn't sufficiently precise to explain attraction.

## Trading theories

In Chapter 12 we talk about the use of models in psychology to explain how something we can't yet investigate directly might work (see pages 260–9). The theories offered here also suggest models for how interpersonal relationships might work. They aren't necessarily to be taken literally.

### Equity and exchange theory

*Equity* means fairness and balance, and *equity theory* suggests that successful relationships exist where each member derives an amount of benefit from the relationship in proportion to the amount of effort they put in. Obviously these benefits and efforts aren't concrete, tangible things that can be measured. They are per-ceived by the people in the relationship. If both think they are getting a good deal, the relationship will be attractive.

▶ I might think that I contribute enormously to my family. The other members may disagree. This isn't to say that every action necessary to maintain the relationship has to be shared equally. I might like to don my anorak and go train spotting with my friends every Saturday, thus leaving other people to take charge of domestic duties. This might be acceptable to them if I agree to take full responsibility for domestic concerns on Sunday. A balance is maintained.

Elaine Walster and Ellen Berscheid (1978) suggest that equity theory has important lessons for people who want to enjoy long-term successful relationships. First, each person will try to maximize the amount of reward and minimize the amount of punishment they receive in any relationship, although the members of each relation-ship will work out their own system of fairness. Each member must feel that they receive equal amounts of rewards and punishments. If I constantly benefit from the kindness of members of my family, but give them few rewards, then they will have increasingly less reason to like me or want to do good things for me in the future. Second, where one partner has taken advantage of another the wronged partner will feel personal distress, and the more they were wronged the more distress they will feel. The balance between fairness and injustice must be restored quickly before resentment is allowed to develop. Resentment may well jeopardize the relationship.

▶ These trading theories reflect the American individualist capitalist economic system, where each person is supposedly able to achieve great success if they work hard enough and maximize their opportunities, even at the expense of others who aren't maximizing theirs.

*Exchange theory* takes the trading idea further, applying some principles of economics to human relationships. **Homans** (1974) claims that we view our relationships with others in much the same way as anyone in business might, that is, as a profit and loss account. Our contribution to the relationship is seen as a cost to us in terms of effort. The benefit we derive from it is a reward. If the rewards we receive are greater than the costs then we are in profit and the more attractive the relationship will be to us.

Both equity and exchange explanations regard people as basically selfish, wanting to obtain the best deal they can for themselves, at the least cost. Most people who have been in an intense and loving relationship, or even one involving friends, know that giving, rather than benefiting, is often a pleasurable experience. Supporters of exchange theory might say that the pleasure derived from giving is simply another reward, in which case the theory fails to distinguish satisfactorily between rewards and costs.

### Matching theory

This is a variation on equity theory, but accepts that there will be times when we will benefit more, and less, and attractive relationships are simply those where we get the best deal we can for as much of the time as we can. The computer dance experiments discussed earlier were amongst the first attempts to investigate matching theory – men clearly used physical attractiveness as the most important variable in their dating choice, and tried to date a female better looking than they were. Far from supporting the matching hypothesis that we settle for someone about as attractive as ourselves, these males acted selfishly. However, in these experiments each male was given a partner and was with her during the evening. This isn't the same as a less attractive male asking an attractive female for a date in the normal course of events, i.e. the experiment lacks *ecological validity*. According to **Roger Brown** (1986) we all know what is 'right' and choose our partners from amongst those who are most 'fitting' for us.

Some support for Brown's view comes from a study by Murstein (1972), who showed people photographs of males and females on their own. Each person in the photographs had a steady partner who was also photographed alone. The participants were asked to rate each person in the photographs for their level of attractiveness on a five-point scale. They rated each individual as being about as attractive as their partner.

► *Ecological validity* refers to research that reflects real life situations in which someone could realistically expect to find themselves.

### Evaluation of trading theories

As with reinforcement, how could we know what some people find rewarding, and what they would regard as a cost? How could anyone predict the rewardingness in the future of a relationship anyway?

To explain choice of partner in terms of weighing up the rewards and costs of all the potential partners we can have doesn't really accord with most people's lives. Most of us do not have so many people queuing to make an assessment of our potential rewardingness, nor are we realistically in a queue to assess many others.

The theory is simplistic and reductionist, seeking to reduce complex human social and cognitive processes to an analogy with a profit and loss account.

■ How do trading theories explain relationship formation, and how adequate are their claims?

## Cognitive consistency theory

This suggests that we expect to be treated as well by our friends and lovers as we treat them. When this expectation is met in reality we are said to be in a state of *cognitive balance* (Fritz Heider 1958, Newcomb 1961). To maintain this balance we need to be consistent in what we like and what we don't like. Otherwise our partners wouldn't know whether they were pleasing or annoying us. We also need to reciprocate, that is, give back to our partners as much reward as they give us. Similarity in attitudes and beliefs also contributes to cognitive consistency. We expect our friends to have similar ideas to us, as we mentioned earlier. If we do like something or someone our friends or partners don't, we may feel uncomfortable since this may even challenge our relationship. We are in a state of *cognitive dissonance*. We may downplay our feelings, or try to change our attitude towards the person or object our partner likes.

■ How do cognitive theories explain relationship formation, and how adequate are their claims?

■ Why is it less common to find groups of three being close friends, compared to pairs of friends?

### Evaluation of cognitive consistency theories

Although a balance of attitudes between partners would be ideal, we do not seek to preserve the balance, and can tolerate quite a variety of alternative views and still find our partner attractive.

The notion of cognitive balance is impossible to test. One partner may have different ideas, expectations and beliefs from another, but still regard their relationship as balanced.

The theory is mechanistic. People's relationships aren't predictable like the relationships between parts of machines. We don't automatically adjust, advance, retreat, submit, demand and so on to maintain some imaginary state of cognitive balance.

---

### Summary – Theories of interpersonal attraction

Learning theories stress the importance of reward or reinforcement. If we find someone whose behaviour we find beneficial, we are more likely to be attracted to that person. An extension of this can be seen in trading theories, which say that we are attracted to partners where we receive more, or at least equal, benefit from our relationship to that which we invest in it. Humans have highly developed cognitive skills and, according to cognitive consistency theory, are keen to maintain a balance between their expectations of others, and other people's expectations of them.

---

## THEORIES OF LOVE

Human language has coined words for love and liking, and we all know the difference between the two. Strange how we can't adequately define either term, or explain the difference. Love is somehow 'deeper' than liking, and involves attraction even more. It may have an instinctive basis, driving us to reproduce and preserve our genes through the next generation. The problem for psychologists is to untangle the confusion and seek explanations for what love is, what function it performs for humans, where it originates, how it develops, and finally, why two people fall in love. Different theories have addressed some of these questions.

### Evolutionary theory – the origins of love

According to the evolutionary theory of **Charles Darwin**, anything that promotes the chances of an individual or species to survive is likely to be preserved. If having a thick coat means an animal will be able to withstand the cold, then, as it gets colder, those animals with the thickest coats will live longer, mate more often, and pass on their genes to more offspring. Some might inherit the genes for a thick coat, and they, in turn, are likely to survive to pass on their genes to more offspring until many animals carry the genes for thick coats. A thick coat is said to have *survival value* (so long as the weather stays cold).

Ellen Berscheid (1985) argues that we need to know what is safe for us to approach, what will enhance our prospects for well-being, and what therefore we will evaluate positively. High positive evaluation could explain love. Equally we must know what to avoid, what may cause us harm, ultimately what will limit our chances of survival. The need to evaluate is instinctively driven.

According to **Edward Wilson** (1978) three instincts have evolved in humans that would explain the role of love in survival. First, infants need to be cared for by adults so have evolved instincts for attachment. Second, adult caregivers develop instincts to care for their young. Third, there is the instinctive sex drive. So love is the way we describe the fulfilment of our sexual urges and procreate the next generation. However, romantic love doesn't necessarily last long, and may be replaced by liking and companionship. Much animal behaviour is instinctively driven, but to explain love in humans in simple evolutionary terms is deeply unsatisfactory since it ignores cross-cultural variations (e.g. arranged marriages) and cognitive factors in the choice of a partner.

*Evaluation of evolutionary theory*

One problem with evolutionary theories is that they attribute all sorts of processes to genetic influence way beyond our present understanding of the function of our genes. Genes are molecules of protein which trigger biological, maturational processes such as puberty or the onset of some conditions such as Down's Syndrome. We do not know all about the 'instincts', 'drives', or 'urges' they may trigger. Whilst Darwin's claims about the origins of species and the role of adaptation in survival have attracted much interest, to generalize evolutionary ideas to explain what humans call love is going way beyond the available data.

### Psychoanalytic theory – the function of love

According to Freud, genital maturity is reached between puberty and early adulthood. Hormonal and other biological changes direct young people towards sexual experimentation and sexual expression. This is perfectly normal. Unfortunately, some societies, including our own, place restrictions on what forms of sexual behav-

■ **Why does someone fall in love with someone else?**

▶ *Survival value* is an essential feature of evolutionary theory since it enables individuals to live longest in order to reproduce more and have more opportunities to pass on their genes.

■ **Evaluate the contribution made by evolutionary theory to our understanding of the origin of love.**

iour are acceptable and what are not. So young teenagers may dance, hold hands, even cuddle and kiss, but they are not expected to indulge in sexual intercourse until much older. Also, the place where sexual activity may occur is defined socially. In private is acceptable, on a crowded bus is not. The number of partners one can have also has social implications. One partner at a time is acceptable, three partners at one time is promiscuous. Freud thought that our urges drive us to wanting to have sexual relations with quite a few people and in quite a few places of which society would not approve.

Freud sees 'love' as being the label for socially acceptable sexual activity. It's more acceptable to engage in sexual activity if we're 'in love' than otherwise. So love is the means by which we *sublimate* (see Chapter 1) our sexual drives into acceptable activity such as going on dates, courtship, and the business generally called romance.

*Evaluation of psychoanalytic theory*

This theory was derived from Freud's analysis of his neurotic patients, and has no experimental or any other support. Freud almost regards love as a (usually) traumatic pathological condition that needs to be 'dealt with' using some defence mechanisms. Others see it more as a glorious condition that should be celebrated.

Freud's explanation for love is little more than a cultural definition of acceptable sexual practices. He imagines that people want to indulge in sexual experiences that society would find unacceptable. There is little evidence that huge numbers of people (e.g. paraphiliacs?) do want to engage in such socially unacceptable behaviour, and the definition of acceptability varies with time and place, and between the individuals concerned. Freud's theory is descriptive rather than explanatory.

### Triangular theory – a definition of love

Robert Sternberg (1987) suggests that love comprises three elements: intimacy, passion and commitment. *Intimacy* refers to the need to confide in and share our feelings with someone we are close to. *Passion* refers to the feeling of being 'in love', and the strong desire to be intimate with the partner. *Commitment* is the strength of the intention to remain in the relationship. Couples will have a blend of these three at different stages in their relationship. By attempting to measure the strength of these three elements Sternberg believes one can identify the kind of love that the couple are experiencing (see figure 2.2).

► There are wide cultural variations in the extent of sexual activity that is acceptable between the sexes at different ages. Nor is the recognition of gender completely determined by one's sex, as in our culture.

■ Outline the function of love according to psychoanalytic theory.

| Passion | Intimacy | Commitment | Type of love |
|---------|----------|------------|--------------|
| low | low | low | non-love |
| high | low | low | infatuation |
| low | high | low | liking (friendship) |
| low | low | high | empty love |
| high | high | low | romantic love |
| low | high | high | companionship love |
| high | low | high | fatuous love |

Figure 2.2 Sternberg's classification of types of love

*Evaluation of triangular theory*

Sternberg's identification of different kinds of love, and how they are arrived at, has made a useful contribution to our understanding of relationship formation and maintenance in the West. Different cultures have widely varying arrangements for who can do what with whom that wouldn't recognize the three components, or how they combine in order to explain their partnering.

### The two component theory – defining being in love

Walster and Berscheid (1974) propose that sexual love results from the combining of two processes. First, there are feelings of physical and emotional arousal when in the company of the other person. Arousal refers to a heightened emotional state, and we have many emotions that can be aroused. Second, we label those feelings as love. Of course we don't have to label them as love, we could define them as hate if the arousal they trigger is loathing or envy. It could be sympathy if the arousal is to some perceived injustice. Although the level of arousal may be triggered by many things, we are unlikely to confuse them with love.

*Evaluation of two component theory*

No doubt the components identified are important in the individual's definition of feeling love, but to reduce the complex set of cognitions, emotions and physical states we define as love to feelings of arousal which we identify as love is too simple. It may explain the diagnosis ('I'm in love'), but it doesn't explain the cause ('Why am I in love with that person?').

■ Summarize triangular theory's definition of states of love.

■ How adequately does two component theory define being in love?

> #### Summary – Theories of love
>
> Evolutionary theories (see Chapter 5) explain love in terms of survival value. We need to feel safe and to express ourselves sexually, whereas psychoanalytic theory sees love as being the result of hormonal and instinctive drives that occur during the genital stage of psychosexual development. Triangular theory recognizes social and emotional components beyond untestable assumptions about survival value and instinctive urges. It identifies intimacy, passion and commitment as being the key variables.

## THE MAINTENANCE AND BREAKDOWN OF RELATIONSHIPS

Most of the research has concentrated on the formation of relationships. **Dindia** and **Baxter** (1987) asked a group of married couples who had been together for various numbers of years what they did to maintain their relationship, and what they did when there was friction between them. They identified 49 answers, ranging from being nice to each other by paying compliments, reminiscing about the past, doing things together as a couple to talking over any

▶ Ayres emphasizes the importance of communication in maintaining relationships. Other things are important, too.

problem and even making ultimatums. Noticeably, those whose relationship had already lasted a long time did less to maintain it than those in shorter relationships. Perhaps they had become so used to each other that they didn't need strategies, perhaps they had stopped caring so much and their relationship had become a routine or habit, but not something they thought about much.

**Ayres** (1983) asked a sample of adults how they maintained their relationships and found three broad groupings of strategies. First, those who wanted to maintain the relationship at its present level (NB the three dimensions noted by Sternberg above) used avoidance strategies to anticipate and avoid any change in the relationship suggested by their partner. Where one person wants to detach himself or herself from the relationship he or she uses balance strategies whereby less effort is put into his or her commitment to the relationship. This often results in the first partner working even harder to maintain the relationship. Some people, particularly women, according to **Shea** and **Pearson** (1986), prefer direct strategies where they simply talk about what they want from the relationship.

One frequently cited reason for staying in a relationship was 'for the sake of the children'. Relatives, friends, colleagues and even acquaintances have expectations about people in relationships. We are pigeonholed by our social roles, such as what we do for a living, what our status is, our family life, our hobbies and interests, and so on. These expectations are subtle pressures on us to stay the same. **Hagestad** and **Smyer** (1982) showed how these pressures operate differently on single people compared to couples.

## Separation and divorce

▶ Whilst it is possible to study the social effects of the maintenance and breakdown of relationships, the psychological effects are much harder to study. They vary so much anyway, with some partners equally wanting to end the relationship, whilst for others it is a tragic loss.

Marital breakdown is studied by asking recently separated or divorced people about the events that led up to their separation. **Diane Vaughan** (1986) sampled 103 such people and found that a social separation precedes the physical separation. The usual routine is that one partner becomes dissatisfied with the relationship and unsuccessfully tries to change the other's contribution to the relationship by putting more into it themselves. When this fails the dissatisfied partner finds new situations in which to develop new interests and friends which do not involve the other partner. The final break is usually preceded by discussions with close friends to compare notes, to see if friends think they are doing the right thing and could cope on their own. Vaughan found that they usually conclude that their own self-development takes priority over their commitment to their partner.

**Argyle**, **Henderson** and **Furnham** (1984) identified a series of 'rules' of any close relationship, which, if broken, will cause disruption and possibly breakdown (see figure 2.3). The more seriously, frequently, or over a long period they are broken, the more likely the relationship will fail.

1 Support, defend or promote the other person when he or she is absent.
2 Share news of successes.
3 Show emotional support when it is needed.
4 Show trust and confide in each other.
5 Help in times of need.
6 Try to make each other happy.

*Figure 2.3  Argyle, Henderson and Furnham's rules of a close relationship*

**Baxter** (1986) sees relationships failing because people have expectations about relationships that aren't met. These are summarized in figure 2.4.

1 Each partner should feel free to contribute to making decisions that affect both partners, and free to decide things for themselves.
2 Partners should find that they share many similar ideas.
3 Partners should support each other's self-esteem and feelings.
4 Partners should be loyal and faithful.
5 Partners should be honest and open with each other.
6 Partners should expect to spend time together.
7 There should be a balance in the amount of effort and resources between the partners.
8 There should be a 'magical quality' in the relationship.

*Figure 2.4 Baxter's summary of expectations about relationships*

Whilst these may be some of the causes of the breakdown, **Steven Duck** (1988) identifies four phases in the process of breakdown. These are, first, the *intrapsychic phase*, where the dissatisfied partner thinks about the problems with their partner and the relationship. If they decide to do something about their feelings they may confront or avoid their partner, they may seek to improve, or terminate, the relationship. This involves the other person and is called the *dyadic phase*. The third *social phase* comprises attempts to work out the social details of who will tell families and friends what story. When the breakup finally occurs the couple enter the *grave dressing phase*, where they establish their new relationships, with each other and with their friends.

■ How have psychologists investigated the maintenance of relationships?
Summarize their conclusions.

### *Evaluation of psychological theories of relationships*
We have talked here about breakdown where both partners adapt to a new lifestyle. Other forms of breakdown include death of a partner; the psychological implications of this are beyond the scope of this book.

It would be misleading to think that there are several explanations of the formation and maintenance of interpersonal relationships, and we have yet to discover the right one. As we shall see in Chapter 10, different therapies are effective with different problems; the same is true here. Exchange theory is useful for understanding the early stages of friendship, but not for romantic love or family relations. Bowlby's ideas about attachment (see Chapter 14) are more useful for understanding love. Equity theory helps explain the breakdown of close relationships.

Most of the research described here has used college students and other adults to investigate the role of attraction in the formation of 'straight' relationships during early adulthood. As Steven Duck (1995) said, 'Something may have been learned from these studies, though not as much as was, and still sometimes is, claimed for them'. Only in the 1990s have researchers widened the study to include attraction amongst old people, lesbians and gay people, people in various non-traditional marriages (such as 'commuter marriages'), and amongst children in various dysfunctional situations. The issue of interpersonal relationships is now being seen as part of the wider social context beyond the role of physical attraction in dating choice or judgements about how attractive people appear in photographs. However, all research has to start somewhere, and it seems reasonable to start by conducting the kind of research that was possible and usual at the time, using the student participants most readily available.

### Summary – The maintenance and breakdown of relationships

Researchers have interviewed couples to identify why their relationship had endured, or why it had broken down. Many factors were identified, including emotions, physical feelings, social and financial needs, and intellectual compatibility and stimulation. Relationships fail when the factors that drew the couple together, or that bound them, are no longer regarded as important.

## COMPONENTS OF INTERPERSONAL RELATIONSHIPS

As we said earlier, Steven Duck (1973) argues that the main objective in maintaining a relationship is similarity. This includes the members or partners sharing similar goals and aspirations. An early goal of a couple in an emotional relationship will be setting up home together, perhaps starting a family. Inevitably, goals will change with time. Later goals might include taking on different pastimes, including separate activities. The pressures on each partner change too, with career advancement and the demands of other family members. For a relationship to survive it must be able to adapt to these changed goals.

Organizations have goals which may change too. They have a distribution of roles which members occupy to fulfil these goals. The goals of a large educational establishment may be spelt out in its mission statement, or similar document. It will include providing top-quality learning environments and experiences for students in a supportive and helpful environment, offering the same opportunities to all regardless of their background. To achieve these goals there are roles. Directors and managers respond to the demands of those who pay for the services by providing appropriate courses in as economic and efficient a way as possible. The teacher's role is to deliver the learning experiences such as lectures, handouts, essay marking, visits, videos and so on. The catering staff contribute by keeping everyone healthily fed, whilst caretakers ensure that the buildings and grounds are in good order.

Sometimes goals can come into conflict. The goals of staff include making students work hard to pass their exams at high grades. Students' goals are sometimes to do as little work as possible and still get top grades. Opposing conflicts must be resolved, and compromises may be acceptable. Sadly, conflicts that can't be resolved lead to one set of goals being achieved whilst the other may be modified or sacrificed. So long as enough of the organization's goals can be achieved the organization will continue. If they can't, the roles and rules may change.

Roles and responsibilities are distributed throughout the organization and become its hierarchy. Inevitably, there will be rules enforcing compliance to the organization's wishes. Students may have signed a contract or charter, specifying what the college will provide for them, and what they must do in return. Failure to comply may result in punishment of one sort or another.

A similar process of negotiation, conflict resolution, goal modification and so on can be seen in family relationships. One partner may sacrifice their goals now so that the other may be able to achieve theirs. Hopefully the favour will be returned, if this is what the other members want. Mutually supportive relationships amongst animals of various species are discussed in Chapters 5 and 6. If one partner's goals change and the other partner's don't change in the same way, conflict occurs. If it cannot be resolved the relationship becomes strained, and may eventually fail.

Gender roles between couples have changed greatly since the days when 'men went out to work' and 'women stayed at home to look after the children', despite the best efforts of some politicians and psychologists to maintain it (see John Bowlby's work discussed in Chapters 14 and 15). The extent to which responsibility for childcare, for example, is shared may depend on the occupations of the parents. **Biernat** and **Wortman** (1990) interviewed parents with similar professional backgrounds who had young children to discover how they organized running their home and having responsibility for childcare. If the couples worked in business or commerce, it was seen as the wife's overall responsibility, with help from her husband. If they were involved in education, it was determined by which partner was available at the time.

▶ All organizations contain people who have relationships, sometimes based on their status in the structure of the organization, sometimes based on friendships that develop inside and continue outside the organization.

### Summary – Components of relationships

Many relationships involve goals, roles and rules and some members have more power over others to set and change them. If all members agree on the appropriateness of the structure and implementation of the roles and rules, the relationships should be harmonious and successful. Where they do not, conflict may occur.

## EFFECTS OF INTERPERSONAL RELATIONSHIPS ON HEALTH AND HAPPINESS

▶ We behave *altruistically* when we behave in ways that put someone else's needs above our own. Giving directions to a stranger or money to charity are examples of altruism.

It seems obvious to say that people need people. Most people are friendly and sociable, and will often behave in pro-social, *altruistic* ways (see the debate on the factors involved in altruism in Chapter 4). If members of a particular group or partnership are happy together, share common goals, have responsibilities and benefits equally shared between them, and agree on the fair distribution of roles, then they should feel happy, and happiness should contribute to their general mental health.

Successful loving relationships are the most rewarding (and possibly the rarest) that humans can have. In *The Psychopathology of Everyday Life* Freud claimed that love was a manifestation of the life force which he called libido (see Chapter 1). The sexual drive is sublimated into love, which is a more socially acceptable means of expressing the sexual instincts. So a man is supposed to substitute his wife for the woman who was the object of his earliest sexual feelings, his mother. (Freud said that, when a man marries, he divorces his mother.) A woman sees in her husband the strong, dominant qualities she first saw in her father. **Averill** (1980) advanced a theory of emotions that claims that loving relationships serve a positive social and emotional role. Loving someone means idealizing them. We feel a strong attachment and passion towards them, and we hold them in high esteem. If they love us, we feel wanted and respected too, and this helps make us feel good about ourselves. Feeling good about oneself should reduce the likelihood of a person becoming depressed or unhappy.

▶ Freud believed that the force for life is essentially sexual, since one of the major functions of life is reproduction. Opposing this urge for life is an urge towards self-destruction, which Freud called the death instincts.

**Brown** and **Harris** (1978) conducted a long-term study of depression amongst people trying to raise a family in London. They found that those who had a close relationship with someone such as a good friend or partner were much less likely to suffer than those who felt themselves to be alone.

### Family relationships

Family relationships are the most persistent that humans experience. They occasionally create problems that can't be resolved using the family's usual communication processes. Family therapy began in the 1960s, and is still offered by some clinics and organizations. It sees the family as a social system, which contains members fulfilling various roles that, between them, maintain the efficient working of the system. Where an individual experiences problems with their role, often because of the expectation made of them by other family members, the problem is regarded as being of the family, rather than of the individual. Members are encouraged to talk about their concerns, attitudes and expectations to try to restore the efficient working of the system.

▶ A systems approach is one that sees the members of a group not simply as individuals, with their own views and behaviour, but sees the group as an organized whole with contributing members. The emphasis therefore is on the maintenance of the efficient running of the system.

## Social support

One factor in close personal relationships is the extent to which the people involved can provide social support when it is needed. Social support comprises three essential elements: *emotional* support, which includes love, caring, respect, sympathy and loyalty; *material* support, which includes providing accommodation, money, help with work and so on; and *informational* support, which includes advice, information on where to go, who to see, and what to do, and personal feedback such as answering questions.

**Berkman** and **Syne** (1979) sampled almost 7,000 adults in 1965 to discover their general state of health, and other health-related behaviour such as what and when they ate, their sleeping habits, levels and type of exercise, smoking and so on. They also asked about the extent of their social networks. The follow-up study showed a very clear trend. Those with the least widely spread social networks were more likely to suffer more illnesses, less likely to improve with treatment, and more likely to die sooner than those with wider social networks. This trend was found regardless of the age or sex of the adult when surveyed. The extent of the social network was also found to be a better predictor of illness and death than was the person's health-related behaviours.

Similarly, **Achterberg** and **Lawlis** (1977) conducted a study amongst people who were suffering serious illness. They identified some patients who had a strong network of social relationships amongst family and friends, whilst some others lacked many close friends or relatives to talk to. They compared the progress the patients made, and found that those with good social networks tended to improve quicker and live longer than those who did not.

### Summary – Effects of interpersonal relationships on health and happiness

Evidence shows that people need people. Those who have relationships with people they can rely on are more likely to live happier and longer lives.

### Exam question – 60 minutes

1  Critically evaluate attempts by psychologists to explain the formation and breakdown of relationships. (*25 marks*)

# (3) *Social influence and persuasion*

**Chapter objectives**

Having studied this chapter you will:

▌ appreciate the importance of norms to social interaction, and how norms are adopted;

▌ be able to describe the different ways in which conformity has been defined and classified, and give a critical review of the major experimental studies of conformity;

▌ be able to describe and evaluate the major studies of obedience;

▌ be able to discuss the ethical dilemmas raised by studies of conformity and obedience;

▌ be able to compare and contrast different psychological approaches to the study of leadership and review the experimental evidence associated with them;

▌ be familiar with the debate concerning the nature of crowds, and understand some of the research evidence for each point of view.

## *Introduction*

In this chapter we will be offering some explanations for why aspects of our behaviour sometimes alter when we are with other people. As we shall discuss in Chapter 16, we draw information about ourselves, and so build our self-concept, from the way other people seem to treat us. Social learning theory says we need them to be models for us to imitate, and to guide, approve of and discipline us (see Chapter 1). At the same time, we try to create the right impression of ourselves. Most of us want other people to think highly of us. Children, and many adults, sometimes 'show off' in order to gain approval.

## THE FORMATION OF NORMS

*Norms* are patterns of behaviour that are typical of a certain group of people. We all acquire social norms, which are somehow representative of our society. When to say what to whom, what to do, when to do it, and what not to do are all governed by social norms. Some norms aren't particularly important, such as attending a bonfire and fireworks display on Guy Fawkes night; others are enforced by law, such as not stealing. We acquire most of our social norms through our *socialization*. Socialization is the name of the process by which each new member of society learns what is expected of it as a member of that society. British children learn to speak English, to dress in British clothes, to eat British food, whilst Japanese children learn Japanese social norms.

There are several types of norms. **Michael Argyle** (1982) identifies task norms relating to the 'method, rate, and standard' of work. Norms of group interaction 'make the behaviour of others predictable, prevent conflicts and ensure fair distribution of rewards'. Experts in the group express attitudes and ideas that lead to the norm to which group members adhere, rather than to ideas from non-group members. **Irving Janis** (1972) warned against the over-conformity that can occur in a crisis or when the issue before the group is serious, which he called *groupthink*. Members are so concerned with the issue under discussion that the dominant view prevails and no one presents alternatives. Finally, group membership produces norms of appearance of clothes, hair and so on, which project the group's identity.

## Psychological studies of norm formation

Norm formation was one of the first features of interpersonal relationships to be studied by social psychologists. Farmers had noted how chickens who had already eaten their fill would start to eat again if placed in the midst of hungry chickens. Their 'eating behaviour' is automatically triggered by the sight of others eating. Many such automatic *fixed action patterns* have been observed by animal researchers. Amongst human sporting competitors the norm is to do one's best. Athletic records are usually broken when an audience is watching, footballers play harder in front of a crowd, and the first night in the theatre always brings out that little extra from the actors than in the rehearsal. In each case the presence of others leads to an improvement in activity. This process is called *social facilitation*. (To facilitate means to enable, or make it easier, for something to happen.) The question is, how much social facilitation is learned through the encouragement of the team manager or theatre director (*nurture*), and how much is a part of our biological make-up (*nature*)? Do we have a need to compete, to excel, to impress? Would such a need help us to survive (i.e. have *survival value*)?

Social facilitation was observed by **Norman Triplett** (1898). Triplett noted that cyclists who raced each other rode faster than when riding the same distance against the clock. He believed that the element of competition would emerge whenever the opportunity for it occurred. It was probably a basic human need. To test this he asked children to wind a fishing reel 150 turns as quickly as they

► Some parodies of social norms are that the Welsh all sing when they're not coal mining, the Scots wear kilts and talk like Rab C. Nesbitt, the English are a nation of shopkeepers and stand in queues all day (possibly wearing bowler hats and pin-striped suits). Notice how most of these apply to men?

► *Groupthink* results in norms of agreement or acquiescence, where no one challenges the dominant view. One example is the British government's policy of the late 1930s under Neville Chamberlain to appease Adolf Hitler, believing that giving in was the best way to avoid conflict.

► A *fixed action pattern* is a reflexive response over which the animal has no voluntary control. It is said to be triggered when an appropriate stimulus is perceived.

could, both on their own and in pairs. When in pairs the children wound their reels faster. We have somehow acquired a norm for improving performance when others of our own species are present.

Triplett stressed the importance of competition. **Floyd Allport** (1924) claimed facilitation would occur in the presence of others regardless of any element of competition. He had participants perform a variety of pencil and paper tasks such as simple arithmetic, crossing out certain letters in a written article, and so on. People performed better when they could see other people around them doing the same thing, even though Allport had told them not to try to compete. He described this type of social facilitation as a *co-action effect*. Performing differently in front of an audience is called an *audience effect*.

▶ Social facilitation comprises *co-action effects* and *audience effects*.

However, the presence of others doesn't always lead to social facilitation. It can lead to social inhibition, i.e. performance worsens. Allport found that in working co-actively people make more errors in the more difficult tasks, possibly because of the distraction of having other people around. We might say that quantity increases but quality decreases. Allport concluded: 'It is the overt responses such as writing which receive facilitation through the stimulus of co-workers. The intellectual or implicit responses of thought are hampered rather than facilitated.' Neither Allport nor other researchers were able to explain why easier tasks are facilitated whilst harder ones are inhibited, and the subject of social facilitation was rather ignored by social psychologists until the 1950s.

■ **Write a paragraph using the following terms in a way that shows that you understand what each term means: social norms, socialization, survival value, social facilitation, co-action effect, audience effect, social inhibition.**

Improved performance in company, even when the task is simple, isn't quite the norm that early research suggests. Sometimes people make less effort, believing that their poor contribution won't be noticed amongst the rest. Many children sing less enthusiastically in the choir than they do when it's their solo! This is called *social loafing* and was demonstrated by **Bibb Latané** and his colleagues (1979). Students were asked to make as much noise as possible, both on their own and in groups. When alone they made rather more than when in groups. It takes some effort to make a lot of noise, so each student let the others make more effort! When students were told that their individual efforts would be tested, they made more effort.

▶ *Social loafing* refers to the way that individuals often reduce their effort when they know that others are making sufficient effort so that theirs won't be noticed.

■ **Make notes on psychological insights into social loafing and social facilitation.**

There are several conditions under which the norms for social facilitation will appear, for example if the individual feels some responsibility for the progress or achievements of the whole group, if the task the group is performing is interesting, and if making more effort would be of some personal benefit.

**Robert Zajonc** (1965) explained why the presence of others produces norms of facilitation or inhibition in terms of *arousal* and *novelty*. The presence of other people arouses our perceptions of ourselves and our performance. Arousal facilitates simple or well-practised responses, such as winding fishing reels, running faster down the home straight, or performing simple arithmetic. However, arousal inhibits performance of novel (newly learned) or demanding tasks such as more complex mental activity, or driving through a busy, unknown town having to watch traffic and read road signs.

However, the mere presence of others does not always improve the performance of even well-rehearsed material, but only if others are co-acting or being an audience. Why make more effort to improve performance if no one will know you've improved? Also, some people tend to get nervous whenever they know they are being watched regardless of how well they know the task.

### Sherif's research (1935)

The first major research into the formation of group norms was conducted in 1935 by **Muzafer Sherif**, who used a visual illusion known as the *autokinetic effect*. Each photoreceptor (the rods and cones of the retina) needs a changing pattern of light if it is not to become saturated and fatigued (see Chapter 11). Retinal fatigue would mean that we couldn't see anything distinctly at all. To avoid this our eyeballs are constantly making tiny movements. This is called *nystagmus*. One consequence of nystagmus is that stationary spots of light will appear to move. The autokinetic effect has been observed, however, even when the eyes do not move.

► *Nystagmus* is the tiny movements of the eyes which change the pattern of light, stimulating individual retinal cells and keeping them from becoming fatigued.

Sherif told his participants that a spot of light that they were about to see in a darkened room was going to move, and he asked them to report the direction and distance of the movement. In the first experimental condition the participants were tested individually. Some said the distance of movement wasn't very far in any direction, others said it was several inches. Sherif recorded each participant's response. In the second experimental condition Sherif gathered his participants into groups of three, and again asked them to report the movement of the light. He gave them no instructions about whether they needed to reach any kind of agreement among themselves, but simply asked them to give their own reports, while being aware of the reports that the other members gave (they could hear but could not see one another).

► The three people in each group would previously have reported quite different extents of movement for the stationary light. Would they now conform to some kind of group norm, or would their reports be quite independent of what the others were saying?

The participants' reports started to converge much nearer to an average of what their individual reports had been. If a participant who had said that the light didn't move very far when tested individually said 'I think it is moving about two inches to the left', then another who had reported movements of four inches or more when tested individually might say 'I think it moved about three inches'. As the number of reported movements continued, the more the members of the groups conformed to an average, group norm score. Sherif asked participants if they felt their responses were being influenced by the scores of the other group members, and they all said absolutely not!

► Despite claiming that they were not being influenced by hearing other group members' reports, each participant conformed nearer to an average of the members' individual scores.

So why were they forming a group norm of the average amount of apparent movement? Remember, this spot of light was in fact stationary, so whatever reports were made were the consequence of the participants imagining they saw something happen. The key is that they were not certain about the movement they observed, and so

► If we express an opinion, and we're not certain of the facts, we tend to look for signs of agreement from others. If someone else expresses an opinion similar to ours, or partly agrees with us, we are usually quite happy to modify our ideas to make a compromise. Perhaps being in agreement and having our ideas confirmed fulfils some psychological need.

■ Why did Sherif's participants in his second experimental condition conform to a group norm?

► Have you ever been on a car journey with other people and none of you was certain of the route? Did you discuss it and come to a best guess, or did you follow the directions of one who was most convinced they knew the way?

■ What have we learned from Sherif's 1930s studies of conformity?

would not feel confident about insisting that their observations were wholly correct. When they heard other reported judgements they may have decided to 'go along' with them. It isn't worth demanding that you're correct if you're not positive that you are. Few people would enjoy being the 'odd one out', being regarded as extreme, dogmatic, selfish, drawing attention to themselves, inexperienced or just plain stupid! It is also possible that there is some psychological benefit in agreeing. It may confirm our self-concept, and make us feel secure that we are in the majority and must therefore be 'right'. It may strengthen our ego and make us more positive in our other attitudes.

In a third experimental condition the participants were retested individually. Their reports should presumably have resembled the scores they had given in the first experimental condition. They were alone, and whatever perceptions made them report the distances they did previously were operating again now. However, this didn't happen. The participants reported movements much more in line with their group norm scores.

Why should this happen? It was their reports, not their perceptions, which were similar. If they benefited from the consensus in condition two, there is no benefit to be gained by agreement in condition three since there's no one to agree with. They probably imagined that a group score was likely to be nearer the correct answer than their own individual perception, since they weren't sure of the movement they saw. Perhaps three heads are better than one when the one doesn't really know!

*Evaluation of Sherif's research*
The problem with this study for our understanding of norm formation is that it is a totally artificial experimental situation. There isn't even a 'right' answer. Requested 'reports of imaginary movements of a stationary spot of light in a darkened room when alone or with two others' hardly reflect situations we come across in our everyday lives. Generalizing from its conclusions to 'real life' might be dangerous, although some of them do have a common-sense appeal.

In addition to the debate concerning the origin of group norms, much psychological research has been put into measuring the extent to which merely being in a social situation can create and maintain conformity to group norms, and the kind of behaviour which holding such norms can deliver.

### Summary – The formation of norms
Norms are the essential knowledge we have about appropriate and inappropriate behaviour. We acquire many of them through our socialization process, by observing, imitating, identifying, being taught, and by trial and error. Others are acquired on the basis of single trial learning (see Chapter 1). There are different kinds of norms, which are affected by the presence of others and the need to compete that some people feel, or the desire to let others work harder than ourselves in a group task.

## CONFORMITY AND INDEPENDENCE OF GROUP NORMS

**Keisler** and **Keisler** (1972) define conformity as 'a change in behaviour or belief toward a group as a result of real or imagined group pressure'. **Richard Crutchfield** (1962) and **Leon Mann** (1969) refer to it as 'yielding to group pressure'. Specifically, conformity has three distinct areas of meaning. First, whether or not to *behave* in ways that other members of the group would think appropriate. Second, whether to express attitudes that conform to those we would expect from a member of the group (NB: people's attitudes and what they actually do aren't always consistent). The third area of meaning concerns personality traits. Most people generally conform to their group's norms, but there are occasions depending on the situation, mood, cognition, state of arousal and so on when they may not. Psychologists have been interested in finding whether some people have a 'conforming personality'.

In general, there's nothing wrong with conformity. It allows us to 'know where we stand', what to think and how to behave. Like stereotypes, conforming and expecting others to conform maintains cognitive balance. A problem occurs when someone's own personality starts to become obscured by their need to conform, as we mentioned with groupthink earlier.

■ What is conformity and why is it generally 'a good thing'?

### Types of conformity

**Herbert Kelman** (1958) distinguishes *compliance* (where the participant goes along with the group view, but privately disagrees with it), *internalization* (where the participant comes to accept, and eventually believes, the group's view), and *identification* (where the participant accepts and believes the group view, because he or she wants to become associated with the group). Several factors have been found to be influential in compliance, including the prestige of the person speaking (Kelman and Hovland 1953), the perceived power and status of the model (Bandura et al. 1963), and the size of the group, as we shall see in Asch's (1951a) studies shortly.

Leon Mann (1969) identifies *normative conformity*, which 'occurs when direct group pressure forces the individual to yield under the threat of rejection or the promise of reward'. This can only occur if someone wants to be a member of the group, or the group's attitudes or behaviour are important to the individual in some way. Mann identifies two kinds of normative conformity. One is compliance, the other is true conformity (similar to Kelman's internalization). According to Mann, 'True conformity occurs when the person both privately and publicly is in agreement with the group'.

Apart from normative conformity there is *informational conformity*, which 'occurs where the situation is vague or ambiguous and because the person is uncertain he turns to others for evidence of

▶ *Normative conformity* comprises compliance (seeming to agree) and true conformity (actually agreeing).

▶ *Informational conformity* occurs when someone copies the behaviour or attitudes of the group in order to appear as a member. Making errors in informational conformity can lead to great embarrassment on the part of the conformist, and great amusement on the part of the competent group members.

► According to Mann there is *normative*, *informational* and *ingratiational conformity*. Mann and Kelman are not disagreeing about the nature of conformity, just offering slightly different variations on its forms.

■ **What are the main types of conformity?**

► Those who behave independently are most likely to be admired, conformers are likely to be accepted, anti-conformers are likely to be rejected.

■ **Why is it inadequate to talk about the conformist personality?**

the appropriate response'. If you're not sure which cutlery to use in a posh restaurant you may copy what someone who seems more experienced than you uses. Otherwise you may appear inexperienced or foolish.

Third, Mann identifies *ingratiational conformity*, which occurs where 'a person tries to do whatever he thinks the other will approve in order to gain acceptance'. If you make yourself appear to be similar to someone else, they might come to like you. (Imitation may be a form of flattery, and flattery does sometimes work.) However, we are usually very aware of ingratiational conformists. As Mann says, 'People are ... reluctant to overdo the conformity technique in case it should rebound against them, promoting dislike rather than acceptance'.

**R.H. Willis** (1963) identified three possible responses when facing a situation in which other people's responses can be seen. First, we can conform to group norms. Second, we can be neutral, conforming if we genuinely believe that it is best, and doing something else if we do not. This is *independent behaviour*. Finally, we can deliberately do the opposite of what is expected, which is termed *anti-conformity*. Anti-conformity is generally thought of as unnecessary and unpleasant, a way of drawing attention to oneself, whereas independence is usually thought of as desirable and mature.

According to Willis, whether our response in one situation is conformist, independent or even anti-conformist, will depend largely on our perception of the situation rather than on whether we have a conformist personality. A person who behaves in a mostly conformist way in some situations or on some occasions may well behave in a more independent way on others.

### Summary – Types of conformity

Different writers identify such different aspects of conformity as compliance, internalization, identification, normative conformity, informational conformity and ingratiational conformity. There is nothing 'wrong' with conformity. Without a large measure of agreement about what we should do in various situations, society would be impossible. It is the rigidity with which we reflect our type of conformity that may create difficulties for us or others.

## Studies of conformity

### Asch's research (1951)

**Solomon Asch** criticized Sherif's experimental design and claimed that it showed little about conformity since there was no 'right answer' to conform to. He designed an experiment where there could be absolutely no doubt about whether participants would be conforming or not, and it was absolutely clear what they were conforming to. He wanted to be able to put an individual under various amounts of group pressure, which he could control and manipulate, and measure that person's willingness to conform to the group's response to something that was clearly wrong.

Asch (1951a) seated seven university students around one side of a large table facing the blackboard, in a classroom. On the left side of the board there was a white card with a single black line drawn vertically on it. On the right of the board there was another white card with three vertical lines of differing lengths. See figure 3.1. The following instructions were given to the participants:

> This is a task which involves the discrimination of the length of lines. You see the pair of white cards in front. On the left is a single line; on the right there are three lines differing in length. They are numbered 1, 2 and 3 in order. One of the three lines at the right is equal to the standard line at the left – you will decide in each case which is the equal line. You will state your judgement in terms of the corresponding number. There will be 12 such comparisons. As the number of lines is few and the group small I shall call on each of you in turn to announce your judgement, which I shall record here on a prepared form. Please be as accurate as possible. Suppose that we start at the right and proceed to the left.

Two of the lines on the card on the right were obviously longer or shorter than the target line. Matching the target line to the comparison line shouldn't have been a difficult task (see figure 3.1). However, as you may have guessed, of these seven students all but one was a confederate of Asch, and they had been instructed to give incorrect responses on seven of the 12 trials. The one *naive* participant was seated either at the extreme left or next to the extreme left of the line of students, so that he would always be last or next to last to answer. He would have heard most of the others give their 'judgements' about which comparison line matched the target line before he spoke. Would he stick to his own judgement, and regard the six other people as poor judges, inconsistent, or just plain odd? Or would he allow himself to be swayed by the others' opinion, doubt his own senses, and conform to the group's judgement even though it directly contradicted the evidence of his own eyes?

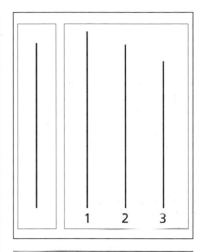

*Figure 3.1  Asch's conformity cards*

► A *naive* participant is deliberately deceived about the nature of the research and their responses form the data from which the research's conclusions are drawn. Do psychologists have the right to treat people like this?

**Table 3.1 Some of Asch's results**

| Length of target line (inches) | Length of comparison line (inches) | | | Correct response | Group response |
|---|---|---|---|---|---|
| | 1 | 2 | 3 | | |
| 10 | 8.75 | 10 | 8 | 2 | 2 |
| 2 | 2 | 1 | 1.75 | 1 | 1 |
| 3 | 3.75 | 4.75 | 3 | 3 | 1 |
| 5 | 5 | 4 | 6.5 | 1 | 2 |
| 4 | 3 | 5 | 4 | 3 | 3 |
| 3 | 3.75 | 4.75 | 3 | 3 | 2 |

In subsequent experiments Asch had between seven and nine participants undergo the experimental procedure just outlined. In the first series of experiments he tested 123 naive participants on 12 'critical tests' (matching the lines), where seven were going to be

► There were 1,476 trials altogether, 861 of them 'rigged'. Over 30 per cent of the sample of 123 conformed on all 861. Only about 20 per cent didn't conform at all.

■ **How did Asch measure conformity in his 1950s experiments?**

▶ *'Debriefing'* is often necessary after research in social psychology, both for ethical and practical reasons. If a participant did something that followed on in some way from the research, then the researcher would be responsible. Some of the participants here may have incurred charges for eye tests or visits to a psychiatrist which they didn't need!

▶ In Asch's experiments the naive participants did not know the confederates, so why would so many of the responses conform to the opinion of just three strangers when the naive participant can plainly see that the response is wrong?

■ **What factors did Asch find to be important in conforming?**

incorrect. Each naive participant therefore had seven opportunities to conform to something he could see to be wrong. One-third of the naive participants conformed on all seven occasions. About three-quarters of them conformed on at least one occasion. Only about one-fifth were independently minded and refused to conform at all.

Just to be certain that the result was due to the influence of the confederates' responses, and not the difficulty of the task, Asch used a control group of similar people, who weren't going to be conned, against which to compare his experimental results. Each control participant was asked to make a judgement individually. There were no pressures at all. Over 90 per cent gave correct responses.

Asch also interviewed each naive participant after the experiment, explaining what had been happening and reassuring them that their judgement wasn't faulty. During this 'debriefing' interview he asked each participant why they had conformed. They admitted that the opinion of the others was a factor, but not the only one. Some blamed their own judgement and were content to believe that the others were better judges. Some had thought that a conforming response was what the experimenter wanted, and they were happy to oblige. Some thought some mistake had been made when drawing the cards and the answer they gave referred to the line that 'should have been' correct. Some claimed that they didn't want to be the odd one out in case they looked foolish or inferior to the rest.

Asch claimed to have found some of the reasons for conformity, at least conformity to an unimportant task like matching the length of lines in a small group. He conducted several variations of this research in the early 1950s to find exactly what factors are involved in conformity. For example, he found that when there was one naive participant and only one confederate, the naive participant did not conform. There was no group or majority decision to conform with. With one or two more confederates conformity increased, although Asch claimed that increasing the number of confederates beyond three made very little difference to the amount of conformity shown. Other research has not confirmed this; the rate of conformity has been found to increase with more confederates, up to seven.

In another variation, if one other member of the group gave the correct answer rather than the wrong one offered by the confederates, then conformity to the majority wrong answer fell to around 5 per cent. Feeling isolated may increase our tendency to conform, but we need only to know that there is one other person on our side, and we refuse to conform to something we don't agree with.

Asch decided to see if the difficulty of the task itself could contribute to levels of conformity. In one experiment he made the three comparison lines very similar in length so that it was difficult to tell which one truly did match the target line. The naive participants would have been less certain. Where there was a majority view expressed by the confederates, conformity by the naive participants rose sharply. This suggests that the less able someone is to make an independent judgement confidently, the more likely they are to accept the judgements of others, either to solve a problem of uncertainty by believing that others are right – an example of informational conformity – or to avoid looking stupid or feeling isolated by going along with the majority judgement – an example of normative conformity or ingratiational conformity.

In his conclusion Asch (1951a) says: 'Independence and yielding are a joint function of the following … factors. (1) the character of the stimulus … (2) the character of the group forces … in particular … the great importance of the factor of unanimity, (3) the character of the individual.' Asch's research has revealed two conditions that promote conformity. One is that individuals can be influenced to say something which they know to be wrong (at least under experimental conditions) when three or more others unanimously say it first. The second is that the presence of just one other person who disagrees with the incorrect decision of the majority is enough to reduce this conformity massively.

Further research has been conducted into why people conform to group norms. Deutsch and Gerard (1955) noted that earlier researchers 'have not distinguished among different kinds of social influence, rather they have carelessly used the term "group" influence to characterize the influence of many different kinds of social factors'. They suggested two reasons for the conformity Asch had observed. These are 'normative social influence' and 'informational social influence'. Normative social influence means that people conform in order to be socially accepted by those in the group. Informational social influence means accepting the group view if you have reason to believe that members have knowledge or evidence that you don't, and which you can't ignore. Other factors that increase the likelihood of conformity are if the naive participant is of a lower status, less experienced, less intelligent and more tired than the confederates.

There are certain problems with Asch's, and Deutsch and Gerard's, studies and conclusions. Like Sherif, they used highly artificial laboratory procedures that do not reflect 'real life' at all. In real life we do not have to make judgements about such things as the length of two lines after having heard a group of strangers give the wrong answer. We could choose to say nothing, or we could ask for help if we weren't sure. In real life 'actions speak louder than words'. Asch's and Deutsch and Gerard's research concerns verbal conformity. Conformity of behaviour – being influenced to do something – is much more important than conformity of speech – being influenced to say something.

Asch assumes that conformity to experimental stimuli somehow represents 'real life' conformity. His measurements of the percentages of naive participants who conformed under various circumstances say nothing about the frequency with which people conform to the opinions or behaviour of others in everyday life. Another assumption of Asch's is that conformity is bad. He

▶ The Sherif and the Asch experiments demonstrated only that people would conform by uttering agreements and not that they would conform by carrying out some action.

► Conformity to some behaviour is demanded by law. We conform to driving on the same side of the road and stopping at red traffic lights too. Are these 'conformities' bad?

■ Summarize the major criticisms of Asch's work.

believed his participants were wrong to conform. But in real life (and in his experiment) conformity is often very useful. We said earlier that agreement may have some positive benefits for us, so unless it is a matter of principle life may be more pleasant if we are generally agreeable. This is hardly bad. Those participants who conformed avoided any stress that could have been associated with resisting the majority view. After all, it was only an experiment.

Finally, Asch's experiments do not identify whether the participants were true conformists, independent thinkers or merely complying with the will of the majority.

---

### Some criticisms of the early research on conformity

Hollander and Willis (1964) have made the following four criticisms of the conformity studies of Sherif, Asch and other early research.

1 The studies do not identify the motive or type of conformity. Do the participants conform in order to gain social approval? Are they simply complying? Do they really believe that their response is correct?
2 They do not identify whether the participants are complying because they judge that it's not worth appearing to be different, or because they actually start to believe that the group's judgement is correct.
3 The studies cannot show whether those who do not conform do so because they are independent thinkers or because they are anti-conformists.
4 The studies seem to assume that independence has to be good and conformity has to be bad. As we found earlier, conformity is often beneficial.

---

*Evaluation of Asch's conformity research*
In the late 1940s and early 1950s Asch conducted what are now described as classic experiments in conformity. That is not to say that they aren't criticized today, or that his conclusions are wholly acceptable now. But they were masterpieces of design and statistical analysis at the time. They showed the rigorous application of the scientific method to social psychology and were used as models of how to conduct psychological research. With the benefit of hindsight Asch's experiments would probably not be conducted now since they have certain flaws, but that is not to detract from Solomon Asch's reply to what he saw as the shortcomings of Sherif's research. Asch's experiments are further examples of psychological research being conducted on American college students.

### Crutchfield's research (1954)

In 1954 **Richard Crutchfield** published the findings of his study of 100 military and business men. Their average age was 34 and they came from a variety of educational backgrounds. They had been unwitting participants in his experiment on the final day of their three-day assessment course. The men had been grouped into fives and seated, side by side, in individual booths. They could not see one another, and were forbidden to talk. Various multiple choice questions were projected onto the wall in front of the men. 'The slides call for various kinds of judgements – length of lines, areas of figures, logical completion of number series, vocabulary items, estimates of the opinions of others, expression of his own attitudes on issues, expression of his personal preferences for line drawings etc.' (Crutchfield 1954). The men had to give their answers by pressing one of five switches which corresponded to the answer they favoured. For example, if they thought the answer to one question was the fourth alternative, they would press switch number four. See figure 3.2.

▶ Crutchfield used highly motivated participants. They were on an assessment course that would have important consequences for their future and they would want to do as well as possible.

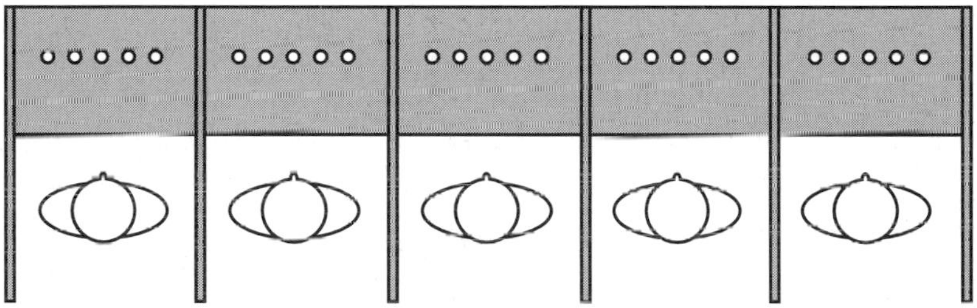

*Figure 3.2  Crutchfield's apparatus*

The men were told that they would take it in turns to answer the questions first, second, third and so on, and that they would be able to see the answers the others gave before giving their own. So on every fifth question each man would see the answers supposedly given by the other four. These 'responses' were in fact controlled by the experimenter from a control panel behind the men. Crutchfield's procedure is an improvement on that of both Asch and Sherif. He used professional adults rather than university students, and he didn't need any confederates. The type of stimuli presented is a great improvement on stationary lights and lines on cards. Each man was able to see the responses the other participants were supposed to have made and the order in which the participants 'answer' can be varied greatly.

▶ Crutchfield's experimental procedures were tightly controlled and little would be left to chance. Are you happy that these participants should have been used, without their consent, in this research?

There were 21 'critical questions' when Crutchfield attempted to induce conformity to a wrong answer. Some men conformed on one or two occasions, one man conformed on 17 of the 21 trials. Crutchfield found that on the judgement questions, such as asking whether one figure was larger than another, and on factual questions, such as asking for the next number in a given sequence,

► 30 per cent conformity is actually quite high in view of the nature of this sample. They were successful military officers and businessmen who were motivated to succeed and whom we would expect to be individual thinkers.

► This description of conformers sounds as though the person possessing such a personality would be a poor creature indeed. However, moderation in all things. All of us have tendencies to be rather weaker than we would like.

■ What intellectual, personality and social characteristics did Crutchfield find characteristic of those most likely to conform?

30 per cent of his participants would conform to the wrong answer when they thought that the others were giving the wrong response too. On matters of opinion one of his more celebrated findings was that 37 per cent of the army personnel he tested agreed with the statement, 'I doubt whether I would make a good leader'. When tested privately none of them had agreed with this statement.

Crutchfield had a mass of data about his participants from the two days of assessment tasks they had completed before becoming involved in the conformity experiment. From this he was able to investigate the question, 'What is it that makes some people more likely to conform than others?' An obvious place to start was with the personalities, intelligence, social adjustment and other social factors of the conformers compared to the non-conformers. Here are his main conclusions.

---

### Crutchfield's conclusions

1 Conformers tended to be less intellectually effective. By this Crutchfield meant that they lacked insight and were less able to apply logical principles to given data. Instead they were more cautious, following 'tried and tested' routes, or imitating other people's solutions.
2 They have less ego strength and are not self-sufficient. This means that they are less sure of themselves, lack confidence in their abilities and are less forceful in expressing opinions or ideas. They are less likely to be able to take care of themselves and need the support of others.
3 They have less leadership ability. Their cautious approach and general indecisiveness would not inspire confidence in their competence and would not inspire respect and loyalty.
4 They tend to have authoritarian views of what 'ought to happen', and what 'should be' done. Their ideas are narrow-minded, simplistic and mostly unworkable.
5 They tend to have inferiority feelings too, and are generally submissive. They know they lack confidence and competence, and so look to others to be strong and decisive. They will not defend their ideas with enthusiasm and tend to agree with whatever the most determined person in the group says. They are usually inhibited in their personal relationships.
6 They have rather limited friendship networks and their social relationships are often rather shallow.
7 They are not widely liked, although they may be widely tolerated. They can be relied upon to 'make the numbers up', but may not often be wanted for themselves.

---

*Evaluation of Crutchfield's research*
Unlike Asch, Crutchfield attempted to conduct a field experiment (see Chapter 17) in which participants are studied in a familiar environment (his participants had to be in these sessions). His procedures were still highly controlled and highly artificial, however, although his findings are detailed and revealing.

**A comparison of Asch's and Crutchfield's techniques**

| Asch | Crutchfield |
| --- | --- |
| Participants can hear each other's responses. | Participants are told how others respond. |
| Participants can see and read each other's non-verbal cues (NVC). | Participants are isolated from each other. |
| Participants have personal contact, which produces a greater pressure to conform. | Participants are anonymous and feel less pressure to conform. |

Whether this description constitutes a 'type of personality' that conformers have, and whether someone with such a personality could be relied upon to conform in all situations, is unclear. What can be demonstrated in experimental studies tends to rely on verbal or anonymous responses to fairly artificial stimuli. What might happen in 'real life' when actual decisive behaviour is required is much harder to demonstrate.

So why do we conform in 'real life'? **Donald Campbell** (1967) noted that we gain our information about the world through personal, direct experience (our 'personal modes') and through what other people tell us (our 'social modes'). Usually these two confirm each other. Campbell suggested that conformity can be explained as a consequence of conflict between these two modes. If the naive participant sees (personal mode) that line 1 is the same length as the target line, but everyone else (social mode) says it's the same as line 2, then the naive participant has to decide which to use. All those factors that make it likely that the personal mode will be used (e.g. intelligence, independence, high status) increase the chances that the participant will not conform. All those that increase the chances that the social mode will be favoured (e.g. members of the group having higher status, higher intelligence) increase the likelihood of conformity.

► Where a discrepancy occurs between what we know personally and what we find out from other sources, we have to decide which to believe. According to Campbell, the more confident and mature we are, the more likely we are to believe our own judgements.

■ **What kind of people are least likely to conform?**

> ### Summary – Studies of conformity
>
> Asch and Crutchfield's experimental research has shown that situational factors influence the likelihood and level of conforming responses, especially the stated opinions of other people. There are strong social bonds that either encourage people to feel part of the group, or stop them from being the 'odd one out'. Those that refuse to conform to situational pressures either do so because they are independent thinkers, or because they are anti-conformists. However, both these experiments used highly artificial procedures to gather their data, and we must be cautious in accepting their findings unreservedly.

## OBEDIENCE

Compliance simply means going along with the decisions, opinions, rules or conventions of a group. Obedience is a special form of compliance where we generally do not want to comply, implying that someone is in power or authority over us giving us specific orders, requests or suggestions that require us to obey. Obedience, like conformity, may be beneficial or destructive, can contribute to the efficient achievement of some goal, or may result in cruelty and evil. As with conformity, psychologists have asked 'is there an obedient personality?' Are there some people who are willing to do the most wicked acts, such as those performed by some Nazis in extermination camps during the Second World War? Or are all of us capable of doing such things, if put into such a situation?

## Studies of obedience

### Milgram's study of obedience

The first major studies of obedience began in the late 1950s and early 1960s in a series of controversial experiments by **Stanley Milgram** at Yale University. Milgram had been working on various aspects of conformity, such as cross-cultural differences, and became especially interested in obedience, since it was being suggested after the Second World War that the German people must have some national character defect that made them especially susceptible to obeying orders – and hence able to follow orders to exterminate people from other cultures. It was said that no other race could have performed such atrocities.

Milgram designed an experiment on 'the role of punishment in learning', whereby pairs of male participants would draw a piece of paper from a hat deciding who would act as the 'teacher' and who the 'learner'. They were told that if the learner gave an incorrect answer to the teacher's question he would receive punishment in the form of an electric shock. This would be administered by the teacher pressing a switch on an electric shock-generating machine. With each incorrect answer the severity of the shock would increase, in 15-volt stages, up to 450 volts. If the teacher showed any reluctance or concern, the experimenter would give him a verbal instruction to continue, i.e. a direct order to obey.

Milgram asked various groups of professionals what they thought the outcome of such an experiment might be. A group of psychiatrists suggested that most people would refuse to participate once they realized what was involved and that less than 1 per cent of those that did would continue administering shocks to the end. A group of psychology students agreed that most people would drop out by half way, although a few might continue right to the end. Milgram had intended to run this experiment among men and women from several nationalities, including German. If the historians were correct then the students' and psychiatrists' predictions for the high rates of early refusals among the American people would not be found among the Germans. If the Germans were more responsive to authority many more of them should continue to administer the shocks right to the 450-volt maximum.

An advertisement was placed in local papers in New Haven, Connecticut, and a postal questionnaire also sent out, asking for men between 20 and 50, and from all walks of life, who would be

▶ The 1950s saw the application of scientific techniques to social psychological issues. One of the first to be studied was conformity, and by the early 1960s Milgram had extended work on conformity to include the study of obedience.

▶ This was a very controversial experiment. Can you identify any reasons why?

*The learner is strapped into the chair and electrodes are attached to his wrist. Copyright 1965 by Stanley Milgram. From the film* Obedience, *distributed by Penn State Media Sales*

paid $4.50 to take part in an experiment at Yale University, lasting for about one hour, 'to investigate the relationship between personality and learning'. Milgram selected 40 respondents, including engineers, teachers, salesmen, clerks and manual workers, and arranged appointments for the men to arrive at the Yale Interaction Laboratory.

▶ This is a *self-selected* sample of participants, and although all such samples may appear biased, Milgram was careful to select as representative a group from his respondents as possible.

On arrival each participant met the experimenter and the other participant, who was introduced as 'Mr Wallace'. He was a rather overweight, very mild and pleasant man in his late fifties. And he was, of course, a confederate of Milgram, although the other man believed he was a naive participant, just like himself. To decide who was to be the teacher and who the learner, and make it appear authentic, the two men drew a slip of paper from a hat. Both slips had TEACHER written on them, but Mr Wallace claimed that his said LEARNER. Mr Wallace was strapped into a chair in the next room, in the presence of the naive participant. Electrodes were placed on his hands, at which point he told them that he had recently been in hospital for a heart condition and the doctors had told him to avoid stressful situations. The young, determined-looking experimenter told him that although the shocks may be painful, they would cause no lasting damage.

▶ A naive participant is led to believe that someone is about to receive painful electric shocks as part of a psychology experiment. Any further thoughts about the controversial nature of this experiment? Any thoughts about the ethics of this research?

The 'teacher' was taken into another room where he could not see the learner and was seated in front of the electric shock generator, a rather intimidating machine with a row of 30 toggle switches along the front that were clearly marked in 15-volt steps. Above the switches were the following eight labels:

| 1 | 2 | 3 | 4 | 5 | 6 | 7 | 8 |
|---|---|---|---|---|---|---|---|
| slight shock | moderate shock | strong shock | very strong shock | intense shock | intense to extreme shock | danger: severe shock | XXX |
| 0–60 | 75–120 | 135–180 | 195–240 | 255–300 | 315–360 | 375–420 | 435–450 |

The teacher was instructed to read out ten words in five, unrelated pairs, e.g. 'Door – grass', 'book – carrot', 'brother – sky', 'radio – spoon', 'hill – sail'. After a pause the teacher would say one of the paired words and the learner would have to signal its pair by pressing a switch which illuminated a light on the generator. If the answer was correct the teacher would pass on to the next set of paired words. If not, the teacher had to announce the intensity of the shock, starting with 15 volts, and increasing by 15 volts each time he heard an incorrect answer.

The teacher believed he is to administer increasingly painful electric shocks to another human being. He received a 45-volt sample shock himself at the start of the experiment, just to convince him that the machine was working.

The machine made a grinding sort of sound, as though it was working, although in fact the learner's electrodes weren't connected to it. The teacher heard a tape-recorded series of answers so that every naive teacher always heard the same answers in the same order. The next incorrect response would be punished by 30 volts, the next by 45 volts and so on.

■ Why did Milgram use a tape-recorded series of answers?

As the shocks grew more intense the learner started to complain.

► The experimenter had four 'prods', each one more insistent than the previous one, to try to make the participant continue to obey the instruction to give the next set of words or the next shock.

At 75 volts he began moaning and groaning. At 125 volts he shouted out, 'That really hurts'. At 150 volts he asked to be released from the experiment. At 180 volts he shouted, 'I can't stand the pain, don't do that'. At 195 volts he yelled, 'Let me out, my heart's starting to bother me now'. At 285 volts he screamed in agony. At 300 volts he kicked and hit the wall, and pleaded with them to let him out. At 315 volts he fell silent, and was not heard from again.

During this period most of the teachers became uncomfortable. Clearly they weren't happy at inflicting pain on someone they hardly knew. They looked to the experimenter for guidance. He had four responses that he could give. First he would say 'Please continue' or 'Please go on'. If the teacher still complained about what he was asking them to do, he would reply, more insistently, 'The experiment requires that you continue'. If that failed he would say, 'It's absolutely essential that you go on' and, finally, 'You have no choice, you must go on'. These were the 'special prods' to try to make the participants obey, and continue giving the shocks. In addition the experimenter could accept responsibility for what was happening if the naive participant demanded it. After 315 volts, when the learner stopped responding, the participants were to be told that no answer was to be treated as a wrong answer and that they must continue to administer the shocks.

To summarize, 40 ordinary American men, aged between 20 and 50, were being goaded into continuing to give electric shocks of up to 450 volts, marked as intense shock, severe shock, dangerous shock etc., to a mild and pleasant fellow participant whom they knew to have had a heart condition, beyond a point when they had reason to believe they may have killed him, in return for $4.50. And all because a 30-year-old, rather severe, unfriendly experimenter, dressed in a grey laboratory coat, told them, 'You have no choice, you must go on'. Surely no one would?

### Milgram's conclusions

► All of the participants continued to administer shocks until the learner begged to be released, screamed in agony and kicked the wall as the shock (supposedly) threw him across the room. Only five of the 40 refused at this point.

Of the 40 men in the first experiment, 26 continued to give the shocks, right up to the maximum of 450 volts. That is, 65 per cent of the sample allowed themselves to be bullied into (as they believed) causing pain, continuing to the point of possibly causing death, to a fellow human being, just because a man in a grey laboratory coat whom they had never met before and weren't likely ever to meet again, told them that they must. None of the participants refused to give shocks at the beginning, and all continued until 300 volts ('intense shock'), and even then only five finally refused. Nine more dropped out between 315 and 375 volts. The rest continued to 450 volts.

Lack of refusal to continue did not, however, mean lack of concern. Most participants sweated, complained to and swore at the experimenter, several had seizures (one so violently that the experiment was terminated and medical assistance was sought). They trembled and stuttered, bit their lips and clenched their hands so tightly that they dug their nails into their flesh. But despite their distress most of them still continued to obey.

Milgram couldn't believe that his findings were correct. His sample must surely be hopelessly biased? Could people so easily be made to inflict pain on others? His findings suggest that the same is true of obedience as of conformity, that there isn't an 'obedient personality character' any more than there is a 'conforming personality character'. Rather, there are circumstances under which most people can be made to obey and to conform. Milgram decided to investigate further the factors that promoted obedience, using variations of his experimental design.

### Variations of Milgram's research

Some of Milgram's main conclusions about the situational factors involved in obedience are described below.

One factor in the likelihood of obedience seems to be the confidence the participant has in the institution in whose name the orders are given. If we believe that the orders come from a legitimate, trustworthy source, we are more likely to obey them. In debriefing sessions some of Milgram's participants said that they continued giving shocks because they knew they were involved in research at a famous university where nothing bad would be allowed to happen. Milgram (1974) says: 'A substantial proportion of people do what they are told to do, irrespective of the content of the act and without limitations of conscience, so long as they perceive that the command comes from a legitimate authority.'

Milgram rented some offices in a rather run-down block in nearby Bridgeport, Connecticut, which he regarded as an 'average' American town. His newspaper adverts asked for volunteers to take part in some privately funded market research. Apart from that, the experimental procedure was identical. This time half of his sample refused to give shocks, but nearly 50 per cent still went on to the end.

Showing participants that other courses of action are possible also seems important. Milgram introduced a similar variation to that used by Asch ten years previously. He arranged for the naive participant to associate with two other teachers (who were confederates) who refused to continue at 150 and 210 volts respectively. In this situation, only 10 per cent of the naive participants obeyed up to 450 volts. Having a model or someone to take the lead in non-obedience seems important. Many of the participants said things like 'I didn't realize I could refuse'.

Having someone else to blame for the consequences of one's obedience appears to be important, too. In another variation there were two teachers, one being a confederate. The real naive participant read out the word pairs, and the confederate gave the shocks; 95 per cent of the naive participants now went to 450 volts. They reasoned that it wasn't their fault, they were only reading words. They argued that the man who was giving the shocks should have taken some action if he was worried about what he was doing to the other fellow.

Another influential factor is having the authority figure close at

■ **Summarize the conclusions from Milgram's first experiment on obedience.**

► People still tend to obey if they perceive that the person giving the orders has the authority to do so, even though the organization doesn't appear to have any authority at all.

► Where someone else behaves in a non-compliant manner, others may also refuse to obey.

► Being able to place responsibility for the consequences of our action elsewhere increases the likelihood that we will obey the orders for that action.

► The nearer the person who gives the order is to the person who is expected to obey it, the more likely it is that it will be obeyed.

■ How would Donald Campbell's theory (see page 55) explain why closing the distance between the teacher and the learner in Milgram's experiment decreases the likelihood of obedience? What are the main social or situational factors affecting the likelihood of obedience?

► Milgram explains the high levels of obedience in terms of the hierarchical structure of society, and the demands of the particular situation.

■ How does Milgram explain obedience?

hand to give the orders. In another variation, the experimenter left the room after explaining the procedure and issued all instructions by telephone. Considerably fewer participants now obeyed the orders to give increasingly painful shocks. In a third variation the experimenter was never present, but left instructions on a tape-recorder. Only about 20 per cent now obeyed, and many gave lower shocks than those required by the experiment. Why do something they found upsetting when no one could know if they obeyed fully or not?

The distance between the teacher and the learner was varied in later experiments. It was found that the closer the learner was placed to the teacher the greater were the refusals to obey. Even so, at half a metre distant, 40 per cent continued to give the maximum shock and when the teacher actually had to put the learner's hand onto an electric plate 30 per cent still continued to the end.

Variations on Milgram's research have been conducted in other countries. Mantell (1971) sampled German males and found 85 per cent went to the end. This isn't as significant as it might seem, and doesn't really support the idea that Germans are much more susceptible to authority than Americans.

A cautionary note: Milgram tested over 1,000 participants, almost all of whom were male. Only in one of the variations did he test women, and then only 40 of them. Any conclusions we draw from Milgram's research ought therefore to be confined to males. When Kilham and Mann (1974) repeated the experiments in Australia, 40 per cent of males obeyed, and 16 per cent of women did.

So why do people obey? Milgram offers several explanations. One is the 'foot in the door' technique employed by some sales people. They start by asking for a little – Milgram simply wanted co-operation and an hour of their time. He made the participants feel committed by paying them and telling them they were helping in scientific research. The first stages only involved giving a few, painless electric shocks and, once started, it became difficult to refuse – after all, they were only giving an extra 15 volts, and if they didn't object previously, why object now? There was also the authority figure who would ultimately take responsibility. By the time they were half way through they had become desensitized to the effects of their behaviour on the victim. These situational factors can be seen in other areas of social life, and they are the single most important factor in why we conform and obey.

In addition, we live in a hierarchical society where orders are always handed down to us – from parents, teachers, older children, other adults, the police. These rules and conventions come to represent our culture. Neighbourly living demands co-operation and we are 'programmed' to obey. Milgram identifies two 'states' of mind which we must adopt in order to accept the responsibilities and rights of social living. In the personal state we have autonomy to choose what to do. In the agency state we are acting on behalf of someone else and must do what we are told. Milgram's participants said that they wouldn't have given those shocks if they hadn't felt that they were required to – it was what they were there for.

There seemed little point in contrasting other nations' willingness to obey since it became apparent that there wasn't an 'obedient personality type', but rather that situational factors were responsible. If anything, Milgram's findings are even more disturbing than those of Asch. The percentage of people who could be made to behave in such an extreme way was higher than in Asch's experiments, and the consequences of their obedience were so much more serious. They protested and became disturbed, but only the minority refused to obey.

## Some criticisms of Milgram's work

### Ethical unacceptability

**Diane Baumrind** (1964) complained that Milgram's work was unethical since he exposed his participants to unacceptable levels of stress and discomfort, and that the research should have been stopped. Milgram wrote: 'In a large number of cases the degree of tension reached extremes that are rarely seen in sociopsychological laboratory studies. Participants were observed to sweat, tremble, stutter, bite their lips, groan, and dig their fingernails into their flesh. These were characteristic rather than exceptional responses to the experiment   on one occasion we observed a seizure so violently convulsive that it was necessary to call a halt to the experiment.'

Baumrind claims that research that can have these effects should not be conducted. Who can say what the long-term effects of knowing that one is capable of such behaviour might be? Milgram made the following points in his defence.

First, he had not foreseen that so many participants would obey to the end, or that those who refused would take so long to do so. He believed that most would have refused to obey the 'authority' long before 300 volts was administered. He did not intend his participants to suffer such distress, and did not anticipate that they would. He also pointed out that participants were free to stop at any time; all they had to do was refuse to obey the experimenter.

Milgram denied that any permanent harm would be caused to the participants. They were all debriefed after the experiment, and reunited with the learner confederate. These were usually very emotional scenes, sometimes with the naive participant embracing the confederate as though he were a long unseen brother. Milgram also sent out a summary of the conclusions and a follow-up questionnaire asking each participant for their feelings and opinions. He claimed that 80 per cent said they were pleased to have taken part in the research, and that more research of this nature should take place. Only 1 per cent said they were sorry to have been included.

### Representativeness of the sample

Although Milgram chose a cross-section of the population, they were male volunteers who read a particular paper. Some groups are

► Baumrind claims that Milgram's research should have been abandoned on the grounds of ethics, and the harm he was causing to his participants.

► Milgram claimed that he never intended that his participants should suffer and that they didn't come to any real harm in the long term. On the other hand, he claims that we have learned a great deal about the nature of conformity from his studies.

► Milgram's experimental situation may not have reflected real life, but he claims that it does reflect the processes involved in real life decisions about obedience.

■ Outline Baumrind's criticisms of Milgram's research, and the points Milgram makes in his defence.

less likely, however, to volunteer to take part in this research, for example, few wealthy people would volunteer. Further, even a representative cross-section of the population of one town may not be a valid measure of American behaviour, since that town may not be typical of all American towns.

However, Milgram used a relatively large sample and we have no reason to believe that the male residents of New Haven are much different from other American males: similar results have also been found by other researchers in other countries. Even if we reject Milgram's precise figures, we can't deny that a disturbingly large number of people were prepared to obey in a frightening way, on the instructions of a man who appeared to represent some kind of authority.

*Generalizability of findings to everyday obedience*
Milgram argues that the processes involved in obeying the authority figure in his experiment are much the same as those involved in obeying people generally, and that there is a correspondence between his findings and 'real life'. He points out that the situation certainly felt 'real' to his participants at the time.

► Whether you accept Milgram's justification or believe that Baumrind's first impressions are correct, Milgram's research has taught us a great deal about how humans perceive authority, and how willingly they obey it.

### Evaluation of Milgram's research
Although much criticism has been levelled at Milgram's research, he has provided one of the most fascinating and controversial psychological experiments. The usual criticisms of social psychological research concern the ethics of its conduct, the representativeness of its sample, and its applicability to 'real life'. However, Milgram has alerted us to the ease with which those who give the orders can have them obeyed, and for us to be vigilant in ensuring, as far as we are able, that power is given only to those people who will exercise it for the good of all of those who are subordinate to it.

■ Summarize the objections to Milgram's research and the benefits of doing the research. Do the benefits outweigh the objections?

## Other studies of obedience

Situational obedience was also investigated by **Bickman** (1974), and more recently by **Beattie**. For example, Bickman had confederates approach strangers on a New York street and ask them either to pick up some litter, or to give some money to someone who had none. Beattie had a confederate act as a stranded motorist in Manchester, and another ask passers by for 20p for the parking meter. Both researchers had the enquirer wearing either everyday clothes or some kind of uniform. Bickman found that 40 per cent of people obeyed when the enquirer was normally dressed, increasing to 80 per cent when the enquirer was in uniform. Beattie found that when the stranded motorist was a woman, almost all people gave the money regardless of the enquirer's dress. When it was a man, 30 per cent gave 20p when asked by a normally dressed confederate, increasing to 60 per cent in uniform. A uniform is a badge of power, and we have learned the response to power is obedience. (Would researchers obtain the same results if they asked for a pound or more?)

**Hofling** (1966) also demonstrated the importance of power. He placed capsules containing glucose in the medicine cupboards of 22 American psychiatric hospitals. The labels read 'Aastrofen' and stated the maximum daily dose was 10 milligrams, which must not be exceeded. A confederate, calling himself 'Doctor Smith', telephoned the duty nurse instructing her to give 20 milligrams to one of his patients. Apart from being twice the maximum dose, hospital regulations also demanded that drugs can only be given after written authority from a known doctor; 21 of the 22 nurses prepared to administer the drug (before being stopped by a hidden observer). They said that doctors often prescribed drugs by telephone and they were frightened to disobey the doctor's authority.

## Zimbardo's study of obedience

During the 1960s stories appeared in the American press about alleged brutality in some American prisons. It was claimed that some prisoners had been robbed and humiliated, beaten and tortured, and even killed by some of their homicidal guards. Could it be that American prisons were staffed by sociopathic sadists? If so, why weren't masses of prisoners and ex-prisoners complaining to every possible civil rights and government organization? Are American criminals naturally submissive and accepting of injustice and hardship? In view of the claims so far that social and environmental factors are more influential than personality types in explaining conformity and obedience, could it be that the social environment, roles and relationships within prisons create the tendency for guards to be aggressive and prisoners to be submissive?

In 1972 **P.G. Zimbardo** published the findings from his experimental study of a 'mock prison', known as the Stanford Prison experiment. Zimbardo believed that the 'social psychological environment' of the prison experience would explain the dominant and submissive roles adopted by guards and prisoners. To test this he set up a mock prison, using paid volunteers, and he observed how their relationships changed.

▶ Zimbardo believes that social psychological pressures make people dominant and aggressive or submissive and dependent.

We will examine Zimbardo's experiment under three headings, representing the three stages: preparation, procedure and conclusions.

### Preparation (the sample)

Zimbardo placed national newspaper advertisements for male university students to take part in a functional simulation of a prison. They would be required for eight hours a day and would be paid $15 a day for their trouble. The research was to take two weeks. Zimbardo received over 100 replies. He gave personality inventories and various tests and interviews to ensure these middle-class and well-educated people were psychologically 'normal', had no history of drug abuse or major convictions, were emotionally stable and physically healthy. From the original sample he chose 25 healthy, stable participants. All said they would prefer to play the role of a prisoner, but they were randomly divided into prisoners

■ Compare Zimbardo's method of recruitment with Sherif's, Asch's and Milgram's. Why did Zimbardo place adverts where he did?

and guards. There were therefore no differences between the students playing the part of either.

*Procedure*

Zimbardo went to great lengths to create the impression that the participants were undergoing a 'real prison experience'. The 'prisoners' were arrested, without warning, by police on a Sunday morning (much to the surprise of their neighbours!). They were accused of some crime, read their rights, handcuffed and taken to the local police station. Here they were treated like every other criminal. They were fingerprinted, photographed and 'booked'. Then they were blindfolded and driven to the psychology department of Stanford University, where Zimbardo had had the basement set out as a prison, with barred doors and windows, bare walls and small cells. Here the *deindividuation* process began.

Zimbardo (1988) defines deindividuation as 'a psychological process in which a set of antecedent variables reduces one's identifiability and self awareness'. There are two kinds of antecedent variables. First, there are cues that inform the individual that they will be held accountable for their action. If a group of people are all doing something, then any individual member may feel less responsible for their actions. (Diffusion of responsibility is discussed in the next chapter.) The second set of variables operates to reduce our individual perceptions and standards of morally acceptable behaviour, and we may allow ourselves to behave in ways we wouldn't behave when not part of a crowd.

When the prisoners arrived at the prison they were stripped naked, deloused, had all their personal possessions removed and locked away, and were given prison clothes and bedding. Their clothes comprised a smock with their number written on it, but no underclothes. They also had a tight nylon cap, and a chain around one ankle.

They were only to be allowed visits from the chaplain and from their relations. They were to be locked in their cells all the time, except when let out for work, toilet privileges or head counts. Toilets were allowed only until 10 p.m. After that the prisoners had to use buckets. There were no shower facilities. Each cell measured two by three metres, and was to sleep three men. Apart from the cells there was 'the hole', a small converted storage cupboard where men could be kept in solitary confinement for fairly short periods if they broke one of the prison 'rules'.

To assist in the deindividuation process, feelings of dependency on the guards were fostered. The prisoners needed a guard's permission for almost everything. They were not allowed to smoke, use the toilet or write a letter (which they could only do on prison notepaper) without a guard's permission. They had no knowledge of the time either. All clocks, radios and so on were removed.

Just as in a real prison, the guards were also deindividuated. They wore authentic khaki uniforms and had silver reflector sunglasses (making eye contact and any kind of personal relationship

▶ *Deindividuation* is the loss of one's sense of individuality as one becomes just another member of a group. Institutionalized mental patients, prisoners and people who work in prisons, or people who do things as part of a mob which they wouldn't do when alone, are said to be deindividuated.

▶ Removing the prisoners' personal possessions and dressing them in identical clothes makes them more anonymous. Anonymity is an essential part of deindividuation.

▶ The conditions in Zimbardo's prison were primitive and unpleasant, and were thought to be fairly realistic.

▶ Most prisons have lists of rules, many of them quite petty and probably unnecessary, which are often strictly enforced. They also have a role in deindividuation since they encourage prisoners to become dependent on the guards. The guards in Zimbardo's prison were allowed to encourage prisoners who were slow to obey by pushing them, but any stronger physical violence was forbidden.

that is facilitated by eye contact impossible). They also had short clubs, whistles, handcuffs, and the keys to cells and the main gate. The guards worked shifts and were allowed home in between. They had offices along the corridor.

When they first arrived the guards were instructed to maintain law and order in the prison, and to make the prisoners aware of the 16 prison rules which they would enforce. For example, there must be silence after lights out, prisoners must eat at mealtimes and not eat at any other time. Tampering with walls was forbidden, and prisoners had to address each other by number only. Meanwhile, they had to address a guard as 'Mr correctional officer, sir'. The final rule was that the failure to obey any of the rules might result in punishment. Having explained the set-up, the investigators left the prison and went into other areas from where they could observe and record what went on through spy holes and one-way mirrors.

## Zimbardo's conclusions

Within a very short time both guards and prisoners were settling into their new roles, the guards adopting theirs quickly and easily. Within hours of beginning the experiment some guards began to harass prisoners. They behaved in a brutal and sadistic manner, apparently enjoying it. Other guards joined in, and other prisoners were also tormented. The prisoners were taunted with insults and petty orders, they were given pointless and boring tasks to accomplish, and they were generally dehumanized.

The prisoners soon adopted prisoner-like behaviour, too. They talked about prison issues a great deal of the time. They 'told tales' on each other to the guards. They started taking the prison rules very seriously, as though they were there for the prisoners' benefit and infringement would spell disaster for all of them. Some even began siding with the guards against prisoners who did not conform to the rules.

The result of the changing perceptions producing changing relationships was that the prisoners became depressed and began belittling themselves, which increased their feelings of hopelessness. A vicious circle was set up. The more the prisoners thought of themselves as useless and without hope, the more the guards despised them and increased their humiliation. As the prisoners became more submissive, the guards became more aggressive and assertive. They demanded ever greater obedience from the prisoners. The prisoners were dependent on the guards for everything, so they tried to find ways to please the guards, such as telling tales on fellow prisoners. As the prisoners were so dependent on the guards' good will, the guards sought more authority and new ways to degrade the prisoners. So the vicious circle went on.

One prisoner had to be released after 36 hours because of uncontrollable bursts of screaming, crying and anger. His thinking became disorganized and he appeared to be entering the early stages of a deep depression. Within the next few days three others also had to leave after showing signs of emotional disorder that

■ **What is deindividuation?**

▶ Overall, Zimbardo's simulation bears a strong resemblance to a real prison and the relationships between prisoners and guards that exist there.

▶ The guards had expectations of their own superior role, and of the prisoners' inferior one, which they soon exploited, and some guards began dehumanizing some of the prisoners. Yet all these people were educated and emotionally stable, with perfectly 'normal' personalities, and had been randomly allocated the role of guard and prisoner.

▶ In a real prison with real prisoners and real guards (all of whom aren't intelligent and stable and where people are together for years, the relationships and interpersonal behaviour between guards and prisoners will probably be worse than described here.

■ **How did the social relationships between guard and prisoner change?**

could have had lasting consequences. (These were people who had been pronounced stable and normal a short while before.)

Zimbardo had intended that the experiment should run for a fortnight, but on the sixth day he closed it down. There was real danger that someone might be physically or mentally damaged if it was allowed to run on. After some time for the researchers to gather their data, the participants were called back for a follow-up debriefing session.

*The follow-up*

Most of the participants said they had felt involved and committed. The research had felt 'real' to them. One guard said: 'I was surprised at myself. I made them call each other names and clean the toilets out with their bare hands. I practically considered the prisoners cattle and I kept thinking I had to watch out for them in case they tried something.' Another guard said: 'Acting authoritatively can be fun. Power can be a great pleasure.' And another: 'during the inspection I went to cell 2 to mess up a bed which a prisoner had just made and he grabbed me, screaming that he had just made it and that he was not going to let me mess it up. He grabbed me by the throat and although he was laughing I was pretty scared. I lashed out with my stick and hit him on the chin, although not very hard, and when I freed myself I became angry.'

Most of the guards found it difficult to believe that they had behaved in the brutalizing ways that they had. Many said they hadn't known this side of them existed or that they were capable of such things. The prisoners too couldn't believe that they had responded in the submissive, cowering, dependent way they had. Several claimed to be assertive types normally. When asked about the guards they described the usual three stereotypes that can be found in any prison: some guards were good, some were tough but fair, some were cruel.

Zimbardo was convinced that anyone was capable of the stereotyped behaviour of the guards. His participants had been randomly allocated to play the part of guard or prisoner, so such differences in their perceptions of one another must be a function of the situation, and not of their personality.

In any situation where one group has power over another there is a tendency for the superior group to dominate the inferior group. The greater the gap between the two groups (as in this experiment), the greater will be the tendency to dominate. At the same time, the inferior group will try to protect or improve its status by appeasing the dominant group, even including rejecting dissident members of its own group. Far from appeasing, however, this has the effect of making the dominant group more resentful of the inferior group, and more harshly disposed towards it.

### Evaluation of Zimbardo's research

Zimbardo attempted to overcome the highly controlled procedures for investigating obedience that Milgram had used. Since it wasn't

► Zimbardo concludes that any social situation involves certain roles, e.g. prison guard, teacher, mother. When someone starts to play the roles their perceptions of what is the other's role – prisoners, pupils, children – becomes distorted.

■ What is Zimbardo's explanation for how some people can behave so brutally towards others?

feasible to conduct a natural observation (see Chapter 17) in a real prison, he showed the usefulness of role play. Whilst the participants may well have known that 'this was just a study', the extent to which their behaviour changed was enough to illustrate the importance of situational factors, and the relative lack of influence of personality factors, in obedience.

■ Identify the ethical objections that might be made of Zimbardo's research. How could the research be defended against these objections?

### Summary – Studies of obedience

Milgram's 'electric shock' experiments were radical and alarming. Combined with the findings from Hofling, Bickman, Beattie and Zimbardo, we have a convincing picture of the influence of power and authority in society, and how we internalize obedience to it.

## POWER AND LEADERSHIP

Power refers to a person or group's ability to have their will obeyed. Most groups, from large nations to small friendship groups, have leaders. According to **Max Weber**, leadership results from such factors as possessing rational, legal authority, by being elected or promoted within the police or military. Charismatic leaders have engaging personalities that people are drawn to follow. Traditional leaders can be found in family firms, where the owner's son becomes the next leader. Bureaucratic leaders draw their authority from the structure of their organization. Psychological research has investigated leadership as a function of the individual personality and so looks for leadership characteristics within certain people, and leadership as a function of the situation, where the requirements of a successful leader vary with the context of the group.

► Power is the ability to have your wishes obeyed. Authority is legalized power.

## The leadership characteristics approach

Early psychological studies supported the nature view, claiming that leaders possessed certain characteristics or *traits* that made them leaders, and which non-leaders therefore did not possess. These traits are fairly fixed and do not vary with the situation. This is sometimes called the 'great man theory'. If there were identifiable personal characteristics or personality traits to leaders, then potential leaders could be spotted early and groomed for leadership. The future performance of their organizations could be predicted and measured. This might improve the efficiency of the whole management process.

Of all the studies that have been conducted on leaders and leadership, no particular personal characteristics have been found that explain why the person who possessed them became the leader. Early studies claimed that leaders were usually slightly more intelligent, more actively involved, more dominant, more self-confident

► A *trait* is our understanding of someone's characteristics that allows us to know what they are like, and what they are likely to do. NB traits are not the characteristics themselves.

▶ Borgatta's conclusions are an example of a *circular argument*. Air Force officers are leaders. They score high on tests of leadership traits. People who score high on such tests must therefore be leaders.

and concerned with achievement. They also come from higher social class backgrounds (Stodgill and Coons 1957). Borgatta (1954) claimed that US Air Force officers scored higher on tests of leadership traits than others. However, since we don't know what 'leadership traits' are, we may assume that Borgatta was measuring those characteristics that successful military officers possess, so his findings are hardly surprising. The only factor that could contribute to someone being seen as a leader is physical attraction, since we are more likely to be attracted to people who are good-looking, truthful, sincere, honest and loyal (see Chapter 2). They may find themselves being regarded as the natural leader in some groups. But not all attractive, intelligent, sincere, loyal or honest people become great leaders.

**J.E. McGrath** (1964) gives five reasons why the idea that leaders are born rather than made is false. First, psychologists do not agree about which personality traits are involved in leadership with which to compare leaders with non-leaders. Second, different observers may believe that different members of the same group could appear to be its leader. Third, the 'great man' idea ignores the relationships between members of the group that will determine how effectively things are done. Fourth, in concentrating on the individuals, the influence of the situation in which the group operates is ignored. And finally, groups often have different leaders for different tasks.

Further, different leaders have different styles of leadership, even if we cannot identify these styles as personality characteristics. **Ronald Lippit** and **Ralph White** (1947) investigated the effects of different leadership styles on groups of 11-year-old children in four boys' clubs over seven weeks. The relationships between club members and leaders were recorded for comparison later. Three leadership styles were employed. *Democratic* leaders ensure that 'decisions are a matter of group decisions and group discussion', and they discuss and direct, they listen and judge, they encourage and praise. *Authoritarian* leaders issue instructions and do not welcome questions or suggestions. They expect obedience and performance, and punish where this is not forthcoming. For them, 'all policies … should be determined by the leader'. *Laissez-faire* leadership 'leaves complete freedom for group or individual decisions', so fails to provide guidance and help, suggestions for achievement, or discipline. When children had democratic leadership they were better adjusted, sociable and co-operative. When they had either of the other styles they were aggressive and unco-operative. They couldn't organize themselves and appeared generally discontented.

How far does this reflect a leadership trait as opposed to an effective style of leadership? Brown (1985) said the democratic leadership style was most effective because it was the dominant style of government and leadership in America at the time, although to what extent 11-year-old children would be aware of this is questionable, even if American government and leadership could have been regarded as democratic.

▶ One problem with interpreting psychological research is that we must be on guard against cultural biases. Because some result is found in the West does not mean that it would necessarily be found elsewhere. It may be a function of culture, not of human psychology.

■ How successful have psychologists been in identifying the personality characteristics involved in leadership?

## *The situational approach*

During the 1950s the nature view was declining in the face of opposition from behaviourist, cognitive and humanist forces in psychology, although interest in personality traits was still popular. Attention shifted from what personal characteristics make a good leader to what the features of the particular situation are that make this particular leader effective. This approach was partially adopted by **Fred Fiedler** (1967). He doesn't reject the idea that leadership is a personality factor, but looks for the situational factors that make and maintain leadership.

Fiedler suggests a *contingency model*. This means that the most effective leader is the one whose personality and leadership style best suit the needs of the organization he or she leads. Sympathetic and understanding leaders are most effective in running organizations that involve sympathy and understanding, such as those in the caring professions. Aggressive and competitive leaders thrive in organizations that have to compete to win, such as business. The contingency model suggests that a sympathetic and relaxed leader would be hopelessly ineffective in a competitive organization.

► Fiedler's *contingency model* stresses the important role of the particular circumstances in the organization which influence both 'leadership' and 'following' behaviour.

Fiedler argued that an effective leader must be able to keep his or her '*psychological distance*' from the co-workers. The leader 'must be willing to reject co-workers who do not adequately perform their jobs. This requires emotional independence and detachment from others. The person who readily forms deep emotional ties with his subordinates, who needs to be liked or supported by his men, will find it difficult to discipline or discharge them, since this may decrease his popularity or cause him to lose their friendship'. To do this requires psychological distance. Further research among many different kinds of groups, from farming co-operatives to aircraft bomber crews, revealed that there are grades of psychological distance.

► *Psychological distance* is a vague concept that Fiedler needed to refine. There must be degrees of it, and it must vary over time and as conditions change.

Fiedler developed the 'Least Preferred Co-worker' (LPC) scale, whereby leaders rate their most and least preferred co-workers. *Relationship-oriented* leaders give a fairly high score, even to their least preferred co-workers, and tend to be more considerate, lenient and indulgent towards all their workers. *Task-oriented* leaders (low LPC) were most successful in organizations where the leader was either highly regarded by his followers, or they thought very little of him indeed, where the tasks to be accomplished were either clearly structured or very unstructured, or where the leader occupied quite a powerful position, or had very little effective power (to give rewards to his followers). Where the situation was intermediate between those variables, relationship-oriented (high LPC) leaders did best.

► *Relationship-oriented* leaders are considerate towards the needs and feelings of co-workers and clients. They will be most effective in the caring professions.

► *Task-oriented* leaders are more concerned with achieving targets and maintain the greatest psychological distance.

■ **How does Fiedler's contingency theory explain leadership?**

Critics of Fiedler's model suggest that the LPC score method is too unreliable since it varies with time. As leaders mature, or are influenced externally, their perceptions of their task and their co-workers may change. Psychological distance alters with greater interaction. A subordinate who had never seemed very appealing may do something that makes him or her more highly favoured.

**Rice** et al. (1980) reviewed Fiedler's and other studies which used the LPC and found inconsistencies and variations in what the LPC was supposed to be measuring. They also argued that Fiedler puts too much emphasis on the leader as a fixed personal characteristic, and too little on the interactive nature of leadership. However, the contingency model does suggest a useful distinction between emergence of leaders, and their effectiveness, and we shall use this distinction now.

### Emergence of leaders

We mentioned Weber's categories of leadership earlier (see page 67). Collins and Raven (1969) identified six sources of social power from which leaders emerge. These are: the ability to give various kinds of rewards, to punish rebels, to appear as someone with whom the others wish to identify, possessing expert knowledge about the task, having the position because of legitimate authority, and possessing particular knowledge about the situation which only the leader knows.

Bales and Slater (1955) observed several discussions amongst small groups of people. They found that those who contributed most often were more likely to be perceived as one of two kinds of leader, one who contributes to the topic of the discussion, and one who works to maintain group coherence, leading Bales (1970) to suggest that most groups have a 'task specialist', and a 'social emotional specialist'. Few leaders managed both roles. Hamblin (1958) suggests that crises also bring out qualities of calm and efficient organization in people who wouldn't otherwise have been thought of as leaders.

One observable factor in the emergence of leaders is that leaders talk more than other people. (This is sometimes called the 'blabbermouth theory' of leadership!) So long as what they are saying is reasonably intelligent, those who talk the most are most likely to be perceived by other members of the group as being most intelligent. In an experiment conducted in the early 1960s, Bavelas divided his participants into discussion groups, with four people in each, and asked them to discuss various topics. He noted how much each of them spoke. Some people dominated the conversation, others were more reticent. Most of the group members had more favourable impressions of those who spoke most.

Bavelas wondered whether contributions to the discussion could be increased by feedback, and if so, whether this would alter the group's perception of the speakers. Bavelas told each group that the contribution of each of its members was to be evaluated by the experimenters, and the members were to receive feedback on their performance. A green light meant their contribution was valuable, a red one signalled that their contributions were unhelpful. The lights actually had nothing to do with the quality of the contribution at all.

▶ Inevitably, LPC will vary with time and experience and has been criticized for being unreliable.

Each time a previously reticent person spoke, the green light came on. They began to participate more. Their posture changed too. They sat more upright and looked more confident. After the session the other group members rated them higher on aspects of leadership such as ability and the quality of their ideas.

Spatial position is also significant. The person who stands in front of the fire, with his or her back to it, may be assumed to be an important person. In offices the occupier usually sits in a slightly higher chair than that provided for visitors, looking down on them as they sit in front of him or her. Superiors are more likely to walk around their desk to stand beside and look down on them. Looking down on someone may give the leader some kind of psychological advantage.

In 1961 Sommer published the findings of an experiment in which five or six people were formed into groups and one was appointed leader. They were asked to enter a room in which there was a rectangular table, and take their seats. The leader usually chose to sit at one of the ends of the table. The position next to him was occupied by the next 'most important person'. This had implications for the choice of foreman of juries in criminal trials. A study by Strodtbeck and Hook (1958) showed that the jury person sitting at the end position is over four times more likely to be elected foreman than anyone else.

## Effectiveness of leaders

Effective leaders use their personal skills, such as verbal and non-verbal communication, and rewarding personality to ensure compliance with their requests. They also use and modify the environment in order to maximize their effectiveness. Having a bigger office and larger desk are signs that the occupier is superior. Fiedler's contingency model says that the most effective leader is one whose leadership style fits the needs of the organization; however, Lippit and White found the democratic style of leadership was generally more effective at producing happy and productive children.

In discussing attraction in Chapter 2 we described the exchange theory, which suggests that we act in selfish ways by trying to have our partner invest more in our relationship than we do, so that we are 'in profit'. This is a (capitalist) economic analysis. Something similar has been used here, whereby the effectiveness of the leader is judged by the productivity of the group. Roethlisberger and Dickson (1939) studied groups of workers at the Hawthorne works of the Western Electric Company in Chicago, and found that the groups headed by task-oriented managers were less productive compared to those with relationship-oriented leaders.

Stodgill and Coons (1957) suggested that leaders could be measured on two scales, and their outcomes could predict their effectiveness as a leader. These were the *initiative–structure dimension*, referring to how flexibly they organize the worker's tasks and

▶ Bavelas found that increasing the amount of participation of a given member also increased the other group members' favourable perceptions of him or her.

■ (a) In view of the evidence, list the main points for and against the view that leaders are born not made.
(b) What environmental and situational factors contribute to the emergence of leaders?

▶ The contingency model says the most effective leader is the one whose approach reflects the needs of the part of the organization that they lead. Lippit and White's research suggests that generally the most effective leader is one whose style is democratic. Both ignore the contribution of the non-leaders. What do they want and expect from their leaders?

► The research on leadership has sometimes failed to take account of the nature of the group. How useful is it to assume that research on 11-year-olds, factory workers and military officers will have much in common? They all ignore the dynamic interaction that occurs between members of groups at many levels.

► A funeral director who referees football matches in his spare time had better bring the appropriate style of leadership to these two situations!

► Successful leaders must provide direction, but also be aware of the needs and feelings of the people they lead. Otherwise they become distant and unapproachable, and their popularity (and probably their influence) declines.

■ What makes an effective leader?

provide guidance and support. The *consideration dimension* refers to how they viewed their relationships with their members. They claimed that leaders who were either task- or relationship-centred were most effective, although Blake and Moulton (1982) argue that the leader who is both driven by the needs of the task and concerned with the welfare of group members is most effective.

House (1971) claims that these views are too simple, portraying leaders as passive individuals who bring their only approach to the groups they lead. Yet most people are dynamic and can vary their responses to suit the needs of the situation. House suggests the *path–goal* theory of leadership, which claims that the leader's expectations and the group members' understanding of them will be the main influences on the leader's effectiveness. A leader who treats members as important individuals with their own skills to contribute and who expects commitment and achievement is likely to get it. One who expects laziness and lack of commitment will get that. So the most effective leaders organize the group's activities so that members can fulfil their own personal goals. Effective leaders therefore have high expectations, provide realistically achievable goals, foster supportive relationships, and convincingly communicate the organization's goals.

Successful leaders, therefore, are popular with their followers, inspiring them to work well, at the same time as bringing success to the group. They are also influenced by their followers. They must be attentive to their followers' ideas and needs so that they can respond flexibly and with understanding to them. According to Turner (1991), almost anyone can be an effective leader, depending on the group they are leading, the task or activity, and the situation in which the group operates.

### Summary – Power and leadership

Leaders exercise power over those they lead; remembering the relative willingness most people have shown in the past to obey orders, psychologists have been interested in whether leaders are born or made, and what factors are involved in leaders remaining effective. As with conformity and obedience, situational factors including verbal and non-verbal communication, spatial positioning, physical appearance, the use of language, and the extent of task or relationship orientation have been found to be more influential than innate or early acquired personality traits.

## COLLECTIVE BEHAVIOUR

William Shakespeare said that 'No man is an island'. We are all members of groups that make up our society, and we all participate in necessary activities such as acquiring food (shopping?), going to work (on buses and trains?), entertainment (in pubs, restaurants, cinemas, theatres?), going on holiday (from airports in aircraft?), and so on. Few of us can avoid being a member of a crowd sometimes, and for most of us this isn't a problem. Most people go about their shopping, business, entertainments, holidays etc. in peace. Some people find being in a crowd a pleasant experience, for example football fans supporting their team, or fans of a pop group at their concert. Sharing your emotions with like-minded people can be rewarding.

Unfortunately, some crowds become destructive mobs, and it is these that have attracted most psychological research.

## Crowd behaviour and aggression

**Gustave Le Bon** (1895) suggested the first theory of crowd activity. He thought that crowds generally were potentially, if not actually, bad. Le Bon had studied crowd behaviour during the French Revolution. He thought that crowd behaviour takes on primitive, destructive forces of its own. People, he thought, act irrationally in large groups, allowing themselves to be influenced and led by the behaviour of the others, to the point of losing their own sense of individuality or decency. Despite there being very little further research, or evidence for Le Bon's theory, it became very popular and has been quoted to justify strongarm police tactics against New Age travellers, groups of young people at Notting Hill Carnivals in the past, industrial disputes, and other action involving crowds.

### Studies in crowd behaviour

Philip Zimbardo supports Le Bon's idea that crowd behaviour can lead to aggression. He quotes several research studies that support his belief that 'conditions which foster anonymity lead people to behave aggressively, or in other anti-social ways which they are given the opportunity to do so' (Zimbardo 1988). Earlier we described how Zimbardo deliberately deindividuated the participants in his prison simulation experiment (see pages 64–5).

To illustrate the role of deindividuation and aggression in groups, Zimbardo had two groups of four, similar, female college students. The members of one group were dressed in 'baggy lab coats and hoods that covered their faces. They sat in a darkened room and were never referred to by name'. The members of the other group wore their own clothes, saw each other's faces, and were referred to by their name. They also wore name badges to make them easily identifiable. Each was asked to give electric shocks to two other female volunteers to see 'their ability to perform under stress' (Zimbardo 1970).

All the participants heard tape-recorded interviews with the two 'volunteers' (who were actually confederates of Zimbardo). One of them was portrayed as obnoxious and 'bitchy', the other as warm and kind. The deindividuated group gave shocks to both the volunteers that were twice as long as the clearly identifiable group, regardless of whether they imagined the 'victim' was pleasant or horrid. The easily identified group gave even shorter shocks to the warm, kind volunteer.

If the police accept Le Bon's and Zimbardo's ideas, then they would not try to reason with members of crowds, or to explain what needs to happen, since they wouldn't believe that people in mobs would be rational enough to understand or respond to their requests or orders. Rather, they would use riot gear and officers on horseback to break and disperse the crowd. Phil Banyard (1989), writing of the tragedy at Hillsborough, where almost 100 football fans died by being crushed against fences and barriers, suggested that the police may have regarded the crowd as a mob rather than trying to allow people to disperse by opening locked gates.

Although there is plenty of theory and speculation, and some fairly contrived experiments, not everyone agrees that deindividuated individuals create aggression and anti-social behaviour in crowds. According to an American government agency, the typical rioter during the 1960s civil unrest that led to Black people gaining equal rights was a worker in a responsible and well-paid job, who was well informed about the inequalities Black people were suffering. Their behaviour was deliberate and intentional, and directed towards a democratic goal. They were not criminals behaving irrationally. (Only white-owned businesses were looted!)

A sociological study of the fans of Oxford Town football club (Marsh 1978) showed that the fans' language and behaviour concerning the opposing team's fans, before and during the match, was not matched by their behaviour when they came face to face. Threats and taunts were issued, with promises to murder and kick the other fans' heads in. What this usually meant was the majority group would chase the others to the railway station (making sure they never quite caught up). Very little real fighting was done. Marsh identified three groupings within the fans, relating to the fans' age and experience. Membership of the youngest group required name calling and other non-violent behaviour. With age and experience these apprentices moved to the next group, where more confrontation took place, but this was much less likely to be 'mindless hooliganism' – it was more likely to be planned and pre-determined. The older group were the planners and organizers. Marsh's study suggests a socially constructed hierarchy within the supporters, a far cry from Le Bon's claims for deindividuated, mindless rioters.

■ **Contrast the two views of the nature of crowds.**

### Summary – Crowd behaviour and aggression

Early researchers claim that people act more irrationally and aggressively when they are members of large groups. One explanation for this is deindividuation, which involves anonymity, the lack of accountability for one's own actions, and a suspension of one's own standards of acceptable behaviour. Others claim that much crowd behaviour isn't random and the result of deindividuation. It is organized or ritualized, and can best be understood in terms of the goals the members wish to achieve, and the only way they feel that they are going to achieve them.

## *Exam questions – 60 minutes each*

1 Critically consider what psychologists have learned from their studies of audience and co-action effects. (*25 marks*)
2 Outline and evaluate psychological findings from the experimental study of conformity. (*25 marks*)
3 Discuss the major psychological research into obedience in humans and consider the implications of this type of research. (*25 marks*)

# 4  *Pro- and anti-social behaviour*

**Chapter objectives**

Having studied this chapter you will:

▌ understand what is meant by pro-social and altruistic behaviour, and why research in this area began;

▌ understand the nature of pro-social behaviour, aggression and violence in humans and other animals;

▌ appreciate the benefits and limitations of the major studies of altruism and aggression in humans, and understand their contribution to understanding the factors involved in the likelihood of altruism and aggression;

▌ appreciate psychological insights into promoting pro-social, and reducing anti-social, behaviour.

## Introduction

*Pro-social behaviour* refers to anything someone does that has a beneficial effect for someone else. A particular form of this is *altruism*, which occurs when someone else's needs are acted upon at some cost to oneself. It ranges from 'low-cost' altruism, such as giving directions to a stranger, to 'high-cost' altruism, such as donating one of your kidneys (Roger Brown 1986), thereby risking your own life to save someone else's (heroism). Exchange theory (see Chapter 2) says we are more likely to help when the cost to us is least, or when the benefit is likely to be greatest. Altruistic behaviour and heroism are, surprisingly, not rare amongst humans. For example, after disasters such as car, train and plane crashes, earthquakes and floods, ordinary people, who had never thought of themselves as brave, help others, even though they may be at risk. Anti-social behaviour is the opposite – any behaviour that causes disruption or harm to another individual or group. Aggression and discrimination are obvious examples of anti-social behaviour.

## PSYCHOLOGICAL STUDIES OF ALTRUISM

### Bibb Latané and colleagues

Several horrific reports of brutal acts, where witnesses did nothing to help the victim, appeared in the American press during the

1960s. For example, in 1964 Kitty Genovase was returning to her apartment in Queens, a district in New York, at 3 a.m. after an evening shift at work. As she reached the steps to her building she was attacked and stabbed by a man. Her screams woke many neighbours in surrounding buildings. Lights went on and blinds parted. Her assailant fled, only to return twice more to continue the attack, until he was certain she was dead. The attack took half an hour, and the police investigation revealed that 38 neighbours had witnessed the attack, as had some passengers on a bus that passed by. None did anything to help at all, and only one phoned the police after the woman was dead and the attacker had gone. This has become known as the *bystander effect*, and it was investigated by **Bibb Latané** and **John Darley** (1968, 1970).

The *New York Times* asked what it was about New Yorkers that made them so careless about others. Was it the fact of living in a big city? Latané and Darley's brainstorming suggested that this was too simple. Rather, the presence of so many other witnesses seemed to be the main factor in why none of them helped. Latané (1990) says 'Witnesses to emergencies are not simply apathetic and uncaring, rather they are strongly influenced by people around them... What's at issue is not moral character but social impact.' Latané (1990) describes the typical witness's reaction as 'Well gee, this isn't up to me, perhaps somebody else will do it'. He calls this *audience inhibition* and conducted a series of experiments to test it.

In the case of an obvious emergency, particularly where lives are in danger, many people will try to help without thought for themselves. However, not all situations requiring action are emergencies. In these cases our perceptual and cognitive systems have to pass through a series of steps. Latané and Darley (1970) define them as follows.

---

### The process leading to the likelihood of bystander intervention

1 Did someone observe an incident?    If no ——> Do nothing
If yes:
2 Did they define it as an emergency?    If no ——> Do nothing
If yes:
3 Did they decide to do something about it? If no ——> Do nothing
If yes:
4 Did they decide exactly how to help?    If no ——> Do nothing
If yes:
5 Did they then do it?    If no ——> Do nothing
If yes:
Help

---

In one of the first experiments naive participants completed some questionnaires in a waiting room before being called for an interview. Shortly after they began (artificial) smoke entered the room through the heating vents. When tested alone three-quarters of them went to find help within a few minutes of noticing the

► The *bystander effect* was discussed throughout the American media, with questions being raised about the decline of the American national character and the effects of living in a big city. Latané and Darley were social psychologists at Columbia University, New York, and their opinions were sought by journalists.

■ What is meant by the 'bystander effect'?

► *Audience inhibition* refers to the way that witnesses are less likely to become involved in a potentially unpleasant situation if they know that there are others who could just as well act as they. A descriptive comment could be 'I do not feel that I want to do anything where there are other people around who have seen the same that I have, and are just as able to act as I am, yet they are doing nothing'. Presumably they would add, 'If they did something, I would too'.

■ **What is audience inhibition?**

▶ A *trial* is a single run-through of an experimental procedure. Each time a participant (or group of participants) is tested under a particular experimental condition, this is called a trial.

Figure 4.1 The effect of group size on helping behaviour with an epileptic

▶ *Diffusion of responsibility* refers to the way individuals who are members of a group feel less responsible to others in need, since the responsibility of helping is shared by the other members. *Pluralistic ignorance* refers to the way in which individuals rationalize their lack of action.

smoke. Clearly they had no difficulty in defining the situation as an emergency and were able to act. In another condition there were two naive participants, one or both of whom reported it in half the experiments. The other half sat there filling in their forms, possibly hoping that the other might do something. Two confederate participants, who were instructed to ignore the smoke and continue filling in their questionnaires, were tested with a naive participant. When the smoke filled the room so that they couldn't see their papers they were to fan it away from their eyes. Ten naive participants were tested in this condition. Only one tried to report it.

Latané and **Rodin** (1969) had participants hear a female assistant fall over, hit a chair, and moan in pain in an adjoining room. When alone they all went to help. The more people (confederates instructed to do nothing) there were, the less likely the naive participant was to act.

In another experiment 52 students took part in a discussion about the problems of college life (Latané and Darley 1968, 1970). As some of their revelations might be embarrassing they were told that they would be anonymous and the conversation would take place in separate rooms via an intercom. In fact, each participant was tested alone, the other contributions were tape-recorded. One participant commented early in the 'discussion' that he suffered from epilepsy, and soon after the start of the discussion he had a seizure. Some naive participants were told that their discussion would be with one other, others were told that five others were involved. When female students were tested, 85 per cent of those who thought they were the only person involved went to find help. When they believed there were two others this figure fell to 65 per cent, and when there were supposedly four others, only 31 per cent intervened. See figure 4.1.

| Group size and composition | Number of trials | % responding by end of seizure | % responding eventually | Response time in seconds |
|---|---|---|---|---|
| 2 (naive and epileptic participants) | 13 | 85 | 100 | 52 |
| 3 (naive and epileptic participant and one other) | 26 | 62 | 85 | 93 |
| 6 (naive and epileptic participant and four others) | 13 | 31 | 62 | 166 |

Source: adapted from Latané and Darley (1970)

Latané and Nida (1981) explain the results of these two experiments in terms of '*diffusion of responsibility*'. The more people who have as much information about the urgency of an event as any individual, the less likely any one of them will become involved. Latané claims that 'psychological motivation' to do anything is reduced by being shared amongst others. In addition, there is *pluralistic ignorance*, which claims that we gather information about any unfamiliar or ambiguous situation from the reactions of others. If no one else acts then each individual thinks that the others do not regard action as appropriate. This is an attempt at rationalizing the situation so as to avoid guilt feelings for having done nothing.

## Clark and Word

Some of Latané and Darley's early experiments have been criticized by **Russell Clark** and **Larry Word** (1974), who claim that they weren't really testing people's responses to an emergency at all. For example, participants in the room filling with smoke could see two others who were calmly completing their questionnaires; the situation couldn't have been defined as that desperate, since no one would stay if it really was dangerous. Clark and Word claimed that the likelihood of someone becoming involved is determined by how obvious the emergency is and how dangerous becoming involved might prove.

Clark and Word had an actor playing the part of an electrician who appeared to receive an electric shock from a faulty control box and fall from his ladder. They used three experimental conditions. First, the electrician was in full view of passers by, and called for help before passing out. Clark and Word called this the 'unambiguous condition'. Second, he fell behind a counter, but was still heard asking for help. This was the 'moderately ambiguous condition'. Although it seemed likely to be serious the observers couldn't be certain that it was a real emergency. In the 'ambiguous condition' the electrician fell behind the counter, but although people could hear him fall, he made no sound afterwards, so he may or may not have been seriously hurt. Onlookers wouldn't have to define this as an emergency situation.

In a further modification Clark and Word tested the danger element by having the electrician in the unambiguous situation fall onto a live wire whilst still holding the faulty control box. He may have the live electric current running through him, and anyone who touched him could also have received a shock! This was the 'high danger condition'. Alternatively, the electrician dropped the control box and fell some distance from the live wire so wouldn't have posed any danger. This was the 'low danger condition'.

**Summary of Clark and Word's findings**

|  | *Number of participants who assisted* | |
|  | *Low danger* | *High danger* |
| --- | --- | --- |
| Unambiguous | 100 per cent | Over 90 per cent |
| Moderately ambiguous | Over 50 per cent | Less than 50 per cent |
| Highly ambiguous | 50 per cent if in pairs | Very few if alone |

It seems that where there is little risk to ourselves, we are more likely to offer help. We will still offer help where the danger is higher, so long as the situation is clearly an emergency. The less

■ **How do diffusion of responsibility and pluralistic ignorance explain bystander apathy?**

► Clark and Word's explanation implies a rational choice being made by people, according to a logical deduction based on observable features in the situation. It avoids untestable predictions about vague notions of 'psychological motivation'.

■ **How do diffusion of responsibility and audience inhibition explain Latané and Darley's research? How do Clark and Word extend this explanation?**

obvious the emergency appears, the fewer people will offer help if it involves risk to themselves.

## Other studies

Clark and Word suggest that *situational ambiguity* and *perceived danger* are major reasons why people don't involve themselves in emergencies. **Shotland** and **Straw** (1976) were interested in explaining the bystander apathy in the Kitty Genovase murder (see page 77). They investigated onlookers' reactions to two people who were arguing loudly and looked as though they would turn to aggression by having men and women stage violent arguments. When onlookers heard the woman say that she didn't know the man she was arguing with, many attempted to stop the fight. When she said 'I don't know why I married you', most did not. Some of the Genovase neighbours said they thought that she might have known her attacker.

Another factor is any feeling of commitment one might have to the victim of any misdeed. **Moriarty** (1975) had a confederate ask someone to keep an eye on his belongings while he was away for a few minutes. Another confederate soon tried to steal them. Those asked were much more likely to stop the thief, or report the theft, than those who witnessed the incident but hadn't been asked. Moriarty is saying that we are more likely to help when we feel a commitment to the victim of some misdeed. We are more likely to help people we know, or like the look or sound of, or we think need our help, or who can do us some good, than people who appear less deserving.

People may also behave more altruistically when in familiar environments than in situations which are strange or new. Latané and Darley (1970) conducted an experiment in which a man on crutches fell in the familiar environment of the New York subway, and the less familiar one of a departure lounge in New York's La Guardia airport; 65 per cent of passers by went to help on the 60 trials in the subway compared to 40 per cent in the airport. However, there are other explanations for these findings. Airport lounges are familiar places to many of the people who use them. There may have been other differences between people who frequently use airports compared to those who use the subway which could explain this result.

**Irving Piliavin** and his colleagues investigated factors to do with the victim that influenced the likelihood of being helped. They had students falling over in subway trains in New York. In one experiment the students dressed up as infirm or disabled people, using a walking stick. They were helped by other passengers on 90 per cent of the trials. Presumably they deserved help. When the students wore a jacket that smelled of alcohol, and were carrying a bottle in a brown paper bag when they fell over, they were only helped on 20 per cent of the occasions. Now they are seen as at least partly responsible for their own misfortune. Another possibility here,

► Is it possible that people who live in small communities feel more committed to one another than people who live in large cities? Could the bystander effect seen in the Kitty Genovase case have occurred in a small village?

► Much of the type of research (e.g. Moriarty, Piliavin) uses 'field experiments' because they take place in the participants' own natural habitat (see Chapter 17). The natural habitat of a frequent subway passenger is the subway.

though, is Clark and Word's idea that perceived danger is a factor. If a bystander thinks the drunk might be aggressive or be sick or something equally unpleasant, then he or she may not want to help. Bearing in mind the importance that people place on physical attractiveness, in another experiment the students were made up to appear to have an ugly birthmark covering half their face. The offers of help fell from 90 per cent to 61 per cent.

Piliavin increased the potential seriousness of the subway helpers experiment. When the confederate fell he would bite a capsule of red dye in his mouth and the fake blood would trickle down his chin. Clearly this is a serious situation and has implications for the level of support that may be necessary (calling the guard, giving a statement, accompanying the victim to the hospital, etc.). Offers of help fell from 90 per cent to 60 per cent, i.e. someone offered help on 60 per cent of the trials, although others looked around to find someone else who might be more useful in a medical emergency.

All the research mentioned so far is into why people don't generally behave altruistically. However, Huston and Korte (1976) found that some people will always offer to help if they possess the expert knowledge required. Nurses and doctors do volunteer if there's a medical emergency, an electrician may step forward in Shotland's experiment. Baron and Byrne (1991) also found that the presence of others makes no difference to the likelihood of assistance being given where the volunteer felt able and qualified to help.

> ► It seems sad that people's looks, over which they have little control, are such an important factor in levels of pro-social helping. Yet it provides further evidence that looks are important in interpersonal perception.

> ■ Show how knowledge of relationship of the partners, commitment to the victim, location familiarity, perception of the victim and seriousness of the situation influence the likelihood of helping behaviour.

---

**Summary – *Psychological studies of altruism***

Several suggestions are made to explain the reluctance of many people to become involved in incidents that do not directly concern them. These include the knowledge of the presence of others who may be more capable of offering help than any individual; the way that responsibility is diffused amongst members of a group; the lack of any feeling of commitment to the victim; and the role of the environment.

---

## The likelihood of altruism

Latané (1990) proposes an almost mathematical explanation for the likelihood of bystander intervention or bystander apathy, which he is still developing, called *social impact theory*. It says that there are 'three central aspects of other people's presence that affect the individual'; these are 'strength, immediacy, and number'. He gives the example of stage fright. The amount of fear is determined by the strength of the audience, 'how important they are, their expertise, and their power over your future'. Second, their immediacy, 'their closeness to you, the type of seating arrangement'. Third, their number, 'how many people there are'. Latané (1981) proposes 'psychosocial laws' that govern the relationship between these three. One such 'law' is *social loafing*, discussed in Chapter 3, where the amount of effort each individual contributes declines when there

> ► According to Latané and Darley the reasons why people do not become involved include perceived diffusion of responsibility, pluralistic ignorance and apprehension about how others will evaluate them.

are greater numbers in the group. (Contrast social loafing with the effects of deindividuation on the behaviour of crowds discussed in the previous chapter.) Another may be 'psychological motivation to help', mentioned earlier on page 78.

■ **Outline and comment on social impact theory.**

*Figure 4.2 Factors in the likelihood of intervention*

| **1 Characteristics of the victim** | |
| --- | --- |
| Similarity of bystander and victim | increases likelihood |
| Relationship or commitment to bystander | increases likelihood |
| Appearance | increases likelihood if attractive, decreases otherwise |
| **2 Characteristics of the situation** | |
| Increasing numbers of bystanders | decreases likelihood |
| Perceived seriousness of the situation | increases if alone, decreases if others are present |
| **3 Characteristics of the bystander** | |
| Possesses specialist knowledge | increases likelihood |
| Strongly motivated to help (mood, personality, etc.) | increases likelihood |

► Altruism means behaving in a way that will benefit another at some cost to oneself. If the individual behaves in a way which results in some benefit to someone she has no knowledge of, and at some cost to herself, is this altruism? Surrendering pocket money to a bully fulfils this definition, but it is hardly altruistic. Altruism must have some *intentionality*.

By proposing psychosocial laws Latané is implying a role for biological forces in pro-social behaviour. Evolutionary and ethological evidence exists for what looks like altruism in other species, too (see Chapter 6). For example, duck and goose mothers will often show themselves to a fox or wolf to distract it away from their offspring. Some have been observed appearing to have a broken wing, and unable to escape from the predator. A full-grown bird is a better kill than some infant goslings, so will be followed. The adult is risking her life to save her offspring. All is not lost for her – when the predator is a safe distance from her family she stops hopping and squawking and flies home! Is this mother behaving altruistically, according to the definition we gave earlier? Or just a mother protecting her genetic investment in her offspring? Does she know that she is acting selflessly? Can we behave altruistically without knowing that we are doing so? Probably not.

How about this example? One male baboon might distract a superior baboon who is about to mate, and whilst he is being chased (or worse), his accomplice might mate the female. What possible motive might the first baboon have for risking a fierce attack by the alpha male, when he can obtain no benefit from it at all? Unless we believe that the favour might be repaid in the future. This, and many other kinds of 'caring behaviour', is described as *biological altruism*. **Roger Davies** (1995) maintains that it is just the kind of behaviour that would be called *psychological altruism* if it occurred in humans. He says: 'It is a result of their aversion to biological explanations that psychologists separate altruism into biological and psychological types.' In humans it is said to result from 'sophisticated and moral upbringing rather than something brought forth from a genetic package'.

Davies claims the distinction is misguided. If, however, we claim that the altruist must have some notion about the effects of his or (probably more usually) her behaviour, then either animal behaviour can't be altruistic since animals don't have the kind of cognitive skills of recognition, memory, turn taking, giving and receiving favours etc. that would be required, or many species do, and we drastically underestimate their powers. **Sue Savage Rumbaugh** has created conditions under which a pygmy chimp called Kanzi demonstrates quite remarkable cognitive skills. Davies claims that what we lack is the open-mindedness to approach animal research such that animals can demonstrate the skills they do possess rather than being made to do things (such as communicate in sign language) that they find difficult.

For evidence Davies cites the universal tendency of humans to organize themselves into family units, and people usually treat members of their family more favourably than non-members. Where non-family members are helped, such as individuals donating to worthy charities, or communities looking after the sick and elderly, Davies suggests that this behaviour may only be an extension of our genetically inherited tendency to put family first. However, the problem with claiming that something is genetically inherited is that we would expect it to occur in the vast majority of cases. Whilst Davies is right that people in all societies form themselves into families, the variety of forms is very wide indeed, usually for excellent socioeconomic reasons. Some preclude the possibility of treating members more favourably (particularly females). Second, there are countless examples of families that do not treat other members more favourably than their friends. More, perhaps, than would be explained by genetic tendencies.

Whether there are genetic influences on our altruistic behaviour, there can be no doubt that learning plays an important role in its likelihood, too. Similar explanations have been offered for anti-social, aggressive behaviour, as we shall see now.

### Summary – The likelihood of altruism

Social impact theory claims a relationship between the importance of the audience to the individual who may want to behave altruistically: how close the audience is and how many people there are in the audience. Evolutionary evidence suggests that altruism may be to do with promoting the survival of the altruist's genes, although this may be difficult to see in human behaviour.

▶ Davies is arguing that we ought to approach the study of animals from the point of view that they are capable of a greater degree of conceptual, cognitive processing than we have so far believed.

▶ *Genes* are microscopic bits of protein that carry messages about when to trigger aspects of human growth. We must be extremely careful when we claim that some aspect of behaviour is 'instinctive', or 'genetically inherited'.

■ Outline the case that altruism is species-specific to humans and that it can be found in other species. Use the concept of survival value in your answer.

■ Make a list of all the reasons given here for (a) bystander apathy and (b) bystander intervention.

► Aggression can take several forms. *Hostile aggression* is impulsive and, at least for a moment, intended. *Instrumental aggression* occurs in pursuit of something else. A child who knocks another whilst taking the other's toy isn't intending to hurt the other child.

► How might this distinction between hostile and instrumental aggression influence parents' attitudes towards their children's aggressive acts?

► The *limbic system* was one of the earliest parts of the brain to evolve. Scientists are a long way from understanding exactly what its various structures do, much less how they work. They appear to be involved in emotional states (e.g. anger) and motivation, the urge to do something about the emotion (e.g. behave aggressively).

## AGGRESSION

### What is aggression?

At an individual or small group level, *aggression* is usually regarded as anti-social, unless used in self-defence. At a national level it may take the form of warfare and the aggression may be justified. Aggression usually includes hostility and ranges from name-calling – *verbal aggression* – to murder. *Hostile aggression* (violence) is usually impulsive and emotional, and is intentionally directed towards the person who suffers it. We want to hurt them for something we think they have done to us. *Instrumental aggression* is often planned and a part of some other activity, and is not deliberately directed against the person who suffers it. A bank robber who injures a guard doesn't have anything personal against the victim.

Aggression has been studied by psychologists from several backgrounds. Some regard it as a personality trait, or dominant characteristic. The classification of behavioural disorders used by counsellors and clinicians in the West (*DSM IV* and *ICD 10* – see Chapter 9) recognizes the aggressive personality as a dysfunctional condition. Other psychologists regard aggression as a motivational state, so are more interested in the interaction of physiological factors. Social psychologists look for environmental and personal interactions. We will summarize the evidence using the nature versus nurture approach discussed on previous occasions.

### Biological bases of aggression

Biological theories include those that refer to structures and processes in the brains of animals (including humans) which are involved in aggressive behaviour, ethological studies of animal aggression, and psychoanalytic theories which suggest the existence of instinctive drives that urge us to behave aggressively.

The first recognizable humans appeared on the planet about 70,000 years ago. For most life would have been a constant struggle to find enough food, shelter and safety to survive. Aggression would have played an important part in human evolution, since those who could obtain all their needs would survive longer than those who could not, and history teaches us that the strongest were more likely to win in the race for survival and evolution.

#### Brain structures and hormones

The *limbic system* is a complex set of brain structures (the hippocampus, anterior thalamus, amygdala, septum and hypothalamus) that evolved very early in human evolution. The precise functions of each organ, or of the whole system, aren't known, but do appear to be involved in emotional and motivational states, including aggression. Laboratory experiments with animals show that aggressive responses can be deliberately triggered by electrical or chemical stimulation of this part of the brain. Animals as large as bulls have been stopped from charging, and passive kittens have been observed to extend their claws and hiss. It is also probable that people with brain disorders of the limbic system are more likely to be aggressive than others.

*Hormones* are chemicals which are synthesized and released into the bloodstream by various organs or glands. They are absorbed by other organs and usually trigger some response in them. Males have more androgenic hormones, such as *testosterone*, whilst females have more oestrogenic hormones. There appears to be a link between testosterone levels and the likelihood of aggression. Delgado (1969) found that men and women who had the highest testosterone levels were also the most aggressive. People with high testosterone levels in prison were more likely than others to have been convicted of violent crimes. High-testosterone females are more aggressive just before menstruation, and least aggressive whilst ovulating. Reinisch et al. (1991) found that children of mothers who had been given testosterone to prevent miscarriage during pregnancy were more aggressive than others. However, we can't assume that the testosterone is causing the aggression. Other variables are involved, too.

► *Testosterone* promotes tissue growth, genital maturity, sperm production, facial and pubic hair, the development of muscles and the male voice breaking with puberty.

■ **Summarize the biological explanation for aggression.**

### Ethological explanations of aggression

*Ethological* explanations of aggression look for causes of aggressive behaviour in the animal's (including human's) natural habitat. Although there are individual differences between members of the same species in their levels of aggressive response, much wider differences are observed between different species. Lions and tigers must kill to eat (instrumental aggression). Zebra and horses don't, as they're vegetarian. Some animals also use aggression for defending their territory, protecting their offspring, attracting and keeping a mate, and defending themselves.

► *Ethology* is the study of animals in the wild. Television programmes that show animals living in their natural habitat such as those presented by Richard Attenborough are good examples of ethology.

Aggression can be seen in animals and humans at quite young ages, although animal aggression is usually competitive and rarely violent (Konrad Lorenz 1966). Animals use *ritualized* threatening displays, including making deep noises to sound powerful, puffing out their chests to look imposing, lifting their heads to look tall, and running and jumping to seem strong. All of this is intended to frighten a competitor. These displays aren't deliberate or conscious attempts to elicit fear and avoidance in the other. They are automatic, reflexive, ritualized responses which will be triggered by the perception of the competitor. Only if all displays and warnings fail will most animals resort to physical contact.

► *Ritualizing* means performing a sequence of behaviour which has (or had) some specific function or meaning. The behaviour is fairly fixed and inflexible. So, when a lion begins his ritual of baring his throat, of dropping his tail between his legs, of stumbling away from his adversary, the ritual conveys the message that he accepts defeat and is no longer a challenger.

One major difference between humans and lower-order animals is the use and extent of ritualized aggression. A ritual is a stereotypical and often repeated behaviour associated with a particular activity. In Chapter 1 we referred to obsessive compulsive disorder, such as constant hand washing. This is ritualized behaviour. Freud described some neurotic patients who had to observe a series of fixed behaviours before they could, for example, go to sleep. However, ritualized violence is not usually thought of as a common feature of human behaviour.

In 1950 Konrad Lorenz defined aggression as 'the fighting instinct in beast and man which is directed against members of the same species'. Instinctive energy to behave aggressively builds up with each new frustration, until it is finally, automatically elicited. Lorenz describes this as a psycho-hydraulic model for aggression (see figure 4.3). The analogy is with a tank (brain centres for aggression) which is slowly filling with water (frustrations and annoyances). Some of the water will be drained off by a tap, and so long as the tap can drain off (release through competitive activities) more than is pouring in, the animal will not behave aggressively. Otherwise the tank will fill up and the water will flood out (the animal behaves aggressively). Once released the next thing that makes us angry will begin the build-up of aggressive energies again.

*Figure 4.3  Lorenz's psycho-hydraulic model*

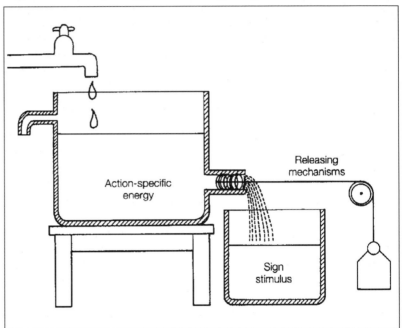

The idea of storing aggressive energy and of the release of pressure after an aggressive act making us feel better may sound plausible, but there is no evidence that brain centres can store 'aggressive energy' in this way, or that it will automatically be released by the 'final straw'. What if the final straw was the sight of a mean-looking 18-stone six-foot tall bloke staring at you?

### Psychoanalytic explanations of aggression

Psychoanalytic explanations of aggression derive from Freud. Freud claimed that we inherit several instinctive urges including aggressive impulses which drive us towards danger, excitement and risk. These are the death instincts, and are ultimately self-destructive. They try to make the child expose itself to danger, and this conflicts with the libido's instincts for preserving life.

If the child is not to destroy itself, it must use defence mechanisms to reduce the destructive urges. (Defence mechanisms are

■ How do ethologists regard aggressive behaviour in (a) animals and (b) humans, especially with regard to ritualized aggression?

▶ *Death instincts* are supposed to be drives that urge us towards risk and destruction. The *libido* is the opposing drive towards success and fulfilment.

discussed in Chapter 1.) For example, we might displace or sublimate our destructive urge by trying to destroy something (or someone) else. Hopefully, children are being brought up (*socialized*) to think that aggression is usually wrong. If the child's ego and superego are not strong enough to resist the aggressive instincts, they might break through into consciousness as aggression.

> ► *Socialization* is the name of the process of watching, listening, copying and learning through which we all acquire our understanding of what our family and our group is like, what it expects of us, and what we shouldn't do.

---

### Summary – Biological bases of aggression

Most animal behaviour is reflexive and driven by instinctive urges. Comparative psychologists look for biological or behavioural adaptations that would promote the animal's survival to pass on its genes. Forms of aggression are used by some species to catch prey for food, or compete with others for a mate or for territory, all of which might enhance the individual's (and thus the species') chances of survival. Psychoanalytic theory says aggression is inevitable since it is an instinctive part of human functioning.

---

> ■ **Briefly outline Freud's explanation for aggression.**

## Behaviourist explanations of aggression

There are several theories which support the idea that social experiences influence the likelihood of aggressive responses. **B.F. Skinner** (see Chapter 1) rejected biological, ethological and psychoanalytic explanations for human aggression since they were untestable, unconvincing and unnecessary. He argued that most antecedents will have a variety of possible behavioural responses. For example, when I was threatened by another kid during school play time (*antecedent*), I could have given in, run to tell teacher or bashed the bully (*behaviour*). Whichever response I found most beneficial the last time I was in a similar antecedent (last time I was threatened), I'm likely to try again, in order to obtain similar benefits. If I bashed a bully before, I'll have a go at this one now. Skinner explains aggression as a learned response to a situation which has been found effective previously. However, how did I first learn to bash a bully? How do we explain behaviour when there has never been an antecedent?

Skinner's explanation is too simplistic. During the 1960s **Albert Bandura** and his colleagues developed social learning theory based on observation, imitation and modelling (see Chapter 1).

Bandura (1973, 1977) conducted several experiments to test whether children who observe powerful or attractive models behaving aggressively are more likely to behave aggressively themselves, particularly if they see the model being rewarded for their behaviour. The ethics of this research is highly suspect, since Bandura is deliberately exposing children to acts of violence in order to test their response. Similar research has been conducted using a variety of stimuli, although it is doubtful whether they would be permitted now.

In one experiment three groups of nursery school children watched a film of an adult male behaving aggressively towards a

> ► Modelling comprises the two elements of observation and imitation. Bandura and others believe that it is the fundamental process in socialization.

large Bobo doll (a rubber toy with weights which made it keep bobbing upright, no matter how it was pushed). The adult hit and kicked the toy, threw it around and punched it. The outcome of the film was different for each group. One group saw the adult being rewarded with praise and sweets for his aggression. Another saw the adult being smacked for his wicked behaviour. The third (the control group) didn't see anything happen to the adult. When given a Bobo doll of their own to play with the first group and the control group were equally aggressive towards it. The children who saw the adult being punished were much less aggressive. (See figure 4.4.)

*Figure 4.4  A Bobo doll*

In order to test the role of reward Bandura and his colleagues conducted another experiment in which all the children were rewarded if they behaved aggressively towards the Bobo doll, no matter what had happened to the adult model. They all soon began behaving more aggressively.

Bandura's experimental situations are rather artificial, watching adults behaving in strange ways towards an inflatable toy. In real life people aren't likely to be rewarded with praise and sweets for being aggressive. Since the Bobo doll wasn't a toy that many children would be familiar with can we be sure that they understood that they were being aggressive towards it when they hit it? (You aren't being aggressive to a drum when you beat it, you are simply behaving appropriately. Perhaps some of these children were behaving in what they thought was an appropriate way towards the doll?)

A prolonged debate about the role of aggressive and violent media images, and people's reactions to them, has continued since the 1950s. Countless experiments have exposed children to violent *Tom and Jerry* cartoons, Superman and Batman socking and powing their way out of a tight spot, and no doubt Mutant Ninja Turtles and Power Rangers appear in some researchers' experimental tool bag now. Observations have been made of children and adults immediately after they have been watching violent images, including men watching violent pornographic images (Donnerstein 1981). Most suggest a link between what people watch and the likelihood that their attitudes, and often their behaviour, will change. Also their sensitivity to the suffering of the victim declines as they see more members of the same group suffering. Similar findings exist in many countries, so it appears that observation is a powerful tool in shaping attitudes towards violence.

To say that children model their behaviour on images they see on TV would only be a cause for alarm if TV programmes did show frequent violent scenes. Guy Cumberbatch analysed all programmes on all four channels that were broadcast in four weeks in 1986. He found that 30 per cent of programmes showed some violent scenes, lasting on average 25 seconds. This amounted to about 1 per cent of broadcast time showing acts of violence. However, TV isn't the only source of violent observations. Some people may be attracted to watching violent videos, or repeat viewing of those TV shows that do contain violence.

■ Contrast Skinner's and Bandura's explanations for the emergence of aggressive behaviour.

> ## Summary – Behaviourist explanations of aggression
>
> Behaviourists claim that aggressive behaviour, like most other behaviour, is learned as a consequence of selective reinforcement. If children are reinforced for behaving aggressively, or if they see others getting their own way through aggression, then they are more likely to behave aggressively.

## Environmental explanations of aggression

Clearly aggression existed long before TV and video, so there must be other causes. One is the violence itself. Violence creates violence. If someone attacks someone else, the second person may attack the first in return. Children talk about 'getting someone back' for something they've done.

Second, Gerald Patterson (1978) found that the submission or crying of a child who has been attacked can become reinforcing to the attacker. Philip Zimbardo found the same reaction amongst the adult guards in his Stanford Prison experiment (see Chapter 3). Bullies continue bullying because they find they can achieve their own ends this way. Most bullies are cowards, too, when confronted by someone stronger.

Third, making people uncomfortable increases their aggression. Alello (1979) found overcrowding led to increased aggression and competitiveness. Anderson et al. (1987, 1989) found that exposure to heat above tolerable levels increases violent outbursts. They plotted the number of violent crimes committed throughout the year in several US cities and found that they rose on the hottest days, during the hottest months, in the hottest cities. Baron and Bell (1975) found that riots were more likely to occur on long hot summer evenings. Other environmental influences on aggression include exposing non-smokers to someone else's smoking, and exposure to noise and other pollution. Imposing such discomforts on undeserving victims may well increase their aggressive responses.

The problem with environmental explanations is that they imply that factors such as heat or overcrowding simply cause the aggression. The government can dismiss public unrest in terms of the environmental factors that will soon subside, or that the rioters are led by a few, politically motivated troublemakers. These claims are widely publicized and allow us to ignore the social unrest that really caused the riot. Early demonstrations against the poll tax were dismissed in this way.

> ### Summary – Environmental explanations of aggression
>
> Aggressive behaviour may increase where others are behaving aggressively, where aggression seems to be appropriate or effective, and where people are made to feel physically or psychologically uncomfortable.

## Motivation and aggression

Motivation is also important. The *frustration–aggression* hypothesis contains elements of both instinctive and learned behaviour and was proposed in 1939 by **John Dollard** and **Neal Miller**. They claim that much of our daily life involves trying to achieve something like catch a bus, get to college, phone a friend, complete an essay, and so on. Things sometimes go wrong. We miss the bus, the phone is engaged, we are stuck with the essay. Our goals become frustrated. According to Dollard and Miller aggression is an instinctive drive that will result from frustration. It is almost automatic.

However, frustration does not necessarily lead to aggression. If someone twice your size is frustrating your desire to achieve something, aggression towards him may be a very risky strategy! Or you may simply become exhausted by your attempts. Albert Bandura points out that different people have their own ways of reacting to frustrations. Some of us are long suffering and very patient. We are tolerant and don't become overexcited. We do not behave aggressively when we are frustrated. However, we might snap if, for example, our child's life is in danger. Other people's normal response to any frustration is aggression. Yet even they are in a good mood sometimes. Martin Seligman (1975) describes a condition he called *learned helplessness*, where people who feel they are constantly being frustrated learn that they can't do anything about it. This often leads to depression rather than aggression.

Schacter and Singer (1962) suggest a modified form of the frustra-

---

■  How convincing are environmental explanations for the causes of aggression?

►  *Frustration* means interfering with or inhibiting someone from achieving their intentions. The *frustration–aggression hypothesis* says that frustration produces aggression.

►  Seligman placed laboratory dogs in cages from which they could not escape, and gave them uncomfortable (though not dangerous) electric shocks. After a few trials they gave up even trying to avoid the shocks. Seligman claims that helplessness is learned (and can be unlearned).

tion–aggression hypothesis which they call *arousal–aggression*. It says that frustration leads to arousal. If social and cognitive factors permit, we may turn to aggression. Delgado interpreted his findings from studies of monkeys in a similar way. He stimulated the hypothalamus of several monkeys who occupied different positions in the status hierarchy of the troupe. The dominant monkeys behaved aggressively, those nearer the bottom found other ways of acting. Perhaps cognitive considerations based on previous experience stop the animal behaving aggressively when it is likely to lose the 'fight'.

---

### Summary – Motivation and aggression

When we are unable to achieve some important goal, we may behave aggressively by swearing or lashing out. Different people have different normal levels of arousal and these may predispose some to behave generally more aggressively than others. The frustration–aggression hypothesis cannot explain all aggression. Arousal–aggression suggests that frustration increases levels of physical arousal, and behaving aggressively is one way to release this arousal.

---

## Deindividuation

Deindividuation is the process of becoming so absorbed into the activity of the group, or one's role in it, that one loses one's sense of self, i.e. who one really is. When Zimbardo questioned the participants after his mock prison experiment (see Chapter 3), many said they couldn't believe that they had done what they did. They were absorbed by their role, they 'became' the prisoner or guard. Their real self seemed to have been suspended. They became *deindividuated.* Something similar might happen in some mob behaviour, although this is far from certain (see Chapter 3 for a summary of the debate). Deindividuation may well explain some violence, but not all.

■ What are the roles of motivation and deindividuation in aggression?

## Putting the theories together

Human aggression takes many forms, and has many causes. Most are socially constructed from the way we perceive and integrate our perceptions about how others are relating to us. For example, I may have formed the impression that you don't like me, and I see you whispering to a friend of yours. I conclude that you are plotting against me. Consequently, I may be aggressive towards you. My understanding and perception may have been quite wrong, but my social construction led me to attack you. In Chapter 11 we describe Robert Gregory's theory of perception, which says that what we experience is the result of the process of perceiving it, rather than the perception of what is actually there (see page 254). We must infer, imagine, or even guess at the meaning of our perceptions.

All the explanations have something to offer in explaining different aspects of aggression. We know that there are brain centres and differences in hormone levels which are involved in aggressive behaviour. Psychoanalysis and Lorenz's ethological theories see the urge for aggression building up slowly until it finally breaks out. A particular event may trigger the aggression, and nature does provide such triggers. For example, something causes birds to migrate, squirrels to wake up from hibernation and most animals to want to mate. The biological approach would say that certain species inherit a predisposition or readiness to behave aggressively. If the necessary event occurs then ritualized aggression will be triggered.

Early behaviourist theories show how learning some aggressive responses occurs through reinforcement, and social learning theories identify the role of observation, imitation and modelling. Environmental factors emphasize the role of discomfort and injustice in triggering aggressive responses.

Cognitive scientists have yet to pay attention to human aggression. Our cognitive system provides information that will help us to survive, for example, by not responding aggressively. You may plot to get your own back on someone who uses their superior strength or power to threaten you. You are not automatically triggered to fight back if fighting means you will be hurt badly. You make an assessment of the situation and judge what is the best course of action based on what you know. You acquire this information through social learning.

## Reducing and controlling aggression and violence

The evidence suggests that the likelihood and level of aggressive behaviour is influenced by a combination of biological (nature) and social (nurture) forces. The biological component could be controlled by such radical measures as deliberately altering hormone levels by brain surgery or drug treatment. However, this is unacceptable in most Western and other societies today. In the past brain surgery has been used in this way (NB see the discussion on Egas Moniz and the use of prefrontal lobotomies in Chapter 10).

If reinforcement promotes and maintains aggression, then removing its association with aggressive behaviour whilst reinforcing non-aggressive, pro-social responses should reduce the likelihood of aggression. This is known as the *incompatible response technique* and was successfully used by Brown and Elliot (1965), who had primary school teachers ignore aggressive acts and praise the children for behaving pro-socially. Beneficial effects appeared within a fortnight. Ron Slaby (1977) found that encouraging young children to say nice things about other children was enough to decrease anti-social and increase pro-social acts. Reinforcing co-operative behaviour makes more sense. If people learn that it pays to co-operate we may reduce the appeal of achievement through aggression.

If people learn through observing, imitating and modelling, as social learning theory claims, then we must provide positive, co-

► Reinforcement is a powerful motivating force in children. Sadly, parents threaten and punish their children for wrongdoing far more than they praise and encourage them for good behaviour.

operative images of people relating to each other. We should encourage and educate parents (and teachers) to behave less aggressively and more co-operatively. They should try to help children find other means of solving their problems and achieving their ends. Restricting children's access to violent TV programmes could also be helpful.

Aggressive responses are often triggered by unfortunate, accidental body contact during children's play. Providing a larger area, or reducing the competition for existing resources (especially toys), at the same time as providing non-violent playthings, should also contribute to lessening aggression. Parents could also encourage *empathy* in their children. This is an understanding that people often have of the feelings and needs of other people. Even quite young children are capable of showing some understanding and sympathy towards others who are clearly in distress. This caring approach could be reinforced.

► *Empathy* is a caring and understanding approach whereby one person seems to be able to share the feeling of other people's misfortunes.

Rather than reducing aggression, Lorenz and Eidesfieldt (1970) suggested that society should provide appropriate channels for our aggressive energies to be released. Active sport such as team games or boxing should be encouraged. People should be able to watch others behaving aggressively to help them release their own feelings. This is what Freud meant by *catharsis*. Unfortunately, as with Freud's claims, the opposite of what Lorenz claims appears to be true. Far from releasing energies, Walters and Brown (1963) found that watching others, or being involved in competition oneself, tends to make people more aggressive, as it had in Bandura's experiments.

► Like Freud, Lorenz claims that aggressive energies can be stored and released through *catharsis*. Catharsis is the release of repressed ideas and emotions that should lead to relief from tension.

Perhaps the single biggest contribution we could make to a non-aggressive society would be by reducing aggression in children, and much psychological research into childrearing style indicates that the largest influence on how children think and behave is the actions of their parents. As **David Shaffer** (1985) says, 'One of the most reliable findings in the child rearing literature is that cold and rejecting parents who apply physical punishment in an erratic fashion and often permit their children to express aggressive impulses are likely to raise hostile aggressive children'. Unfortunately it would be the job of government, not psychologists, to attempt a programme of parent training beyond post-natal classes.

■ How far would it be possible to reduce the incidence of aggressive behaviour in humans?

**Summary – Reducing and controlling aggression and violence**

Since aggression may be habitual if someone has learned that aggression is an effective way of achieving their ends, or biologically triggered by some brain chemistry or instinctive urges, or the result of some cognitive processing, or sudden, uncharacteristic urge, it is very difficult to be able to suggest how to control or reduce it. Since we may not be able to do much about biological transmission it may be more useful to work on the things that we can do, for example control the amount of aggression that people can watch on TV and promote pro-social activities. Educating parents into the need to encourage caring and co-operative behaviour amongst their children, at the same time as reducing the amount of aggression shown them, might also help to reduce the amount of violence in society. However, the decision to implement such policies is a political, not psychological, one.

## Exam questions – 60 minutes each

1(a) Discuss TWO social psychological theories of the origins of aggression. (*10 marks*)
(b) Critically consider the implications of social psychological theories for the control and reduction of aggression. (*15 marks*)
2 Critically consider the claim that the media might contribute to levels of aggressive behaviour. (*25 marks*)
3 Evaluate psychological insights into the likelihood of people behaving in altruistic ways. (*25 marks*)

# *Part 2*
# *Comparative psychology*

*In the early twentieth century Pavlov, Watson and Thorndike's work with dogs, chicks, other birds and rats developed into behaviourism (see Chapter 1). Its emphasis was on how these animals acquire learned habits. Many learning theories have been advanced and are combined with aspects of several disciplines including genetics (the biological bases of life), zoology (the study of animals), physiology (the study of the structure and functioning of living things) and ethology (the study of animal behaviour in its natural setting) to produce* comparative psychology. Comparative psychology identifies, and tries to explain, the similarities and differences that exist in the behaviour and functioning of animals of different species. It is not concerned with comparing aspects of animal functioning to human functioning, or using explanations for human behaviour in explaining animal behaviour. It insists that animal behaviour is a valid and interesting area of study in its own right. In this section we shall examine what evolutionary perspectives have contributed to understanding animal behaviour, kinship and social behaviour, and several other features of animal behaviour.*

**5** *Evolutionary determinants of behaviour*

**Chapter objectives**

By the end of this chapter you will:

▌ discover the relationship between genetic and evolutionary forces in shaping animal behaviour;

▌ understand how competition for essential resources has influenced behavioural adaptation in non-human animals;

▌ understand how the relationship between predators and prey shapes the behaviour of both;

▌ appreciate the behaviours involved in symbiotic relationships.

## Introduction

Information about each member of a particular species is carried in the individual's genes. Your mother and father passed thousands of human *genes*, carried on 23 pairs of *chromosomes*, on to you. Of the 23 pairs of chromosomes, 22 carry genes which contain information about your physical structure, such as your size, hair, skin and eye colouring etc. One pair carries genes containing information about which sex you will be.

Each chromosome carries about 2,000 genes. Each gene is a microscopic bundle of DNA and RNA. These substances are the essential 'building blocks' of life. They carry information about what sort of cells will be constructed, when they will begin to work, and the ways in which they will work. For example, most people are born with genes that will permit them to have sufficient control of their legs, and adequate balance and co-ordination so that they can walk and run. But they cannot walk immediately after birth or hatching, unlike many other animals such as ducklings, goslings, lambs, foals and elephants. The genetic instruction to start walking isn't triggered until the organism is mature enough.

The characteristics of any species may stay remarkably consistent over countless thousands of generations if they are well adapted to their environment and the environment doesn't change. For example, crocodiles haven't changed much in 200 million years. Others change more rapidly. Humans that lived just one hundred

▶ Maturation here refers to the biological process of physical growth.

thousand years ago would have been quite different from humans today. The way these changes come about is called *evolution*.

## WHAT IS EVOLUTION?

Evolution is the process by which plants and animals have descended from their earlier forms. The planet Earth has existed for about four and a half thousand million years. Evolution began when the first living things appeared on the planet. Micro-fossils of some bacteria which existed three thousand million years ago have been discovered. We know that single-cell protozoa lived 1,200 million years ago. Jellyfish fossils have been found from 650 million years ago.

Since life began on Earth countless different life forms have appeared, inhabited the Earth for some time, and disappeared. The dinosaur era lasted for about 140 million years, from around 205 million years ago to about 66 million years ago. Many species of dinosaur became extinct, often when the climate changed and their food supply disappeared. Other life forms were able to adapt to a changing climate, terrain or food supply. Other successful species survived not only because they could adapt, but also because enough of their members were able to avoid their enemies. We know all this largely because of the 'fossil record'. This is the rather patchy, though extensive, collection of the remains of animals. Unfortunately, fossils only tell us approximately when, and with what others, various animal species lived. We might learn some things about them such as their diet, their survival techniques, or their living patterns. Much of our understanding of their behaviour is based on guesswork, since ultimately their bones are almost all we have to study.

Evolution is not a theory, it is a fact. Inevitably, it has attracted a great deal of theorizing about animal and human ancestry. During the last few hundred years several quite different evolutionary perspectives have developed to explain animal behaviour. The French philosopher **René Descartes** (1596–1650) argued that a distinction should be made between the human mind and the human body. This idea is called dualism. The body, he believed, was simply a machine, although made out of organic material such as bones and muscles which make them move. Understanding the rules of mechanics would enable us to understand the functions of the body. One of the functions of the body is, of course, behaviour. The mind was much more difficult to understand.

### *Theories of evolution*

**J.B. Lamarck** (1809) was one of the first to advance a theory of evolution. His basic idea was that each individual animal (and human) will have to work hard during its life if it is to achieve success. Hunting, gathering food, mating, protection and so on are all essen-

▶ *Adaptation* in this sense is the process of modifying one's behaviour in the light of new experiences. Eating a poisonous butterfly will allow the bird to be rather more selective the next time. The bird will make an adaptation that should help it to avoid dangerous or undesirable situations in the future.

▶ According to Descartes, the mind was separate from the body, and worked on different rules and principles. Descartes suggested a part of the brain where the mind and the body would interact, each influencing the other. This idea is referred to as *Cartesian dualism,* or *interactive dualism.*

tial feats of survival. Lamarck claimed that the characteristics that each individual acquires through such effort could be passed on to its offspring. Although the theory was popular for many years (into the twentieth century in Russia), most modern evolutionary theorists reject the idea that acquired characteristics can be biologically transmitted after one lifetime.

### Charles Darwin's evolutionary theory

**Charles Darwin** (1809–82) proposed an evolutionary theory that revolutionized the way biologists regarded the origins and development of animals, including man. Darwin published his theory of *natural selection* in 1859 in *On the Origins of the Species by Natural Selection or the Preservation of Favoured Races in the Struggle for Life*. In the introduction he states: 'As many more individuals of each species are born than can possibly survive; and as, consequently, there is a frequently recurring struggle for existence, it follows that any being, if it vary however slightly in any manner profitable to itself, will have a better chance of surviving, and thus be naturally selected.'

In Chapter 3, entitled 'Struggle for Existence', Darwin says:

> Owing to the struggle for life variations, if they be in any degree profitable to the individuals of a species, in their infinitely complex relations to other organic beings and to their physical conditions of life, will tend to the preservation of such individuals, and will generally be inherited by the offspring. The offspring will also thus have a better chance of surviving, for, of the many individuals of many species which are born, but a small number can survive. I have called this principle, by which each slight variation, if useful is preserved, by the term Natural Selection.

It had been known for centuries that if one individual lives longer than another, or is generally more fertile than another, then that individual will have a greater chance of leaving more descendants than another. Darwin suggested that if there were genetic *traits* for 'living longer' or 'greater fertility' (amongst other things that also influence survival rates), then those traits will be inherited by the offspring of the most fertile or those who live longest, possibly allowing them to be slightly more fertile or live slightly longer in their turn, thus passing those traits on to their offspring.

So if an animal has some physical structure, such as a slightly longer tail, or slightly larger claws, or a slightly bigger wingspan, and this helps the animal to survive, then genes for that structure will be passed on to its offspring. The offspring may have a slightly greater chance of having slightly longer tails, larger claws or bigger wingspans that assist them in surviving too. The animals with the 'regular' tails, claws or wingspans may well continue for many generations, whilst some descendants of those who were more fit to survive may come to dominate the rest, or might cause the rest to become extinct by taking all the available food. Or they might move elsewhere where the conditions are more beneficial.

That is not to say that those who inherited the most advanta-

► The principle of *natural selection* simply means that those individuals and those species which are physiologically and behaviourally most fit to survive are most likely to pass on their characteristics to their offspring.

► In biology a *trait* is any distinguishing anatomical feature or inherited characteristic of an organism.

► It is important not to exaggerate the effect of receiving particular genes from our parents. They are usually very slight and may take many generations before they become significant. Or the receiving offspring may die before reproduction so any benefits will be lost. Occasionally a change may occur between one generation and its offspring, for example the shape of the beaks of Galapagos finches vary slightly between generations.

► For Darwin 'fitness to survive' meant 'had most offspring'.

■ **What is evolution?**

■ **Explain what Darwin meant by natural selection.**

► Darwin believed that all species had evolved from other, earlier forms, and that many species had become extinct when they finally couldn't compete with better adapted species.

■ **What did Darwin mean by 'survival of the fittest'? In your answer make it clear what 'the fittest' are most fit to do.**

► *Reductionism* was a major influence in early psychology, reflecting its roots in biology. It underlies much of the thinking of the behaviourist traditions of Watson and Skinner.

■ **Where does an animal's behaviour originate, according to Darwin?**

■ **What is the difference between Lamarckian and Darwinian theories of evolution?**

► During the middle decades of the twentieth century Konrad Lorenz and Niko Tinbergen introduced a new way of studying animals called *ethology*. Early ethology maintained the reductionist perspective implied by Darwin's explanations of evolution. Ethologists study and describe animal behaviour in its natural setting and most now see it as an interaction between biology and environment.

geous genes were necessarily superior to others. As far as Darwin was concerned, if an organism is suited to the environment in which it lives, and could reproduce in sufficient numbers to perpetuate the species, then it was well adapted or *fit to survive*. Darwin wasn't even happy with the idea of 'evolution' since it implied that all living things are 'progressing' towards some inevitable, specific ideal state, with each generation becoming a little closer to achieving it. He rejected this idea. He wrote: 'No country can be named in which all the native inhabitants are so perfectly adapted that none of them could be still better adapted or improved.'

Those individuals (and those species) who were less able to survive were more likely to die sooner, thus not passing on their less well-adapted genes to very many descendants. Like the better adapted organisms, those descendants would either die, or mature and reproduce. Thus, after many generations, a whole new species could emerge from another, the old one simply continuing as it always had, becoming extinct, or finding other ways to survive, and the new one being much more fit to survive and evolve further.

Darwin's theory implies that all the behaviour that any species exhibits is the result of its genetic inheritance. This principle is called *reductionism* (see Chapter 17), and it dominated evolutionary thinking for several decades, although Darwin himself couldn't have known about the existence or function of genes so we couldn't describe Darwin as a reductionist in this sense. Most contemporary psychologists are highly doubtful that reductionism could ever explain all behaviour, even all animal behaviour. More recent developments in evolutionary thinking investigate the possible interaction between behaviour and physiological states.

### Sociobiology

Sociobiology is a radical alternative evolutionary theory, first proposed by the zoologist **Edward Wilson** in 1975. In *Sociobiology: The New Synthesis* he tried to integrate material from ideas about evolution and population control, zoology, genetics and ethological studies of animals into a single theory that would encompass *ethology* and comparative psychology. The new theory adds several points to Darwinian evolutionary ideas. For example, sociobiologists maintain that what is important is the survival of the genes of the species, not the survival of each individual member. (We will return to this idea later when we consider the biological basis for altruism.) Second, it attempts to explain the biological bases for social behaviour, as well as for how bodily structures and functions may change over time. This claim has attracted a great deal of controversy.

Wilson claimed that genes influence behaviour. If the behaviour they promote contributes to the species' survival, and so ultimately to its ability to reproduce itself, those genes will be naturally selected. If sociobiology's claim is correct, it follows that each individual will tend to behave in ways that maximize its (and therefore its group's) fitness to survive.

Sociobiologists claim that there is evidence that most of the behaviour of most animals can be interpreted as maximizing their chances of surviving. Avoiding predators, selecting a mate, caring for the offspring, forming social groups, establishing and defending a territory, and so on can all involve behaviours that contribute to survival. However, not everyone accepts that behaviour can be naturally selected in this way, and behaviour is seen as a result of evolution, not an influence in it.

The major criticism of sociobiology concerns the application of its claims to human behaviour. If people behave in ways that maximize their own chances for passing on their genes, then we could understand women whose partners aren't willing or able to make them pregnant having sexual relationships with men who are. Equally, men might be expected to behave in ways that would lead to them having as many sexual partners (and therefore offspring) as possible. Sociobiologists aren't recommending, or condoning, such behaviour. They are saying that there might be some biological justification for it. Supporters of various religious organizations, supporters of the family unit, many women's organizations and various others have attacked such implications.

One of sociobiology's critics is **Nicky Hayes** (1986). Her criticism is not so much on moral, religious or ethical grounds, but rather on what she sees as sociobiology's lack of scientific credibility. She describes the theory as 'magical and unscientific'. By magical she means that the theory does not rely on 'material evidence' such as scientifically gathered 'facts', but is somehow 'self-sufficient' and precludes the need for further investigation. Scientific explanations rely on data that have been carefully gathered and analysed, and that can be rejected, refined or supported by other investigations. They allow predictions to be made, which themselves can be tested. Hayes claims that sociobiology is not open to scientific analysis in this way.

Despite such criticisms, sociobiology gathered many supporters all over the world during the 1970s and 1980s, and Wilson continues to refine and publish further insights into behaviour gained from applying a sociobiological perspective. Sociobiology continues to attract supporters and critics and we will return to the debate in Chapter 7.

► Sociobiology maintains that behaviour that contributed to survival is just as likely to be naturally selected as physical characteristics are.

■ How does sociobiology differ from Darwinian views of evolution?

### Interaction of genetic and environmental factors on adaptation

Here is a summary of the way contemporary evolutionary theorists regard the interaction of genetic and environmental factors on the successful adaptation of animals:

(a) The genes that convey information about when and how each individual will develop its characteristics are inherited by each offspring from its parents.

(b) The transmission is normally, but not always, perfect.

(c) Occasionally the offspring will not receive an exact set of its parents' genes.

## Summary – Evolution

Evolution is a process in which individuals of every species compete for the resources necessary to stay alive and reproduce themselves. Darwin's theories have influenced many psychologists, particularly his claims for animals being naturally selected for their fitness to survive longest to pass on their genes to their offspring. Sociobiologists argue that behaviour can also be selected for, and any behaviour which promotes the likelihood of the genes themselves surviving will contribute to the members of each species' chances of survival.

▶ Claims from one side or the other of the nature versus nurture approach have appeared, and still do, as the results of new research are revealed, or old research is reinterpreted.

▶ Supporters of the nature view claim that each individual animal's behaviour is the result of the evolution of its species. Supporters of the nurture view emphasize how behaviour is adaptive, according to learning based on experiences.

(d) Many species have large numbers of genes, and many populations of animals are also very large.

(e) So that, although all the members of any one species will be very similar in most respects, none of them is likely to be the same.

(f) Therefore, some members of any species will be better adapted than others at any one time, and some not at all well adapted.

(g) Those who are least well adapted are least likely to thrive.

(h) This process of 'survival of the fittest' constantly pressures all members of a species to adapt themselves to the needs of their environment.

(i) Environments keep changing as climates, land use, tides and so on all change, forcing animals to extend their range, change their habitat, and generally modify their behaviour in order to survive.

(j) The process begins again (go back to (a)) – all species are thus constantly in a state of evolution since all must adapt to their environment, which is itself constantly changing.

## EVOLUTION OF BEHAVIOUR IN NON-HUMAN SPECIES

There is disagreement between supporters of the idea that many animal behaviours were instinctive or genetically inherited (the nature view), and the argument that many are acquired through exposure to situations and experience (the nurture view).

Supporters of the nativist view claim that living things inherit the essential behaviour patterns that will allow them to survive. Many animals do not live very long, and would simply not have the time to learn the skills necessary for survival before passing on their genes to the next generation. A female digger wasp must emerge from her pupa, mate, dig a hole to lay her eggs in, line it with individual cells, catch food and place some in each cell, lay an egg in each cell, seal each cell, and do all of this in a few weeks before she dies. It seems unlikely that she could have learned this behaviour from another digger wasp (her own parents would have died, as she will, before the offspring emerge). Dung beetles have much the same experience.

Even those who live longer inherit bodily structures such as wings or gills that allow them to function in certain ways such as flying and swimming under water. For example, if flying around a particular area does not yield a good supply of nectar-bearing flowers, the honey bee will return to the hive where it receives signals about where to hunt from bees that have been more successful (see under signalling systems in Chapter 6, pages 124–8, for other examples). These behaviour patterns are claimed to be directed by instinctive drives or genetic forces.

Supporters of the nurture view do not dispute that animals are born with certain physical structures such as wings and gills, but put much more emphasis on how they develop and change their behaviour in the light of experience. Larger animals such as monkeys and chimps, lion cubs and calf elephants spend quite a large percentage of their lives in an immature state (for example, they cannot protect themselves, feed themselves, and are not sexually mature). They have much to learn by observing their parents and their elder siblings, and by interacting with each other. They appear to be 'playing'. They may be establishing their place in their group and learning about who occupies other places, learning about courtship rituals, about feeding, and even learning from their mistakes. Learning is a flexible strategy that allows animals to deal with similar objects in appropriate ways.

In evolution theory any change in the physical structure of an animal or any modification of its behaviour that has *survival value* is called *adaptation.* Being able to see a mountain hare or red grouse will enable a golden eagle to catch its prey and either eat it, or bring it back to feed its family. The co-ordination of sight and flight obviously has survival value for the individual eagle. Survival value also refers to the degree to which the whole species may be helped to survive. Being able to share information about where nectar is to be found will contribute to the survival of the whole colony of bees, and to the survival of all other bee colonies, too.

► It was observed that some chickens expressed what appeared to be their superiority over other chickens by pecking at them. This was called the '*pecking order*'. Individuals of many other species also display dominance over others, and these were also called 'pecking orders'. Many psychologists now prefer the term '*dominance hierarchy*'.

► One way of conceiving of bits of an animal's behaviour is in terms of its *survival value*. Survival value refers to the contribution the behaviour or physical structure makes to the likelihood that the individual or whole species will survive

### Summary – Evolutionary determinants of behaviour

The behaviour of those animals that do not live long enough to learn how to acquire or adapt behaviour must be better explained by biological transmission. Animals that do live longer, and who live in social groups, have the opportunity to learn behavioural adaptations. Learning is a flexible process that allows individuals to make beneficial adjustments to their environments, and may enhance their chances of survival.

■ Summarize the nativist and nurturist view of the relationship between nature and nurture.

## COMPETITION FOR RESOURCES

According to evolutionary theories, members of each species will seek to maximize their chances of survival in order to pass on their genes to as many offspring as possible. At any moment in evolution, therefore, those animals that are alive are the product of the best adapted members of their species. Krebs and Davies (1984) describe them as 'survival machines'. Survival demands such things as having enough food, being able to mate, and living long enough to reproduce. For territorial animals it also means having somewhere to live. Each need has led to each animal species evolving its own particular strategies for achieving it.

## *Finding food*

In order to survive many animal species will have to compete for scarce resources such as food. For example those animal species which have to hunt, such as wolves, jackals and lionesses, must find, chase, catch, and then overpower and kill their prey. Chasing uses energy, which must be replaced by eating food. Using excessive energy without eating will weaken the animal. Becoming weak makes the predator more vulnerable to other animals that mightn't otherwise prey on it.

Any strategy that makes hunting more likely to succeed will benefit the hunter. An obvious example here will be stalking the prey. A successful hunter may use its sight or hearing to detect the presence of prey before the prey detects its presence. By staying upwind, and moving nearer slowly and silently, the prey may still not detect its presence until it is quite close. Minimizing the distance of the chase makes success more likely at minimum cost in effort. The various activities used in stalking will contribute to the individual hunter's survival.

Strategies useful in chasing include watching the fleeing quarry, and noting if it starts to turn to the left or right. Cutting the corner or taking short cuts will shorten the gap, and possibly the effort of the chase. Having caught the prey hunting animals need effective strategies for killing it at minimum risk to itself. This often involves killing the prey as soon as possible (unless it has no means of defence, attack or escape). Wolves and jackals will bite the throat of their prey.

Not all animals hunt. Some simply take their food from a defenceless neighbour. Skuas, for example, are large, aggressive sea-birds that prey on colonies of neighbours. A maturing kittyhawk chick will make a good meal for their own chicks. Some skuas have also developed strategies for taking an adult kittyhawk in flight as food for themselves. They plunge into the sea with the kittyhawk in order to drown, or at least weaken it. They then attack it with their powerful beaks. The main prize is the kittyhawk's liver, since this will contain a rich supply of nourishment. Those skuas that have developed the most effective means of taking food for themselves and their offspring will be most successful at exploiting their environment and competing with other species and with each other for success in survival.

Other animal species, such as many crab and spider species, simply wait for their food to come to them. The trapdoor spider finds a convenient hollow, hides in it, pulling a leaf over the entrance, and waits for a small insect to drop in. Finding such a place in an area that attracts many insects will be an effective way of obtaining food. The most successful members of web-spinning spiders species will make their webs in places where insects are most likely to be found. Where other species also exploit any one species' food, the most successful animals will be those that have developed the most effective strategies for finding and keeping it.

Some animal species have developed a strategy of using tools for obtaining food. For example the angler fish waves a lure in front of its prey, attracting the smaller animal which swims into the angler fish's mouth. Sea otters lie on their backs with a mollusc shell wedged on their fronts which they break open using a stone. An insect-eating monkey might find that pushing a stick into an ants' nest then withdrawing it results in food, since ants will have moved onto the stick. Those members of the species that can adopt these strategies are most likely to be successful at obtaining food.

## Mating and rearing the young

Not all species require males and females to mate. Some fish and frog species, for example, produce eggs that may be fertilized by others who never come into contact with the egg producers. For others finding a mate may involve singing to identify an opposite-sex member of the same species, followed fairly automatically by mating. For these species few strategies are required. For those species that have evolved elaborate courtship rituals, such as grooming skills, precision flying to show off flying skills, or leaping into the air to impress with their strength, those animals that can perform the activities most effectively are most likely to be rewarded.

Having found a mate, the parents of those species that live long enough to see their offspring develop may have evolved strategies for ensuring successful rearing. An interesting example is the cuckoo. Different cuckoos will produce eggs of different sizes and colouring. While the adult birds are away, cuckoos will leave their eggs in a nest of a species of bird which is smaller than they are, and which already contains eggs that look similar to their own. By removing one of the existing eggs, and substituting one of their own, the deception may not be noticed by the returning adults. It is an instinctive reaction for nesting birds to feed their young. The hatchlings call for food by turning their beaks upwards, opening their mouths, and exposing the red patch around their throats. Seeing this patch acts as a trigger for the parent bird to feed the young by putting food that they have gathered into the offspring's mouth. The young cuckoo will eject any unhatched eggs from the nest, soon followed by the other nestlings. Having eliminated the competition, the unwitting parents spend all their energies feeding this large and ever-hungry parasite.

## Living space

Competition for living space is another significant factor in survival for many territorial animals. A territory needs to be large enough to contain the necessary elements of food and shelter, but be small enough to be defensible. Members of a territorial animal species will compete where a potential living area, such as a nest site, is near a high concentration of food items. Hummingbirds have been found to compete for territory only when the territory contains enough food items to justify the effort involved in competing for, or defending it.

Lions will defend their territory against other males who may seek to challenge for possession of the territory and the lioness. If the challenger is successful the defeated lion may slink away with its tail between its legs. The victorious lion will need to start reproduction with his new mate. He will often kill any cubs that belonged to his predecessor, which may bring the lioness into breeding condition, whereby she will be able to mate and become pregnant. Killing the cubs is simply a strategy for promoting his chances of passing on his own genes.

Many species of birds, including penguins, have been able to survive by developing the strategy of exploiting the resources of two geographically separate areas by migrating between them. Migration is one response to changes in the climate with the seasons, and when the food supply in one area is nearing depletion. The Arctic tern probably has the longest journey, flying about 12,000 miles twice a year from its nesting sites in Europe and Asia to the coasts of Antarctica for the winter. Whilst birds are the best known for migrating, some insects also migrate (Biblical stories of swarms of locusts are well known).

Reptiles such as the green sea turtle have nest sites on land to which they return every two or three years to lay their eggs. Apart from this they live in the sea. The exploitation of different areas by marine mammals such as humpback whales appears to be influenced by the availability of their food. They live near the North and South Poles when food is plentiful, and, as the weather grows even colder and the food supply diminishes, they swim to more tropical seas. The 300,000 wildebeest of the Serengeti Plain in East Africa migrate to Lake Victoria as the dry season begins and their food supply reduces.

## Survival by predicting other's behaviour

Each member of an animal species has a limited number of behaviours that it could perform at any one time. It may be able to eat, drink, attack another, run away, make a home, rest, copulate, and so on, but usually only one at a time. Knowing what any other animal in the vicinity is likely to do would be of enormous advantage in deciding what it actually does. If a wildebeest (a large antelope) needs to drink, but a lioness is lying between it and a waterhole, the wildebeest would be unwise to risk its life by approaching the lioness. If, however, the lioness has eaten recently, the wildebeest is less at risk. Knowing that a well-fed lioness lies in a certain way, breathes in a certain way, and looks in a certain way, compared to a hungry animal, would be of enormous benefit to the wildebeest. Some animal behaviour may be predictable, and being able to make these predictions will help others who share the same environment to survive.

▶ The extent to which animals are likely to migrate depends largely on the availability of their food, their requirements for reproduction, and how much the weather changes in their environments.

■ In your own words, explain why some species of animals migrate.

■ Name another species of animal that has found a different way to deal with the factors you suggested in the previous answer (here's a clue: NUTS). How does this animal survive without migrating?

■ How might being able to predict the behaviour of another species be beneficial to an animal?

**Konrad Lorenz** (1966) claimed that these skills of prediction would either have been naturally selected from amongst today's animal ancestors, or would be learned during the lifetime of any animal. So those wildebeest who ran away when they saw a crouching lioness were more likely to have survived than those who didn't. It was argued that 'genes for running away from perceived danger' would be passed on to future generations, who, in turn, would have survived longer and passed on the genes to their offspring. Critics argue that this idea about what genes are and how they work is misleading. Of course, a lioness might have found that lying still and looking asleep is a successful way of luring an unfortunate wildebeest to pass nearby. Springing onto the unsuspecting wildebeest would save the lioness from having to chase it, and run the risk of wasting a lot of energy, and possibly still not catching it. Luckily for wildebeest, few lionesses have adapted the way they look when hungry or well fed.

There are many occasions when it is in an animal's best interests to have its behaviour accurately predicted, and so the question of exploitation doesn't arise. For example males of many territorial species will attack any other member of its species that enters its territory, including females. Any female, therefore, that may be in mating condition may stay away from the territory in case she is attacked. If the male can signal whether he will attack or be receptive to mating, this would save them both unnecessary effort.

A very effective survival strategy has been developed by many warm-blooded animals who live in areas where the winters are cold and long, and food becomes very scarce. Ground squirrels, hedgehogs, shrews and some bats will hibernate and become dormant, in a cave, burrow or some other enclosed space. Since they possess brain centres that allow them to control their body temperature, they can control their body's heat loss so that they can survive in near-freezing temperatures. They are effectively becoming coldblooded. Their body's functioning, such as heart rate, breathing and movement, are all reduced, so they do not need much food or water. When fully hibernating they are virtually unconscious and inactive, and can survive a long winter on the fat that they have built up when food was available, although some may wake from time to time to eat food stored for that purpose.

Full hibernation isn't the only form of dormancy. For example, brown and black bears sleep for days and weeks during winter, but wake occasionally to eat and prowl, and cubs are often born during one of these periods. Another type of dormancy, called *estivation*, occurs for the opposite reason. When desert temperatures soar and food and water become especially scarce, some desert animals reduce their body activity in order to conserve what resources they have.

► Lorenz's ethological theory is claiming that some behavioural adaptations can be naturally selected, as did sociobiology.

■ **Ethologists and sociobiologists both claim that behaviour can be naturally selected. How does this compare to Darwinian theory?**

► Hibernating animals aren't 'asleep', which is often how hibernation is portrayed.

**Summary – Competition for resources**

The most important resources for any animal are food, protection and the availability of a mate. Competition for resources from within the same species is likely to lead to the best adapted being most successful. However, many strategies have been developed to maximize the survival of the group as well as the individual, from using tools and other animals, to migrating to exploit other territories.

## PREDATOR–PREY RELATIONSHIPS AND THE EVOLUTION OF BEHAVIOUR

Throughout our discussion of animal behaviour we have stressed the importance of food. Food provides the energy necessary to live, some of which will be spent on getting food. For some animals, such as wildebeest, their food supply is vegetation. For others, it is other animals. Many spiders spin webs to trap any animal small enough to become caught. Lionesses crouch, chase and pounce on inexperienced or immature, elderly or injured antelopes, gazelles, zebra and so on. Most large fish eat smaller fish, as do many birds. The female praying mantis even kills her mate during mating. His body will be a valuable source of nourishment for her later.

Predator–prey relationships can be seen from the point of view of the predator and the defender. Predators need to be skilled at running, flying, diving, biting, stinging or whatever other devices they employ for conquering their prey. Some animals resort to all kinds of trickery to catch their food, and all manner of adaptations to avoid being eaten. For example, female Photuris fireflies lie in wait for a male of another species to pass by. Males attract a mate by flashing their light until they find a female who flashes back. The predator firefly gives the signal, and the unfortunate male ends up as a meal rather than a parent.

### Anti-predator strategies

In order to avoid being killed by predators, some species have evolved many effective anti-predator strategies and adaptations. The most obvious are trying to get away, for example by running, flying or swimming in the opposite direction. Hiding or camouflaging (the chameleon) are also used by some. Having an effective warning system in place so that predators can be detected and avoided at the earliest moment is used by some social animals. Here are some examples of anti-predator strategies.

*1 Protecting the weakest members*
Groups of Yellow Baboons who live on the plains of East Africa travel with the females, the old and the immature baboons surrounded by the younger, stronger males. If a predator lioness or a

▶ Some animals are vegetarian (for example horses, cows, deer, antelope); most are predators or prey. Few animals prey on healthy elephants!

leopard is seen the strongest males will distract and even attack the predator. The rest form a tight defensive circle to protect the rest of the troupe. Dolphins have been known to circle an injured dolphin, which they help to the surface for air.

Some social insects live in colonies and have evolved specialized forms to fulfil specialized functions. A good example is the soldier ant. Soldier ants can produce pheronomes that alert other soldier ants to danger when the colony is being attacked. The soldier ants will close in upon the predator and bite with their large and powerful jaws. Others can spray harmful chemicals such as formic acid, and, in one extreme case, some defenders have thrown themselves at the attacker, at the same time bursting their bodies open and rupturing a gland in their stomach that secretes a sticky substance over their enemy. (This kind of sacrificial behaviour is discussed as *altruism* in Chapter 6.)

*2 Distraction displays*

Some ground-nesting birds such as the pipit will flutter down to the ground in front of a predator that is approaching the nest. Hopefully the predator will be distracted and attempt to catch the adult bird. As it does the bird will take off and fly away from the nest. The pipit may seem to fall to the ground several times, drawing the predator to follow. When the predator is sufficiently distant, the pipit will fly back to the nest. Some ducks and waders appear to go even further. They distract a predator by appearing to be injured. One wing is drooped as if broken. The animal may appear to be an easy catch for the predator. When the 'injured' bird has drawn the predator far enough away she appears to enjoy a miraculous recovery and flies back to her young!

Some mammals such as seals also use distraction displays. An adult seal will show itself to a killer whale, presumably in order to lead it away from its young. Distraction displays sound almost charming, but sadly nature isn't always kind, otherwise all predator species would become extinct. Often the adult will be caught and killed by the predator.

*3 Flocking, herding and shoaling*

If one member of a group becomes aware that a predator may be nearby it might start to run. This appears to signal to the others to run too. Members of other species who are preyed upon by the same predators will also start to run. Staying close together makes sense, since a group of animals who are flying, running or swimming together deters a predator who needs to single out a particular individual to attack. A lioness who becomes entangled in a herd of running wildebeest may be trampled and injured. It appears that there's safety in staying together, which is also reflected in imprinting and bonding behaviour, which we will review in Chapter 6.

*4 Alarm calls*

Most flocking or herding animals use alarm calls to warn others in their group that an enemy is nearby. Many small songbirds such as chaffinches, robins, titmice and thrushes make a reedy whistle to

► *Altruism* refers to any behaviour where one individual sacrifices or risks some aspect of its own well-being in favour of another individual.

► Animals that use distraction displays would have little or no conventional defence against an attacker, so the distraction display may be the only thing that they can do.

► Tape-recordings of the distress calls of gulls are played at some airports to clear the gulls from the runways before an aircraft takes off or lands.

► Alarm calls from one species will often excite members of other, unrelated species too. In the jungle, when the birds flock, other animals scamper for safety as well, even though they may have no idea what the danger might be.

signal the approach of a predator. When any of the small songbirds hear the call they will all seek cover, regardless of the species the caller belongs to. Many species of monkeys give out a high-pitched screech, ground squirrels chatter loudly, and rabbits drum their feet on the ground, all appearing to act as warnings to others. The most elaborate alarm calls are probably given by vervet monkeys. They use a different call for different groups of predators. So if one spots an airborn predator it will give a call that alerts the others to hide in thick undergrowth. If a ground-based predator is suspected, a different call results in the animals climbing a tall tree. Vervets have four distinct alarm calls.

### 5 Alarm displays
These are made by some animals to alert others. Thomson's gazelles, for example, raise their tails and display their tail patch. This alerts other Thomson's gazelles that a cheetah, or other predator, is nearby.

### 6 Warning the predator
Thomson's gazelles are efficient runners and can keep up their speed for long distances. Cheetahs can run faster than a Thomson's gazelle, but not for long. If the cheetah can get sufficiently close without its prey noticing, it may well catch and kill it. If the gazelle is alerted, it could outrun the cheetah. Since it's in neither of their interests to have an energy-consuming race, the gazelle has evolved a display called stotting in which it stiffens its legs and jumps vertically into the air, landing in the same place. Cheetahs observing this behaviour are much less likely to attempt to chase a gazelle.

### 7 Mimicry
Some prey species can fool their predators by appearing like the predator, or like another species that the predator does not prey upon. This was first recorded in 1862 by **H.W. Bates**, and is called *Batesian mimicry*. He noticed that if a species of butterflies that could be eaten by a predator looked like species that were poisonous or distasteful, they were much less likely to be eaten. The Monarch butterfly is large, orange and flies slowly. It is also poisonous to birds. The Viceroy butterfly has evolved similar colouring and characteristics, and is also less likely to be attacked by a bird who has had any experience of Monarchs.

Batesian mimicry can be found among many species of animals, including fish and birds. However, it can be seen most frequently amongst insects such as wasps, bees and flies. Several species of fly have evolved black and yellow markings and so resemble bees. Predators who avoid painful stings will avoid animals that look like they can sting.

■ How have some species of animals evolved to avoid being prey?

### Summary – Predator–prey relationships
Many of the animals that eat other animals have evolved some ingenious strategies for catching their prey. Many of the animals they eat have evolved mechanisms for avoiding their predators. These include stronger or more skilled individuals defending

weaker ones, parents distracting predators by sacrificing themselves, joining together into large groups, calling or moving in ways intended to warn others or summon assistance, warning the predator that it has been spotted, and mimicry.

## SYMBIOTIC RELATIONSHIPS AND THE EVOLUTION OF BEHAVIOUR

*Symbiosis* refers to any kind of close relationship, temporary or permanent, that exists between members of two or more species. The individuals in a symbiotic relationship (*sym* means together, *bios* means life) may be entirely dependent upon each other for survival, or that life is at least made easier by the presence or behaviour of the other. There are three kinds of symbiotic relationship. *Mutualism* occurs when both partners benefit from the relationship. In *commensalism* one partner benefits and the other isn't particularly affected. When one partner benefits and the other loses out we have *parasitism*. To varying degrees commensalism and mutualism may appear *altruistic* (see Chapter 6).

■ What is meant by a symbiotic relationship?

■ How would Darwinian evolutionary theorists explain how symbiosis comes about?

### Mutualism

Mutualism has been observed in the behaviour of some insects, vertebrates and fish. Here are some examples.

One species of small flatworm that lives buried in the sand on the seashore allows green algae to live in its tissues. When the tide is out during the day the worm lies on the sand so that light can stimulate the green algae to manufacture starch. This starch is the flatworm's only food. The algae benefit by having somewhere to live, the flatworm has something to eat. Lichen is the result of a mutual partnership between a fungus and an algae.

Some caterpillars excrete a sugary substance called honey-dew, which is eaten by some species of ant. This secretion is a normal part of the caterpillar's digestive system, and it would secrete the substance regardless of whether any other organism ate it. The ants sometimes stimulate the caterpillars to produce the honey-dew by stroking them with their antennae. Some species of caterpillar have been surrounded by their ant partners for so long that they have lost their own external covering and rely on the ants to protect them.

Ox-pecker birds spend much of their lives feeding on the tics and fleas that live on the backs of large grazing animals such as giraffes throughout Africa. The larger animal derives two benefits. First, it loses its parasites and any dead hair, which the birds use for their nests and which could otherwise cause damage. Second, it has an early warning system of the approach of a predator, since the birds will fly away. However, there is a downside too. If the large animal has damaged skin caused by the blood-sucking tics, the birds will often peck at the damage and stop it from healing. The wound may even become infected and cause more harm to the animal. The benefit to the birds is that they receive a plentiful food supply.

The crocodile bird appears to be rather more adventurous. It enters the open mouth of the crocodile and feeds off the food that is stuck between the crocodile's teeth, and any leeches that are clinging to the crocodile's mouth. At any moment the crocodile could close its mouth and have an instant meal of birds. Yet it doesn't since, again, both are benefiting. The behaviour contributes to the survival of both species.

Many small fish perform a similar 'cleaning operation' in the mouths and on the bodies of larger fish. Manta ray also have trouble with lice on its skin. Other fish swim with it, and, when they can, they eat the lice from the larger fish's body. Most cleaners are brightly coloured to warn the larger fish not to eat them as they are 'friendly'. They usually have long snouts and small teeth. In the waters off southern California groups of opal-eye fish gather and wait for their clean-up by the golden brown wrasse. The large fish have evolved a behaviour pattern that recognizes and responds to the cleaner fish. Although the cleaners can deal with up to 50 larger fish an hour, the larger fish return every few days for the service.

## Commensalism

This usually refers to the way some species feed together.

Some hermit crabs protect their soft abdomen by surrounding them in an empty whelk's shell. Some sea anemone often cling to the whelk's shell and eat scraps of the crab's food. The anemone receives food while the crab doesn't derive any particular benefit. There's no reason to imagine that the crab associates the presence of the anemone on the whelk shell with itself, and the anemone only receives food that the crab has let go.

Sponges contain numerous passages through which water filters, depositing particles of edible plankton on the passage walls. Some small worms also pass through the sponge. Some cling to the walls and eat the plankton, causing them to grow until they are too large to pass through an exit hole. They spend their lives being fed and protected by the sponge, which receives no benefit at all from their presence. The sponge didn't 'invite' the creatures to move in, nor is its survival enhanced by their presence.

## Parasitism

A parasitic relationship involves one species of organism living in or on another, and depending on it for food and other needs. Almost all life forms, including humans, have parasites living in or on them. We've all seen cats and dogs scratching. Fleas are flightless animals with strong hind legs that allow them to jump onto a host. Lice are also insects. Within a few weeks after birth most birds could be parasitized by 20 or 30 different species of lice and other parasites. Mites are tiny relations of spiders that can be parasites on other parasites. Like all others they contribute nothing to their hosts' survival, yet couldn't exist without them.

---

### *Summary – Symbiotic relationships*

Symbiotic relationships exist where several animals co-exist. Mutual symbiosis occurs where both benefit. Commensal symbiosis occurs where only one member benefits, and there's no significant effect on the other. In parasitic relationships one organism benefits at the cost of another.

---

### *Exam questions – 60 minutes each*

1  Describe and evaluate the role of evolutionary ideas in understanding the behaviour of non-human animals. (*25 marks*)

2  (a) Identify and explain the main resources non-human animals need for survival. (*6 marks*)
   (b) Describe, with examples, some of the ways in which animals have to compete for resources. (*8 marks*)
   (c) Analyse evolutionary perspectives on the competition for resources. (*11 marks*)

3  Critically discuss the effects of predator–prey and symbiotic relationships on the evolution of behaviour in animals. (*25 marks*)

# 6 Kinship and social behaviour

> **Chapter objectives**
>
> By the end of this chapter you will:
>
> ▐ understand the nature of apparent altruism in animals;
>
> ▐ have recognized some examples of sociality in some species of animals, and the potential benefits of social living;
>
> ▐ appreciate the interaction of genes and social factors in animal altruism, as well as problems of interpretation in this research;
>
> ▐ appreciate research findings underlying the nature and consequences of imprinting in precocial animals, and bonding in altricial animals;
>
> ▐ appreciate the nature and variety of animal communication, and how different signalling systems are used.

## Introduction

Some animals, such as the giant panda, live solitary lives, rarely encountering others of their own species. Others live in social, often co-operative groups, and some aspects of group life will be discussed here. Some members behave in ways that appear to help others whilst putting themselves at greater risk. These are examples of *apparent altruism*. Research into altruism in human subjects is discussed in Chapter 4. Each new member of a group must be integrated into the group, and some do so by forms of bonding with their caregivers. Bonding behaviour in humans is discussed in Chapters 14 and 15. Group members use *signalling systems* for communication between themselves, and sometimes their signals are also interpreted and acted upon by members of other species. Comparative psychologists look for any clues that the principles and practices that underlie animal behaviour may explain similar processes in humans.

## SOCIALITY IN NON-HUMAN ANIMALS

To be *social* animals that stay together must do things together. This is perhaps best seen in the division of labour that exists in a beehive or termite mound. Each member of the whole group has specialized functions that serve to protect and promote the survival of the group. When people live together they find security, companionship, help and a division of labour to achieve things such as making goods, providing services, rearing children and running the home. Humans can usually see the benefits of such co-operation. When animals form a herd, when they swarm or flock, they may also be benefiting from their social behaviour. If there's safety in numbers then a herd of zebra may be more likely to survive an attack by a hungry lioness than a single zebra. Chimpanzees live in family groups, with the young learning from their mothers. If a young chimp loses its mother it may well be adopted by its older brothers or sisters.

► Not all behaviour involving a group of the same species is necessarily social behaviour, however. A swarm of insects may be attracted by a bright light on a dark night, and may swarm around it. They are together, but they are not behaving socially.

## Some examples of social behaviour

We said in the last chapter that there are several essential needs that all animals must satisfy if they are to survive and thrive. These include finding sufficient food to eat, finding somewhere safe to live, and satisfying the needs of reproduction. In Chapter 5 we described some ways in which social animals alert other animals to the presence of a predator, for example herding, flocking and shoaling, and by giving alarm calls and alarm displays. The members of some animal species such as dolphins make distress calls if stranded or lost, or in some other kind of distress (see the discussion later in this chapter on pages 124–8 under signalling). In this section we will concentrate on social behaviour involving the other needs – sharing food and helping others to reproduce.

■ Identify the main needs that all animals have if their species is to survive.

Many birds, including penguins, eat fish. Some eat meat, including golden eagles. Most birds will catch their food and bring it back to their nests, where they will share it with their young and sometimes with other members of their species. Some animals, such as the jackal, sometimes hunt in packs and may catch large prey such as sheep, antelope or a Thomson's gazelle between them. They carry or drag parts of their prey back to their dens. African wild dogs seem very sociable. The pack will bring food which they regurgitate for all the members of the pack to share, including those that are injured or orphaned. Vampire bats will often share their meal of blood with another bat who has been unsuccessful at hunting. Lionesses often hunt in pairs and catch larger or faster prey, which they share with the rest of the pride. Such a co-operative picture of animals sharing with each other may be misleading. When food is scarce the lion will bully his way to the kill, and the lioness gets what's left. Only if she leaves some food do the cubs feed. They often starve, but at least she can produce more cubs.

► Sharing food with one's offspring will not aid individual survival. Yet many animals share food with their offspring when it is plentiful.

In most baboon troupes there will be a dominant male who will have his pick of the females. When he is preparing to mate two younger males have been observed acting co-operatively to mate the female instead. One distracts the alpha male, the other mates with the female. Being the dominant male is not always an advantage. He may have to spend energy guarding his position that he could otherwise spend on mating. Being a subdominant may be

► Darwin's ideas about the laws of natural selection do not seem adequate here. They would demand that each member must survive to pass its genes to future generations. Helping others to reproduce and become rivals to one's own offspring seems contradictory to Darwin's view of natural selection.

■ List some examples of social co-operation which animals use as part of their defence (you may need to look back at the last chapter).

► *Pro-social* behaviour supports and promotes the well-being of the majority of the members of a given group. It is the opposite of *anti-social* behaviour, which threatens wider group interests.

► Not all human behaviour that helps someone else is necessarily altruism, either. You may have been involved in some activity for Children in Need, or Red Nose Day, which you enjoyed, and had a brilliant time. You were sponsored and so someone else benefits. Were you behaving altruistically?

■ What is the difference in the definition of altruism when applied to animals compared with its application to humans? Why is this difference important?

more advantageous! Lionesses who have young of their own will suckle the young of another lioness who isn't able to feed them herself, possibly because she is hunting for the pride's food. Black-backed jackals do not breed themselves, but guard and help to rear another pair's pups. Worker bees will spend their lives bringing up the queen bee's offspring. They will even die to defend the hive against attackers, yet they are sterile and unable to reproduce at all.

> ### Summary – Sociality in non-human animals
> Survival demands meeting the needs for food, protection and safety, and reproduction. Some species find that living socially is an effective means of satisfying these needs. Some animals hunt in packs, rear their young collectively, and have organized themselves for defence.

## APPARENT ALTRUISM

One feature of sociality is *apparent altruism*. As we said in Chapter 4, altruism in humans involves doing something for someone else and putting someone else's needs, interests, happiness or even survival above one's own. For humans altruistic behaviour is thus *pro-social*. As far as altruism in animals is concerned it involves behaviour that promotes the chances that the group to which the individual altruist belongs will survive to pass on its genes to future generations.

When humans behave in caring ways, for example by giving time or money to charity, by being a blood donor, or by helping those less fortunate than themselves, they are behaving altruistically. The behaviour implies an intention or motivational state in which we make a judgement about other people's needs relative to our own, and our ability to help them. If you have some time, and someone else needs your help, you may well give it. When the term is applied to animal behaviour it means something slightly different. Non-human animals do not have the higher cognitive centres that humans have for understanding the consequences of their actions, for paying attention and remembering, for acting sympathetically towards others in need, or for planning and implementing their own courses of action. Much non-human animal behaviour is largely directed by biologically transmitted instincts and drives. Altruism in non-human animals is only recognized by its consequences. If an animal behaves in a way which seems to help another, whilst putting itself at some disadvantage in satisfying the basic needs described above, then its behaviour is interpreted as altruism.

### Some examples of apparent altruism in non-human animals

The most obvious example of altruism, using the definition above, is parental care. Not all animals rear their young (e.g. cuckoos, frogs, fish and dung beetles). Of those that do (many birds and mammals), parental behaviour involves expending a great amount of time and energy feeding and protecting the immature offspring. Caring for the young can expose the parent to danger (see the discussion under distraction displays in Chapter 5, page 109.)

Perhaps the best known examples of social animals behaving altruistically are found amongst ants and termites, wasps and bees. Their populations have evolved individuals who are suited to performing specific roles. For example, there are soldier ants, who are large and ferocious, and worker ants, who are specialized in caring for the grubs and caring for the colony's structure. The workers are usually sterile, so their entire lives are devoted to helping rear the offspring of the queen of their group, or to cleaning ventilation shafts and so on without any opportunity to pass on their own genes.

The most extreme examples of altruism occur when the individual dies in order to help satisfy the needs of other members of its species. Some worker ants will form a bridge across a stream in order for others to cross in pursuit of food. They will drown in the process. Such behaviour poses a special problem for Darwinian evolutionary theory. In the introduction to his book *Sociobiology* (1975), Edward Wilson says it is 'the central theoretical problem for sociobiology'. Darwinian theory says that all individuals must behave in ways that promote the opportunities of passing on their own genes.

## Some explanations for seemingly altruistic behaviour

To be altruism, when an animal gives an alarm call or display it must promote the interests of others over its own. The other members of the species may freeze or flee, making themselves less available to the predator. This may reduce distractions, leaving the predator free to concentrate on the animal that gave the call. Also giving an alarm call, for example, may give the predator extra information about exactly where its prey is.

### It's not altruistic at all
However, Charnov and Krebs (1975) suggest that by giving an alarm call or display an animal may actually surround itself with lots of others, thus protecting itself. Tilson and Norton's (1982) research on antelopes being hunted by jackals suggests that the jackals gave up the chase as soon as they realized that the antelopes had detected their presence. Jackals cannot outrun an antelope, so there'd be no point in giving chase. In this case it appeared that the alarm call was more for the benefit of the predator than the rest of the antelopes! Neither of these cases supports the claim that animals behave altruistically.

### The altruistic gene
Nevertheless, some defensive tactics may well put the signaller at risk. Sharing your food may lessen your own chances of survival. And helping others to reproduce may threaten the survival of your genetic

▶ Limiting one's own chances of reproducing and thus passing on one's own genes contradicts evolutionary ideas that individuals strive to survive.

▶ Seemingly altruistic behaviour such as giving an alarm call can be explained as a survival strategy.

► *Inclusive fitness* refers to all the measures an organism may use to ensure that its genes continue. It includes both personal genetic success and the success of the survival of the genetic stock of a close relative.

► If each infant has 50 per cent of its genes from its mother then two infants comprise the same amount of their mother's genes as their mother has herself. Since the infants may not survive to pass those genes on, and the mother is sexually mature and could probably have more offspring, sacrificing oneself for two offspring isn't good odds. Three offspring represent 150 per cent of the mother's genes. Sacrificing oneself to protect one and a half times one's own genes may make better sense.

material to the next generation. So how can Darwin's theory of the survival of the fittest explain such altruistic behaviour? To answer this we need to shift the focus from individual fitness to survive to group fitness (called *inclusive fitness*) to survive. This idea was developed by **William Hamilton**, a population geneticist, in 1964.

William Hamilton developed a theory of kin selection from the gene's point of view. It used a formula to describe the gene relationship between members of the same family. Each offspring comprises a combination of genes from each of its parents, and shares the same combination as its siblings (siblings are 'brothers and sisters'). Assuming that each offspring inherits 50 per cent of its genes from each parent, then a mother who sacrifices herself to save more than two of her offspring will be increasing the chances of her genes surviving.

The third generation have one-quarter of either of their grandparents' genes. A mother might need to be able to save at least five 'grandchildren' to cause her to sacrifice herself. So the calculation went for all the other relations an organism could have. Hamilton is not, of course, suggesting that animal parents are mathematicians, simply that natural selection could favour the characteristic for maximizing the chances of passing one's genes on, and this would include inclusive fitness. **Robert Hinde** (1982) claims that the 'altruistic gene' would increase if altruists sacrificed themselves for only two of their offspring since those two will inherit genes that promote their survival. Inclusive fitness explains the likelihood of altruism between family members being determined by how close the genetic relationship is.

---

### Two examples of inclusive fitness

Langurs are long-tailed monkeys which inhabit parts of India. They live in colonies. If attacked the colony will be defended first by the elderly females, often getting killed themselves. This reduces the numbers of offspring who could be born and seems to serve as a form of population control. They may be killed whilst fighting off their attackers, but at least their daughters and granddaughters might survive through their sacrifice.

Common vampire bats are small, furry creatures with pointed ears that spend their days hanging in caves, old mines, crevices in rocks and such like in parts of Mexico, Chile, Argentina and Uruguay. They feed at night on larger, sleeping animals (including humans) by using their 20 sharp teeth to cut a hole in the skin through which they drink some of their victim's blood. (Unfortunately, they also carry several diseases such as rabies, sometimes killing themselves and their prey.) While the parents leave the cave to hunt and feed, the offspring stay in the nest. Parents bring food back for their offspring, but they also share it with other family members who haven't been successful in finding a victim, including parents of offspring who will be rivals in the hunt for food with their own. Inclusive fitness may explain this behaviour.

## Inclusive fitness or selfish gene?

There is an argument between those who claim that it is possible that natural selection has favoured group survival over individual survival and that altruistic behaviour promoted the continuation of the group. Altruistic genes would be inherited by members of the whole group (to varying extents). In 1962 the ecologist **Wynne-Edwards** pointed out that animals generally do not overexploit their habitat's food supplies since this would lead to overcrowding, which would threaten the survival of all the members of the group. Wynne-Edwards produced evidence which showed that animals higher up the pecking order (and presumably, therefore, 'most fit to survive') continued to reproduce, whilst those further down either started to reproduce later, or didn't engage in sexual behaviour at all. He claims that animals use a number of methods to keep themselves informed of the numbers of their group, and this somehow triggers mating behaviour (or lack of it).

The problem for this explanation is that group selection might not work if it opposed individual selection. This is the *'selfish gene'* theory advanced by sociobiologists such as **Richard Dawkins** (see Chapter 7). The rejection of the theory of group selection did more than anything else to promote the idea of sociobiology. The argument goes: individual animals have genes which must survive at all costs, and will urge the individual to do everything it can to survive and reproduce, to ensure the genes survive. If an animal cheats, for example an animal further down the group hierarchy didn't share its food when food was scarce (therefore behaving selfishly), it may produce more offspring. Those offspring will be inheriting 'cheat genes'. They would continue to mate on other occasions when food was scarce, and would continue to produce selfish breeders. Later the selfish breeders would also breed when they shouldn't, and within a few generations selfish breeders would dominate the group. The group will overexploit its environment, and either die out, have to move to another environment (if it can find an uninhabited one), or change its diet.

Whilst inclusive fitness seems to resolve one flaw in Darwin's ideas about survival, it doesn't explain why members of quite unrelated families also sometimes help others. Humans help other humans because we have each developed certain moral codes. It seems unlikely that non-human animals such as jackals and vampire bats would have such refined cognitive skills. One possibility is that animal altruism is the consequence of altruistic genes. Those animals that benefited from good turns by others were more likely to have survived. However, this only explains how benefiting from altruism could have been naturally selected. Perhaps doing another animal a good turn increases the likelihood that they'll do one in return in the future. So perhaps behaving altruistically might also have become naturally selected amongst today's animals' ancestors.

▶ It may be more realistic to talk in terms of group survival rather than individual survival. The emphasis is moved from genes promoting the survival of the individual to the survival of the group.

▶ It seems the emphasis is moving to the importance of the survival of the genes themselves.

▶ If we accept the principle of fitness to survive explaining the continued adaptation of species, then 'cheats' would have to adapt to a changed diet or changed environment if they are to survive.

▶ According to Darwin, those animals which survive longest must possess characteristics that make them more 'fit' to survive. Fitness of an individual equates to the number of relatives it leaves. Because they live longer they reproduce more offspring, thus passing on the 'fitness to survive' genes to successive generations. If behaving altruistically towards non-relatives contributed to that fitness to survive then it, too, could be passed on to future generations.

## Reciprocal altruism

*Reciprocal altruism* is the animal equivalent of 'you scratch my back and I'll scratch yours'. So long as the monkey who's just had his back scratched returns the favour, the pair might groom each other in the future. This is *intra-species altruism* (intra-species means within the same species). **Craig Packer** (1977) has found in the olive baboon that those males who willingly go to the aid of others in fights (and therefore risk being hurt) are most likely to receive aid in return, and that those who show reluctance to become involved in someone else's battle are least likely to be helped if they are attacked.

**R.L. Trivers** (1971) claims that an animal will assist another if the cost to itself is not high, and if there is a strong chance that the act will be reciprocated in the future. This is called *delayed reciprocal altruism*. The olive baboon studied by Craig Packer has a long life expectancy, and it lives in close-knit groups where members would recognize one another and might be able to remember who they owe favours to, and who the 'cheats' are. This explanation for reciprocal behaviour assumes that baboons have significant cognitive skills of perception, recognition and memory.

So, in order for reciprocal altruism to occur, two conditions must be met. First, the animals must live long enough to provide opportunities for the debt to be repaid. Smaller insects such as digger wasps live only a few weeks. They're unlikely to have evolved much altruistic behaviour. The altruists must also stay together for long enough. Some animals such as swans, geese, eagles, foxes and gibbons are perenially monogamous, i.e. they stay together for life. Animals that stay in the same group for a long time are most likely to show altruistic behaviour.

Second, the animals concerned must be able to recognize each other individually, or all be programmed to help all others who have a known appearance, or who behave in a certain way. If an animal helps all others who presumably are like it in some way, then cheats, who take but do not give, are more likely to survive. Cheats have all the benefits of others' altruism with none of the costs of helping others. They become prime candidates in the survival of the fittest. Eventually such altruism will disappear, and the species will be much more vulnerable to extinction as a result.

For animals to recognize each other they require a degree of cognitive processing that is unlikely to be present in the smaller animals such as insects, fish and birds. They may be genetically programmed to recognize their own species, and (usually) prefer their own species for mating, but that isn't the same as recognizing individual members, and remembering that they had performed some service that may now be repaid.

► If an animal possesses *delayed reciprocal altruism* it must have some reasonable cognitive abilities. Some psychologists researching monkeys' capacity to understand human language claim that they do (see Sue Savage Rumbaugh's work in Chapter 7, pages 139–40). Others are unconvinced.

► For reciprocal altruism to occur animals must live together for long enough for the favour to be repaid, and the animals concerned must be able to recognize who to repay the favour, and who not to.

■ What is meant by (a) the altruistic gene, (b) the selfish gene?

■ What is delayed reciprocal altruism and how does it challenge evolutionary theory?

**Summary – Genetic explanations for apparent altruism**

Some animals behave in ways that promote the needs of other members of their own species at some cost, at times fatal, to themselves. Although altruism contradicts Darwinian evolutionary ideas about natural selection and adaptations for survival, others have explained it as an altruistic gene, which others, who possess selfish genes, will exploit.

## IMPRINTING AND BONDING

Some animals acquire skills such as standing, walking, following and so on very soon after birth or hatching. Animal species that mature quickly are described as *precocial* species. *Precocity* refers to the early appearance of skills or abilities. One of the things they need to learn soon after birth is what their caregiver looks like so that they can stay close to it. This special kind of learning is called *imprinting* and is seen when a newborn animal follows its caregiver in order to stay close.

Other animals (including humans) take time to mature. (Humans take almost a quarter of their entire lives before becoming fully mature.) Those slow to mature are called *altricial* animals. Altricial animals cannot imprint since they are not mobile for some time after birth. However, they do need to form *bonds* with their caregivers. These bonds may encourage the caregiver to stay near to the offspring, and provide for its needs. Altricial birds bring food back to the nest, mammals provide breast milk for their young, whilst lionesses take their cubs to the carcass of an animal they have killed.

### Imprinting

When an animal first perceives something new it will take time and exposure to learn whatever associations exist between the new stimulus and itself. So if you take a dog home to live with you it will take the dog some time to learn to recognize you, its new surroundings and so on. This is *perceptual learning* and just about all organisms are capable of some form of it. The process of imprinting has a similar outcome to that of perceptual learning. It occurs, very quickly, soon after birth in precocial animals. The animal appears to be biologically predisposed to make the adaptation. Imprinting usually lasts for the individual's whole life, and is resistant to extinction (see Chapter 1). Ethologists use this term to describe how the newly born of some species of animals such as sheep, horses, geese etc. learn to recognize and follow their caregivers, since they are the first thing the newborn will see.

► Behaviour towards the bonded object will be different in some important ways from behaviour directed towards any other objects. For a bond to occur amongst adults some courtship may be necessary (for those species that use courtship and bonding as part of the way they reproduce). The special behaviour may be elaborate courtship displays, usually with the male trying to attract the female. The result will be mating, reproduction, and therefore the transmission of the pair's genes.

► Ethologists observe animal behaviour in its natural context (although this didn't stop Lorenz conducting carefully controlled experiments!) to see how biology and environment contribute to animal behaviour.

*Konrad Lorenz*

► The idea of there being a sensitive period became popular amongst child developmental psychologists, too. Some believed that human infants are especially sensitive to forming emotional bonds with their parents during a sensitive period (between six and 60 months was proposed). We will discuss this in Chapter 14.

### Studies of imprinting

**Konrad Lorenz** (1935) noted how some newly hatched birds, such as greylag geese chicks, will imprint on the first thing they see, presumably because the first thing they see will be their caregiver. We say an animal is imprinted on another animal if it follows it, as soon as it is able to follow anything, shortly after birth. Lorenz tested to see if animals would imprint on other things apart from their caregivers. He deliberately exposed some chicks to a variety of objects tied on the end of some string, such as rubber gloves, matchboxes and a large canvas bag. The chicks imprinted on them and followed them when Lorenz pulled the string. He allowed some to imprint on him, and they followed him too. Two types of imprinting were described by Lorenz. *Filial imprinting* allows the birds to recognize and form some kind of a relationship with their parents, while *sexual imprinting* allowed them to choose a mate from the opposite sex of their species.

Lorenz also experimented with the timing for imprinting. He found that chicks would imprint successfully so long as they see the imprinting object during a certain period of time, starting a few minutes after birth, and ending several hours or days later. He called this the *critical period*. If the animal was reared in the dark for the first two days, it would not imprint successfully, and was more likely to show fear of the first object it saw. The idea that there was a critical period during which exposure must occur was not supported by others. There is a period when animals are most sensitive to external influences, and the idea of there being a *sensitive period* soon replaced the idea of the critical period.

Hess (1972) added the importance of primacy and recency. Where animals are exposed to two objects to imprint on at the onset of the sensitive period, the first one it sees will become the imprinted object, even though it may have imprinted on a second object for a time. He also pointed out that imprinting isn't exclusively visual. He noted how mallard mothers and their unhatched chicks made reciprocal noises during the later stages of incubation, which he claimed marked the onset of the imprinting process.

So far we have referred to studies of imprinting which have relied on visual signals, with the animal following the first thing it sees. Different species have other senses that mature quickly and that can provide information about what to respond to. For example, herding animals such as sheep, goats and deer use their sense of smell as the basis for their imprinting. European shrews are small, mouse-like creatures who rely more on touch than sight or smell. Wood ducks use sight and sound as the basis for their imprinting.

The fact that precocial animals are able to imprint soon after birth suggests that some biological mechanism may be operating. The nervous system in the newborn is receptive to all sorts of stimulation. Nerve pathways don't develop until the individual has had some social experiences, and some feedback from environmental or parental influences. Perhaps the nervous systems of such animals are biologically prepared to make early behavioural adaptations, with the neural pathways that are involved already prepared, just waiting for the first perceptual experience.

If some early evolutionary ideas about natural selection and the survival of the fittest are correct, then we could look to imprinting as survival value. In this case it has three distinct benefits. It makes sense in survival terms to stay near to the parent, since those individuals that did stood a better chance of being kept warm, fed and protected from predators than those that did not. So an urge to imprint may have become biologically transmitted.

Some of Lorenz's early claims for imprinting haven't been confirmed. The precise timing of the critical period depends rather on how imprinting is measured, and the term sensitive period is preferred. Bateson (1979) shows that the factors which cause it to start and end aren't well understood. For example, birds of a few days old (and therefore supposedly outside the sensitive period for imprinting) can't actually be tested for it since they will try to escape from a new object which they haven't seen before. Just because they won't imprint on something doesn't mean they can't imprint on it.

Second, Lorenz thought that imprinting was permanent and irreversible, presumably because the animal had passed the end of the sensitive period for it. However, if a bird has imprinted onto a matchbox, it will try to stay close to that matchbox, so it won't have many opportunities to transfer its attachment to another object such as another goose. Research with other species doesn't reveal many consistencies either. For example, turkeys imprinted on humans will attempt to mate with other turkeys if the human imprinted object is absent. Sluckin and Salzen (1961) used a controlled laboratory experiment to test reversibility of imprinting. One group of chicks was imprinted onto a green ball suspended nearby. Shortly after they were exposed to a blue ball. Another group of chicks saw the blue ball first, then the green. Three days later they were all exposed to balls of both colours to see if they had any preference. They preferred their first choice. Three days later they were exposed to the balls again, and preferred to stay close to their second choice. This preference remained for a long time afterwards. These animals seemed to have changed their preference.

> ▶ Note that, even though precocial animals probably have biological predispositions to adapt their behaviour in line with experience, the form that adaptation takes (imprinting and following) is a special form of learning.

> ▶ What animals can be shown to do in the laboratory does not necessarily reflect what they would choose to do in their natural habitat.

> ■ What is the relationship between precocial and altricial species, and imprinting and bonding behaviour?

---

### Summary – Imprinting and bonding

Many animal species form bonds between individual members, or individuals and features that are associated with safety. The consequence of forming such bonds include remaining safe, learning appropriate behaviour, courtship and reproduction. Imprinting is a special form of early learning that doesn't rely on reinforcement or reward; it seems to be biologically driven, and its nature varies between different animal species. Its purpose may be to contribute to each individual's survival.

> ■ What are the consequences for successful imprinting and bonding?

## SIGNALLING SYSTEMS

► Several apparently altruistic types of behaviour are examples of signalling.

Individual members of many animal species communicate with each other. Earlier in this chapter we listed several as examples of apparently altruistic behaviour. Examples include dogs barking to warn other dogs to stay away, bees rattling their wings to signal the whereabouts of a useful supply of nectar to other members of the hive, and rabbits drumming their feet to warn other rabbits that a predator has been spotted.

Solitary species use signals to warn others to stay away. However, it is amongst animals that live in social groups that signalling seems to be most highly evolved. Those species that live in social groups need to communicate with each other, and sometimes with members of other species, too. Animal communication generally refers to anything that one individual does that has any effect on the behaviour of another. It includes the exchange of information between individuals, although the individuals concerned are usually members of the same species. Communication is interaction, so both the sender and the receiver need to know what the signals mean.

► All social interactions result from the capacity two or more individuals have to communicate the need to co-ordinate their behaviour.

Before looking at possible examples of animal communication we must appreciate a major problem researchers face in discovering the specific meaning any animal communication has. Whilst they can often observe and record the signal itself, they can't always see its effects. A male whale's singing in the presence of a female whale may be interpreted as courtship. Since we can't know how the female is interpreting it, or even always what she actually does, we can only guess the meaning of the communication. Anyway, the appropriate response may not occur for hours or days after the communication, or its meaning may be to instruct the receiver not to do something that it might otherwise have done.

### The origin of signals

► Any behaviour that was associated with a particular event may have become highly specific and stereotyped, and always appears in the presence of that stimulus (even though it has long since lost its original significance). This is *ritualization*.

During their evolution some behaviours would have become a *ritualized* response to some stimuli. (Ritualized means automatic, without the need of being aware of what is causing the response.) Those behaviours that became associated with the presence of predators, availability of food, desire for mating, building a home etc. would have adopted some survival value. Many have become signals for communication.

Ridley (1986) identifies three classes of behaviours that are the source of signals. These are *intention movements, displacement* and *behaviour controlled by parts of the animal's nervous system*. Intention movements are the behaviour that the animal starts to show to some stimulus, but then does not complete. A lion may suspect a stranger approaching his territorial boundary and start to adopt the aggressive behaviours intended to frighten the intruder away. However, the signals that alerted him to the possibility of the intruder weren't strong enough to rouse him fully and he returns to his rest. A bird might suspect danger and spread her wings to take flight, but the signals weren't sufficient to fully motivate the bird to take off. Adopting aggressive stances and spreading the wings may become signals to other lions or birds that the individual is preparing to fight or fly. Seeing this behaviour might signal the observer to do something too, such as escape!

Displacement behaviour is any behaviour that seems inconsistent or irrelevant to the task in hand. Hinde (1982) gives the example of a chaffinch who is adopting threatening behaviour towards a rival chaffinch, then suddenly breaks off the threat to wipe its bill. Bill wiping in chaffinches may come to be recognized as signalling a threat.

Activity in the *autonomic nervous system* may result in movements in feathers or fur, changes in skin colour, urinating, defecating, scratching and preening, and so on. These actions may become signals in courtship, mate attraction, marking of territorial boundaries, threat etc.

## Different types of signals

Just as precocial animals have some senses that provide information about their immediate environment sooner than other senses, so different animal species use different senses to send and receive their signals. The most widely used systems include sight and sound, but also smell.

### Pheronomes

Secreting chemical signals, called *pheronomes,* is probably the most basic communication system animals employ. Ants mark their trails by scent-marking points along them. Following the pheronome scents allows all the ants to find their way back to their colonies. They also use pheronomes as alarm calls to alert other ants to an intruder, or if the colony is under attack. Female dwarf Siberian hamsters secrete a scent to attract potential mates from up to half a mile away. Female silkworm moths use such a powerful pheronome that males up to two miles away have been observed rushing to mate with her!

When a queen honey bee is about to lay her eggs she secretes a pheronome that reduces the possible production of new queens. However, when the colony grows so large that her scent will not be detected by all the worker bees, those that do not detect it will start the production of new queens. The presence of a new queen may act as a signal to the existing queen to leave the hive and form a new colony. Several workers accompany her, still, presumably, attracted by her scent.

The main benefit to using a pheronome as a trigger is that it can spread a specific message to all individuals able to receive it in a given area. The size of the area is determined by the strength of the pheronome and the sensitivity of the receiver. If the message is simple and urgent, as with the Siberian hamster, then it is an effec-

▶ Seeing a lion stand up may be all that a younger lion challenger needs to decide that a challenge would not be a sensible move at this time.

▶ The nervous system of most animals consists of several subsystems. The central nervous system usually comprises the brain and spine (in those animals that have spines). The *autonomic nervous system* involves those automatic functions that occur within the body (such as digestion, heart rate, blood sugar levels) over which the animal has no control.

■ Outline Ridley's explanation for the origin of animal signalling.

▶ *Pheronomes* are used to convey specific signals to other animals whose senses are tuned to detect them. They are the most primitive form of communication.

tive means of spreading the message. It would have evolved in those animals who live in close enough proximity to each other, where weather conditions aren't so unpredictable that the pheronome will be scattered by storms. The cost could be that predators may learn to detect traces of the pheronome, or associate certain climatic conditions with movements of prey animals. Pheronomes are disrupted by the weather, and insufficient numbers of others may detect the message.

### Sight

Rather more complex signalling uses sight. Many species use courtship displays to attract the attention of a possible mate, including the highly visual acrobatic flight patterns of birds of paradise and butterflies, whilst peacocks strut about displaying their glorious (and otherwise completely useless) fans. Ethologists have studied small freshwater fish such as sticklebacks. When male sticklebacks are in breeding condition their bellies turn bright red. This attracts the female (and other males to attack it!). Many animals change their appearance to indicate threat or warning, too. The tomato frog glows red to warn any potential predators that, if they have eaten a tomato frog before, they should associate the sight of this one with the effects eating the last one had on them. They secrete a powerful poison.

Visual signals are immediate and clear, but do have one limitation: they are only useful if the individual for whom the message is intended is able to see the sender. They are not likely to have evolved in species that live in deep water or dense forest, or in the relative dark. A further problem is that if the receiver can see the sender, so might a predator!

### Sound

Sound is useful when the receiver can't see the sender, such as in dense vegetation, in the oceans, or under the cover of darkness. It is useful in communication over distances, since sound travels well in the air, though less well under water. The common house cricket chirps in a different rhythm that seems to indicate whether it is signalling courtship, aggression or warning others not to invade its territory. Fish-eating birds such as sooty terns make a distinctive call when returning to their chicks with food. Each parent has its own call that only its chicks recognize, and chicks don't respond to the calls of other returning adults.

Marine mammals such as cetaceans (whales and dolphins) have been extensively studied, both ethologically and in captivity. They mostly use sound for communication with each other, presumably since sound travels better through water than any other signals they could produce. They are difficult animals to study in the wild since it's impossible for humans to get close enough, or keep up with, a whale swimming and singing, possibly as part of its courtship behaviour.

Singing humpback whale males have been observed approach-

▶ Pheronome signalling is fairly safe, since only members of the same species can detect the scent. Visual signalling does have the potential danger that predators may detect a prey species' signals.

▶ It simply isn't possible to study cause and effect in those animals that live in what humans find to be less accessible parts of the Earth.

ing females (Tyack 1981). If the females allowed the male to approach, he may follow her. If she doesn't swim away he may swim alongside her, and stops singing. Whether this really is courtship behaviour is impossible to know, especially since humpback whales copulate deep below the surface where observers are unable, or unwise, to venture.

Probably some of the most communicative animals are dolphins, since they rarely stop making sounds. In fact they make two different types of sound: one is called a click and is a short, pulse-like sound which is beamed forward and is used for echolocation of objects around them, including other dolphins. It is possible that dolphins also use their clicks to deliver an acoustic shock for stunning or killing small prey. The other type of sound is a high-pitched squeal or whistle. They are single tones that appear to be used to communicate the dolphin's emotional state such as fear or sexual arousal, which may influence the behaviour of other dolphins.

Earlier we mentioned how dolphins will whistle when they need help, either because they are separated from the rest of the group or because they are injured. It is possible that these whistles have social significance to the other members of each individual's group, although the difficulties in conducting this kind of research don't permit any certainty. Bright (1984) reported the case of a dolphin who was caught and its whistles were recorded and played back to members of its group. They fled. Perhaps they interpreted this as an alarm call rather than a distress call (see page 115). When the calls were played to members of a different group they appeared curious. Perhaps the sounds one group uses as alarm calls aren't interpreted in the same way by members of other groups.

Sounds fade quickly. This can be both a limitation and an advantage. Predators will find it more difficult to get a fix on where the sender is if the sound they make fades rapidly. At the same time a member of the same species whose ears are tuned to hearing other members' calls may be able to locate the source of the sound more easily.

## Comments on communication systems

As we said earlier, evolution demands that survival is an ongoing process of adaptation to changing environments and needs. Individuals and species that are most able to use effective communication systems are most likely to survive longer and pass on their genes to future generations. If an existing form of communication becomes less effective as climate, terrain, predator–prey relationships and so on change, those most likely to survive will be those who can modify their means of communicating.

An important reminder: as we mentioned previously, these examples of animal behaviour which we understand to be communication are seen to be associated with some direct consequence, so we assume that the behaviour is a signal, and that the response is the function that was intended by the signaller. It is important to remember that these are assumptions, not certainties. They are

► It is tempting to explain animal behaviour that may have evolved over countless generations in fairly simple terms, as though we can know for certain what behaviour is a signal and exactly what it is signalling. To be more certain simple observation isn't enough. We may need controlled experiments. However, these may not be practical, or ethically (morally) desirable. We will return to the ethics of animal research in Chapter 17.

inferred from the behaviour and the circumstances of the sender and the receiver. To make matters even more difficult, the function of any signal may vary according to the situation in which it occurs, or amongst different members of the species. For example, a vervet monkey might signal others to climb trees to escape from a wolf. However, not all of them do. Other vervets may not recognize the meaning of the signal.

■ Outline some of the ways in which animals signal to each other, with an example of each.

■ What are the problems that researchers face in studying animal communication?

---

### Summary – Signalling systems

Signals are mostly used by social animals to communicate with members of the same species. The signals are probably to do with the satisfaction of animals' basic needs for food, safety and reproduction, although in some animals such as monkeys and chimps, it may be for fun and practice. The main kinds of signals are the release of scents, visual signals and sound signals.

---

### Exam questions – 60 minutes each

1  Discuss genetic explanations for apparent altruism in animals. (*25 marks*)
2  (a) What is imprinting and how is it different from bonding? (*10 marks*)
   (b) To what extent has research into the consequences of early experiences in animals helped us to understand their behaviour in the natural environment? (*15 marks*)
3  What insights into animal behaviour have we gathered from studying their signalling? (*25 marks*)

# Behavioural analysis

**Chapter objectives**

By the end of this chapter you should:

❚ understand the distinction between learning and biological transmission in animal skills;

❚ realize the need for interaction between biology and experience for survival;

❚ understand the main ways in which animals acquire experience leading to successful adaptations of their behaviour;

❚ appreciate the contribution of evolution and experience in foraging and homing behaviour;

❚ know some of the research that has been conducted into animal language, and be able to evaluate its conclusions;

❚ understand some of the implications of evolution for human behaviour.

## Introduction

In previous chapters we have discussed evolutionary and biological influences on behaviour between members of the same and other species, and their implications for kinship and social behaviour. This chapter is mostly to do with learning. In Chapter 1 we discussed classical and operant approaches to learning, and you should be familiar with them when reading this chapter. They explain how animals can acquire some aspects of learning in the laboratory, and, no doubt, in the wild. Classical conditioning explains how involuntary responses can become stamped into the animal's memory by its previous associations with some rewarding stimulus. Operant conditioning emphasizes the importance of the consequences of an animal's actions on the likelihood of similar action being repeated in the future.

## LEARNING IN THE NATURAL ENVIRONMENT

## Types of learning

### Classical conditioning and operant conditioning

If an animal learns that when the daylight goes it gets cold, it will have learned a simple association. In future, its previous experi-

▶ *Learning by association* is an illustration of classical conditioning. Although Pavlov demonstrated it using the salivation response in his laboratory dogs, it is found in the natural environments of most animals.

▶ In operant conditioning some behaviour occurs first, and if it is followed by a reinforcer it will tend to be repeated.

▶ A *trial* is a single run-through of a procedure associated with changing some behaviour. Every time you try to co-ordinate the clutch, accelerator and gear stick when you're learning to drive is a trial.

▶ Some authors claim that there are several kinds of learning, although, since we can only recognize learning in terms of its consequences, we may be unwise to suggest that there are different forms of the process itself. Learning may result from different circumstances; this isn't the same thing as there being several kinds of learning.

▶ Crows and other threats to farmers' crops have been frightened off by scarecrows and other devices. The birds soon habituate them, too, and they fail to frighten the birds away.

ences of cold will cause it to seek shelter when the daylight begins to go. This is an example of *association learning*, and it was first tested by **Ivan Pavlov** on his laboratory dogs.

If an animal behaves in a certain way that results in a rewarding or pleasant experience, it may behave in the same way again. Monkeys who find that jumping (an aspect of their natural behaviour) into the sea (sea water is not a part of a monkey's usual natural environment) is rewarding, may scamper up the rocks to do it again. The first time they ventured near water they may have felt protected by a parent's presence, or the safety of being in a group. It may have been accidental or unintentional. However, Skinner (see Chapter 1) would say that they must have found the experience reinforcing because they repeated it. Equally, if an experience is unrewarding or unbeneficial, it will not be repeated. If a bird eats a Monarch butterfly of the Amazonian region in South America, it will vomit. Monarchs are poisonous to birds. If it sees another (or a Viceroy mimic – see Chapter 5) it appears to prefer to go hungry.

Seeing each of these examples leads us to conclude that the bird has learned something new, and changed its behaviour accordingly. These are examples of operant conditioning that could occur in the wild. Avoiding Monarch butterflies and their mimics may be learned through a single exposure to the undesired stimulus. This has been called *single trial learning*. Other learning may need several trials. This is *trial and error* learning. Learning is therefore recognized when a change has occurred in an animal's performance that increases its likelihood of success.

### Perceptual learning and imprinting

Learning occurs in the natural environment as a result of the combination of several events, apart from behaviour becoming associated with a reinforcing or unreinforcing consequence. In Chapter 6 we described two of them. *Perceptual learning* involves a gradual process by which an animal learns to recognize objects in its environment. A cat may take quite a time to learn to recognize a cat flap, and what to do with it. Imprinting leads to a rapid form of learning by which a precocial animal learns to recognize its caregiver (or some other object if an experimental scientist is involved!).

### Habituation and sensitization

Another way in which learning occurs in the natural environment is habituation. When young chickens and turkeys first observe something flying overhead, they crouch. This isn't necessary since the birds flying above have no interest in the crouching birds. The young birds soon learn not to waste their energy performing pointless acts. They habituate the birds overhead. However, if an unfamiliar shape (such as a bigger bird, or a kite), flies overhead, they will return to crouching. When sheep, horses, cows or any other animals are first put in a field near a railway line, they quickly move away from the line when the first train passes. After a few trains have passed, and they have learned that trains do them no harm, they habituate the trains. People who live near railways also say they stop noticing the trains after a few days.

Seemingly the opposite of habituation is *sensitization*. An animal may grow increasingly wary of something that causes it discomfort. An electric fence is intended to give an animal that touches it a modest electric shock. It is sufficiently painful to discourage the animal from trying to get through. Several trials may be necessary for the animal to be made sufficiently sensitive to the fence that it avoids contact.

### Imitation

Imitation forms a large component in the learning of songbirds. **William Thorpe** studied chaffinch song in the Cambridgeshire countryside in the 1950s. Thorpe (1961) concluded that the basic patterns of male chaffinch song are genetically inherited, as a kind of template for appropriate sounds. Each new member learns its particular dialect from hearing adult birds from several species singing, and comparing these sounds to its own template. By a process of listening and copying the dialect that most closely fits their template, so they slowly improve their own song until they sing the characteristic song of their species.

|  | Learned in the environment | Interaction between biology and environment |
| --- | --- | --- |
| Classical conditioning |  |  |
| Operant conditioning |  |  |
| Perceptual learning |  |  |
| Imprinting |  |  |
| Habituation |  |  |
| Sensitization |  |  |
| Imitation |  |  |

Animal behaviour between, and within, species varies greatly. It is impossible to classify bits of animal behaviour exactly into that which is biological and that which is learned because the environments in which they live influence their behaviour in complex ways. For example, Marler (1973) isolated birds so that they couldn't hear the male adults of their own species singing. They still developed their own characteristic song, based on their template, although they had never heard the male adults of their own species singing it.

Not all species of animals are equally able to adapt their behaviour in line with experience. Thorndike's work with rats and cats showed they made many errors in learning simple tasks (trial and error learning), and often took many trials to accomplish simple behaviour such as pressing a latch to open a puzzle box door. In the natural environment those species which are most exposed to danger will need to adapt their behaviour as each new threat occurs if enough members of their species are to survive to reproduce the species.

### Foraging behaviour

*Foraging* refers to how animals acquire, use and store their food. This will vary enormously according to the species. Some species

▶ *Sensitization* explains how learning comes about. It is not a type of learning since if it was, it would be indistinguishable from a form of operant conditioning.

▶ Birdsong is essentially for courtship. Male birds sing to attract a partner from the same species as themselves. Few songbird species have females that sing, since they do not need to use song to be courted by the male.

■ **Several of these forms of learning also involve biological transmission. Which ones?**

■ **Why do you think male songbirds have different dialects?**

■ **Define, using your own words, each of the ways by which learning can come about in the natural environment.**

► Factors in the likelihood of animals actually eating include how motivated they are to eat (how hungry), and whether food is available or would require effort to obtain. The hungrier the animal is, the more likely it is to seek food.

► Darwin believed that the most important factor in survival was food. If an animal species that eats a particular type of food finds a plentiful supply of it that isn't exploited by any other animal, it has found an ecological niche.

► Short-lived animals need to be able to find food quickly or they will not survive. This appears contrary to evolutionary ideas about survival. However, one solution to the problem is for such animals to have large numbers of offspring, some of whom should survive, even if most perish.

► Salmon return to the place where they were born to give birth (spawn) their young. They will endure all kinds of hardships, and attempt to overcome huge barriers in order to reach their spawning area. Once spawning has been accomplished the adult salmon die. The fertilized eggs develop into young salmon, and the life cycle begins again.

hunt, chase and catch food. For example, cheetahs are solitary hunters and have to stalk their prey until they can outrun them. Jackals, hyenas and wild dogs hunt in packs and co-operate to catch and overpower their prey.

Apart from hunting one's food, foraging also includes such feeding behaviours as taking the food that is readily available, e.g. grazing amongst vegetarian animals. A tapeworm, which has a symbiotic relationship (see Chapter 5) with a sponge, merely hooks itself onto the inside of the sponge's digestive system and absorbs the sponge's food as it passes by. The worm doesn't even have a mouth! Foraging also includes behaviour involved in the acquisition of food, such as web building amongst many spider species or hole digging amongst the trapdoor spider.

The range of behaviour used in foraging is enormous. Birds such as the coal tit peck at insects deep in between pine needles in conifer forests. A wrong move could be dangerous. Several species have evolved behaviour that reduces competition from other animals who take the same kind of food. Several species of warblers, for example, have been found to divide where in the trees they will look for insects. The green warbler searches the higher, outer branches, the bay-breasted warbler hunts amongst the middle height branches, and the myrtle warbler feeds amongst the lower, inner branches. This co-operation presumably minimizes competition and maximizes the chances all have to survive.

For some short-lived animals foraging skills are almost non-existent. The animal is born, and if it cannot find a food supply quickly enough, it will die. Others are more adaptive. As they repeat their foraging behaviour they learn, usually through trial and error, to improve their performance. Being as efficient as possible is important to animals whose survival depends on a frequent supply of food. Bumble bees are a good example of adaptive learning in the natural environment.

Bumble bees can be seen and heard in meadows searching out, and taking nectar from, the flowers there. Extracting nectar isn't a straightforward process since several activities are involved. If they are not performed efficiently the bees will use up a lot of energy and achieve modest amounts of nectar. As each bee gains experience of the species of plants it visits it will become more successful. It is learning through experience. Each bee tends to collect nectar only from one or two species of flower, although it will visit others occasionally.

Those animals with complex hunting techniques and strategies will improve their performance with age and experience. The brown bear doesn't usually spend much time in fast-flowing rivers. However, when salmon are leaping upstream to return to their spawning grounds, bears do plunge in to try and catch some. Salmon are obviously a pleasant addition to the bear's diet. The younger bears thrash about, rarely catching anything. The more experienced bears will adopt a strategy that works for them. Some lie quietly with their mouths open, hoping for a fish to venture in, others study and pounce, catching the fish with their claws.

Birds such as oystercatchers need to co-ordinate their behaviour quite finely, and this can only come with learning and experience. They must spot their prey, time their flight, precisely control their dive, and take off having caught their fish. Young, inexperienced birds are spectacularly unsuccessful. More experienced birds are much more successful. An even more striking example is the elaborate flying skills of the parasitic frigate bird of the South Pacific. It tracks smaller birds who have caught a fish and are bringing it back for their offspring. It swoops on the smaller bird and harasses it until it drops its food, which the frigate bird then catches and takes to feed its own offspring.

> ### Summary – Foraging behaviour
> Foraging is behaviour associated with acquiring and using the appropriate food for the species. Since there are so many different species of animal on the Earth, it's not surprising that there are many different kinds of food, and many different means of foraging for it. Like all skills, foraging must be learned through the mechanisms of animal learning in the wild.

## Homing behaviour

Those species that have to travel in order to find their food are then faced with the task of returning home again. If the animal rears its young, it needs to be quite efficient at returning with the family's food. Those animals that exploit the resources in two territories by migration will have two sets of homing behaviour.

Some species have apparently amazing capacities for finding their way home, and almost certainly use more than one source of information to do so. We have all read incredible stories about animals such as cats and dogs travelling enormous distances and crossing dangerous obstacles (such as motorways) to get home. Most of the research in this area has been conducted on birds, and of all the birds, pigeons are probably the best known homers. Pigeon fanciers train their birds from when the birds are about three months old. They are allowed to fly around their loft, and presumably take in whatever information they need about how to find it. Over a period of several months they are taken increasingly further away from their home, in closed baskets, and then released to see if they can find their way back. Some are lost (to predators or blown off course by strong winds). Most find their way home.

Many other birds, such as the albatross, have incredible homing skills. Since food is scarce, and fish isn't plentiful in the cold, one of the parent birds may be away from the nest for weeks at a time, and cover distances of several thousand miles, before returning to allow its partner to hunt. Finding one's own nest after a round trip of four thousand miles across the featureless ocean is quite a feat of homing skill.

■ What is meant by foraging behaviour?

■ Give some examples of how foraging behaviour is mediated by experience in non-human animals.

■ There are several reasons why animals can be seen moving around. The most obvious one is foraging for food, but movement may also be triggered by changes in the external environment (e.g. the weather changes and the animal isn't equipped to cope with it), or for finding a mate, establishing a new territory, or seeking somewhere safer when predators appear.

▶ Could you make any suggestion at all to explain how the green sea turtle is able to navigate between nesting and feeding grounds?

▶ We're not saying that some birds such as pigeons don't recognize landmarks, only that recognizing landmarks isn't the only means they have for homing.

▶ Research into how animals use internal and local time is very revealing. However, evolution has often provided animals with supplementary or back-up systems, and homing animals probably have several sources of information which they use to find their way.

In Chapter 5 we mentioned the green sea turtle. The female lays her eggs in the sand of an Ascension Island beach. The island is less than five miles across and is in the middle of the Atlantic Ocean, yet she finds her way back a few years later to lay another clutch of eggs.

The most obvious explanation for how these animals can find their way home is that they have phenomenal memories, and store an impression of where they are going as they fly or swim away, and remember the route for when they come home. This seems highly unlikely. A similar possibility is that they store landmarks by which they can navigate, rather than storing the whole journey. What would a turtle, on her way to or from Ascension, or a salmon returning to its birthplace to spawn its own young, see en route? An ingenious experiment by Schlichte and Schmidt-Koenig (1971) had homing pigeons fitted with translucent goggles before releasing them 90 miles from home. The effect of this is that they could see very little at any distance (including obstacles or predators in their paths), although some did still manage to arrive home. Landmark recognition wouldn't explain the albatross's ability, since there aren't many landmarks in the sea! One suggestion is that homing pigeons have a concentration of iron in parts of their skull bone which allows them to use the Earth's magnetic fields.

One important factor in homing is time. Most animals (including humans) have an internal time clock. This is set according to where we spend some time. We know when we are feeling tired or feeling aroused. If you go to America your body clock will have to adjust to being a few hours earlier than you are used to. We know about local time, too. The airport clock when you arrive in New York might say that it's only 8 p.m., but your body clock tells you that it's after midnight. We call this phenomenon *jet lag*. France is an hour in front of us, so there's not much problem adjusting there.

Some birds and ducks have been shown to use their internal clocks too. They can also tell what the level of daylight suggests about local time. By comparing their internal perception of time with local conditions, they have some perception of how far they are from their normal place. If a bird is deliberately kept in artificial conditions, its internal clock will re-set to the time the conditions reflect. When released away from home these animals make many errors of navigation and many do not return. Some animals also use the position of the sun and stars as a part of their navigational equipment for returning home. Obviously, flying towards the sun on the way out should be matched by flying away from it to return. However, the position of the sun changes with the passage of time and rotation of the Earth. This doesn't appear to pose a problem for navigational birds, or honey bees, who use levels of polarization in the sky when the sun is obscured by clouds. Visual and time clues are obviously helpful, but they are not the only sources of information animals use as part of their navigational equipment.

Pigeons are able to detect *infrasound*. This is a form of sound that is well below the threshold of human detection. (See Chapter 11 for a discussion of human abilities to detect sensations.) Large structures such as mountain ranges contribute to infrasound, as do stretches of water. The sheerwater is a homing bird that will only fly across water. Its infrasound detection must be sensitive to the way water distorts the sound. Salmon can detect minute traces of minerals in the water where they were spawned, and they seek these same minerals when they come to spawn themselves.

Animals who could find their way back to the safety of their familiar home range, to their hungry offspring or to others in their group (if they were social), would probably have lived longer than those that did not. An animal who is lost may be an easy victim to a predator on its own range. So homing behaviour would have become naturally selected, and it is likely that homers use more than one homing system. This suggests that today's animals are the descendants of successful homers, and that many of them will be successful homers too. However, even animals who have some kind of biological capacity to develop any skills will need the social experience to practise it. Those who survived their attempts at practice would have become successful homers.

### Summary – Homing behaviour

Animals use a variety of sources of information about where they are, and which way they need to go to return home. The capacity to detect these sources is biologically programmed, possibly as a consequence of natural selection. As the animal gains experience of its environment these biological influences are modified. The precise mechanisms of how they do it are a fascinating area of study, but it's important not to lose sight of the power of the motivation that these animals have to return home.

## ANIMAL LANGUAGE

We have seen that animals are capable of some skills that humans can only achieve with sophisticated technology such as navigational aids used by air traffic controllers and ship and aircraft captains. Some are stronger, faster and physically better adapted to the environments in which they live. Humans have superior cognitive skills and can process sensory information and respond to it in vastly superior ways to any non-human animal. Or so, at least, it was thought until some recent research into trying to teach animals to communicate in a symbolic form seemed to suggest that some non-human primates do possess cognitive centres which are far more like our own than was generally believed.

This issue divides psychologists into those who believe that chimps, gorillas and orang-utans do possess cognitive centres that could understand vocabulary, and even grammar, and can therefore communicate meaningfully with humans, and those who believe that they do not possess such centres, and that language is a highly complex, *species-specific* skill, and that what animals do isn't real language.

► As animal biology is so diverse it is hardly surprising that those who move around on land, in the sea or in the air have different mechanisms of finding their way.

■ What is homing behaviour and why do many animals exhibit it?

■ Outline some of the explanations offered so far for how animals are able to navigate over long distances.

► Symbolic language refers to language which uses shapes, pictures, signs or sounds to stand for bits of meaning. Spoken or written language, non-verbal waves and gestures, and sign language used by hearing-impaired people are all symbolic language.

► *Species-specific* means only occurring in the named species.

If we are to review the research evidence on whether animals can use language to communicate, we need to offer a detailed definition of what we mean by language. Before the investigation of animal language, and the division over whether they can use language or not really began, **C.F. Hockett** suggested a model of the major features of human language in 1959. Here is a summary:

**C.F. Hockett's design features of language**

| Design feature | Meaning |
| --- | --- |
| 1 Vocal/auditory | Transmitted between people by sound |
| 2 Broadcast/directional | The sound is broadcast, but the listener knows the direction it is coming from |
| 3 Rapid fading | The sound fades quickly |
| 4 Total feedback | Speakers can hear what they are saying |
| 5 Interchangeability | The same person can send and receive information |
| 6 Specialization | Language is intended only for communication and is not a by-product of any other behaviour |
| 7 Semanticity | Language communicates meaning |
| 8 Arbitrariness | Language doesn't always communicate its meaning clearly |
| 9 Traditional transmission | Language is passed down the generations, from adults to children |
| 10 Learnability | New forms of language can be learned |
| 11 Discreteness | Language is coded into separate units (sounds and letters) which can be organized into bigger units |
| 12 Quality of patterning | Sounds can have meaning when combined into words, and words extend their meaning when combined into sentences |
| 13 Displacement | Language allows users to refer to objects and events that are not present at the time or which may not exist in a concrete form (e.g. justice) |
| 14 Openness/productivity | Language allows new meanings to be created |
| 15 Prevarication | Language allows users to invent stories which are not true (tell lies) |
| 16 Reflexiveness | Language can be used to talk about itself (e.g. by writing about it) |

## Research into animal language

Most of the research has been conducted using the three groupings of apes, gorillas, chimpanzees and orang-utan. However, other species have shown capacities for copying human behaviour and language. For example, **Lilly** (1965) trained a dolphin to imitate English syllables and shaped them into words, which the dolphin did with a modest amount of training. However, the dolphin only ever imitated, it never said anything original or spontaneous. **Pepperberg** (1983) trained an African grey parrot called Alex to use 50 spoken English words by a combination of imitation and reinforcement (see Chapter 1). One researcher held a picture of an object and asked 'what is it?'; the other would say what it was, and receive a reward of playing with the object (or eating it) if he said the correct answer. Alex was then shown the object and asked the question. If he imitated the researcher he received the reward.

Both of these studies show that some animals have considerable capacity for imitation. However, what they imitated was a sound

▶ Some animals, such as parrots, are great imitators. Alex was able to name objects, so has some recognition and learning capacity.

approximating English speech when presented with a particular stimulus. The first attempt to teach an animal to use English was conducted by **Kellogg** and **Kellogg** (1933) when they reared Gua, a female chimp, alongside their own son Donald for six months. Gua learned to make three speech-like sounds and applied them to three objects, although she was quick to learn to solve other problems. The experiment was ended when Gua was becoming rather strong and boisterous, whilst Donald was barely able to walk. **K.J. Hayes** and the Hayes family (1950) spent six years trying to teach Vicki, a chimp, to speak, but she too only learned to apply four words (cup, up, mama, papa) to the correct object or event.

► The Kelloggs thought that Gua was able to produce nearly a hundred words. Perhaps they all sounded the same.

In 1980 **Laidler** spent eight months trying to teach Cody, a young male orang-utan, to speak, but he only learned to say four words, although he was developing other ideas, for example about food and drink, which he may have learned the words for had the experiment been allowed to continue for as long as the study of the chimp Vicki.

It is now known that attempts to teach animals to talk are doomed, not because they lack the necessary cognitive structures but because they lack the necessary physiological structures in the speech-producing parts of the throat. Apes cannot produce the variety of sounds that would be necessary to speak. So, in all the ape studies that followed Gua and Vicki, the apes were taught an association between the name of the object (such as parts of their body), action (such as open doors and windows), or person (such as their trainers), and a visual or other symbolic representation of it. The researchers then note how well the animals can use their symbols to make meaningful communications.

► The base of an ape's skull, where the vocal cords leave the brain and connect with the spine, is flat. The equivalent area on a human skull is angled. The orientation of the bones may allow humans to control and produce a range of vocalizations that can be used for speech. Apes cannot produce anything like the range of sounds that humans can.

### The Gardners' experiments with Washoe

One of the first projects to investigate whether apes can use language was Project Washoe (1966–70). **Allen** and **Beatrix Gardner** had Washoe, a female chimpanzee, living with them from when she was ten months old until she was five years, when she returned to the research centre for mating. By the time she was 18 months old she'd learned four signs. By two and a half she knew 30 signs. She eventually learned more than 130 American Sign Language (for the deaf) hand-signs. The Gardners modelled the signs for her to imitate, moulded her fingers and hand into the right shape, and reinforced her with food, praise and tickles when she made the sign and applied it correctly.

► Washoe's skills sound impressive, and she could understand more signs than she could use. However, compared to a human baby, Washoe's communication was very limited.

As Washoe couldn't learn about time she never understood past, present and future. She didn't understand the rules of grammar, that words need to be put in a particular order. On seeing her living area in the Gardners' yard locked she was likely to make the signs for home, locked, gimme and key in any order. There is disagreement about her ability to create original utterances. When walking in the park, for example, and seeing a duck for the first time she was asked 'What's that?' and she signed 'water bird'. A cigarette lighter was signed as 'hot metal', and Alka-Seltzer became 'hear

► Sadly, Washoe lost her own baby, but eventually adopted another baby chimp and was observed teaching him some of her signs. She talked to herself in signs, too.

water'. Critics say that this is no more than the chimp saying 'water', which the duck was on, and 'bird', which is what the duck is, rather than 'water bird', implying that the two go together as an original utterance.

### The Oklahoma colony and Lucy

**Roger Fouts** and the Gardners set up a further study of signing in young chimps in the early 1970s in what became known as the Oklahoma colony. Assistants who had used sign language all their lives, and so were highly proficient, taught young chimps, who learned the signs and were filmed signing to each other when no humans were around. Lucy, a member of the colony, started combining her own signs for objects. For example, she knew the sign for watermelon, but used her own sign combination to describe it as 'fruit drink' or 'candy drink'.

### The Premacks' experiments with Sarah

One problem with this research is that it is attempting to assess one skill (the use of language) and does it through measuring another (proficiency with hand-signs). Although chimps have considerable control over their hands, it did seem unnecessary to have them demonstrate one skill via another. **Ann** and **David Premack** (1972) used operant conditioning to teach their chimp Sarah to use plastic shapes to represent objects and ideas. After two and a half years of training at an hour a day, the chimp was able to arrange the magnetic-backed shapes on a metal board in two- and three-word sentences, and she could create complex requests and answer quite difficult questions. Like Washoe, she couldn't learn to arrange the shapes in a grammatically correct sequence. If asked 'Is the banana bigger than the apple?' she might communicate 'bigger apple banana is' or any other combination of those shapes. She would respond enthusiastically enough by arranging the shapes when her trainer asked a question, but she never started a 'conversation' with them.

### Duane Rumbaugh's experiments with Lana

**Duane Rumbaugh** trained Lana to operate a large, vertical keyboard, rather like an old-fashioned shop cash register. She could press keys that would cause symbols to appear in the window. If she pressed the keys in the correct order she would be rewarded, often with food or drink. Rumbaugh suggests that Lana is capable of some grammatical construction. She became quite skilled at controlling aspects of her environment with the apparatus, for example she could tell the difference between 'Tim tickle Lana' and 'Lana tickle Tim'. However, there is great doubt whether she is learning language at all. She could be described as doing no more than an elaborate sequence of key presses in the right order in order to obtain a reward. This is operant conditioning (see Chapter 1) and could be seen in any circus ring.

► Being able to create new signs is a feature of language. It is said to show that the animal has some cognitive capacities.

■ Look back at Hockett's design features of language (page 136). Pick out those which support the idea that Washoe and Lucy are using language in the way that animals use it.

► Sarah isn't really using a language that would satisfy many of Hockett's design criteria at all. She is learning to associate a pattern of shapes with a particular outcome.

■ How many of Hockett's design features of human language are Sarah and Lana using?

### Francine Patterson's experiments with Koko

**Francine Patterson** and her deaf assistants (1979) taught a gorilla named Koko American Sign Language (ASL). After a year she introduced a younger gorilla called Michael into the programme. For a further six years the animals were taught signs, and rewarded when they used them correctly. Koko learned over 400 signs accurately, and knew another 300, which she used occasionally.

This ambitious project yielded some fascinating results. First, both animals appeared to learn signs quite quickly and were able to answer quite complex questions when asked by the researchers. Second, they communicated with each other using signs, although they didn't always wait for one to stop signing before the other began, and often they just signed almost oblivious of the other. On one occasion Michael wasn't permitted to enter the caravan being used by Koko and Patterson until he made the sign asking to enter. Koko showed him the sign through the window, Michael made it, and on entering Koko signed 'Nice sign Michael'. Third, and unlike the other apes tested so far, they would actually start a conversation with the researchers. Koko also invented about twenty of her own signs for words she did not know, and used some she did know as swear words, including the signs for 'dirty' and 'toilet'. Fourth, she lied! She also seemed able to express emotion. When she was displeased with someone she signed 'red mad gorilla'.

### Herbert Terrace's experiments with Nim Chimpsky

**Herbert Terrace** (1979) was also convinced that animals could use a form of language that could allow them to communicate with humans. An eminent American philosopher and linguist is **Noam Chomsky**. Chomsky advanced a theory of language acquisition in humans that relies heavily on biological structures, especially brain structures, that only humans possess. Terrace, and the other researchers discussed so far, disagreed. Terrace named his chimp Nim Chimpsky, and set about teaching him ASL. However, he began to realize that Nim wasn't actually learning the signs and realizing that they had some significance in communication. Rather, he was performing a trick to obtain a reward. This was operant conditioning. He reviewed the hours of film that the other researchers had taken and concluded that most of the animal language that they had reported could also be explained as clever chimps learning to behave in ways that meant they obtained some reward, and that they wouldn't have any idea about what their hand-signs actually meant. He said: 'I could find no evidence of an ape's grammatical competence either in my own evidence or that of others' (Terrace 1979).

### Sue Savage Rumbaugh's experiments with Kanzi

Despite Terrace's objection, there is evidence from **Sue Savage Rumbaugh**'s research with a pygmy chimp called Kanzi that apes are capable of much greater skills of comprehension than had been

► Gorillas, chimps and orang-utans are all great apes, and are human beings' closest evolutionary relatives.

► Gorillas are rather large and powerful creatures. Whilst generally fairly solitary they can become co-operative and communicative.

► Terrace became a determined critic of the view that animals were capable of using language in a way that humans would recognize, having realized that Nim Chimpsky was cleverly imitating his signs in order to obtain a reward. The Gardners, and others, completely reject his interpretation of Washoe's signing.

■ Outline Terrace's view of language skills in animals.

► All the research into animal language until this point involved trying to make the animals produce language in order to communicate with humans. The Kanzi research attempted to see if animals could understand human language when it was directed at them.

► It does seem that Kanzi is able to obey simple instructions and requests when he hears them. He also appears to enjoy communicating with humans.

■ How many of Hockett's design features for language does Kanzi have?

imagined. The early studies had all tested apes' abilities to mould their hands or place a shape or press a key in response to some direct stimulus. Sue Savage Rumbaugh claims that this is simply imposing an unnecessary level of performance on an ape, and what we are measuring is their performance, not their understanding of language. She has concentrated on measuring Kanzi's understanding of spoken English. In 1991 Kanzi understands over 200 words and can obey quite complex instructions such as 'fetch Sue the apple that is on the table near the window'. Despite there being apples on other tables he fetches the one requested. 'Can you go to the colony room and get the telephone?' posed no problem at all. He can recognize his trainers by sight and by photograph.

His skills are developing all the time, and he is now beginning to understand subtle differences in the ways in which instructions are phrased. For example, with an orange placed in front of him he is asked 'go to the colony room and get the orange'. There are two simple instructions here – 'go to' and 'fetch'. Kanzi obeyed most of the time, but the orange right in front of him was confusing. When the instruction was rephrased 'get the orange that's in the colony room', he got it right every time. However, Terrace and others are still not convinced. They say that Kanzi's abilities are impressive, but they do not measure up to human language skills. Savage Rumbaugh replies that since his brain is about one-third the size of an adult human brain it's hardly surprising that Kanzi's language skills are limited. His language is at about the same level as that of a young child.

Kanzi had originally been taught to communicate by pointing to symbols that he had learned had some meaning on a large board called a *lexigram*. As his comprehension skills increased he seemed to want to communicate more with humans. Savage Rumbaugh says that he gets very frustrated because his lexigram symbols cannot say all that he wants to communicate. **Roger Lewis** (1991) asks: 'And if Kanzi were to talk, what would he say? Maybe the first thing he'd say is that he's fed up with Terrace claiming that apes don't have language.'

*Kanzi practises 'blind syntax' of vocabulary words*

### Summary – Animal language

Although some animal species can imitate and can recognize objects, most of the research is conducted amongst the three groupings of apes, gorillas, chimps and orang-utan. Much research has shown that they possess great skills at imitating and communicating with ASL, or by pressing keys or moving objects. However, these skills may be little more than complex operantly conditioned responses. Research with Kanzi has gone beyond what could be explained by simple operant conditioning. However, Kanzi is only one chimp. His skills need to be demonstrated in others before the claim that animals are capable of human language can be accepted.

## *EVOLUTIONARY EXPLANATIONS OF HUMAN BEHAVIOUR*

Before discussing the application of evolutionary concepts to human behaviour let us review the basic principles discussed in Chapter 5. First, the idea of 'evolutionary time' is rather different from the everyday meaning of time. In evolutionary terms ten thousand years is what we think of as a moment. So when we say that the environment in which many animal species live is constantly changing, we mean that changes may take thousands of years to occur. The climate may have grown colder, bringing in the Ice Age, or the ice may have been receding, carving out the terrain that animals will inhabit. Over thousands of generations the animal species will have to adapt its lifestyle, habitat, diet, and so on in order to survive. Some will be unable to adapt, and will become extinct. Dinosaurs are an obvious example. Others will adapt successfully. For example, penguins are now flightless birds, presumably because they stopped flying in favour of swimming to catch their fish. For others the environment didn't change at all, for example crocodiles.

Those animals that adapt their form (polar bears growing a thicker coat, albatross developing a wider wingspan, anteaters having a longer tongue, Monarch butterflies evolving a warning display, etc.) to be most appropriate to the environment they are living in are likely to survive longer. Their successful adaptations lead to them being *naturally selected*, particularly if they can make any behavioural adaptation, too. Some animals will use aggression, cunning, cheating and stealing in order to benefit in some way over others. The benefit often results in them living long enough to have the maximum possible opportunities to mate. The individuals of some species (notably humans and other primates) live well beyond their reproductive capacity. In nature only the fittest are likely to survive when resources are scarce. Living longer provides the opportunity to pass on the animal's genetic material to more offspring, and so natural selection results in the offspring of those who are fittest to survive inheriting the genes (or imitating the behaviour) of the best adapted models.

## *Sociobiological explanations of human behaviour*

In essence, then, all members of any species are often in competition with each other to pass on their genes to as many offspring as they can, and will use whatever means they can to achieve this. Applying this sentiment to human behaviour has always been very controversial. A 'Social Darwinian' would say that the rich and powerful should enjoy all of life's benefits since they or their forefathers have obviously adapted well, and there's no point in helping the poor and disadvantaged since they are least fit to survive. This

▶ Changes that occur as a result of evolutionary adaptation can take thousands or millions of years, and countless generations of animals.

▶ Adaptation of form and function, the process of natural selection, and the survival of the fittest to produce many offspring are fundamental concepts in the evolutionary approach to explaining many aspects of animal functioning.

■ Define these terms as used by students of evolution: natural selection, adaptation, and survival of the fittest.

▶ Wilson made proposals about how we should approach an understanding of human behaviour from an evolutionary biological perspective. As such the attempt was intellectually challenging, and his suggestions are well argued.

▶ There are many examples in human behaviour where we can see the effect of being well adapted to our environment. Whether this can be explained in simple evolutionary terms (with the absolute minimum of evidence in support) is another matter.

▶ Wilson is arguing from the point of view of detached scientific speculation. He is not making prescriptions about how people should behave, only the mechanisms by which (he claims) biology has fitted them to behave.

▶ In Chapter 5 we discussed how emphasis within evolutionary theories has shifted from the importance of the survival of the individual to the importance of the survival of the group. With sociobiology the emphasis is on the survival of the genes themselves.

controversy was brought out with the publication of **Edward Wilson's** *Sociobiology: The New Synthesis* in 1975, and later in *On Human Nature* in 1978.

Towards the end of the first book Wilson claimed that human behaviour has been shaped by natural selection to promote the genetic success of each individual. So all sorts of anti-social behaviour such as aggression and male dominance of women suddenly appeared more acceptable, and ultimately inevitable. Many groups were fiercely opposed to such ideas. However, Wilson and supporters of 'human sociobiology' say that all they are doing is attempting to test the relevance of evolutionary ideas for explaining aspects of human behaviour. They want to take any aspect of human functioning, such as any we noted in our examination of social psychology, or from cognitive or developmental psychology.

For example, people work more quickly at low-demand tasks when others are present. In Chapter 3 we called this a *co-action effect*. Sociobiologists would try to explain this in terms of its adaptive significance. Perhaps it contributes to efficient co-operation so that tasks that might have exposed people to danger, such as hunting or crossing open countryside, may have been accomplished faster. Those who did it faster were less likely to attract the attention of predators. In Chapter 11 we discuss how humans can attend to only a narrow range of stimuli at any one time, although we can 'tune in' when we hear someone talking about us, or about something we know about. This is called the 'cocktail party effect'. It also has survival value, since allowing us to detect anything that is relevant to us would warn us of potential danger. In Chapter 14 we note how babies form emotional attachment bonds to their caregivers. As with imprinting in the animal kingdom, it serves to keep the child close to its attachment object (usually a parent), since that person is most likely to defend and care for it.

Let us be clear – Wilson does not say that all human behaviour is no more than a series of genetically inherited adaptations over which individuals have no control. Nor do sociobiologists believe that people (men) should behave in ways designed to help them to have as many children as possible. When groups of people live together and form societies they evolve a culture which includes expectations about acceptable behaviour (called norms), and acceptable beliefs (called values). Different societies have different norms and values associated with childrearing, and these values are often reinforced by law. Wilson would agree that they must be respected. Anyone who transgresses social norms and values, or the law, in order to maximize his attempt to make babies, deserves whatever sanctions that society will impose. We may be constantly evolving to make better adaptations to our environments, we are not prisoners of our genes.

### Richard Dawkins and 'the selfish gene'

In 1976 **Richard Dawkins** published *The Selfish Gene*, in which he proposes an extension of sociobiological theory based on the idea that the most important feature of biology, and the single thing that is supposed to direct our behaviour, is the continued existence of our genes. The genes themselves must survive, humans are merely 'survival machines' who carry them. Dawkins quotes some (usually rather negative) examples from animal behaviour and claims that they reflect similar experiences in human behaviour, since their existence can be explained by the contribution they make to the continuation of the selfish genes. Such behaviour as aggression and violence generally, being hostile to strangers, lying and cheating, treating stepchildren less well than one's own, are all inevitable. They can all be found in nature, and are all said to promote the success of the selfish gene.

### Some criticisms of sociobiological explanations

Much human behaviour isn't negative. Most of us aren't habitually aggressive, manipulative and dishonest. Most of us don't cheat, lie and continually try to win over others all the time. We are usually co-operative, generous and helpful. In Chapter 4 we described how some people will go to considerable lengths to help others, often at great cost to themselves. This could even diminish their own chances of survival. Sociobiologists say that altruistic behaviour can be explained in terms of inclusive fitness (see William Hamilton's ideas in Chapter 6). It seems that just about any behaviour could be explained by inclusive fitness if one tries hard enough to find an explanation. Positive, pro-social behaviour could equally as well have been naturally selected.

Although sociobiological analysis sounds helpful, and likely to yield useful insights into human functioning, some critics still believe that this approach can lead to misunderstanding and misuse. For example, critics of human sociobiology fear that adopting an evolutionary approach to human behaviour may encourage a belief that male aggression and male discrimination against women shouldn't be discouraged since they are supposed to have some adaptive significance.

Critics of sociobiology claim that it isn't supported by much actual evidence. We do not know the biological mechanisms by which genes regulate the development of the human (or any other animal) nervous system. Few successful studies have been conducted into how neural and hormonal activity controls even a single behaviour pattern. Much research needs to be conducted into how information carried in the genes influences or determines the organism's physiological structure. Natural selection sounds fine as a description, but inadequate as an explanation. How does it work to shape the size, colouring, mode of feeding, mating and defence?

Until we have some understanding of the relationship between genes and physiology we can only guess about any relationship between genes and behaviour. Only when we have some understanding of these relationships will we have any evidence for how natural selection shapes behaviour by influencing genetic transmission between generations.

■ **What does Dawkins mean by 'the selfish gene'?**

► According to sociobiology, altruistic behaviour is designed to promote the likelihood that the genes will survive. However, if one person is going to die in an accident his genes will be lost. Another could help but doesn't. The genes therefore survive. Had the witness attempted to help, he may have died too, thus losing both sets of genes. Altruism has been counter productive here.

► Explaining complex behaviour as being genetically determined may be tempting, but there is no real evidence or understanding for how it works. To say that adaptive behaviour would be naturally selected doesn't explain how such behaviour becomes encoded into molecules of protein called genes.

► Evolutionary theories suggest the biological mechanisms through which behavioural and physiological adaptations take place. It will take many years of patient enquiry before we have any real understanding of how this may occur.

■ Summarize sociobiology's explanation of human behaviour.

■ Outline some of the criticisms that have been made of current evolutionary explanations of human behaviour.

*Summary – Evolutionary explanations of human behaviour*

The main evolutionary explanations of human behaviour come from two sources. First, Darwinian ideas about how natural selection shapes animal physiology, especially the notion of survival of the fittest. Second, sociobiological explanations for the adaptive functions of human behaviour becoming encoded into genes and transmitted to future generations. Both offer interesting insights. Both claim evidence in support. However, we know very little about the actual mechanisms of genetic transmission and how it influences behaviour.

*Exam questions – 60 minutes each*

1  (a) Describe some of the ways in which animals have been shown to learn in the natural environment. (*10 marks*)
   (b) Assess the effectiveness of animal learning in the adaptation of behaviour in non-human animals. (*15 marks*)
2  Describe some of the attempts to teach language to a variety of species of non-human animals, and discuss the extent to which these attempts have been successful. (*25 marks*)
3  How far have evolutionary ideas been successful in explaining human behaviour? (*25 marks*)

# Part 3
## Adjustment and abnormality

*We all know what we mean by people behaving 'normally', although we may have difficulties defining or explaining what we mean. Yet our ideas about what is normal have changed over the centuries. Since medical and psychological researchers began their studies they have identified groups of behaviours which they claim are symptoms or signs of some condition or 'illness'. In Part 3 we examine the major classifications of abnormal behaviour used today, including the practical and ethical implications of 'mental illness', and the major forms of treatment or therapy for dealing with them.*

# *Conceptions and models of abnormality*

---

**Chapter objectives**

By the end of this chapter you should have:

▌ a knowledge of the advantages and disadvantages of various definitions of normality and abnormality;

▌ an understanding of the ways in which society responds to normal and abnormal behaviour;

▌ an appreciation of ethical implications for dealing with people with abnormal responses;

▌ an awareness of the assumptions made by medical and psychological approaches to abnormal behaviour.

---

## Introduction

Some people have been, and still are, regarded as 'abnormal' because what they say and do, or how they look, is different from the rest. In the West, during the last two centuries, the 'mentally ill' have been forced to live apart from other people since they were 'schizophrenic', or 'delusional', or 'obsessive', or in any other way 'abnormal'.

There are at least four problems with labelling someone in this way. First, people become so used to treating the individual according to his or her label (e.g. 'he is schizophrenic') that they no longer regard that person as a fellow human being with all the rights and liberties that others enjoy. The individual is eventually 'dehumanized'. Second, our behaviour changes with age and experience. Someone once labelled 'abnormal' may continue to be thought of as different, even though any differences have long since disappeared. Third, behaviour often changes in different situations. How we behave with close friends who know and like us may not be how we behave at work. Further, some situations promote abnormal behaviour. We may not normally behave in the same ways as we do, for example, when attending a job interview, being questioned by the police, or even consulting the doctor. Fourth, abnormal behaviour is often a result of interaction between particular people, for example two people who are calm and pleasant when apart may fight and argue when together. The first two problems here relate to defining the individual as abnormal, the other two show

▶ *Labelling* occurs when we define someone in a certain way. Calling a child 'stupid' is applying a label. The more people that regard the child as stupid, the more likely it is that the child is seen to be behaving in stupid ways, and the child might eventually see itself as stupid. (NB Cooley's 'looking glass world', discussed in Chapter 16.)

how abnormal behaviour results from someone being in a particular situation.

We must distinguish between three things when discussing abnormal behaviour. First, the individuals themselves; second, what they do (their behaviour); and third, the situation they are in when their 'abnormal' behaviour occurs. Humanist psychologists such as **Carl Rogers** and **R.D. Laing** are more concerned with individuals and their perceptions of themselves and others. Psychoanalytical psychologists are concerned with the individuals (their previous experiences) and what they do (their 'symptoms'). Behaviourist psychologists are concerned with what people do in different situations.

## WHAT IS 'ABNORMAL BEHAVIOUR'?

### Some definitions of normality and abnormality

One behaviourist claim is that there is no such thing as 'abnormal behaviour' since all behaviour is socially defined. If so, then behaviour is not being defined as 'abnormal' because of what someone did, but rather when, where and how they did it. This is a cultural or subcultural definition. Davison and Neale (1994, reported in *In Search of the Human Mind* by Robert Sternberg, 1994) report the behaviour of Eskimo religious leaders (called shamans) who use magic and mystical incantations, spells and wild behaviour to promote the good of an individual or the whole society. By Western standards their behaviour is quite abnormal or would be defined as 'severely disturbed'. Before the fall of Communism Russian poets and writers who spoke out against the system were 'dissidents' and were put into Siberian mental hospitals. Critical writing is not, in itself, abnormal; it becomes defined as such because of the situation in which it occurs.

Socially defined abnormal behaviour is not confined to individuals. Wider social paranoia must have gripped seventeenth-century communities that hunted and burned often elderly peasant women as 'witches' in Europe, or supported the Spanish Inquisition, or the attempted elimination of the Jews in Nazi Germany. This view would claim that abnormal behaviour is *any behaviour that is inappropriate to the social or cultural context in which it occurs*. This is a social definition and not everyone agrees with it. Anthropologists, for example, claim that some behaviour must be considered abnormal regardless of the circumstances under which it occurs. Any act that reduces the chances of the group to survive must be considered 'abnormal'. Incest, child abuse, prolonged self-mutilation and suicide are examples of behaviour which 'weakens' the group. These acts are forbidden in almost all cultures on Earth. This view claims that *some behaviour is universally abnormal*.

The problem with defining 'abnormality' is that it is supposedly somehow different from 'normality', and we can't actually define

---

► Humanism is a branch of psychology concerned with human needs and helping people to achieve them, to come to know themselves as best they can, and to fulfil their potentials. We will discuss the humanists' approach later in this chapter.

| Psychologists | Concern |
|---|---|
| Humanist | individual |
| Psychoanalyst | individual and behaviour |
| Behaviourist | behaviour and situation |

■ **In your own words describe some of the problems in labelling someone as abnormal.**

► If critical writing was a cause for being locked away there would be precious few writers of any merit left, and news reporting would be very dull indeed.

► There are some acts which are socially defined as normal and acceptable and others which must be considered abnormal and unacceptable under any circumstances. These latter are more likely to be defined as psychiatrically abnormal.

■ **What is meant by the phrase 'abnormal behaviour is any behaviour that is inappropriate to the social or cultural context in which it occurs'? Explain the objection to it.**

that either. Behaviour thought normal in one culture (e.g. acquiring status, individual competitiveness, not always telling the truth, and so on) might be quite unacceptable elsewhere. The most obvious definition of normality is 'typical' or 'average', i.e. what most people in the group do. Any behaviour which only a minority exhibits must therefore be abnormal. There is an obvious problem here – most large groups are made up of many minorities. In Britain we could be differentiated by countless variables. We could use age: the majority of people are aged below 65. So is anyone who draws an old age pension behaving abnormally? Or we could define people by job or profession. Most people don't paint great pictures, design great buildings, create great music or fashion. Are those that do behaving abnormally? Or we could define by ethnic origin. Scottish people are in a minority, so is their behaviour abnormal?

Clearly crude statistics aren't going to help us since they don't take the effects of the behaviour into account. Some behaviour is simply more desirable than other behaviour. So we could define abnormality as behaviour which differs from that which we expect of someone playing a particular role. So a student who doesn't behave in 'student-like' ways (whatever they are) would be defined as deviant and his or her behaviour would be abnormal. The precise role need not even be defined. People generally would regard crime as abnormal since not to commit crime is regarded as the normal state of affairs in many countries (else why have a police force?). Anyone committing crime (not the norm) is therefore behaving abnormally. Even if the statistical majority of the population did commit crime it would still be defined as abnormal, since it deviates from the desirable, supposed norm of not committing crime.

### A 'mental health' definition

Jahoda (1958) proposed a 'checklist' of features of mental health that all 'normal' people would have, and people whose behaviour is abnormal would not. These include a realistic view of oneself and of the world, acceptance of oneself for what one is, a solid sense of identity, and competence in coping with life generally. The problem with this is that we can't know that such a checklist does constitute a statement of mental health. For example, what exactly is 'competence in coping with life'? How can it be measured? How much of it do we need to have in order to be 'normal', and who says that someone whose behaviour isn't always 'competent' is therefore behaving abnormally? This is a very value-laden view, in other words, it reflects very middle-class, conservative ideas that the way society is at the moment is the way people want it to be and to remain. Anyone who conforms to these values will be normal and anyone who doesn't must be abnormal.

### Humanist definitions of abnormality

Rather than attempt a broad definition of abnormality from society's point of view, humanist psychologists see 'abnormality' from the sufferer's viewpoint. For example, someone who reports

► This is a simple statistical model whereby what the majority do is normal and what minorities do is abnormal.

■ In America one in three people is obese (i.e. they weigh about 30 per cent more than they should). Is obesity 'abnormal'?

■ 20 per cent of Americans admit to being homosexual. Is homosexuality 'abnormal'?

■ About 20 per cent of Americans are disabled. Is disability 'abnormal'?
Explain your answers.

► This is a 'deviation from the desired norm' explanation, but it still assumes that there are universally shared norms of desired behaviour without questioning where they come from, how they are maintained, and for whom they are desirable.

► 'Mental health' is a concept, like 'intelligence' and 'personality', that psychologists put forward to describe a condition that they believe exists, and then treat as though it was 'real' and existed just as they described. 'Mental health' is, at best, culturally defined, since people in different societies have different ideas about what constitutes 'mental health'.

► This view claims that conformity is always a good thing. See Milgram's work in Chapter 3 for a discussion of this.

■ Summarize the argument for and against the usefulness of a mental health definition of normal and abnormal behaviour.

feeling very depressed for long periods, who is constantly listless and unable to settle to anything, feeling agitated, profoundly unhappy, and can't see that things can ever get better, may well define themselves as abnormal. Physical symptoms that often support these reported feelings include insomnia and lethargy (lack of energy), no interest in food or exercise, and general aches and pains. A humanist definition of abnormality could be: '*abnormality is those symptoms which someone who regards themselves as behaving abnormally reports suffering*'. However, even this more qualitative, less judgemental approach wouldn't include all people who could be defined as abnormal, since many have no idea that there is anything wrong with them at all.

So far we don't have a definition of abnormal behaviour that avoids *value judgements* about what is desirable and undesirable with which most psychologists could agree. Most definitions rely on the extent of the maladaptiveness of the behaviour. By maladaptive we mean behaviour that is a response to some problem with living, but which avoids rather than deals with the problem. In this way the problem never gets solved and the person who can't cope with it may feel frustrated and unhappy with themselves. This may make matters worse. For example, someone who feels inadequate in some way may be highly critical of someone else. This could create other problems for themselves since the other person may not respond as flexibly or helpfully as they could. Also the victim of the criticism may have lowered self-esteem, which could lead to other problems for them.

### Medical definitions of abnormality

Our last definition of abnormality comes from supporters of the medical approach. It sees abnormal behaviour as a symptom of 'mental illness'. This view was popular amongst health professionals for most of the twentieth century, but has been attacked recently. According to Maher (1966), even the language we use to describe people whose behaviour is abnormal is entirely 'medical'. We have *patients* who exhibit *symptoms*, which are *diagnosed* by *doctors* and *psychiatrists* who work in *clinics* and *mental hospitals* where they are *treated* and given *therapy* to *cure* them of their *illness*. This is the process of *psychopathology*. But to assume that abnormal behaviour is necessarily a symptom of an illness that can be treated with the tools of medicine is regarded by many psychologists as completely misguided, as we shall see in the next section.

It seems that, even if we can't adequately define abnormal behaviour, we often know it when we see it. Whilst we've all done something a bit mad on occasions, to be thought of as abnormal behaviour it would have to be something very serious, or persistent.

## How has our understanding of abnormal behaviour changed?

The earliest conceptions of abnormality were that the unfortunate person was possessed by some kind of evil spirit. The idea of spirits

▶ *Value judgements* are the opinions of people which imply that their way of seeing and doing things is superior or 'more civilized' than those of other people.

■ Note the way that supporters of the medical approach regard abnormal behaviour.

■ How useful is the distinction between normal and abnormal behaviour? What are the advantages and disadvantages of describing behaviour in this way?

## Summary – Models of abnormal behaviour

| Definition | Assumptions | Implications for treatment | Ethical implications |
|---|---|---|---|
| Statistical | Minority behaviour is deviant. | Everyone would need treatment for some minority behaviour. | Can everyone in the group really be abnormal? |
| Deviation from the norm | There are social 'norms' of desired behaviour. | People who do not conform to social norms need re-education and other treatment. | Who defines social norms? Are people abnormal because they do not conform? |
| Mental health | It is possible to define and measure mental health. | Those who fail on the test items need some treatment to improve their mental health. | Who decides what constitutes mental health and what is the alternative to health? |
| Personal distress | Individuals can feel when they are behaving in maladaptive ways. | People can 'check in and out' of treatment depending on how they feel. | Can't provide treatment when feelings change over time and across situations. |
| Maladaptiveness | There are underlying problems that cause maladaptive behaviour. | Retrospective therapy can find the origin of the inadequacy that creates the maladaptive behaviour. | Retrospective therapy (e.g. Freud's) is highly subjective and interpretive, and not to be trusted. |
| Mental illness | Problems with living are symptoms of an illness that may be treated. | Behaviour can be classified and effective treatments prescribed. | The individual may be labelled as 'mentally ill' and treated differently. |

probably goes back many thousands of years. If the individual is serene and calm, or energetic in doing 'good' things, then the spirits would be thought of as beneficial and the individual could be treated with reverence. If their behaviour was anti-social, then the spirits would be evil and people were generally afraid of them. It is thought that one way in which possession was treated was by drilling a hole in the head (called trepanning) in order to let the spirits escape (an unfortunate side effect of this treatment would probably have been the death of the sufferer, of course). Not really an acceptable approach to dealing with 'abnormal behaviour' (even if we knew exactly what it was) now! In the fifth century AD, **Hippocrates,** the founder of modern medicine, was the first known writer to claim that abnormal behaviour was better seen as a symptom of an illness.

As Christianity spread throughout Europe from the Middle Ages people whose behaviour was different were thought of as having troubled minds, or were even possessed by demons or the devil. 'Witches' were burned and other means of exorcism were employed by the Church. Disturbed people were regarded as 'anti-Christian' and their evil influence had to be removed from society. By the 1500s doctors began to claim that abnormal behaviour was a symptom of 'mental illness', not possession. St Mary of Bethlehem

► Earlier we made a distinction between the individual and his or her behaviour. No such distinction would have been recognized until very recently.

► The idea of a hospital was quite different then from what we know about hospitals now. 'Bedlam', as St Mary of Bethlehem was called, would have been a sorry place for the unfortunates who lived out their miserable lives there, often chained and manacled, often lying in their own mess, with few visitors and nothing to do.

opened as a hospital for the 'treatment' of such symptoms in 1547, although the Church continued to claim that abnormality meant possession. At this time medical knowledge, especially about the origins of disturbed behaviour, was non-existent, so 'treatment' really meant being locked away and looked after by attendants.

For the next two hundred years doctors speculated about the biological, physical cause of mental illness. They worked on a trial and error basis, trying different treatments to see what their effect would be. Some unfortunate patients were whipped, flogged, starved, dipped in freezing water, purged, bled and vomited to see if these treatments would improve their behaviour. During the nineteenth century **Jean Martin Charcot**, **Sigmund Freud** and other physicians interested in 'nervous diseases' attempted to classify the symptoms of their patients to differentiate between different types of 'illness'. Freud suggested classifying abnormal behaviour into three parts: *neuroses, psychoses*, and *personality disorders*. We will discuss this in Chapter 10.

The 'mentally ill' had no rights, no public sympathy and few who wanted to protect them. Some refuges were offered, by the Quakers for example, but most of those who behaved differently from others were the victims of experiments to see the effects of treatment, with very little regard for the suffering of the 'patient'.

Into the twentieth century the Church's explanations and responses have changed to be more compassionate and there has been vast expansion in the influence of medical explanations and treatments. The influences of both the mind (Freud) and the environment were discounted and mental illness was regarded as a problem in the body (more specifically, the brain). This is a *somatic* explanation (from *soma* meaning the body) and underlies the medical model's approach to abnormal behaviour. The medical model uses drugs (chemotherapy), psychosurgery and electroconvulsive therapy (ECT) as its main methods.

More recently in the West, a movement away from the somatic approach that originated two thousand years ago in the Far East has grown. This *alternative medicine* includes acupuncture, reflexology, aromatherapy, iridology, the use of crystals and so on. Where the medical model reduces symptoms to specific causes, alternative approaches claim to be *holistic,* taking the individual's whole life experiences into account and attempting to treat the whole person – body and mind.

*Holistic* medicine reflects the view that the body, mind and environment are all linked and that the whole person has to be treated, not just the specific symptoms.

According to Bailey (1979), medicine began by classifying conditions such as tuberculosis and typhoid which had some physical, biological symptoms. More illnesses were added as organic symptoms were identified. Unfortunately, medicine also classified conditions that do not have any organic symptoms at all as if they were also diseases. Psychiatrists recognize this and refer, for example, to 'functional' psychoses as opposed to organic psy-

## Summary – Changing attitudes towards abnormal behaviour

| Date | Causes | Treatment | Social responses |
|------|--------|-----------|------------------|
| up to 1500s | Possession by demons | Trepanning, burning, religious exorcism | Fear of 'devils' and probably of the Church. Avoid or report sufferers. |
| 1700–1900 | Physical (something inside the body) | Vomiting, bleeding, flogging, starvation, containment in asylums | Few knew or cared – lock the demented away to protect the rest from their madness. |
| 1900–1940s | Somatic (problem with the brain), psychological (childhood experiences) | ECT, brain surgery, psychoanalysis for mild problems, containment in asylums | Some marvelled at medical break-throughs (ECT and lobotomies), and hope for psychoanalysis. Lock the mentally ill away to protect others and for their own benefit. |
| 1940s– | Organic, somatic (body's organs, including the brain), psychological (symptoms and behaviour) | Drugs, surgery, ECT, psychoanalysis, behaviour therapies, containment in asylums | Most people have faith in medical intervention and hope for psychological therapy. Lock the mentally ill away so they can be treated. |
| 1950s– | Organic, somatic, psychological (behaviour, symptoms, and faulty self-perception) | Drugs, surgery, ECT, psychoanalysis, behaviour therapy, humanist therapies, containment in mental hospitals | Continued hope for medical and psychological treatment, but continue to lock the severely mentally ill away so they can be treated. |
| 1960s– | Organic, somatic, disruption in whole life experience, psychological (faulty self-perception) | Drugs, surgery, ECT, therapy, counselling, holistic medicine, fewer locked wards in mental hospitals | Continued hope for medical and psychological treatment, tolerance of and some enthusiasm for alternative approach to orthodox medicine. Continue to remove the 'mentally ill' from mainstream society. |
| 1980s– | Organic, somatic, psychological (faulty self-perception) | Drugs, surgery, ECT, counselling, holistic medicine, care in the community (closing mental hospitals) | Continued hope for psychological treatment. Initial hope for care in the community, but tragic incidents suggest under-resourcing. The NIMBY (not in my back yard) principle. |

■ Summarize social reactions to those whose behaviour was described as abnormal.

choses, where there are physical symptoms. In this way conditions that Thomas Szasz (1974) calls 'problems with living' become 'mental illness'.

### *Mental illness or abnormal behaviour?*

It is certainly preferable to think of alcohol abuse as a disease rather than an immoral act, as it was during Victorian times, and it's certainly preferable to think of someone as being ill than to have them tortured or burned at the stake! The medical model has provided a useful alternative. However, it does have its problems.

First, as we mentioned earlier, the medical model assumes that some behaviour is 'normal' and that those people who behave 'normally' are mentally healthy; other behaviour is 'abnormal' and people who behave abnormally are 'ill'. This is too simple. We can't define 'mental health' in our own culture, and acceptable behaviour varies enormously between cultures as well. It also varies over time. We don't regard homosexuality as an illness now, though it was defined as such not too long ago. It would be impossible to measure how much 'mental health' any one person at any one time enjoys, or define the cut-off point between being 'mentally healthy' and being 'mentally ill'.

Second, there are several problems associated with being defined as 'ill'. It enables the individual to put the blame for their condition on circumstances beyond their control. After all, it's not their fault that they are ill, and it is a psychiatrist's job to diagnose their condition and make them better. This also removes the responsibility from the 'patient' to participate much in their own treatment. Humanistic therapies such as Rogers' client-centred therapy (see Chapter 10) require the individual to be actively involved in their recovery. A part of this is the reduction of the differences in status between doctor and patient which the medical approach maintains.

A third set of questions concerns the nature of psychiatry itself. Doctors involved in diagnosis of organic conditions such as appendicitis or heart tremors use two broad sources of information, called signs and symptoms. Signs are the results of their own tests, such as blood tests, taking a pulse, examining X-rays etc. Symptoms are the answers the patients give to the doctor's questions, such as 'where is the pain?', 'when did it start?', 'have you had it before?', and so on. Psychiatrists have very few, if any, reliable signs, and are forced to rely on symptoms. Fransella (1975) says that psychiatristic diagnosis ultimately rests on whether the psychiatrist believes the patient's claims or not. Cooper et al. (1972) showed psychiatrists in Britain and the USA filmed diagnostic interviews and found that the American psychiatrists were between two and ten times more likely to conclude the patient was schizophrenic than the British psychiatrists. For these reasons Fransella and Szasz describe psychiatry as 'quasi-medicine'.

## Summary – Mental illness or abnormal behaviour?

*For the medical model*
Defining someone as suffering from a particular illness gives a more precise categorization of behaviour into 'normal' and 'abnormal'.

*For 'abnormal behaviour'*
At different times and in different places the same behaviour has been thought of as 'normal' and 'abnormal'. Most behaviour is culturally defined.

'Mental illnesses' often have an organic base, and can often be treated by drugs and surgery.

This is only true of some conditions. Many 'illnesses' are *learned*, not *caught*. Treatment is often inappropriate and can have side effects.

'Symptoms' are usually self-evident, and diagnosis can be made by a skilled psychiatrist.

Unlike in other areas of medicine, psychiatry has few valid objective tests. 'Interpretation of symptoms' isn't as accurate as 'analysis of objective test results'.

The medical model raises two issues: the cause of the 'illness' and providing the most appropriate treatment.

Since we know relatively little about the structure and functioning of the brain, we can't always identify causes. Different systems of classification may result in different diagnoses for the same symptoms.

Describing someone as 'ill' implies that they can be treated, and possibly cured. This avoids the social shame of being seen as 'mad', 'weird', or 'crazy'.

If you're 'ill' it is up to someone else to 'cure' you. You need not feel any responsibility for your own actions, and so make no contribution towards changing your own behaviour.

Similar percentages of people suffer similar symptoms, no matter how they are classified, in different parts of the world.

All societies have customs and rules about social living, and some people will have problems with making appropriate responses. That doesn't make them 'mentally ill'.

In *The Manufacture of Madness* (1973), **Thomas Szasz** insists that a distinction must be made between 'illness', which is the domain of the medical profession, and problems with living, which is a much broader social issue. Illness is the organic consequence of infection, genetic inheritance, neurochemical imbalances and trauma. Those which concern behaviour must have an organic base and can be regarded as 'diseases of the brain'. Psychiatrists recognize that the absence of any known organic base for 'mental illness' poses a problem for the medical profession, so claim that there is an organic problem, but it hasn't been discovered yet, and in the meantime refer to the functional nature of the condition.

A final issue concerns the future of societies that continue to use the concept of 'mental illness'. People whose behaviour is inconvenient will continue to be labelled as schizophrenic (R.D. Laing 1965), and continue to feel dehumanized as a result. R.D. Laing argued that society ought to try to recognize schizophrenia as a valid and possibly beneficial alternative way of viewing the world, although few people take this view seriously now. Szasz (1972) says the medical model takes no account of interpersonal and social causes of abnormal behaviour, thus preventing society from understanding and dealing with crime, delinquency and other deviant behaviour. To describe criminals as being 'born evil' and 'mad' is to misunderstand the social circumstances under which they live.

From what we have said so far you might form the mistaken impression that psychiatrists and psychologists take entirely opposing views on the nature of the people they deal with. This isn't generally true. Partly because of the issues raised by Szasz, Cooper, Laing and others, psychiatrists now are recognizing the importance of stress in the environment and between people contributing to state of mind. Equally, psychologists do recognize the usefulness of brain surgery in the treatment of conditions such as epilepsy and that the only way in which some people can exist outside an institution is by taking drugs.

■ Summarize the arguments in favour of, and against, the concept of 'mental illness'.

## EXPLAINING ABNORMAL BEHAVIOUR

In the first part of this chapter we noted the difficulties in arriving at a satisfactory definition of abnormal behaviour. These have not stopped supporters of the major approaches in this area from offering their explanations. The main perspectives here are the *psychodynamic* approach from Sigmund Freud; the *behaviourist* approach from drawing on the work of Ivan Pavlov and B.F. Skinner; the *humanist* approach advanced by Maslow, Rogers and others; and the *somatic* approach taken by the medical profession generally.

► See Chapter 1 for a fuller discussion of Freud's theory.

### The psychodynamic approach

Psychoanalytic theory sees the central role of instinctive urges in explaining normal and abnormal behaviour through shaping the adult personality during key stages in childhood. Life is characterized as a conflict between those urges which promote our well-being and drive us to express ourselves through our achievements, which Freud describes as libido, and those which drive us towards our ultimate destruction, which are the death instincts. Underlying this struggle is the unconscious interaction between the three components that will, more than anything else, shape our personalities and the 'battlefield' for our libido and death instincts.

The id is the primitive source of all psychic energy. Throughout life its function is to drive the individual to seek ways of satisfying its needs immediately and at all costs. At some time around the age of two years ego emerges through id's frustrations. It is a more rational drive and seeks strategies to satisfy its needs. If needs remain unsatisfied then neurotic anxiety is produced. This conflict will be inevitable occasionally. Over the next three years, to resolve Oedipus and Electra complexes, children begin to identify with their same-sex parent, leading to the formation of the child's superego. This reflects the child's moral feelings; conflict between ego and superego is also inevitable and produces moral anxiety. Freud suggested that the psyche has three means of dealing with neurotic and moral anxiety. These are through dreams, through the appearance of neurotic symptoms, or through defence mechanisms.

Freud (1900) thought that, during our everyday lives, thoughts, hopes and desires pass through our mind, many of which must not be expressed or acted upon since that would break our moral or social codes of behaviour. Sometimes we consciously refuse to recognize the thought, so we *suppress* it. Neurotic and moral anxiety is produced. If the thought or impulse is too bizarre or extreme we unconsciously *repress* it into our unconscious mind. These repressed anxieties may cause some neurotic symptoms to appear later in life.

Neurotic symptoms include temporary paralysis of a limb, temporary blindness or deafness, migraine headaches, various phobias, multiple personalities, obsessive behaviour such as arranging every object in a room into exactly the right place before being able to sleep, hand twitching, and so on. Any of these could provide a clue as to what has been repressed into the patient's unconscious.

Defence mechanisms are the third of ego's methods for dealing with anxiety and are quite unconscious (and normal). Where someone is unable to deal with reality, for example a child who is punished by its parents for something it hasn't done, that person may *displace* his or her anxieties by kicking the cat! Repression and displacement are two common defence mechanisms that help us deal with anxiety. All defence mechanisms involve some distortions of reality so that ego can deal with its anxieties. Other defence mechanisms include denial, where we refuse to accept that something is true; *rationalization*, where we give a seemingly acceptable excuse for otherwise unacceptable behaviour; and *sublimation*, where we channel all our energies into some acceptable activity so that we don't recognize or act on the unacceptable thoughts or impulses we are having. There are dozens of other defence mechanisms.

Freud's therapeutic approach (see Chapter 10) makes several assumptions. These are that we are born with competing instinctive

► By anxiety Freud meant what we would take it to mean now – an unpleasant, hard to define, emotional state characterized by uneasy feelings of apprehension that something unpleasant, or threatening, is about to happen, a general fear, without being quite sure about exactly what we are afraid of.

► *Suppression* is a conscious desire to avoid thinking about something that may embarrass us, cause us alarm, or be traumatic. *Repression* is an unconscious defence mechanism, as we shall see shortly.

► Freud claimed that conflicts between imagined instinctive urges can create observed symptoms. There are, of course, other explanations for these symptoms than those Freud offered.

■ **Outline the role of the instinctive urges in Freudian psychoanalysis.**

■ **Outline the strengths and weaknesses of the psychodynamic approach to abnormal behaviour.**

urges that are expressed through three parts of personality. Conflict between the demands of the id, ego and superego produces anxiety, which must be dealt with at the time, otherwise it will enter the unconscious part of our mind where it may trigger various neurotic symptoms to appear later. We have three ways of dealing with this anxiety. If they fail we may need psychoanalysis. Therapy involves isolating and dealing with these conflicts using the methods of psychoanalysis. However, no matter how attractive some aspects of this approach seem, there is no scientifically acceptable evidence that any of these structures or processes in personality do actually exist. Therapy may actually benefit some people (apart from the therapist), but they may equally have benefited from talking to someone with no knowledge of psychoanalysis.

### Evaluation – Implications of the psychodynamic approach

| Assumptions | Implications for treatment | Ethical implications |
| --- | --- | --- |
| There are instinctive urges and structures in personality formation. | Explore them through one-to-one therapy sessions, which will be time-consuming and costly. | Since the theoretical assumptions have no scientific basis the therapy may be a huge con. |
| Personality growth is driven by conflict and resolving anxieties (this is very pessimistic). | Conflicts must be resolved by exploring the patient's past relationships and experiences through retrospective methods such as hypnosis. | Exploring the patient's memories of childhood involves discussing the behaviour of other people such as parents. This isn't ethically acceptable. |
| Unresolved anxieties produce neurotic symptoms. | The job of psychoanalytic therapy is 'to make the unconscious, conscious to the patient'. | If there is no such thing as 'the unconscious mind' then the aim of therapy is a deception. |
| Freud assumed that studying the spoken memories of neurotic adult patients was an acceptable way of gathering data about healthy personality development in children. | Dealing with adults requires different therapeutic approaches than would dealing with children. Allowance must be made for the adult-therapist relationship. | To suggest that childhood experiences explain the symptoms of hysterical neuroses in adults is misleading and possibly deceptive. |

## The behaviourist approach

Ivan Pavlov's studies of association learning in dogs led to the emergence of classical conditioning. Pavlov claimed that all learning originated as complex sets of conditioned reflexes (see Chapter 1). Few people would agree with this, although some behaviour is learned in this way. For example, some stimuli naturally (or otherwise) elicit anxiety. Aeroplanes which might crash, a high tower from which you might fall, and spiders which might bite you are examples. Neutral stimuli that are associated with them, such as the airport departure lounge, the upper windows in tall buildings, and the thatch on an old cottage, might also trigger the anxiety. *Behaviour therapy* may be necessary to help reduce or eliminate the anxiety.

Proponents of operant conditioning prefer a system of *behaviour modification*. They maintain that all *voluntary behaviour*, including undesired or maladaptive behaviour, is learned (and can be unlearned) in just the same way. The process involves deciding exactly what behaviour is to be changed and how, then discovering what stimuli are triggering it under which circumstances, and finally, finding out what consequences are reinforcing, and thus maintaining it. Behaviour modification can now begin by removing the stimuli and changing the consequences. This may need to be completed gradually so that the individual is weaned away from his or her previous response in favour of a more desired one.

Social learning therapists advocate modelling therapy. They assume that maladaptive behaviour is being maintained by fear. People who know what they are doing is wrong in some way are unable to change because they fear the alternatives. I may know that being afraid of snakes isn't sensible since I'm unlikely to come into contact with many, and extremely unlikely to encounter any that would harm me. That may not remove my fear. Watching someone else handle snakes (i.e. model snake-handling behaviour) has been found to be effective in reducing the symptoms of snake phobia.

The main assumptions that underlie the behaviourist approach are that all behaviour is learned and can be unlearned. It does not result from unconscious urges to resolve imaginary conflicts. The symptoms of the condition are therefore the condition itself, since when the symptoms are removed the condition no longer exists. According to H.J. Eysenck (1960), if you 'get rid of the symptom … you have eliminated the neurosis'.

## The humanist approach

**Abraham Maslow** (1958) believed that psychology, dominated at the time by psychoanalysis and behaviourism, was becoming sidetracked from its true purpose. Psychoanalysts seem to characterize people as being one step away from being neurotic and are over-

▶ See Chapter 1 for a fuller discussion of behaviourist theory.

▶ *Behaviour therapy* is a technique for reducing the learned association between a stimulus and a response.

▶ *Voluntary behaviour* is anything you have the choice to do. *Involuntary behaviour* involves those reflexes or habits that you can't break. The behaviour of someone who is scared of spiders when they see one isn't reflexive, but it's certainly involuntary!

■ **Explain this quote from Eysenck for behaviourist responses to abnormal behaviour.**

■ List the major assumptions made by (a) behaviour therapists, (b) behaviour modification therapists and (c) modelling therapists.

■ Contrast the assumptions made by behaviourist and psychoanalytic approaches to abnormal behaviour.

► A *mechanistic* approach is one which claims that it is useful to compare some of the principles of human functioning with those of machines. A determinist approach is one which argues that certain external forces determine human responses. Both seem to challenge the idea that humans have some elements of 'free will'.

► *Self-actualization* means reaching the final level in a hierarchy of needs, from basic survival needs to having achieved all of one's creative potentials.

## Evaluation – Implications of behaviourist approaches

| Assumption | Implications for treatment | Ethical implications |
|---|---|---|
| All behaviour is learned. | Discover what triggers the learned response. | Ignores that which is spontaneous, creative or caused by physical trauma. |
| Symptoms are the problem. | No need to look further than the symptoms. | Ignores psychological conditions where the symptoms are manifestations of the condition. |
| Remove the reinforcer and the symptoms disappear. | Discover how patients appear to benefit from the consequences of their actions. | Looking for a reinforcer to remove may overlook other, more urgent, clinical considerations. |

concerned with neuroses and anxieties. Maslow thought behaviourism was simplistic and misguided. Both traditions were *mechanistic* and reductionist whilst both claimed to be scientific. Maslow, and later **Carl Rogers** and **Rollo May**, thought psychology should be about understanding people's needs and finding how these needs can be achieved so that every individual can reach his or her full potential. Maslow described this objective as '*self-actualization*'.

The major assumptions here are that human needs can be divided into two groups. First, there are basic physiological and psychological needs, for food and shelter, safety and security, and for giving and receiving love and belonging. These ensure the survival of the group. Maslow claimed that these needs must be satisfied before the next needs can be achieved. Additionally we have psychological needs for 'becoming everything that one is capable of becoming' (Maslow 1970). These needs are for the respect of others and self-esteem, for knowledge and understanding, the appreciation of beauty in all its forms, and for realizing that one has reached one's full potential. Another assumption is that psychology is about individuals, and should not be concerned with discovering (probably non-existent) universal laws or principles of human functioning. Third, Maslow assumes that psychology is capable of being a science concerned with higher human motives, self-development, knowledge and understanding.

Carl Rogers (1961) agreed with Maslow about the need for self-actualization, which he saw as closely linked to the need for other people to think well of us (see Cooley's looking glass theory, discussed in Chapter 16). Without positive regard from others we feel isolated and rejected, and this forms the basis for 'mental illness' according to Rogers. He proposed client-centred therapy, which aims to help the client rebuild his or her social relationships. (See Chapter 10 for a discussion of these therapies.)

### Evaluation – Implications of humanist approaches

| Assumption | Implications for treatment | Ethical implications |
|---|---|---|
| Each person is unique. | Individual therapy is essential, but is time-consuming and costly. | None, so long as the 'client' isn't suffering from a condition that needs a different kind of treatment. |
| Each individual needs to feel that he or she is respected and valued by others. | Therapy will aim to show unconditional regard for the individual. | Therapy might create a false impression of how an individual is to be regarded outside. |
| Everyone is entitled to their own personal values. | The therapist will have to suspend his or her own personal opinion to appreciate the client's values. | Conformity to socially approved values is essential for the regard of others in many societies. |

■ Outline how humanist views of abnormal behaviour differ from those of the more determinist and reductionist approaches.

## The medical approach

As knowledge about biology grew the medical profession became increasingly interested in studying people whose behaviour was abnormal. Researchers can learn much about 'normal' functioning from studying people whose responses are different. They assume that psychological disorders such as anorexia, phobias, obsessions, depression and so on must have biological causes. Such disorders are therefore examples of mental illness. Treatment must involve finding which biological structures are concerned and treating them. The medical approach claims that mental illnesses arise from one of four causes.

First, infection by germs or viruses. A virus might lead to a recognizable set of symptoms, or what is called a *syndrome*. (The Robertsons identified the syndrome of distress to describe how children separated from their usual childcare routines without adequate alternative care suffer – see Chapter 14, pages 311–12.) Second, genetic inheritance might produce symptoms of psychological maladjustment that are taken to be 'mental illness'; Down's Syndrome or autism are examples. Third, neurochemicals in the brain such as dopamine (involved in schizophrenia), epinephrine (involved in depression), or serotonin (involved in failure to form new memories) may become unbalanced, giving rise to abnormal behaviours. Finally, physical trauma (e.g. accidental brain damage) or psychological trauma (e.g. the effects of neglect or abuse) can lead to psychological conditions such as depression, which are claimed to be mental illnesses.

### *Evaluation – Implications of the medical approach*

| *Assumption* | *Implications for treatment* | *Ethical implications* |
|---|---|---|
| The origins of abnormal behaviour are physical and biological. | Understanding the biology of the human body is all that is required to understand and treat mental illness. | Physical differences are not always found in the brains of people whose behaviour is abnormal, and treatment based on this assumption will be inappropriate. |
| The causes of mental illness are similar to the causes of other physical illnesses. | The same approach towards medical intervention is required for mental as well as physical illness. | There is no evidence for these claims and therefore physical intervention is the wrong treatment for the patient. |
| Mental illnesses can be classified in the same way as physical illnesses can. | Adopt a system of classification such as 'neuroses, psychoses, personality disorders'. | If abnormal behaviour is not a symptom of mental illness, classification will produce misunderstanding and potentially dangerous treatments. |
| Mental illnesses can be treated in the same way as physical illnesses. | The methods of medicine include drugs, surgery and ECT, and these are appropriate. | Drugs often have side effects, psychosurgery can cause more harm than good, ECT involves causing harm. |

## Summary – Approaches to explaining abnormal behaviour

Psychodynamic approaches offer theoretical explanations of how the interaction of instinctive urges and early experiences shape personality and behaviour later. The behaviourist approach rejects such intuitive, interpretive approaches and suggests that scientific investigation has revealed the principles upon which all behaviour, including maladapted behaviour, is learned. Humanists are equally scornful of attempts to apply science to human experience. Each individual has many social relationships, and people's unique experiences produce their individual perceptions of themselves and their behaviour. Supporters of the somatic approach see behaviour as symptoms of conditions, diseases or illnesses that can be understood and treated with the tools of orthodox medicine, as we shall see in the next two chapters.

## Exam questions – 60 minutes each

1  Discuss the practical and ethical implications of *either* the behaviourist *or* the psychoanalytic approaches to defining abnormal behaviour. (*25 marks*)
2  (a) Describe the main ways in which psychologists have defined abnormal behaviour. (*10 marks*)
   (b) Evaluate these attempts in terms of their usefulness. (*15 marks*)

# 9  *Psychopathology*

**Chapter objectives**

When you have read this chapter you should have gained:

▌ a knowledge of the advantages and disadvantages of definitions and classifications of normality and abnormality;

▌ an appreciation of the categories of abnormal behaviour in the major Western classifications and an idea of the symptoms of some of these syndromes;

▌ the ability to evaluate the current models in abnormal psychology, especially their ethical and practical implications;

▌ an understanding of genetic, biological and environmental forces which act upon people and shape their behaviour, and the difficulties researchers face in untangling these influences;

▌ an appreciation of schizophrenia, depression, eating disorders and paraphilias as examples of disorders with complex causes.

## Introduction

According to Bentall (1991), 'The main goal of psychopathology … is to render comprehensible behaviours and experiences that are ordinarily incomprehensible'. He claims that the traditional way of identifying symptoms, diagnosing them as a disease, then treating them as though they actually were that disease, is mistaken.

## CLASSIFYING NORMAL AND ABNORMAL BEHAVIOUR

Everyone occasionally becomes anxious, nervous, depressed, worried, unable to think clearly, excited and elated. This is perfectly 'normal'. If someone was acutely or permanently anxious, nervous, depressed etc. so that they couldn't act reasonably, their behaviour would be 'abnormal'. From Thomas Szasz's point of view, we are having some 'problem with life'. The symptoms of such behaviour, e.g. stopping eating, inability to sleep, persistent crying, disorganized thinking, and so on, would be taken to indicate a form of 'mental illness' by supporters of the medical model. Either way there are enormous practical and ethical problems associated with defining some behaviour as 'ill' and some as 'normal', as we saw in Chapter 8.

The medical profession is dedicated to identifying the causes of 'illnesses' in order to find 'cures' for them. This process begins with discovering which symptoms occur together that can be regarded as part of the same condition. So streaming eyes, a runny nose, a headache, aching limbs, and feeling tired and listless are some of the symptoms that are included in the diagnosis called 'the flu'. Doctors use the *British National Formulary*, a book which classifies symptoms under headings for the stomach, the skeleton, the blood system, digestion, the sense organs and so on. Psychiatrists have developed their own systems of classifying the symptoms of the major 'mental illnesses'.

The first system of classification was the clinical classification. It emerged as groups of clinicians, such as **J.M. Charcot** (1880s), **Emile Kraepelin** (1883) and **Sigmund Freud** (1890s) argued that psychological conditions have biological causes and symptoms. If the symptoms can be identified as belonging to a particular disease, then that disease can be treated using medical techniques. For the next century psychologists and psychiatrists have been identifying symptoms and naming diseases, as we saw in Chapter 8. For example, psychotic disorders (fairly extreme mental states where the individual is unaware of the effect of their behaviour) became subdivided into schizophrenia (see pages 172–6), depression (see pages 176–80), eating disorders (see pages 182–4), and so on. Clinical classifications suggest four main groupings of disorders. The first three were suggested by Freud's psychoanalytic model:

1 *Neuroses* are generally not too serious, often temporary, and may not need medical attention at all. The symptoms include anxiety, which may have a specific cause such as spiders or the objects of the other phobias. Phobias are often described as irrational fears, although sometimes the fear may be perfectly rational. 'Free floating' anxiety occurs where there isn't a particular cause for the anxiety but the individual is generally anxious. Obsessive behaviour occurs where the individual thinks about something a great deal, sometimes so that they can't think of much else. They may also have a compulsion to do certain things in connection with their obsession. Frequent bouts of mild depression are also regarded as neurotic symptoms.

2 *Personality disorders* are general reactions which can be seen in anti-social behaviour, e.g. aggression, violence, stealing, being obsessive about everything (hoarding), and behaviour resulting from an overwhelming feeling of inadequacy. These reactions are fixed and inflexible, and apply to the whole of a person's behaviour. They may well need psychological intervention and are resistant to change.

3 *Psychoses* such as schizophrenia (where reality and fantasy become

▶ Behaviour is more likely to be regarded as abnormal, and the person exhibiting it as 'mentally ill', if it is more extreme, permanent or handicapping, and if the individual doesn't realize the effect their behaviour is having on those around them.

▶ Although we characterize 'psychiatrists' as supporting the medical model, this doesn't imply that they refuse to recognize the importance of social, environmental influences such as the family. Far from it. Psychoanalytic insights, which emphasize the importance of family relationships, still have a role in psychiatric practice today, as we will see in Chapter 10.

▶ The *clinical model* for classification of mental or behavioural disorders is a part of the medical model, which sees such disorders as 'illnesses'.

► Schizophrenic symptoms include a distortion between reality and fantasy. Paranoia is a delusion of being persecuted, that people are against you and that they seek your destruction. Manic depression refers to a state where a patient's moods swing from being wildly, uncontrollably elated to being in deepest, miserable depression.

► 'Psychosis' used to refer to the whole mental condition of a particular person at a specific time, usually implying that their condition was abnormal in some way. Organic psychosis refers to a psychosis that has a physical cause, which is known. Functional psychosis refers to disordered thinking or maladapted behaviour whose physical cause is not known.

confused – see pages 172–6), severe depression (intense sadness and feelings of frustration and hopelessness – see pages 176–80), and paranoia (a mistaken belief about oneself, for example that one is deliberately being persecuted) result in an inability to recognize and deal with reality. Symptoms of psychotic disorders include hallucinations, delusions, rapid changes of mood, incoherent speech and severe regressive behaviour (the person acting as though he or she were a child). Psychotic disorders are also serious and may require treatment, often in a 'mental hospital'.

4 *'Brain syndrome'*, or 'organic psychoses', includes those conditions resulting from accidents, illnesses, addictions and diseases that have caused actual brain damage. They can be temporary (such as recovery from addiction to alcohol), or permanent (such as Alzheimer's disease, an example of senile dementia). They are the kinds of conditions where we would expect medical intervention.

There are several more detailed systems of classification in use in different countries today, since psychologists and psychiatrists still haven't reached agreement about the extent to which the presence of precisely which symptoms constitutes a particular condition. In 1994 the American Psychiatric Association published its latest version of the *Diagnostic and Statistical Manual* (*DSM IV*), which American psychiatrists use as the reference book for diagnosing dysfunctions. It avoids the term 'mental illness' or 'disease', preferring, where possible, the term 'disorder'. Clients (patients) are diagnosed on each of five dimensions. These follow with examples in brackets:

1 *Clinical syndromes*, which include the major disorders such as schizophrenia, anxiety disorders (free floating anxiety), mood disorders (manic behaviour), childhood disorders (autism), somatoform disorders (belief that something is wrong when it isn't), sexual disorders (paraphilias), substance use disorders (drug addiction), eating disorders (anorexia nervosa), sleep disorders (inability to sleep), and cognitive disorders (amnesia).

2 *Personality disorders*, which might overlap with those on the first dimension. Examples include paranoid (persecution complex), histrionic (immature and self-centred), narcissistic (self-obsessed), anti-social personalities (hyperaggression), obsessive compulsive disorders (hoarding), dependent and inadequate personalities.

3 *Physical disorders* include general medical conditions such as brain malfunction and body problems not ordinarily associated with mental illness, such as asthma, heart problems and physical handicaps. Physical conditions can contribute to psychological ones.

4 *Psychosocial and environmental problems* can cause stress and their intensity can be a major factor in 'mental health'. The client's exist-

ing and previous case histories are studied to assess the severity of any stress that the individual is experiencing. Some of the factors considered are present support systems (parents and others), any problems associated with education, occupation, housing, economic situation, health, legal and other psychosocial problems.

5 A *global assessment* is made of the person's overall state in terms of how violent or vulnerable they are in their particular circumstances. Someone who scores highly has 'superior functioning in a wide range of activities'. A low scorer will be in 'persistent danger of severely hurting self or others' and will need a more urgent response, including hospitalization.

■ **Summarize *DSM IV*'s approach to investigating abnormal behaviour.**

On the basis of the diagnosis on each of these dimensions psychiatrists claim to be able to classify an individual's problem, leading to an accurate diagnosis and treatment.

In Britain we have the tenth version of the World Health Organization's (1992) *International Classification of Diseases* (*ICD 10*). Like *DSM IV* it avoids the term 'mental illness', and has also abandoned the distinction between neuroses and psychoses (which was present in *ICD 9*). Neuroses were supposed to be minor, temporary and a response to stress, which could be dealt with through counselling. Psychoses were more severe where fantasy replaces reality. Gelder et al. (1989) give four reasons for losing this distinction. First, there are too many exceptions to the claim that neuroses are minor and psychoses have more extreme effects. Some neuroses need medical intervention with some people, and some psychotic disorders do not have serious consequences for the individual or society. Second, the conditions listed as either neurosis or psychosis have little in common; for example, psychoses were supposed to include paranoia, schizophrenia and acute depression. Such conditions may not have the same cause, nor are their effects similar. It may be preferable to talk in terms of 'schizophrenic symptoms' rather than schizophrenia. Third, any distinction is simply unnecessary since identifying an individual with a particular disorder such as 'exhibiting schizophrenic symptoms' tells us more than simply saying someone is psychotic. Fourth, any benefit such a distinction offers can be maintained, for example in naming disorders such as hysterical neurosis and categories of drugs such as antipsychotic treatments, without reinforcing an arbitrary distinction between neurosis and psychosis.

*ICD 10* lists ten major categories of disorder. These are:

1 *Organic mental disorders* caused by injury or disease, infection or genetic inheritance. Viral infections can destroy brain tissue, leading to problems with living, as we saw in Chapter 4. Brain tumour, cancer of the pancreas and an overactive thyroid gland can appear as symptoms of depression or anxiety. A skilled psychiatrist should know when to treat and when to refer patients with medical conditions and clients with mental and behavioural disorders.

2 *Schizophrenia and delusional disorders.* A discussion of schizophrenia follows on pages 172–6. Delusions are beliefs that something is true, even though there is no evidence for it. For example, someone who is not generally popular may start making up stories about themselves that make them appear more important, brave, skilful and so on. If this continues over the years they may start to believe the stories themselves. Freud thought that these delusions resulted from a lack of power, which he believed everyone feels they need. Every time you make a decision you exercise power. Someone who never gets to contribute to the decision-making process feels insecure and worthless. This can lead to delusions.

▶ A general principle might be that it has taken evolution over two million years to develop and fine tune the marvel of biological engineering called your brain. It doesn't make sense to use substances with the intention of making it malfunction. It's the only one you've got, and without it ...?

3 *Mental and behavioural disorders caused by psychoactive substance use.* There are many compounds that will affect the brain's normal functioning. Drugs such as Ecstasy seem to trigger the mechanisms that produce energy and a feeling of calm and well-being. Others, such as heroin, create bizarre hallucinations and delusions. Many drugs are prescribed for use under medical supervision and some of these might be psychoactive, for example when prescribed as anti-depressants or sleeping pills. Research into new drugs, both legal and illegal, continues as multi-million pound industries produce new compounds each year. Many will prove beneficial in the treatment of some disorders.

4 *Mood, or affective, disorders.* Symptoms of hyperactivity, rushing all the time, but not actually achieving anything, being highly elated etc. are associated with mania. The opposite symptoms are associated with depression. A combination – sometimes hyperactive, sometimes depressed – is manic depression. We will discuss depression later in this chapter (see pages 176–80).

5 *Neurotic, stress-related and somatoform disorders.* Neurotic disorders were described as less serious, although whether this definition referred to the severity of the symptoms of the disorder, or the outcome for the patient, wasn't clear. Someone who is convinced that they have cancer, their arm is incredibly painful, they are blind, or they have unimaginably painful headaches, when none of these symptoms is actually true, is suffering a somatoform disorder. They are the symptoms that Freud described as hysterical neurosis (see Chapter 1) upon which he developed psychoanalytic theory. The defining characteristic is that the individual concerned is convinced that they genuinely do have the condition. In the worst case it has led to suicide when it appears that no one except the individual seems to believe that they have a problem, and they know they can't get help. The 'painful arm', where there is no organic cause for that pain, may not appear very serious and is a symptom of neurosis. The suicide that results is rather more serious for the sufferer and their family.

6 *Behavioural and emotional disorders usually occurring in childhood or adolescence*, such as hyperactivity, conduct disorders and pervasive developmental disorders, which we discuss at the end of this chapter.

7 *Mental retardation resulting from failure to develop intellectual skills and leading to special learning difficulties*; 80 per cent of those who are defined as retarded have IQs between 50 and 70 and are described as mildly retarded. About 12 per cent are moderately retarded, with IQs between 35 and 49. About 7 per cent are severely retarded, with IQs between 20 and 34, and about 1 per cent are profoundly retarded (IQs below 20).

8 *Developmental disorders* form a broad category, including such characteristics as failure to develop physical skills (such as language), cognitive skills (including recognition and memory), affective skills (such as appropriate displays of affection), and social skills (such as co-operation).

9 *Disorders of adult personality and behaviour*, such as the anti-social, psychopathic or sociopathic personality. Such people are often charming and entertaining, and enormously manipulative. They also have no sense of right and wrong, are entirely insensitive to anyone else's feelings, and are incapable of feeling guilt or remorse. Someone with a paranoid personality is a loner, often with an inflated sense of their own importance, who can't trust people not to be attempting to trick them, to get the better of them, or to lie to them all the time.

10 *Behavioural and mental problems associated with handicap, physiological problems or hormonal imbalance*. This is another broad category covering people with physical handicaps such as spina bifida, hydrocephalus and muscular dystrophy, physiological difficulties such as cretinism, Down's Syndrome and the result of brain malfunctions through disease, accident or injury, and hormonal imbalances such as testicular insensitivity and andro-genital syndrome (see Chapter 16).

▶ The system of classification used in Britain is substantially different from *DSM IV*, but this does not mean that someone would necessarily be diagnosed as having a different condition using the two systems, merely that the route to arriving at a diagnosis is rather different.

Having classified the patient as having the symptoms of one or more of these categories, further diagnosis takes place. *DSM IV* has more sub-categories than *ICD 10* since it treats some disorders such as anxiety disorders, dissociative disorders, somatoform disorders and adjustment disorders as separate conditions, whereas *ICD 10* lists them under the same major category (number 5 above, 'Neurotic, stress-related and somatoform disorders'). Dissociative disorders include some forms of amnesia and multiple personality disorder, where the sufferer takes on more than one personality and switches between them depending on the circumstances. Psychosexual disorders and eating disorders are regarded differently by each system, too.

▶ Since the two major systems of classification used in the West do not agree on exactly what symptoms constitute what 'disorder', we may have cause to question just how useful they are.

■ Summarize *ICD 10*'s approach to defining abnormal behaviour and mention how it differs from *DSM IV*.

► A *dysfunction* is any disruption to the normal functioning of an individual.

## Evaluation of systems of classification

There are practical issues involved with diagnosis. Psychiatrists have the symptoms of mental and behavioural *dysfunctions* classified into syndromes. They have to interpret (they call it 'diagnose') what their experience tells them about what the patient is like to make it fit what would characterize a particular syndrome or condition. One early study (Aaron Beck 1962) had 153 patients diagnosed separately by two experienced psychiatrists on admission to hospital. They diagnosed only 83 patients (54 per cent) as having the same condition. When the reasons for such wide discrepancies were examined, 5 per cent were because the patients gave different responses when asked about their symptoms, 32.5 per cent were because the psychiatrists interpreted what they heard differently, and 63.5 per cent were because the early version of *DSM* being used was inadequate. Although the current classification systems are much improved, we can't be sure that psychiatric diagnoses are much more reliable now.

In a classic study **Rosenhan** (1973) investigated the validity of psychiatric diagnosis. In 'On being sane in insane places' Rosenhan describes how, over a three-year period, eight normal, healthy, 'sane' people turned up at various American mental hospitals, complaining that they could hear voices in their heads which kept saying 'empty', 'hollow', or 'thud'. These 'patients' included a housewife, a painter, a graduate, three psychologists and a psychiatrist (Rosenhan himself). They all used invented names, and lied about their jobs (and their 'symptoms'). Apart from this they answered every question they were asked as truthfully as they could. They performed whatever tests they were asked to, to the best of their ability. The psychiatrists who saw them therefore had only the patients' reported symptom on which to base their judgements. Despite having no other evidence than the 'voices', every one was admitted to the hospital, and all but one were diagnosed as being schizophrenic.

Immediately after their admission they stopped 'hearing the voices', and started asking to be released from the hospital. None of the hospital staff suspected that they were actually sane, 'normal' human beings, despite the fact that they were behaving 'normally' at all times. Several of the real patients did suspect the truth, that they were sane people conducting a study. (So the patients could make an accurate diagnosis, even if the staff couldn't!) On average the 'pseudopatients' saw a member of the psychiatric staff for seven minutes each day. One patient was released after seven days, another was kept in for 52 days. The average stay was 19 days. After release each 'patient' was diagnosed as having 'schizophrenia in remission' (i.e. the patient still has the condition but the symptoms have disappeared for the time being). It appears that once having been labelled by a diagnosis the psychiatrists were determined to see the diagnosis confirmed.

Another problem involved in diagnosis concerns just how

► Labelling is a process that involves someone (possibly in authority) defining someone else. For example a teacher might label a child as bright. The child, and people around it, come to expect the child to behave in intelligent ways. People often respond to other people's expectations, so the child does well at school, perhaps partly because of the expectations associated with the label.

'severe' does any behaviour have to be before it becomes diagnosed as a 'symptom'? This varies between psychiatrists. Would just hearing a 'voice' say one word have been enough to become diagnosed and admitted? How often do the words need to be heard? If I report feeling depressed, just how 'depressed' do I have to appear to the psychiatrist before I become diagnosed? There may well be a stigma attached to being diagnosed 'mentally ill', or being a resident in a mental hospital, so I might try to hide my symptoms or make them appear less severe when I visit the psychiatrist. There are obviously practical difficulties involved in accurate diagnosis.

*ICD 10* and *DSM IV* have been developed without regard to any particular theory or therapeutic system. They are 'atheoretical'. The problem with this is that they offer no clues as to the causes of the symptoms they classify, although they offer useful labels for the groups of symptoms they identify as a syndrome. For example, behaviourist psychologists claim that all behaviour is acquired in the same way, and is therefore essentially the same. It cannot be divided into 'normal', which is somehow different in kind from 'abnormal' behaviour. It can only vary by degree or intensity. Most psychiatrists (and psychologists now) would be highly sceptical on this point. All the same, without an idea of cause, effective treatment is less likely.

Richard Bentall (1991) identifies methodological problems, too. He claims that evidence from biological studies has been regarded as more scientifically acceptable than evidence from psychological research. He argues that 'in comparison to the achievements of psychological investigators the results of biological researchers have often proved disappointing or inconsistent'. He says that the traditional approach's insistence on pursuing 'cures' for 'diseases' has also diverted us from studying the important things, which are the behaviour that the traditional model calls 'symptoms'. It is the symptoms that are abnormal, and so it is these that should be 'treated'.

There are ethical implications here, too. Society recognizes that some people are ill, including 'mentally ill', and employs people called psychiatrists to define and help those who need it. As we have seen, the systems of classification may be inadequate to allow a recognition of the individual's particular difficulties and psychiatrists don't always agree on diagnoses, either. Being medically trained, psychiatrists may place too much trust in the validity of their classifications and label someone as having a particular condition where the label may not exactly fit. Once labelled a 'schizophrenic', or a 'depressive', someone may feel locked into a pattern of behaviour almost because it is what other people expect of them. The help the psychiatrist provides may be inappropriate. The drugs they prescribe may have known and unknown side effects, the surgery may have unseen and unintended consequences, too. The doctor could worsen rather than improve the patient's quality of life.

► The symptoms of some conditions, such as colds and flu, are so well known that treatments include remedies for each symptom. Each sachet of Lemsip 'contains paracetamol, EP 650 mg; phenylephrine hydrochloride BP 10 mg; Vitamin C (ascorbic acid EP) 50 mg'. No doubt these are decongestants, pain killers etc. Psychiatric treatments may not address all the symptoms that each individual sufferer has.

► Psychiatrists are accused of assuming that they know the principal symptoms of mental disorders and so treat the disorder as a whole rather than treating the symptoms themselves.

■ What are the practical and ethical implications in classifying some behaviour as abnormal?

■ Would there be any advantages to abandoning systems of classification?

► A classic illustration of the schizophrenic's conviction that something obviously untrue is actually true was the patient who was convinced that he was dead. As a last desperate measure his therapist asked: 'Can dead men bleed?' The patient replied that of course they could not. Taking his paper knife the therapist made a small cut on the patient's hand, which began to bleed. The astonished patient saw the blood, paused and said 'Wow, dead people *do* bleed'.

### Summary – Classification of mental and behavioural dysfunction

Collections of symptoms are taken to be evidence that someone is experiencing a particular syndrome, i.e. that their experiences can be described with a particular label. This diagnosis is problematic, with psychiatrists varying in the extent to which they will define some symptoms as evidence and not others. The problem exists because psychiatrists have very few reliable signs of the condition. Opponents of the medical model say these difficulties are sufficient to abandon this model except for those conditions where there are organic determinants such as the destruction of brain tissue.

## GENETIC, BIOLOGICAL AND ENVIRONMENTAL FACTORS IN EXPLAINING ABNORMAL BEHAVIOUR

Abnormal behaviour can result from a genetically inherited condition, such as Down's Syndrome, biology, such as memory problems caused by viral infection, environmental factors, such as a head injury resulting from a car crash or blow on the head, or withdrawal from a substance to which someone was addicted. They can be short term or permanent, and may be stable (staying the same) or progressive (getting worse). Four groups of disorders are reviewed here.

## Schizophrenia

Schizophrenia refers to a group of disorders characterized by a deterioration in emotional and cognitive responses, including auditory hallucinations (hearing 'voices'), a loss of knowledge about one's 'self', and loss of ability to deal with reality. The symptoms in *DSM IV*'s syndrome of schizophrenia include (1) problems that make work and relationships with people very difficult; at the same time self-care skills (washing, cleaning teeth, keeping clothes and hair in good order etc.) are reduced; (2) a failure in two or more of the cognitive, emotional or physical characteristics of 'normal' people, such as memory failure or perceptual problems; and (3) the individual has had these symptoms for at least six months. *ICD 10* only requires symptoms to have persisted for one month and the diagnosis can be made if the individual has one or more of what Shneider (1959) called 'first rank' symptoms. These are that the individual's thought processes are operating at a lowered level (resulting in slow thinking and responding), and that their thoughts are controlled by some external force. Second, they have auditory hallucinations (NB Rosenhan's pseudopatients feigned this symptom). Third, they insist that something is true, despite all evidence to the contrary.

## Some explanations for the causes of schizophrenia

Since the classification systems offer no clues as to what causes schizophrenic symptoms to appear, other factors have been considered. These include genetic transmission, social class background and environment. One problem in researching the cause of schizophrenia is that we are assuming it is a distinct condition, like a dislocated kneecap, that would be reliably diagnosed by any doctor in the world. This doesn't appear to be true, even between users of *DSM IV* and *ICD 10*. Since psychiatrists have few, if any, reliable signs that a particular patient actually has a particular condition, they have to rely on their own judgements, and people's judgements aren't always the same.

### Genetic transmission

One suggestion is that 'schizophrenia' runs in families. **Irving Gottesman** (1991) found that relatives of someone with schizophrenic symptoms are ten times more likely to be defined as suffering the condition than non-relatives. Can you see why this claimed family link is only a suggestion? Is it the case that schizophrenia does run in families, or that those who are related to schizophrenia sufferers are more likely to be diagnosed as schizophrenic themselves, while non-relatives with similar symptoms are less likely to be defined 'schizophrenic'? Gottesman also found that where one identical twin was diagnosed schizophrenic the other was as well in 44 per cent of cases. In non-identical twins, if one is diagnosed schizophrenic so is the other in 12 per cent of cases. The figure is 7 per cent for siblings of schizophrenics. Some 9 per cent of schizophrenic parents have schizophrenic children and 3 per cent have schizophrenic grandchildren. Is it possible that psychiatrists who 'know' that schizophrenia is genetically transmitted are more likely to use this knowledge as part of their clinical judgement?

Family studies suggest that people who have schizophrenic family members inherit the potential for developing schizophrenia, according to **Zubin** and **Spring** (1977). Whether they do develop schizophrenic symptoms depends on environmental circumstances such as levels of stress. Whilst this is an attractive idea, and may be applied to the origin of several human skills and capacities such as intelligence, aspects of personality and perception, it is quite impossible to find evidence in support. How could we know that we inherited the characteristics until they appeared? If they show we say it is because we inherited them. Yet there are people who develop the symptoms who do not have any history of schizophrenia in their families. How could their symptoms be explained?

One problem with 'nature–nurture' studies that attempt to show the importance of genetics (nature) amongst families is that families also tend to live together and therefore share the same environment (nurture). So children of 'schizophrenic' parents will see their parents behaving in schizophrenic ways. Skinner argues that the role of reinforcement is important here. Parents whose children behave appropriately will either be rewarded, or at least will avoid

▶ Having a detailed checklist of the symptoms of schizophrenia isn't a guarantee that someone who exhibits some of them will be 'a schizophrenic'. What if some of the symptoms are temporary, or mild, or only appear when with particular people, or in specific situations, or at particular times? How many symptoms, and how often do they appear, and how severe are they when they do, are all a matter of judgement.

▶ Genetic inheritance refers to the transmission of genetic material from parents to their offspring. The biological mechanisms are extremely complex and we are only just beginning to understand some of them. It will be some time before we can know what material is being carried on which genes.

▶ The nature–nurture debate is an early example of a controversy that is long past its sell-by date. Most researchers recognize that most human skills and capacities are forged as a result of their genetic, biological make-up interacting with their social experiences. Much abnormal behaviour is probably the result of such an interaction as well.

punishment. Such reinforcements continue to shape schizophrenic behaviour. Bandura claims that modelling is the essential process in childrearing. (See Chapter 1 for a fuller discussion of these ideas.)

*Psychoanalytic explanations*

According to psychoanalysts schizophrenia is linked to developmental and family experiences. Freud said it originates during the oral stage, when the irrational and pleasure-driven id dominates personality. Hence people with schizophrenic symptoms have little conception of reality and are self-absorbed. Children may identify with their same-sex parent in order to resolve anxieties and conflicts. By taking on and internalizing the parent's norms and values the child learns that its parents' feelings are appropriate, and the child acquires 'schizophrenic' emotional responses.

► According to psychoanalytic and learning theories generally, children acquire their schizophrenic behaviour through social experience rather than genetic inheritance.

*Cognitive explanations*

Cognitive theory explains schizophrenia in terms of individuals attempting to interpret their own sensory perceptions of themselves, and explain them to others. If their perceptions are wrong, then their interpretations will be distorted, and their explanations appear quite unreal (hence 'out of touch with reality'). Sensory overload is one suggestion by which the schizophrenia sufferer is thought of as having limited cognitive abilities in filtering important information about who and what they are from irrelevant details (Payne 1959). All sensory input is processed, regardless of relevance (see Chapter 12 for a discussion of cognitive filtering and selective attention), leading to confusion.

*Humanist explanations*

Humanist psychologists offer quite different explanations. **Thomas Szasz** wrote *The Myth of Mental Illness* (1972), in which he claimed that so-called mental illnesses are merely alternative ways of experiencing the world. In their book *Sanity, Madness and the Family*, **R.D. Laing** and **Aron Esterson** (1964) give case studies of the family circumstances of a number of people diagnosed as suffering from schizophrenia. These case studies were produced through interviewing the schizophrenia sufferer and members of their families, alone and together, building up a picture of the way each family member saw the others, and of how they often said different things in different company. The case studies give a picture of the schizophrenia sufferer as someone locked into a family which gives them contradictory messages, so that they cannot gain a coherent picture of themselves. Looked at as an attempt to come to terms with the contradictions of their experience, the behaviour of schizophrenics becomes understandable.

► Dissatisfaction with the medical model during the 1960s led to a number of psychiatrists, including Laing, Cooper and Esterson, forming what has become known as the *anti-psychiatry movement*.

One case study, for example, concerns Maya Abbott, who feels that she is not in charge of herself and is driven by forces beyond her control so that she cannot understand her own behaviour. She says that she feels that her parents try to influence her every movement. Her parents say this is nonsense, but they pray for her, and if they sit and think hard about her she will come into the room, and that they have to keep a close watch on her since she is unable to look after herself. She says her parents try to stop her reading. Her parents say this is nonsense, and anyway she reads too much. She says she masturbates and has sexual fantasies. Her parents say she does not. When she says she feels well enough to do things for herself her parents say her attempts to act independently are symptoms of her condition deteriorating.

Like everyone else Maya Abbott has two sources of evidence about what is real and what is not: her own experience and other people. Her parents constantly invalidate her own experience – is it any wonder, say Laing and Esterson, that she has a 'reality problem'?

Laing claimed that schizophrenia is not an illness but rather a label that society gives to people whose behaviour is different, possibly even threatening to the way that most of us live. On the basis of this label those different people can be removed and 'treated' to make them 'more normal', by which we mean 'more like us'. Laing has been accused of viewing the 'straight' world as mad, and the mentally ill as sane. He doesn't quite say this, but he does query the sanity of a world dedicated to weapons of mass destruction and environmental pollution that then needs to protect itself from some of the people it has created.

### Biological explanations

For further clarification we look for evidence that links brain structures and biochemicals to schizophrenic symptoms. There are two sources of evidence so far from brain studies that suggest that schizophrenic symptoms do have an organic basis. In 1982 Andreasen published his findings from brain scans of the four interconnected ventricles in the human brain. The ventricles are cavities that contain *cerebrospinal fluid*. We do not know what this substance is for, although it is thought to be involved in tissue regeneration. Patients exhibiting acute schizophrenic symptoms have enlarged ventricles compared to non-schizophrenics. Second, people exhibiting schizophrenic symptoms have excessive amounts of a *neurotransmitter* brain chemical called dopamine, according to Seidman (1990). Post-mortems on schizophrenics have found high levels of dopamine (Iversen 1979) in their brain's *limbic system*. The favoured treatment for schizophrenics is antipsychotic drugs. However, diagnosed schizophrenics do not respond to them consistently. None of these sources of evidence proves that schizophrenia is caused by chemical imbalances or altered structures, since both could be the result of the schizophrenia rather than its cause. Or they may all be linked in another way which we have not discovered yet.

**Richard Bentall** (1988) has summarized the available research data on schizophrenia and finds it contradictory and misleading. He says that 'the concept of schizophrenia should represent a cluster of symptoms that tend to occur together'. No such cluster can be found in the evidence. In other words, the people diagnosed

▶ *Neurotransmitters* are substances which are created by the nervous system to assist the movement of electrical 'messages' around the body.

▶ The *limbic system* is a complex set of brain structures that appeared early in human evolution and are probably involved in emotion and motivation, although scientists can only guess at how they operate.

as schizophrenic don't all share the same symptoms. But the definition of a disorder is that it is a group of symptoms that do appear consistently. Having defined a disorder it would be reasonable to predict the effectiveness of the treatments given. However, according to Bentall, 'the outcome of psychotic disorders is highly variable and seems better predicted by social factors than symptom variables'. He concludes: 'Given that schizophrenia is a disease with no particular symptoms, which follows no particular course, has no particular outcome, and responds to no particular treatment, it is unsurprising that … research reveals it to have no particular cause' (Bentall 1988).

■ What is schizophrenia and what causes have been suggested for it?

### Summary – Schizophrenia

Schizophrenia is a group of psychotic disorders in which a person fails to distinguish between reality and fantasy, especially concerning themselves. Social relationships become impossible and cognitive functions are disturbed. Various suggestions have been made for its cause, including contributions from psychoanalysis, behaviourism, cognitive theory and biology. Different patients have slightly different symptoms that may have had different causes, so different aspects of each suggestion may be correct, and therapies based on them may be more effective. According to Bentall, the disorder is so vague that it is pointless to use it and we would do better to focus on particular experiences of particular patients in order to understand the way they view the world.

## Depression

Depression is characterized by feelings of inadequacy, inactivity, loss of appetite and diminished sex drive, frustration, pessimism, lowered self-esteem and feelings of helplessness, worthlessness and sadness. We all have some of these feelings occasionally. In this sense they are normal and temporary. Where the symptoms are more intense and permanent they could result in a psychiatric diagnosis of depression. For example, a depressive patient may report feeling ugly and unloved because they are worthless, that there is no point to life and they may have suicidal tendencies (if only they could summon the energy!).

► Depression can take many forms, can be acute and render the sufferer incapable of doing anything. The British wartime prime minister Winston Churchill suffered frequent bouts of depression, which he called his 'black dog'.

### Forms of depression

The term *unipolar depression* is applied to cases where the symptoms described above are constant and unremitting. In about 20 per cent of cases, however, they alternate with episodes of intense activity. This is *bipolar depression*, sometimes called manic depression. Symptoms of mania include wild excitement over nothing important, constant talking, the sufferer often claiming much more importance for themselves than they deserve, hysterical laughter, ideas rushing into and out of the mind far too quickly to express, and making little sense anyway. Manics have enormous energy and rush about, rarely achieving anything, and seem to lack the inhibitions that most of us have.

More specific forms of depression have been diagnosed. These include agitated depression, where the patient can't remain still. They are listless, restless and irritable, as well as having other symptoms mentioned above. Mostly they rush about, achieving nothing but whatever satisfaction they find in being on the move. In psychotic depression their condition is so severe that they have lost touch with reality and all reasoning has gone. Reactive depression occurs where the patient views events in their lives as signifying something quite different from what they meant to anyone else. They react to any change as though it were deliberately intended to put them down, to demote them in some way, even to attack them for no reason. People whose motor development is some way behind others may become so accustomed to (habituate) their condition that they cease to strive to make progress. They may become inactive and lethargic. These are the symptoms of retarded depression.

## Some explanations for the causes of depression

Because depression varies so much it is more difficult to be certain about cause. For example, unipolar depression seems to involve low dopamine levels whereas the manic episodes in bipolar depression involve high levels (Iversen 1979). It is unlikely that an important neurotransmitter could be produced in such excessive amounts triggering mania, and on other occasions be at sufficiently low levels to trigger depressive symptoms. Further research in this area is needed. For now it makes more sense to regard unipolar and bipolar depression as different conditions with different causes. Bipolar depression is probably triggered by biological factors, whereas unipolar depression can have psychological causes (which could trigger biological states).

### Freudian explanations

In 1917, Freud made an interesting observation that there is a notable similarity between depression and mourning involving intense sorrow. Freud noticed that mourners often feel confused, on the one hand intensely sorrowful for their loss, while at the same time blaming the deceased for leaving them. One way in which Freud thought people attempt to resolve this confusion was to try to incorporate aspects of the departed person into their own personality. In this way they haven't really 'left' and are still somehow 'there'. Symptoms of depression may occur when a relationship breaks down, either amongst colleagues at work, friends or family, producing a similar sense of sorrow and loss, which we try to resolve in the same way, by incorporating aspects of the person we partly blame for leaving us into our own character. Turning this anger upon ourselves, Freud thought, could cause depression. As with most of Freud's ideas, this one contains elements of truth. Mourners do feel depressed and angry. To believe the whole explanation, though, would be more an act of faith than of evidence.

► There are many categories of groups of symptoms generally referred to as depression. Each may have a different mix of social and biological factors causing them.

► Since the mid-1960s there has been a decline in the popularity of many of both Freud's and behaviourists' claims.

*Behaviourist explanations*

Just as Freudian explanations require complex twists of imagination, so behaviourist accounts require the suspension of judgement in favour of simplicity. Behaviourists explain depression in terms of scarcity of rewards. The fewer pleasant, and the more miserable things that happen to you, the more depressed you are likely to become. In other words, doing something which is reinforced increases the likelihood that you will do something similar again. Not getting reinforced decreases the likelihood that you'll do anything in future. The less you do, the less likely you are to be reinforced. Eventually you have low energy levels and other symptoms typical of depressed people. This explanation also accounts for the fact that depression can be self-sustaining. If someone is behaving in a depressed way other people are less likely to respond positively to them. Gotlib and Robinson (1982) found that non-depressed people smiled less, were generally less pleasant and more negative when interacting with depressed people than when interacting with others like themselves. Finally, depressed people believe that other people are behaving negatively towards them, even when they are not, and, at the same time, give themselves fewer rewards, too (Nelson and Craighead 1977).

**Rene Spitz** (see Chapter 14) found severely deprived children in poor orphanages who seemed to have no interest in anything or the energy to do anything. Spitz described their condition as *anaclitic depression*. This came about through a severe lack of stimulation of any kind, not just lack of reward or reinforcement.

*Cognitive explanations*

► Cognitive psychology has offered many useful insights into the way people see themselves and how those perceptions influence their behaviour.

Cognitive explanations combine elements from behaviourism to explain depression. Since women are 60 per cent more likely to be admitted to a mental hospital than males, and twice as many females as males are defined as depressed, and this has remained consistent over time and place in Western countries, it is likely that either hormonal factors explain the difference or that the ways in which the two sexes regard themselves do. Cognitive explanations (and sociological ones) suggest that the traditional roles that women play are regarded by society, and by the women themselves, as inferior to men's roles. They have less control over their roles. For example, babies still need feeding, changing, stimulating and so on, and these responsibilities fall mainly to women. This also involves women in feeling financially dependent on men, who go to work and earn the money to support them all. Even when the woman does work her earnings (in Britain) are typically two-thirds those of men. Women are often expected and encouraged to be emotionally dependent on men, too. These perceptions are said to cause frustration and feelings of helplessness, both of which are symptoms of depression. As **Raymond Cochrane** (1995) concludes, 'It does seem that some clues to the particular vulnerability of women to depression lie in the … circumstances surrounding the experience of motherhood and child-care – what it gives to women and what it takes away'.

This explanation as to why women are more likely to feel depressed than men assumes that women are sufficiently aware of the inhibitions, frustrations and injustices that shape many of their lives. However, it is likely that the very women most at risk from this rather gloomy lifestyle are least likely to be able to manipulate the system to become defined as needing help or support. Women with young children simply can't afford to be ill. Who will provide the things the woman does if she isn't there?

Aaron Beck (1991) suggests that depressed people generally are most likely to misperceive their situations because they make five logical errors in the way they think. These are: (1) the tendency to draw conclusions with minimal evidence (*arbitrary inference*); (2) emphasizing insignificant aspects in a situation whilst ignoring important ones (*selective abstraction*); (3) drawing conclusions about their overall ability based on a single unsuccessful experience (*over-generalization*); (4) emphasizing the importance of single, small, unfavourable experiences leading to negative evaluation (*magnification and minimization*); (5) blaming themselves for situational events beyond their control (*personalization*). These categories overlap and several may be involved at once. Their purpose is to show how some people's cognitive reasoning is faulty, leading them significantly to undervalue themselves and hence to depression. However, not all depressed people exhibit these illogical thought processes, and, as we saw earlier with schizophrenia, these distortions in logical thinking may just as easily be caused by the depression, rather than be the cause of it, or other factors (biology, environment, stress) could cause both.

► There is no doubt that depressed people misperceive their situation according to the standards of non-depressed people. However, the depressed person is not in a position to make that (or any other) coherent judgement.

*Biological explanations*

The case for biology comes from three sources. First, particularly low levels of neurotransmitters are found in the brains of depressives. Excess *norepinephrine* is found in the manic phase of bipolar depression and levels decrease during the depressive phase (Bunney et al. 1970). Second, as we said earlier, precise outcomes of particular treatments have been speculative. Some drug treatments have been found to be effective in reducing some of the symptoms of depression by acting upon different neurotransmitters, notably norepinephrine and serotonin, and the most effective treatment for depression so far is a drug called *lithium*. How it works is unknown. It affects sodium levels and changes the composition of body fluids, and does reduce the manic aspect of bipolar depression. Third, relatives of people suffering from bipolar depression are more likely to have the condition, compared to relatives of people with other depressive illnesses.

► *Norepinephrine is a* neurotransmitter substance that is necessary for the flow of electrical impulses around various parts of the nervous system, especially the brain.

► *Lithium salts* are classified as anti-psychotic or anti-depressant drugs. They are also extremely dangerous unless taken in precisely prescribed doses.

## Summary – Depression

There are several categories of depression, but all include intense feelings of hopelessness and helplessness. In unipolar depression the symptoms are continuous; in bipolar depression the sufferer exhibits manic symptoms some of the time. There are

■ Outline some of the major types of depressive disorder and comment on the main explanations that have been advanced so far to explain the origin of the disorder.

biological and sociocultural factors involved in cause, although it is impossible to find a single, predominant causal factor present in all the forms of depression.

## Disorders of childhood and adolescence

Three categories of abnormal behaviour appear before adulthood. These are *attention deficit disorder* (hyperactivity), *conduct disorders* (behaviour problems), and *pervasive developmental disorder* (autism).

### Attention deficit disorder (hyperactivity)

According to the American Psychiatric Association (1987), between 3 per cent and 5 per cent of children exhibit enough of the symptoms to be diagnosed as suffering from attention deficit disorder each year. Typically, this condition affects males rather than females before the age of seven years. Symptoms include an inability to pay attention to anything for more than a few moments, vigorous, impulsive and disruptive behaviour, and constant attention seeking. The symptoms reduce after puberty, although the adolescent may still seek attention and remains impulsive. Although the cause is as yet unknown, it seems likely that there is some structure in the brain which is malfunctioning.

### Conduct disorders

There is some dispute as to whether this should be regarded as a clinical condition at all, since some claim that its cause is entirely social, and so should be its treatment. It is also a predominantly male phenomenon and occurs in middle and later childhood; in some cases, it can go on into adolescence and adulthood. The 'symptoms' are behaviour that is entirely socially unacceptable. It can be committed alone or in groups or gangs. It may be committed under circumstances that do not involve anyone else, such as cruelty towards animals or destruction of trees, shrubs or property when alone, or it could involve others, such as fighting and being cruel to other children. Stealing or destroying someone's property, truancy from school, and lying about one's behaviour are generally common. If this is a clinical condition its organic origin is unknown.

### Pervasive developmental disorder (autism)

The word autism literally means 'self-absorbed', deriving from *auto* meaning 'self' and *ism* meaning 'state'. Autism is an extremely rare condition affecting less than one child in 200, with boys being four times more likely than girls to have the condition. Three categories of symptoms may be identified. First, autistic children don't seem to recognize or show willingness to interact with their caregivers and have no interest in their surroundings. Second, they have very poor communication skills, both verbal and non-verbal. Third, they prefer inactivity or rocking backwards and forwards, sometimes quite violently. At other times they stare blankly into space. They are generally withdrawn, and often fixate on an inanimate object such as a corner of a blanket. As infants they do not co-operate in attachment behaviour (see Chapter 14), and rarely if ever cry or smile.

### Some explanations for the causes of childhood and adolescent disorders

Several suggestions for the cause of disorders of childhood and adolescence have been offered. Psychoanalytic theory suggests that childhood disorders are caused by failures in family relationships. Effective progress through the stages of personality development requires emotionally warm and supportive parents. Those parents who are cold and distant, who substitute discipline for love, are likely to have children who have problems in adjusting to the norms and values of society. However, this explanation isn't widely supported by studies of actual parents of children with these disorders, who appear as loving and caring as any other cross-section of parents.

Behaviourist psychologists suggest that undesired behaviour has been accidentally reinforced, leading to the child behaving in increasingly strange ways in order to receive further reinforcement, until finally their behaviour includes the symptoms of a clinical condition such as conduct disorder. Since all learned behaviour can be unlearned (we shall see how in the next chapter), then subjecting the child to some form of behaviour therapy should modify its behaviour. Whilst this has been successful for some behavioural conduct disorders it has been remarkably unsuccessful in treating autistic or attention deficit disorder children.

According to cognitive theorists children have some malfunction in their perceptual system such that they perceive their behaviour as being consistent with their thoughts and feelings. If their perception of their environment, family, friends and so on results in them feeling insecure and anxious, then refusing to co-operate with it, or withdrawal from it, makes sense. There may be some merit in this explanation, but the symptoms of autism occur before the infant could have formed much of an impression about the world at all.

On balance, biological explanations for what appear to be pathological conditions are preferred. Research has found, for example, that the brain stem in some autistic children has injuries, possibly caused by disease or genetic inheritance. Others have enlarged ventricles, which suggests that the parts of the brain surrounding them have degenerated. There are signs of chemical imbalance and the right-hand cerebral hemisphere appears to have more neural activity than the left hemisphere, but we have little idea about how these signs actually explain the disorders described.

■ **Consider some of the influences that biology and the environment may be having on disorders of childhood and adolescence.**

### Summary – Disorders of childhood and adolescence

Three main groupings of symptoms into syndromes have been identified. These are attention deficit disorder, where a child is unable to attend to one stimulus for more than a few moments;

conduct disorders, where the majority of a child's behaviour is unacceptable; and pervasive developmental disorder, for example autism, where there is an emotional and cognitive detachment from almost all environmental influences. The cause of each of these is probably a mix of malfunctioning brain structures or processes combined with some distorted cognitive and behavioural responses.

## Eating disorders

There are several eating disorders which have been classified as neurotic conditions. Examples are anorexia nervosa, bulimia, obesity and pica. In anorexia and bulimia the individual is concerned with staying thin, and these have received most attention from researchers. Obesity is the result of overeating, and becomes a psychological problem when the obese person's life is affected by the condition. Pica is a condition in which the individual has an enormous craving for unnatural foods such as the soil on potatoes, chalk or clay, and various kinds of rubbish.

### Anorexia nervosa

Anorexia nervosa, sometimes called 'the slimmers' disease', typically affects young women between the ages of 15 and 30. Only 5 per cent of known anorexics are male. Mostly known anorexics come from rather well-off home backgrounds and are often described by their parents as 'model children'. The diagnosis occurs when someone has lost 25 per cent of their normal body weight. In Britain about 20 per cent of anorexics die from their illness, whilst the figure in America is nearer 30 per cent. However, in the majority of cases the symptoms of the disorder disappear, without treatment (spontaneous recovery). This is just as well because the disorder is extremely resistant to treatment. The incidence of the disorder is increasing in other countries such as Japan, where it was not previously noticeable.

The symptoms of anorexia nervosa include reporting a loss of appetite, followed by a loss of weight. Anorexics are good at disguising their condition, so the weight loss may be masked by wearing hairstyles, make-up and clothes that would hide it. Some show great interest in food, in shopping and cooking, in fact in everything except eating it. If the anorexic can't avoid eating some make themselves sick in order to get rid of the food. Sleep patterns become disturbed and anorexics often wake early. Menstruation stops in the later stages.

### Bulimia

Bulimia is another eating disorder found predominantly in female adolescents and young adults. Some anorexics also have the symptoms of bulimia, in fact bulimia is more widespread than anorexia nervosa. The symptoms typically include repeated binges, often

► Someone who is grossly overweight through overeating, e.g. 120 kg, who then attends a slimmers' club and sheds 30 per cent of their body weight, is not going to be diagnosed as anorexic. It's their 'normal' body weight that matters, i.e. what they 'should' weigh. However, this definition is as much culturally as medically defined (largely by insurance companies in America and Europe).

eating high-calorie food, followed by vomiting, or purging by swallowing laxatives. Bulimia sufferers do not chew the food more than is necessary to swallow it. Bouts of eating and vomiting often occur when the sufferer is feeling depressed and is often followed by feeling guilty. The guilt can contribute to a further bout of depression, and possibly further binging and vomiting. Like anorexia, bulimia is extremely difficult to treat, partly because of the determination of the sufferer to maintain their behaviour.

### Obesity

Obesity is diagnosed when someone weighs over 30 per cent above their 'normal' weight. One-third of Americans are obese and obesity in the US is becoming a major national concern. Abnormal eating patterns can be acquired through childhood and many obese children have obese parents. Overeating appears to be a response to depression, loneliness and a lowered self-image, whilst normal eaters tend to eat more when in company. Eating more is also associated with the variety of food available: the more there is, the more we will have. Obese people may be more responsive to external cues, e.g. the sight and smell of food may trigger their desire to eat, even though they aren't hungry.

The obvious response to overeating is to diet. Diets often fail because overeating has become a habit which, like all habits, is hard to break. Polivy and Herman (1985) found that dieters also ate more when they drank alcohol, were anxious, depressed, felt stressed, and when high-calorie food was available. Non-dieters are much less likely to eat more under these circumstances. Scientists may have found a brain chemical that resists the person's attempts to eat less too, but research is continuing.

### Some explanations for the causes of eating disorders

Several suggestions have been offered for the causes of eating disorders. An obvious explanation for dieting disorders is the fear of becoming obese, but most people who wouldn't want to be obese don't become anorexic or bulimic instead.

Psychoanalytic theory suggests two possible reasons. One is that young women have not successfully resolved all the conflicts and anxieties of the Electra complex. They do not regard womanhood as a state that they are anxious to reach. Eating as little as possible, or even not eating at all, is seen as one way of staying a child. A second suggestion is that fatness is associated with pregnancy. By remaining thin the girl cannot be pregnant, therefore cannot become a woman. These issues are explored in psychotherapy, where that is seen as the best way to deal with an anorexic.

Behavioural explanations concern the reinforcing consequences of the eating or non-eating behaviour. For anorexics and bulimics it is the thinness which is presumably regarded as the desirable norm. For obese people the food produces an instant reinforcement that will sustain future eating behaviour. If this explanation were correct, then inappropriate eating behaviour could be unlearned,

▶ If someone really does not wish to give up smoking, biting their fingernails, excessive drinking or not eating, very few things are going to make them. Most 'treatments' are more likely to be effective with the willing co-operation of the sufferer.

and appropriate behaviour substituted using the principles of behaviour shaping (discussed in the next chapter). Unfortunately, they don't seem to work! Habitual behaviour will not be lost so easily.

Cognitive psychologists such as Agras et al. (1974) suggest that people with eating disorders such as anorexics and bulimics misperceive the signs of hunger and don't realize that they need to eat. Not eating then becomes a habit which is hard to break. They also misperceive their own body image, seeing themselves as fat, or become convinced that if they eat they will become fat.

Environmental effects include Western society's obsession with being slim. Western media reflect slimness as the ideal and overweight people are either to be made fun of or pitied. One explanation for the increasing incidence of eating disorders in Japan is the Japanese people's exposure to Western influences. Another explanation identifies the dysfunctional family, where tensions may not be visible to the outsider. Abnormal eating may become the means by which a powerless child expresses anger and frustration and takes revenge on its family (usually its mother). Liebman et al. (1974) suggest *family therapy* may be effective in treating some eating disorders, particularly if it emphasizes the importance of positive communication between family members.

▶ *Family therapy* is a system whereby counsellors help family members to share their perceptions and feelings about other family members in socially acceptable ways in order to settle grievances and promote family harmony.

Biological explanations of eating disorders have been derived from animal experiments as well as studies of human sufferers. Gelfand et al. (1982) suggest that a complex brain structure called the hypothalamus contains self-regulatory systems which maintain the balance between food intake and energy needs. Damage in the area that houses one of the systems leads to overeating and obesity, whilst damage in the other leads to starvation. An extension of this might explain anorexia and bulimia. The effect of the damage is that the individual is unable to recognize the need to eat more. However, this explanation ignores social factors such as cultural norms of ideal body shapes and the effects of the media on people's perceptions.

> ### Summary – Eating disorders
> Biological studies suggest that animals have an ideal body weight, determined by their fat cells and a number of brain chemicals. Maintaining that weight can be upset by eating disorders which either lead to weight loss or weight gain. In the extreme forms, anorexia nervosa and bulimia involve a determination to lose weight that becomes an obsession. It overrides brain chemicals which inform us about our state of hunger. Obesity is a compulsive disorder which is often found in association with unhappiness, boredom and depression.

## Paraphilias

*Paraphilia* is a general term for any manner of sexual expression in which arousal depends upon forms of stimulation that are socially unacceptable; for example, someone who needed to be driving a fast motorbike before they could achieve arousal might have some difficulties (and not just in finding a partner!). The true paraphiliac is someone who needs that type and level of stimulation, not someone who has a passing fancy to do something crazy, daring or adventurous. The true paraphiliac is fairly obsessed with the source of their arousal. There are as many examples of paraphilia as there are objects, processes or events that people (probably mostly men) can become obsessed with.

---

### Examples of paraphilias

**dyshomophilia** – arousal results from the overwhelming fear that the individual possesses homosexual feelings, regardless of whether they are homosexual or heterosexual.

**exhibitionism** – arousal results from the exhibitionist's compulsion to expose parts of their body, usually the genitals, in public.

**fetishism** – arousal results from association with a particular object, such as an item of clothing, or a part of the body not normally associated with sexual arousal (e.g. the hair or feet).

**frottage** – arousal results from rubbing the body (especially the genitals) against other people in public places such as the crowded London Underground. This is a form of exhibitionism.

**masochism** – arousal results from causing what others regard as pain to oneself, especially the genitals, for erotic pleasure.

**necrophilia** – necrophiliacs find dead human bodies fascinating and erotically arousing.

**sadism** – sadists are aroused by causing pain to others, either directly or by watching someone else do it.

**troilism** – troilists are obsessed with having sexual relations in the presence of others without their knowledge.

**voyeurism** – voyeurism means watching and voyeurists gain arousal from spying on other people.

**zoophilia** – zoophiliacs are sexually aroused by contact with animals.

---

Although these paraphilias are listed under the same heading they do not necessarily have the same cause, nor are they necessarily similar in any way other than their association with sexual arousal. Although regarded as abnormal in this society at this time some may not only be regarded as normal, but possibly even required in some others. What we defined as masochism was seen as necessary by some religious orders to punish the believer for their evil thoughts or other sins. Anorexia nervosa was seen as a spiritual experience by others. Some fashions such as clothes made from see-through materials and skimpy swimwear may come close to exhibitionism. Perhaps those who stare at the wearers come close to being 'social voyeurs' too. Others, such as necrophilia, aren't so easy to explain socially and may well have cognitive or even biological components.

► If a group of like-minded sado-masochists practised their art on each other, should it still be socially unacceptable? It may still be illegal, so should 'acceptability to those who make the law' be the definition of 'socially acceptable'?

### Some explanations of the causes of paraphilias

Depending on the exact symptoms, psychoanalysts would look to inadequately resolved Oedipal conflicts (since most paraphiliacs are probably male). Obsessions with females may originate in the child–mother relationship, whilst fear of homosexual feelings may have something to do with the boy's father being overprotective or physically loving. Freud saw the phallus as symbolic of power. The objects of the paraphiliac's obsession become substitutes for power which the paraphiliac is unable to gain in his everyday life. Behaviourists would claim the object of the paraphiliac's obsession has been associated with some other reinforcing stimulus in the past, and has now taken on reinforcing properties of its own. One problem in discussing paraphilias is that few dependable studies have been conducted (Jeffrey Dahmer possibly excepted). Because of the unacceptable nature of paraphilia far more people may have some of the symptoms than would be prepared to admit it. It is quite possible that some are simply 'for kicks', so a behaviourist explanation would be adequate. Others are probably better explained cognitively, as a distorted desire for power, either to exercise it over others, or to submit to it. The mass murderer, Jeffrey Dahmer, claimed that he never wanted to kill any of his 17 male victims. He just wanted them to stay with him so that he could use them for his own pleasure, and the only way he could control them was by killing them. Whether scientists will ever find brain chemicals to be involved in paraphilias remains to be seen.

### Summary – Paraphilias

Paraphilias are sexual dysfunctions or obsessions where arousal can only be satisfactorily reached by association with a socially unacceptable stimulus. Most are culturally defined and vary with time. No doubt precise causes will depend on the particular condition; some are probably cognitive distortions involved in the desire for power.

### Summary – Explanations for some psychological disorders

| Disorder | Explanation | | | |
| --- | --- | --- | --- | --- |
| | *Psychoanalytic* | *Behaviourist* | *Cognitive* | *Physiological* |
| Schizophrenia | dominant id during oral stage | symptoms learned through modelling and inappropriate reinforcement | misinterpretation of own sensory perception and failure in explaining it to others | genetic inheritance demonstrated through family connections. Also brain abnormalities and abnormal dopamine levels |

| Depression | internalizing aspects of someone you blame | inactivity or low levels of functioning become reinforced | perception or misperception of own situation | imbalance in neurotransmitter chemicals, successful drug treatments, family connection |
|---|---|---|---|---|
| Disorders of childhood | disturbed family relations causing anxiety states | undesired behaviour accidentally reinforced, leading to further bizarre behaviour | perceptual malfunction produces distorted self-concept | brain malfunctions, as yet barely known |
| Eating disorders | avoidance of adulthood | eating behaviour becomes habitual | misperception of hunger signs and distorted body image | damage to hypothalamus |
| Paraphilias | inappropriate identification, a means of exercising power which is denied otherwise | consequence of paraphiliac behaviour is beneficial and reinforcing | misinterpretation of appropriate sexual signals and symbols | unknown |

## Summary – Approaches to abnormal behaviour

Psychodynamic theories offer theoretical explanations for the interaction of instinctive urges and early experiences on the individual which will influence their adult behaviour. Abnormal adult behaviour reflects disturbances earlier. Behaviourists reject such intuitive and interpretive explanations. They claim that scientific studies have revealed the universal principles that govern the acquisition of all behaviour, including abnormal behaviour. Humanist psychologists are equally scornful that science can reveal anything about complex human behaviour, which is the result of each individual's unique experiences and perceptions. Supporters of the somatic approach prefer to regard instances of abnormal behaviour as symptoms of a medical condition.

## Exam questions – 60 minutes each

1  Discuss the ethical and practical difficulties in the psychodynamic approach to defining abnormal behaviour. (*25 marks*)
2  Discuss the ethical and practical difficulties in the behaviourist approach to defining abnormal behaviour. (*25 marks*)

**Therapeutic approaches**

## Introduction

In Chapter 8 we looked at the historical development of abnormal behaviour and how society has responded to it. In this chapter we turn to the specific therapeutic systems that have developed as a result of the way in which supporters of the various models have viewed abnormal behaviour. Inevitably this has meant attempting to change the patient's or client's behaviour, and possibly their understanding of themselves. This is always problematical and may have ethical implications. We must not allow ethical issues about who has the right to do what to whom to be ignored in psychiatric or psychological therapy any more than we should in any other areas of social life.

► *Ethics* is that branch of philosophy concerned with 'good' and 'bad', 'right' and 'wrong' amongst groups of people in different places and at different times.

## DESCRIPTION AND EVALUATION OF SOMATIC (MEDICAL) APPROACHES

The somatic approach generally regards the more extreme symptoms of abnormal behaviour as being caused by some biochemical imbalance, or some malfunction in the brain. As such there is little discussion between doctor and patient, since the doctor diagnoses and prescribes, and the patient receives the treatment. It offers three broad approaches to treatment: *psychosurgery* (brain surgery), *electroconvulsive therapy* (ECT), and *drug treatment* (chemotherapy), although they may well be used in conjunction with more psychological therapies.

# Psychosurgery

Psychosurgery involves making lesions (cutting into brain tissue) or removing (ablating) various parts of the brain. If we know, for example, that a certain part of the limbic system is responsible for levels of aggression, and if we have a patient with a pathologically aggressive personality, we could surgically remove all or some of that part of the system, and hopefully the aggression should be removed. Unfortunately, things are rarely so simple and patients who have had such operations have suffered all kinds of side effects. Some have been made so docile that they are incapable of normal emotional responses. Other organs were sometimes damaged during surgery as well, and many patients died. Whatever the effects of the psychosurgery, they will probably be permanent (unless offset by chemotherapy) since the brain may not be able to regenerate lost tissue.

We said in Chapter 8 that many early investigations were experimental. This was true of the first attempts at brain surgery. The first psychosurgical operations were performed on people whose behaviour was severely dysfunctional. They involved making lesions in the white tissue (corpus callosum) which connects the brain's frontal lobes (where the major thought centres are found) with the major organs, the thalamus (the relay centre for co ordinating sensory input) and the hypothalamus (which controls vital functions such as heart rate, feeding, sexual arousal, temperature and emotional state). Tens of thousands of such prefrontal lobotomies were performed. For most of the patients – mainly schizophrenics and acute depressives – their abnormal behaviour did cease, but so did much of their personalities. Many of them were made into little more than human cabbages. The general consensus is that the technique does not produce acceptable results, and it would be extremely unlikely to be used today.

Recent advances in the techniques used in other psychosurgery, such as using low-intensity lasers as surgical instruments, allow surgeons to destroy precise and tiny pieces of brain tissue, such as tumours, without having to make a hole in the skull and risking destroying unintended brain tissue. They have also increased the ability to treat specific symptoms such as severe (grand mal) epilepsy, and reduced the likelihood of undesired side effects, making it much more acceptable and effective.

# Electroconvulsive therapy (ECT)

Electroconvulsive or 'shock' therapy is highly controversial. It is used mainly with patients suffering severe depression or schizophrenics with severe mood disorders. They are given a drug to relax their muscles and are anaesthetized, and an electric shock of between 80 and 150 volts (depending on the judgement of the psychiatrist in charge) is passed between their temples for about one-tenth of a second. The patient has a minor convulsion,

▶ *Psychosurgery* is a physical intervention inside the skull. Such surgery is always dangerous and many patients have not survived it, or have suffered terrible side effects.

▶ The prefrontal lobotomy was regarded as a major breakthrough in psychological treatment and in 1937 its inventor, Egas Moniz of Portugal, was awarded the Nobel Prize. One patient whom Moniz had operated on couldn't have agreed – he shot Moniz!

▶ During an epileptic seizure the victim may have convulsions and may lose consciousness and control over motor functions. Excessive amounts of neural activity are often involved in the cause.

▶ ECT was first used because it was noticed that schizophrenics didn't have epilepsy. There might be something about epilepsy that inhibits schizophrenia, so some schizophrenics were given electric shock treatment to produce an epileptic-type seizure.

although in the past some patients have injured themselves during their semi-epileptic convulsions. Some have died, whilst others who have had repeated treatments over longer periods have suffered permanent brain damage. Patients usually lose their memories for the period of the treatment, although sometimes the amnesia can be more profound and the patients become quite disoriented. The treatment is usually repeated three or four times a week for about a month.

Studies suggest that ECT is generally effective (Abrams 1988), although it doesn't work for all patients. The problem in judging effectiveness is, would the severity of the symptoms have reduced anyway without the electric shock? ECT involves the patient in being the centre of attention in a serious medical procedure. Additionally, having had the shock and its associated seizure, memory loss and disorientation once, the patient will try hard not to behave in ways that will earn another dose! Experiments to test this would involve putting the patient through the ECT procedure except for administering the actual shock. However, treating depressed people as human guinea pigs in an attempt to discover why a controversial, painful and potentially dangerous procedure that we are giving them works, is ethically unacceptable to many. Several studies have attempted to measure the effectiveness of ECT, compared to psychotherapy and chemotherapy (Fink 1978). Between 60 per cent and 90 per cent of severely and manically depressed patients show less depressed behaviour in the weeks following a series of ECT, and the suicide rate amongst ECT patients declined compared to those receiving psychotherapy.

No one knows why it works, and this has led some organizations that support and represent people with symptoms of depression to call for its abolition. It is used mostly when everything else has failed. Advances in drug therapies have allowed many depressives to be treated without ECT.

## Chemotherapy (drug treatment)

▶ Many drugs are self-administered, many are prescribed by doctors. Concern is being expressed that people generally are becoming too dependent on drugs, including drugs prescribed by doctors.

Until the mid-1950s psychiatrists used combinations of psycho-analysis, containment, psychosurgery and electroconvulsive therapy to 'treat' their patients. Since then increasing numbers of drugs have been refined that can control aspects of people's behaviour, and even their personality. Many perfectly 'normal' people buy drugs to relieve their headaches, help reduce the symptoms of their colds, reduce their travel sickness, give them energy and contain their allergies. Most homes in the West probably have medicine cupboards or drawers where drugs can be found. Psychiatrically prescribed drugs have largely replaced the use of strait-jackets and locked cells, and have allowed many people to live fairly normal lives who otherwise might have needed hospitalization.

There are three categories of psychiatrically prescribed drugs: anti-depressants, anti-psychotic drugs and tranquillizers.

### Anti-depressants

Anti-depressants, sometimes called psychic energizers, are of several kinds. Tricyclic anti-depressants stimulate the production of serotonin and epinephrine, two neurotransmitters, in particular brain centres involved in mood. Monoamine oxidase (MAO) inhibits destruction of neurotransmitters, but this can have serious side effects and is not widely used now. A third, more modern variety of anti-depressant works by inhibiting the absorption of serotonin and norepinephrine after they have been used, thus increasing their concentration in the synapses. Prozac is the best known example. They all take about three weeks for their beneficial effects to show, and they all have side effects, including feelings of nausea, and increased nervousness and agitation.

In 1949 lithium carbonate, or lithium salts, was found to have a major beneficial effect in treating the manic symptoms in manic depressives (bipolar depression). No one knows why it works, but the effects are almost immediate in three-quarters of patients. It is an extremely dangerous drug if not taken in precisely the quantity and frequency prescribed.

### Anti-psychotic drugs

Anti-psychotic drugs such as chlorpromazine (Largactil) revolutionized the way severely dysfunctional people were treated. They inhibit the production of dopamine, which is associated with schizophrenic symptoms. They also have unfortunate side effects such as a dry mouth, stiffened joints, jerky movements and uncontrolled shaking. The severity of these effects varies enormously between patients, but some are badly affected and it becomes debatable whether the patient was better off with the symptoms of schizophrenia than with the side effects of the medication. Some patients do not improve anyway, so have all the side effects without any alleviation of their schizophrenia. Other drugs, such as clozapine, are available, but they are only effective in treating about 10 per cent of patients who didn't respond to chlorpromazine (Kane 1988). Clozapine also has serious side effects, such as immune syndrome breakdowns.

### Tranquillizers

Tranquillizers are anti-anxiety drugs such as Valium and Librium, which reduce anxiety and cause drowsiness by inhibiting neural activity in parts of the brain and by relaxing muscles. They can be useful in treating phobias, problems with sleeping and other somatoform disorders (somatoform refers to problems with the body). Valium is thought to be the most widely prescribed drug in many countries. The problem with such drugs is that people can sometimes become physically addicted to them or come to depend on them emotionally, and they may need to be weaned from them.

### Evaluation of the somatic approach

You will remember from Chapter 9 that there are fierce debates about the nature of abnormal behaviour, and whether it can usefully be regarded as 'mental illness' or a 'disorder', or whether we should simply try to alleviate the symptoms rather than treat a possibly non-existent syndrome. Some symptoms will be the manifestations of brain malfunctions caused by infection, injury and so on. Others are caused by problems with living. Some will continue as a combination of both. For those that have an organic cause chemotherapy may be appropriate, bearing in mind the ethical implications in possibly worsening someone's condition by prescribing drugs whose function we don't really understand, and whose side effects may be worse than the symptoms of the disease. ECT and surgery are also questionable in some cases. The somatic approach doesn't often address the cause of the 'illness'. On balance, medical treatments are beneficial to many, inappropriate to some, and have been a disaster for others.

## DESCRIPTION AND EVALUATION OF PSYCHOANALYTIC THERAPY

Psychoanalysis is a therapeutic system based on psychoanalytic theory developed by Sigmund Freud between the 1890s and 1930s. It became enormously influential and was the dominant psychiatric approach (mainly because there weren't really any others). Psychoanalytic theories see the origins of abnormal behaviour as having been built into the individual's personality during their early development. Psychoanalytic therapy therefore tends to look backwards for the origin of a problem, rather than looking at the individual's present symptoms. Psychoanalytic theories are sometimes called *insight theories* because they aim to give patients insight into the cause of their problems. Freud was mainly concerned with the emotional rather than the intellectual components of the cause of abnormal behaviour, so the patient's final understanding mustn't simply be theoretical. Patients have to 'feel' the cause of their problem. (Simply understanding it in theory is a *defence mechanism*.) Psychoanalysis proposes that if we feel what is causing our problem we may be able to do something about it, and the problem should disappear.

### Freudian psychoanalysis

Freud saw personality developing through the interaction between its three components: the id, which is the irrational, instinctive urge; the ego, which is the urge to be rational; and the superego, which is the learned, moral component of personality. This interaction would occasionally include conflict, which can produce anxiety. The rational ego reduces anxiety through a number of defence mechanisms, such as displacement, sublimation, projec-

▶ Insight is rather like intuition, an inner knowledge or understanding. The aim of *insight theories* is to give people a better understanding of the causes of their own problems. Once they have insight they are likely to improve. Psychoanalytic and humanistic therapists rely on insight.

▶ *Defence mechanisms* are unconscious and entirely normal devices by which we protect and maintain our image of ourselves, and avoid the embarrassment of discovering that we are less valuable and infallible than we think.

■ Why should it be necessary for a person to feel rather than just understand the cause of his or her disorder?

tion, rationalization, and so on. This uses a great deal of psychic energy.

The psychoanalyst has to uncover the original sources of the conflict, many of which will have a sexual element. Freud used a variety of methods to investigate the unconscious mind, including the interpretation of dreams, through which we live out our deepest wishes and fantasies. Free association is where patients relax and are prompted to recall any incidents they can from their childhood (called 'the talking cure'). Freud thought slips of the tongue ('Freudian slips') reveal what we really think as our unconscious thoughts are made conscious. Analysing the individual's sense of humour reveals insights into an individual's true nature. Freud tried using hypnosis through which patients might relive their most painful experiences, but found it contradictory and unhelpful.

The patient will often try to resist the therapist at first, by missing appointments, remaining silent during free talk, not recalling any slips of the tongue or what has made them laugh, or claiming to have no dreams to report. This resistance is considered to be a defence mechanism, since the patient unconsciously avoids the anxiety that exposing their neuroses would create. The analyst explains the cause of the patient's behaviour until the patient finally gives in to the analyst and therapy can continue.

Freud used a variety of methods in his clinical therapy, but favoured free association, dream analysis and the analysis of common mistakes such as slips of the tongue. Therapy today often involves one-hour sessions, up to five times each week, sometimes for years. The analyst and patient slowly build up a picture of the dynamic workings and development of the patient's childhood and past and present experiences until they feel that they understand the causes of the patient's present conflicts.

The techniques of psychoanalysis are intended to lead to *transference*. Patients begin to recall early events in their childhood, and how they felt about them and the people involved. They express their attitudes and feelings towards these early experiences, which is sometimes like 'reliving' them. (The process of reliving early experiences is called *abreaction*.) The analyst remains neutral and aloof at all times. Slowly patients are encouraged to express their feelings to the analyst. If they felt anger, say, towards their father, they must say how they felt, almost as though the analyst was their father. Attitudes and feelings that could be the source of conflict and anxiety are thus transferred to the analyst. Present-day problems may be caused by repressed childhood emotions, and the analyst may also 'play the part' of the people – boss, spouse, lover, child – with whom the problem exists.

The analyst will explain the inappropriate nature of the transference until the patient eventually experiences *catharsis*. This is a great release of emotions as the patient realizes the nature of his or her relationships, both with the therapist and with the people who had caused such emotional 'blockages'. The analyst and patient

▶ The id, ego and superego are hypothetical components of the personality in psychoanalytic theory. Freud did not intend them to be thought of as real entities, any more than hypothetical concepts like time, justice or logic are real.

▶ *Transference* is the process by which the patient projects and displaces (both defence mechanisms) his or her feelings onto the analyst.

▶ *Catharsis* refers to the release of anxiety and tension that occurs when past events are brought into consciousness. Catharsis is necessary if a patient and analyst are to work through the events that caused the repression.

■ **Show how Freudian psychoanalysis as a treatment follows logically from Freud's view of the development of the personality.**

■ **What is the role of transference in Freudian therapy?**

▶ Adler became quite a favourite of Freud's while attending his weekly session on psychoanalysis in Vienna. In 1910 Freud had him made president of the Psychoanalytic Society, but Adler criticized some of Freud's ideas and he was forced to resign in 1911.

▶ According to Adler a general inferiority complex develops out of feelings of inferiority about our bodies, or some of its organs.

▶ Unlike Freud, Adler is not concerned with biological drives or unconscious forces. He sees the development of personality occurring as the result of conscious knowledge and feelings about ourselves.

▶ Freud believed that a patient's symptoms would simply disappear after catharsis. Adler deliberately attempted to change the patient's future.

■ **Contrast the aims of Freudian and Adlerian therapy.**

then work through the events that gave rise to these emotional blockages (repressions). This reduces the anxiety they produced originally, and removes the need for further repression. After sufficient working through of these problems the analysis can be stopped, although the symptoms may reappear at times of stress in the future, and will need further working through sessions.

## Alfred Adler's 'individual therapy'

**Alfred Adler** was a colleague of Freud's until they disagreed about the types of forces acting on early development. While Freud emphasized sexual motives lying behind many early anxieties, e.g. Oedipal conflicts, Adler emphasized social and interpersonal relationships as having more influence on self-perception, and hence personality growth.

According to Adler all people have a will to have power over others. When this can't be achieved we experience feelings of inferiority. Right from early childhood we will all experience inferiority feelings at some times. We may have the impression from others that we are too small, too big, too unattractive, too noisy, too greedy, and so on. Later, feelings about the development of our genitals or breasts might give rise to inferiority feelings as well. We must learn to cope with these inferiority feelings or we may develop an inferiority complex. Equally, overcompensation for feelings of inferiority can lead to a superiority complex.

Since these feelings that the child develops about itself are extremely important, so the main sources of information – parents, siblings, friends – are important influences on development. Adler isn't concerned with probing the unconscious mind, but rather seeks to discover how patients feel about themselves. The Adlerian therapist conducts intensive interviews to discover the early communications between the parents and their child, whether the child was first, second or third born, the age of the other siblings, the lifestyle the child enjoyed, and anything else that could give an insight into the child's early feelings about itself. Having made these discoveries the therapist can begin to explain to the patient the background to his or her behaviour.

Having explained where the patient's feelings came from in the past, the Adlerian therapist sets out to change the patient's future feelings by establishing a sense of worth, value, achievement and importance. The therapist establishes some areas in which patients have some skill and builds on them, showing the patients that they can make a valuable contribution and that they have something they can feel good about. These two goals, understanding the negative aspects of past experiences and emphasizing a positive future, are the characteristics of Adlerian individual therapy.

## Other therapies influenced by psychoanalysis

Such was the popularity of psychoanalysis that many therapies originating in its principles have been developed. They each have their supporters and critics. Two of the more popular ones are described here.

## Transactional analysis

This is derived from **Eric Berne**'s psychoanalytically inspired book, *Games People Play* (1968). Berne argues that most of our interactions with each other involve us in social games, competing, being assertive, cheating, losing, and so on. In these games we are sometimes fun-loving, careless, immature and irresponsible. We are playing the role rather like an emotional child. This is similar to Freud's concept of the id. Sometimes we are more strict, severe and serious, exercising control and being critical, rather like the role of parent. This corresponds to Freud's superego function. And occasionally we are more rational, sensible and perceptive, more like an adult. This resembles Freud's concept of ego. The aim of transactional analysis is to make the person more aware of their three components and how they appear in their everyday lives.

People are encouraged, both alone and in group meetings, to be aware of the effect that their behaviour is having on others, to realize the influences that the id, ego and superego are having, and to try to make their behaviour more like an adult and less like a parent or child. The ego is to be made stronger, particularly at the expense of the id.

▶ Berne was a psychoanalytically trained therapist who believed he recognized the influence of the three hypothetical parts of the personality identified by Freud at work in our everyday social encounters.

▶ Transactional analysis uses several techniques to make people aware of the influence of their id, superego and ego, and lessen their more destructive elements.

## Primal therapy

From the mid-1960s there was something of a social revolution in the West. The 'hippie generation' flocked to the West coast of America to wear flowers in their hair, beads around their necks, and to practise their ideals of making love, not war. This spirit of liberation from the traditional values of seeking success, advancement and prosperity reflected itself in some academic areas too. In California **Arthur Janov** invented primal therapy around 'the primal scream'.

Primal therapy accepts that we experience anxieties during childhood, which can become repressed. Every time parents fail to satisfy a child's wishes it suffers some anxiety. Repressed anxieties can appear as neurotic symptoms in adulthood. The neurotic symptoms will relieve some of the repressed anxieties, but the only way to eliminate them altogether is to relive the experiences that caused them in the first place – the withholding of parental love.

People are encouraged to remember these occasions and to relive them, but this time letting their parents know what they want and need, what they think and feel. They must speak out loud, shout, scream, cry, rage, groan, moan, whimper, sob, howl, beg and generally expose their deepest feelings. They must run, jump, roll, writhe, twitch, kneel, crawl, wriggle and make any other movement that expresses the way they were feeling. These feelings are called 'primals'. This is supposed to produce catharsis by 'getting it out of the patient's system'.

▶ Reliving an emotional experience is called *abreaction* in psychoanalytic theory. It is supposed to produce catharsis. Whether it does or not depends on many factors, including the person's ability and desire to 'let it all hang out'.

### Evaluation of psychoanalytic therapy

Most psychoanalytic therapies rely to varying extents on Freudian views about the structure and functioning of biological and social forces in development. Psychoanalytic approaches propose that emotional and personality disorders are caused by childhood experiences. If we reject this theory then techniques designed to relive childhood cannot produce a 'cure' for an 'adult' problem. It is sometimes argued that by always looking backwards for the origin of problems psychoanalysts may miss real causes of problems in the here and now. For example, if being trapped in a tower-block with two young children is what is making me miserable, there seems little point in analysing my early relationships with my mother. Psychoanalytic approaches can appear as ways of helping people misunderstand the true nature of their problems in the here and now. However, Davenhill and Osborne (1991) claim 'an informed understanding of psychoanalytic principles and an ability to apply these principles flexibly in different situations can be of benefit to ourselves, our clients, and the staff with whom we work'. Indeed, many clinics still employ psychoanalytically inspired therapists.

## DESCRIPTION AND EVALUATION OF BEHAVIOUR THERAPY

While the medical model seeks to treat and even 'cure' problem behaviour by surgery, ECT or chemotherapy, and while psychoanalytic theories try to put patients in touch with the cause of their problems, behaviourists believe that any maladapted behaviour is likely to be the result of an inappropriate association of an act and a reinforcer. According to behaviourists the cause of the maladapted behaviour is less important than its consequences.

▶ Behaviourists' only concern with the cause of maladapted behaviour is in the nature of the reinforcer that maintains it.

▶ According to the supporters of the behaviourist tradition, any learning (including maladapted learning) that has come about through association can be removed in the same way.

The cause of the act could be external, such as a broken relationship, the death of a friend or failing an exam. This external factor could induce an internal state of stress, conflict, anxiety or frustration and these emotional states could bring about behaviour which has the symptoms of depression, anxiety, obsession and so on. Other people's sympathetic or understanding reactions might provide reinforcement for the symptoms.

Three broad areas of learning theory have been applied to changing maladapted behaviour. These stem from classical conditioning, with its concern for physiological explanations for behaviour. **Hans Eysenck** developed the applications of classical conditioning in the 1950s, calling them 'behaviour therapy'. A year later **B.F. Skinner** also used this term to describe his techniques for modifying behaviour based on operant conditioning principles. Later the term 'behaviour modification' was used for operant techniques. These two approaches are discussed below. The third broad area of theories that have been applied to changing some problem behaviour are the social learning theories developed originally by **Albert Bandura** and his colleagues, which propose modelling therapy.

▶ Learning theory covers a vast range of approaches in psychology, from those that seek a physiological explanation for learning to those that reject the influence of physiology altogether.

# Classical conditioning and behaviour therapy

Many learned responses that both humans and animals make are the result of an association being formed between some act and a reflexive response. So if the smell of cooking fish and chips makes you salivate you may associate the sight of a chip shop with feeling hungry. For some adults some neutral events, people, animals or objects may have become inappropriately associated with such emotional reflexes as fear and anxiety, pleasure and need, so the sight of a spider may cause you to show fear.

Sometimes the association results in abnormal behaviour. For example, someone might have an irrational fear of cats because a cat was involved in some frightening previous experiences. This means they cannot visit friends who have cats and are constantly on guard against being near a cat. An alcoholic has learned to associate alcohol with a compulsion to drink it. This abnormal behaviour needs therapy either to change a negative behaviour (avoiding cats) to a neutral or positive one (accepting the presence of cats), or to change some positive behaviour (alcoholism) into a negative one (not being addicted). Each type of behaviour change requires a different type of therapy. The first requires systematic desensitization or implosion therapy, the second requires aversion therapy or stimulus satiation.

▶ Responses become conditioned to a neutral stimulus when the stimulus that naturally elicits them is associated with it.

## Systematic desensitization

Desensitization works by the therapist providing a stimulus which has a pleasant response. The stimulus is usually some kind of relaxation. The client's unpleasant response is gradually associated with it. The pleasantness of the first response must always have a more profound effect on the client than the unpleasantness of the second. The two responses are incompatible, and the weaker of them should disappear.

Let's take as an example a man who had several frightening encounters with birds as a child, and is now a zoophobic. The therapist provides a pleasant unconditional stimulus (a relaxation technique), which will elicit in the client a pleasant unconditional response (comfort). A second, unpleasant, conditioned response (the man's anxiety reaction to birds) is then gradually paired with the comfort he feels from the first. At all times the conditioned anxiety response must be weaker than the unconditional comfort response. Since the two responses (comfort and anxiety) are incompatible, the weaker of them will fade away.

There are several kinds of relaxation and the techniques can be learned in a few hours. The stimulus to trigger the pleasant reaction response might be the sight or sound of the therapist, or simply entering the therapy room.

It is impossible to feel two incompatible emotions at the same time. You may cry because you're happy, but this crying is not seen as a symptom of unhappiness. You can't feel relaxed and comfortable at the same time as feeling anxious and afraid.

▶ Systematic desensitization and aversion therapy are examples of *counterconditioning*. This means taking a powerful conditioned stimulus which elicits a pleasant response and associating it with a less powerful (undesired) conditioned response.

## Systematic desensitization with a zoophobic

| Stage | Aim | Example |
|---|---|---|
| 1 The therapist explores the thresholds of tolerance of the anxiety-producing stimulus. | To discover the shortest distance the phobic can tolerate between himself and a bird. What other bird-like stimuli cause anxiety? | 20 metres |
| 2 The most desirable outcome of the therapy is established: the 'target behaviour'. | To establish the distance the phobic would find acceptable. What other stimuli would the phobic want to tolerate? | Pictures, photographs Actual bird at 1 metre |
| 3 Relax the client and make him imagine being in the presence of various bird-like objects, from least feared to most feared. (This is an 'anxiety hierarchy'.) | To achieve a relaxed state incompatible with being anxious. | Pictures, photographs Client can tolerate thoughts of birds |
| 4 Continue relaxation and introduce some simple bird-like sketches on the other side of the room. | Same as above | No anxiety in the presence of the sketches |
| 5 Bring the sketches nearer until the client shows some anxiety reaction, then stop. | As above | As above |
| 6 Repeat the last stage until any anxiety reactions to the sketches have disappeared (been 'extinguished'). | As above | As above |
| 7 Replace the simple sketches with a more realistic drawing of a bird at some distance, and bring it closer as before. | As above | No anxiety in the presence of the drawing |
| 8 Replace the drawing with a photograph and repeat. | As above | No anxiety from a photograph |
| 9 Replace the photograph with a stuffed model of a bird and repeat. | As above | No anxiety from a model bird |
| 10 Replace the model with a small caged bird and repeat. | As above | No anxiety from a small bird |
| 11 Use a larger bird and repeat until the bird is 1 metre from the former zoophobic. He has now been desensitized to birds. | As above | No anxiety from a larger bird at 1 metre |

### Evaluation of systematic desensitization

Systematic desensitization is an effective technique for treating people with minor phobias. They need to be able to allow themselves to imagine the anxiety-producing stimulus, and the therapeutic situation must be so controlled that they can tolerate the phobic object. They may also need to learn to use a relaxation technique. Such an approach couldn't be used with people whose behaviour is more deeply dysfunctional, such as those with psychotic disorders or severe personality disorders.

There is some disagreement about whether it is necessary to arrange the anxiety-producing stimuli in an 'anxiety hierarchy' from least distressing (the bird-like sketch in our example – see box) to the most distressing (actually being close to the bird). There is also disagreement about whether it is necessary to have the pleasant, unconditional response at all. Merely exposing clients to the source of their anxiety may be enough to reduce the anxiety, particularly where clients are well motivated to want to reduce their anxiety reaction.

### Implosion therapy and flooding

The idea behind implosion therapy is that no one can maintain any response indefinitely, including an anxiety response to a stimulus about which one is phobic. A fear of birds can only persist when the client generally avoids birds and is able to escape from them on the rare occasions that he or she comes into contact with them.

With implosion therapy the aim is to achieve extinction of the fear response very quickly. There are no relaxation exercises and phobic clients are not gently and systematically exposed to the source of their fear. Instead they are simply made to imagine that there are, for example, masses of birds all around them. The therapist describes the scene in great detail. Some of the birds touch the client, wings flap, beaks peck at the ground, and eggs are laid all over the place. This should be enough to produce a fair amount of anxiety! The therapist goes on and on, despite the client pleading with him or her to stop. After a time the client should no longer find the descriptions so frightening.

Clients can't escape from the descriptions of the birds and the theory is that they will eventually become exhausted, even bored, by them. When next confronted by a real bird it is hoped that the response in the therapy session will be *generalized*, and the client will not feel afraid of them. Similarly, someone who is afraid of heights will be shown photographs or videos taken from high places in an attempt to lessen the client's sensitivity to them. When next in a high place the person's anxieties should be lessened.

An even stronger version of implosion therapy is flooding therapy. Here the client is actually exposed to the objects themselves, rather than to hearing verbal descriptions of them. An arachnophobic could be shut in a room containing jars and glass-cases full of all kinds of spiders, with pictures of spiders lining the walls. The initial anxiety attack (assuming it doesn't provoke instant heart failure!) should, in theory, eventually subside.

Someone who has a phobia about aeroplanes, perhaps having been involved in a plane crash, might be made to watch a few hours of films featuring planes, including war films, documentaries about aircraft, flight simulators, and so on. An agoraphobic could be made to walk around a busy shopping precinct, buy things in the

► In a faster-working version of desensitization called *graded exposure* clients are not taught relaxation but have to find their own way of coping with the phobic object.

■ Outline a systematic desensitization procedure for reducing an agoraphobic's fear of open spaces.

► Escape and avoidance behaviour are important sources of learning and allow us to maintain many of our normal daily routines.

► *Generalization* means making an induction from examples of something, and applying the same principles or conclusions to other, similar objects. Having learned the principles of servicing one car engine you may generalize your knowledge to other car engines.

► Compared to desensitization implosion therapy can be very speedy (and therefore cheaper), though it can also have some dangers.

► In implosion therapy the client's experiences happen inside his or her own head (they implode). In flooding the experiences are real and exist outside the client.

shops, have a coffee in a coffee bar, and so on. Someone afraid of heights could be made to ride on elevators or lifts up and down tall buildings.

### Evaluation of implosion and flooding

Implosion and flooding are successful with some clients, although there are ethical and practical implications. The client's motivation has to be very strong. An agoraphobic who would consent to spending some hours in a shopping precinct must be so well motivated to overcome his, or more usually her, phobia that the phobia can't be regarded as extreme, and the client may well have improved without therapy. Anyone who would willingly stay in a room full of feared spiders is unlikely to have that severe a phobia. A further problem is that the therapy may backfire and make the client's phobia even worse. Exposure to the phobic object during flooding might confirm or reinforce the phobic response.

### Aversion therapy

Aversion therapy can be thought of as being the opposite of desensitization. It doesn't try to eliminate the fear response, it tries to trigger it. The behaviour that is to be eliminated is associated with an unpleasant response so that the unpleasant response will be elicited if the client begins the behaviour in the future.

A common problem that has been successfully treated by aversion therapy is alcoholism. Clients are given a drug that has an unpleasant effect when combined with alcohol, such as causing vomiting or eliciting a fear response. They are then asked to smell, sip, savour and finally swallow the alcoholic drinks to which they are addicted. As they are enjoying their drink, the drug begins to make them feel ill or frightened. The pleasure soon disappears in the face of the effects of the drug. An association between drinking alcohol and being ill or frightened should be formed, and any time they think about having a drink in the future they should start to feel ill or scared.

Aversion therapy has also been found effective with paraphilias and other sexual dysfunctions, from sexual fetishes such as transvestism, to homosexuals who feel uncomfortable with their sexuality and desire to be heterosexual. Transvestites (men who derive sexual pleasure from dressing as a member of the opposite sex) will be asked, in the privacy of a room in a clinic, to dress up in their favourite female garments. As they do so they will probably experience some sexual arousal. Unknown to them, their dressing will be recorded on video. Later they will be given a nausea-inducing drug and shown the film. They should learn to associate the thought of themselves dressing in women's clothes with feeling sick. After several such pairings the association should be so strong that the mere thought of 'cross-dressing' should induce nausea. Since it is impossible to feel sick and sexually aroused at the same time, the desire to achieve arousal through cross-dressing will, in theory, be eliminated. (The fear-inducing drug would not be used

■ Contrast implosion therapy with desensitization techniques.

▶ Unlike the other therapies described so far, aversion therapy pairs the undesired behaviour with an unpleasant response so that, if the stimulus for repeating the behaviour occurs in the future, the unpleasant response will be elicited.

▶ As with systematic desensitization, two opposing emotions cannot be felt simultaneously. The strongest will win. The fear or dread of vomiting should be greater than any enjoyment that one might have from a drink.

▶ Aversion therapy works on the principle that a positive response, e.g. sexual arousal, will be replaced by an incompatible, negative one, e.g. feeling sick, if several pairings are made.

in this treatment since fear and sexual arousal are not incompatible: fear can sometimes increase sexual arousal.)

### Evaluation of aversion therapy

A major ethical problem with aversion therapy concerns deliberately giving someone a treatment (the drug) that is intended to make them ill. This goes against the whole of clinical practice, where drugs are administered to make people better. Second, there are problems with generalization. A former transvestite who feels sick at the thought of dressing in female clothes may generalize this to feeling sick whenever he is near a female who is wearing clothes. This could severely limit his social life! Former alcoholics may generalize their fear or sickness response to being in any place where alcohol can be seen or smelt. Supermarkets, hotels, aeroplanes, restaurants and even other people's homes may all elicit vomiting. Some alcoholics have been known to drink themselves insensible to avoid feeling sick!

## Operant conditioning and behaviour modification

Operant conditioning (see Chapter 1) is founded on the idea expressed by E.L. **Thorndike**'s 'law of effect', which states that any action that has pleasant consequences is likely to be repeated, while any action that has unpleasant consequences will be avoided. These consequences are termed *positive* and *negative reinforcement*. This has obvious significance to therapy. In the early 1960s, for example, Ayllon and Houghton asked the attendants on a ward for psychotic patients to ignore the patients' descriptions of their hallucinations, delusions and erratic ramblings. Instead they were to reinforce (with attention, praise and any other appropriate reward) any of the more sociable or sensible utterances. The results were quite dramatic. The number of sensible comments increased, and the number of signs of disordered thinking decreased, quite markedly.

Before deciding on a course of therapy it is first necessary to establish exactly what the problem behaviour is, what are its consequences, and which circumstances in the client's environment trigger it. Behaviourists such as Skinner argue that antecedents (the situation, environment or circumstances in which people find themselves) provide stimuli which trigger certain behaviour (actually doing something in response to the stimuli). The behaviour will inevitably have some consequences (be they great or small, pleasant or unpleasant). It is the consequences of our behaviour that largely determine the likelihood of us repeating the action. For example, the smell of freshly baked cakes as you walk past the bread shop are antecedents to the behaviour 'buying and eating some cakes'. The consequences of your behaviour – your enjoyment in eating the cakes, your weight, your complexion, your bank balance – will influence whether you buy cakes again the next time you pass a bread shop.

■ How does aversion therapy differ from the other behaviourist techniques?

■ Show how desensitization, implosion therapy and aversion therapy follow from the theory of classical conditioning.

▶ A *positive reinforcer* is anything a person finds beneficial in some way. It could be primary (essentials like food and sleep) or secondary (anything, such as money, which can be exchanged for primary reinforcers). *Negative reinforcers* are either escaping from an unpleasant stimulus or avoiding it in the first place.

▶ Behaviourists identify ABC (Antecedents, Behaviour and Consequences). According to Skinner it is the consequences, not the antecedents, that determine behaviour.

► Some of the symptoms of some of the patients in Ayllon and Houghton's research appear to be caused by their treatment, i.e. they are social symptoms and not part of a medical condition or mental illness.

► Discovering precisely what each person finds reinforcing and what is reinforcing particular behaviour is not as easy as it might seem. If you don't buy a cake, can I infer that you do not find cakes reinforcing? A cake is only a positive reinforcer if you're hungry, or have some money, or are not off cakes, or not on a strict diet.

■ **How does behaviour modification based on operant conditioning differ from the methods employed in classical conditioning?**

► The programme of reinforcement to be used with autistic children has to be much longer than with 'normal' children, and substitution of reinforcements must be made very gradually.

In Ayllon and Houghton's experiment, the ward, the behaviour of the attendants and the other patients were all antecedents for each of the patients. Their dysfunctional behaviour occurred (partly at least) in response to those antecedents. The consequences (before the experiment) were that the patients who exhibited the most extreme symptoms received the most attention. A behaviourist would claim that a 'vicious circle' has developed in which the most attention is paid to the patients whose behaviour is most dysfunctional, and the patient knows, therefore, that to obtain attention he or she must behave in a dysfunctional way. To put it simply, the caring behaviour of the attendants is actually causing some of the problem!

The therapist must discover exactly what each client would find positively and negatively reinforcing. People vary in their likes and dislikes, and what one would find reinforcing another might find distressing. For example, would you find smoking a cigarette positively reinforcing? Would all your friends? (Some of Ayllon and Houghton's patients stayed unnaturally quiet for most of the day, seemingly absorbed in their own pursuits. Attention was not a positive reinforcer for them.) Having found what is presently reinforcing the undesired behaviour, and what the client would find rewarding, the therapist must remove the reinforcer from the undesired behaviour and apply it to the desired behaviour.

The following are some examples of problems where behaviour modification techniques have been used.

### Infantile autism

(See Chapter 9.) Autistic children are generally preoccupied with their own perceptions and have no interest in other people, which makes them difficult to train in basic skills such as washing, dressing and using the appropriate utensils to eat with. In therapy they often appear to be ignoring the therapist, and do not make or keep eye contact with him or her. Chemotherapy cannot improve their condition, and insight theories are impractical when the subject cannot or will not co-operate.

**Ivar Lovaas** (1968) adapted and applied a behaviour modification approach – specifically 'behaviour shaping by successive approximation' – to training some autistic children in California in the 1960s. It isn't necessary, or possible, to establish the antecedents of autistic behaviour and Lovaas simply reinforced every aspect of any behaviour that was vaguely sociable, such as making eye contact, making sounds, imitating the therapist's actions, cuddling, etc. He used encouragement, praise and pieces of chocolate as reinforcers.

After a while the children had to make more speech-like sounds and had to hold eye contact for longer, or imitate more complex action, in order to gain reinforcers. Cuddles were now a normal part of the child's repertoire of behaviour and could be used as a reinforcer. As the children's behaviour continued to become slightly more 'normal', verbal reinforcement, e.g. 'good boy' and 'well done', was all that was necessary to maintain progress. By now the children had learned to make combinations of sounds into words, although correctly applying them required immense patience, many months of training, and countless reinforcements.

Lovaas found that considerable improvements could be made, with tremendous and constant effort on the part of the child's carers. Autistic children are unlikely ever to be able to compete with normal children in language, creative skills, co-ordination, and so on. For a child who is completely isolated to become even slightly more sociable has to be seen as great progress. Luckily the principles of behaviour modification are not difficult for parents to understand, and they are usually the people most highly motivated to strive for improvements in the child.

► Many parents of autistic and other retarded or behaviourally dysfunctional children have been taught the principles of behaviour modification with some success.

### Behaviour modification and children with pervasive conduct disorders

Children whose behaviour in school or at home causes acute problems for their carers, and indirectly for themselves, are sometimes treated by a *'time out'* procedure. For example, a child may be uncontrollable, attention seeking, aggressive or hyperactive. The frustration, anger or distress the child is causing its carers may be reinforcing the child's behaviour. In 'time out' the child is removed, forcibly if necessary (and it often is necessary), from the situation where it is behaving badly and placed in an unstimulating part of the classroom, away from anyone else, or in a separate, empty and bare room. The child is told what is happening, and that it will only be released when its behaviour has been acceptable for a period of, for example, five minutes.

► *Time out* is a quite extreme measure and is usually used only when other, less severe attempts at control have failed.

► Time out was developed from operant conditioning and attempts to extinguish undesirable behaviour by removing the child from the situation that could be reinforcing the undesired behaviour.

In most cases the child's behaviour becomes more extreme in the time out. The child may scream constantly, wreck the place, appear to hurt itself or do anything else that might tempt its carers to release it. This has to be resisted at all costs, despite the carer's urge to give in to the child, who seems to be in such distress. After a while in time out the child's behaviour will usually subside for long enough for it to be returned to the company and activity of the class or family. The child is told that if its behaviour becomes unacceptable again it will be returned to time out.

### Severe retardation and behaviour modification

In 1971 Azrin and Foxx published the results of their procedure for toilet training severely retarded children. The children were given extra drinks and taken to the toilet every half hour. When they used it successfully they were given sweets, biscuits, praise and lots of attention. When they 'had an accident' they were strapped into a chair for half an hour, away from the rest of the class. (This is a time out procedure.) On the whole the number of 'accidents per week' declined fairly dramatically.

Severely retarded children have been taught to dress using an application of operant conditioning called 'prompt and fade'. They were first taught to dress themselves in large, loose, elasticated smocks. As the children were helped to dress themselves, each operation was explained to them, and they were told what they would have to do. Each time the child had to get dressed, the helpers would tell the child what to do, but reduced the amount of help actually given. As each operation was mastered the child was praised and given reinforcers such as spoonfuls of chocolate pudding. When they could put on their loose smocks without any help, they were then taught how to dress in conventional clothes. This technique has worked with children with IQs of below 10.

### Evaluation of behaviour modification

Positive and negative reinforcement are most effective when used with specific symptoms rather than entire disorders. Eliminating specific, simple problems and then successively removing the next simplest until eventually the more complex symptoms have been extinguished is an ideal goal for behaviour modification therapy. It isn't, however, always possible because of the nature of the client's personality or condition, the antecedents or the therapy situation, the resources available, and so on.

Time out procedures involve the deliberate withdrawal of a child's civil liberty (freedom). On the other hand, the child's disruptive behaviour may be interfering with the adult's rights to expect reasonable behaviour. If the child's behaviour is simply 'naughty', then time out may be a useful method for discipline. If it is a symptom of a dysfunctional state, then time out becomes imprisonment. Is it ethically acceptable for use with retarded children? Or will the benefits they will gain from being more able to control themselves justify the use of this technique? A time out procedure called 'pin-down' used by Staffordshire Social Services was recently severely condemned as cruel, and is no longer used.

### Institutionalized adults with psychotic disorders

An application of operant conditioning that was widely used in the 1960s to prepare some patients for life in the outside world was the 'token economy'. Patients had to start doing things for themselves, as one does in 'real life', in order to gain some tokens. For example, chores such as tidying, cleaning, washing up, dressing and helping to prepare food were all rewarded by tokens that could be exchanged for privileges. The more complex or demanding the task, the more tokens could be given.

### A token economy programme (based on Ayllon and Azrin 1968)

Examples of how tokens can be earned:

| Job | Reward in tokens |
| --- | --- |
| Make own bed and clean area | 1 |
| Brush teeth once a day | 1 |
| 10 minutes waiting on table | 2 |
| 10 minutes washing up | 6 |
| 30 minutes writing names of other patients brushing teeth | 3 |

**Examples of what tokens can be exchanged for:**

| Cost | For |
| --- | --- |
| 1 token per day | the use of a personal chair |
| 1 token per day | the choice of a bedspread |
| 2 tokens | a 20-minute walk in the grounds |
| 3 tokens | choosing a TV programme |
| 1–10 tokens | toiletries, e.g. toothpaste, comb, lipstick |
| 10 tokens | attending a religious service off the ward |
| 20 tokens | a private meeting with the ward psychologist |
| 100 tokens | a private meeting with a social worker |
| 12–400 tokens | clothes and accessories, such as slippers, skirt, handbag |

There is no doubt that well-run token economies have led to improvements in the behaviour of even quite severely dysfunctional schizophrenics, but they have not led to anything that can be remotely thought of as a 'cure'. Although some patients have been able to cope with life outside the institution, for example in 'halfway houses', nearly all of them have needed great assistance and supervision. Once the token system is removed, improvements in behaviour tend to disappear. This shows that the token economy is treating the symptoms of maladapted behaviour and largely ignoring its cause.

Also, a number of problems have been found when running token economies. Some patients stole others' tokens, other patients hoarded them. Some were simply unable to understand the benefits of changing their behaviour, or unable to control their behaviour sufficiently to make it change.

Token economies are not widely used today in the West, partly because it is recognized that mental patients have the same human rights as anyone else. These rights (to see a psychologist or social worker, to sit in a chair, etc.) have been tested in the courts. In America legal action has been taken against institutions that denied patients the right to attend religious ceremonies unless they had enough tokens. Also there are legal limits on the minimum wages that can be paid for many of the duties that patients had to perform in order to earn tokens. The value of the work in dollars amounted to rather more than that to which the tokens would entitle a patient. A few psychiatric wards were run as token economies in Britain, but with limited success.

## *Social learning theory and modelling therapy*

Observational learning has been researched by Albert Bandura since the 1950s and is part of social learning theory (see Chapter 1). We often watch someone else who is doing something better than we can, and imitate their performance as a means of improving our own. If a person's responses (for example towards spiders) are maladapted (i.e. they have a phobic reaction), and he or she sees someone else behaving appropriately, then the maladapted

► Most forms of treatment, even those based on the principles of conditioning, at least attempt to 'cure' the problem. The token economy has had some success in changing some aspects of behaviour, but never offered a 'cure'.

► Patients who were sufficiently aware of themselves to be able to control their behaviour and benefit from the tokens were often on the same ward with even more severely dysfunctional patients who were unable to earn any tokens. This seems like discrimination.

► Token economies bring some improvements in the behaviour, and the quality of life, of some patients (and staff), but possibly at the expense of some basic human rights.

■ **Explain how behaviour modification illustrates the principles of operant conditioning.**

► *Modelling therapy* comprises showing the client someone behaving appropriately in a situation in which the client's responses are inappropriate. It has been used both to extinguish unwanted behaviours and to rebuild appropriate ones.

► The *live modelling group* had some direct experience with the object of their fear, the snake.

► The *symbolic modelling group* saw others interacting with snakes, but had no personal experience.

► The *desensitization group* were relaxed and were gradually exposed to images of snakes and eventually to a live snake.

► *Self-efficacy* involves some cognitive restructuring from 'I can't do ...', to 'I can do ...'.

response could be replaced by an appropriate one. This technique is known as *modelling therapy*.

Eliminating inappropriate behaviours, such as phobias, by modelling someone without the phobia interacting with the phobic object, has been demonstrated many times. The best known is Bandura's experiment with severe snake-phobic subjects. They were first tested by seeing how closely they would approach a glass tank containing a snake. Their attitudes towards snakes were also tested. They all had negative images of snakes and found snakes disgusting. Bandura then divided the participants into three experimental and one control group.

The first experimental group, called the *live modelling group*, saw a therapist handle a live king snake without fear. The participants were encouraged to touch the snake, first while wearing gloves, then with their bare hands, finally touching near to its head. Gradually all the participants allowed themselves to be touched by the snake's body, even allowing it to crawl over them. The second experimental group, called the *symbolic modelling group*, watched a film of children and adults interacting with various snakes. In the film the stimuli were fairly mild to begin with and became progressively more frightening to the phobic viewers. In the early scenes the people played with plastic snake toys; later they touched and handled a live king snake without any fear; and in the final scenes the king snake slid across their shoulders and around their necks. The people on the film obviously enjoyed their experience with the snake. If the participants became too aroused they could stop the film, rewind it and watch any parts of it again if they wanted to. The third experimental group, the *desensitization group*, had a systematic desensitization procedure as described earlier under classical conditioning (see pages 197–9). The control group received no therapy at all.

After the modelling sessions all the participants were asked to approach the snake in the tank again. Those in the control group were still unwilling to go very close and refused to touch the snake. More participants in the desensitization group were now able to touch the snake, and many more still in the symbolic modelling group were now prepared to handle the snake. However, the greatest change occurred in the live modelling group, many of whom were even able to have the snake placed in their laps while they sat with their hands down by their sides. Each experimental group's attitude towards snakes had also changed in relation to their experience with the live modelling group now having quite positive attitudes towards snakes. Bandura claims that 90 per cent of snake phobias can be cured using a live modelling technique.

According to Bandura the explanation for the success of this and other cognitive behaviourist therapies lies in *self-efficacy*. By this he means the change in our cognition which says 'I can do this'. Much maladapted behaviour is the result of negative views of what the sufferers can't do or what they are afraid of. The best way to achieve self-efficacy is to encourage people to come face to face with the object that frightens them and encourage some interaction with it. The more we know about some things, the less likely we are to fear them.

Social learning theory uses the principle of operant conditioning, but it gives the participant another person as a model to identify with and the main reward for showing a desirable behaviour is usually the participant's sense of achievement.

### Evaluation of behaviourist therapies

Behaviourist therapies have had considerable success in dealing with phobias. They have sometimes been successful in dealing with addictions and with psychosexual problems, but their use in this context sometimes has unfortunate side effects. Behaviour modification has been used to shape and change the behaviour of autistic, retarded and psychotic patients. But in these contexts it cannot be said to offer a cure: rather, it makes their behaviour more socially acceptable.

A common criticism of behaviourist therapies is that they are based on a grossly oversimplified picture of human behaviour. In the behaviourist model people react to stimuli and act because of learned associations. They do not seem to reason, think or make sense of their experiences. This criticism is most telling with regard to the failure of behaviourist therapies to effect improvement in psychotic patients whose problems probably lie in thinking and interpreting things differently from other people.

In treating any conditions like phobias, a major limitation of behaviourist therapies is that they usually require a highly controlled environment if the improvement is to persist. It is easy to arrange things in a treatment room so that undesirable behaviour is followed by an unpleasant experience, or desirable behaviour is rewarded with a pleasant one, but once out in the real world it all too often happens that the alcoholic overcomes his or her nauseous association with alcohol and returns to drinking for pleasure, or the badly behaved child relearns the joys of being naughty.

Another line of criticisms of behaviourist therapies is moral rather than practical. Humanistic psychologists in particular object to people being treated like laboratory animals.

## DESCRIPTION AND EVALUATION OF COGNITIVE THERAPY

During the last 30 years or so there has been a movement in psychology away from some of the more rigid ideas of behaviourism such as behaviour being 'the result of situational antecedents and previous consequences'. This is now seen as a rather narrow view of the causes of human behaviour. We do things for all kinds of reasons, including 'for the hell of it' and 'because we just felt like it'. These may not be logical reasons, but humans aren't the logical robots that some behaviourism implies.

▶ Every branch of science should be dynamic, with new ideas, new theories, even whole new perspectives emerging as knowledge leads to speculation.

► Dysfunctional does not mean ill. Ill implies a breakdown in structure, which causes a breakdown in normal functioning. Dysfunctional means a breakdown in normal functioning for which there is no organic cause.

► A *personal construct* is a general term for each of the ways in which people try to understand, predict and control their situation.

In other areas of psychology there has been a trend towards seeing human cognition and human interaction as the key to a better understanding of human behaviour. Our thoughts, understanding, reasoning, memories, guesses, intuition, perception, imagination, motives, intelligence, abilities, self-concept and other mental processes all contribute to explaining human behaviour. This has relevance for therapies to deal with the 'mentally' (or 'behaviourally') 'dysfunctional'. If behaviour is the result of mental, cognitive processes, and behaviour is 'dysfunctional', then the mental processes must be 'dysfunctional'. What is needed is not behaviour shaping, but rather some cognitive restructuring. Some examples of cognitive therapies are described below.

## Personal construct theory

During the 1950s **George Kelly** was among the first to reject both the medical and psychoanalytic models, with their assumptions of 'illness' which has a 'cause' and which can be 'cured'. He also rejects the behaviourist emphasis that the consequences of previous behaviour determine future behaviour. He regards each person as a unique 'scientist': we test our ideas each day, and adapt our behaviour accordingly. For example, you might express your ideas about some current item in the news, and others around you may give their response. You might learn something you hadn't realized before, and you may modify your ideas in the future. If you do something to achieve some aim which is ineffective, then you won't do it to achieve the same aim again. Kelly sees this as *adaptive functioning*. If most of your ideas about your world allow you to function effectively in it then you have an effective *personal construct system*.

If some of our personal constructs about ourselves, other people or our situation repeatedly appear to be wrong, we may consider that we have a problem. If I believe (have a personal construct) that if I eat anything I will put on weight and be unattractive, then I will try to arrange my life so that I do not have to eat. This will include refusing all offers of food, or vomiting as soon as possible after eating. Since I may be in no danger of becoming overweight, if anything the opposite is true, my personal construct is clearly wrong, but I still believe it. I have a problem called anorexia.

According to Kelly the aim of therapy is to reconstruct those ideas that are clearly producing an inadequate or inaccurate response. The client and therapist work together, using whatever therapeutic techniques seem appropriate (including those of Freud, Adler and Skinner among others). They seek out what clients think about themselves, others and their environment that could explain their particular problem. They are then shown that it is possible to change their constructs. Unfortunately, by the time the dysfunctional behaviour is recognized and the individual needs help, it may be too late for this approach to work. Many anorexics know how ill they are, but simply cannot eat food any more than you could eat a plate of worms and spiders.

## Ellis' rational emotive therapy (RET)

In the early 1960s **Albert Ellis** suggested one of the first therapies that attempted to 'restructure' part of a person's cognition by emphasizing the rational, problem-solving aspects of cognition and the appropriate role of emotions in thinking. He believed that one of the main causes of maladaptive behaviour was that people developed some irrational ideas about themselves or their situation. For example, people who have an obsession about cleanliness and a compulsion to keep washing their hands may have the idea, without ever admitting or even realizing it, that the environment is grubby and grimy, that their hands inevitably become dirty, and that filthy hands are a major threat to health. Ellis' aim was to make the person confront his or her 'irrational' ideas in order to replace them with more 'rational' ones. One's hands do not necessarily become filthy, and dirty hands do not necessarily pose a major threat to health.

► Ellis doesn't use the term 'irrational' literally. It isn't irrational to think that the environment is dirty or that washing hands isn't a good thing to do. It's the hand washing in response to the obsession that needs to be eliminated. The obsession is an irrational cognition that needs restructuring.

People may also develop distorted views about relationships. For example, people who are convinced that they should be the centre of everyone's attention may become very depressed when it appears that some people ignore them. They may begin to feel a failure, worthless and incompetent. The therapist has to make them recognize that they have an irrational idea; that no one should or could be the centre of attention all the time, that we are all ignored sometimes, and that they need to have a more optimistic, positive outlook on life.

► Rational emotive therapy is highly directive and fairly aggressive: it tells clients what to think and do, and challenges them to do it. It emphasizes positive thinking such as 'be happy', 'pull yourself together', 'look on the bright side', 'you can do it'.

Ellis identified 11 basic irrational beliefs that lead to dysfunctional behaviour. These include: it is necessary to be loved by everyone, it is necessary to be thoroughly competent in everything if one is not to be considered worthless; some people are essentially bad and should be punished; things should be the way one would like them to be; past history will always determine present events; I am unable to control my emotions; unhappiness is always caused by other people; we are each responsible for other people.

## Beck's cognitive restructuring

At about the same time that Ellis was developing RET, **Aaron Beck** had abandoned his psychoanalytic training in favour of cognitive social learning theory. He adapted cognitive restructuring for use with depressives, believing that depression is often caused by people's faulty ('depressogenic') cognitions – beliefs, expectations, fantasies, etc. – about themselves and their failings. These ideas dominate the clients' thinking about themselves (helpless and worthless), their world (insensitive, empty and unpleasant), and their future (hopeless and limited).

Beck's therapy involves asking specific questions about how

► Beck uses the depressed client actively to explore his or her cognitions both during therapy and between therapy sessions. He regards the client as a 'colleague' and they explore the client's cognitions together.

▶ Other research on depressives supports Beck's idea about how they see themselves, their world and their future. Note the contrast between the cognitive view of depression, and the biological, somatic model noted earlier.

▶ According to Meichenbaum faulty perception leads to a failure to self-instruct and results in faulty cognition.

▶ Meichenbaum insists that people describe to themselves what the problems are and how they are going to overcome them in a positive, optimistic way. This is a deterministic, directive therapy.

▶ Familiarity with the situation helps take the anxiety out of anxiety-producing situations. This is achieved by role play and verbal descriptions of thoughts and feelings.

■ **Summarize the main cognitive restructuring therapies.**

■ **What kinds of problems can cognitive restructuring therapies work on?**

clients feel about themselves and helping them to realize how wrong they actually are. Between therapy sessions Beck sets his clients homework, which is intended to make them achieve something enjoyable and positive every day. Depressed people often deliberately avoid pleasant experiences. They have to keep a log of their feelings and anything that causes them to change their mood. Such things are explored further in therapy to see how they affect the client's cognition. In Beck's therapy, changing the cognition is all important since if cognition changes behaviour will surely follow.

## Meichenbaum's self-instructional training (SIT)

During the 1970s **Donald Meichenbaum** speculated that people hold 'internal dialogues' with themselves. We talk to ourselves, describing our thoughts and feelings. We tell ourselves what we should do next. These are *self-instructions*. Sometimes these discussions can be very negative and by focusing on these negative thoughts, levels of arousal are increased. If this continues then various neuroses result.

Meichenbaum's therapy is even more directive than Beck's. He insists that people talk to themselves in a positive way, emphasizing the power of positive thinking in training sessions. Having been faced with their negative thoughts, clients are taught various practical coping skills such as relaxation techniques, breathing exercises for controlling heart rate and arousal, and planning strategies for adapting appropriate behaviour.

One coping strategy is advance role play. Here the client runs through the situation that will produce anxiety, talking out loud and describing what he or she is doing. If you know you will be anxious and nervous outside the exam room, then several days before the exam you could go to the exam room and familiarize yourself with it, saying out loud what you see and how you feel. Explain what you intend to do on the day of the exam, how you intend to relax, be fresh, be prepared, and be positive. If necessary do this several times on subsequent days.

### Evaluation of cognitive therapies

Cognitive restructuring theories tend to direct the client's perceptions and cognitions wherever possible, and focus on positive rather than negative images. At first sight, whilst it may seem obvious that gaining a better understanding of ourselves is good, understanding our thoughts isn't the same as changing our actions. The emphasis in therapy must be on changing undesired behaviour into desired behaviour.

Thought influences behaviour, and behaviour influences thought. Since these two are inseparable, cognitive therapy should emphasize behaviour as well as thought processes. Most modern therapies are better described as 'cognitive behaviour' therapies, and there is mounting evidence that they are successful in treating depressive and anxiety disorders, and those where low self-image and poor self-control lead to difficulties in coping with life.

## DESCRIPTION AND EVALUATION OF HUMANISTIC THERAPY

Humanistic psychology is deliberately non-scientific; it rejects behaviourism as having an inhumane, mechanistic view of human beings, and rejects psychoanalysis because it treats adults as the victims of their early childhood experience. Humanistic psychology places great emphasis on the uniqueness and creativity of each individual (i.e. it is *idiographic*), their potential for self-improvement and for taking charge of their own lives. As with cognitive approaches humanistic psychology sees people as thinking and reasoning beings rather than as objects moved by biochemistry, by psychological complexes or by stimuli. It is central to humanistic psychology that the individual with problems – who is never called 'a patient' – should be treated with respect as a fellow human being, and however odd their way of thinking about the world may seem, it should be treated seriously as an alternative rather than as a faulty way of understanding.

> ▶ *Idiographic* refers to the study of the qualities of the individual as a valid subject for psychological research.

> ▶ Humanism developed out of the work of such people as Alfred Adler (see page 194) and Abraham Maslow (see pages 16–17).

Humanistic psychology comprises a rather diverse group of theories. One of the ways in which they vary is in the degree to which they are critical of society. Most other theories tend to take society for granted and see 'abnormal behaviour' as a problem, and conformity as desirable. Humanistic psychologists, by contrast, do not necessarily see normal behaviour as healthy behaviour. Humanistic psychology has generated many different therapies, some of them bordering on the mystical and spiritual. Here we will deal with the three more common humanistic therapies.

## Gestalt therapy

**Fritz Perls** was a German psychoanalyst who rejected most of the traditional Freudian ideas. He developed and used Gestalt therapy in the 1960s in America, and after his death in 1970 the techniques were used and extended by others. There are three major differences of approach between Gestalt therapy and psychoanalysis. First, Gestalt therapy is not based on any particularly explicit theory, unlike Freud's (or Skinner's). It is a system of therapy rather than a doctrine of development. Second, it is not particularly concerned with the cause, origin or development of the condition or problem. Its primary concern is with the here and now. (It shares this view with the behaviourist theories.) Third, it does not rely on the therapist interpreting the clients' condition, but rather on the clients becoming aware for themselves.

> ▶ Perls invented his own techniques designed to remove emotional barriers to self-expression and to make people more aware of themselves as whole beings so that they could move towards self-actualization.

> ▶ Gestalt therapy is much more about the here and now. It is less concerned with the origin of the condition than with its future.

The basic assumption that Perls made was that we sometimes erect emotional barriers to 'block out' things that we would find distressing. These barriers, which are like Freud's defence mechanisms, also stop us from really 'knowing' our 'true' selves. Gestalt therapy aims to remove the barriers by using techniques originally designed by Perls.

People are instructed to talk in the present tense. Everything must be about how they think or feel here and now, and they are sometimes asked to add the statement 'and I take responsibility for that'. If, for example, someone says 'I feel depressed', they might have to add that they were responsible for that feeling.

One of Perls' games or exercises uses the 'empty chair'. Two chairs are placed opposite each other, and clients play the role of themselves in one of the chairs, and imagine that the person they have a problem with is in the other chair. Clients express their fears, hopes, anxieties, hatred, loves, and so on to the person whose reaction to them is causing a problem in order to gain insight into themselves. Clients may then swap chairs and take the role of the other person. The clients may later talk with the therapist about the experience, and the idea is that people gain insight from analysing how they interact with these 'important others'. As with all of these therapies, the technique could work for some people who want it to work for them.

► Helping people to take responsibility for their feelings and behaviour is a major step towards them becoming more aware of themselves.

## *Carl Rogers' client-centred therapy*

**Carl Rogers** was a psychiatrist and psychotherapist who noted that his clients often referred to their symptoms as coming from within their sense of themselves, who they were, what they were like, how they saw the world, and so on. Their actual feelings and behaviour often fell short of what they would like to be like. Like Freud, Rogers distinguishes between 'actual self' and 'ideal self'. The greater the distance between the clients' understanding of their own actual and ideal selves, the greater would be the problems they experienced. Rogers concluded that the sense of self is the source of our knowledge about ourselves, and this knowledge contains evaluative as well as factual information – whether you are a 'nice' person, an 'arrogant' person, a 'superior' person, and so on. According to Rogers, how people view themselves is the most important aspect of the functioning of the personality. His theory of personality is based on a set of principles which may be summarized as follows.

► Rogers would have agreed with Cooley that we live in a 'looking glass' world (as we will see in Chapter 16).

► Client-centred therapy was a dramatic challenge for the medical profession. Many psychiatrists preferred to keep their distance from their patients and preserve their professional status. Rogers' ideas were met with considerable hostility.

### *Rogers' theory of personality*

1 Individuals can only see their particular world from their own point of view and each person is therefore the centre of his or her own world.
2 Each person's perception of the world is real to that person. Since each individual is unique, each one's perception is also different from anyone else's.
3 We all share the same basic desire to survive and get ahead, and much of our behaviour will be an attempt to satisfy our various needs (ultimately for self-actualization: see Chapter 8).

4 Knowledge of our self is part of our view of the world and comes from interaction with the environment, particularly with other people in it. How they treat us is built into our knowledge of what we are like and how we value ourselves.

5 We tend to behave in ways that reflect what we know we are like. If we know we are generous (because people have told us so, and treated us as though we are generous), we tend to behave in a kind and giving way. If we know we are aggressive, we tend to act in an unpleasant, anti-social way.

6 We are each strong enough to understand our own perceptions if we can be helped to review them, and we can change our views if we can be encouraged to examine them.

7 If we are to understand each other we must first understand the other person's perception of his or her world. A good way to do this is through open and honest discussion. The first aim of client-centred therapy is to achieve this understanding so that reorientation of a distorted self-perception can begin.

In client-centred therapy the first aim is to build a co-operative, trusting relationship between therapist and client (not patient). The therapist must appear supportive, emotionally receptive, and not judge the client in any way. He or she must genuinely regard the client as a valuable person, and not be interested only because the person is a client. The therapist must try to understand what the client is thinking and feeling, so must concentrate deeply on what the client says, asking for clarification where appropriate. Rogerian therapy is very demanding of the therapist.

The second goal of the therapy is to help clients think about their problem, which is encouraged by the therapist reflecting back what the client is saying, so that the client is enabled to see his or her problems differently.

In client-centred therapy the client takes the lead, the therapist simply supports and tries to be understanding, helping the client to come to terms with his or her own perceptions and feelings. The clients may then grow to 'know themselves better'. Each client is quite unique. No two clients described the same set of perceptions as leading to their particular views. (This has led Rogers to reject all systems of classification of diagnoses since he sees everyone as unique.)

## *Existential therapy*

Existential psychiatry represents the most radical wing of the humanistic psychology movement. Most other forms of psychology tend to see socially acceptable behaviour as desirable, and the person who deviates from it as being, or having, a problem. Existential psychologists by contrast do not make this assumption. Psychiatrists such as R.D. Laing see madness as understandable

► The two goals of client-centred therapy are to establish a supportive, caring relationship between therapist and client, and to help clients develop towards actualization as they realize their true feelings. The therapist aims to help clients come to terms with their feelings, and the first step might be to enable clients actually to face their emotions by stating them out loud.

■ Outline the principles upon which client-centred therapy is based.

■ What would a client-centred therapist aim to provide and why?

► Existentialism is an important school of philosophy which became very popular in the 1960s.

responses to 'insane' social circumstances. Existential psychiatrists have taken a particular interest in schizophrenia. More orthodox psychiatry views the schizophrenic as someone who has a faulty grasp of reality. Laing, by contrast, argues that the schizophrenic may be someone who has a better grasp of reality than most people, and that this is the schizophrenic's problem. In a world in which most people behave inconsistently, lie to each other, fool themselves, and avoid facing up to their responsibilities, the schizophrenic is someone who is unable to do this, and confronts the awfulness of the human condition directly.

Since existential psychiatry does not assume that the symptoms of schizophrenic behaviour are abnormal, then success in therapy doesn't necessarily mean 'becoming more like non-schizophrenics'. Rather, the task is for the individual to find a personality and lifestyle for themselves with which they can live without undue distress. Since the problems experienced by the 'mad' person derive from normal society, it is logical that existential therapy often involves creating new and better societies for them to live in, in the form of therapeutic communities.

Laing and others claim that if you treat people with equality, dignity and respect, regarding them as important individuals with the right to exercise their free will within the framework of a caring community, then most mental problems will resolve themselves. In the kind of therapeutic community in which this is supposed to happen, all reasonable distinctions between staff and other residents are removed. They usually live in the same place, eat the same food, and are participant to the same general 'rules', which the community as a whole decides at regular meetings. At these meetings issues are discussed which are of concern to any of the members. No one is obviously 'in charge' and the aim is to make the whole atmosphere supportive and non-threatening.

► Existentialists put most emphasis on free will, participation and individuality. It is what people themselves think that is most important.

### Evaluation of humanistic therapies

Many people who have undergone Gestalt therapy or client-centred counselling claim that they have benefited from it. As with other therapies there is always the possibility that they would have felt better irrespective of any therapy at all, and the vast majority of people who receive these kinds of therapies are not suffering from very serious complaints. However, since the humanistic approach shows considerable respect for the opinions of clients, expressions of client satisfaction are regarded as important evidence of success.

Existential therapies are virtually impossible to evaluate in their own terms. This is because they reject the idea, and/or the desirability, of 'normal behaviour', hence it is impossible to judge their success or otherwise in terms of whether or not they help someone to behave normally. For R.D. Laing, for example, 'madness' can be a valuable voyage of self-discovery, equivalent to a religious quest, so that whether or not existential therapies promote sanity is irrelevant. Other kinds of therapists who see the object of therapy as curing behaviour problems would not agree.

## *Community and occupational psychology*

People generally live in social groups, and many psychological problems arise because of difficulties in social interactions. Rather than offer therapies for problems, community and occupational psychologists attempt to prevent problems arising in the first place. Psychologists are employed by many agencies that deal with people, from education departments, police forces, large employers and the military, to advise on the design of situations that will minimize the stress that can lead to problems.

Two aspects of any situation can promote or minimize stress. These are the physical characteristics, such as the areas in which activities take place, and the social relationships that exist between people. The layout of a workplace, the decoration of prison cells, the routines of school and army life, can all be analysed to discover areas of potential stress, and strategies may be suggested to reduce this. Also, the way teams are organized and treated can influence the relationships between their members and the chances that they will work harmoniously together.

Rearranging an organization to reduce stress and conflict is a possibility if resources can be found to do so. Reorganizing life in the community for the same purpose is much more difficult. Studies of the distribution of some kinds of mental problems suggest very strongly that social causes are to blame. For example, **George Brown** has shown conclusively that depression is diagnosed much more frequently among young working-class housewives with young children than among any other single group. If it is the social situation of these women that causes their depression, prevention may mean radically changing their lives in terms of income, housing, childcare facilities and marital relationships. Resources for such grand social engineering are rarely made available. However, community psychologists can give advice on the design of housing estates, the provision of meeting places and other amenities and facilities for housebound mothers to make their lives less depressing.

Brown and Harris (1978) compared 458 working-class women in England with 100 similar women being treated in psychiatric hospitals for depression. They found the same factors to be common to most of those in hospital and many of the others: little communication with their husbands, having three or more young children at home, lack of a mother to help or confide in, and lack of outside employment.

Since community psychologists tend to see many problems arising from community life (or the lack of it), it is understandable that they usually favour treatment in the community rather than in hospitals or therapy rooms. There is not much point in curing someone in hospital and then returning them to the same situation that caused their problem in the first place. Community psychiatrists favour treatment in the community, often using half-way houses where patients can be supported by staff, while living as near a normal life as possible, or day centres where people living in their own homes can visit during the week for support or treatment. Day centres are sometimes organized so that groups of fellow-sufferers meet together to support each other.

## Summary – The major therapies

| Therapies | Assumptions | Techniques |
|---|---|---|
| **Medical therapies** | *Like physical illness, mental illness is caused by bodily malfunctions, in this case of the brain or nervous system.* | |
| Psychosurgery | Brain surgery can cure mental illness | Remove or cut into brain structures |
| ECT | Brain needs electrical stimulation | Apply mild electric shock |
| Chemotherapy | Chemical imbalance in the brain needs to be stabilized | Giving drugs |
| **Psychoanalytically inspired therapies** | *Problem behaviour has an identifiable cause in previous experience.* | |
| Freudian psychoanalysis | Conflict between parts of personality can lead to repressed anxiety | Analysis of early life through free association, dream analysis, Freudian slips, etc. |
| Adler's 'individual therapy' | Inferiority feelings develop during childhood because of inadequate relationships | Reconstruct early experiences to build sense of worth |
| Transactional analysis | Influence of 'parent' or 'child' state interferes with healthy 'adult' responses | Games, contracts and other dealings within groups aid cognitive restructuring |
| Primal therapy | Parents cause repressed childhood anxieties, resulting in adult neuroses | Expose true feelings by shouting and moving around |
| **Behaviour therapies** | *Better patterns of behaviour can be learned.* | |
| Systematic desensitization | Treating symptoms will effect cure | Gradual exposure to feared object |
| Implosion therapy | Prolonged exposure to a fear-inducing stimulus eliminates neurosis | Full exposure to stimulus until neurosis subsides |
| Aversion therapy | Pairing undesired CS with an unpleasant CR eliminates the undesired CS | Administer drugs to induce fear or nausea at the idea of the undesired CS |
| Behaviour modification | Maladapted behaviour is learned by associating a reinforcer with a response | Remove reinforcer from undesired response and positively reinforce desired response |
| Modelling therapy | Irrational fear comes from lack of knowledge. Actual exposure eliminates fear | Seeing someone else doing what scares us and then doing it ourselves removes anxiety |
| **Cognitive therapies** | *Problems arise from people having faulty ways of interpreting experience.* | |
| Rational emotive therapy (RET) | Problems result from misinterpreting present events | Replace incorrect interpretations with appropriate ones |
| Cognitive restructuring | Depression is caused by mistaken beliefs about what we ought to be like | Direct questioning and discussion to alter mistaken beliefs |

| Self-instructional training (SIT) | Internal dialogues may be faulty, leading to mistaken ideas about self-worth and interpersonal relationships | Make internal dialogues positive, and teach coping skills to help face problems |
|---|---|---|
| **Humanist therapies** | *Everyone is unique, so it is nonsense to talk about normal and abnormal behaviour. People experience problems with living. Many of these problems arise from the way they treat each other.* | |
| Client-centred therapy | Self derives from unique experiences | Therapist supports client, urging him or her towards self-actualization |
| Gestalt therapy | Problems result from clients not being fully aware of their whole selves | 'Games' increase self-awareness |
| Existential therapy | People are frustrated by the way other people treat them | Therapeutic communities encourage freedom and responsibility |

## DIFFICULTIES IN ASSESSING THE APPROPRIATENESS AND EFFECTIVENESS OF THERAPIES

As we have seen, we have biological, somatic approaches, with their medical, 'scientific' status, which have used treatments based on trial and error testing of drugs and brain surgery, observation, experience and guesswork as the basis for their interventions. The history of prefrontal lobotomy (psychosurgery) between the 1930s and 1950s isn't a lesson in how to conduct scientific research for the betterment of humanity. For many patients and their families it was a disaster and a disgrace to the medical profession.

In many cases the doctors do not know what causes the dysfunctional symptoms, or exactly what their intervention is doing to the cells of the brain that are being treated. In the case of ECT, the intention is to induce a seizure in the patient, i.e. deliberately to cause harm. In addition medical treatments require the informed consent of the patient, which, in the case of schizophrenic or acutely depressed patients, can't be given. Despite these qualifications, medical intervention does often work to improve the quality of life for patients who couldn't manage otherwise.

Critics of psychoanalytic approaches have to face the fact that these therapies sometimes seem to work, too. Yet there is no scientific support for many of Freud's claims. It's likely that many neuroses are caused by a combination of mind and body experiences and if the condition is not too severe, then almost any therapy, including talking to your best friend, could be effective. A neurotic symptom could easily be a cry for attention, so any therapy that provides attention could well remove the symptom. For lonely, depressed, anxious people with low self-esteem there can be something very gratifying about being listened to by a psychoanalyst, or being a valued member of a transactional analysis group. In this way psychoanalytic therapies may work by trans-

► Medicine and the somatic approach to abnormal behaviour is taken seriously because of its claim to scientific status. However, this claim could be challenged.

► Freud is accused of having an answer for everything, and where 'the facts' didn't fit psychoanalytic theory, he'd claim the facts were wrong. Psychoanalysis is a therapeutic application of the theory, so Freud would insist that the therapy works.

forming the patient's life, rather than for the reasons therapists claim.

Attempts to test the effectiveness of psychoanalysis are also likely to fail since they could involve taking a group of people with very similar symptoms, dividing them into one group who will attend regular psychoanalytic therapy, another who will receive another therapy, and a third who will receive no treatment at all. How could such a sample be found? Who would decide which person would be placed into which group? What is meant by 'regular' therapy sessions? How long would they need to continue? What exactly do we mean by cure? Jacobs (1984) claims that each patient may have different definitions of 'cure' anyway. **Anthony Storr** (1966) says that the symptoms of neurosis are merely indicators of what repressed urges inhabit the unconscious, therefore 'curing' the neurosis wouldn't have removed the cause of the neurotic symptoms.

Hans Eysenck is a strong supporter of behaviourist principles and has made frequent attacks on psychotherapy, comparing it to mysticism and religious faith rather than science. In 1952 Eysenck reviewed the results of five studies attempting to measure the effectiveness of psychoanalysis. He claimed that only 44 per cent of patients 'improved'. Bearing in mind Storr's comment, 'improvement' would be a difficult matter to judge. Eysenck also reviewed the success rates of 19 other treatments, finding about two-thirds of patients improved. He claimed that about two-thirds of people with minor symptoms recover without therapy of any kind, so psychoanalysis achieves nothing. However, Eysenck includes all those who dropped out of psychoanalysis. If these are excluded the success rate goes up to 66 per cent. Some of the studies Eysenck chose included patients whose symptoms were not typical of those who would ordinarily be in analysis, and for whom this treatment was not ideal.

Like the somatic and psychoanalytic approaches, behaviourists are accused of reducing complex human behaviour to its elements (ABC and reinforcement, observation and modelling), and deriving therapies intended to ignore the cause and eliminate the symptoms which someone has decided are maladaptive. There are some dysfunctions where this is enough. An acute agoraphobic may be less interested in what caused their fear of outside than in being able to conquer it, and for these people behaviour therapy is effective.

Behaviourist approaches have had some success with autistic children (Lovaas 1968) and people with special learning difficulties (Matson 1982 and Azrin and Foxx, noted earlier), although any improvement might need thousands of reinforcements, and often disappeared when the individual stopped receiving the reinforcement. Token economy programmes have been less successful, with improvements not being sustained off the programme.

Cognitive and humanist therapies are generally more effective in reducing anxiety and improving self-esteem, but less so for psychotic conditions. Cognitive restructuring, changing personal

▶ Behaviourism was a dominant psychological approach in the 1940s and 1950s, but its popularity has declined since then. However, many of its therapeutic practices have been remarkably resistant to extinction!

constructs and striving for self-actualization would only work with highly motivated and co-operative clients.

Several major problems exist for attempts to measure the effectiveness of psychological therapy. One is, who defines effectiveness? The answer is usually the person supplying the treatment or the person receiving it. It could be that they want their treatment to be regarded as effective, or why else are they doing it? Indeed, why are they working in or attending psychotherapy at all? Second, many symptoms show spontaneous remission, i.e. they diminish, irrespective of which treatment is given. Third, any attempt to measure the effectiveness of any therapy must take the length of time the individual is undergoing the treatment into account. Kenneth Howard et al. (1986) reviewed many studies of the effectiveness of different kinds of psychotherapy, taking into account 'dropping-out' rates. They found that over a third of patients improve after three sessions, over a half by the seventh session, over two-thirds by 16 sessions, and 85 per cent by the first 100 sessions.

Attempts at meta-analysis have been made. Meta-analysis means incorporating the results of previous studies in order to gain overall conclusions. Smith and Glass (1977) and Smith (1980) sampled over 400 studies which had used just about all the major approaches to therapy. They agree with Howard et al.'s meta-analysis, that undergoing any kind of therapy is better than not undergoing one at all. However, it doesn't seem to matter which kind of therapy one has. One reason for this is that no treatment will work unless clients feel that they have a positive relationship with the therapist, and this relationship accounts for some of the initial improvement regardless of which therapy is applied. William Stiles et al. (1986) identify the therapists' 'warm involvement with the client' and their 'communication of a new perspective on the client's person and situation' as the major factors. Andrews (1993) also found that clients who received psychotherapy are 75 per cent more likely to have seen their symptoms reduced compared to those who received no therapy.

The overall conclusion is that cognitive therapies (including cognitive behaviourist approaches using modelling therapy) are highly effective in eliminating simple phobias and associated anxieties and fears. At the moment pioneering advances are being made in hypnosis which are quicker, cheaper, and just as effective as some of the behaviourist therapies for eliminating these symptoms. Humanist therapies are useful in restructuring attitudes and increasing self-esteem. Psychoanalytically inspired therapies were effective with patients exhibiting psychotic symptoms.

There are critical voices claiming that therapists are so convinced of the benefits of their treatments that they ignore, or see as irrelevant, attempts to assess and evaluate the outcomes of their treatments. In *Psychotherapy: Who Benefits?*, Ian Howarth (1989) argues that therapists seem to ignore the outcome of their treatments. If the clients' own reports alone are to be believed, about

► The concept of cure is a particularly difficult one. If I'm not ill, can I be cured? If I do odd things, how many fewer do I need to do before I'm 'better'?

■ **Explain why therapies produce beneficial effects.**

▶ Ethics is a branch of philosophy concerned with culturally defined conceptions of desirable and undesirable states.

half say they feel better with therapy than without. However, 'success is much less impressive when assessed objectively'. Howarth concludes: 'I challenge any psychotherapist to say directly to a client "I can probably make you feel better, but I am unlikely to be any more effective than a friend, a priest, or a good variety of less qualified persons. Moreover there is a real possibility, which we must choose to ignore, that I will reduce your chances of promotion, and make you more likely to become physically or mentally ill." At the present time that is the honest thing to say.'

## Ethical implications for therapy

In addition to the specific ethical issues associated with particular therapies, there are some overall implications of attempts to change the behaviour of others, and of the process of therapy itself. First, Alison Wadeley (1991) makes the point that it isn't only the person whose behaviour or self-concept is being changed by therapy who is involved. Their parents, spouses, siblings, offspring, relations, friends, neighbours and workmates are also likely to be affected. No one lives in a social vacuum and we are all affected by the way others respond to us. Changing one of us has implications for the rest and therapists would do well to bear in mind these external influences and possible support systems.

Psychotherapists are in a uniquely powerful position. By definition they enjoy higher status than the client during the therapy session, at least as far as the client is concerned. They ask the questions, they analyse the answers. They know more about the client's intimate details than the client knows about them. Therefore they owe the client absolute confidentiality and are expected to behave with respect towards each client. They should not allow any sexual relationship to develop and, wherever possible, they must have the informed consent of the client, or the client's spokesperson, before embarking upon any procedure that may affect the client in significant ways. Fortunately, the British Psychological Society, the American Psychiatric Association and other psychological governing bodies publish guidelines and principles of good practice in the treatment of people with symptoms of abnormal behaviour.

## THE WAY FORWARD

In mid-1995 the British Psychological Society and the Royal College of Psychiatrists published their first joint statement called 'Psychological therapies for adults in the NHS', which 'heralds the importance of psychological therapies ... in the National Health Service ... [and] confirms [their] position as an integral part of psychiatry and psychology and as an essential provision within the NHS'. The professional bodies clearly see that there is more to gain from co-operation and integration than from conflict over the labelling or nature of abnormal behaviour. However, it does not overlook the issue of effectiveness of the therapies. It calls for 'specialist teams [to] develop and disseminate research, audit, and evaluation methods in the psychological therapies'. Perhaps in a few years we will be in a better position to judge the effectiveness of the treatments psychologists offer.

## Exam questions – 60 minutes

1 Discuss ethical and practical implications of the psychodynamic and behavioural approaches to abnormal behaviour. (*25 marks*)
2 (a) How does the somatic approach regard abnormal behaviour? (*5 marks*)
  (b) Describe treatments offered by the somatic approach. (*5 marks*)
  (c) Discuss the difficulties involved in evaluating the effectiveness of these treatments. (*15 marks*)

# Part 4
## Cognitive psychology

*So far we have noted the rise of academic psychology and its preoccupation with personality and learning. During the last 40 years psychologists have become increasingly interested in how humans take in, process, store and retrieve information. This has become known as the information-processing approach. In the next three chapters we will review its development and the current state of psychological knowledge.*

# 11 Perceptual processes

## Introduction

Most animals have sensory systems that they can use to help them survive in their own environment. Some have abilities which humans lack, for example bats have echolocation, and migrating birds can use the Earth's magnetic fields. However, humans are capable of acquiring, storing and using more information about the world around us than any other animal. In this chapter we will review the sensory basis of perception and comment on the origin of some of our perceptual skills.

## THE SENSORY BASIS OF PERCEPTION

We have many senses to gather this information. The senses usually quoted are sight, sound, smell, touch and taste. We also have a sense of balance, a sense of our body and where our limbs are, senses of heat and cold, wet and dry, and pain and pleasure. Having detected forms of stimulation we may need to interpret them according to what we know already. We will return to this in the next section. Levine and Shefner (1981) define perception as 'the way in which we interpret the information gathered (and processed) by the senses'. Notice the two stages here. First, gathering information from the world around us through our senses, and second, interpreting that information according to our previous knowledge stored in our memories. In this section we will discuss the first of these – the sensory basis of visual and auditory perception.

## Vision

Textbooks sometimes say that about 90 per cent of all the information that enters our perceptual system is detected through our eyes, although there must be very wide variations in this. The human eye responds to light energy from the visible spectrum, a tiny part of the whole electromagnetic spectrum (see figure 11.1). There are broadcast radio and TV waves, mobile phone radio waves, microwave oven waves, infra-red and ultra-violet waves all around us, which we cannot see with our eyes. All this energy is part of the electromagnetic spectrum and is measured in waves (see figure 11.2).

► Wavelength refers to the distance between the same point (e.g. the top) on two adjacent waves. So we have microwaves, and the BBC used to broadcast on the 'medium wave', and still does on 'long wave'.

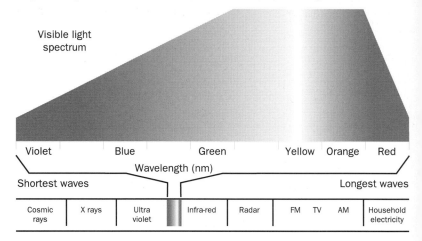

*Figure 11.1 Electromagnetic and visible spectrum*

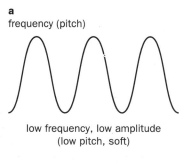

**a**
frequency (pitch)

low frequency, low amplitude
(low pitch, soft)

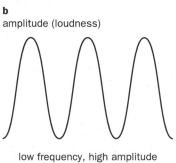

**b**
amplitude (loudness)

low frequency, high amplitude
(low pitch, louder)

*Figure 11.2 Wavelength*

Light energy enters the eye through the corneal lens, which bends to focus the light. The amount of light is controlled by the pupil and the iris, which opens (up to 8 mm diameter) to allow more light and closes (down to 2 mm diameter) to restrict light. The light is further focused by the curvature of the inside of the lens onto the retina at the back of the eye (see figure 11.3) The retina comprises three broad layers of cells. One layer contains the photoreceptors, which detect the light. These are the rods and cones. Each eye contains approximately 115 to 120 million rods, and 6 million cones. The rods are densely packed around the outer edges and become less so towards the centre of the retina. The cones are concentrated in the inner area, particularly in an area called the fovea, where there are about 50,000 cones and no rods at all. Rods are about 500 to 1,000 times more sensitive to light than cones, so enable us to see in fairly dark conditions. However, they do not respond to colour.

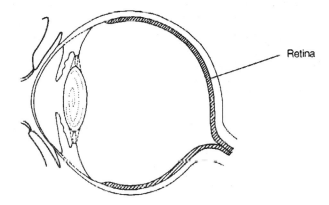

Retina

*Figure 11.3  The eye and retina*

Cones are able to detect colour and fine detail. There are three types of cone, each responding to light of shorter, medium or longer wavelengths from within the visible spectrum. Add to that the amount of light being reflected from the object and we have our experience of colour. A bunch of flowers looks different in bright sunlight compared to how they look on a dull day.

Light is a form of physical energy. However, a different form of energy flows through our visual system. It is the job of the photoreceptors to change one form of energy into another. This is called *transduction*. Here is a simplified description of how transduction works. The rods and cones contain pigments which change their chemical (molecular) structure when they absorb light. These changes trigger tiny electrical charges. If enough rods or cones have absorbed enough light their energy (called potentials) will combine to trigger the next layer of cells on the retina. These are the million or so ganglion cells, although there are other, interconnecting cells as well. They seem to have a role in organizing or co-ordinating the information in some way. If enough electrical energy has stimulated enough ganglion cells it will be passed on to the bipolar cells, which form the beginning of the optic nerve. Transduction will have trig-

▶ The light that we see is called the visible spectrum and can be measured in wavelengths.

▶ It is possible to say that humans have two visual systems, the rod system (for dark conditions) and the cone system (for bright conditions). This is called the duplicity theory of vision.

▶ The kind of energy used in the brain includes positively and negatively charged potassium and sodium molecules, and many other chemical structures. Each sensory system uses its own (unknown) 'code' or pattern of nerve impulses.

■ **Summarize what happens before and immediately after transduction of light.**

gered some early processing of the information before it has left the retina along the optic nerve, and so before the brain has been informed. Information processing seems to start very early in the perceptual system.

At a point called the blind spot (so-called because there aren't any photoreceptors there) the million or so ganglion and bipolar cells leave each retina, pass through the back of each eyeball and form the *optic nerve*. The two optic nerves form the visual pathways. As you can see from figure 11.4, the visual pathways meet at the optic chiasma and some information crosses to the pathway that connects the other eye. Each optic nerve then passes through a part of the brain called the thalamus. The thalamus is a very complicated set of nerve fibres (called neurons) which act as a relay centre for most of our senses. The part of the thalamus that deals with vision is called the lateral geniculate body, and it integrates the information from both eyes before sending it to the visual cortex for further processing.

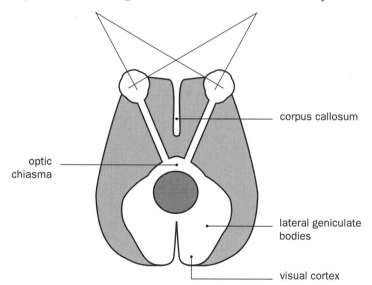

*Figure 11.4 Visual pathways*

► Hubel and Wiesel suggest that cells on the retina are linked directly to cells in the visual cortex (there is a 'point to point' connection).

In the visual cortex there are specialized cells for detecting the elements from which our experience of sight is made up. There are cells that detect colour, line, orientation and so on. Our understanding of the activity in the visual cortex began in 1962 when **David Hubel** and **Thorsten Wiesel** used the single-cell recording technique with cats and monkeys. They suggested the existence of three types of cell in the visual cortex: simple cells, complex cells and hypercomplex cells. Simple cells detect lines of a particular direction which are detected in a specific part of the retina. Complex cells are similar, although they can respond to lines regardless of where they fall on the retina. Hypercomplex cells respond best to lines of a particular length. Hubel and Wiesel thought that simple cells acted together to become complex cells, although this claim seems unlikely now.

Since Hubel and Wiesel an enormous amount of basic research has been conducted on the visual system. Models and theories have been suggested to explain how it works and countless experiments with animals have been conducted to test them. Research on colour vision, different kinds of perception, the way visual skills develop or appear at birth and many aspects besides have been studied. Scientists now have sophisticated high technology in the form of brain-scanning devices and ways of recording brain activity to enable this research with human participants, both those whose perceptual systems function normally, and those whose functioning is damaged in some way. The picture that emerges is that perceptual information processing involves very complex brain activity in many different parts of the brain, and that to understand perceptual functioning we need to have some understanding of the way the system works.

## Hearing

The auditory system is also quite complex. Sound, like light, is a form of energy. It is caused by molecules of air being pushed together, which, in turn, pushes other molecules together. They form a pressure wave and it is this wave that is detected by our ears. Although air is the best medium for transmitting sound, any other medium that has molecules (e.g. water) will also transmit sound. Since water molecules are much denser they cannot move so freely and sound will appear distorted.

The auditory system has three components. The first is the outer ear (or pinna), which collects the sound waves and passes them down the auditory canal to the eardrum (or timpanum). This vibrates, depending on the intensity of the sound wave. Each ear will detect those waves that fall on it first (see figure 11.5). Combining the sounds gives us our impression of stereo sound, and is a cue to judging distance. Since our ears are physically separate it is possible, with headphones and tape-recorders, to play different messages into each ear. This led psychologists to study the way humans selectively attend to some stimuli and not others, as we shall see in Chapter 12.

▶ Scientists often use models. They are mini-theories or illustrations of what something might be like, or how it might work. A model may provide the basis for some research to find out if the model really does represent the structure or process being explained. A theory usually takes the form of a statement that may then be tested in some way.

▶ Our perceptual system can take in a vast amount of sensory data, but our cognitive systems cannot attend equally to all of it. Interesting questions are: what capacity for paying attention do we have, how many things can we pay attention to at the same time, and how is the decision about what is selectively attended to and what is left out made?

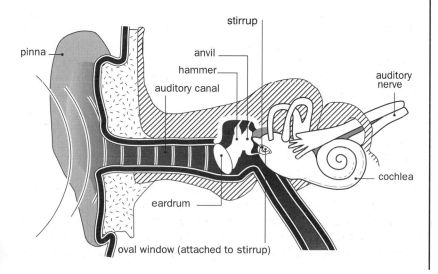

Figure 11.5  *The ear*

▶ *Cognition* is the general name of all those processes by which we 'know' things. Direct experience, thinking and reasoning, language, attention and memory are all part of cognition.

■ **Summarize what happens before and immediately after transduction of sound.**

The second area is the middle ear, which begins at the inside of the eardrum. The ossicles are three tiny bones, the hammer (malleus), the anvil (incus) and the stirrup (stapes), which amplify or reduce the vibrations, passing these modified vibrations through the oval window into the inner ear. As with vision, the auditory system itself seems to be processing and dealing with some aspects of the information before it reaches consciousness. These mechanisms have led psychologists to describe the whole of human perceptual processing as an 'information-processing system', which starts with sensations and ends with *cognition.*

The principal structure in the inner ear is the cochlea. This looks like a snail, but is about the size of a peanut. Inside there are three fluid-filled channels running its length from the broad outer end at the oval window to the small inner end at the centre of its spiral (see figure 11.5). One of the channels is separated from another by the basilar membrane, which is covered in microscopic hair cells. These cells transduce the physical energy caused by vibrations on the oval window (which trigger waves in the fluid to move the hair cells) into the kind of chemical energy the auditory system uses.

Nerve fibres (neurons) leave the cochlea and form the auditory nerve. As with the optic nerve, the auditory nerve passes through relay centres on its way to the auditory centres, where complex sounds such as language will be interpreted. First stop is the medulla oblongata (a group of cells at the point where the spine enters the brain which is involved in vital bodily functions such as breathing and blood circulation). Next is the midbrain (further vital bodily functioning) before it reaches the thalamus and finally the auditory centres.

## Summary – The sensory basis of perception

After 2.5 million years of human evolution we have acquired many highly complex biological structures in the brain. These allow sensory processing to begin at the level of the sense receptors themselves. The photoreceptors on the retina and the hair cells in the cochlea transduce physical energy into a biological code which can be further processed in other brain structures. Human perception begins with sensory input and often ends with cognition.

## THEORIES OF PERCEPTION

All our senses provide information about our immediate surroundings. We also have memories of what things that surround us are like. **Herman von Helmholtz** (1821–94) suggested that information provided by our senses is extended by unconscious inferences. Most psychologists probably argue that we use both these sources of information to know what we are perceiving at any particular time. This would make sense, otherwise there may not be much point in having vast memories. However, not everyone agrees. Another explanation for perception is that we build up our knowledge about what is going on around us directly from fairly minimal processing of sensory information. There are enough cues in what we experience directly to enable us to make correct judgements about what we perceive. This is called perception from the 'bottom up'. The opposite is perception from the 'top down', which says that we need those previous experiences stored in our memories in order to make sense of perception.

## Bottom-up theories

**James Gibson** (1950) rejected previous theories of perception (see the next section on top-down theories). Most had been developed from laboratory studies, which tested people's perception under very controlled conditions, quite unlike how we see things in real life. He claimed that our sense receptors could detect enough information about objects in our everyday environment for us to make perfectly good sense of them. For example, as we move around any object such as a chair its relationship to objects around it changes. Our eyes take in all of this constantly changing information, giving us all the visual stimulation that we need to make sense of the chair. Gibson claimed that perception is *direct* with no need for input from other thought processes. For example, there is no need for intelligence to be involved.

Gibson claims that all life forms have evolved within a particular environment (for many fish the underwater environment, for many birds the air is the environment). Having developed such a close and meaningful relationship with one's environment there seems little need for further processing. Indeed, many relatively simple life forms have sufficient perceptual skills to allow them to thrive, yet aren't capable of thought as we know it at all. Gibson believed that many species genetically inherit the abilities to decode their perceptions in their everyday existence. His theory is sometimes referred to as an *ecological theory of perception* for this reason.

Perception of objects and events always takes place when we are in some physical situation such as in class, at home, on a plane or in a car. Gibson also notes that we are in a psychological state such as happy, angry, upset or hopeful, and we are in a physiological state, such as wide awake, hungry, exhausted or excited. Add to these our constantly changing perception of the object and this information together allows us to know not only what the object is, but also what it does. Gibson calls this the *'affordance'* of the object. So you know things like how inviting the chair is to sit on, depending on where it is (physical), e.g. in your sitting room at home or beyond a barrier in a stately home. Second, you know how you feel about sitting down (psychological), e.g. knowing that you'd love to but must prepare a meal instead. Finally, you know how tired you are (physiological). Note that Gibson does not say that no processing of sensory information occurs in the perceptual system. Obviously it

▶ According to bottom-up theories what you see is what you get. Top-down theorists argue that what you see is the result of some perceptual processing.

▶ *Ecology* is the study of the relationships between members of a particular species and their environment.

■ **Look at Levine and Shefner's definition of perception at the beginning of this chapter (page 225). How far does Gibson's view agree with or differ from theirs?**

does. He does claim that this processing is unnecessary for the immediate perception of the meaning that objects that we see have for us.

Gibson claims that the senses detect a huge amount of information from the environment and perception is available as soon as it is registered on the retina. **David Marr** (1982) offers a computational model of how we recognize objects in the visual system (based on how computers could be programmed to recognize objects). Recognition starts with identifying the edges, borders or boundaries between one thing and another. Before you can recognize your friend when she enters a room you must be able to tell what lines, colours, textures and so on belong to her, and which belong to the furniture, wallpaper or bookcase. Marr claims that information from the retina can be organized into two kinds of features. First, *contours* are the edges of shapes in three dimensions. Your friend's face shows different contours if she is looking straight at you, or is sideways on to you. You still recognize her. The second feature involves *regions of similarity*, where an area (such as a painted wall or field of grass) doesn't have many distinguishing features.

Having made some computations about contours and boundaries the visual system is supposed to perform an algorithm. This is a form of testing which tries every possible solution until it reaches the one that is most likely to work. If several solutions might work it will find the one most likely to be successful. Finally, there is the implementation level at which the system is supposed to test itself to make sure that all the nerve cells and so on are actually present so that the algorithm will be able to be implemented.

► As human behaviour, especially mental behaviour, is highly complex, psychologists often use models to help understand it. The development of computing has been a primary source of such models in cognitive psychology.

■ How do (a) James Gibson and (b) David Marr explain human visual perception?

> ### Summary – Bottom-up theories
> Bottom-up theorists argue that our sense receptors are able to detect enough information to know all that we need to know about objects around us, and that this skill has evolved as we have adapted to our environments. This approach has posed a fairly radical challenge to other theories, but relatively little experimental evidence has been gathered to support it.

## Top-down theories

Gibson and Marr's theories are challenging but cannot explain why, for example, we perceive visual illusions (see pages 253–5). If all you needed to make sense of your surroundings was instantly available on your retina then you wouldn't be fooled by visual illusions that appear to result from the way that information is processed in the perceptual system. Top-down theories which suggest that our perceptions are constructed as a result of perceptual processing may be more convincing. They are sometimes called *constructivist theories* and began with Herman von Helmholtz, who believed that it was necessary to look for the influence of thoughts and unconscious mental processing only when the detection of the

► *Constructivist theories* say we build up our final interpretation or impression of what we see based on making judgements from previous experience.

sensations early in the perceptual system alone could not explain the perception. So, if something was highly visible and obvious, such as a large brown horse at 10 metres distance in the midday sun, the perception required little processing. If it was dark, and there were many distractions such as other horses and fireworks going off, it would require more processing.

Probably the best known advocate of top-down perception is **Richard Gregory**. Like Marr, Gregory was interested in how patterns of light falling on the retina are interpreted as objects. Usually there is sufficient information for us to know what we are looking at. When the information received isn't what was expected, as with visual illusions, the perceptual system seems to search for clues that allow it to infer what the perception means. Inference refers to the way we draw conclusions about something that we couldn't reasonably know, such as whether a stranger 'looks intelligent', whether an apple 'looks juicy', and so on. Gregory's theory is sometimes called *inference theory*. Perception is seen as the result of a process that begins with a stimulus, but then requires information from our thought processes such as the expectations that we have of what an object looks like, and our previous experiences. These will interact with the stimulus to help us to infer what we can see. All this processing is unconscious, instant and automatic. Since perceptual processing relies on inferences deriving from previous experiences and so on, we occasionally make mistakes, for example being fooled by visual illusions.

Gregory claims perception results from inference and interpretation, but if so, we would probably make more mistakes than we actually do. Remember that Gregory was trying to explain why visual illusions work in the controlled laboratory conditions to which Gibson's ecological theory objected. Gibson maintains that in everyday life we rarely experience such illusions.

> ► It may be hard to see how a process of inference can also be described as automatic. The process is triggered automatically and runs through automatically, i.e. without the conscious intervention of the perceiver.

> ■ Write one sentence that would explain to a non-psychologist how James Gibson would explain perception, then one more to explain how Richard Gregory explains it.

> ■ Write one sentence for each of the two explanations that identifies their significant weakness.

---

### Summary – Top-down theories

Top-down theorists argue that there isn't enough information available at the level of the sense receptors to know everything that is necessary to know about what an object is like, what it is for, what one can do with it or how to react to it. Instead there has to be cognitive processing of that information based on one's existing knowledge, expectations and ability to infer. We will return to these ideas at the end of this chapter.

---

## So which theory is best?

Neither direct nor constructivist theories of perception can explain all perception all of the time. Gibson's ecological theory assumes that people can view objects in their environments under good viewing conditions. The objects are being viewed for long enough and provide plenty of visual information. However, one of the best known theories of perceptual organization, Gestalt theory (see pages 247–9), was investigated in the laboratory. Gregory's inference or constructivist theories have investigated viewing under controlled conditions. **Endel Tulving** et al. conducted an experiment involving word recognition. He suggests that under perfect viewing conditions we don't need to use other sources of information and there may be little processing. Where the conditions were poor we do look for other cues to aid processing. This supports von Helmholtz's suggestions of a century earlier.

A theory which tries to combine the strengths of both direct and constructivist theories was suggested by **Ulric Neisser** (1976). He says that we create perceptual expectations about what we are likely to see in given contexts (top-down processing). So, we expect to see our friends in our classroom for our psychology lesson. These expectations combine with what we actually see (bottom-up processing). The expectations are checked against the reality. If the reality matches the expectations then perception is complete. Checks are made if any aspect of the perception changes. If the two do not match then they must be modified until a match is found. This is called *cyclic theory* because of the checking and double-checking.

▶ In *cyclic* explanations the process of perception is constantly being checked against reality so that perceptions are constantly being modified.

Alternative bottom-up explanations of how we know what we are seeing are *feature detection theories*. These were first suggested by **Oliver Selfridge** in 1959. Selfridge says that, as we acquire new knowledge of what things are like, we build up libraries of features that we know belong to them in memory. So a friend may have the following features: medium height, fairly slim, green eyes, blonde hair, long hair, straight hair, dresses in black. If you see someone with some of these features you will look to see if there are more features that match until you can decide whether that person is your friend.

Selfridge had developed a computer programme called Pandemonium, which was used for reading Morse code. It read the features (dots and dashes) and when enough of them matched Morse code letters it displayed the Morse message. It used a system called **TOTE**, which stands for **T**est (look for a particular feature), **O**perate (attempt to make the actual features fit the ones being sought), **T**est (try again), **E**xit (if it now fits, or exit this trial and start again). Lindsay and Norman (1972) modified the programme to read some letters of the alphabet (assuming that we recognize features that make up letters when we read).

▶ Models of how perception works have often been derived from understanding how computers work. They are useful as starting points but are often limited by the inadequacy of computing machines compared to highly evolved human brains.

Based on the Pandemonium programme Selfridge suggests that there are four levels of detectors called demons. If the feature they are designed to detect exists in the sensory information they are said to 'shriek'. The lowest level of demons (*image demons*) simply detect the existence of an image or pattern on the retina. *Feature demons* analyse this pattern for the features that they recognize. So those demons that detect round lines shriek after the image demons have shrieked when the photoreceptors were stimulated by a capital D. Those that detect vertical lines also shriek. But is it a D or an O? Other demons detect other features about size and orientation until enough shrieking is going on to stimulate the third level of demons. These are the *cognitive demons*, which shriek when they detect the letter they recognize from all the shrieking feature demons. Those that detect an O are shrieking, but those that detect a D are shrieking louder. At the top level, the *decision demons* respond to the loudest shrieks and we perceive the capital D. This process is consistent with what Hubel and Wiesel claimed for the point to point connections between photoreceptors on the retina and some cells in the visual cortex (see page 228). This explanation is all very well for recognizing letters, but its origin in a computer programme makes it very 'mechanical', since early computers did work on TOTE principles. The theory does not explain everyday perception or how perception would be modified by psychological factors.

## PERCEPTUAL DEVELOPMENT AND HOW IT IS STUDIED

The job of all our senses is to provide perceptual information from which we can know, understand, and be able to survive and thrive in our environment. The process of perception will combine information from several of the senses. For example, we mentioned how vision and hearing are both relayed through the thalamus. Some of us may have a vast, flexible and highly efficient perceptual system, others of us may be slower in our thinking and perceiving. Some of the differences and similarities between people will have been caused and others influenced by our genetic inheritance. Some will result from our social experiences. To ask the question 'are perceptual skills in humans innate or learned?' is really to misunderstand the complexities of the perceptual system. Still, if you want an answer to the question asked, it's 'yes'. In this section we will review some of the main psychological interests in perceptual development, and in doing so, will note how experiments have been used to investigate them.

## The nature–nurture debate

Those who supported the view that many human capacities, including perceptual skills, are present at birth or develop gradually according to a pre-set programme of maturation, are called *nativists* and are said to support the nature side of the nature–nurture argument. Those who believed that a variety of sensory experiences (light, colour, form, pattern, texture etc.) are necessary for the perceptual system to operate are called *nurturists*. They claimed that we learn from our experiences. This dispute has underpinned a great deal of research in the area of perceptual development.

One of the founding fathers of academic psychology, **William James** (1890), said that all the senses are integrated at birth and any experience will be interpreted by all those senses that are stimulat-

■ **Outline attempts to combine ecological and constructivist explanations for visual perception.**

► Innate means present at birth and only requiring a reasonable diet in an environment that is not too threatening for the skill to appear with maturation (i.e. as we develop towards physical and psychological maturity).

► The nature–nurture (or heredity–environment) debate goes back a long way in psychology. It concerns the relative contributions of experience, environment and learning on the one hand, and genetic inheritance, biological factors and 'nature' on the other, to the making of human beings.

► An *interactionist* believes that those structures and functions that are present at birth will be modified by the environment in which one grows up. The state of functioning anyone achieves depends on the quality of the interaction between innate forces, such as genetic inheritance, and environmental forces, such as socialization.

► Whilst no one would dispute that human neonates (neonate means newborn) have some visual abilities, their perceptual world may be quite different, and require some learning, in order to make sense of it.

■ How would (a) a nativist, (b) a nurturist and (c) an interactionist explain a human infant's abilities to recognize its primary caregivers?

► The word 'infant' comes from a Latin word meaning 'before speech'. Since human infants don't talk much before their first birthday we can think of infancy as the first year of life.

ed by it. Only as the child gains experience will it learn what sensations are to be interpreted by which senses. Nativists are more sympathetic to bottom-up explanations, whereas nurturists would favour top-down theories of perception. Few psychologists now would regard themselves as either nativist or nurturist. Most are *interactionists*. We will review the main contributors to the debate.

### The nature view – perception is innate

Perceptual development has been speculated about by philosophers for hundreds of years, but its systematic study really began in the 1960s, when some original and inventive psychologists began to devise ways in which perception in very young babies could be studied. There are several problems associated with studying infants – they can't answer your questions, they aren't necessarily co-operative, and just because they don't do something doesn't mean they can't. So testers have to be particularly inventive! One of the first was **Robert Fantz**, who investigated how clearly babies of different ages could see, and whether they could distinguish various patterns.

*Pattern perception*

Do infants perceive objects as whole shapes? Do they have any preference for looking at one pattern of colours, lines or textures rather than another? Fantz designed some apparatus called a *looking chamber* (see figure 11.6), which would allow him to observe children's gaze and time how long they looked in a particular direction. He thought that children will gaze longer at things they find more interesting. They will quickly look away from things they find uninteresting. He could also judge their facial expressions and body movements to see if they looked interested.

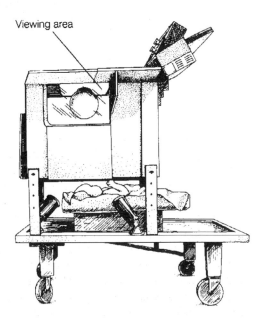

Viewing area

*Figure 11.6 Fantz's looking chamber*

In one experiment Fantz tested 30 infants at weekly intervals, from when they were one week old until they were 15 weeks old. Various objects and pictures were placed in the looking chamber. He showed them different shapes and patterns such as a bull's eye pattern, stripes of various thicknesses, a cross, a chessboard design, plain triangles and plain squares. Fantz found that even the youngest infants generally preferred the more complicated shapes, such as the bull's eye and the chessboard. Therefore some degree of form perception may well be innate. Ethologists (who study behaviour in its natural environment – see Konrad Lorenz's work in Chapter 5) claimed that human infants are born with a preference for seeking out the human face. Fantz investigated this claim.

In a very early experiment (1961) Fantz showed 49 infants between four days and six months of age three pictures (see figure 11.7). The first was a crude drawing of a face with black features on a pink background. The next was the same as the first, but the features were all jumbled up, and the third was a pink face shape without any features except for the hair. Most of the infants ignored the face without features altogether. The six-month-olds barely glanced at it. The children up to about three and a half months of age seemed interested in the scrambled features. The infants all appeared slightly more interested in the picture that was closest to a real face. Although the differences were quite small Fantz did conclude that human infants are born with a preference for looking at the human face. This claim appeared to support the nativists, who believe that infants have innate capacities to recognize other humans, although the differences were too small to justify the claim.

▶ Fantz claimed to have shown that human infants as young as one week can perceive form or pattern and that, during the next six months, their vision improves so that they can see increasingly complicated patterns of lines and shapes.

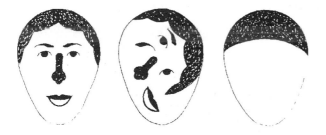

*Figure 11.7  Fantz's face shapes*

Several criticisms can be made of Fantz's early experiment. Although the looking chamber provided an ingenious way of experimenting on babies and recording their responses, the pictures of the 'faces' were two-dimensional black and pink drawings that didn't look anything like 'real' faces. They didn't move, either, whereas human faces are always changing expression. Other researchers have used Fantz's methods and repeated his experiments, but either have not made similar findings, or have offered other explanations for them. **Marshall Haith** (1980) suggests that the reason why the infants looked at the picture of the 'scrambled' face and the face drawings was that they both contained the same amount of contour. David Marr maintains that contour is one of the

▶ Here we have two contrasting methods for finding the truth of the origins of form perception. One is the experimental method, with a looking chamber apparatus and various stimulus objects, a carefully controlled procedure and a specific sample to test. The other is the natural observation and speculative theory. Haith and Marr have made observations of the topic and offered possible explanations, which may then form the basis of experiments.

▶ *Schemas* are strategies, plans, frameworks or basic ideas about action – about what goes with what.

■ Would Fantz be described as a supporter of top-down or bottom-up theory? Explain your answer.

■ Why is a combination of experiment and theory very useful for psychological research? In your answer distinguish between basic and applied research and give examples.

main features that humans perceive. Haith claims that human infants are 'information seekers' who use the following strategy:

1  If sufficiently aware, open your eyes.
2  If possible, scan the surroundings.
3  If no contours are found, continue the search.
4  If contours are detected, study them.
5  Keep scanning for more contours and study any found.

If Haith is right, the infants in Fantz's experiment were just studying contours, not preferring faces. Fantz and various colleagues have investigated other factors involved in infants' visual preferences. For example, Fantz and Hagan (1975) found that one-month-old neonates prefer to look at rather simpler objects. They used two stimuli, one had eight 1-inch squares, the other had 32 1/4-inch squares (same amount of contour). By two months the infants prefer the more complex shape. Similar findings were made about curvature. At one month infants showed no preference for round or straight objects, by two months they preferred round ones.

**Jerome Kagan** (1971) offers an alternative explanation for why two-month-olds spend longer looking at one object rather than another. His theory is that, at birth, infants have no idea about what anything looks like. Soon they acquire basic ideas about 'roundness', 'contour' and so on as they look at their caregivers' faces. A basic idea about what something is like is called a *schema*. Simply, two-month-old infants (and babies of any age) spend longer studying things for which they have no schema (in order to acquire one) than objects of which they already have some experience.

Whether Fantz's findings do support the nature approach is difficult to argue. It could be that maturation triggers the infants' preferences, or equally they could have gathered enough experience by two months to know what round things are like, and to associate them with pleasure perhaps? Kagan would certainly say so. (NB Pavlov was the first to investigate association learning in dogs – see Chapter 1.)

### Depth, distance and direction perception

Another original experiment was conducted by **Eleanor Gibson** and **Richard Walk** in 1960. They wanted to test whether human infants were able to judge depth soon after birth (if so, it was probably genetically inherited), or whether this had to be learned later. One principle of evolutionary adaptation (from Charles Darwin, 1809–82) suggests that animals evolve those skills that they need in order to survive in their environment. The animal will show those skills when it is mature enough to use them. If so, then it is unlikely that human infants would have depth perception soon after birth. Since they can't move around on their own, and couldn't do anything to stop themselves from falling even if they could perceive depth, it seems unlikely that they would have inherited any ability to judge it.

On the other hand, the ability to judge depth and distance is very important to visual perception. The majority of things you look at will have depth. People and things will be nearer to or further from you. How could you reach for something and pick it up if you couldn't perceive distance? In this case it does make some sense that the ability to judge depth and distance might be present from birth just waiting to be used.

Gibson and Walk constructed some apparatus known as the visual cliff, which comprised a sheet of non-reflective glass covering a table top. Half of the table top had been removed. A piece of chequered cloth covered the remaining table top, fell to the floor where the top was removed, and lay along the floor. The illusion would be that the apparatus had a shallow side and a deep side. A shelf was placed along the edge between the deep and shallow sides (see figure 11.8).

Some newborn animals were placed on the shelf, and Gibson and Walk recorded their responses. Most of the animals tested would not move over the deep side. Even one-day-old chicks never strayed onto the deep side. Lambs and kids placed on the deep side refused to stand, and kittens either froze or circled backwards. Rats were the only animals that would venture onto the deep side. Rats rely on their whiskers as guides and so touch is more important to them than vision. When the researchers trimmed their whiskers and they were forced to use vision, they also wouldn't move onto the deep side. This seems to confirm the view that animals have innate depth perception.

Just because other animals possess some innate perceptual skills does not mean that humans possess them too. The problem for Gibson and Walk in testing humans is that their apparatus needs the subjects to be mobile, to see whether they would cross onto the deep side. Humans aren't mobile before six months or so. By this time they could have learned about depth and distance. However, Gibson and Walk did try 36 human infants of between six and 14 months of age on the visual cliff. They were placed on the shelf between the shallow and deep sides and a parent called them from one side, then from the other. Nine infants refused to move at all, but the 27 infants who did would crawl to their parents over the shallow side, and only three crawled over the deep side. Some crawled away from their parents when they were being called from the deep side, others just cried because they couldn't reach their parent. Some of the infants fell onto the glass on the deep side, and started to crawl towards their parent until they looked down. Once they saw the chequered cloth at some distance below them they became distressed. Before looking down these infants were presumably using their sense of touch, which told them that the surface they were crawling over was safe. As soon as they looked down their sense of vision must have overruled their sense of touch. Vision is a powerful source of information for babies.

**Joseph Campos** and some colleagues (1970) had sensors which would monitor heart rate fitted to infants below six months of age,

▶ Even very young infants will try to reach and grasp things that are offered to them. Within a few months they have learned what sort of things they can grasp and what they cannot.

*Figure 11.8 The visual cliff*

▶ Psychologists have sometimes used animals in their experiments in the past where, for various reasons, it would not have been possible to use humans. Although the findings may be interesting they don't necessarily help us to understand human behaviour.

▶ Whether depth perception is innate or not isn't certain; what is shown by this experiment is that human infants certainly have it by six months.

and had them lowered over each side of the visual cliff. At one month the heart rates did not fluctuate over either side of the cliff, probably because the infants hadn't developed an ability to recognize depth, or to associate it with danger. By two months the heart rates decreased over the deep side, suggesting greater interest being shown. Perhaps they were developing a schema for depth? **Michael Eysenck** (1993) suggests that we should be very cautious in accepting the findings of the visual cliff experiments. He points out that nine-month-old infants' heart rate increased when placed over the deep side, suggesting that they perceived the 'drop' and were frightened by it.

**Tom Bower** (1977) has also devised some ingenious experiments to investigate infants' visual abilities to judge distance and direction. Babies are born with about 50 reflexive responses. Doctors use one of them, the defensive reaction, to test whether babies are blind. An object is moved towards an infant's face. If the babies are blind, they will not react. If they can see the approaching object they will try to lean out of the way or lift their arms to protect their faces. This suggests that the ability to judge direction is innate. Judging direction of movement is an essential ingredient in judging distance or depth. So why do the infants lift their arms or try to move away from the oncoming object? There are two possibilities. Either the ability to judge direction is innate, or they are responding to the movement of air towards their faces as the object approaches. Bower experimentally tested this possibility. He arranged three experimental conditions.

*Condition 1*: A foam rubber cube is slowly moved towards the baby's face (and the air around it is displaced in the normal way). This produced the classic defensive response.
*Condition 2*: The air was displaced but there was no cube. The infants didn't appear to take any notice.
*Condition 3*: The baby saw a film of the object slowly moving towards it. Obviously no air was being displaced as the film is two-dimensional. The infants showed no defensive reaction here either.

Bower's experiment supports the view that an infant's ability to judge direction is innate. Infants show distress if an object appears to be heading straight for their face but do not show concern when the same object would miss them, even by just an inch or two! The defensive reaction is also probably innate. (For evidence from Tom Bower on infants' early perceptual skills, see the discussion on pages 252–3 on size constancy.)

These experiments also indicate some of the limitations of the baby's visual system. Infants can take in a great deal of information, but cannot process it as quickly as an adult can. Jerome Kagan and Jean Piaget (see Chapter 15) said that babies have relatively few schemas and those that they do have are quite limited. If the object in the defensive reaction experiment was heading for the baby at any speed, then the baby didn't respond at all. The information

■ Evaluate Gibson and Walk's contribution to our understanding of depth perception.

■ What evidence does Bower give for his view that direction perception is present soon after birth?

would probably have been sent to the brain, but the brain isn't mature and well organized enough to respond very quickly.

### Summary – Depth perception

Gibson and Walk's clever experiments do not allow them to claim that depth perception is innate in humans. The visual cliff experiment requires that the human participants can crawl, so they have to be six months old or more. Much learning occurs during the first few months of life, as Kagan and others have shown, so the infants could have learned depth perception. Gibson and Walk did say that the results support their view that depth perception is innate in animals. Tom Bower finds more convincing evidence that direction perception is innate in his 'defensive reaction' experiments.

*Experiments with animals*

Before we leave the nature view, some strong evidence in support of some visual skills being innate in origin comes from another aspect of the development of perception – experiments with animals, as Gibson and Walk demonstrated. Here is another example.

The first visual perception experiments with animal subjects were conducted in the 1960s by Robert Fantz. He hatched some chicks in total darkness. Since chicks will peck at grain soon after birth, and well before they could have learned that grain is their food, it seems reasonable to assume that they have an instinctive knowledge of what their food looks like. Fantz gave his chicks eight tiny, different-shaped objects and recorded the number of times they pecked at each of them. The objects were different shapes ranging from a small round object, similar to a grain, to pyramid-shaped objects (see figure 11.9). The chicks pecked ten times more at the round objects than the ones that didn't look anything like grains. Fantz concluded that chicks innately recognize round shapes and objects with three dimensions. This supports the nature view that shape recognition in chicks is innate.

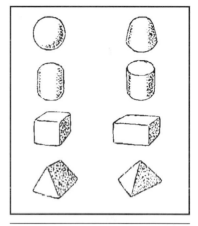

*Figure 11.9  Fantz's chicken food*

► Like most animals, chicks rely much more on instinct and are much more mobile soon after birth than human infants. Being able to recognize food would obviously be of great benefit to survival. It is likely to be genetically inherited. Human infants can't feed themselves anyway, so recognizing food wouldn't help much. Human infants have a rooting reflex, where touching their cheek (perhaps with a nipple?) causes them to turn their heads towards the touch, and they open their mouth.

■ List as many advantages and disadvantages as you can think of for psychologists using animals in their research.

### Summary – The nature view

Whilst infants may not have many innate recognition skills they may have some other visual skills present from birth. Depth perception is difficult to demonstrate in human babies, although we do seem able to predict direction (and appear to have an understanding of relative size, as we will see later in this chapter).

### The nurture view – the case for learning

If perceptual skills have to be learned, then people who had been blind since birth, who then had their sight restored, would take some time to learn to recognize all the things that normally sighted people recognize straight away. Studies of sight-restored patients showed that they need very little time to learn to recognize familiar objects, judge depth and distance, and so on. However, learning to recognize unfamiliar objects by sight alone proved more difficult. In 1932 von Senden found that adult patients who had their sight restored had basic perceptual skills such as distinguishing an object from the background, but they had difficulty in naming objects using sight alone.

In 1963 Gregory and Wallace reported the case of a 52-year-old man who had eye surgery to give him sight, having been blind from birth. He quickly learned to recognize and judge things which he had experienced before through his senses (unlike von Senden's patients). For example, he could tell the distance between objects such as his bed and the door, and he knew the size of objects that he knew from touch. He did have problems learning to recognize new objects, though, and understanding distances between things of which he had no previous experience. He never learned to interpret what people were thinking or feeling by looking at their faces, although he could interpret well using their tone of voice.

▶ Here we are using a case study of an adult to give us insights into visual skills which we can then investigate in infants. This is another useful technique for studying perceptual development.

There are several problems with these kind of studies to untangle the influences of nature and nurture. First, they use human adults who can explain and answer questions on what they see. They may have learned from previous experience and so their answers may not reflect nature's or nurture's separate contributions. Second, having had considerable experience using their other senses adults come to rely on them so don't need to use their new visual skills. Gregory and Wallace's subject would sometimes sit all evening in the dark rather than turn the light on. Finally, even if sight-restored adults did learn visual skills, this doesn't necessarily solve the nature–nurture riddle. Just because adults can learn visual skills, such as judging distance, this doesn't mean that infants have to learn them. They may well still be innate.

▶ A *readjustment study* is usually an experiment in which people have some aspect of their normal routines changed to see if they can adapt their behaviour, and how long it takes them to do so.

If human visual skills have to be learned, then they can be relearned. This idea is tested in *readjustment studies*. Altering the way in which someone perceives the world, for example by making them wear goggles with lenses that distort their view, shouldn't cause long-term difficulties. They should be able to learn to adjust their behaviour. The following experiments seem to suggest that this is true.

▶ An *inverting lens* turns everything one sees upside down, and also reverses left and right.

**George Stratton** (1897) wore a patch over one eye so that he couldn't see anything through it, and an *inverting lens* over the other eye, which made everything he looked at appear upside down and left to right. Objects that were to his right looked as though they were on his left. He walked into things that he was trying to avoid, and looked to his right to try to recognize a noise he could hear coming from his left. He wore the lens for eight days to discover if he could make a visual adjustment. By the fifth day he was able to walk around without bumping into things. While he was moving around everything appeared fine. When he stopped, and concentrated on an object, it appeared to be upside down.

Stratton claimed that his eyes had adjusted to his altered perceptions, but many researchers were not convinced.

J. and **J.K. Peterson** (1938) used inverting lenses on both eyes of a sample of people, and found similar results to Stratton, although not all of the subjects could adapt to their new perception. Eight months later they retested their participants and found that they adapted to their upside-down world more quickly than before. They quickly learned to avoid furniture and do most things that others could do. Clearly learning is involved in perception. In another study an Australian professor was so confident in his new skills that he used to ride his bicycle to college. When a participant in this type of research was asked whether what he was looking at really appeared upside down he replied: 'I wish you hadn't asked me … when I recall how they did look before I put on these lenses … they do look upside down now … until … you asked me I was absolutely unaware of it.'

In the mid-1960s **Ivo Köhler** tested different lenses that distorted sight in several different ways. Some had different-coloured lenses, some turned the line of sight slightly to the left or to the right. After a few hours of wearing each of his distorting lenses he was able to adapt his behaviour to cope with his changed visual experiences.

These readjustment studies seem to support the nurture view, that perception results from learning. If it was innate then we would never be able to adjust it. However, things aren't quite as straightforward as they seem to be. People do seem able to make some adaptation to changes to their visual experiences. These adaptations are in their responses, not in their perceptions. They do not start seeing the world the right way round; rather, they begin to learn how to behave in an upside-down one. In other words, it isn't their vision that is readjusting, it is their behavioural response to it. They are simply learning what to do to compensate for their visual distortions. For example, you know that your lenses make everything on the right appear to be on the left. So if you see something on your left, you know that you have to turn your head to the right to see it.

> ► All of the experiments discussed so far have failed to solve the nature–nurture debate. It is unlikely that any ever will. Human perception is very complex and is bound to be affected by all sorts of influences.

> ■ What are the advantages of studying sight-restored adults over studying infants when investigating visual perception? What are the findings from such studies? How useful are they in contributing to the nature–nurture debate?

> ■ Evaluate the contribution of readjustment studies in understanding the learning of visual skills.

---

### Summary – The nurture view

Studies of blind people who have their sight restored show that they quickly learn to recognize things that they knew by touch. Readjustment studies show that humans can adapt their behaviour to take account of new visual experiences, although this isn't the same as making a visual adaptation.

---

The research so far has either used adults or children. There are inevitably problems in using humans in this type of research. One way to investigate the contribution of biology and learning is by experimenting on animals.

## Further studies with animals

In 1950 **A.N. Reisen** reported his study in which he kept a male and

► Deprivation studies such as these were carried out before people became more concerned with animal rights. They probably would not be allowed now.

► Several experiments in dark-rearing have been conducted. They have proved inconclusive, despite the obvious suffering of the animals involved.

► Reisen's experiments were often carried out on very few subjects (and sometimes only one), and so we must be cautious about any generalizations we make from them. His subjects did have some visual experiences, too. He turned the light on for 45 seconds each day to allow the animals to feed.

► A *critical period* is a period of time, usually shortly after birth, when something must be experienced if normal development is to follow.

a female monkey in the dark, so depriving them of sight, for their first 16 months of life. He reasoned that if perception is innate, this early deprivation won't make any difference, they'll still be able to see well enough. When they were exposed to light at 16 months they couldn't open their eyes like normal monkeys, they appeared scared by bright lights, they had no blink reflex when something moved towards them quickly, and they had no interest in their toys unless they touched them first. This suggests that perception isn't entirely innate.

One monkey remained in the normally lit conditions. Over the next five months its visual skills developed until its sight was normal. It had good hand-to-eye co-ordination and could recognize objects by sight. The other chimp was returned to the dark for another 16 months. When exposed to normal light it behaved in the same way as it had earlier. Its abilities improved slightly over the next few weeks, then declined.

**Michael Weiskrantz** (1956) showed how rearing in the dark stops normal development of retinal cells and cells in the visual pathway, so these chimps had poor visual skills because their visual system was damaged. Weiskrantz claimed that light was necessary for the normal development of the visual system. Consequently Reisen reared another monkey who was made to wear a translucent mask, which allowed one and a half hours of diffused, unpatterned light to enter the eye each day. Translucent means that light can pass through, but not distinct patterns or shapes (like looking through greaseproof paper). The mask was removed at seven months. This animal also did not develop normal sight. It seems that patterned light was necessary for the development of a normally functioning system.

**Colin Blakemore** and **Grahame Cooper** (1970) showed how important early visual experience is in developing normal visual skills. They reared some kittens in the dark, except for periods when the kittens were placed inside large drums that were painted on the inside. Some cats were in a drum which had vertical black and white stripes, while the other drum had horizontal black and white stripes. When they stood up the kittens reared in each drum could only see either vertical or horizontal black and white lines. The *critical period* for kittens developing visual skills was thought to be from three to 15 weeks of life. Blakemore and Cooper tested their visual abilities from when the kittens were five months old.

If visual skills are simply innate, then the animals' early experience wouldn't have much influence and the kittens would be able to see normally when removed from the drum. If it was the result of nurture they wouldn't be able to see anything different from the lines inside their drums. At first the kittens could not recognize anything with edges that were different from the ones they had seen inside their drum. However, this does not entirely support either side of the nature–nurture debate, because it could be that all of the cells necessary for normal vision are present at birth but need stimulation from light in various patterns to make them work.

There is another problem. Like most kittens, the subjects in this experiment would have rolled around in their play. A vertical stripe will appear to be horizontal when the kitten is lying on its side! They would have seen the stripes from many angles. Several independent judges were asked to say which cat had been reared in which drum. Most couldn't!

At the same time as Blakemore and Cooper were rearing their cats, **Richard Held** and **Alan Hein** had designed some apparatus to overcome the problem of the cat's movement changing its visual experiences. Their apparatus, called the *kitten carousel,* made two kittens share the same visual experiences, although only one of them could move fairly independently. They were connected by pulleys and strings so that the movements of the active kitten were transferred to the passive kitten (see figure 11.10).

*Figure 11.10 The kitten carousel*

The kittens were allowed three hours each day for several weeks on the apparatus. When their paw-to-eye co-ordination was finally tested the active kittens had far better abilities. For example, after 30 hours in the apparatus all of the active kittens could move their paws deliberately in a particular direction. None of the passive kittens could. It seems that experience in the environment is necessary for normal visual development.

These findings do appear to suggest that the environment is very important in the development of certain kinds of perceptual ability. However, as animals are unable to tell us what they see, we can only *infer* what their perceptual abilities are from what they do. A

■ What was the point in conducting deprivation studies using animals? Summarize the findings of two such studies and say how their findings have contributed to untangling nature and nurture.

▶ Some of the neurons in the brain have a white, fatty insulation called a *myelin sheath*, which appears to speed up transmission of brain activity by 20 times compared to unmyelinated neurons. Myelination occurs gradually after birth.

▶ Being able to see and interact with one's caregivers early in life will have a strong binding influence on them. We return to this, and the work of Genevieve Carpenter, in Chapter 14.

second problem arises from the use of animals in the first place. It is by no means readily accepted within psychology that animals are appropriate in the study of human behaviour.

> ### Summary – Animal studies
>
> There is a significant problem with all experiments that involve animals behaving in some way or another after we have altered some feature of their environment. We can describe what they do, we can't know whether they are capable of doing other things. Just because an animal behaves in one way does not mean that it can't behave in another way. Animals can't describe their experiences, and much of their behaviour is fairly reflexive or learned by association. Since they lack consciousness we must be cautious in drawing any inferences from their behaviour to human experience.

## Combining the two views – the need for biology and learning

So far we've reviewed the case for the nature view and the nurture view. Most modern psychologists would think that visual perceptual skills result from an interaction between the two. For the first few months of life a baby's visual system isn't fully developed. The nerves in those parts of the brain involved with vision take time to develop their insulating layers. The result is interference (a bit like a radio that isn't quite tuned properly). Some of the signals are lost, others are confused. The baby's vision is blurred. As the baby's visual system matures, so its ability to see will improve. Biology influences perception at this early stage.

Despite these limitations infants can see reasonably well right from birth. We can do tests to measure how far a baby can see, and even what sorts of things it can see. However, we cannot know what the baby makes of the things it sees. **Genevieve Carpenter** showed that by two weeks of age infants may have learned to recognize their mother (and father?), and will expect her face to move and change expression. Learning from early experience is also necessary for the infant to make sense of what it can see.

On many occasions when psychologists have re-examined the contributions of either biology or the environment, they have concluded that both are involved and that there's little to be gained from trying to decide which is responsible for what. This is true here. Rather than trying to claim some skill for biology or the environment it makes more sense to see how the two interact to produce the skill.

In conclusion, human babies have impressive visual skills such as depth perception, size constancy and pattern recognition. They also have the ability to imitate facial expressions and to copy behaviour. When a caregiver sticks their tongue out, the baby may well return the gesture. Although this simple copying may seem fairly obvious, it really is quite amazing. How does the infant know what is being stuck out, and how does it know what part of its own anatomy to stick out?

It is unlikely that there will ever be a simple solution to the nature or nurture question. Most psychologists now support the nature modified by nurture view. Babies are probably born with the capacity to develop all the visual skills that they will show later. If the environment they grow up in allows those skills to develop, they will.

■ Summarize the evidence for each side of the nature–nurture debate on visual perception.

## PERCEPTUAL ORGANIZATION OF SPACE, MOVEMENT, PATTERN RECOGNITION, CONSTANCIES AND ILLUSIONS

Human visual perception includes a number of abilities such as the ability to recognize shapes (pattern perception), and the knowledge that things do not change their shape, size or colour when they change their distance or position, or when the light falling on them alters. These visual skills are called shape, size and colour *constancy*. James Gibson argues that evolution has provided us with the abilities to organize our perception to provide instant feedback about the environment and affordance of objects in it. Richard Gregory claims that highly complex perceptual processing relies on well-organized, meaningful and accessible previous experience. Either way, psychologists agree that the perceptual system is highly developed and relies on certain principles of organization. These can be best seen in the work of the Gestalt school of psychology.

► *Constancy* means unchanging. Jean Piaget gave the term conservation to the knowledge that objects do not change their essential features when their appearance changes, as we shall see in Chapter 15.

### Gestalt psychology

One of the concerns of the earliest academic psychologists was explaining the structure and function of human consciousness. To do this, **William James** in America and **Wilhelm Wundt** in Germany (both 1870s) attempted to isolate a single human experience and to reduce it to its smallest elements (its 'atoms') to try to see how these elements combine to become an experience. Gestalt (meaning 'pattern', 'form' or 'configuration') psychology emerged in Germany in the early twentieth century, partly as a reaction against this reductionist, atomistic approach. Gestaltists claim that we do not hear music as a series of individual notes or regard a scene as shape, colour, texture or form. Instead we hear the melody and see the whole picture.

Gestalt psychologists such as **Max Wertheimer, Wolfgang Köhler** and **Karl Koffka** suggest that perception is governed by the innate and universal 'law of pragnanz'. Pragnanz loosely means 'looking good', or 'pleasing to the eye'. More technically, it is the idea that anything we perceive will be seen in a way that requires the least amount of perceptual processing. You can see from this that Gestalt psychology reflects James Gibson's bottom-up idea (see

► Reductionism is an attempt to describe any event in more basic terms. According to Skinner, all behaviour can be reduced to ABC and reinforcement (see Chapter 1).

page 231) that perception is direct and needs the minimum of processing.

In order to make the perception of the *figure* (object that is being regarded) stand out from the ground (background) require minimum processing, there are several 'laws' or principles within the law of pragnanz. These include:

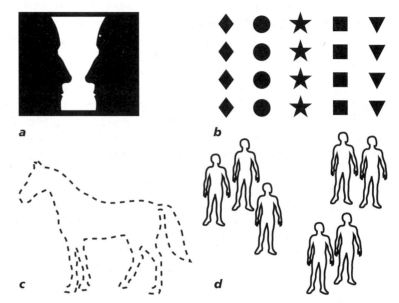

**a** *Figure–ground principle;*
**b** *law of similarity;*
**c** *law of closure;*
**d** *law of proximity*

- The figure–ground principle (what is the object and what the background).
- The law of similarity (similar objects will be seen as being together).
- The law of closure (missing parts of a figure are ignored and the figure seen as a whole).
- The law of proximity (objects that are close together will be regarded as being part of the same perception).

### Summary – Gestalt psychology

Gestalt psychology of perception was partly a reaction against reductionism and atomism of human experience, and partly a promotion of the role of genetic inheritance in perceptual functioning. Claims for laws of perceptual organization are rather overstated and, whilst they can be easily demonstrated in two-dimensional illustrations, they may lack ecological validity.

### Evaluation of Gestalt psychology

Gestalt psychology was popular at a time when great emphasis was being placed on the role genetic inheritance plays in directing human functioning. There is no evidence that innate factors are involved in perceptual organization (see earlier comments on the inconclusive nature–nurture debate). Michael Eysenck (1993) makes the point that the 'principles' and 'laws' of Gestalt are only descriptions of perceptual organization; they do not explain why such organization occurs. By ignoring the role of visual experience

Gestalt psychologists have offered a limited number of explanations for all visual experiences. Eysenck says the processes proposed by the Gestalt psychologists perhaps account for the early stages of perceptual processing which will be organized later by previous experience.

In any science researchers look for ways of investigating claims made by theorists. **David Navon** (1977) thought that some of the principles of Gestalt psychology were so 'global' that they would be the first stage in processing. He showed his participants stimuli, which were large letters made up of small ones. They had to identify either the small letters or the large ones as quickly as possible. For example, he had a large letter H made up of small Hs and another consisting of Ss. There was also a large S made up of small Hs and another of small Ss (see figure 11.11). He found that the large letters were identified equally quickly, regardless of what they comprised. However, it took longer to identify the small letters when they were different from the large letter. Participants already had some information about letters (the large one), which interfered with their perception of the small ones. If this supports the Gestalt claim that there are principles of perceptual organization, then Eysenck's claim that, at best, they explain the first stages in perception is correct. Early processing provides the building blocks of 'what is there' for further, detailed (top-down) processing later.

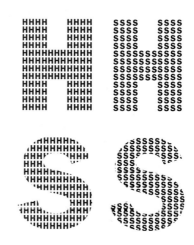

*Figure 11.11 Navon's experiment*

## Perception of space

Gestaltists imply that what we see in our perceptual field is a series of figures in the grounds linked by similarity, proximity and so on, all perceived in ways that require least processing. However, when you look around the room you see real people with real lives, real things with real uses. They are three-dimensional, have colour and texture, distance and orientation. The environment provides various cues as to what is where and what is bigger or brighter than what else. Here are some of the cues to perception in three-dimensional space when the objects and the viewer are stationary. Some are monocular cues (i.e. only require one eye to be looking), and some are binocular.

▶ There is rather more to judging the relationship between objects in three-dimensional reality than the principles of perceptual organisation offered by the Gestaltists.

### Cues to perception in three-dimensional space

**Interposition.** If our view of an object is obscured by another object we assume that it is further away from us (see figure 11.12).
**Shadowing.** If one object casts a shadow on another we can judge which one is nearest to us.
**Relative size.** If we know how big something is (e.g. a car), and the image it projects onto our retina is quite small, we know that it is a long way away.
**Distinctiveness with distance.** Things which are slightly less distinct are inferred as being further away.
**Retinal disparity.** Each eye sends a picture to the cortex. The

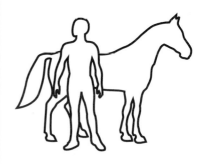

*Figure 11.12 Interposition*

■ **Which of the cues to perceiving objects in space are monocular and which binocular?**

more similar the two pictures are the further away the object must be.

**Height in the visual plane.** Objects that appear to be higher than others as we look are seen as being further away (particularly if they are less distinct).

If the viewer is moving (e.g. riding in a car), objects that are closest to us (a hedgerow) appear to be moving more slowly than objects further away (the barn across the field). This phenomenon is called *motion parallax*. As objects move closer than about 50 metres to our faces our eyeballs, which are about 6 cm apart, turn inwards to focus on them. This is *convergence* and the muscles that control it provide information about how close an object must be.

## Perception of movement

Perceiving and responding to movement are essential to our survival (how do you judge it is safe to stroll or dash across a busy road?). Some psychologists do not believe that the perception of movement is anything more than inferences taken from our perception of something in one place, then in another, then another. This seems unlikely, since illuminated adverts often have a series of stationary lights which turn on and off in just the right timing to give the impression of movement. This is called the *autokinetic effect*. Cinema films are a series of (24) individual frames shown every second. We don't see 24 individual pictures from which we infer movement – we see what looks like movement. This is called *apparent motion*.

One explanation for movement perception is that the image of the object being cast simply moves across our retina, stimulating different rods and cones as it goes (assuming that you don't move your head much to 'track' the object). This is called *image displacement* and seems fairly unlikely too. Where we do track the object the muscles that move the eyes send information which is used to infer movement. This is called *ocular pursuit*. A third possibility is movement against a stationary background. When we know that the background (a house) is stationary we infer that someone coming down the path must be moving.

## Pattern recognition

How do you recognize your friend from across a crowded room? How do you know which car on the car park is yours? How do you know that this is an A and this is an H? This part of the perceptual process is called *pattern recognition*. It involves matching the information from the visual image with information stored in our long-term memories. This association between what we see, what we store, and how we match new perceptions to existing memories must be very complex. However, this hasn't stopped psychologists suggesting explanations!

*Template-matching* approaches take an analogy from machines that can recognize objects by comparing them to known examples. The police use fingerprint-matching computers to help associate a suspect with the scene of the crime. Their computer contains templates of known criminals' prints. The post office is developing character recognition systems to read people's handwriting in order to automate letter sorting.

The implication is that our memory stores miniature templates of everything we've ever known. Imagine the capacity that would be needed to have a template for every thing or person you ever knew. It would be vast. Since you may never see some of them again it would be a rather uneconomical use of your brain's capacity. A second problem concerns the way that we can recognize objects even when they are confused, incomplete or have bits missing. You would recognize a picture of your friend even if it was upside down. (Look at the examples under our discussion of Gestalt psychology.) You will recognize your friend from several angles. Surely we don't have templates for every one?

An alternative is *prototype theory*. Rather than having templates for everything we are said to have prototypes, which are generalized categories of objects with similar features. So you may have a prototype for 'youngish, blondish females' to which you can match your best friend. This theory still ignores the context in which recognition takes place, as we will see shortly.

Third, there are *feature-matching theories*. These suggest that we identify key features of the visual stimulus (contours, shades, areas of similarity etc.), which we store as defining characteristics of that object. These explanations are consistent with Hubel and Wiesel's physiological findings, and Selfridge's Pandemonium model discussed earlier. Feature demons represent what Hubel and Wiesel described as functions of simple and complex cells. Selfridge's model goes way beyond Hubel and Wiesel's actual findings, however. (The idea of all these demons shrieking is giving me a headache!)

However, these theories still ignore context and experience (M. Eysenck 1994). In experiments by Palmer (1975), participants were shown a context-setting scene, such as an Alpine mountain view. They were then shown a number of related objects (snow shoes, skis, goggles etc.) and unrelated (e.g. a boat, a football, a typewriter). They had to say what the object was as quickly as possible. They could name the related objects (since presumably their *perceptual set* was switched to Alpine-related material) more quickly than the unrelated ones. However, naming an object is not necessarily the same as recognizing it.

Form and pattern perception are highly complex and rely on the integration of many brain centres. It is hardly surprising that we do not have a convincing theory to explain all of it yet.

▶ We said at the beginning of this book that psychology involves the study of human behaviour. As new aspects of behaviour have been identified psychologists have turned their attention to them. Where explanations based on observation and prediction were all that was possible, they were made. When predictions could be investigated, they, too, were made. Some of the explanations have not stood the test of time and have either been rejected altogether, or been replaced by something better. This is the normal process through which all sciences gather their body of knowledge.

▶ *Perceptual set* refers to the way that our perceptual system may be especially receptive to one kind of material rather than another, e.g. being engrossed in *Coronation Street* may mean you don't hear the phone ringing straight away. Factors in perceptual set include the situation you are in, your expectations of what should happen based on previous experience, your emotional state, your level of motivation, and whether the situation is rewarding or threatening to you.

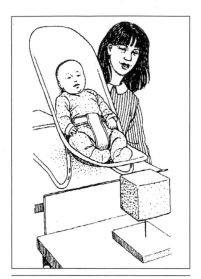

*Figure 11.13 Bower's experiment*

▶ A trial is a run-through of an experimental procedure.

## Constancies

Can you recognize a door when it is closed, ajar and wide open? Would you know that you are picking up a cup, even when it is upside down? Would you recognize a chair when it is on its side? Yes? You know that something doesn't change its shape just because you see it from different angles. You know the colour of your front room curtains don't change, regardless of whether you see them on a sunny day or returning home in the middle of the night. These are examples of visual constancies such as size constancy, shape constancy and colour constancy.

### Is size constancy innate or learned?

In 1966 **Tom Bower** conducted an experiment to investigate whether size constancy was innate or learned. (See earlier discussions in this chapter on the nature–nurture debate.) Nurturists argue that infants could not show size constancy because they would not have learned it. Nativists argue that infants would show size constancy because it is an innate ability. One at a time, infants of between six and 12 weeks of age were placed on a table in a comfortable cot from which they could see a screen (see figure 11.13). Behind the screen was a 30-cm cube at a distance of about 1 metre from the infants. When the screen was moved and the infants saw the cube they were called by their mothers, who were on one side of the cot. If the infants turned to look at their mother she would pop up and say 'peek a boo' and tickle the child. The infants enjoyed this form of reinforcement. Bower is using operant conditioning (see Chapter 1) to teach the infants to perform a simple task, turning their heads to one side when they saw a 30-cm cube in order to gain a reinforcement. After several trials the infants were conditioned to turn their heads towards their mothers when they saw the 30-cm cube.

Bower had three other experimental conditions. In the first the 30-cm cube was moved back until it was 3 metres away from the infants, and the screen was removed. If the infants had size constancy they would look at the cube, recognize that it was the same cube as before, and turn their head to receive their reward. In the next condition the original cube was removed and one three times as large (90 cm) was placed 3 metres from the infants. It would now cast the same size image on their retinas as the original 30-cm cube had at 1 metre. If the infants perceived this new cube to be the same as the original cube, they should turn their heads for their reward. In the third condition the 90-cm cube was placed 1 metre from the child. Such a cube would look three times as big compared to the original cube. Would the infants think that this was the original cube and turn their head for their reward? In each experimental condition the number of times the children turn their heads for a reward is used as a measure of how similar the infants thought the cube was to the 30-cm cube at 1 metre distance that they were conditioned to turn from.

If the nativist view is correct and infants are born with size constancy, they should respond most to condition 1 since it uses the original cube. They should respond rather less to condition 2 and least to condition 3. If the nurturists are right and infants have to learn size constancy, then they should respond most to condition 2, since it cast the same size image on their retinas. Condition 1 and condition 3 should trigger the fewest head turns.

### Bower's results

| Original condition | a 30-cm cube at 1 metre | |
| --- | --- | --- |
| *Experimental condition* | | *Average number of head turns* |
| 1 | a 30-cm cube at 3 metres | 58 |
| 2 | a 90-cm cube at 3 metres | 22 |
| 3 | a 90-cm cube at 1 metre | 14 |

Bower's findings appear to support the nativist view. The infants seemed to recognize the 30-cm cube as the original stimulus, and turned their heads most for their reward. Less than half that number of head turns was recorded for the 90-cm cube at 3 metres, and less than a quarter of that for the 90-cm cube at 1 metre.

Certainly size constancy implies the ability the brain has to recognize an object from a retinal image regardless of how large that image is. Colour constancy shows that inferences taken from our perceptual system by those brain centres that analyse for meaning (by accessing memory banks) are interpreted as the colour we know the object should be, rather than what it looks to be. How these mechanisms work is still unknown, but research is proceeding.

## Illusions

A final area of perceptual processing that has fascinated psychologists (and artists) for centuries is that of *optical illusions*. Optical illusions occur when there is an inexplicable difference between what something looks like and what it would be like in reality.

Richard Gregory (1983) identifies four types of illusion:

1 Distortions which are the result of an actual perceptual error, e.g. the Muller–Lyer illusion, the horizontal–vertical illusion, and the Ponzo illusion. In each case some important information about size or distance is missing.
2 Ambiguous figures such as the Necker cube, Leeper's 'old/young lady', and Rubin's vase.
3 Paradoxical figures such as Penrose's impossible objects. These could not exist in reality, so why do we try to perceive them as real objects?
4 Fictions such as the Kanizsa triangle, in which what we 'see' isn't actually there at all.

Richard Gregory maintains that we need to use information about size and distance during perceptual processing to make perceptual

*Leeper's 'old/young lady'*

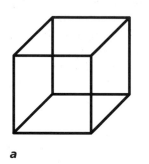

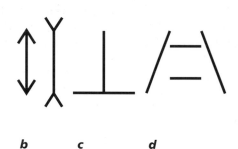

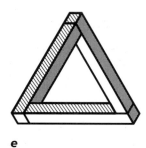

*a Necker cube;*
*b Muller–Lyer illusion;*
*c horizontal–vertical illusion;*
*d Ponzo illusion;*
*e Penrose's triangle;*
*f Kanizsa triangles*

► James Gibson claimed that perception is direct, and that although further perceptual processing does occur it isn't generally required. This explanation cannot easily explain perceptual illusions.

► The study of optical illusions provides support for Gregory's view of perception as a process of inference. If we constantly test hypotheses about our perceptional world, then occasionally these hypotheses will be wrong, and we will experience an illusion.

judgements. When these cues are absent, conflicting or confused, then mistakes, possibly illusions, will follow. In each illusion our brains are trying to find the best explanation for what we are 'seeing' (or think we are seeing?). Gregory (1972) says that 'perception is an active process of using information to suggest and test hypotheses' (hypotheses are predictions).

Gregory suggests one reason for why we see illusions. He says that our brains are actively trying to make sense of the perception by using all those cues that are so useful in three-dimensional space. This is especially true for distortions such as Muller–Lyer and Ponzo. Unfortunately, they lead to errors when applied to two-dimensional objects. (Most visual illusions are presented two-dimensionally.) For example, the Muller–Lyer illusion works because in three-dimensional space the fins that face outward appear to be coming toward us, and the fins that point inward mislead our size constancy into thinking that the vertical bar is further away. So we say it is shorter. Segall, Campbell and Herskovits (1963) suggest that in the West we live in a 'carpentered world', i.e. our environment is full of right angles, such as the corners of the room you are in. How many Muller–Lyer lines with fins are there in the room? Marshall Segall and his colleagues sampled over 1,800 people from places in Africa, the Philippines and America. Those who lived in rural areas, with presumably fewer right angles, were less likely to be fooled by the Muller–Lyer illusion. This explanation has been criticized and isn't wholly accepted now. For example, when the fins are replaced with circles, thus removing the 'carpentered world' explanation, the illusion persists (and the size constancy explanation no longer applies).

If distortions are explained by applying depth and distance cues, ambiguous figures such as the Rubin vase and Necker cube work because they do not provide enough cues about what should be the figure and what should be the ground, or which face should face forward. Penrose's paradoxical objects are rather clever artist's creations, and so aren't really visual illusions at all. You see exactly what there is, it's just that what there is has been carefully crafted to be impossible to exist in reality. Fictions can be explained in terms of expectations. These include context and several Gestalt principles such as closure and proximity.

■ Summarize the explanations for why we see the four categories of 'visual illusions' that Gregory identified and show how they relate to top-down and bottom-up explanations.

## Other factors that contribute to perception

It seems that visual perception isn't simply the consequence of what we see and how we see it. Humans have consciousness and cognition. They have thoughts such as feelings, expectations and beliefs. We don't approach any situation as though we were in a psychological vacuum. Here are some other factors that contribute to perception. Most of us are influenced by our needs, such as our knowledge of how hungry we are. Hungry people perceive food in different ways (and recognize food-related words more quickly in experiments!) than non-hungry people. A football fan's perception of the quality of the opposition and how the game is played will be influenced by his or her support for one of the teams.

Your norms (standards of behaviour that you set for yourself) and values (standards of acceptable beliefs) are influential, too. If you do not believe that aliens visit our planet then you won't accept that corn circles are messages from them. You might think that any society that is technologically advanced enough to have mastered space travel would have found rather better ways of communicating with us than knocking over corn in the middle of a summer's night some distance from wherever they might be seen! If you regard Parliament as the home of democracy then you may regard Guy Fawkes as an enemy of the people who deserved his fate. If you see him as one of the few people ever to have entered the Houses of Parliament with honest intentions your perceptions of what happened to him will be different. After all, one person's terrorist is another person's freedom fighter.

Your emotional state will affect your perceptions, too. If you are really miserable then you mightn't even want to watch your favourite soap opera, and if you do watch, you won't regard any of the characters in a very happy way. It's hard to make someone who is very unhappy see the funny side of anything!

Our previous experiences also lead us to expect what things look like. Have you ever been told about, or spoken on the phone to, someone you haven't met? You probably form impressions of what that person looks like. If you meet the person, how do your impressions fit reality? We might imagine that famous war leaders are tall and imposing. Churchill, Stalin, Mussolini and Hitler were not tall. Napoleon Bonaparte, the Emperor of France, was about 150 cm tall.

The value that something has for us will also influence our description of it to others, and possibly our own perceptions too. When I'm describing the fish I nearly caught in the angling competition, I might have perceived it to have been as long as Napoleon, when it was actually nearer half a metre. If you received your £20 million National Lottery win in pound coins, how big a vehicle would you need to carry it home?

### Summary – Perceptual organization

Gestalt psychologists identify several features in our visual field, such as shadowing and relative size, that contribute to our ability to understand how objects relate to one another. Cues for understanding movement include ocular tracking and comparison to something which we know not to move. As we experience new objects we may build up databases of templates which we search to find cues to interpret new visual experiences, whilst prototype and feature detection theories claim that we store the main features which similar objects have in common. Some evidence, such as Bower's work with young children, suggests that visual constancies such as size constancy are innate, and so aspects of visual organization can be explained in terms of biological inheritance, although research into visual illusions emphasizes the role of experience in perceptual organization.

### Exam questions – 60 minutes each

1 'Perception is an active process.' Discuss. (*25 marks*)
2 'There is more to visual perception than meets the eye.' How do theories of perceptual organization explain visual perception? (*25 marks*)
3 (a) Describe the findings of TWO pieces of research into the development of visual perception. (*10 marks*)
  (b) Describe and evaluate the methods used in such studies. (*15 marks*)

# Attention and performance

**Chapter objectives**

By the end of this chapter you will be able to:

■ appreciate the nature of human perception and cognition, and its relation to perceptual processing;

■ understand the early and later models of selective and divided attention;

■ understand the research methods employed in gathering attentional data and their limitations;

■ appreciate the difference between partial and total processing approaches;

■ understand the relationship between action slips and modes of control of thinking;

■ contrast the models based on different computer analogies in the information-processing approach.

## Introduction

As we noted in Chapter 11, we can see or hear something, recognize it, and respond to it automatically and instantly. According to Gibson's bottom-up theory, each perception provides just about all the information we need to make sense of objects in our environment. Gregory and others claim this requires cognition. Cognition is the name of the mental process by which we come to know and understand things. It is influenced by our emotional state and our general level of arousal. Selectively attending to one or two messages is one of the first stages in the cognitive process. We have several sensory systems that provide information about an object, such as what it looks like, sounds like, feels like, and so on.

Research into human attention has used two similar approaches. One investigated the way that we can *selectively* attend to one source of information when presented with two or more sources. Another approach has been to present several sources of information at once and see how much or how many can be made sense of. This is *divided attention*. We will discuss both in this chapter.

▶ Perception is the process by which we take in information about our external (and internal) environment and make sense of it.

► *Habitual* means the ability to do something without having to think about it.

► As you are reading these words many things are going on around you. People may be talking, cars may be passing, phones may be ringing, birds may be singing, etc. If you're 'paying attention' to your reading you should be unaware of most of them. That's not to say that you can't hear them, just that you are not attending to them. You can often choose what to pay attention to and what to ignore. Attention must be selective.

■ **Describe what is meant by perceptual set.**

■ **In your own words outline what is meant by a low-capacity, single channel system for selective attention.**

► During the course of your day you will have moved through several environments – home, work, college, shopping, bus etc. Each contains people, objects and events. Many of these will be available to your senses for you to see, hear, touch and so on. For the purposes of this discussion, we're going to refer to all those sources of information, stimulation, sensations etc. as 'messages'.

## SELECTIVE ATTENTION: THEORIES AND EVIDENCE

No matter how acute our perception is, we cannot pay equal attention to many things at the same time. We may be able to sing and play guitar at the same time, or knit and watch TV. With practice these skills become fairly *habitual* and don't require great attention. But could you watch two basketball games at the same time, paying equal attention to both? Or add up your shopping list at the same time as completing a jigsaw? Or do your homework competently whilst plugged into a personal stereo? (If you think you can, you're wrong!) The way humans pay attention has been described as a *single channel system*, i.e. we can only concentrate on information through one sensory channel at a time. Moreover, we can't handle too much information in that single channel. If this is correct, we may have a *low-capacity* system.

Inevitably, some stimuli are more likely to be attended to than others. Things that are different from what we expect, for example a loud noise or sudden flash of light, will certainly attract your attention. Things that you are expecting to see will be quickly perceived compared to the time it takes to perceive something unexpected. This is an example of *perceptual set* (see Chapter 11).

The early explanations for how selective attention works refer to some kind of a physiological filter, which allows one source of information through into consciousness while not allowing other sources through. The theories differ in where and how they see that filter occurring. Some explanations, such as those of **Donald Broadbent** and **Anne Treisman**, suggest that all stimulation is partly processed and those which aren't important are filtered out (the *partial processing approach*). The alternative, from **Deutsch** and **Deutsch**, suggests that all stimulation is processed and decisions about what is important or not are made later. This is the *total processing approach*.

### How have psychologists investigated attention?

With the availability of the tape-recorder during the 1950s researchers could control auditory information into each ear. Different messages are played in each ear (called *dichotomous presentation*) and the participant is asked to shadow, or repeat, one of the messages. The messages can vary depending on the sex of the speaker, the language spoken, the content of the message, and so on. After speech shadowing the message in the 'attended ear' the participants were asked about the messages from both the attended and unattended ear. Apart from dichotomous presentation there is *binaural presentation*, where two or more sources of information are played into both ears at the same time. This leads to confusion.

Inevitably, research can only be conducted if we have the appropriate technology. Sometimes our attention is dominated by our own thoughts and memories, feelings and level of arousal. We have no way of investigating this yet, although with the rapid advances being made in neuropsychology (the study of how psychological processes are organized in the brain) we may be able to do so eventually. At other times our attention is taken by watching or playing some sport, watching a film and so on. Most research is into external influences (auditory and visual) on attention.

## Early research in selective attention

Psychologists were becoming interested in how people such as aeroplane pilots and air traffic controllers manage to attend to a mass of information and take in and respond to the most important data. At the time computers were often regarded as miracle machines that could solve all sorts of problems if they were fed the right information. Psychologists were quick to look for analogies (comparisons) between how computers work and how aspects of human cognition work. This has become known as 'the *information-processing approach*', which we shall review at the end of this chapter.

The earliest research on selective attention was conducted in the 1950s by **Colin Cherry**. Cherry played tape-recorded material to his participants, through headphones. Some heard two stories at the same time, through both ears (*binaural presentation*). They found it very difficult to understand either story, even after hearing the tapes 20 times. Others heard two stories, but one story in each ear (*dichotomous presentation*). They had no difficulties in shadowing the message in the 'attended ear' and could describe the story afterwards. However, they had very little knowledge of the story being played in the unattended ear. They knew what was being presented was speech, but couldn't even be sure whether it was in English or any other language.

Cherry concluded that early selective attention was largely determined by the physical characteristics of the message, e.g. the sound of the speaker's voice – how loud or deep or fast-speaking and so on. The likelihood of a message being selectively attended to had little to do with the meaning of what was being said. Cherry identified three other factors. First was redundancy. This refers to how predictable the rest of an utterance in the attended ear was. If someone is talking about the weather it's pretty obvious what they'll be saying for the next few seconds, so it's easier to attend elsewhere. Second, the position of the unattended speaker in relation to the listener is important. If the message was being spoken nearby it would be easier to eavesdrop. Third, the tone of the unattended speaker's voice is significant. Voices that were muffled or unclear were harder to follow than clear voices.

Other researchers have modified Cherry's experimental procedures. **Anne Treisman** (1964a) had the language spoken in the unattended ear changed from English to German, and found that the participants didn't notice. They couldn't tell what language was being spoken, or whether it was English played backwards. **Neville**

> ► We mentioned the idea of information processing in Chapter 11. The visual system and the auditory system are involved in the early stages of processing light and sound at the level of the sense receptor itself.

> ► Early experiments in selective attention used carefully controlled experiments using tape recorders and headphones. In 'real life' we don't hear messages through one ear, since the auditory system is integrated in the thalamus (as discussed in Chapter 11).

> ► We may see a comparison with the computer even here. Data (messages) which are unambiguous, relevant and in the appropriate format will be recognized and processed by the computer. If the information to be input is inappropriate, processing and any subsequent answer will be confused. In American slang 'garbage in, garbage out' (GIGO).

> ■ **Explain what is meant by binaural and dichotomous presentation.**

**Moray** (1959) had the same word repeated up to 35 times in the unattended ear while the participants were shadowing the other ear's message, and the participants later said they hadn't heard the word at all. But if the voice speaking the unattended ear was of the opposite sex to that heard speaking in the attended ear, or if other sounds than speech were played, then participants could tell that something different was happening in the unattended ear. This suggests that the participants could detect the physical properties of the unattended sound – its pitch or tone – although they could not process it very deeply for meaning. We will return to this idea shortly.

## Partial processing approaches

### Donald Broadbent's early filter model (1958)

Donald Broadbent (1958) also used dichotomous presentation in his 'split-span' experiments. He played his participants a series of three pairs of numbers. One number from each pair was played in one ear at the same time as the other number was played into the other ear. For example:

|  | Number |  | Number |  | Number |
|---|---|---|---|---|---|
| Left ear | 3 | Pause | 9 | Pause | 5 |
| Right ear | 7 | Pause | 2 | Pause | 8 |

The participants recalled what they had heard in each ear, e.g. 3 9 5 7 2 8. They didn't seem able to switch from ear to ear to recall the numbers as pairs, e.g. 37 92 58. This seems to confirm Cherry's claim that the meaning of unattended messages is not important, we can only recognize physical characteristics. Also perception treats each ear as a separate (single) channel and only one channel can be processed at a time. Non-attended information rapidly decays from the sensory buffer which holds messages received in the other ear.

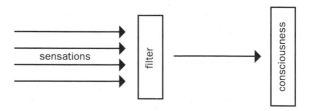

■ Summarize the early experimental studies conducted by Cherry, Treisman and Moray.

*Figure 12.1 Broadbent's early filter model*

► A model is a simplified way of describing what something might be like. It may be thought of as a 'mini-theory'. It is useful only if it allows useful, possibly testable, predictions to be made from it.

Broadbent's was the first model to propose the idea of a filter to explain why some messages are processed after selective attention whilst others are not. He suggests the existence of two related systems. The *sensory system* includes each of the senses – sight, hearing, taste, touch, smell, etc. – and exists at the level of the particular sense organ. The sensory system interprets the simple physical characteristics of a stimulus, such as its volume, brightness, temperature, pressure, etc. It can hold many different kinds of stimuli in a *sensory buffer*, but for a very short time. If not selected, information in the buffers will rapidly decay and be lost. The *perceptual system*, which involves what we mean by 'consciousness', 'attention' or 'short-term memory', is aware of the individual's current state of attention. It 'scans' the sensory buffers, allowing information relevant to current needs to pass, while anything that is irrelevant is filtered out. Hence Broadbent's is an early *filter* and *single channel model* (see figure 12.1).

### Evaluation of Broadbent's model

Broadbent's model is simple and elegant. However it has some flaws. It is rather 'mechanistic', suggesting that we can only process messages through one channel at a time. We said earlier that people can attend to more than one thing at a time, although it may be easier not to! Also, Broadbent's findings derive from some fairly contrived laboratory experiments that may not reflect 'real life' situations at all. Third, the idea of two separate systems, and a sensory buffer that loses most of the information it holds very quickly, seems rather wasteful. Why would we have evolved a capacity to store something if it will only last a moment and then be lost? However, Broadbent's model inspired other researchers to challenge the early claims, and this, after all, is one of the prime functions of scientific research and theorizing.

A further problem is that Broadbent's model cannot explain some aspects of the cocktail party effect. This is the phenomenon of being able to hear someone mention your name or something important to you across a room, when you are actually attending to someone else. Cherry and Broadbent claim we do not process meaning from unattended messages – clearly we do!

Amongst the first to challenge Broadbent's claims were **Gray** and **Wedderburn** (1960). They modified a dichotomous listening task by presenting three pairs of words and numbers at the same time, e.g. left ear: 'Dear', right ear: '6'. They asked their participants to say what they heard (either in each ear or in any other way they wanted). Here is one possible sequence of word/number combinations:

| Left ear | Dear | Pause | 3 | Pause | Jane |
|----------|------|-------|------|-------|------|
| Right ear | 6 | Pause | Aunt | Pause | 8 |

If Broadbent were correct participants would say 'Dear 3 Jane 6 Aunt 8'. After all, Cherry and Broadbent claimed that we can only process physical characteristics in one channel (ear) at a time, and since meaning isn't a physical property participants won't recognize Dear Aunt Jane as a meaningful message. However, most of Gray and Wedderburn's participants did report 'Dear Aunt Jane' and '638'. Obviously people can hold information for long enough to interpret it for simple meaning and it doesn't immediately decay from a sensory buffer.

Neville Moray (1959) tested the cocktail party effect directly in one of his experiments. Participants speech shadowed a story in the

► Unfortunately the simple ideas aren't always the best. What they offer in ease of understanding they lose in simplicity and failure to explain the whole phenomenon.

■ Outline Broadbent's early filter model of selective attention and summarize the objections made to it.

attended ear whilst other messages were played in the unattended ear. At some point their name was mentioned in the unattended ear, followed by an instruction to change ears. About a third of them did. Broadbent's insistence that only one channel (one ear) can be receiving information at one time is wrong.

### Anne Treisman's attenuator model (1964)

Gray and Wedderburn showed that selective attention does take note of meaning, as well as physical characteristics. Anne Treisman (1964a, b) also investigated the extent to which meaningful messages could be detected in the unattended ear.

In one experiment using dichotomous presentation, participants were played two statements. For example 'Viv is married to Bill and they have three children' and 'The film finished at 11 o'clock so we all went home'. However, the last few words in each message were switched to the other ear. So participants might be played in the attended ear 'Viv is married to Bill so we all went home' and 'The film finished at 11 o'clock and they have three children' in the unattended channel. If Broadbent's early filter idea is correct, then the message shadowed will be just as stated, making no sense. If Gray and Wedderburn are correct, and messages are processed for meaning, then the participants will switch ears in order for their utterances to make sense. They did. This shows that messages in the unattended ear are still being processed for meaning, even though the participants are quite unaware of it. Findings such as these led Anne Treisman to suggest an *attenuator model* of selective attention (see figure 12.2).

▶ Anne Treisman says that two of the greatest influences on her psychology were Richard Gregory's top-down theory of perceptual processing, and Donald Broadbent's idea about human attention being an information-processing system.

▶ The discussion here concerns the extent to which we can recognize physical characteristics and meaning in our attentional system.

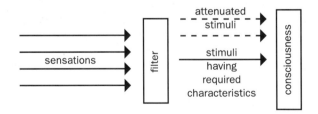

*Figure 12.2  Treisman's attenuator model*

Treisman proposed that all the messages detected by our senses will be analysed by an early filter for their physical characteristics. Those that are relevant to our state of awareness (what we are doing and how we are feeling at the time) will pass through the filter for further perceptual processing for meaning. By 'relevant' Treisman means that the sounds are of the right pitch and volume, coming from the right place, and so on. So messages are analysed for their physical characteristics in the first instance, and their meaning afterwards. Those messages that aren't relevant are attenuated, but still receive some processing for meaning. This could explain the cocktail party phenomenon. Your name is detected but attenuated, since you are attending to the messages all around you. However, it is important enough to pass through the filter.

▶ *Attenuation* is rather like gradually turning the volume down. All messages are analysed, those which aren't immediately relevant are turned down. They might become relevant and be further processed.

### Evaluation of Treisman's model

Broadbent suggested an early filter which only allowed one channel to be selectively attended. Treisman proposed that there were several levels of processing, beginning with filtering for physical characteristics, then meaning, and so on. Messages in the attended channel were processed whilst unattended messages are attenuated.

There are two problems with Treisman's attenuation model. First, why bother to have two systems of filter, one to assess the relevance of the physical characteristics of a message, and one for processing relevant messages for meaning? If messages can still be selected after first being attenuated, why bother filtering them in the first place? Second, each filter must have access to very complex sensory processes in order to decide which messages are relevant and which are to be attenuated. Treisman does not explain how the attenuator works. Quite simply, the attenuator doesn't seem to be very necessary. However, the idea of an attenuator has received some support from neuropsychological research. Posner and Presti (1987) found structures in the brain that do appear to attenuate non-attended messages.

> **Summary – Partial processing models**
> Broadbent's early model proposed the existence of a filter which removed input that hadn't been judged to be relevant to the individual's immediate situation, although critics complained that a decision about relevance can only be judged when the input has already been processed to some extent. Various ingenious experimental procedures have been employed to assess the extent to which messages in unattended channels are processed. None of the theories is entirely convincing, which shows how complicated cognition is, and how far psychological research still has to go to understand it.

■ Contrast Broadbent's and Treisman's models of selective attention.

## Total processing models

### Deutsch and Deutsch's pertinence model (1963)

Anthony and Diana Deutsch suggest a pertinence model, which attempts to explain how unattended messages can be processed for meaning (e.g. Gray and Wedderburn, Moray). The pertinence model is a type of attenuator model where attenuation occurs very late in the filtering process. All messages are processed to quite a high degree, for both their physical characteristics and meaning. For example, visual stimuli are recognized as people, houses, and so on. Auditory stimuli are recognized as words or other sounds. Selective attention will only occur if they are pertinent (relevant) to whatever the individual is doing at the time of perception.

▶ If you are waiting outside the cinema for your friend you may scan the faces of the people in the street, recognizing them as people but not really noticing much about them, looking for your friend. If someone looks rather like your friend (pertinent), you will attend further to them to decide if they are your friend or not.

### Evaluation of the pertinence model

There is some experimental evidence to support the idea of late processing as explained by either attenuation or pertinence models.

Neville Moray (1969) classically conditioned (see Chapter 1) some participants to associate a particular word with a mild electric shock. In classical conditioning a stimulus (a target word) is paired with a mild shock. The shock elicits a galvanic skin response (GSR), which was slight sweating. After several such pairings the appearance of the target word elicits the stress response without the shock being given. When Moray's participants heard the word later they exhibited the stress response. Later they were attending to some auditory message on a dichotomous listening task when the stimulus word was played in the unattended ear. They gave the GSR stress response. However, this doesn't necessarily imply that unattended messages are processed for meaning in the way that Deutsch and Deutsch predict. Classically conditioned responses do not require meaning to trigger them, they are almost reflexive and automatic.

Three years after Moray's research was published **Corteen** and **Wood** reported their similar research, which does support the idea of processing for meaning in the unattended channel. Rather than play the stimulus words they played synonyms (words that mean the same) in the unattended channel. This elicited a GSR response. So someone conditioned to expect to receive a shock when they heard the word 'pertinence' might also give a GSR response if they heard 'relevance'.

There is a problem with the pertinence explanation. It seems a rather inefficient use of our cognitive system to have to analyse every message around us. Evolution has usually provided us with the most efficient way of achieving most things that we can reasonably hope to have. On the other hand, if the most efficient system demands that we do process for meaning as much as possible (since that most important factor, our safety, might depend on it), then we would expect it to be organized as efficiently as possible, and the pertinence model may be it.

Treisman and Riley (1969) set out to test the pertinence model against the attenuator model. Participants were to dichotomously shadow a message. Every time they heard a target word (e.g. 'picture') they were to stop shadowing and tap the table. The target word could appear in either the attended or unattended ear. Treisman's attenuator model predicted more target words would be detected in the attended than the unattended ear. In the unattended ear they would have been attenuated. More correct responses were made to the attended message. The pertinence model would predict that as many correct responses would be detected in the unattended ear since both messages should be being analysed for meaning. Broadbent (1982) agreed that total processing models do not explain the research findings as well as the attenuation models.

■ Make notes on how the pertinence model differs from the other models of selective attention.

### Summary – Total processing models

Partial processing models claim that filtering out of irrelevant information occurs fairly early in the perceptual process. Total processing approaches claim that decisions about processing input for detailed meaning, and filtering that which is irrelevant, are made only after a considerable amount of processing has already occurred. This may seem inefficient by our understanding of efficiency. However, we do not know enough about human capacity or need for complex cognitive processing.

## Dynamic processing models

Early filter models such as Broadbent's are not supported by research evidence. Treisman claims the filter is rather later, Deutsch and Deutsch say it is later still. **Johnstone** and **Heinz** (1978) argue that to pinpoint the position of a supposed filter is too rigid and mechanistic. It may be simple to represent the position of a fixed filter in a diagram, but it ignores the flexibility and sophistication in the way that human cognition probably works. Johnstone and Heinz claim that messages can be attended to at almost any stage in processing, although generally the earlier the better. If the message is simple it is possible (and makes sense) to attend to it early so as not to take up other processing capacity. The later something is attended to the more capacity it is likely to demand.

Johnstone and Heinz conducted a laboratory experiment involving participants repeating target words and ignoring non-target words. When the target words were read by a male, and the non-targets read by a female voice, shadowing was easy; Johnstone and Heinz claim that selection is early since all it requires is the sex of the speaker. Participants couldn't remember many of the target words when questioned later, suggesting that they hadn't been processed for meaning. When both sets of words were spoken by a male voice there needed to be more processing to decide whether it was a target word or not. Participants were able to remember more of the words later, which suggests that they had processed these words for meaning.

> ► All of the models so far assume that we have a certain amount of 'processing power' or 'mental capacity'. Computing power was a big issue at this time in the computer industry, with an ever-increasing need for more powerful machines that could process more information more quickly.

### Summary – Dynamic processing models

The decision about what to process and what to filter isn't simply a question of timing, but rather a question of the complexity of the message, the medium through which it is received, the responsiveness of the recipient to receive and understand the message, and other factors beyond.

## Comments on studies of selective attention

There have been numerous experimental studies of selective attention, most supporting some form of attenuator model. Most of the research has investigated the auditory channel, since it is experimentally convenient to separate the two ears (under headphones) and much easier than trying to separate the visual channels. In Chapter 13 we will note **George Sperling**'s work on the duration of visual attention. Also the techniques for investigating auditory attention are tried and tested. Consequently we know more about auditory attention than any other kind.

Early models of selective attention suggest that we can only process one source of information (one 'message') at a time. This was probably inspired by the computer analogy, since at that time computers could only process one thing at a time. This is called *serial processing*. Since computer technology has moved on to include *parallel processing* (processing several messages at the same time), so the psychological models will change.

### Summary – Selective attention

Selective attention refers to our ability to focus our attention on one message, and studies have tried to discover the circumstances under which attention will switch to other messages. The first models saw some kind of filter operating early in the perceptual process, removing all stimuli that were irrelevant to what the individual was doing at the time. Models which claim that a filter operates later during perception claim that all messages are analysed at quite a high level. Both ideas have serious flaws, and the concept of a simple filter operating at a given point in the process of perception, and analysing only for physical properties or for meaning, is probably far too simple.

## DIVIDED ATTENTION: THEORIES AND EVIDENCE

An alternative to the attenuator or pertinence filter models of selective attention is the *limited-capacity model* suggested by **Norman** and **Bobrow** in 1975. They claim that the human perceptual system can take in only a small amount of sensory information at any one time, not because other messages are filtered out, but because we don't have enough 'processing power' to handle more.

Norman and Bobrow identify two reasons why selective attention is limited. One is because the *data themselves* are limited (if everyone in the canteen around you is talking it's difficult to selectively attend to someone talking two tables away). The other is because some tasks are very complicated and our *resources* are limited. When learning to drive you can't hold an intelligent conversation with your passenger. If you try to spread your attention too thinly you may be trying to exceed your limit and might make a disastrous mistake. When you become an experienced driver you won't be using all your capacity so will have some spare to hold your conversation. If you are coming to some diversion signs you will need to concentrate on driving so will 'lose' what your passenger is saying.

The limited-capacity model was also developed by **Daniel Kahneman** (1973). He suggested that we have a certain amount of 'mental energy' for processing in attention, which varies according to how tired or wide awake we are. The more alert you feel the

▶ William James first suggested the idea of there being a limited capacity for human processing over 120 years ago. He said we could perform one demanding task, or several undemanding ones, at the same time.

▶ Norman and Bobrow identify two limitations that inhibit processing for attention. These are data-limited features and resource-limited features.

▶ We might think of mental energy as being the amount of biological activity that may be going on in parts of the brain. The assumption is that we only have a certain amount of biological mental energy in the same way as we only have a certain amount of physical energy, although Kahneman claims that the amount can vary with alertness or fatigue.

more 'mental energy' you have and therefore the more processing capacity you will have. You can attend to several simple things or concentrate harder on one or two more complex ones.

When several tasks demand our attention a decision has to be made about how to allocate our mental resources (mental energy and processing capacity). According to Kahneman, somewhere in our cognitive system there is a *central processor*, which allocates our processing capacity to the various tasks. The more demands being made the fewer the resources available for any of them. What we do take notice of depends on three things. First, the maximum capacity that we have available for processing (influenced by our physiological state). Second are our general attitudes and behaviour, our personality and general disposition, any habits or long-term aims. Third are any short-term influences, such as our mood at the time, whether we find any of the tasks relevant or interesting, any feelings we have about the tasks, and so on.

### Comment on divided attention models

Divided attention models assume that we have a fixed capacity for processing that can be allocated in some way. These explanations still reflect the idea of serial processing from the computer analogy. They use terms such as 'resources', 'energy', 'processing capacity', 'storage' and so on, all of which imply a mechanistic view of the way in which a fundamental human process works. In a culture dominated by machines and technology it isn't surprising that psychologists use models derived from the ways that machines work. These models are useful only in so far as we accept that human perceptual processing does somehow reflect the way that machines work.

## How have psychologists studied divided attention?

### Multichannel models

The models proposed so far describe human perceptual processing as though it relied on a single perceptual processing system with a fixed overall capacity, which integrated information from the various senses. **D.A. Allport** et al. (1972) suggested the *multichannel processor* theory of attention. It says that we have several different types of processors involved in perception. Each sensory system has its own, and they do not need a central processor to control them. If two tasks are similar they will use the same processors and will interfere with each other. If the tasks are different we can use different processors.

Allport had participants wear headphones through which they shadowed one message whilst trying to learn a list of words that they heard at the same time. This proved impossible, Allport says, because the same processors were involved. When asked to shadow a message at the same time as learning the content of a set of pictures (different processors for auditory and visual processing), over 90 per cent was recalled. The participants could even remember

■ Contrast the role of the filter in attenuator and pertinence models with the role of capacity in models of divided attention.

► Notice that most of these experiments use hearing something through headphones and doing something else. Is this a realistic way to learn about the way we pay attention to things around us?

lists of words when they were presented visually. Allport found that experienced pianists could sight read and play music they were not familiar with, and speech shadow a story perfectly well. Both skills are said to use different processors.

Shaffer (1975) described a skilled audio-typist who illustrates Allport's point. When asked to speech shadow a story in one ear whilst audio-typing the messages received in the other ear she made many mistakes and expressed confusion. The similarities in the way she was receiving the messages meant that she used the same processors and the tasks interfered with each other. On another occasion she was asked to read some information from a card whilst audio-typing. She had difficulties with this too, since similarities in the way she was having to output the information (typing and speaking out loud) also produced interference. However, when asked to copy-type in German (which she did not know) she had no difficulties in speech shadowing some messages presented through headphones.

To what extent, though, do these kinds of studies show active processing in different processors? Or do they really show the effects of experience and practice so that at least one, if not both, of the skills is not particularly demanding? A skilled pianist should be able to sight read and play without much 'mental effort', and speech shadowing doesn't take much capacity, either.

On regular occasions during a college term Spelke et al. (1976) had two students practise performing two tasks, which should interfere with each other, at the same time. One involved writing a list of words that were being read to them, the other was simply reading stories. They soon learned how to do these tasks simultaneously. To test their capacity for a different kind of processing they now had to write down a word that had something in common with each of the words they heard, whilst still reading the stories. So on hearing 'house' they might write 'apartment' or 'bungalow'. With about 90 hours of practice the students learned to perform these two tasks simultaneously.

### Automatic processing

There is some suggestion that practice and habituation (adapting to the new situation) will extend the upper limit of processing capacity. Shiffrin and Schneider (1977) disagree. They argue that Allport's participants weren't actively performing two equally demanding tasks at the same time, but that one of them had become automatic through practice. Shiffrin and Schneider suggest that two kinds of processing are occurring here. One type is *controlled processing*, where there is limited capacity which would only allow serial processing. The other is *automatic processing*, which might be quite unconscious and performed in parallel.

Norman and Shallice (1980) suggest that to describe task performance as either automatic or needing attention is misleading. They proposed three levels of functioning in the need for attention. At the first level functioning requires no attention at all. We have

■ Summarize the evidence from multichannel models of attention. To what extent do they explain human ability to do two things at once?

■ How does Shiffrin and Schneider's explanation relate to William James' suggestion of over a century ago?

schemas (see page 238), which are organized plans or strategies of what to do, so processing is fully automatic, and the individual might not even be aware that messages are being detected and processed. At the second level some processing capacity for attention is required, since processing is partially automatic. We have some conscious awareness of paying attention, but it is momentary, or switches between different messages very quickly. At the third level we exercise deliberate control, by concentrating on certain messages, by choosing what to attend to, and by acting on the results of those attentional processes.

Whilst this model does recognize the diversity of processing compared to Shiffrin and Schneider's, it doesn't explain why practice leads to automatic functioning and why some processes become fully automatic whilst others are less so. Logan (1988) says that practice combines the individual tasks (such as reading the music, and pressing individual fingers on individual piano keys for a particular period) into one task (called playing the piano). Before practice each of these skills required separate processing. With practice the skills combine into one, and so the schemas that represent them in memory also combine, requiring less processing. Cheng (1985) goes further, claiming that practice actually changes the schemas themselves and therefore how they combine. The process of restructuring schemas actually changes our understanding of the task or message.

A challenging view was offered by **Ulric Neisser** (1976). He actually rejects the whole idea of limited capacity or attenuator models of attention. He believed that we automatically process whatever we need to know about from all the objects and events around us. His theory is based on James Gibson's ideas about direct perception, discussed in Chapter 11. We choose whatever else to attend to according to our expectations and needs at the time. However, others insist that we do not passively attend to whatever is there; we are active in attending to that which we consider relevant. Deciding what to attend to is a skill that will be acquired over time, like any other.

■ Make notes on Shiffrin and Schneider's objection to Allport's experiment, Norman and Shallice's alternative, Logan's schema combination model and Cheng's qualification.

### Summary – Divided attention

Early explanations for selective attention were developed from an understanding of the way that computers worked, and some highly artificial experiments. They couldn't explain how we are able to attend to several things at once. Divided attention theories still use an outmoded computer analogy, but have begun to reflect a more sophisticated appreciation of the way that cognitive functioning might work.

## ACTION SLIPS

Sometimes we do things that we did not intend to do. These are *action slips*. They have been investigated by asking people to keep diaries of the mistakes they make, and the circumstances under which they make them. **J.T. Reason** (1979) identified five categories of action slips from over 400 such slips recorded by 35 people. Some 40 per cent of these slips resulted from *storage failures*, where an action just performed is repeated with the individual being quite unable to recall that they had just performed it. Reason quotes one participant who started to pour boiling water into a teapot to make a pot of tea, not realizing that he had already filled the pot moments earlier. A further 20 per cent are *test failures,* where we set out to do something and become side-tracked half-way through. One participant went to drive his car out of his garage, but as he was leaving the house he saw his gardening clothes, and put them on as if to start gardening. A further 18 per cent were *subroutine failures*, where we mistakenly forget something, or add another stage, or reorder the stages in a larger action plan. Starting work is an action plan requiring one participant to sit down and begin writing. He interrupted this to lift his hand to his face to take his glasses off, only to find he wasn't wearing them. Another 11 per cent were *discrimination failures*, where we mistake one object for another, e.g. coffee for gravy granules or toothpaste for shaving cream. Finally, 5 per cent were *programme assembly failures*, where our behaviour will not lead to the effect desired, like throwing the sweet away and putting the wrapping paper in your mouth.

### Evaluation of diary research into action slips

Diary research is very useful for revealing categories, although the percentages of types of slips in each can be ignored since we cannot know how many of each type of slip weren't recorded. It could be that people are better able to remember what Reason calls storage failures, and so are more likely to write them down. Also, we can't know the total number of occasions when any of the slips could have occurred, only the number when they did, so we can't compare the frequency of one category of slip compared to another. Finally, diary studies don't reveal any underlying psychological reason for why any of the slips occurred.

## Laboratory studies of action slips

It is possible to create action slips under controlled conditions. Eysenck and Keane (1995) quote Reason's (1992) discussion of two groups of participants who were asked to answer the following question: 'What do you call the white of an egg?' The correct answer is albumen. One group was first asked:

'What do we call the tree that grows from an acorn?' They answered 'Oak'.
'What do we call a funny story?' They said 'Joke'.
'What noise does a frog make?' … 'Croak.'
'What is another name for cape?' … 'Cloak.'

This group answered the egg question 'Yolk' compared to 5 per cent of the group who had not been set up to make the action error.

### Evaluation of laboratory studies of action slips

Creating such slips under artificial laboratory conditions doesn't really help us explain why they occur in our everyday lives. In the laboratory we are being forced to think in certain ways, whilst in everyday life we may be thinking about something else, or anyway not concentrating on what we are doing when a slip may occur.

## Theories of action slips

The main theories (Reason 1992, and Sellen and Norman 1992) suggest the existence of two major modes of cognitive operation. The first resembles Norman and Shallice's first two stages. Processing of sensory data is automatic and behaviour results from the well-learned plans that we have acquired, which are quite beyond our conscious control. We are on 'autopilot'. The advantage to this mode of control is that it is fast and doesn't use up mental resources that could be better employed elsewhere. For example, walking a very familiar road doesn't require conscious mental processing. We may find ourselves at our destination quite unable to remember much about how we arrived there. The disadvantage is that automatic processing is inflexible and allows us to make action slips. A friend walks past and says 'Hello' and we reply 'Hello Bob', only to realize five seconds later that he was Mark.

In the second mode of control we cognitively process sensory data in the ways suggested by the filter or attenuational theories discussed earlier. This is more flexible since we are aware and paying some attention to what is going on. It is essential to activities such as crossing busy roads. We make fewer slips, and it is more flexible. However, it takes up more mental resources, which aren't therefore available for thinking about other things. Early research into selective attention showed that we can't remember much about unattended messages since we are attending elsewhere. Similarly, if we are preoccupied with some thoughts that are unrelated to what we are doing, it would be easy to make an action slip such as repeat an action that we have only just performed. Someone might chide us to pay attention and stop daydreaming.

Sellen and Norman (1992) propose a more specific schema theory. This says that we have numerous major schemas for tasks we must accomplish. Some are major intentions and these are seen as being at the top of a hierarchy of schemas. For example, I'm attending my sister's wedding next week in Banbury. This involves several lower-level schemas. I have to book my dinner suit at the hire shop, get my lounge suit cleaned, find out the times of the Banbury trains on Saturday, organize a taxi to Bodicote House for the service, and the Bell Inn for the wedding lunch. These lower-level schemas reflect the actions involved in achieving the overall schema of being a wedding guest. Action slips can occur at various stages in the achievement of my overall schema. For example, I might misunderstand the intention and make an action slip in implementing it – I may have the wrong date or it may not be a 'black tie' do and I'll be inappropriately dressed. Or I may make a slip in implementing a lower-level schema such as get on the wrong train or leave my case with the wedding present on the platform.

### Evaluation of theories of action slips

The theories suggest that action slips aren't caused by any particular mechanism that some people may have more or less of than others. Rather, they result from a combination of conscious and automatic processing of sensory messages which we all do. According to Sellen and Norman, they are 'the normal by-products of the design of the human action system'. Critics argue that this is a very simple way to view complex human functioning. If the claim that we have an automatic mode of control is true, then we would expect more action slips to occur when we are in this mode. However, this is far from certain. Most action slips may occur when the task we are performing is regarded as trivial rather than when the mode of control is automatic. As is often the case in psychology, the need is for more research.

## THE INFORMATION-PROCESSING APPROACH

How humans acquire and use all the information that is available to our senses (messages) and all the information that we already possess (schemas in memories) has occupied hundreds of cognitive psychologists in thousands of hours of theory and research. Their efforts have been described as adopting the 'information-processing approach' to understanding cognition. Different psychologists use the term in a variety of contexts. For example, cognitive scientists use it to mean the development of applications such as models of artificial intelligence or the way humans reconstruct their recollection of perceptions for eye-witness testimony. Other psychologists use general terms from computing to reflect what human processing is like, so talk about 'input' and 'output'.

As we said earlier, the development of the computer has had a considerable effect on how psychologists have attempted to understand cognitive processing. Rebok (1987) identifies three stages in computer processing which have parallels in human cognitive functioning, outlined in table 12.1.

**Table 12.1  Parallel stages in computer processing and human cognitive functioning**

| Process | Computer | Human |
|---|---|---|
| Input via | keyboard, mouse, joystick, scanner, etc. | senses and previous memories |
| Throughput | processing in working memory | cognitive processes, e.g. thinking, reasoning, remembering |
| Output to | screen, printer, plotter | behaviour, decision making, long-term memory storage |

As Michael Eysenck (1993) summarizes it, the information-processing approach includes the following assumptions:

1 Information made available by the environment is processed by a series of processing systems (e.g. attention, perception, short-term memory).
2 These processing systems transform or alter the information in various systematic ways (e.g. three connected lines are presented to our eyes, but we see a triangle).
3 The aim of research is to specify the processes and structures (e.g. long-term memory) that underlie cognitive performance.
4 Information processing in people resembles that in computers.

The information-processing approach became popular with cognitive psychologists during the 1970s. In its earliest form it comprised a stimulus in the environment (1) being detected and (2) attended to by an individual's perceptual system, (3) being thought about, and (4) being acted upon and/or being stored for later retrieval. According to Eysenck, this version implies two things. First, that attention and perception are 'stimulus driven', i.e. that environmental influences trigger perception. We described this in Chapter 11 as a bottom-up theory. Second, it implies that although processing in each stage may be very fast indeed, only one process can be occurring at any one time. This is serial processing. As we have seen in our discussion of parallel processing and divided attention, this early model is inadequate.

> ► Remind yourself, if you need to, of the major claims in the bottom-up and top-down debate (see Chapter 11, pages 231–3).

More recently, technological advances in brain-scanning devices such as positron emission tomography (PET) and magnetic resonance imaging (MRI) have allowed neurological and cognitive psychologists to study specific areas of cognitive processing. Brain-damaged as well as healthy patients are studied doing various cognitive tasks, such as mathematics or recognition of familiar objects, to enable brain mapping. Useful models are being derived about how information is processed in the brain, such as Ellis and Young's (1988) model of reading and Mishkin and Appenzeller's (1987) model of recognition.

> ► For a description of the information-processing approach applied to perception, see the discussion in Chapter 11 of bottom-up and top-down theories.

The information-processing approach has been reflected in the models and experimental procedures that psychologists have used to study attention. Broadbent's early filter model reflected the serial processing capability of early computers and isn't helpful now. There is so much evidence that humans can *multitask* now that it isn't likely that humans have much use for serial processing, except when deliberately attending to a logical problem such as working through a statistical formula. Treisman, Deutsch and Deutsch, and Johnstone and Heinz offer more sophisticated explanations, with varying degrees of support from often contrived and highly controlled shadowing studies. However, they are also based on the idea of serial information processing and ignore our ability to divide our attention between two or more tasks.

The first models to explain divided attention came from Norman

> ► *Multitasking* refers to the way that computers can perform different sets of calculations in different parts of their working and storage memories at the same time. So a computer could be working out a small firm's wages bill at the same time as calculating how many new parts the company needs to order. Humans can drive and talk, run and think, plan a meal and get dressed.

and Bobrow, and Kahneman. They suggested that we have a limited capacity to process information, although Kahneman does claim that capacity can vary. Processing capacity must be divided between the competing demands. These models do not recognize human capacity for parallel processing and multitasking. By the late 1970s and early 1980s computer technology was moving towards parallel processing capacity. Allport was one of the first to apply a multichannel model derived from the new technologies. It said that multitasking in different perceptual modes occurs without the need for an overall 'executive' decision maker. Some support for Allport's parallel processing model has come from neuropsychological research using PET scan data. The brain location for some aspects of the ways different senses attend to certain messages has been discovered (Posner and Peterson 1990).

Shiffrin and Schneider's automaticity model allowed for both serial and parallel processing and, combined with Norman and Shallice's and Logan's ideas, is at least able to explain how practice leads to automatic processing. The usefulness of the computer analogy is now being questioned. Computers aren't yet 'intelligent' in any sense that would be recognizable to students of human cognitive processing. We are some way from Hal in *2001: A Space Odyssey*, Kit in *Knight Rider*, or 'Computer' in *Star Trek*.

■ What is meant by the information-processing approach to (a) perception and (b) attention?

■ Outline the contribution the approach has made to the usefulness of each of the major models.

---

### Some differences between computer and human processing

| *Computers* | *Humans* |
| --- | --- |
| are machines | are organic |
| are manufactured | have evolved over hundreds of thousands of years |
| require external input | can direct themselves |
| have limited perceptual skills | have advanced perceptual skills |
| require programmes of instructions | can think for themselves, have some 'free will' |
| use algorithmic logic (finding the 'best fit') | use heuristic logic (make 'educated' guesses) |
| can repeat a set of programmes instructions faultlessly | get better with practice or become overconfident or careless |
| can go on until they break down | get tired, bored or simply refuse |
| have a limited range of responses | can do many different things |

---

► If the limitations lie in perceptual, not cognitive, processing, is it time we had a second look at William James, Donald Broadbent, Anne Treisman and the others?

### Evaluation of the information-processing approach

If by the 'information-processing approach' we mean the process of perception from sensation to cognition, then the information-processing approach offers many neurological challenges. We already know something of perceptual processing. There is increasing evidence from neurological studies to show parallel processing in different senses and that attenuational processes appear to be operating. However, there is no support for limited-capacity models. Researchers have found no evidence for a central processor allocating resources to different demands, nor do we believe that there is a limit to how much information particular structures can process. The reasons why we don't take everything in is more likely because our senses and perceptual systems can't handle everything rather than any limitations in our brain's ability to process.

If we can separate the information-processing approach as applied to attention from the computer analogy, then it, too, may challenge psychologists such as Neisser or supporters of the inferential models to provide explanations based on neurological evidence. However, as long as information processing is synonymous with the computer analogy, we are going to have problems.

---

### Summary – The information-processing approach

The information-processing approach is a useful and challenging way to characterize human perceptual and cognitive processing. Neurological studies are producing some support for models derived from this approach. The extent to which it is helpful to compare human information processing with machine processing rather depends on how similar we imagine human and machine processing are likely to be.

---

### Exam questions – 60 minutes each

1 Discuss the contribution that research on information processing has made to our understanding of attention. (*25 marks*)

2 (a) Describe techniques that have been used in the study of selective attention. (*5 marks*)

(b) Describe and evaluate two theories or models of selective attention. (*20 marks*)

# 13 *Memory processes*

**Chapter objectives**

By the end of this chapter you should be able to:

▌ define the term memory and see how it relates to selective attention;

▌ appreciate the development of memory research during the last century;

▌ outline, compare and contrast, and evaluate two major psychological models of memory;

▌ comprehend the ways organization of material affects storage and retrieval in memory;

▌ understand some of the recent advances in memory research;

▌ appreciate some biochemical and physiological bases of memory;

▌ describe and evaluate the major psychological explanations for why we forget;

▌ know some practical applications of memory research.

## Introduction

Crowder (1978) offers a simple definition of memory which says that memory is the *dynamic* process associated with the retention and retrieval of information about past experiences. Being able to take in sensory information, transduce it, code and store it, and later retrieve it enables us to make sensible adaptations to our environment and to pass on our knowledge to our children. The term memory has three variations of meaning. It can refer to the mental function of processing and storing information that can be recalled later. It is used to mean the storage system that we actually use, and which has been experimentally investigated. And it can mean the actual information that is remembered.

In this chapter we are interested in the ways in which psychologists have described human memory, what they know about its biology, why we forget, and what practical implications are there for our everyday use of memory.

▶ *Dynamic* means constantly in a state of change.

## APPROACHES TO THE STUDY OF HUMAN MEMORY

### Early studies of human memory

Some 120 years ago **Hermann Ebbinghaus** applied an introspective approach, and careful measurement and recording techniques, to measure his own (and an assistant's) memory capacity. They learned lists of 2,300 German nonsense syllables. He chose nonsense syllables because he thought that learning actual words wouldn't be a true test of memory capacity since words have meaning and it may be the meaning that he was remembering. The alternative approach – to investigate how people store and use meaning – was developed from 1932 by **Frederic Bartlett** (1886–1969). We will return to Bartlett's contribution later in this chapter.

During the early part of the twentieth century most of the research on memory was performed on laboratory animals. It was assumed that memories were formed from numerous conditioned responses. Apart from Ebbinghaus' attempts to measure memory capacity, other work involved patients with *amnesia* (memory loss) or people in specialized occupations such as air traffic control. Some studies proposed the existence of a short-term memory store where attention was paid to various kinds of stimuli (visual, auditory, etc.) for a few moments (see Chapter 12 on selective attention). Other studies were explaining long-term memory storage in terms of simple associations between stimuli and responses.

### Modern approaches to studying human memory

We now believe that memory is a much more complex process than could be investigated by experiments. Most early research was confined to artificial and highly controlled experiments that tried to identify how selective attention worked and how memory stored information. This lacks what James Gibson would call ecological validity (see Chapter 11), as we shall see in the work of Ulric Neisser later in this chapter.

During the 1960s and 1970s a *multistore* model of how human memory works was widely adopted. It involved three distinct but interrelated stages. First, we perceive something (sensory registration) which is transduced into neural activity. We referred to this under the general heading of 'selective attention' in Chapter 12. The second stage answers the question, 'how do we remember things?', i.e. how is the coded information stored? Are there different types of memory, just as there are different structures in the brain associated with different senses? (See Chapter 11 for a discussion of brain structures and processes in the visual and auditory systems.) The type and duration of different stores will be discussed later. Third, memory requires retrieval, since there's no point in storing something unless we can recall it later. Questions about forgetting are relevant here.

Breakdowns may occur in any of these stages. We may misperceive, and hence store and recall wrong information. Or we may

▶ Unfortunately, knowing the capacity one scientist had for memorizing meaningless verbal material tells us little about 'normal' human memory concerning things that do have meaning for us.

▶ *Amnesia* refers to a loss of memory, either due to an inability to process and store information, or to a failure to retrieve previously known information. It can be caused by physiological factors, including old age, accidents or substance abuse. Or it can be caused by some psychological problem which blocks recall.

▶ Regarding memory as a dynamic process is another aspect of the information-processing approach to human cognition discussed in Chapter 12.

▶ Most of the experiments in memory research have been conducted to test the duration, capacity or speed of processing of various kinds of material. This *psychometric* (measuring human mental abilities) approach may be useful for explaining how some system works in theory, but it doesn't necessarily help psychologists explain real life memory in real life situations.

■ **What are the stages in the dynamic process called memory?**

▶ A model is a mini-theory, an untested prediction about what form or set of procedures something might take.

▶ You might find it helpful to see a distinction between a memory 'store', implying a group of cells and systems somewhere in the brain which houses the memory traces, and memory 'processes', implying how information is selected, transduced, coded and processed for storage, and the biological processes involved in how storage itself is achieved.

▶ Before we can process information we must first receive it. Cognitive psychologists refer to a sensory store where this process occurs. It is one of the first stages in the information-processing system.

perceive accurately, but the coding process is inadequate so we store the information in the wrong place, or in a mistaken form, so that later recall is confused. Or we may perceive and code the scene correctly, but still fail to recall because of some 'retrieval failure'.

Even this summary sounds as though the job of memory could be performed by a mechanical device such as a computer. Each of the stages is, in fact, more complex than it seems, and psychologists have hypothesized about what kind of activities are occurring in them. We shall describe in the following pages two of the best known information-processing theories: the *two-process model* first suggested by **Richard Atkinson** and **Richard Shiffrin** in the 1960s, and the *levels of processing* approach proposed by **Fergus Craik** and **Robert Lockhart** in the early 1970s.

> ### Summary – Approaches to the study of human memory
>
> The study of memory began, and has remained for most of the twentieth century, a laboratory affair. The earliest attempts to study the capacity and duration of memory weren't particularly successful, since they ignored 'everyday memory'.

## MODELS OF MEMORY

Those interested in the information-processing approach, from Broadbent on, have mostly supported a view that memory comprises several 'stores' or stages of processing. These have been called multistore models of memory. They usually begin with registration of some sensory data and end with long-term storage and retrieval.

### The sensory store

Humans have many senses, which provide them with information about their world. The main ones include the visual sense, the auditory sense, several aspects of the sense of touch, the sense of smell, the taste senses and the senses of balance and body position. Each probably has its own sensory store, although only the visual and auditory senses have been studied in any detail. The sensory store may lie in the system of nerves that links the sense organ with the brain. Broadbent's early filter system (see Chapter 12) described this as a sensory buffer, which each of our senses has. It holds information for a few moments until it is either processed further, or it decays and is lost.

Since information can only be held in the sensory stores for a few moments, new information coming in will displace any already there. Imagine we arrange an experiment during which you see a picture of a street scene with people and traffic for a fraction of a second. Then we ask you some questions about the picture. You should be able to hold the image in your sensory store (or buffer – a computing term) for long enough for most of it to pass to the short-term store and long-term store, and so allow you to answer our questions. If we showed you other pictures immediately following the first, then the first picture would be 'overwritten', and wouldn't pass to the other stores. You wouldn't be able to answer many questions about it.

The first major laboratory-based research into visual sensory decoding was conducted in the late 1950s by **George Sperling**. Sperling had a difficult experimental problem to solve. If people remember some things for only very short periods, how can you find out what they remember if they forget it more quickly than it takes them to tell you about it? Sperling found an ingenious solution.

His experiment used an apparatus called a *tachistoscope* to show participants visual stimuli for one-twentieth of a second. He showed them 12 letters in three rows of four and asked them to recall one of the rows. He did this by sounding a tone to indicate which four-letter row out of the three rows they should disclose. A high tone indicated that they should recall the top row, a middle tone the middle row and a low tone the bottom row. He reasoned that if participants could announce any row of four letters out of 12 then there was a brief period when they could remember all twelve, although that period might be shorter than it would take to say all 12 letters

The inset shows Sperling's experimental procedure and figure 13.1 shows some of his results. He found that if the tone was sounded immediately after the presentation of the letters, participants could remember 3.3 letters on average. He took this to mean that participants could actually remember 9.9 letters out of 12 on the sounding of the tone, but would have forgotten some of them had they had to announce them all. This is shown as a recall of 82.5 per cent on the bar chart in figure 13.1.

■ In your own words describe what happens in the sensory store. How does this relate to (a) Broadbent's sensory buffer, (b) Treisman's attenuator and (c) Kahneman's limited-capacity model of selective attention?

▶ *Tachistoscopes* are machines that allow people to see particular objects or words, possibly superimposed on various backgrounds, for precisely timed periods from one millisecond (one-thousandth of a second). They used to be quite widely used by experimental psychologists to test the thresholds of human perception.

*Figure 13.1  Bar chart of Sperling's results*

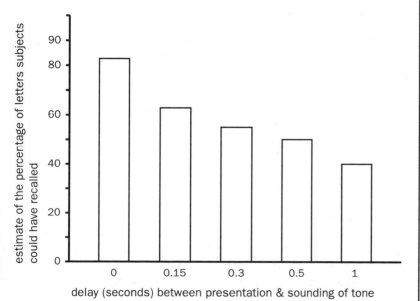

estimate of the percentage of letters subjects could have recalled

delay (seconds) between presentation & sounding of tone

Note: *The bar chart shows that the number of letters recalled declines as the delay between presentation and recall increases. Sperling took this to represent the fading of an afterimage of the presentation.*

▶ According to Sperling's research, visual sensory registration lasts for about half a second in ideal laboratory conditions, using very simple stimuli which the subjects were told to expect. In 'real life' the duration of sensory registration will be affected by all kind of things, including its intensity, importance, novelty, duration, and so on.

**Sperling's experimental procedure**

| Stage 1 | Stage 2 | Stage 3 | Stage 4 |
| --- | --- | --- | --- |
| Becoming accustomed to looking into the tachistoscope | Presentation for one-twentieth of a second | Sounding of tone § | Recall |
| | Q F H T | High | Q F . . . |
| | Z M K E | Medium | |
| | C B V R | Low | |

§ The tone could sound before, during or after the presentation

Sperling concluded that his participants held an afterimage of the display in their perceptual system from which they recalled the letters. This is an example of *iconic imagery*. The afterimage (*icon*) would quickly fade, so that the longer after the tachistoscope presentation the tone was sounded, the fewer of the letters participants could recall. This is confirmed by the results in figure 13.1. With a half a second delay between presentation and the sounding of the tone, participants could only remember just over two letters on average from a row of four. This is equivalent to an afterimage of just over six letters out of 12. After a delay of one second they could only remember the equivalent of five letters out of 12. The results in the bar diagram as a whole show the speed at which the afterimage fades.

Sperling thought each sense would have its own sensory store. The visual sense has an iconic store, the auditory sense has an acoustic (or echoic) store, the sense of touch has a haptic store, and no doubt taste has a taste store, and smell has an olfactory store. This idea was also accepted by Atkinson and Shiffrin, who suggested further processing and storage systems.

**Summary – The sensory store**

Each sense modality has a system of transducing physical energy into the kind of chemical energy that our perceptual system can handle. Shortly after transduction the messages are held in a 'store' (or are on their way to the brain). They are either processed further towards consciousness or are lost. Sperling attempted to measure the capacity and duration of a sensory store for vision using his ingenious tachistoscope experiments.

## Atkinson and Shiffrin's two-process model

William James referred to primary and secondary memory, equivalent to our conceptions of short- and longer-term memory over a century ago. Others, from Ebbinghaus onwards, have claimed that a clear distinction can sensibly be made between two memory storage systems. Richard Atkinson and Richard Shiffrin proposed a 'two-store' model of memory (1968, 1971). Short-term store is roughly equivalent to the processes of selective attention for meaning, and long-term store is for 'lifetime' memory.

## Short-term store (STS) or short-term memory (STM)

According to the two-process model selective attention is paid to some feature in the environment. For example, the fire bell rings while you are concentrating on preparing an essay in the library. The feature (the sound of the bell) will be held for a few moments in a sensory buffer or store while processing takes place. You recognize it within a second as the fire bell.

Atkinson and Shiffrin propose a pattern-matching explanation for how the decision is made about which information in sensory store becomes further processed. Template matching, feature detection and pattern matching were discussed in Chapter 11. Information about the feature that is recognized will be passed on to a short-term store (STS), which is more or less what we mean when we talk of 'consciousness'. In the STS the coded information about the feature will be further processed for up to 20 or 30 seconds. Its importance may be evaluated in some way. You may ponder, 'Is it a real fire, or is it a fire drill?'

If it is relevant the information may then pass into long-term store (LTS), where it may last for years. If it doesn't appear to be relevant it will simply be lost as new information enters the short-term store. Although we talk of two stores, Atkinson and Shiffrin do not mean that they will be in two different locations in the brain. This is only a model to characterize the memory process, not a guide to the functions of parts of the brain. Information entering our sensory store depends entirely on what is going on in our environment at the time. We have no conscious control over what enters, or whether it will be processed to any extent. The same is not true of the short-term store. Atkinson and Shiffrin suggest that the STS is our everyday 'working memory'. You can consciously try to remember something that will help you solve some puzzle, such as using landmarks to find your way around an unfamiliar town on the first day of your holiday abroad. Listening to conversations, reading an article, playing games or following the story in a TV soap opera all require you to use your short-term memory. If you couldn't remember what had happened in the last few seconds you would not be able to follow any activity very well!

Atkinson and Shiffrin say that the STS contains some *control processes* which enable us to exercise some control. For example, we may choose to *rehearse* some information so that it will be transferred to long-term memory. After parking in the multi-storey car park you may say to yourself, 'The car is on Level Four, by the Market Street entrance, down the alley with the café and bridal gowns shop'. This is *verbal rehearsal*. If you take a look over your shoulder at the alley when you're some distance from it, this is *visual rehearsal*. Both should help you find your car later. Rehearsal is a control process.

Another example of control processes are the *retrieval strategies* we employ to find relevant information in our long-term stores (LTS) that will help us decide the importance of the information

▶ Short-term memory (STM) is the memory we use for dealing with everyday experiences. It is what we mean by 'consciousness'.

▶ A *control process* is a strategy we use for directing our knowledge in some way to achieve some greater understanding.

▶ *Retrieval strategies* search for information in long-term memory to enable interpretation or evaluation of the present contents of STS.

■ Describe the role of the STS in Atkinson and Shiffrin's two-process model of memory.

currently in STS. When all the processing and 'coding' are finished, decisions are made in STS about any action that may be required. After your shopping trip you look down the left-hand parade in the precinct, and see a bridal gown shop. Is this the way to the car? STS searches LTS for other clues that might confirm or reject the possibility. You might look down the right-hand parade to see if there's more than one bridal gown shop. In almost conscious consultation with LTS, our STS makes a decision, and we behave accordingly. See figure 13.2 for a diagram of Atkinson and Shiffrin's model.

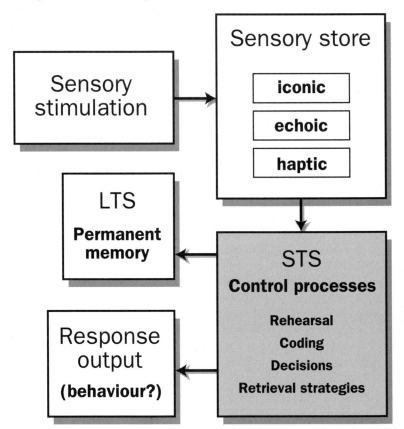

*Figure 13.2 Atkinson and Shiffrin's control processes and short-term storage*

▶ Although psychologists talk of long- and short-term memory as though they were 'real' and known to exist, the evidence for the distinction is not conclusive.

STS can process information very quickly, but it can only process a few items of information at a time. This was confirmed independently in the late 1950s by **J.M. Brown** in England and **Lloyd** and **Margaret Peterson** in America. They were actually investigating forgetting rather than memory, and the technique they devised demonstrated, really for the first time, that short- and long-term storage could be seen as two processes within memory. Until then researchers investigating the process of forgetting were either behaviourists (see Chapter 1), who believed that learning occurred by association (and therefore forgetting results from a breakdown in these associations), or they were clinical psychologists studying problems of short-term memory loss in patients suffering from various kinds of amnesia, which we shall discuss later in this chapter.

The Brown–Peterson method is another carefully controlled laboratory method. They tachistoscopically flashed a three-letter nonsense syllable such as VEL and a three-digit number, e.g. 486, simultaneously. The subject had to look at the number and nonsense syllable, and immediately start to count backwards from the number seen, in multiples of four or three, e.g. 486, 483, 480, 477, 474, etc., to ensure that no rehearsal of the letters could occur. After a delay of several seconds, called the *retention interval*, the participants were to stop counting and try to recall the nonsense syllable. The Petersons found the duration of the STS for this kind of material was about 18 seconds. If the retention interval was longer than 18 seconds, recall was impossible.

The amount of information that can be held in STS can also be made to vary. **George Miller** (1956) argues that the maximum capacity of STS is 'The magical number seven, plus or minus two'. So whether it is sometimes five and other times nine depends on the nature of the information. An 'item' of meaning can be a combination of smaller units of meaning. A letter of the alphabet has some meaning. 'C', 'A' and 'T' are thus three items, but they can be *chunked* together to make a 'one word item' – 'CAT'. This is sometimes called Miller's *chunking theory*. Miller says that STS capacity is determined by the number of chunks of meaning, rather than the amount of information taken to establish that meaning. Words can be *chained* into sentences. So 'The cat sat on the mat' could count as 17 'letter items', six 'word items', or a 'one sentence' item. Chunking and chaining are useful techniques for expanding memory.

**Alan Baddeley** and **Graham Hitch** (1974) disagreed with other descriptions of the short-term memory. Agreeing with Broadbent that 'if we are to get anywhere we have to build things that will last', Baddeley and Hitch slowly developed their ideas about STS based on experimentation and observation. They were more interested in the question 'What is memory for?' rather than what was being asked until then, 'What is memory like?' They thought that short-term memory was better understood as a *working memory* that had several functions beyond control processes. There is a *central executive*, which makes decisions about what demands are being made and allocates attention accordingly in much the same way that Kahneman's model of selective attention does (see Chapter 12). There are also now three slave systems. The *primary acoustic store* is where all sounds are initially received and await processing for meaning. Second, the *articulatory loop* is for verbal rehearsal, for example of a telephone number we've just looked up and repeat to ourselves. Third is the *visuo-spatial sketch pad* for visual rehearsal or for recall of familiar visual information, for example when giving someone directions to somewhere you know well by sight. These three interact with the central executive to decide what gets attended to, processed and stored. With further research no doubt other 'slave systems' will be discovered.

■ **Explain what Miller means by 'the magical number seven'.**

▶ *Working memory* is a limited-capacity model which does allow some processing of information to occur before processing it into long-term memory.

### Summary – Short-term memory

One way of characterizing short-term memory is what we think of as consciousness. Atkinson and Shiffrin suggest that messages can last for about 30 seconds, by which time they must have been acted upon, or will be lost. STS contains some processes that will decide the fate of the messages it holds. These include retrieval strategies for checking long-term store for relevant information, and rehearsal, which enables information that needs to become long-term memory to be put there. Brown and Peterson suggest that short-term processing can last for about 20 seconds. Miller suggests that the magic number seven, plus or minus two, explains STS capacity.

## Long-term store (LTS) or long-term memory (LTM)

The long-term store can hold information for any period of time up to one lifetime. As far as we know, there is no limit to the amount it can hold. It contains all our knowledge (and misunderstandings) of physical objects (their use, size, colour, weight, etc.), social relationships (where each person stands in relation to others), locations and how to move from one to another, and so on.

One interesting finding from studies of long-term memory is that what is recalled after a period of time isn't necessarily exactly what was perceived in the first place. Our long-term memories are dynamic. They tend to 'reconstruct' past events in terms of our present understanding. **Frederic Bartlett** moved out of the laboratory to conduct slightly more ecologically valid research over 50 years ago. He told his students stories that were from another culture, and which weren't always easily understood by people from this culture. At various intervals afterwards he asked his participants to recite the story back to him. The best known example of Bartlett's stories is probably 'The War of the Ghosts'.

► Some writers believe that after material has been transferred to long-term store, certain changes take place in the structure and chemical balances in those parts of the nervous system where the learning has occurred. The phrase 'metabolic consolidation' is used to mean the transfer of information between short- and long-term store.

### The War of the Ghosts

One night two young men from Egulac went down to the river to hunt seals, and while they were there it became foggy and calm. Then they heard war cries and they thought, 'Maybe this is a war party'. They escaped to the shore and hid behind a log. Now canoes came up and they heard the noise of paddles and saw one canoe coming up to them. There were five men in the canoe and they said: 'What do you think? We wish to take you along. We are going up the river to make war on the people.'

One of the young men said, 'I have no arrows.'

'Arrows are in the canoe,' they said.

'I will not go along. I might be killed. My relatives do not know where I have gone. But you,' he said, turning to the other, 'may go with them.'

So one of the young men went and the other returned home.

And the warriors went up the river to a town on the other side of Kalama. The people came down to the water and they began to fight, and many were killed. But presently the young man heard one of the warriors say: 'Quick, let us go home: that Indian has been hit.' Now he thought, 'Oh they are ghosts'. He did not feel sick, but they said he had been shot.

So the canoes went back to Egulac and the young man went ashore to his house and made a fire. And he told everybody and said, 'Behold, I accompanied the ghosts and we went to a fight. Many of our fellows were killed, and many of those who attacked us were killed. They said I was hit and I did not feel sick.'

He told it all, and then he became quiet. When the sun rose he fell down. Something black came out of his mouth. His face became contorted. The people jumped up and cried. He was dead.

► 'The War of the Ghosts' is an American Indian folk story, and would make sense to the Indians. Their ideas about death and spirits are quite different from ours.

The versions Bartlett's participants gave of 'The War of the Ghosts' were different from the original in several respects. They were generally shorter, since details and aspects that did not conform to the subject's own culture were usually omitted. Details were also added to make sense of, or rationalize, the parts of the story that were difficult to understand. Some parts, usually the death scene, were taken to be more important than others, and much more detail was provided about them. Some of the words were changed and events were taken out of sequence to make more sense.

Bartlett concluded that all new learning is based on previously existing schemas. His participants would try to understand the story in terms of what was normal in their culture and experience. When they tried to remember it they reconstructed it according to their existing knowledge about the world. What they recalled was reconstructed from what they thought they knew.

**Marcia Johnson** suggests that what we remember is what we 'reconstruct' from the meanings we have stored in our memories. She presented participants with a series of sentences. One was: 'John was trying to fix the birdhouse. He was pounding the nail when his father came out to watch him and to help him do the work.' Later she presented the participants with several sentences. They included the original sentence, and all had similar meanings. She asked them to pick out the one they had heard originally. Most chose the following sentence: 'John was using the hammer to fix the birdhouse when his father came out to watch and help him do the work.' The original sentence doesn't mention a hammer, but that was the meaning the participants remembered. If the participants were given the choice immediately after hearing the original sentence, then they would probably have chosen correctly. However, the passage of time leads to meanings rather than actual details being stored for later recall.

■ Try Bartlett's experiment on your friends. Get them to read 'The War of the Ghosts' and test their recall in a week's time.

■ What is meant by 'reconstructive memory'?

### Summary – Long-term store

Long-term memory can hold vast amounts of information for many years. Many parts of the brain are involved, and many brain processes involved in storage and retrieval ensure that what we remember isn't necessarily what happened, although it can often be remarkably close, depending on how meaningful and impressive it was when the experience first occurred.

### Organization in memory

We could not hope to remember everything that goes on around us. One of the factors that influences the likelihood of something being remembered is how it is organized. **Gordon Bower** and his colleagues (1969) showed that when verbal items were organized into meaningful hierarchies they could be learned and recalled more quickly and accurately than when the same material was not organized. An example of their organized hierarchies is shown in figure 13.3.

▶ A hierarchy is any group of items that are placed in rank order, from the most general to the most specific, or from the highest to the lowest, e.g. 'Animal, vertebrate, mammal, feline, cat', or '90 per cent, 78 per cent, 45 per cent, 30 per cent, 23 per cent'.

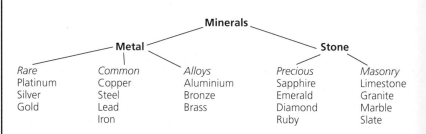

*Figure 13.3 Example of Bower et al.'s organized hierarchies*

One group of participants (the 'organized' group) saw the words to be recalled set out in hierarchies, like the one shown in figure 13.3. Another group (the 'randomized' group) saw the same words in lists that only appeared to have some structure. Altogether there were 112 words to be remembered. When tested later the 'organized' group could remember 65 per cent of the words in the hierarchies, while the 'randomized' group could recall only 19 per cent.

Further support for the idea that memories are organized according to the meaning of the material comes from **Brown** and **McNeill**'s (1966) 'tip of the tongue' experiments. They gave participants a list of definitions of words that were rarely used. When recall was tested later many of the participants couldn't remember the target word, but 'knew that they knew it'. Sometimes they could remember the first letter, or what the word sounded like. They could give words that were similar in meaning, too. This does suggest that information about words is stored according to their meaning and sound.

During the 1960s **Allan Collins** and **Ross Quillian** concluded that meaningful information was stored in a hierarchical way, with ideas that 'go together' being stored together. For example, there would be a hierarchy for 'people'. Below 'all people' might be knowledge about different races, each divided by knowledge about men, women and children. Further down would come sets of ideas about family members. Figure 13.4 shows one of Collins and Quillian's best known hierarchies. Each hierarchy starts with some general categories, and becomes more specific as we move through it. Having our knowledge stored in hierarchies allows easier access to appropriate information.

► If items are stored hierarchically, and items in each hierarchy are 'cross-referenced' to other relevant items in other hierarchies, could 'intelligence' be the physiological efficiency with which these hierarchies are made, maintained and accessed?

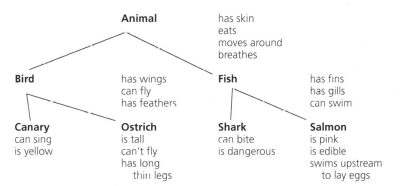

*Figure 13.4 Example of Collins and Quillian's semantic hierarchies*

Collins and Quillian tested their model by asking participants to say whether a series of statements they were shown were true or false. If the theory is correct, then statements that are closely related in where they are stored will be processed, and a response made, more quickly than statements which are from different parts of the hierarchy. Thus the statement 'Canaries are yellow' involves very little processing time, since the information about the colour of canaries is very close in the hierarchy. The statement 'Canaries have skin' involves several levels of processing, and the response should take longer. Collins and Quillian tested the response time, and found that it did increase with the number of levels that would have to be processed. However, it takes longer for most people to recognize an ostrich than a canary anyway, so this delay may be caused by the need for further perceptual processing rather than processing for meaning.

Apart from information being stored according to its meaning, it is also stored according to the relevance it has for us personally. Some researchers, such as **Endel Tulving**, suggest that there are at least two types of long-term storage. These are the *semantic store*, where events are stored by the meaning they had for us at the time, and the *episodic store*, where memories of particular episodes in our lives are stored. Episodic memory does not require hierarchies for retrieval. (This might explain why some items stored in episodic memory are more likely to be forgotten than semantically stored information.) The two types of store will inevitably be interlinked. Not everyone agrees with Tulving's semantic/episodic distinction, since it would be impossible to recall incidents from our lives (episodic memory) without the meaning (semantic memory) they had for us at the time.

► Suggesting two types of long-term storage does not mean there are two different parts of the brain where these different stores are found. It is a model that is being proposed, a way of understanding memory processes, and not a guide around the brain.

► Tulving's distinction between episodic and semantic long-term storage is not shared by all cognitive psychologists. Perhaps we only remember episodes in our lives in terms of the meaning they had for us at the time.

■ **Compare Collins and Quillian's conclusions about the nature of long-term storage with those of Gordon Bower.**

### Life without long-term memory

Without long-term memory life would consist only of brief impressions of where we are at the moment, with no understanding of ourselves, our personality, our family or our background. We would have very little knowledge of the world and wouldn't know anything about the people we were with, apart from what they had said and done in the previous 20 seconds. Meaningful conversation would be impossible. We couldn't play any games because we'd have no understanding of rules. In fact, life would be altogether meaningless. This is why the study of memory is important in psychology and why memory is regarded as one of the central cognitive processes.

### Summary – The two-process model of memory

Short-term memory provides our conscious awareness of the world around us. Control processes allow us to rehearse information or effect decisions. Brown and Peterson found that information in STS can't last for more than 18 to 20 seconds without rehearsal. Miller claims that up to seven items can be chunked and chained for meaning to increase STS capacity. LTS has unlimited capacity and is reconstructive in nature. Early research has tested the duration, capacity or speed of processing of various kinds of material, but it doesn't necessarily help psychologists explain 'real life' memory in everyday situations.

### Evidence for the two-process model

Earlier we discussed the Brown–Peterson technique, which seems to indicate the existence of a short-term store. Information in it will be overwritten by new information coming in if rehearsal and further processing are frustrated by a task such as counting backwards. The Brown–Peterson method is taken to support the view that memory comprises two (hypothetically) distinct types or levels of processing.

Another way to demonstrate the distinction is to ask people to read aloud a list of words. Immediately afterwards they are asked to recall as many of the words as they can. Most people were said to be able to recall the first few and the last few, but rarely many from the middle of the list. Plotting the number recalled and the position in the list that they occupied provides a *serial position curve* (figure 13.5). The first words that are read are supposed to have been processed into LTS, from where they can be recalled later. The last words read are supposed to be recalled from the STS. This demonstrates what psychologists call the *primacy* and *recency effects*. Primacy refers to what we experience first, and recency to what we experience last.

None of this evidence actually confirms a distinction between a short- and long-term memory store, since there is no obvious need

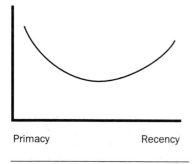

Primacy                    Recency

*Figure 13.5  Serial position curve*

► If we do not know very much about something, the first information we have is likely to have the greatest effect on us. This is the *primacy effect*. If we already have some knowledge, but are uncertain, the last information we receive is likely to have most influence. This is the *recency effect*.

for any distinction to exist. Why should the primacy effect suggest a separate, long-term mode of storage from the recency effect? Perhaps we are simply more receptive to the novelty of the words at the beginning, so they are remembered. And the words we heard last can be recalled simply because we heard them last. Why should they be being remembered from a different (short-term) type of store? Further, why aren't the words in the middle of the list remembered well at all? If we have a long-term store, why aren't they being stored there along with the ones we hear? At the very least we have to accept that the case is not proven.

Craik and Lockhart (1972) summarize the case against the multi-store model by quoting the following researchers: Tulving and Patterson (1968), who dispute the idea that information has to pass from one store to another; Shallice and Warrington (1970), who 'presented evidence against the idea that information must "pass through" STS to enter LTS'. Craik and Lockhart continue: 'In our view the criteria listed … do not provide satisfactory grounds for distinguishing between separate stores.' They conclude: 'Whilst multistore models have played a useful role, we suggest that they are often taken too literally and more fruitful questions are generated by the present formulation' (i.e. their levels of processing approach).

## The levels of processing approach to memory

As Gordon Bower and others have shown, new items are stored in memory in terms of some association they have with existing memories. For example, any new knowledge about motorbikes will be stored with existing 'motorbike knowledge'. When we need to recall it we will only need to search the 'manufactured', 'machine', 'transport', 'motorized', 'motorbike' hierarchy to find the information. If items were stored according to when we first discovered them we'd have to remember everything that happened to us for the last few years before finding the motorbike information. This would take ages, be completely uneconomical, and probably threatening to our survival.

In the early 1970s **Craik** and **Lockhart** proposed a modification of the two-process model. They see no particular need for separate systems of short- and long-term store, but rather see memory as the (almost accidental) by-product of the level to which information has been processed. Some stimuli that are barely or briefly perceived will hardly be processed at all. They will produce a faint *memory trace*, which will soon decay from sensory store as new information enters. They may be attenuated, or simply overwritten. Other information will be processed more deeply, depending on a number of factors, such as how relevant it is to the perceiver, how much time there is available before other stimuli are perceived, and the nature of the stimulation. The more deeply an item is processed, the more durable will be the memory trace it produces. The most durable traces last the longest time, and become longer-lasting memories.

► Atkinson and Shiffrin have presented a neat and attractive model of two, separate memory storage systems, each with its own functions. There may indeed be two systems, but the case is far from proven.

► When information becomes stored in memory it is said to alter the biochemical structure of (probably millions) of brain cells. These changes are called *memory traces* or *engrams*.

► Attenuation is the process of reducing the strength of an unwanted signal. The signal is not eliminated altogether.

► Like Atkinson and Shiffrin, Craik and Lockhart are attempting to explain highly complicated physiological relationships in the human brain in terms of some relatively simple psychological principles.

► Cognition (knowing) means selectively attending to one stimulus rather than another. It results from perception (the senses responding to it in some way) and remembering (the memories and previous knowledge required to interpret it have been used). Cognition requires that information must have been deeply processed.

► Craik's theory does not reject the possibility of a dynamic 'working memory' (which may be the same as 'consciousness' or 'attention'), but it only accounts for what we attend to, not for the type of active processing, especially rehearsal, which Atkinson and Shiffrin proposed.

► Craik and Watkins' findings do not mean that rehearsal isn't important for things to be remembered for longer periods of time. If you wish to pass your exams, then you will need to remember the material, and one way to do this is to rehearse it.

If you see a photograph of someone you know well, first your eyes recognize a two-dimensional form with a pattern of lines and colours on it. It has taken some visual perceptual processing of the structural parts of the picture to achieve this level of pattern recognition. (This is what Craik and Tulving describe as 'structural processing'.) An instant later further cognitive processing occurs, and the lines and colours are interpreted as representing a human form. (If the stimulus was a word, not a picture, this stage would involve phonetic processing – processing for sound.) Finally, memory processing occurs to find a match for the patterns in the picture, and we 'recognize' our friend. (The word would be processed semantically – for meaning.) Even this rather simple description of three levels of processing should give you an idea of just how complex and interrelated perception, cognition and memory are. And yet we recognize the person in the photograph, or know the meaning of a familiar word, in a fraction of a second.

Craik and Lockhart identify at least three different stages in the depth to which stimuli will be processed. If the stimulus presented is the word 'octopus':

| *Level 1* | Processing Structural level | What does the shape or form of the word 'octopus' look like? |
| *Level 2* | Processing Phonetic level | When spoken aloud, what does the word 'octopus' sound like? |
| *Level 3* | Processing Semantic level | What is the meaning of the word 'octopus'? |

Other skills also require increasingly complex levels of processing, probably including varieties of pattern recognition, feature detection and template matching, as discussed in Chapter 11. Reading, for example, involves several stages of processing. First, to recognize the letters that make up a word requires limited sensory processing. Then follows recognizing the word itself. So far the level of processing required is small. The next stage involves storing the meaning of the word, and this requires much deeper processing. This must happen for each word in a sentence. Understanding, and being able to work out a response to each sentence you hear or read, requires very deep processing.

An experiment by **Fergus Craik** and **Michael Watkins** supplies evidence for a levels of processing approach. According to the two-process model, if information is to pass from short- to long-term storage it must be rehearsed. Craik and Watkins asked participants to listen to a series of word lists and remember the last word beginning with a particular letter. For example, if the 'target letter' was 'l', then in the list 'grass, level, rejoin, potato, wolf, carpet, lady, launderette, legal, aim, stable, bungle, lurid, tadpole', the word 'lurid' should be easily remembered. It was.

Craik and Watkins also asked the participants to recall as many of the other words beginning with 'l' as they could. If rehearsal was important they should have remembered 'level', and also 'legal', since there was time to rehearse them while 'non-target' words were being heard. There wouldn't have been time to rehearse 'lady' or 'launderette', since these words were immediately followed by another target word which would be rehearsed. In fact, Craik and Watkins found that all the target words were equally likely to be recalled. Rehearsal alone clearly does not explain what is remembered and what isn't.

> ### Summary – Levels of processing approach
>
> Fergus Craik and his colleagues question the idea that there need to be separate 'stores' in memory: why not see the process of memory as a continuity of processing for different features of the message? If so, then memory is rather an incidental by-product of processing. Those messages that are processed deepest become best remembered.

### Comments on the two-process model and levels of processing model of memory

*Two-process model*

| Claims | Criticisms |
|---|---|
| Logical system of stores reflecting different functions of storage. | Implies two separate locations for different memory functions. There is no reason or evidence for this. |
| Concentrates on explaining verbal memory. | Memory has visual, non-auditory, spatial and other aspects, too. |
| Suggests that memories are coded for particular features such as sound and meaning. | A rather simplistic view of the functions of memory. Cognitive processing is probably far more complex. |

*Levels of processing model*

| Claims | Criticisms |
|---|---|
| Memory is seen as an integrated part of the perceptual system. | Avoids considering the function of particular kinds of memory. |
| Has empirical psychological support, e.g. Craik and Watkins. | Studies of brain-damaged patients and patients with amnesia do not show evidence of a unified system, but rather of separate stores with different functions. |
| Shows how events which have most meaning will be best remembered. | Rather obvious, and doesn't confirm the correctness of any theory. |

## Latest approaches to memory research

The whole field of cognitive psychology has been facing challenges recently on a number of fronts. Martin Conway (1992) says: 'The study of human memory is currently evolving and changing at a rapid pace. Issues on which researchers were once silent such as

■ **Summarize the role of rehearsal in memory.**

■ **Using your previous notes on memory, compare and contrast the two-process model and the levels of processing model with particular reference to the experimental evidence supporting and undermining each.**

emotions, the self, autobiographical memories, collective memories, consciousness and recollective experiences now feature large in the major cognitive psychology journals.'

A major challenge to the contributions to our understanding of cognitive processes that can be made by laboratory research has come from ecological ('in the field') research. Much of the early work in memory, as in selective attention, involved contrived experiments designed to provide support for a hypothesis (an idea that is to be tested scientifically) that the researcher has. Experiments can find evidence for which no parallel could be found in everyday memory functioning. As Graham Davies predicted (Davies and Logie 1991), 'Researchers would look to the real world for a source of validation for laboratory derived ideas in an effort to produce more ecologically valid psychology. Traditional laboratory research would continue, albeit in a more restricted form'. By 1991 they find that 'Laboratory work continues with considerably more vigour than was predicted, but increasingly with an eye on the ecological relevance of the work'.

A major reason for this shift goes back to **Ulric Neisser**, who, in 1976, was arguing that psychological knowledge was being obscured rather than helped by laboratory-based research, since it ignores the obvious fact that human cognitive functioning has evolved over the last two million years to equip us to thrive in 'the real world'. If psychologists want to study memory, it is to the real world they should go to make their observations. This, and subsequent critical reviews of laboratory-based research, led to a recognition of the importance of ecological research (based in the 'real world') which has become known as *everyday memory*. Laboratory research still dominates, however, as those who cling to the scientific tradition (e.g. Banaji and Crowder 1989) insist that everyday memory research is unscientific and of little value. The argument seems to have centred on the usefulness or otherwise of *discourse analysis*, a means of studying how people use their knowledge of past events to share their ideas through communicating in the present. It is a technique employed by supporters of everyday memory, and dismissed by supporters of the laboratory-based approach. (If you want to read how psychologists attack each other, get hold of *American Psychologist* for January 1991.)

## PHYSIOLOGICAL AND BIOCHEMICAL BASES TO MEMORY

▶ All our brain activity depends on electrochemical and other messages being passed around very quickly to various locations in extremely complex systems. We do not fully understand how they all work, and any physiological explanation relies on much educated guesswork.

The area of cognitive psychology that is investigating the physiological (to do with the nerves and organs in the brain) and the biochemical (how these structures work and relate to each other) is receiving a great deal of research attention at the moment. We still know surprisingly little about it, despite technological advances in brain-scanning devices. This merely underlines how immensely complex the human brain is.

Rather than applying models of how memory works, and constructing methods to investigate them (sort of 'from the outside in'), psychologists interested in the biology of memory start from the neurons and chemicals in the brain where memories are formed and stored ('from the inside out'?). The essential question is, how do all the experiences that each person has become part of their memory? Three general strategies to answering this have been taken: first, by finding where memories are formed and then stored; second, by studying changes that occur in the nerve cells in the brain that become the memory traces; third, by studying how memories are altered or modified once formed. We will review some of the evidence gathered in these areas so far.

## Investigations into the formation and loss of memory function

Humans have evolved memories for the skills they perform such as running, swimming and jumping. These memories house *procedural knowledge*. More recently in our evolution we have acquired the ability to learn facts. This is *declarative knowledge*. It would seem logical to assume that each skill or fact exists in a 'brain chemical' form in a particular location in the brain. The memory trace for each bit of knowledge was called an 'engram', and the search for it dates back to Karl Lashley's experiments using rats in the 1920s.

Lashley conditioned some rats successfully to escape from a maze or to recognize a ledge in a tank of water from which they could get out. He then removed parts of the animals' cerebral cortex (the outer part of the brain – see figure 13.6), since this was the obvious place to search for the engrams for 'maze running' and 'ledge recognition'. The animals still performed well, though, regardless of which part of their cortex was removed. The more of the cortex he removed, the worse the rats performed. Lashley concluded (partly correctly) that memory traces do not exist in a single location, but are located at various centres around the cortex. Some 20 years later, Wilder Penfield, working with epileptic patients, believed that he had found the location in the human cortex for some specific memory traces. For example, stimulating some areas led patients to imagine they heard music.

Speculation about the areas of the brain involved in integration of memories began with studies of brain-damaged patients. For example, 'H.M.' (studied by Brenda Milner et al. 1957 and 1968) was given an experimental surgical technique for the control of severe epilepsy. He suffered acute *anterograde amnesia*. In this condition patients can remember events up to the time the condition began, but nothing from then on. In the worst cases it is as though the ability to form new memories is destroyed. The tragic case of Clive Wearing also illustrates this point. His brilliant career in classical music ended in 1985 when a rare viral infection destroyed the hippocampus and other areas of his cortex. He now lives in a state of

► Neurons are individual nerve fibres. They carry messages in specialized codes around the brain and body. They are the 'telephone network' or 'neural net' of all biological functioning.

► Studies of the brain have found that it comprises many structures that have now been named. We know some of the functions that many of them perform, we know that some are interconnected, and we have some idea about how messages flow around many of them.

► *Procedural knowledge* is to do with how to perform some task or other, and would be very difficult to describe in words. How would you explain to someone how to run?

► *Declarative knowledge* refers to that which we know (and can declare) to be a fact, e.g. 'a pen is a tool for writing with', 'the United States is a large country' and 'snow is cold'.

► Rats will swim (like most animals), but given the choice most would rather not!

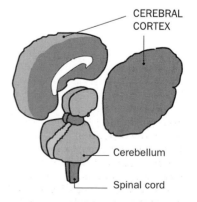

*Figure 13.6 The cerebral cortex*

► It is an unfortunate fact of life that we sometimes learn far more about what some aspect of human functioning is for, or how it works, from studies of unfortunate individuals whose functioning is abnormal in some way. We will see examples of this with children whose early lives have become disturbed in some way in Chapter 14.

► Looking at an attractive, simplified, two-dimensional diagram of the human brain inevitably invites us to think that its structures and functions are well researched. Names like amygdala and hippocampus could easily lead you to imagine that they are researched and understood. Regrettably, as yet, this is far from the truth. It took evolution about two and a half million years to create the first humans, and the last seventy thousand to produce the modern brain. It'll take scientists a few more years yet to understand much about how it works.

*Figure 13.7 Brain structures involved in memory*

► It makes evolutionary sense to accept that those skills which were acquired soonest are most deeply housed in the brain, and that knowledge acquired later would involve structures nearer the surface.

constant 'here and now', with very few memories of his earlier life, and no understanding of the future. Every moment of his life is like the first moment. He writes constantly in his diary that this is the first moment in his consciousness – he is conscious for the first time.

### Brain structures involved in memory

The brain structures that we know are involved in memory so far are the hippocampus, amygdala and cerebral cortex (see figure 13.7). The hippocampus is a (relatively) large structure that seems to be involved in emotions, motivations, learning and the recall of long-term memory (McCormick and Thompson 1984). People whose hippocampus has been damaged have problems with long-term memory, but not necessarily so with short-term memory. The amygdala is a part of the larger limbic system. It is closely interconnected with the hippocampus and other brain structures, and has an important role in emotional states, especially aggression. Its role in memory is not really understood as yet, although it is probably involved in coding neural messages to do with emotion into memory traces for storage. The cerebral cortex is probably involved in storage of long-term memories. It is the 'crinkly' outside covering of the brain that would be about the same size as a pillow case if ironed out! The cerebral cortex houses much higher-order human functioning such as language, problem solving and thinking as well as memory.

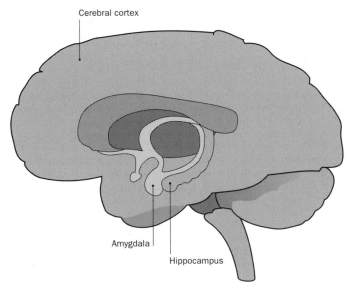

Studies with amnesic patients and those suffering after electro-convulsive therapy (see Chapter 10) have shown a distinction between two broad categories of learning and two levels of storage which we touched on earlier. In evolutionary terms, we first learned certain skills essential to our survival, e.g. finding food, climbing trees, making fire and so on. This is procedural knowledge and its engrams or memory traces may be located in a group of structures called the basal ganglia, which evolved before the limbic system of which the hippocampus is a part. Declarative knowledge would have accompanied the development in communication in human evolution. These traces exist in the cortex, and the hippocampus, amygdala etc. may act as relay and integration centres.

It appears that memory can be disturbed by a blow to the head, a psychological disturbance to consciousness, sudden shock, diseases etc. We may be able to detect exactly where the damage is, and what structures are involved. We may also be able to record exactly what memory disturbances someone exhibits afterwards. It would be tempting, but quite misleading, to assume that damage in those structures caused the memory damage, although we might conclude that at least those areas are involved.

Since we don't know too much for certain about which brain structures are responsible for what kinds of memory function, have scientists been any more successful in knowing what happens at the level of the nerve cells themselves? One area that has been investigated is that of memory consolidation.

### Hebb's cell assemblies

When a new experience is processed through the cognitive system it is linked to existing long-term memories by some retrieval strategies (in short-term memory according to Atkinson and Shiffrin). The hippocampus has a role in integrating these new memories into existing ones. This integration is called *consolidation* and can take minutes, days, weeks or even years. One of the earliest explanations for this comes from **Donald Hebb** (1949). The cerebral cortex consists of millions of tiny neurons. Each is capable of transmitting some information to a nearby neuron. Even such microscopic neurons don't actually touch one another – a tiny gap called a *synapse* separates them. The information flows across this synaptic gap. Typically, a brain neuron could make a synaptic connection with 60,000 others. Hebb suggests that when a memory is being formed a neural pathway is being forged through possibly millions of neurons. By repeated use this becomes a 'closed circuit' (the physiological equivalent of the engram). Hebb called this pathway a *cell assembly*. Add thousands of cell assemblies together and he suggests we have the physiological basis for memory.

Hebb went on to suggest how each particular group of neurons form a particular cell assembly. As the coded impulses of chemical energy which carry the information reach the synapse, they trigger a neurotransmitter substance such as adrenaline or acetylcholine. A neurotransmitter is one of many substances that act as the 'vehicle' that carries a nerve impulse across a synaptic gap. These substances help to project the impulse to the receiving neuron, where other substances (such as acetylcholinesterase) help it arrive, project it on its way towards the next synapse, and help eliminate any residue of the transmitter substance. As the impulses whizz round the cell assembly (at anything between 2 and 200 miles an hour!), the structure of the synapse begins to change. See figure 13.8.

Support for these ideas has come from many experimental sources. Latest ideas are that neural networks of cell assemblies

▶ Studies of people with different types of brain disorder do not support any single explanation for memory function. The human brain seems to be extremely adaptable, and when some dysfunction occurs in one part, other parts appear to try to compensate for them.

▶ An individual neuron can only transmit a single coded impulse. Many neurons make up a nerve, such as the optic nerve or auditory nerve. Triggering a single neuron in the circuit would trigger the whole circuit.

▶ Hebb's speculations were fascinating and have inspired scientists to seek evidence either to support or reject them. So far, some evidence does show that Hebb's ideas about changes in synapses were right.

■ **What are cell assemblies and how do they explain the formation and maintenance of memory?**

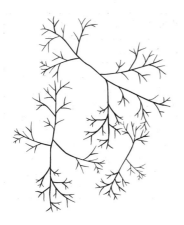

In a real cell assembly the number of neurons might be in the thousands.

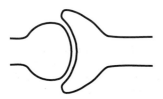

A synapse before it becomes established in a cell assembly (according to Hebb).

After it has become established (structural change occurs to increase surface area for efficient and speedy neural transmission).

*Figure 13.8 Hebb's cell assemblies*

▶ Alcohol disrupts the production of serotonin, which impairs memory formation. This is one reason why heavy drinkers sometimes experience memory problems.

■ **Comment on the role of (a) the hippocampus and amygdala, and (b) neurotransmitters in memory.**

form as the location of particular memories. However, it is the activity across the whole network that is important (John 1972 and Lynch 1986), not activity in specific neurons. This could explain why Lashley's rats were able to solve their maze-running problems. Despite parts of their nets being removed they could still use the rest to provide the information they needed. McGaugh (1983) used a high-frequency device for bombarding the hippocampus with a range of stimuli. It led to an observable change in synapse structure and an increase in the number of synapses. At the same time learning was enhanced. The effect accompanied a rapid increase in calcium levels in the stimulated neurons which break down the cell membrane, thus creating more synapses.

### The role of neurotransmitters and hormones

Apart from brain structures we are also beginning to appreciate the role of certain neurotransmitters and hormones in the formation and loss of memory function. For example, acetylcholine and serotonin enhance memory formation. Lower than normal levels of acetylcholine are found in the hippocampus of Alzheimer sufferers. However, we do not know whether Alzheimer's disease triggers the reduction of acetylcholine, whether it is the other way round, or whether a much more complex relationship exists between them. There is evidence to suggest that hormones play a role in memory formation, too. Epinephrine levels, for example, have a role in both stimulating learning and storing memory. However, epinephrine doesn't directly enter brain cells. Rather, it stimulates glucose production and utilization in the blood. Since proteins are essential for hormone production, and hormones are involved in memory, it seems logical that proteins are important in forming memories, too.

### Summary – Physiological and biochemical aspects of memory

The search for the 'engram' and speculation about where memories were stored dominated early research. We now realize that various types of memory require different brain activity and involve several locations within the brain. Searches for location of memories have been abandoned in favour of studying actual memory function, both in brain-damaged and, increasingly, in 'normal' people. The more we learn about physiology, the more complex it seems, with the involvement of hormones, proteins and other brain chemicals.

## WHY DO WE FORGET?

It is important not to confuse 'forgetting' with 'never knowing in the first place'. If you paid insufficient attention to something, such as learning about 'memory' for a psychology test, and you then fail the test, you can't claim that you 'just couldn't remember', or 'you forgot' the details. Information in the STS or the lower levels of processing may not be passed for further processing, in which case you wouldn't have known it, so couldn't have forgotten it. Pay special attention to the practical applications section.

Psychologists who believe in a particular perspective, such as psychoanalysis or behaviourism (see Chapter 1), have offered their explanations for why we forget. Those more interested in biological explanations for aspects of human behaviour advance neurophysiological explanations. Others are more interested in the practical implications for learning, remembering and forgetting.

## Repression – the psychoanalytic view

Throughout life we all experience worries and upsets. Some will be serious enough to cause anxiety. Freud believed that the process of normal personality development created additional problems since it involves the erogenous zones and includes feelings of pre-genital sexuality, with associated fear and guilt. Anxieties that might threaten our personality could become repressed into our unconscious. Repression is said to be one of the more effective defence mechanisms.

According to Freud, our unconscious mind contains two groups of impulses. One comprises those psychic urges that drive our thinking and behaviour, which were always unconscious and which have been there since birth. The other comprises all those fears, worries, memories, desires and wishes that produced too much anxiety when they were conscious, and so were repressed into the unconscious during development. Freud said 'forgetting, in all cases, is founded on a motive of displeasure'. We will have problems if we try to remember events that produced such anxiety for us.

It may be true that it is easier to remember pleasant events in more detail than unpleasant ones. We may more easily forget things or people we do not like. However, Freud's explanation cannot be tested experimentally, doesn't explain why we do also forget pleasant things, and doesn't explain why we forget more as we grow older.

## Interference – the behaviourist view

This was a popular idea around the 1950s, but by the end of the 1960s behaviourism, on which it is based, was being largely discredited. Young people often have fantastic memories – sometimes to the embarrassment of their parents! As we grow older our memories start to fail. We say we can't remember. We suffer increasing retrieval failures. According to interference theory, as we gain more experience, more and more items will need to be stored. Some items will inevitably be similar to ones already stored. Occasionally, the similar items will interfere with each other. We will become confused about the precise details, making accurate retrieval impossible. This is called *retroactive interference*. Sometimes the exis-

---

**Memory research**
Research is stimulating and promises many discoveries that could have immense value to humans. As technology advances for brain scanning, so studies of normal experimental participants can replace the animal subjects or brain-damaged participants used in most research to date. At the moment our exploration of the physiological and biochemical basis of memory is in its infancy.

▶ A defence mechanism is an unconscious, and entirely normal, automatic response that we make to issues that might otherwise threaten our personality development.

▶ For a fuller discussion of Freudian ideas see Chapter 1.

■ Explain the role of repression in wider Freudian theory.

tence of some knowledge will distort the learning of some new, similar knowledge. We may confuse the new information with the old when we try to retrieve it. This is called *proactive interference*. Interference theory is based on the behaviourist view that memory consists of associations made between specific stimuli and responses.

Numerous experiments using lists of words and lists of nonsense syllables have demonstrated proactive and retroactive interference in the laboratory. One of the first was from **McGeoch** and **Macdonald** (1931). They tested retroactive interference by first asking participants to learn a list of words, followed by an interference task. The interference task involved reading another list of words. If the second list was similar in meaning to the first, more of the target words weren't recalled. Another group was given a list of numbers to read as its interference task. The group could remember most target words. This experiment suggests that meaning is important in memory (which no one would dispute), and that new material interferes with old (which can be shown in a laboratory but probably doesn't occur in everyday experience).

However, these experiments do not seem to be applicable to 'real life'. In fact just the opposite could occur. Having a fairly specialized knowledge of something which has built up over the past few years, e.g. a car enthusiast might know the specification of modern cars, shouldn't provide any problems for recalling relevant information, e.g. whether it's the Escort XR3i or the Astra SRi which has the higher torque or goes from 0 to 60 m.p.h. in the shortest time. If a new model is added to the range the enthusiast may enjoy increasing his or her knowledge. When it comes to learning about the new range of Golf GTis (which would be an example of proactive interference), the enthusiast's knowledge of the Escort and Astra might positively help because it provides points of reference against which to compare the Golf. As Atkinson and Shiffrin claim, the concept of interference may be better at describing what can be shown to occur under particular laboratory conditions, rather than explaining what actually does occur in 'real life'.

## Trace decay and displacement – the physiological view

Neither of the previous explanations deals adequately with one of the most obvious features of forgetting – why does it increase with time? According to the physiological view, new experiences are coded into memory traces, which are carried by groups of neurons in 'memory circuits' or 'cell assemblies' (Hebb 1949). With the passage of time, biological processes in the brain cause the trace to decay until eventually the message it carried – the procedural or declarative knowledge – is lost. Decay only occurs through disuse, so the way to stop it is to recall the event.

This explanation has the attraction of being quite simple, but

▶ This is an example of just the kind of experiment that really doesn't help us understand everyday memory at all. It's as though we could find experimental evidence to support any idea we have if we just design it in such a way that it would produce that result. Far from being unbiased and objective, experiments can be highly subjective. We will return to this theme throughout the book.

■ Outline the behaviourist view of forgetting.

▶ This explanation is based on the conviction that memories are stored in actual physical traces somewhere in the brain. If the brain were a computer this would be true. But it isn't.

▶ Neurons are individual nerve fibres which carry the signals around nervous systems. The brain is composed of millions of neurons, each being able to pass messages to an average of 60,000 other neurons.

unfortunately it doesn't really fit the facts. Many elderly people can recall incidents from their youth in great detail. Unless they have recalled the instance many times throughout their lives the trace should have decayed. Skills learned in childhood, such as swimming or riding a bike, and not practised for many years, are often quickly relearned by adults, for example when they come to teach their own children.

If trace decay theory is correct, and you hadn't played the guitar for 20 years (the trace had decayed), then not only would you be unable to recall the chord sequence for a particular song, but it would also take you as long to learn the song the second time as it did the first. This simply isn't true. If you haven't ridden a bike since you were young (and the trace has decayed), could you not ride one now? Surely 'you never forget' to swim, ride a bike or play the piano once you've learned? People under hypnosis can often recall things that they haven't thought about for years, so their traces may still be there. Freud tried several techniques to encourage his patients to recall their earliest memories, presumably with some success.

Perhaps the biggest problem for trace decay theory is that it can't explain why some people seem to have poor recall of even recent events, while others have incredible memories going back for decades. Such physiological processes must be fairly similar in most people, so why such huge individual differences?

■ Outline the trace decay explanation for forgetting and say why it isn't adequate

## Retrieval failure – the 'tip of the tongue' phenomenon

(See Brown and McNeill's study, page 286.) The theories outlined so far are called *trace dependent*, since they see the memory trace as the main cause for forgetting. If our memories are difficult to recall because of their unpleasant associations, or are 'interfered with' by new information entering memory, or are decaying with time, then some traces must still be there, but we can't gain access to them. Retrieval failure refers to a temporary inability to make a mental connection between two events. Have you ever put something down, then forgotten where you put it, and tried to visualize where you were when you had it last? This visualization provides you with information to help you find the object. We have retrieval cues, which are either stored with the information, or applied later, which help us find the memory. This is called *cue-dependent theory* (after Tulving 1974). It doesn't so much explain 'forgetting', but rather 'how not to forget'! Cue-dependent forgetting supports the idea of hierarchical organization in memory (e.g. Collins and Quillian), which suggests that information that has things in common is stored together in the 'neural net'.

One form of cue dependency is state dependency. Numerous studies have found that recall is better if the physical state of the person is the same when recall occurs as it was when the learning first

▶ While other explanations for memory loss look for problems in storage, *cue-dependent theory* looks for problems in how we try to remember the information. Just because we can't find it doesn't mean it isn't there!

■ **Name some cues that could improve recall.**

occurred. For example, Overton found that participants who had drunk a large amount of alcohol could recall what had happened to them the last time they were drunk rather better than they could when they were sober! Another cue to remembering is where we were when we did the learning. D.R. Godden and Alan Baddeley had 16 divers learn lists of 40 (unrelated) words under two experimental conditions. They were either on shore or 20 feet under the sea when the learning occurred. Later the divers were asked to recall each list either in the context where it was learned or in the other context. Recall was 50 per cent better in the situation in which the learning had occurred.

Having category names for groups of items to be recalled is another cue. Tulving and Pearlstone asked two groups of participants to learn lists of items in named categories, e.g. a category name could be ANIMAL, and the list would contain one, two or four words such as 'monkey', 'grass snake', 'ostrich', 'starling'. One group was given the category name when asked to recall the lists, the other was not. Predictably, those who were given the category name remembered far more of their lists. The group who weren't cued by hearing the category name missed out entire categories. Later the two groups were tested again. This time both groups heard the category name cue. The second group now performed almost as well as the first. This shows that retrieval cues are very useful to recall.

■ **Using your previous notes on forgetting construct a table of contrasts showing the differences between the major explanations of forgetting. Note the major shortcomings of each.**

**Summary – Why do we forget?**

Psychoanalytic views that loss of memories are motivated by defence mechanisms, ultimately repression, are not taken seriously by many psychologists now since so few of our experiences of loss of memory involve early traumas. Behaviourist claims that new associations interfere with existing ones imply that memory capacity is limited. There's no evidence for this. Trace decay doesn't seem to fit the facts, either – we can remember things we haven't thought about in years and forget things whose 'trace' should be fresh. Ideas about cue and state dependency may explain some aspects of retrieval failure, but is retrieval failure (usually temporary) the same as 'forgetting'?

## PRACTICAL APPLICATIONS OF RESEARCH INTO MEMORY AND FORGETTING

Memory research was almost exclusively based in the laboratory until Bartlett started giving his students strange stories to remember. One of Ulric Neisser's complaints was that laboratory research findings do not generally explain 'everyday memory'. Eysenck (1993) says that laboratory-based research has concentrated on *retrospective memory*, i.e. 'the ability to remember some event from the past' such as a list of words or a strange story. However, in 'real life' we use *prospective memory*, which is the knowledge about how and when to do something in the future. Remembering that your lift home leaves at 5 o'clock enables you to be there in time. Prospective memory may not work in the same way as retrospective memory. Baddeley and Wilkins (1978) gave participants tests involving both kinds of memory task and found that those who did well on one didn't do particularly well on the other. If they are correct, then laboratory research can only reveal insights into retrospective memory.

### Summary of the major practical applications of memory research

1 **Organization:** The most obvious practical lesson we can draw is the need for organization of material to be placed into memory. Evidence comes from Bower, Collins and Quillian, Collins and Loftus, etc. Regrettably, the things we have to learn during our lives aren't always able to be organized in the ways that material in an experiment can be.

2 **The method of loci:** We could try to impose some organization on things we want to remember, such as information for an exam. One way is to imagine that you are in a familiar place, your room at home perhaps. Take the first things you need to know and imagine them to be on, in or near the first thing you see when you enter your room. The theories of selective attention could be on a chair, just inside the door perhaps. The next items are to be imagined around the next feature of your room. Maybe the sensory store can be imagined on the mantelshelf above the fireplace. Information on STS and LTS could be on your pillow and the end of the bed. Organization in memory might lie near the waste bin. Eventually you will have arranged all the material around the room. To recall it, just mentally open the door and walk round the room!

*Figure 13.9 An example of number mnemonics*

3 **Number mnemonics:** With practice you could remember quite long numbers (should you ever need to). Memorize a picture that rhymes with a number from nought to nine (or ten). So, for example: nought – port, one – bun, two – shoe, three – tree, four – door, five – hive, six – sticks, seven – heaven, eight – gate, nine – line, ten – hen. Then combine these mental images to represent the number. So the phone number 223586 could be like figure 13.9.

4 **Letter mnemonics:** You could make a silly sentence out of the first letters of important words in the order you need to recall them. For example, the first major schools of thought in psychology were structuralism, functionalism, associationism, psychoanalysis, behaviourism, cognitive theory and humanism. One student's sentence for remembering this was:

'Science Fiction Annoys Psychologists But Can't Hurt.'

5 **SQ3R:** Written material presents a special case (particularly for students!). It's easy to let your eyes run across the printed page (if you're doing it now, STOP, you're wasting your time). After a while you may realize that you haven't taken in a word of what you've read. Hopefully you won't simply congratulate yourself on your

► A mnemonic device is anything which aids the memory, such as a silly sentence featuring the initial letters of what we want to remember.

► Never aim to learn something, always aim to understand it. We often forget what we have learned, we rarely forget what we have understood.

► This might sound rather long-winded, but SQ3R REALLY DOES WORK. When you've done it a few times it becomes quite quick and very effective. It takes about twice as long as just reading and is about five times more effective.

■ What have psychologists contributed to understanding how humans can improve their ability to store and recall material in memory?

efforts and believe you've understood or will remember your reading! If you need to learn something you have to take it into consciousness in as clear a way as possible so that your hippocampus can find connections with existing memories to aid understanding rather than just learning.

Morris (1979) describes the technique for reading important material as SQ3R, which stands for **S**urvey, **Q**uestion, **R**ead, **R**ecite, **R**eview. For example, take a section in your book and quickly scan it to get an impression of what it's about. When you've done this, ask yourself 'what is this about?' You must answer this question (in your head). Go back to the beginning and read the material properly. Then put the book aside and recite to yourself what you have just read. If you can't remember anything important, go back and read that bit again. When you're happy that you understand most of it, go back and link it to previous sections or other material such as lesson notes or handout material. Review the whole topic at the end.

6 **Cue and state dependency:** Material is best recalled under the same conditions under which it was acquired. So take your revision notes into the room that the exam will be held in a few days before, have a good look around, then read through your notes (even SQ3R?).

---

### Some general principles to help you improve your memory

1 Have confidence that you can learn the material and that you will not blame others for stopping you or blame yourself for not being bright enough.
2 Try to form an impression of the whole topic in general, and where it fits into other, related items before trying to learn the details.
3 Learn the details, but always relate them to the whole topic, rather than seeing the details as ends in themselves.
4 Use rhymes and mnemonics to group related items together. Try to see the topic as a picture.
5 Use the information in another way as soon as you can afterwards, e.g. if you've read it, then talk about it, if you've heard it, write it down in your own words.
6 Having learned it, test yourself on it. For example, relate to yourself the major theories of forgetting, explaining how they fit into our understanding of the functioning of human memory.

### Summary – Practical applications of memory research

Laboratory-based research has shown the need for organization and consolidation of learned material. Material may be stored in memory so that links to similar or related material are facilitated. Organizing the material to be recalled is important. Everyday memory studies emphasize the effectiveness of projective as well as retrospective memory. Presentation, mnemonic devices, method of loci and SQ3R are all useful ways of improving memory function.

### Exam questions – 60 minutes each

1 Discuss psychological understanding of the organization of information in memory. (*25 marks*)
2 Describe the application of psychological research in memory and evaluate the studies upon which these are based. (*25 marks*)
3 Why do humans forget? (*25 marks*)

# *Part 5*
# *Developmental psychology*

*Physical development starts with conception. Psychological development starts shortly after birth. Researchers have investigated the nature and influences upon these psychological processes, particularly early emotional bonding, and the effects of disruptions to it, which we shall discuss in Chapter 14. In Chapters 15 and 16 we shall discuss the development of cognitive skills, and the emergence of social and individual development in children.*

# 14 *Early socialization*

> **Chapter objectives**
>
> By the end of this chapter you should be able to:
>
> ▌ describe the early development of sociability in humans;
>
> ▌ discuss psychologists' claims about the importance of attachment bonding;
>
> ▌ appreciate and evaluate the research and evidence associated with these claims;
>
> ▌ understand the human infant's capacity for attachment bonding, including forming multiple attachments;
>
> ▌ understand the distinction between short- and long-term effects of early experience;
>
> ▌ evaluate the nature of theory and evidence which claims a link between early experience and later behaviour;
>
> ▌ comprehend the contribution of nature and nurture in similarities and differences in behaviour found in cross-cultural research.

## Introduction

Some early psychologists believed that humans are genetically 'programmed' to think and behave in certain ways. Freud, for example, claimed that we inherit various instinctive urges that will shape our personalities. The idea that the origins of our behaviour and thought are genetically determined is known as the *nature view*, and those who support it are called *nativists*. During the twentieth century there has been a movement away from this idea. Behaviourists, for example B.F. Skinner (see Chapter 1), argue that most of our behaviour is learned and influenced by social experiences. This is known as the *nurture view*, and those who support it are called *nurturists*. Some biological functions (e.g. breathing and sucking) are genetically inherited and are present at birth. Others, such as walking and talking, require maturation and experience before they will appear. Other features of our behaviour, such as playing an instrument or acquiring an understanding of psychology, are learned. The nature–nurture debate has influenced a great deal of psychological research and theory, particularly in the area of child development.

▶ *Norms* are socially acceptable or appropriate standards of behaviour which are typical, or representative of, members of each social group.

▶ *Values* are general moral principles that we use in making judgements about right and wrong.

■ Write some reasons for why socialization is so important for humans and not for other animals.

▶ Temperament refers to the aspect of an individual's personality concerning changes in moods, level of emotionality, and level of general sensitivity.

## EARLY SOCIALIZATION

Each human infant is born into a society which has its own particular culture, language, style of dress and behaviour, and set of acceptable attitudes, all of which the individual will have to learn. The infant will start on this huge learning task within a few weeks of birth. Different societies have different standards of behaviour which are typical of, and acceptable to, most of its people. These are *norms*. Norms are not simple rules that can easily be written down as instructions for correct behaviour. Appropriate behaviour varies from time to time, place to place and social group to social group. For example, behaviour that is appropriate at home (watching TV, listening to music, having parties) would not necessarily be appropriate in college! Not only do people have to learn norms, they also have to learn when, where and for whom they are appropriate. We also acquire *values,* which are socially acceptable standards of thought. Beliefs such as honesty, freedom, democracy, truth and decency are important values in many Western societies. *Socialization* is the process of learning the rules of social life and how to apply them.

### Summary – Socialization

Socialization is the name of the process by which individuals learn the ways of behaving and thinking – norms and values – which are thought appropriate by other members of their group. The family, education and the media are the principal agencies of socialization in Western societies. Each member of society will benefit from learning what is appropriate as early as possible.

## THE DEVELOPMENT OF SOCIABILITY AND ATTACHMENT

Socialization begins as soon as the baby is sufficiently aware of other people. However, infants vary enormously in their temperaments. Some are happy, sleep well, and are generally easy to manage. These are more likely to be aware of, possibly even interested in, their caregivers and their environments. Others are generally irritable, slow to respond, and cry a lot. They may be generally less willing to communicate and respond to stimulation. Others are sometimes happy and sometimes irritable. There are probably some genetically inherited reasons for this, and so even the most devoted mother may have a 'difficult baby'. Helen Bee (1989) estimates that about 10 per cent of babies might have 'difficult temperaments'.

According to Rudi Schaffer (1977), human neonates (newborn infants) prefer the company of humans to inanimate objects. They reach and smile and cry and wave and do whatever they can to attract someone's attention. It takes a month or so before they can clearly distinguish between different people. From that time the face and voice of their main caregiver should elicit a smile from the infant. **Genevieve Carpenter** (reported in T.G.R. Bower 1977) showed infants of two weeks combinations of (1) their mother's face and voice, (2) a stranger's face and voice, (3) a stranger's face and their mother's voice, (4) their mother's face and a stranger's voice. The infants showed interest in (1), less so in (2), and actively turned away from (3) and (4). Babies of just a few weeks could tell the difference between their mother and a stranger, and that faces and voices should go together.

After a few more weeks the infant will start to show distinct preferences between the people who care for it and others. This is the beginning of *bonding*. A few months later infants start to make a firm emotional *attachment*. **Mary Ainsworth** (1978) defines attachment as 'the affectional bond or tie that an infant forms between himself and his mother figure'. (The idea of the 'mother figure' is disputed now, as we shall see later.) Generally, an attachment is an emotional bond that develops between an infant and the person or people who are closest to it. A child is said to be attached to someone if it shows anxiety when that person leaves it, or when a stranger approaches it.

## Sociability and attachment

Mary Ainsworth and her colleagues (1971 and 1978) devised 'the strange situation' experiments to show whom babies are attached to. The infant, its caregivers and strangers are placed in a room, then mother, father or a stranger leaves and re-enters the room, and the child's reaction to each event is recorded. Two responses indicate the infant's attachments, *separation anxiety* and *stranger fear*. If the infant shows anxiety when mother or father leaves the room, then this is taken as a sign that the infant is attached to that person. If the infant shows anxiety when approached by a stranger when mother or father is present, this is also a sign that the child is attached to its caregiver.

Ainsworth identified three patterns of behaviour. About 25 per cent of her sample of children were *avoidant* (Type A). They weren't especially concerned whether their mother was present or not and didn't show much concern when approached by a stranger. Approximately 65 per cent were *secure* (Type B). They cried when their mother left and preferred her contact when she returned. *Resistant* (Type C) children cried for their mother and approached her on her return, but didn't seem able to cope with the reassurance she offered and struggled against her. They were about 12 per cent of the sample. This experiment has been repeated many times, although just how much we can learn about the effects of temperament and attachment from such controlled research using some middle-class American families in the 1970s is questioned. In the everyday world of the infant many people come and go in all sorts of situations.

▶ For the first few months of life babies have a great deal to experience. They aren't very aware of anyone else until they start to recognize and respond to some of the people around them. This often takes up to two or three months.

▶ *Attachments* are emotional bonds that provide those who have them with a sense of comfort, security and well-being. In adulthood we call it 'love'!

▶ Symptoms of anxiety include looking away, staring, pouting, frowning, stiffening of the muscles, and generally resistant behaviour, as well as the obvious one, crying.

■ What is an attachment? Give three examples of behaviour which you think would aid attachment formation between an infant and its caregiver.

■ How does Mary Ainsworth suggest we identify whether an attachment has been formed between an infant and its caregiver?

■ Why might babies of differing temperaments have different patterns of attachment?

▶ 'Anaclitic depression' was defined by Spitz as severe withdrawal caused by the lack of mothering and the absence of an attachment bond.

▶ Any behaviour that has *survival value* could contribute to preserving the individual's life. If there is some threat, a baby who is grasping its mother's hair while she seeks shelter is more likely to survive than one who doesn't grasp, and is dropped!

▶ A variable is simply anything that can vary, e.g. the amount of physical punishment used on children, or that comes in more than one form, e.g. sex. Psychologists are often interested in which variables are associated with which others.

## Summary – Sociability and attachment

All babies are born with different genetic inheritances, and will have different predispositions to mature in different ways. They all have different temperaments, too. By temperament we mean emotions and moods that affect babies' reactions to stimuli, such as being touched, cuddled, left alone, or approached by strangers. Differences exist in very young babies, and are probably genetic in origin. Regardless of temperament most babies gradually learn to recognize their own mothers or main caregivers, and begin to prefer them to the company of others.

## The infant's need for attachment

Rene Spitz had observed children in understaffed and overstretched South American orphanages during the 1930s. The staff only had time to tend to the children's physical needs and had little opportunity to play with or stimulate them. The children ate little and were undersize and underweight for their age. They took little interest in anything around them and were unnaturally depressed and passive. Spitz described their condition as 'anaclitic depression' caused by being deprived of mothers or other adults with whom to form attachment bonds.

**John Bowlby** became an authority on early social experiences after his research into motherless children in the late 1940s. Bowlby believed that infants are born with a range of abilities, such as sucking, smiling, reaching and grasping, which are likely to attract and keep an adult caregiver's attention. Such skills would have evolved in humans because of their *survival value*. They might convince the caregiver that the baby was content and happy to be with them, which might strengthen the bond between them.

Bowlby (1951) claimed that making successful attachments is essential for future emotional, social and intellectual development. This idea, that early experiences will have long-term effects, is called *continuity theory* and we will return to it later. Bowlby did not say that children who have unsuccessful attachment bonding will automatically suffer later. Their adult personalities and intellectual skills may be influenced by all kinds of other variables. However, inadequate bonding is certainly a contributing factor. He suggests that about 40 per cent of children whose attachments were inadequately formed in childhood will have problems as adults. Children between six months and five years of age should not be separated from their mothers for a prolonged period, according to Bowlby. A separation of just two weeks could be disastrous for a young child's future development.

Bowlby observed the cases of 44 adolescents who had been referred to his child guidance clinic for stealing during the 1930s. Of the 44, 17 (40 per cent) had been separated from their mother for six months or more before they were five years old. Bowlby diagnosed

14 of the 44 as having the clinical condition 'affectionless psychopathy', the symptoms of which were that they showed no guilt for their crime, or concern for their victims, or themselves. Seven of them had been separated from their mothers during early childhood and two more had been in hospital when they were about two years old. In his report entitled *44 Juvenile Thieves*, Bowlby claims that maternal separation could have contributed to this condition. He wrote: 'There is a very strong case indeed for believing that separation of a child from his mother (or mother substitute) during the first five years of life stands foremost among the causes of delinquent character development.' Delinquency wouldn't be the only consequence of maternal deprivation. Bowlby claims that emotional disturbance, social maladjustment and retarded intellectual growth could also result from being separated from one's mother.

There are flaws in Bowlby's study. He identified two factors, 'maternal separation' and 'delinquency', in a relatively small group of socially maladjusted children, and assumed (with no actual evidence) that one causes the other. A third variable, e.g. poverty, could have caused both. Bowlby didn't take a group of non-thieves to see how many of them had been separated from their mothers. For these reasons we can only appreciate Bowlby's research, but cannot wholly accept his findings.

Bowlby looked to other research on institutionalized children for further evidence to support his claim that maternal deprivation leads to social, emotional and intellectual problems, either by stopping attachments forming, or disrupting ones that had.

In 1946 **Rene Spitz** and **Katharine Wolf** published their study of 123 babies during their first year of life who were being looked after by their unmarried mothers in an American penal institution. At one point the mothers were moved and their babies were cared for by the other mothers or pregnant girls. The 123 babies were between six and nine months old at the time. During the separation 'the child either didn't see its mother at all, or at best, once a week'. Spitz and Wolf noted that the children cried more than they had before. They lost their appetites, and failed to gain weight. When their mothers returned the babies' conditions returned to what they had been before the separation.

Bowlby (1951, 1958) claimed that this study, and other research on institutional children conducted by Spitz and Wolf, supported his hypothesis that babies need their mothers. However, it could equally well be argued that what this study shows is that babies whose routines are disrupted become distressed. We do not know about the quality of the alternative care offered to the babies during their mothers' absence. It may not have been the same as that provided by their mothers, and this could account for some of their distress.

During the 1950s and 1960s **James** and **Joyce Robertson** drew attention to the distress suffered by children in Britain who were temporarily separated from their mothers when they or the mother went into hospital. The usual medical procedure was not to encourage children and mothers to see much of each other if one of them

*John Bowlby*

▶ Spitz and Wolf suggest that separating young babies from their mothers has physical effects on the child, but again, there are other variables that could equally well explain these effects.

■ **What explanation do Spitz and Wolf offer for the babies' worsening condition when their mothers were removed? What other variables might also be involved?**

▶ One type of hypothesis states that two variables, such as maternal separation and delinquency, are related, and that a change in one might cause the other to change as well.

► James Robertson's claim that babies suffered as a result of being removed from their mothers was ridiculed by some members of the medical profession, but he determined to prove them wrong.

► Even after viewing the Robertsons' films many members of the medical profession were still hostile to their warnings. Some said that the films were an untypical and distorted record. They claimed that the children suffered because of inappropriate care, not because they were being separated from their mothers.

► In separation the usual pattern of distress, despair and detachment is called the *syndrome of distress.*

► Most of the studies described here do not necessarily show that there will be any effects of maternal separation. It depends very much on what happens to the child during the separation. We may distinguish possible short-term effects (the syndrome of distress) from possible long-term effects (developmental retardation). However, many other factors are involved.

■ What are Bowlby's conclusions about the relationships between babies and their mothers?

■ Briefly describe some of the evidence he uses to support his claims.

► According to Michael Rutter, conflict and tension in the home can make a child feel insecure, and this insecurity may lead to disturbed behaviour such as delinquency.

was in hospital. The Robertsons were convinced this practice was wrong. Attempts to convince the medical profession failed, so James Robertson bought a cine-camera to film some *Young Children in Brief Separation*, and showed the results to other doctors. The Robertsons made a series of powerful films of children aged between 17 months and 29 months.

One child, John, was 17 months old when he was placed in a residential nursery while his mother was in hospital having a second child. The film showed how John's condition deteriorated as the separation continued. For the first few days John protested as best he could and tried to obtain attention. When this failed he showed distress. He tried to make attachments with the nurses, but the system of group care meant that they had to tend to the most demanding children, and John was unable to compete with the other children who'd been in the nursery for a long time. His father's nightly visits did little to comfort the child.

After a few days John's condition passed from distress to despair. He cried constantly and started to refuse food, and had difficulties sleeping. The nurses were worried about him and tried to comfort him. While he was being held by a nurse he quietened, but the other children demanded attention too and he had to be put down. His condition changed again. He seemed to give up trying to attract attention and appeared less interested in the nurses or his father. This is *detachment*. When his mother finally came to collect him he ignored her and wouldn't allow her to comfort him. We will return to John in the next section.

To show the importance of the mother, or mother substitute, the Robertsons themselves temporarily fostered four children while their mothers were unavailable. The children stayed with the Robertsons between 10 and 27 days. Two were under two years old, the other two were around two and a half. Joyce Robertson provided very high-quality care for each child. The younger ones adapted to their substitute mother, and coped well. The two older ones had more difficulties in settling, but very few compared with the problems that John experienced.

Several researchers have criticized Bowlby's claims. **Michael Rutter** (1979) studied groups of adolescent boys in London and the Isle of Wight. Many had been separated from various people for varying reasons and for various lengths. He found that conflict in the home was more likely to be associated with disturbed behaviour, including delinquency, than was maternal separation. Children who lose their mothers completely, through death for example, are not necessarily going to have a disturbed personality if the alternative care is good.

### Summary – Bowlby and the need for attachment

John Bowlby was an influential child psychiatrist who claimed that humans have evolved a need for a special, close emotional bond with their primary caregivers – their mother or mother substitute. Any disruption of the attachment bond could have adverse effects on personality development. According to Bowlby, our future mental health is influenced by the success of our bonding with our mother during the first year of life, and by the bond not being broken thereafter in childhood.

## Making successful attachments

Since attachments are two-way processes, we can distinguish factors which are important from the caregiver's point of view and those which are important from the infant's point of view. According to **Marshall Klaus** and **John Kennel** (1976) 'intimacy' and 'timing' are the major contribution caregivers make. They studied some premature and full-term babies and their mothers, and found that those who had the most 'skin-to-skin' contact immediately after birth with their caregivers were most likely to develop close attachments with them.

They studied a group of new mothers. Half of their sample underwent the normal maternity hospital routines, with the infant being removed from the mother after birth for the usual tests, then seeing its parents for between six and 12 hours a day while the mother stayed in hospital. The other half of the sample were allowed extra contact with the baby. They had an extra hour of skin-to-skin contact within three hours of birth, then an extra five hours a day while their mothers stayed in hospital. Klaus and Kennel claim that there is a *sensitive period* of six to 12 hours following birth for establishing an early bond. They suggest that there are various hormones associated with giving birth that focus the mother's attention on the baby. Allowing this early contact encourages the mother to express the emotions associated with these hormones.

Klaus and Kennel visited the mother–infant pairs a month after leaving hospital, recording their general activities together. They interviewed the mothers, asking about their feelings towards their babies; they examined the infants, and filmed the mothers feeding them. They reported that the 'extended contact' group were closer and more loving towards their babies. They held them closer during feeding, and seemed generally more involved with them. When the babies were a year old they were visited again, and the researchers concluded that the early effects were still noticeable. Compared to the 'normal routine' control group, the extended contact experimental group were still more deeply involved with their babies.

Mary Ainsworth (1979) studied the Ganda peoples of Uganda. Those mothers who tend the fields normally have their infants with them, in a sling around their necks where the babies experience many hours a day of close physical contact. She claimed that the mothers and babies developed firm attachments by five or six months. However, other research has failed to confirm the benefits

► A *sensitive period* is a period of time after birth when some infants are particularly sensitive to certain stimuli, such as the sight, sound and smell of their caregiver.

► Klaus and Kennel suggest that emotional bonds will be strengthened with the right kind of contact at the right time in the infant's life, and that there is a biological, hormonal need for close physical contact.

► A control group is a group whose members are as similar as possible to the members of the other group being studied. Their behaviour is not manipulated in any way, and the behaviour of the members of the two groups is compared to see if any changes have occurred.

► Klaus and Kennel's studies of the caregiver suggest that timing and frequency of interaction are the most important factors in establishing close emotional ties in early childhood.

of early extended contact, or the existence of any sensitive period for emotional bonding in humans. For example, parents of babies who are kept in intensive care until long after any 'sensitive period' might exist still develop close emotional bonds with them, and Michael Rutter (1981) has shown how parents who adopt children develop very close bonds with them even if they are adopted weeks and months after birth. So, not everyone agrees that extended skin-to-skin contact is essential for close attachments, although the practice shouldn't be discouraged if both partners find it pleasant.

Apart from timing and amount of contact, other factors in successful bonding can be inferred from studying the behaviour of infant rather than the behaviour of caregiver. Mary Ainsworth and Silvia Bell (1972) naturalistically observed 26 mother–baby pairs in their homes for four hours at a time, every three weeks, during the infant's first 12 months of life. They particularly noted the mothers' reactions to their babies crying. It soon became apparent that young babies cried most when separated from their mothers, and least when being held by them. It seemed that some mothers were very sensitive to their babies' needs and responded quickly by picking the baby up. Others let the baby cry for some time before responding. The mothers who appeared to be more sensitive had babies who cried less and seemed generally more content.

► Crying is a sign that something is wrong with the baby, and babies use different kinds of cry for different kinds of distress. Parents soon learn to recognize whether the particular cry indicates hunger, pain, boredom or tiredness.

■ What does Mary Ainsworth mean by the 'sensitive mother'?

■ Name three factors that caregivers provide which have been claimed to aid attachment formation.

### The sensitive mother

According to Mary Ainsworth, a sensitive mother is 'able to see things from her baby's point of view. She is tuned in to receive her baby's signals: she interprets them correctly, and she responds to them promptly and appropriately. Although she nearly always gives the baby what he seems to want, when she does not she is tactful in acknowledging his communication … The sensitive mother, by implication, cannot be rejecting, interfering or ignoring'.

The relationship between parents and babies isn't all one way. Babies are active in the exchange, too. **Daniel Stern** (1977) maintains that babies are good at communicating their needs and thus regulating the amount of social contact they receive. They can start some contact by reaching, waving, gazing and smiling. Smiles are very powerful social signals inviting someone to pay the baby some attention. Babies make and break eye contact as they 'hold conversations' with their caregivers. They stop the interaction by frowning, stiffening and even crying. By three months of age babies are using similar kinds of social signals as adults use.

### An observation by Daniel Stern

A mother is feeding her three-month-old infant. While talking and looking at me the mother turned her head and gazed at the infant's face. He was gazing at the ceiling, but out of the corner of his eye he saw her head turn towards him, and he turned to gaze back at her ... he stopped sucking. He let go of the nipple ... The mother abruptly stopped talking ... her eyes opened a little wider and her eyebrows raised a bit. His eyes locked onto hers, and together they held motionless for an instant. This silent and almost motionless instant continued to hang until the mother suddenly shattered it by saying 'Hey!' and simultaneously opened her eyes wider, raising her eyebrows further, and throwing her head up toward the infant. Almost simultaneously the baby's eyes widened. His head tilted up, and, as his smile broadened, the nipple fell out of his mouth. 'Well, Hello! ... Heello ... Heeelloo' so that her pitch rose and the 'Hellos' became longer and more emphatic on each successive repetition. With each phrase the baby expressed more pleasure, and his body resonated almost like a balloon ... filling a little more with each breath. They watched each other expectantly for a moment ... then the baby took the initiative ... his head lurched forward, his hands jerked up, and a fuller smile blossomed.

**Colwyn Trevarthen** and **Martin Richards** (1978) filmed five babies (sometimes playing alone, sometimes with their mothers) for one hour a week each, over their first six months. The infants behaved quite differently when alone than when with their mothers. The researchers noted how babies move their bodies during interaction with an adult. From around two months, as the adult speaks, the child remains quiet and still. Two months later, if the infant wants to butt in it will raise its arms and babble more loudly. When the adult stops talking the infant begins to make noises and move its body in the way Daniel Stern observed above. Trevarthen and Richards describe this as *interactional synchrony*.

### Summary – The baby–adult social interaction

| The baby | The adult |
|---|---|
| Looks, gazes, stares at caregiver, uses reflexive and social smiles | Returns gaze, is sensitive to baby's needs |
| Exchanges 'conversations' | Participates in 'exchange games' |
| Expresses physical needs, through crying, etc. | Responds to baby's needs quickly |

Most of the evidence for the (supposed) social skills of young babies comes from observational studies. Inevitably, observations are not completely objective because the observer may already have some idea of what to expect and may interpret the observations accordingly. **Kenneth Kaye** (1984) has made extensive studies of the young baby's cognitive development. While he accepts that babies are born with some ability to take turns in their social exchanges, he claims that most of what is seen as being 'social' is probably merely innately driven responses which have some 'sur-

▶ Daniel Stern has applied his psychoanalytic training to the study of babies and concludes that they are much more advanced than was previously thought in the way they regulate social contact.

▶ Stern believes that babies are genetically predisposed to be sociable and to regulate their communication. The actual social contact, and what they derive from it, is purely socially learned, and some is simply for fun.

▶ According to Trevarthen and Richards babies are not the passive, helpless creatures that Bowlby and others believe. Rather, they interact actively in their social contact. The way in which adults and babies co-ordinate their interaction is called *interactional synchrony*.

▶ Daniel Stern, Mary Ainsworth, and Trevarthen and Richards are all claiming that even quite young babies are capable of making social exchanges, and having some control over their exchanges.

■ **What is meant by 'interactional synchrony'?**

■ **What is the evidence in the quote from Daniel Stern's observation for interactional synchrony or mutual reciprocity?**

vival value'. He doesn't believe that some of the social skills claimed for very young babies would actually be acquired until they were many months old.

---

### Taking turns

Kenneth Kaye claims that:

> … mother–infant interaction is characterised by turn taking right from the first, but the roles of mother and infant in managing the turns is highly asymmetrical. The mother's role is a matter of fitting in to those rhythms so as to produce a semblance of dialogue for which she alone is really responsible. Gradually the roles become more symmetrical but adults continue to manage and lead dialogue with children until the children themselves become adults.

---

### Summary – The research on attachment formation

| Researchers | Main conclusion |
| --- | --- |
| Klaus and Kennel | Very early contact is beneficial for making strong attachments later |
| Ainsworth and Bell | Mother's sensitivity to her baby's crying facilitates attachment |
| Stern | Babies can regulate their contact |
| Trevarthen and Richards | Babies' ability to participate in interactional synchrony is socially learned |
| Kaye | Infants aren't capable of much early learning of social skills |

---

Whether babies have early social skills to assist them and their caregivers in attachment formation isn't known for sure. No doubt sensitive, stimulating company is much better than uncaring, unstimulating company, no matter what the baby makes of it.

## Making more than one attachment

Bowlby originally claimed that babies make one essential attachment to their mothers, or mother substitute. Later he admitted that a hierarchy of attachments is possible, but insisted that the mother figure is at the top. In 1964 **Rudi Schaffer** and **Peggy Emerson** published the findings of their *longitudinal study* of 60 Glasgow babies from their birth until they were 18 months old. Every month for the first year the mothers were interviewed and asked about how the baby behaved with the various people with whom it came into regular contact. A final interview occurred when the babies were 18 months old. As their definition of an attachment Schaffer and Emerson used separation anxiety. If the baby showed anxiety when separated from someone, then it could be said to be attached to that person.

Schaffer and Emerson identified four stages in the development of attachments. For the first six weeks the babies had no particular preference about who they were with. Between six weeks and six

► A *longitudinal study* is conducted over a period of time, usually years, and usually involving the same participants, which allows us to observe the effects of time, age and experience on behaviour.

► Rudi Schaffer also stresses the importance for both partners to be equally involved. He calls it *mutual reciprocity.*

months they became increasingly more sociable with anyone who wanted to interact with them. Over the next month or so nearly 30 per cent formed attachments to several people (10 per cent had as many as five attachments by seven months). The rest started to prefer to be near their main caregiver, and to show signs of anxiety if approached by a stranger. This is the beginning of their first attachment. From around eight months the final stage was reached with the babies being content to attach to several people. By ten months nearly 60 per cent had more than one attachment. By 18 months 87 per cent had more than one attachment, and over 30 per cent had five or more. Only a half were primarily attached to their mothers. A third were mainly attached to their fathers.

Bowlby claimed that the bond that grows between a mother (or mother substitute) and her baby is special. It has evolved in us, and plays an important role in survival. However, babies do not always want their mothers and seem to use different adults for different things. When frightened they often prefer to be close to their mother. When they want more robust play, they often prefer their father. Schaffer and Emerson did not find significant differences in the quality of the relationships that the babies developed with each of the people to whom they became attached. As Schaffer says, 'being attached to several people does not imply a shallower feeling for each one, for an infant's capacity for attachment is not like a cake that has to be shared out. Love, even in babies, has no limits'.

## The benefits of making multiple attachments

There are several benefits for the child. As it grows it will have a variety of people to identify with. Its personality will be shaped by the personalities of the people to whom it is closest. It will also have a variety of role models on which to model its behaviour. It has more people to offer it a range of discipline and rewards (and more people to spoil it, too!).

There are also benefits to the adults. If a child is attached to one person, that person must be constantly available to comfort and stimulate the child as necessary. Knowing that the baby is content to be with someone while its primary caregiver is away could encourage many caregivers to return to outside work, or to take up social or other activities, at least for part of the time. If the parent has to enter hospital, then the presence of others to whom the child is attached can help it cope with the separation. James and Joyce Robertson tried to establish some kind of attachment with the children they fostered to minimize the ill effects of the separation. Patient, high-quality care and love did help these children (see page 312).

■ Schaffer and Emerson used 'separation anxiety' as their main method of measuring whether an attachment had formed. Can you think of any limitations this might pose for the validity of their research?

► Older babies seem to be able to recognize different people, associate each of them with different activities or qualities, and prefer the individual that possesses the skill the baby wants at the time. Schaffer and Emerson claim that babies have a large capacity for developing loving relationships.

■ What kind of differences would you expect to find in the behaviour of securely and insecurely attached children?

### Summary – Multiple attachments

In the early research the emphasis has been on the mother–infant relationship. Schaffer and Emerson argue that other family members can be closely involved. In many families it simply isn't possible for one or more of the adults to provide continuous care for the offspring. Increasing numbers of mothers work outside the home, while fathers may stay at home and look after the child, or often a baby-minder or older siblings will be entrusted with the care of the baby. Not surprisingly, the babies are quite likely to form strong attachment bonds with these various caregivers. Schaffer and Emerson found that babies of between six and 18 months could form several attachments to different people, and that each attachment was of the same quality.

■ Outline the conclusions of the following researchers: 1 Colwyn Trevarthen and Martin Richards; 2 Genevieve Carpenter; 3 Daniel Stern; 4 Mary Ainsworth and Silvia Bell; 5 Marshall Klaus and John Kennel; 6 Rudi Schaffer and Peggy Emerson.

### Summary – Sociability and attachments

Humans have a great capacity for learning, and a great deal to learn. Those with generally co-operative temperaments may be more sociable. If they have willing caregivers they will begin to form attachments within a few months of birth and the socialization process will begin within a few months of that.

If a baby is securely attached it will develop some ideas about security and trust. It will feel safe and protected, and more able to explore away from its caregivers. It may be able to treat them as some kind of safe base to which it can return in case of trouble. Knowing that there is this safe base could encourage a child to be more adventurous, and possibly more independent, too. This could be beneficial to cognitive development, as we'll see later.

## LONG-TERM EFFECTS OF EARLY EXPERIENCE

In the previous section we mentioned the Robertsons' study of John, a 17-month-old who was placed in a residential nursery for ten days whilst his mother was having a second child in hospital. He was unable to keep the attention he needed and exhibited the symptoms of the syndrome of distress. John's experiences appeared to have some long-term effects. His personality seemed to have changed. He had more temper tantrums, sometimes refused to walk, and was occasionally hostile and uncaring. One day, when he was six, he looked up to his mother and asked, 'Mummy, why am I so horrible to you?' Some of John's problems could have resulted from the separation.

There are essentially two opposing theories on the relationship between early experiences and later life. The view expressed by the psychoanalysts, including the Robertsons and Bowlby, is *continuity theory*. This says that young children go through sensitive periods or stages when they are especially receptive to certain influences. These influences will affect their personalities as adults. The alternative, *discontinuity theory*, strongly advocated by Ann and Alan Clarke, claims that early experiences are just one link in the 'developmental chain', and are no more influential than experiences gained at any other time. Much research has been conducted in the area of early experience and its long-term effects. The principal questions underlying it have been, 'Will a deprived environment lead to a damaged adulthood?' and 'Will a rich and stimulating early experience lead to a well-adjusted and successful adulthood?'

Studies of the effects of deprived environments have taken the form of controlled experiments using animal subjects, while others are studies of institutionally reared children. Finally, we will discuss some attempts made in America and Britain at social engineering.

## Animal research

We obviously can't conduct controlled experiments on humans to investigate the effects of disrupted or non-existent attachments, but such research has been conducted on animals. **Harry** and **Margaret Harlow** (1958, 1962, 1965, 1966) removed some rhesus monkeys from their mothers just after birth and reared them in isolation. Their cages contained a blanket and the animals spent many hours cuddling up to it. When the blanket was removed they showed violent emotional reactions that lasted for several days. These infant monkeys appear to need something constant, dependable and comfortable in their lives.

► Rhesus monkeys are small animals which have been extensively studied by psychologists. Many are bred in captivity at American universities.

When some monkeys were released into the company of laboratory-reared monkeys after three months' isolation they initially avoided contact, but gradually learned to adapt and became accepted by the other animals. Those released after six months' isolation were severely withdrawn and never fully adapted. They were attacked by the others and had little idea about establishing their place in the group. The males had little success at attracting a mate, and the females that did mate had little idea of motherhood and neglected their offspring.

► Some time between three and six months seems to be a cut off point, after which isolated monkeys appeared unable to adjust to normal life.

To test the psychoanalytic claim that food was more important than comfort, Harlow isolated eight rhesus monkeys just after birth. Each was kept in a cage containing two dolls, which Harlow described as 'surrogate mothers'. One doll was made of wood and was covered in terry towelling. The other was a wire-mesh, uncovered doll. Four monkeys were placed in cages where the feeding bottle was in the wooden doll, and four had the wire model containing the feeding bottle. All the monkeys spent most of their days clinging on to the terry-covered substitute regardless of which one had the feeding bottle. This *contact comfort* was clearly as important for these monkeys as it had appeared to be for the earlier group with their blankets. These animals also had long-term problems with adjusting to life with other 'normally reared' monkeys.

► A *surrogate* is a substitute or stand-in, usually for a parent. Primary school teachers are often used as surrogate parents by the children in their classes. Harlow's wire and cloth-covered dolls were surrogate mothers, although they only provided contact comfort and food. 'Real' mothers also provide stimulation, discipline, and act as models for behaviour.

When the monkeys were frightened (by Harlow putting strange toys, such as a mechanical teddy bear or large wooden spider, into their cage), they all clung to the towelling-covered mother. Eventually they would leave the model briefly to go and explore, then rush

► Harlow and Bowlby rejected the central importance of feeding for infants. Instead, they saw *contact comfort* as far more important. Bowlby claimed that contact comfort would help in the bonding process as well as in survival.

▶ Harlow's early research points to the need for contact comfort, and its role in the animal's independence. The later research shows that animals other than the mother can provide the stimulation for making normal relationships with others.

▶ *Imprinting* is a special form of learning that occurs soon after birth in some animal species. Konrad Lorenz found that many animals imprinted on their caregivers during the few hours following birth. Having an instinctive urge to follow the first thing one sees would contribute to one's survival. In the wild the first thing the newborn sees is likely to be the mother, who will feed and protect it. (See Chapter 6, pages 121–3.)

▶ A *sensitive period* is a period of time after birth when some animals are particularly sensitive to certain stimuli, such as the sight of their caregiver. See Klaus and Kennel's research on sensitive periods in the previous section (page 313).

back to it for comfort again. The terry-covered surrogate served as a safe base from which to explore.

These results appear to support Bowlby's predictions that maternal deprivation leads to unsatisfactory development. However, these animals weren't just being deprived of their mothers (maternal deprivation), but of all social contact (social privation). Isolation from all contact with other monkeys, rather than solely from their mothers, may explain their long-term disturbed behaviour.

In later experiments by Harry Harlow and **Steven Suomi** (1971), three-month-old 'normally reared' females were gradually introduced into the isolates' cages. The behaviour of the isolated monkeys gradually improved over the following months as their exposure to the females increased. When released at 12 months they adjusted to life in the monkey troupe. Over the long term their behaviour improved further. This suggests that young rhesus monkeys need other monkeys around to learn from, and not just their mothers. Also that the effects of severe deprivation early in life can be overcome. (Harlow called the young females 'therapists'.)

One major problem with most laboratory-based research is that it loses touch with 'real life'. Animals (including humans) are influenced by all kinds of things, from the weather, how alert they are, their relationships with others, which often aren't explored in the laboratory. Ethologists study the interaction of genetic and social forces on animal behaviour in their natural habitat and make observations which may be tested experimentally later. **Konrad Lorenz** was an ethologist who observed the events he called *imprinting*. In 1935 Lorenz observed that some newborn animals tend to follow the first moving thing they see after they are born. Since the first thing a newborn will see is its mother, it learns what mothers look like so they can be recognized in the future. Lorenz claimed that this would enable them to recognize potential mates in the long term. Animals who had imprinted on an unusual object (including a matchbox tied to string, a yellow rubber glove, and Lorenz himself) often tried to mate with it later!

Lorenz claimed that there was a *critical period* during which imprinting must occur, otherwise it wouldn't occur at all. The length of this time varies depending on the animal species in question. For ducks and geese it was about 24 hours following birth. For humans it could start after a few months, and might last a few years. Later researchers have challenged Lorenz's ideas of a critical period, preferring instead *a sensitive period*, when animals and people may be particularly receptive to certain stimuli.

### Summary – Animal research

Harlow's privation studies found that monkeys can recover from the loss of their mother if they have other social contact. Lorenz found that certain species have an instinctive need to form a relationship with the first thing they see. For similar reasons humans might have evolved something similar, but this is debatable. These animals' early experiences can lead to long-term problems if untreated.

## *Institutionally reared children*

Earlier we mentioned Rene Spitz's observations of orphans in unstimulating environments. Supporters of continuity theory would claim that such deprived early lives will almost certainly produce disturbed adult personalities. Psychologists have studied children in several institutional settings, and followed them up later to assess the impact such experiences may have made. Some have emphasized emotional and social aspects of development, whilst others have looked more for any effects on intellectual development. Most have taken the form of longitudinal studies, where the same people are tested in some way at different times in their lives. On the whole, what they have shown is that children are generally far more flexible than was claimed by continuity theorists, and that even quite awful early experiences can be overcome.

**William Goldfarb** (1943) conducted a longitudinal study of 30 teenagers, 15 of whom had been fostered before they were 12 months old, while the other 15 had spent at least the first three and a half years of their lives in an understaffed and unstimulating institution. The two groups were similar in age, sex and social background of their biological parents. Goldfarb studied the children when they were three and a half, six and a half, eight and a half, and 12 years old. Those who had stayed in the institution scored lower on Goldfarb's tests (for intelligence, independence, language and speech, self-control etc.). They were more likely to become aggressive, some were hyperactive, and most were more likely to try to deceive their adoptive parents. They had few friends, were emotionally insecure and spent most of their time alone. Goldfarb claimed that all these difficulties were because of the time spent in the orphanage without a mother.

▶ Goldfarb found evidence that late adoption leads to retarded development, where early adoption does not. His study, like Bowlby's *44 Juvenile Thieves*, takes two factors, 'maternal deprivation' and 'retarded development', and sees a relationship between them, assuming one is causing the other.

**Barbara Tizard**, **Judith Rees** and **Jill Hodges** (1989) studied 65 children who had been placed in a residential nursery before they were four months old. Many of their mothers were unmarried, and were unable to cope. By three years of age some of the children were adopted, some had returned to their natural mothers, and some were to remain in the institution. The adopted children had similar difficulties to those in Goldfarb's study. They still coped better than those children who remained in the institution. Those who had returned to their natural mothers seemed least emotionally secure of all. The mothers still had difficulties in coping, and the children appeared to suffer. Tizard et al.'s study showed that mothers weren't necessarily the best people to bring up their children unless they had the ability and adequate material conditions. Those reared by adopting parents did overcome most of their problems later.

▶ Tizard et al.'s study found that those children who were adopted made a good recovery after initial problems. Those who stayed in the institution adapted to their situation. Those who returned to their natural mothers continued to have emotional and social problems.

**Harold Skeels** and his colleagues have conducted several studies of children whose environments have been enriched and whose abil-

▶ What the Skeels studies suggest is that children can overcome deprived early experience with appropriate enrichment, so long as the period of deprivation isn't too long.

▶ Dennis and Dennis' study suggests a sensitive period of around two years for intellectual development.

ities changed as well. Skeels (1939) reported the cases of two children in a state orphanage in America whose development was so poor that they were placed in a special institution for severely retarded children. For example, they didn't speak or walk, they showed little curiosity and spent a lot of time staring into space. There are a number of *developmental* scales that measure how advanced some children's skills are. The average child would score 100. After a few months the two children showed dramatic increases in their recorded abilities. It seemed that they were forming multiple attachments with other children in the institution and the staff 'mothered' them. Within two years both children were able to be fostered.

Skeels and Dye (1939) decided to test the impact of changing environment on changing development more thoroughly. They sampled 25 19-month-old orphans who lived in a deprived and overcrowded orphanage. Of the 25, 13 were so retarded that they weren't suitable for being considered for adoption. They were moved to an orphanage for slightly subnormal older girls who cared for the children for much of the time, acting as surrogate mothers. After another 18 months, the babies' scores on a developmental scale had risen on average by 28 points, from around 60 to nearly 90. The scores of the 12 babies who remained in the orphanage declined further and were now the same as the first group before they were moved. Two and a half years later the differences were still there, and when Skeels tested them again when the two groups were 21 years old those from the more stimulating environment were still ahead. Many had finished college, some had married and obtained useful jobs.

Until 1956 adoption of illegitimate children was not legal in the Lebanon. **Wayne** and **Marsena Dennis** (1960) found the developmental and intellectual scores of some of the teenage orphans from a deprived orphanage to be well below average at 53. Wayne Dennis followed up a group who had been adopted at various ages 15 years afterwards. He found that the longer they stayed in the orphanage after the age of two years, the further below average they remained. Dennis suggests that around two years might mark the end of the sensitive period for intellectual development for these children. He says: 'there is a period near the second birthday which is critical with respect to complete recovery from the effects of … deprivation upon intelligence. Those adopted before age two recover completely … among those adopted later there is a marked persistence of retardation.' This study suggests that enriching a deprived environment has benefits for intellectual development.

**Ann** and **Alan Clarke** are amongst the fiercest critics of continuity theory, i.e. they do not see the first few years of life as being all important for future development. They name several studies which have documented almost miraculous recoveries from the most awful early starts. Here are two of them.

Anna Freud (Sigmund's daughter) and Sophie Dann conducted a case study of six Jewish war orphans at the Bulldogs Bank children's home in the late 1940s entitled *Childhood Survivors of the*

*Holocaust.* Their families had been killed by the Nazis in concentration camps. They were aged approximately three years to three years ten months when they arrived at the Bulldogs Bank. They had almost no language, weren't potty trained, couldn't use a knife and fork, were aggressive and destructive. However, they were totally attached to one another and quite inseparable. When one stopped eating, they all stopped, when one woke up, they all did. The children gradually adjusted to life in the home, and made good progress generally. They were adopted and, as far as we know, went on to make successful lives. What this study does show is that it is not who the child forms attachments to that is particularly important, but that it is able to form attachments with someone.

The Clarkes also report the case studied by Jarmila Koluchova of Czechoslovakian identical twin boys who had been kept isolated from anyone else, often locked in the cellar, and treated very cruelly by their stepmother from when they were about two to when they were seven. They had little to eat, nothing to play with, and she would beat them with wooden kitchen spoons or a length of hose pipe if they cried. When discovered at the age of seven they had severe rickets, were covered in scar tissue from the beatings, could not speak, and were (understandably) frightened of humans. Their intelligence was too low to be measured. It would be difficult to imagine a much worse start anyone could have in life. After intensive hospital treatment and several years of remedial education they were successfully adopted and by 15 years appeared to make a full recovery.

**Albert Kadushin** (1976) studied 91 families who had adopted a child who was five years or older. Six years after the original placement he interviewed the parents and found around 85 per cent of them were highly satisfied with the way the children had formed close relationships with them and that the adoption had been successful. Only two had failed. Other studies have found similar results. Kadushin claims that children are far more adaptive and capable of a far greater range of responses, depending on the needs of the situation, than some of the early research suggested.

▶ The Clarkes see infancy and childhood as the first stages in development. Problems we experience during the first few years can be overcome later as we become more able to understand what has happened to us.

▶ The Bulldogs Bank children had probably never made attachments to any adults, but had attached to each other.

## Summary – Institutionally reared children

Bowlby's version of continuity theory predicts that early experiences will have long-term effects. This view is not supported by the studies quoted here. The Dennis' study of Lebanese orphans suggests that there may be a sensitive period of around two years, during which children should be stimulated emotionally and intellectually, otherwise they may never achieve their full potential. Skeels and Dye found that children placed in more stimulating environments made considerable gains in their intellectual development. The Clarkes quote evidence that shows that children can recover from the most awful early experiences.

## Social engineering

During the 1950s and 1960s in America, many children, often from ethnic minority backgrounds and poor neighbourhoods, were doing badly in school, dropping out, sometimes turning to crime. As adults many were unemployed and generally living in poverty. One suggestion made by Oscar Lewis in the late 1950s was that this lack of success was due to their poor cultural experiences when compared to that of normal American children. Many lived in deprived neighbourhoods without the usual facilities such as libraries, parks or theatres. Many of the children did not speak fluent English. This deprived or impoverished culture would hold those groups of children back in later life, which would be bad for them, and bad for America as a whole, since they could end up in dead-end jobs, or on welfare, or in prison. Lewis describes the culture of poverty which had become a 'design for living', from which so many poor people could not escape.

► Lewis proposed that the reason why many people lived in poverty was because they had developed a culture of poverty. Their expectations were that they would live in poverty and so were unlikely to escape using the acceptable forms such as hard work and educational or other qualifications. This explanation is criticized for failing to explain why people became so poor in the first place.

President John Kennedy stated that the American government was declaring a 'War On Poverty', which became a massive attempt at enrichment aimed at improving the culture of these children. It spent 17 billion dollars on a series of programmes of compensatory education for disadvantaged children. (To 'compensate' them for lacking a 'superior' culture, and to give them the opportunity to become more 'American'.) Some of the programmes emphasized social development, some emphasized cognitive (thinking, reasoning, etc.) development. The general aim was that deprived children would receive some pre-school remedial education. One of the best known programmes of compensatory education was Project (or Operation) Headstart, which started in the summer of 1965.

► Project Headstart comprised dozens of small-scale attempts to improve the life chances of the children who attended the classes.

Hundreds, later thousands, of programmes were set up in different areas in American cities. Some were very education-centred, with children being taught discipline as well as basic skills. Others were more child-centred, trying to help children to be more sociable, co-operative or confident. Most of the children in Headstart and similar programmes would go on visits to parks, and have people come into their neighbourhoods, even into their homes, and teach them about road safety and where to play. They had extra teaching in English and maths, they received free medical and dental check-ups, and generally were encouraged to absorb the competitive atmosphere that dominates American schools. In this way, it was argued, they would be academically as prepared for junior school as their other classmates, and they would be able to join in the games, the competitions and the individual achievements too.

► Although the Headstart children weren't all making the progress in school that had been hoped, some were. Studies showed that the main factor that those who were most likely to succeed had in common was the involvement of their parents in their experiences.

Most of the children benefited from their early enrichment. However, once they were in school many of the Headstart children began to fall behind their native American classmates. Many coped better than they may have coped before, at least for the first few years of schooling, but disappointingly, by nine or ten years of age, the vast majority had fallen behind and few went on to graduate from college or go on to university or other training.

So why didn't more of the children who went through these compensatory education programmes improve in their schooling? Perhaps the influence of the home and family as the children grew was greater than the influence of spending a few hours a day in the programme when they were young. Those Headstart programmes that involved parents did seem to be more successful than others. Enrichment only seems to have any real chance of success when all the areas of one's life are affected, for example when a child is removed from one institution, such as a poor orphanage, and reared by loving parents. A few extra hours of enrichment could not begin to outweigh the disadvantages of being brought up in a poor, deprived environment.

In Britain something on a much smaller scale than Headstart began in the late 1960s. Children in some inner-city areas were leaving school with few qualifications and little chance of worthwhile jobs. Many lived in sub-standard housing in run-down areas. The government recognized that there was a link between children's social experiences and their chances of success in education and directed some money into intervention programmes to improve school buildings and encourage teachers to work in these areas by giving extra pay. Four areas were identified as Educational Priorities Areas (EPAs). These included parts of Liverpool, Birmingham, London and Yorkshire.

These programmes of compensatory education aimed to raise reading and writing skills in pre-school and primary schools. The results were disappointing, as they had been with Headstart. EPAs did not lead to improvements in academic qualifications or employment prospects. As with Headstart, without involving the parents, and even the wider community, in education, specific programmes of education alone are unlikely to succeed in improving the life chances of children.

► More recent studies of those who went through Headstart are more encouraging. Although the children may not have benefited in the ways intended, they do seem to be more likely to be successful citizens, with fewer committing crimes or becoming pre-maritally pregnant, and more holding down a job, finishing school etc.

► Compared to Headstart, the EPAs were not well funded and supporters claim they were not given an adequate chance.

---

### Summary – Social engineering

Large-scale attempts by governments to influence the long-term effects of early social experiences have largely failed, not for the reasons that continuity theory suggests, but rather because the task was too great. Taking a child out of its deprived environment for a few hours a day would not substitute for its experiences whilst in it. Critics have attacked the notion of compensatory education for its assumption that one set of experiences (American culture) is superior to another (e.g. Puerto Rican culture).

---

## Long-term effects of alternative forms of childcare

Bowlby claimed that nature has given the role of childcare to women. Schaffer and Emerson show how others are involved, too. Later research still has included the role of fathers, nannies, childminders and others involved in daycare. There are problems with drawing conclusions from some of the studies, since the children studied were often in above-average centres, and parents were more likely to take an active interest in their progress anyway. Parental involvement is a major factor in the success of many children's activities. Further, what exactly would we mean by success? According to Clarke-Stewart and Fein (1983), who reviewed the research so far, children in good nursery schools have good cognitive skills when they start, and most continue to do so. They are more sociable with other children, and their existing attachments aren't damaged. They are more active and noisy, too. On balance, most children benefit from pre-school experiences in the long term, but it's very difficult to conduct research to support this claim.

## CROSS-CULTURAL FACTORS IN EARLY SOCIALIZATION

Earlier we referred to the nature–nurture debate concerning those skills and abilities that are the result of biology and those that result from environmental influences. One way to solve some of these matters is to conduct cross-cultural research. This involves observing and testing aspects of the behaviour of people from different cultural backgrounds who have different lifestyles, language, attitudes and experiences. If we find that one thing is true everywhere, e.g. that children develop the capacity to talk between the ages of ten and 30 months, then we are justified in claiming that we are biologically driven to develop language then (nature). If we find that some things vary, e.g. that in some societies female children are more aggressive than male children, then the way they are brought up (nurture) is probably responsible.

When psychologists study people from their own society they may be tempted to imagine that what they find would be true everywhere. Bowlby's claim that infants are able to develop their first attachment bonds after the age of six months is an example. Most of the bonds he had studied did develop at this time. However, Mary Ainsworth found that many Ganda children formed their first attachments several months earlier than children in the West. This was facilitated by the close physical contact and the almost constant verbal stimulation between the mother and infant. Although we are biologically driven to develop attachments, the timing of them is influenced by experience. Cross-cultural research shows the effects of different forms of childrearing.

**Urie Bronfenbrenner** (1974) found that American educational systems reflected the individual competitiveness in American society. Individuality is encouraged and groups are encouraged always to compete. Two decades ago the Russian education system emphasized co-operation and mutual support. American teenagers develop a subculture which places value on daring, behaving in anti-social ways, and trying to beat the system. Films that portray

► Few psychologists now would subscribe to EITHER the nature OR the nurture view. Obviously there is an interaction between the two. Psychologists are more interested in the contributions made by biology and experience, and how they interact.

► Cross-cultural studies take a particular aspect of life in different cultures and compare them. In this way we can build up a picture of how cultural expectations influence people's behaviour.

young people behaving like this are often popular. Russian culture did not respect anti-social behaviour. Teenagers behaved in pro-social ways and this was reflected in co-operation and mutual support.

Some people choose to live in communes and collectives, where the children tend to be brought up by the whole community, or by particular people other than their parents. There is no evidence that this pattern of childrearing causes emotional disturbance. In Israel a small percentage of the population chooses to live in kibbutzim (agricultural communes). The success of the group depends on all of its members contributing, so new mothers gradually return to work during the child's first year, and a children's nurse takes over childcare. Eventually, the child will be brought up with all the other children in the Children's House, although most of them will see their parents every day. There is plenty of scope to form attachments with the metepelet (nurse) and the other children. Since the time the parents spend with their children needn't be interrupted by the other demands of parenting such as feeding, the quality of the interaction is maximized, leading to the formation of strong attachments with their parents too. Children in the kibbutz confirm the findings of other studies of attachment bonding, that it is quality rather than quantity of interaction that promotes attachment bonds.

► The kibbutz allows us to make a cross-cultural study of attachment bonding. In the kibbutz children are reared with all the other children by a special children's nurse, and by their parents. They make attachments with other people as well as their parents.

■ **Make notes on the use of evidence from the kibbutz as cross-cultural research.**

■ **What do cross-cultural studies contribute to our discussion of Bowlby's claims?**

---

### Summary – Cross-cultural factors in early socialization

Childrearing practices vary enormously in different cultures around the world. In some, roles and responsibilities are clearly marked out by age and sex. In others, acceptable behaviour is determined by strict rules and enforced by harsh discipline. For those societies that do not have such clear-cut principles, a vast range of childrearing techniques is employed. Some have maternity and paternity leave and the children are reared by both parents; in others parenting is largely left to the mother, yet others share childrearing between a number of people and agencies, and in the kibbutz the commune itself is responsible for all its children.

### Exam questions – 60 minutes each

1 Discuss the evidence for the formation of attachments in early childhood. (*25 marks*)
2 What evidence is there that deprivation of attachment in early childhood could affect future development? (*25 marks*)
3 What have psychologists found out about the long-term consequences of enrichment and/or deprivation in children? (*25 marks*)
4 (a) What is sociability and what is attachment? (*5 marks*)
  (b) Critically discuss psychological evidence in the development of attachment. (*20 marks*)

# 15 Cognitive development

**Chapter objectives**

By the end of this chapter you should:

▌ be able to describe and evaluate Piaget's and Bruner's contributions to our understanding of how cognitive development occurs and the evidence upon which they are based;

▌ understand some of the influences family, peers and others have upon the cognitive development of the child;

▌ understand the nature and function of play and its role in cognitive development;

▌ appreciate the importance of cognitive factors on educational performance and classroom practice.

## Introduction

As we saw in Part 4, humans have an enormous capacity to selectively attend to and mentally manipulate vast amounts of sensory data. We are especially good at making sense of what we experience using complex thought processes and our immense memory capacities. This is one of the main things that separates humans from other animals – our capacity for *cognition*. The *Penguin Dictionary of Psychology* defines cognition as a 'broad term which has been traditionally used to refer to such activities as thinking, conceiving, reasoning … symbolising, insight, expectancy, complex rule use, imagery, belief, intentionality, problem solving and so forth'. You can see from this list that cognition involves many mental skills. Inevitably, some of them are present shortly after birth, while others will take time to acquire. In this chapter we will study two theories that have attempted to explain the development of cognition, and look at other influences on its development, and how cognition relates to education.

## THEORIES OF COGNITIVE DEVELOPMENT

### Jean Piaget's contribution

In 1920 Jean Piaget (1896–1980) was scoring some children's intelligence test papers and noticed that many were giving the same

*Jean Piaget*

▶ Jean Piaget can be fairly described as the founding father of developmental cognitive psychology. His countless hours of detailed study have produced a theory which has had enormous impact on childrearing and educational practices in the West.

wrong answer to certain questions. He asked other children for their answers. For example, five-year-old girls who had sisters were asked 'does your sister have a sister?' Many said 'no'. Eight-year-olds said 'yes, me'. His researches convinced him that children aren't 'little adults' simply waiting to grow up, which was the popular idea at the time. Rather, they seemed to have ways of viewing things that were quite different from those of an adult. This observation has led to one of the major contributions to our understanding of how children think. Piaget spent over 50 years studying children's thinking, until his death in 1980.

### Piaget's methods

Piaget had learned the *clinical interview* technique while studying Freudian psychoanalysis (see Chapter 1), and applied aspects of it when talking to hundreds of children to discover their views on where rules come from, how some things are related (such as chickens and eggs, or clouds and rain), how the appearance of an object influences their understanding of its other properties, and so on. The problem with this is that children aren't always co-operative, they don't always give you the answer to the question you thought you were asking, they get bored quickly, and just because a child doesn't do something doesn't mean that it can't do it. The clinical interview itself is very subjective, that is, it relies largely on the interviewer interpreting what he or she is being told. This method isn't 'scientific' enough for some psychologists.

Piaget also observed children playing alone, and together, in their own natural surroundings (the street, their garden, etc.) to see how they responded to one another and how they would play their games. If all six-year-olds responded in similar ways to things such as taking turns, obeying the rules or changing the procedures they might tell us how six-year-olds think. If eight-year-olds respond differently, their level of cognitive development must be different.

Another method was direct questioning, in which he would show the children something (such as a 25-cm stick and a piece of string the same length) and ask them if the two were the same. Then he'd curl the string up and ask again. Younger ones said the string was shorter now. Direct questions about what windows are for and what can we do with a brick also reveal the way children reason and use what they know. This led Piaget to develop the story-telling technique, which he used to find how children regard good and bad, right and wrong, and so on.

Over a period of years Piaget constructed a model, largely influenced by his knowledge of biology, to explain cognitive structures, and a theory of how they work to allow cognition to develop.

### Piaget's model of basic cognitive processes

Piaget believed that babies are born with a few basic strategies or ideas for receiving information and dealing with it. They build up 'mental structures' about what they experience. He called these mental structures *schemas*. In Chapter 13 we referred to them

▶ Piaget used the *clinical interview* technique to gather information from children about why they thought they did things.

▶ Piaget used clinical interviews, observations, story-telling and experiments to discover similarities in the thinking of children of the same age, and how and when this changed.

■ **What do you think are the advantages and disadvantages of each of the main methods Piaget used to gather his data?**

► Piaget uses the term *schemas* to refer to mental structures which are strategies that we use to handle information. The first schemas are involuntary, reflexive responses, many of which increase the infant's chances of survival. These are *action schemas*.

► Action schemas are joined by *symbolic schemas* from around the age of two years. A *symbol* is an idea that we have that represents an object, such as a traffic sign for a roundabout, or a word which represents its meaning.

► An operation is a mental routine for transposing information. So, imagining what the curled string would look like if it were straightened is an example of operational thought.

■ **What are 'schemas'? Briefly describe the types of schema identified by Piaget.**

■ **Why does Piaget call schemas and operations 'variant mental structures'?**

► Everyone is born with three unconscious capacities. First, to develop schemas; since everyone has different experiences, so each person's particular schemas will be different. Second, to organize schemas for making sense of our experiences. Third, we have the capacity to adapt our knowledge according to our previous experiences.

loosely as 'memory traces', which may be housed in Hebb's 'cell assemblies' (see pages 295–6). There are three types of schema that appear as the child matures. The first, *action schemas*, are the 50 or so reflexes that we have at birth. Breathing, sucking, grasping and crying are fairly obvious examples. Many reflexes involve actions or behaviour (since the young baby isn't mature enough for any other kind) that promote survival value.

By around the age of two the child learns to communicate. The word 'doll' can be used to stand for the object, and two-year-old children will know what you mean if you ask them 'Is that your doll?' They also learn to let one thing, such as a doll, stand for another, such as a 'mummy' or a 'baby'. These are *symbolic schemas*.

After another five years or so the child's thinking becomes more logical. It begins to realize that it can influence objects and events in its environment in a deliberate and meaningful way. It learns that performing some operation produces a predictable outcome. *Operational schemas* allow the child mentally to reverse some process and predict what the outcome will be. The child will realize that rules can be changed, that things aren't always what they seem, and that they can solve problems by thinking about them. Piaget described schemas and operations as 'variant mental structures', because everyone's cognition is different.

### Summary – Schemas

Schemas are basic concepts or mental representations of how to deal with something. Some schemas are fairly simple, such as eating with a knife and fork. Some are more complex, such as playing various games. Others are more complex still, such as playing a musical instrument or driving a car. Operations are more logical ways of combining schemas and do not appear until middle childhood.

Apart from the predisposition to develop schemas Piaget also claims we inherit the unconscious capacity mentally to organize them so that new experiences build on old ones. An infant who has learned that it can 'hold and shake' a rattle will combine this with the 'reach and grasp' schema. Now the sight of the rattle will trigger the 'reach and grasp, hold and shake' schema. The inborn capacity to combine schemas is called *organization*. There is one other inborn tendency which Piaget identified. This is the capacity to adapt our knowledge (and possibly our future behaviour) based on our previous relevant experiences.

Adaptation consists of two interdependent processes, assimilation and accommodation. Assimilation refers to the processes of selective attention and perceptual processing. Information has been taken into the perceptual system to be interpreted for its relevance and meaning. It may be in what Atkinson and Shiffrin referred to as short-term memory (see Chapter 13, pages 281–2). Long-term memories will be searched in order to make whatever sense of the new experience we can. Since young children have relatively fewer experiences, so they have less stored memories to search. For example, the young child may be familiar with bowls from which they are fed. Their first experience of plates will contain some of the same features as their knowledge of bowls, e.g. 'objects from which I eat', 'light in colour', 'round and flattish in shape', etc. The new information, that this is a plate, will modify the baby's existing knowledge about food servers. This modification of existing schemas by new information is what Piaget means by *accommodation*.

When the child has learned from some adaptation it has made, its knowledge is said to be in a state of *equilibrium* or cognitive balance. It has assimilated and accommodated, and now it 'knows'. For example, a two-year-old might know that 'doggies' have four legs, a head at one end and a tail at the other. Then she sees a cat, and logically calls it 'doggie'. Mother explains that it is a cat. Now there is new information to be assimilated and accommodated, and the appropriate mental adaptation to be made. The child was in a state of equilibrium, knowing that all four-legged creatures with heads and tails were called 'doggie'. Then new information about four-legged creatures has to be dealt with, and the child's mental processing is in a state of *equilibration*. A new state of equilibrium has to be achieved after assimilating and accommodating the new knowledge. Cognitive growth is a constant shift between states of equilibrium and equilibration.

> **Summary – Piaget's assumptions**
> Each child develops a unique set of insights gained from its particular experiences of its world. The child constructs increasingly complex schemas through the process of organization. Each schema is subject to adaptation as new information is assimilated and accommodated.

### Piaget's stages of cognitive development

Piaget (1969, 1972) found that we do not acquire new schemas in a simple continuous sequence. Children's ways of thinking change as they mature. Every child passes through the same sequence of stages (i.e. they are *invariant*), although the ages at which they enter and leave each one vary widely. Progress through them cannot be speeded up since it is a maturational process controlled by genetic forces. Piaget identified four broad stages, each with a number of substages. At each stage the child is able to make increasingly complex adaptations.

*1 The sensory motor stage, 0–2 years*
The young child develops action schemas, is preoccupied with itself and involves itself in solitary pastimes. Its thinking is dominated by its direct sensory experiences of the immediate environment, and what it can do with objects in its environment. For its first month the child concentrates on instinctive behaviour

▶ The process of adaptation is central to Piaget's theory. The nature of intelligence itself is the result of this process.

▶ For Piaget, 'knowing' or 'having cognition' is as a state of *equilibrium* between assimilation and accommodation. When a new adaptation needs to be made we are in a state of *equilibration*.

■ Describe Piaget's concept of adaptation.

▶ The four stages of cognitive development are *invariant*, that is, they always occur in the same sequence since they are dependent on the child's state of maturation, which is genetically controlled. Other examples of invariant processes are walking before running, babbling before talking, and passing through puberty before entering adulthood.

such as grasping and sucking. The child gradually begins deliberately to repeat actions that are (presumably) satisfying. By four or five months actions are performed on objects that will not directly satisfy the child's basic needs, but are stimulating in some way. Waving its hands around in front of its eyes may be satisfying, so the child deliberately waves its hands. By eight months the child is developing some idea about objects in the environment being 'real' and still being present, even though they are no longer visible. If the rattle is thrown to the floor the child will know that it still exists, although it is temporarily out of sight. This is called *object permanence*. By 12 to 18 months the child will follow the movement of an object as it disappears from view, and look for it in the place where it was last seen. Between about 18 and 24 months the child first shows signs of insight, the ability to solve problems in its head, i.e. symbolically.

**Tom Bower** (1971) insists that object permanence can be seen in infants long before the eight months that Piaget specified. He has conducted experiments with babies of between one and four months in which they were shown an interesting object placed in front of them. When their attention had been caught the object was hidden by a sliding screen. The object was removed while unseen by the baby. The screen was then retracted and the babies' reactions were observed. If they showed surprise that the object was no longer visible, then they could be said to have some idea of object permanence. Many did. Bower also showed them an object that they might try to take. When they started to reach for it the lights were turned off. Observations with an infra-red camera showed that the babies continued to try and reach for the object, despite not being able to see it. See figure 15.1.

▶ Piaget claimed that the very young child can only respond to things if they can be perceived. If they can't see or touch it, then, as far as the infant is concerned, it no longer exists. *Object permanence* is the knowledge that something still exists even when hidden from view. It was said by Piaget to develop at around eight months.

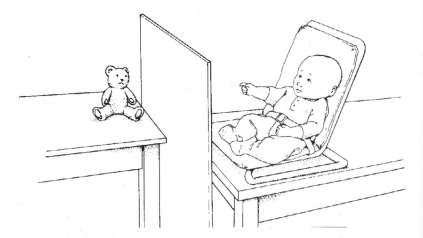

*Figure 15.1 Bower's object permanence experiment*

Bower also quotes research by **Mundy-Castle** and **Anglin** (1974). They sat some four-month-old infants in front of an apparatus that had two portholes (A and B). An object travelled behind the apparatus so that it appeared at the bottom of porthole A travelling upwards, and at the top of porthole B travelling downwards (see figure 15.2). The researchers watched the infants' eyes. After a few revolutions the babies started to anticipate the movement of the object by switching their attention to the next point where it would appear. These infants had object permanence long before the eight months that Piaget predicted it would occur.

■ **Outline the first stage in Piaget's theory of cognitive development.**

■ **Comment on the role of object permanence in Piagetian theory.**

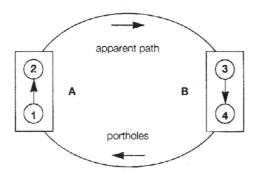

*Figure 15.2  Mundy-Castle and Anglin's experiment*

### 2 The pre-operational stage, 2–7 years

Children between two and seven were extensively studied by Piaget, yet somehow his descriptions of their cognitive skills seem rather negative. He appears to emphasize what children can't do rather than what they can. The title 'pre-operational' tells us that children in this stage can't think in an operational – logical – way. They are improving their symbolic skills, and language is a particularly useful asset to developing cognition. The child asks questions and makes what sense it can of the answers. It might imitate solutions, and apply experiences from one situation to another. Mostly the child cannot learn from being taught, and has difficulty using someone else's knowledge to solve its problems. The child must learn for itself.

During the substage of preconceptual thought (two to four years), thinking is dominated by unrealistic ideas and the child enjoys fantasy or make-believe play. One common unrealistic idea is *animism*. Animism is the child's idea that, since it has feelings, motives and intentions, then everything else, including inanimate objects, must have them too. The child explains the sun going down in the sky in the evening 'because it is tired', and 'smacking the naughty table' for hurting the child who bumped into it is a sensible punishment.

Another characteristic of preconceptual thinking is *egocentrism*. This is the child's inability to see things from any other viewpoint than its own. Sit a four-year-old on your lap facing someone else and ask the child what the other person can see. The child will probably tell you what it can see. Asking a two-year-old not to spill his paint water because you have just cleaned the floor may not make as much sense to the child as you'd hope since an egocentric child can't take your views or wishes into account, only its own. The ability to take other views into account is called *decentring*, and

► Between two and seven years children's thinking is illogical and inconsistent, and yet they seem to learn a colossal amount, without appearing to have been taught very much.

► *Egocentrism* means being able to conceive of the world only from one's own position. Considerable maturation and experience are necessary before the child can put itself mentally into someone else's place and imagine what things look like from there. This is *decentring*.

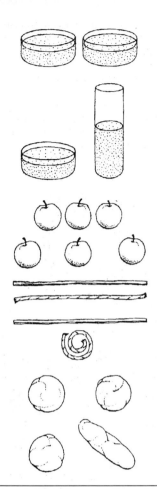

Figure 15.3 *Conservation of volume, number, length and mass*

■ **What does Piaget mean by egocentrism?**

▶ *Conservation* means the ability to maintain a mental image of what something is truly like when its appearance is transformed.

▶ Piaget was conducting this research over 50 years ago. It is likely that children now are more sophisticated and conservation skills may appear earlier.

▶ *Reversibility* is an example of quite complex operational thought. Several schemas about an object and what is happening to it need to be operationalized in order for the child to mentally manipulate them in this way.

Piaget thought it couldn't happen until some time after seven years of age.

The second substage of the pre-operational stage is that of intuitive thought. Between four and seven years children's thinking is still egocentric and animistic, but becomes more concerned with the most obvious feature of any object – what it looks like. The best known examples of intuitive thought are demonstrated in *conservation* tasks (see figure 15.3). Piaget found that children of this age rarely understand that an object can be transformed in its appearance without necessarily changing in any other way. Show a five- or six-year-old two identical balls of plasticine and ask it to agree that they contain the same amount of plasticine. Roll one into a sausage shape and ask the child if they still contain the same amount of plasticine. The intuitive, pre-operational child will often say that the sausage shape has more. This is because it looks bigger. Or try showing the child two identically spaced rows of five buttons. The child will agree that both rows have the same number of buttons. Spread out the buttons in one row, and the child will probably say that there are more buttons in that row (so long as it can't count!).

Piaget offered two reasons why children under about seven years cannot conserve. One is that they can only attend to one process occurring, e.g. the plasticine changing shape as they have seen it. They can't perform the mental operation required to answer the question, 'What would happen if we reversed the process we have just performed?' Quite complex schemas are involved in doing this. The ability to do this is called *reversibility*. The other reason why children under about seven cannot conserve is *centration*. This is the tendency to concentrate on only one aspect of a situation at a time, while ignoring all others which are necessary for the child to solve the problem. The child concentrates on either the shape of the plasticine or the amount of the plasticine, but not both.

One of Piaget's most famous conservation tasks involves two identical tall thin jugs containing the same amount of liquid. The contents of one of the jugs is emptied into a shorter, wider jug, and the child is asked which jug has the most liquid. The pre-operational child will say the tall thin jug contains more. It cannot imagine what the liquid level in the first jug would be if the liquid was poured back into it. Piaget claimed that mental reversibility will not appear until the child is around eight years old.

---

**Summary – Main features of the pre- operational stage**

| | |
|---|---|
| 1 Preconceptual thought | *Animism:* everything has consciousness, therefore has feelings, motives, etc. |
| | *Egocentrism:* one's own needs dominate one's thinking |

| | |
|---|---|
| 2 Intuitive thought | Inability to conserve an object's appearance dominates one's thinking about what it 'is like' |
| | *Centration:* one feature of an object or situation dominates one's thinking about it |

▶ *Centration,* as in concentration, is the fixing on only one aspect of a situation at a time, and ignoring others that could have an important bearing on a solution.

■ **What features of the conservation of liquid experiment does the child need to understand in order to conserve liquid?**

We said earlier that Piaget thought that children continue to think egocentrically right through the pre-operational stage. He conducted a rather complicated experiment to demonstrate this. He had constructed three model mountains from papier mâché, each in a different shape and each with something different on the top (see figure 15.4). A doll was moved to different positions around the mountains and the child was asked to choose one of ten photographs that corresponded to what the doll would be able to see from its position. Pre-operational children couldn't do this, often choosing the picture corresponding to their own viewpoint. This experiment has been criticized for being unnecessarily elaborate. Perhaps children below seven didn't understand what they were supposed to do. Perhaps if Piaget made the task more interesting, or better still, more fun, the children may well have been able to show that they could think non-egocentrically.

**Martin Hughes** (in Donaldson 1975) constructed an experiment which comprised two intersecting model walls and some dolls that could be moved, by the experimenter or a child, into various places behind or in front of the four walls. There was a policeman doll and a boy doll, and the game was to place the boy in various positions and ask the child if he could be seen by the policeman (see figure 15.5). This requires the child to imagine what the policeman can see from its position. The child, too, placed the boy so that he was hiding. If a child can do either of these things it must be able to decentre. Hughes found that children as young as three and four years had little difficulty in playing this game and responding correctly. Even when more walls were introduced, and more dolls, over 90 per cent of the children could still decentre.

**John Flavell** (1979) showed three-year-olds some cards with a drawing of a cat on one side and a dog on the other. Holding the card vertically between the experimenter and the child so that the child could see the dog, he asked them what he could see. These three-year-olds had no difficulty in saying that he could see the cat. In another experiment children between two and a half and five were seated on the opposite side of a table to a researcher. On the table was a Snoopy doll. The children were asked to close their eyes, and then answered questions like 'Can I see you?', 'Can I see your head?', 'Can I see your arm?', and 'Can I see Snoopy?' The youngest children weren't sure whether the researchers could see them, although most said they could see their arm or head. Yet all said they could see Snoopy. Clearly these children aren't egocentric.

If Piaget was rather pessimistic in the age at which he thought

*Figure 15.4 Piaget's mountains*

*Figure 15.5 Hughes' doll experiment*

■ Why do you think children under the age of seven in the 'three mountains' experiment appeared to Piaget to be egocentric?

■ What does Piaget mean by decentring?

*Figure 15.6  Naughty Teddy*

► Hughes' experiment was probably more interesting for a young child than Piaget's model mountains and a selection of photographs. It is more like a 'real game' in which the child can become involved.

► The experiments by Hughes and Flavell do not imply that two- to four-year-olds can decentre to other viewpoints over more complex issues. The tasks being tested were rather simple. Things requiring abstract thought would be impossible for such young children.

► Conservation of number probably occurs at a younger age than Piaget predicted since his experiments may not have involved the child's interest and co-operation.

children can decentre, he may also have been about the age for conservation. McGarrigle and Donaldson (1978) devised a game to test conservation of number in which two identical rows of sweets were placed in front of the child, and a glove puppet called 'Naughty Teddy' then spread the sweets in one of the rows while not moving the others (see figure 15.6). Of the 80 four- and five-year-olds tested, 50 said that the number of sweets remained the same, and so could conserve number. However, when the adult researchers moved the sweets, only 13 out of 80 said there were the same number. It is possible that the children responded more accurately with 'Naughty Teddy' because the experiment was more like an enjoyable game. But it is also possible that some of the children were actually being distracted by the puppet and weren't really concentrating on the conservation task at all, so some may have given the correct answers without being able to conserve.

Numerous experiments have shown that children of three or four can conserve when they have been taught about how number, mass, length, weight, volume, speed, etc. do not change just because appearances do. If they can practise the knowledge they have been taught, they can solve conservation problems. It appears that conservation isn't dependent on the degree of cognitive maturation, which Piaget predicted doesn't occur until later childhood. Whatever maturation is necessary has occurred by four or five years. What seems to be needed is training and practice, and these are socially acquired. **Dorothy Field** (1979) trained some four-year-olds in one conservation task and later found that they could apply their new skill to other conservation tasks in which they weren't trained.

Having challenged the ages at which certain skills occur, **Olivera Petrovich** (in ongoing research at Oxford University) and others have questioned whether conservation and decentring are cognitive events anyway. She claims that four- and five-year-olds can speculate answers to questions such as 'If you were a bird flying above us what could you see?', 'Where does water come from?', 'Where did the first rabbit come from?', 'What is the sky?', 'Who made the clouds?', 'Where do grapes come from?' In most cases children give thought-out and reasoned answers, and not the stereotyped responses Piaget would predict that pre-operational children would give. She claims that children do think competently, they show genuine interest and curiosity, and that their styles of thinking aren't much different from those of adults.

> ### Summary – Egocentrism and conservation
>
> Piaget's observations and experiments led him to conclude that children below the age of seven years weren't maturationally ready to decentre or conserve. Their cognitive development relies on both a state of maturation and a state of experience. When both are present, decentring and conservation occur. More recent research has suggested that Piaget is too pessimistic. Some of his experiments may have been inappropriate for testing children below seven years. When the test is made more relevant or when training and practice are given, children of only three or four years show that they can conserve.

*3  The concrete operations stage, 7–11 years*

By this age many children will be in school. They will be competing and co-operating in play, and must be able to decentre in order to understand the benefits of having mutually agreed sets of rules, or of negotiating other rules. They are rapidly acquiring and practising cognitive skills, and performing mental operations. Objects and events that they have experienced, or at least imagined, will be acted upon through play and manipulation. This is what Piaget means by 'concrete' operations. For example, arithmetic has formal rules which must be learned in a logically progressive way. One of the first things to be learned is 'adding up'. A child who is about to learn to add will want to know what we are adding up. Children can see the point of adding three apples to two apples to see how many apples there are now. It makes sense. They have schemas for apples. It doesn't make sense just to add up. This need for concrete, real objects to manipulate is what Piaget means by concrete operations.

During the concrete operations stage children's conservation skills expand. Most words ending in 'er' will be 'relative' words, i.e. comparing one state with another. Older–younger, faster–slower, longer–shorter, thicker–thinner are all relative words, and will all need to be conserved. Some things are easier to understand and conserve than others, and these will be learned first. Conservation of number, for example, only requires the child to consider one thing when making the judgement about whether there are 'more' or 'less' of something. Piaget claimed that six- and seven-year-olds could conserve number. Mass requires the child to consider both size and shape when making conservation. This will take longer. Weight requires size and mass to be considered, while volume requires an understanding of shape, size and mass. Children will need to be ten or more before they achieve this, according to Piaget.

▶ A formal operational thinker could answer the following question: 'If you go to town to buy a T-shirt during lunchtime, will you be able to get back to college before the first afternoon lesson, and if not, what will the teacher say to you?'

▶ Formal operational thinking is flexible, rational and systematic. It is like mental hypothesis testing involving rapid solutions to 'what would happen if?', and 'if this happens, then what will happen?' type questions.

▶ Physical and mental maturity coincide after puberty. However, the formal operational type of thinking which Piaget described as rational and flexible is not shared by everyone.

■ Outline the main differences in the thinking of children above and below the age of seven, according to Piaget.

*4 Formal operations stage, 11 years on*

During the previous stage children were able to learn to mentally manipulate objects or events so long as they had some direct experience of them. Formal operational thinking does not require this direct experience. Adding up and taking away can now be performed in the person's head, without the aid of apples. The youngster can also now answer hypothetical questions, and concepts such as justice, freedom and conscience can be considered.

Piaget's description of formal operational thinking is that it is the only way in which cognitively mature people can think and it takes several years to achieve. However, not everyone fully achieves it and it's quite possible to think formally for some propositions, but not others. Most people think irrationally about some things sometimes, particularly if they are especially sensitive to them, or are tired, 'in a mood' etc. Nor does everyone agree that formal logic, which Piaget thought would be more or less achieved (in some areas anyway) by 15 or 20 years, is the last stage of development. It could be that there are stages above that which only certain, gifted people (like Piaget himself) would reach. Not all people use what by Western scientists is understood by formal logic anyway. Some societies have their own forms of logic, and reason in ways that are logical but follow a logic different from that of Western scientists.

### Summary – Operational thought

Piaget believed that children acquire operational thought some time after the age of seven. Piaget's methods have been criticized as inadequate, and other researchers have found the kind of thinking Piaget described developing rather earlier. Not everyone acquires fully operational thought in the Western sense of the logical rules of Western science or philosophy.

There's more to human mental processing than solving conservation tasks and the ability to decentre. There are wide individual differences between children in their development of operational thought, and adults sometimes think operationally and sometimes do not. Therefore, to talk about 'operational thought' as if it were a single entity is misleading.

### Evaluation of Piaget's theory

| Theory | Comment |
| --- | --- |
| For the first ten years children are incapable of logical operaitonal thought. | Modern research shows that Piaget underestimated the cognitive abilities of younger children. |
| Operational thought develops from puberty. | Many adolescents and adults do not think formally at all. |
| Cognitive skills change at 2, 7 and 11. | The changes probably occur before these ages. |
| Piaget gave children particular tasks and asked them specific questions which he assumed allowed them to demonstrate cognitive skills. | The tasks may have been too difficult, or lacking interest or relevance to the child, thus producing an underestimation of their abilities. |
| Piaget claimed that cognition develops | Piaget is unclear about why one stage ends |

through four distinct stages.
Piaget describes what the average or typical child of a given age can do.
Piaget emphasized the importance of the child's relationship with the environment for cognitive development.
Piaget's methodology has been criticized, especially that he rarely identified how many children he had studied, nor did he offer much evidence of statistical analysis.

and another begins.
There are wide variations in individual children's abilities.
The child's relationship with other people may be very important too.

A good theory should be derived from research conducted using scientifically acceptable procedures. Much of Piaget's research may have been more intuitive.

## A final comment on Piaget

In such a brief description of Piaget's theory it would be understandable for readers to gather the impression that Piaget's contribution is of little value. Inevitably, those claims that have been challenged have needed to be discussed. However, it would be difficult to overestimate the enormous contribution Piaget's theories and research have made to our understanding of children and how they think. Without his inspiration much other research may not have been conducted. He truly deserves to be called the founding father of cognitive developmental psychology.

## Jerome Bruner's view

**Jerome Bruner** (1966) shares Piaget's view that the development of cognition is the result of continuous, dynamic interactions between maturational and environmental forces, i.e. between nature and nurture. Children are naturally curious, so there must be some genetic force driving us to find out about our world. This force seems to be present from birth. As the higher brain centres develop throughout childhood so the form the child's enquiries take, and what it makes of its findings, will change. Bruner suggests that the ways in which children are able to organize their experiences change as they mature. He describes these as modes of thinking or modes of representation.

Where Piaget was concerned mostly with the stages of cognitive development, Bruner is more concerned with the form that knowledge takes. Piaget thought that we pass through the stages of cognitive development in an invariant sequence, each stage replacing the previous one. Bruner believes that each mode of thought is added to the previous one(s). Essentially, he sees knowledge gained throughout childhood being represented mentally in one or more of three possible forms or 'modes' of representation.

### Enactive representation

According to Bruner, for the first couple of years babies' knowledge of the world is derived through their own actions and movements. The child's ideas about an object or event are based on what it can do with it. This knowledge is a series of *enactive representations*.

► Bruner was greatly impressed by Piaget's ideas and his theory shouldn't be seen as radically different from Piaget's. It differs in emphasis rather than being a rejection of Piaget.

► *Enactive representations* are ideas the baby has, based on its experience of what objects such as people can do with the baby. As we grow older enactive representations are our fairly simple ideas about things which do not need to be thought about in other ways. Knowledge about how to ride a bicycle is in terms of an enactive representation.

Enactive means 'acting upon'. Given a particular stimulus, such as the sight of a caregiver, the baby responds with reaching and smiling. These responses are the result of its enactive representation of that caregiver. The baby knows what caregivers can do. Enactive representation is a fairly primitive type of knowledge. The young child cannot distinguish between a perception of an object or an event, and its own reaction to it.

By adolescence many things concerning action and movement will have been learned enactively. Swimming, running and hiding are things that we have ideas about that do not need to involve words or images. They are simply things that we can do. For adults some aspects of driving a car are fairly automatic. Fluently playing musical instruments or being skilled at a sport have aspects of enactive representation. We don't think about what we are doing, we just do it.

### Iconic representation

► *Iconic representations* are ideas derived from combinations of sensory information.

*Iconic representations* are forms of knowledge derived from our senses. They result from visual, auditory, smell, touch or taste images. (They are exclusively perceptual.) Several experiences will build up to form an iconic representation. For example, seeing a cup of coffee, smelling it and tasting it result in an iconic representation which we don't generally think about in words.

Iconic representations are rather more complicated than enactive forms of knowledge. The 18-month-old child starts to be able to put together ideas about its own behaviour, and what it can do with various toys and people it has experienced previously. The seven-year-old child will have iconic knowledge of plasticine and shapes, mass and size, but has difficulties in making connections between them, so cannot solve the conservation problem.

### Symbolic representation

From around the age of seven children add the third, *symbolic* mode of representation. Bruner was particularly interested in the addition of the symbolic mode, which marks the move to a more logical, systematic type of thinking that comes about through the child's ability to use language and to think in linguistic symbols. Thinking in words is of enormous benefit to the pursuit of logic and the ability to solve problems (which is, after all, what intelligence is all about). To demonstrate this Bruner and Kenny (1966) devised an experimental apparatus comprising a board divided into nine equal squares, plus nine tumblers which would stand on the squares.

Children from five to seven, i.e. both younger ones who used only enactive and iconic imagery, and older ones who would have some symbolic imagery too, were shown the board with the tumblers arranged on it in a certain way. The tumblers were then scrambled and the children were asked to put them back where they had been before. This was the *reproduction* test (see figure 15.7).

Bruner and Kenny then moved all of the tumblers from the board, and put the tumbler that had been in the bottom right-hand corner in the bottom left-hand corner. The children had to rebuild the pattern in a mirror image, using the same principles as before. This was the transpositional test. Children with a symbolic mode of representing the original board should be able to solve this. Those relying on iconic imagery should not. The results are set out in table 15.1, which shows the percentage of successes.

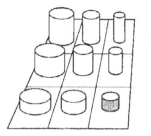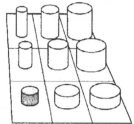

Table 15.1 **Bruner and Kenny's results**

| Age of child | Type of test | |
| --- | --- | --- |
| | Reproduction (%) | Transposition (%) |
| 5 years | 60 | 0 |
| 6 years | 72 | 27 |
| 7 years | 80 | 79 |

These results suggest that the younger children have an inflexible visual representation (icon or image) of the way the matrix looks, and can't do anything to change it since they lack the ability to transform symbolically. Older children who have symbolic thought can imagine, and apply the rules they have perceived.

> ## Summary – A comparison of Piaget's and Bruner's approaches
>
> *Piaget*
> Piaget identifies a series of stages of cognitive development, which occur in a distinct order. When each stage has been completed the child moves on to the next stage.
>
> *Bruner*
> Bruner identifies a series of three 'modes of representation', each with its characteristic style of thought. When the first mode is mastered the next is added to it.

## THE INFLUENCE OF THE FAMILY, PEERS AND OTHERS ON COGNITIVE DEVELOPMENT

Since psychologists started taking an interest in the major influences in children's development the role of the mother was dominant (Freud, Bowlby, Spitz etc.). By the 1960s fathers and siblings were being studied, too. As psychology became more ecologically aware, and researchers came out of the laboratory and into the everyday world of the child, it became clear that other non-family members

■ **Name and briefly describe the three modes of representation in Bruner's theory of cognitive growth.**

*Figure 15.7 Bruner and Kenny's task*

■ **Summarize the main difference between Piaget's and Bruner's view of developing cognition.**

▶ Siblings are brothers and sisters.

also influence children's understanding. Although it is possible to identify some specific influences (such as a mother's sensitivity to her baby's crying) on aspects of development (such as closeness of bonding) in the infant, as the child grows more and more influences act upon it. It is not possible to identify exactly which influence is causing exactly which aspect of cognitive development. If a girl comes from a well-supported home environment, formed good attachments, went to a well-run playgroup, and is now enjoying and succeeding in school, which factor is responsible for her level of cognitive awareness? Probably all of them, and more. Attempts to isolate individual variables and determine their effect on individual features of development calls for the most careful experimental control and is probably not worth doing except in exceptional cases. At worst, it can lead to 'the folly of *mono-causality*'.

▶ *Mono-causality* is the idea that differences in one variable inevitably cause changes to occur in another.

Piaget insists that intelligence, or *adaptation* as he prefers, is a process which unfolds as the child matures and is influenced by the variety of experiences the child has. In the past psychologists have used intelligence tests to 'measure' intelligence as though it were a series of quantifiable skills. This view is seriously questioned today. Each person who sat a test (and there are dozens of such tests) answers questions that are scored and expressed as their Intelligence Quotient (IQ). When we talk here about environmental influences upon cognitive development we will often be referring to studies that have used IQ scores as measures of cognitive capacity. This is problematic since we do not know what intelligence is, either cognitively or biologically (see the discussion of Donald Hebb and others in this area in Chapter 13). Whatever skills our tests do measure are therefore at best only aspects of intelligence.

## The home and family

We saw in Chapter 14 how children deprived of social contact such as those reared in orphanages or other forms of isolation become withdrawn and depressed. Curtiss (1977) reports the tragic case of Genie, who was isolated by her psychotic father from just about all sensory and social stimulation. She was barely recognizable as a human being when rescued. Such tragic cases teach us that people need people if they are to develop healthy personalities. The group usually involved in supplying society's new members is the family.

▶ NB Not everyone agrees that babies are so 'capable' of communicating their needs. Kenneth Kaye believes that this is simply what rather optimistic observers would like to think.

Babies begin their cognitive development as they learn to recognize and interact with their caregivers. Daniel Stern (1977) has shown that babies can signal their needs to their caregivers and help to regulate the type and amount of contact that they received. Trevarthen and Richards (1978) suggest that infants and caregivers move their bodies in interactional synchrony with each other's 'conversation'. Michael Lamb (1977) noted how babies use different caregivers for different activities. Babies appeared to prefer their mother's company if they were distressed, but seemed to prefer their father's for rather more adventurous activities.

There are three variables involved in the chances of the child fulfilling its cognitive potential. The first is the attitudes and responses of the other family members towards the child, and we will discuss this first. Second, the size of the family is important; and finally, the position of the child in the birth order, which will be discussed afterwards.

### The influence of other family members

Some parents have taken this message to a fairly extreme extent. They have been entirely child-centred, and spent a great deal of time, patience and love on their children. They have talked to the children almost as though they were adults, and tried to teach them as much as they could. Mostly they have shown their children that they have very high expectations of their abilities. This process has been called *hothousing* (a 'hothouse' is the American term for 'greenhouse'). In those cases that have been reported (only the most sensational ones?) the results have been breathtaking, with ten-year-olds taking university courses and 16-year-olds who have qualified as doctors.

The home environment obviously plays an influential role in all aspects of children's development since it gets the child first. American psychologists have been keen to find ways of measuring aspects of human functioning and influences upon it. **Caldwell** and **Bradley** (1978) invented HOME (Home Observation for Measurement of the Environment), comprising 45 'yes'/'no' questions which caregivers (usually mothers) were asked, followed by observations of adult–child interaction. HOME is supposed to measure how cognitively enriching or impoverishing a child's home environment is, and the authors claim it is excellent at predicting children's performance on IQ tests later. The factors that HOME identifies as being most important for boys are mothers who are deeply involved with them, who provide an organized environment with plenty of age-appropriate toys and activities. New experiences are introduced gradually as the child becomes familiar with the requirements of the previous one. Additionally, girls benefit from non-punitive caregivers who are sensitive to their needs (see Mary Ainsworth on 'the sensitive mother', page 314).

The clarity of language used around the child is also important. The more accurately something is described and discussed, the quicker the child will develop appropriate schemas for it. Patrick Dickson (1979) found that mothers who used precise and clear language had children who scored highest on IQ tests and appeared to be most cognitively aware.

Fathers are often more playful with their babies, where mothers are often more nurturant. Fathers offer 'rough and tumble'-type activities. They can also be gentle with their infants, and the infants can form strong emotional ties with them. These three things – tenderness, emotional warmth and more physical activities – might help the baby use its father as a 'safe base' from which to explore the world. In Schaffer and Emerson's Glasgow study (1964), about

▶ Caldwell and Bradley have invented a device to measure the level of cognitive stimulation in a home and compare the score it generates with a score from a test that claims to measure intelligence. Is this a case of the unquantifiable predicting the undefinable? Do we need two entirely speculative measures to tell us that good parenting styles are likely to produce brighter children?

half of the sample of 60 made attachments to their fathers or other family members within two months of making their first attachment. Ten years later Barry Lester and his colleagues (1974) found that the babies that they studied had all made strong attachments with their mothers by the time they were nine months old, but had also attached to their fathers by 12 months.

Siblings are probably very important to young children. They often spend more time together than the child does with its parents (Dunn 1983). Children with brothers and sisters are more likely to have to learn to compete and to share than single children. Schaffer and Emerson also found that younger children are quite likely to form 'attachments' with their older siblings in much the same way as they do with their parents. Siblings imitate each other, compete with each other, and protect each other. They learn about love and rivalry, trust and aggression, and many other emotions from these early relationships with other family members.

Dunn and Kendrick (1982) have shown how younger children are often attached to their older brothers and sisters, and how older children look after their younger ones. Children as young as three have been observed changing the ways they speak when talking to their younger siblings. They talk in simpler sentences, repeat themselves and are generally warm and encouraging. All of which would encourage the younger child to respond socially, encouraging cognitive development to proceed sooner than it may have done otherwise.

What, then, do families need to provide in order to stimulate their children's cognitive development? As David Shaffer (1985) puts it, an 'intellectually stimulating home environment is one in which parents are warm, responsive, and eager to be involved with their children. They describe new objects, concepts, and experiences clearly and accurately, and they provide the child with a variety of play materials that are appropriate for her age and developmental level.' The child needs to be encouraged to contribute, too. Shaffer goes on: 'They [parents] encourage the child to ask questions, to solve problems and to think about what she is learning.' They have high expectations of the children, both at home and in school. They make sure their children feel secure and loved.

### Family size and birth order

In general, families with fewer children are better able to provide the ones they do have with the types of stimulation described by Shaffer above. In a large-scale study of the military records of all the males born in Holland between 1944 and 1947 (all 386,114 of them), Belmont and Marolla (1973) found that those from the smallest families tended to have the highest IQs. When the order of birth was analysed they also found that first-born children tended to have slightly higher IQs on average than second-borns, who achieved slightly higher scores than third-born children, and so on. Zajonc and Markus (1974) found similar results in American children. Most researchers would agree that this average difference is probably

■ What evidence is there that babies attach to more than one person?

■ List the items that Shaffer claims would stimulate a child's cognitive development. Provide an example for each.

▶ The differences between average IQ scores of members of different size families or first- or second-borns etc. are really quite small. IQ tests themselves aren't very accurate anyway (especially since no one knows exactly what they're measuring).

explained by caregivers being able to spend more time stimulating fewer children. The more children there are, the less individual attention each can have. First-borns receive all the attention, second-borns have to share their attention with first-borns, and so on.

**Robert Zajonc** (1976) suggests that the level of cognitive competence being less in younger children can be explained in ways that are quite consistent with Piaget's theory. First-born children are attended by adults who are obviously intellectually superior to them, hopefully in the ways Shaffer described above. The next child, however, has only some of its time being stimulated by adults, while some of its time is spent with its older sibling receiving the stimulation. Third-borns have less time being stimulated, since they have to share with their siblings. So the average amount of superior intellectual stimulation each receives declines. As Zajonc says, 'with each successive child the family's intellectual environment depreciates'. However, children in families with three or more adults (parents living with grandparents) do not score higher than children in two-adult homes, contrary to what Zajonc's theory predicts. Also, children who grow up in single-parent households do not have lower IQs than children in similar two-parent homes.

## Peers and play

Play is a normal part of the development of many animal species. It occupies most of the child's time, much of the adolescent's, and some of the adult's. Play consists of three elements: curiosity, exploration and manipulation of objects. There may be a genetically inherited basis for play, but psychologists have concentrated on how play contributes to social relationships and cognitive development rather than on how or where it originates.

During childhood, play is for fun, for practice, for discovery, for developing our knowledge about properties of various things, for discovering what effect we can have on the environment, for playing out our feelings, for expressing ideas and experimenting with them, for developing muscles and co-ordination, for learning about how other people behave, and much more. Play prevents boredom and promotes happiness, and can also help relieve stress. As well as being fun, play can be a very serious business. Children can concentrate for quite a long time on their Lego and Meccano constructions, or completing their jigsaws. In a word, play is for stimulation.

There are different kinds of play activities which children enjoy. Each offers different kinds of stimulation, and the child will switch from one to another during the day. These different kinds of play emphasize different skills. There is *discovery play*, where the child finds out what things are like, and what they can be used for. In *physical play* the child is active and develops muscles and co-ordination. In *creative play* the child expresses its own ideas, tests things

■ **How have psychologists explained the effects of birth order on cognitive development?**

► Peers are 'equals' who see each other frequently, have similar ideas about what sort of behaviour is right for them, and who often have similar aims or goals to achieve.

► Play has many functions, such as soothing emotions, gaining practical experience, promoting social relationships, developing physical skills and advancing intellectual development.

■ **What is play? What is it for?**

► Although these types of play sound as though they involve quite separate activities, that is not necessarily true at all. It is quite likely that children extract their own reasoning from whatever they are doing and the same activity could be satisfying different needs in different children.

▶ Pro-social behaviour includes being co-operative and helpful, sharing and interacting in unselfish ways.

▶ In *solitary play* children are busy practising and mastering basic physical and social skills.

▶ *Parallel play* recognizes the existence of others, but there is no peer-group influence.

▶ *Associative play* is the first stage in the development of play where peers begin to shape the child's thinking about how the game can be extended.

▶ In *co-operative play* children are able to take each other's needs and abilities into account, and can tailor their games to the resources and facilities available.

out, and sees what can be achieved with things. During *social play* the child is learning about itself and other people.

Piaget thought children would be egocentric and thus unable to cope with the needs and wishes of other children. Whilst this may be true in very young children any visitor to a busy, well-equipped pre-school nursery or a well-supported large family will see plenty of examples of children behaving in pro-social ways. Given the choice of a toddler or an adult to interact with, most toddlers prefer the adult. They will play with other children, though, and how this comes about has been described in several stages.

### 1 Solitary play

During the sensory motor stage of cognitive development Piaget sees the role of play as practice leading to mastery of basic motor, cognitive and social skills. For the first few months of life a child's play is largely solitary. Infants are unable to take very much in, so anything requiring them to concentrate or co-operate will be impossible. At best they can join in interactional synchrony and exchange games. During the second year children's motor skills enable them to start making choices about the things they reach for or put down. Manipulative skills lead to more exploration and experimentation with objects. Play may involve adults to some extent, but the child is still mostly engaged in solitary pastimes and there is almost no peer influence.

### 2 Parallel play

By two to three years of age children start to take some notice of peers, and will play alongside other children. Two girls might be playing with toy cars in the sandpit, building roads and bridges in the sand for their cars. But they do not play together. Each has her own roads and cars. One child might try to take over another's game, or sneak onto the other's roads, or take the other's car, but mostly they merely tolerate each other's presence, and ignore each other. This is *parallel play*, and it is an extension of solitary play.

### 3 Associative play

Within a few months children begin to share a toy, or play in each other's area, or agree to some limited co-operation. The sandpit roads may be joined so that one child's car can drive on the other child's roads. The cars might be allowed to crash, or they may be swapped. This is *associative play*. The children are still playing their own game, and wouldn't welcome too much interference from other children, but at least peers are having some influence or impact. However, most humans are sociable creatures, so taking note of other children's existence leads to *co-operative play*.

### 4 Co-operative play

Most children reach this stage some time between three and five years of age, largely depending on the opportunities they have had for interacting with peers. Now children are able to join in with each other's games, or agree to play 'your' game now so long as we play 'my' game later. Simple co-operative play involves two or three children working together, perhaps to build a tower from building blocks. Complex co-operative play features several children taking part in more adventurous games, including imaginative games involving role play. The most important factor in co-operative play is that peers now interact, sometimes sharing, sometimes competing, forming alliances and establishing their place in their groups. Some children become popular and are sought out to join in play activities. Others are less popular, maybe less competent or confident, and they are less likely to be chosen. This in turn influences the child's level of self-confidence, which might then affect achievement in other areas such as school.

### Summary – Stages of play

| Age (years) | Stage | Features |
| --- | --- | --- |
| 0–2 | Solitary play | Simple, repetitive activities helping mastery of skills |
| 2–3 | Parallel play | Playing the same game alongside each other, but not playing together |
| 3 | Associative play | Acceptance of other child, occasional sharing of toys |
| 3–4 | Co-operative play | Increasing acceptance of the benefits of sharing, e.g. taking different roles to make role-play games work |

■ Outline the major stages in the development of play and show how they may reflect Piaget's observations.

### Sex differences in peer play

In most Western societies boys and girls tend not to play together. From around three years of age children know whether they are a boy or a girl, and this will influence some of the ways they will play. Boys tend to play with noisier, more active toys, like balls, drums, bikes and scooters. They are more independent, do not often seek advice or assistance, and frequently play at some distance from an adult. Girls tend to play with the quieter, more gentle toys, often in 'pretend games'. They will often seek to involve an adult in their game, or obtain assistance from one, so will tend to play near to an adult.

From around three years children seek out the company of others of the same sex as themselves. By school age sex differences in play will be firmly established, and any boy who appears to want to play with a girl's toy, or become involved in a girl's game, will quickly be discouraged by other boys. **Judith Blakemore** (1979) found that two-year-old males preferred traditionally boys' toys (trucks, planes etc.). The same-age girls did not show any such preference, nor did they prefer 'girls' toys' when they were three, unless reminded that they were more 'appropriate' by an adult. By three years boys expressed dislike for 'dolls' and 'girls' toys' generally. Many studies have shown that when boys play with their toys in a 'sex-appropriate' way their games were inventive and involving. Being involved seems to increase the enjoyment, and make the children want to play the game again. If a child started to play with

► Most children are treated differently by parents, and different expectations are made of them, according to their sex. They learn that boys and girls are different and so acquire their gender roles.

► There are sex differences in the toys children choose, the ways they play with them, and the extent to which they involve adults.

► Sex differences in play are quite marked by about five years old, although there are always exceptions. A younger brother with several sisters may seek out 'girls' toys' by choice.

the opposite sex's toys, or in an 'opposite-sex way', it was soon 'told off' by its same-sex peers.

■ What differences have psychologists observed between males and females in play?

**Summary – Sex differences in play**

There are genetic differences between boys and girls. For example on average, boys grow bigger and heavier, and girls develop language skills earlier. Girls may be better able to play games requiring verbal communication earlier than boys. These genetic differences probably do not account for all the differences in the ways the two sexes play. We expect different kinds of play activities from our sons and daughters. We dress them differently, speak to them differently, handle them differently, offer them different things to play with, offer them different kinds of discipline. Traditionally boys have been encouraged to be more robust than girls. By about four years old each sex knows what kind of play is expected of it, and will ridicule or isolate anyone playing in a 'cross-sex way'. These differences continue until beyond puberty.

### Peers and school

Pre-school children can still act in egocentric ways, using their friends for what they can get out of them. If not before, then soon after children start school they learn that they must co-operate, and peer relationships become more equal. They learn that they can benefit from giving and helping, sharing and co-operating.

▶ Egocentric children can't take other children's needs into account. They 'use' their 'friends' for their own benefit.

Peers can have two effects on individual children. First, they may be seen as rivals and barriers to the child's own success. Being egocentric a child might believe that only one or two children can 'come top', or gain all the teacher's attention and praise. The more children there are, the less likely any one child is to succeed. This could be a negative influence, causing jealousy and hostility. The child who does best might be disliked or even mistreated. Calling a bright child 'teacher's pet' or abusing the child in other ways may make it less keen to do well in future.

On the other hand, according to Albert Bandura (see Chapter 1), children can learn much by modelling themselves on others. A successful peer may also become a powerful model. Seeing someone else do well and gain some benefit might encourage the others to do well, too. Although peers can be important models, it is important not to overemphasize their role. Children don't always do what their friends are doing!

Children form themselves into 'gangs' or close-knit groups. Being a member of one group or another is especially important to many children. Each group develops its own norms of behaviour, of dress and so on, and its own values of attitude to work, to authority etc. Group members will go to great lengths to ensure that they stay in the group and avoid the risk of being rejected. So a group that is 'pro-school' will encourage its members to work hard and achieve success. An 'anti-school' group will resist authority and penalize any member that might appear to do well.

### Summary – Peer groups

Peer groups are groups who interact frequently, who have similar norms and values, and who have similar aims and ambitions. In the junior and secondary school they can be powerful influences, either pro- or anti-school.

■ Summarize the influences that peer groups can have on children's experiences at school.

## COGNITIVE FACTORS IN EDUCATIONAL PERFORMANCE

Most children in Britain have started school by their fifth birthday and will have to attend regularly for 11 years. During this time they must achieve two goals. First, they must learn to control their behaviour so that it contributes to rather than disrupts the smooth running of school life. So they must know who is in authority, and the importance of recognizing authority and obeying school rules. This is for the maintenance of social order. Second, they must apply themselves to, and try to succeed in, school tasks such as learning to read, write and do arithmetic, learning material for all the other National Curriculum and school-directed subjects, performing in school plays and sports activities, and so on. These are for personal development. Cognitive and social factors are inseparable during schooling.

► As in most aspects of children's development it is impossible to single out particular influences and their effects.

There is evidence that children have a good idea about who is 'in charge' very early in their school life. **Sara Meadows** (1977) interviewed four year-old nursery school children who had already acquired the *script* for what to do in school. They placed 'emphasis on clearing up, and teachers were predominantly organizers and controllers'. As children progress through school the control functions should be well understood and emphasis is on the acquisition of skills such as reading.

► A *script* is a set of expectations about what should happen in what order in any given social event. It implies who does what, when, where and how.

## Piaget on education

Piaget didn't specifically apply his ideas about cognitive development to education, although others have. He drew attention to the interaction between maturation and experience, and this has clear implications for schooling until puberty. If primary school children think and reason pre-operationally and junior school children think in concrete operational ways, then it makes sense that teachers should use this knowledge in helping them construct lessons appropriately. Children learn by manipulating real objects and discovering such properties as their size, shape, weight, mass, colour and functions.

### Evaluation of Piaget's contribution to education

| Piaget's theory | Educational practice |
|---|---|
| Piaget's theory identifies four stages of cognitive development linked to four ages. Piaget concentrated on the influence of environmental and biological forces on how children acquire knowledge. | Children are in school during the second stage onwards. Concentrating on acquiring knowledge ignores how children come to understand and use the information they've acquired. Education is about comprehension as much as acquisition and information. |
| The child doesn't appear to be able to make any active contribution to its own development, rather waiting for maturational forces to prepare it. | Education encourages children's active involvement in their own learning and practising their skills. |
| Piaget claimed that cognitive development was biologically linked to certain ages and that children couldn't acquire skills before they were maturationally prepared. | By involving children in their learning it is possible for them to acquire conservation skills, decentring, reversibility, etc. much earlier than the concrete operations stage at age seven (McGarrigle and Donaldson, Hughes). **Thomas Kuhn** (1979) found that children could acquire operational thought before seven if their present knowledge was challenged whilst giving them the resources to solve their problems. This was called 'optimal mismatch theory'. |
| Piaget regards language as being the consequence of extending schemas. As the idea is learned a word is learned to express it. | There's much more to language than expressing ideas. In school language is used to challenge ideas, and having the words may shape the thoughts. |

Bruner's approach to classroom practice is called 'learning by discovery', since he claims that the most valuable and long-lasting knowledge has to be discovered by the child itself. The process of discovery helps the cognitive system (attention and memory) organize the information effectively and inspires the child to discover more, which in turn promotes self-confidence in the child. Bruner's theory makes recommendations for educational practices, but since, like Piaget's, it is mostly speculative and not based on much scientifically acceptable research, its suggestions may not be entirely valid. For example, discovery learning claims that the most important skills that school should teach the child would be problem-solving ability. This is an important skill, but others would be equally as important.

Children are naturally curious and active. This provides the primary schoolteacher with an excellent opportunity to help them to learn. As the child progresses from stage to stage, so the kind of experiences they are offered should be altered to suit their cognitive needs. It would be inappropriate to 'teach' young children in the formal sense, since they do not think operationally until they are about seven, and even then the operations they are capable of are specific and immediate, according to Piaget.

### Discovery learning
*The role of the first schoolteacher*
1  To provide a safe, warm, secure environment in which the child can feel comfortable.

2  To recognize that each child is an individual whose state of development depends on its unique experiences.

3  To provide the kind of materials and activities that are appropriate to each child in the group.

4  To encourage the children to explore and to think about what they are doing with the materials, and how else they can be used. This assists *assimilation* (see page 330).

5  To encourage a variety of activities that both complement and contrast with one another, thus maintaining variety and novelty. This assists *accommodation* (see page 331).

6  To provide new materials when the properties of previous ones have been explored as fully as seems appropriate. This assists *adaptation* (see pages 330–1). The child must be encouraged, but not pushed, since the child may not be able to learn from things for which it is not maturationally ready.

7  To allow children to discover things for themselves by observing, or competing with others. The teacher may arrange pairs or small groups of children to work together.

8  To know exactly what stage of development each child is in, what skills a child in that stage is capable of, and what skills will be mastered in the next stage. The child must be helped towards its transition into the next stage. This is called the 'readiness approach'.

9  Always to be ready to show the child an alternative strategy for achieving whatever the child is attempting if the strategy being used has no chance of success. Success in achieving goals is important to children's confidence and desire to succeed further.

10  To encourage each child to recognize when it has a problem and to be ready to talk the problem through with each child. Piaget believed the clinical interview to be a useful aid to teachers.

*The role of the child*

The child should be enthusiastic, active, curious and adventurous. It should regard school as a fun place, because learning should be fun to young children. It should see school as a place of adventure and stimulation. The role of the parent is to encourage the child to adopt these ideas about school.

## Summary – Piaget on education

The role of the primary schoolteacher is to give children practice in the skills relevant to the stage they are in, and to prepare them for the skills of the next stage. The role of the child is to be enthusiastic. The role of the parent is to encourage enthusiasm.

■ **What are the implications of Piaget's cognitive theory for how schooling should be organized?**

► By about seven children can speak about 4,000 words and read about 600. Over the next year practice and consolidation of previous knowledge should increase this to about 9,000 and 3,000 words respectively.

► If you view a cup from the top or bottom or side you still recognize it as a cup. This is 'shape constancy'. There are several other constancies, too, including size, distance and colour. Alphabetical letters lay a trap for children because 'a's and 'b's show shape constancy but change their meanings!

► *Dyslexia* is a general term to describe failure to acquire reading skills at the level that most similar people are at which can't be explained by cultural reasons, or mental impairment, or emotional withdrawal etc.

## Cognitive factors and reading

If Piaget is right, by the age of seven children are beginning to decentre (see pages 333–4). They can understand that language can be written as well as spoken. They should also have shape constancy, so realize that an object stays the same regardless of the angle from which it is viewed. However, there are exceptions since 'd' and 'b' or 'p' and 'q' are not the same. They will learn when to use upper- and lower-case letters and how sentences must be constructed to communicate meaning. In reading new material they have to make reasoned guesses about pronunciation. These tasks would be impossible for an egocentric child.

Concrete operational children need hands-on experience of written language materials. Attractive books with simple words accompanying colourful drawings or pop-up objects are most likely to hold a child's attention and encourage it to want to read. Being read stories by adults in primary school may prepare the child for reading. Children like stories involving adventures featuring children, animals, wicked adults, fantasy characters, thrilling action and 'shoot 'em up' storylines.

### Problems with reading

Where children aren't encouraged to read, or where there aren't suitable reading materials available, they may have problems. Piaget sees cognitive development as a reflection of our biological inheritance. Problems with reading, therefore, may be caused by a biological 'breakdown'. This is loosely called *'dyslexia'*. Since several skills are involved in reading, a problem in any one of them could account for reading difficulties. The main skills are visual (recognizing letters and words), visual and auditory (associating them with sounds), auditory (hearing language spoken), memory (remembering what has already happened), and language (being able to recall what was read).

### Chapter summary

Piaget sees the growth of cognition passing through four identifiable, biologically controlled stages which can be grouped into two: pre-operational and operational. Pre-operational thinking is immediate, illogical and uses appearance as the basis for other judgement. Operational thought is logical and appears from about the age of seven. Bruner argues that there are different ways in which people can think: enactive, iconic and symbolic representation. Other influences on the extent to which cognitive development is successful include the home environment, peers and school, although these influences are inextricably linked.

### Exam questions – 60 minutes each

1 Evaluate two theories of cognitive development in terms of their empirical evidence. (*25 marks*)
2 Discuss the applications of any one theory of cognitive development to education. (*25 marks*)

# 16 Social behaviour and individual differences in development

**Chapter objectives**

By the end of this chapter you should:

▌ be able to compare and contrast psychodynamic, behaviourist, social learning and cognitive approaches to the moral development of children, and understand the nature of the evidence upon which these theories are based;

▌ be able to describe self as a construct using the ideas of self-image, self-esteem and self-concept, and appreciate the roles of achievement, approval and the value of friendships in the development of a self-concept;

▌ understand the nature of the evidence from which theories of self are developed;

▌ be able to write a critical review of the nature–nurture debate as it applies to gender roles and their development, and understand the nature of the evidence from which these explanations are derived.

## Introduction

In Chapter 14 we noted that socialization is the process through which we each learn the language, customs, norms and values, moral principles and all the other things we need to know if we are to become an integrated member of the various social groups to which we belong. Much of that knowledge is acquired during childhood, although socialization continues for the rest of our lives. Psychologists are interested in how we acquire this knowledge.

## MORAL DEVELOPMENT

Moral development refers to the way we acquire our sense of what our society believes is 'right' and 'wrong', or 'good' and 'bad'. According to Freudian psychoanalytic theory, behaviourism and social learning theorists, different societies and different groups within a society have different norms and values reflecting that group's traditions of desirable and undesirable behaviour. They argue for *moral relativism*, i.e. that there are no such things as 'right', 'wrong', 'good' or 'bad', and that it depends on where, when and under what circumstances the behaviour takes place. So, for example, killing people is wrong, except in war or where capital punishment is legal. Cognitive developmentalist theorists, such as Piaget and Lawrence Kohlberg, argue that some moral principles may be found in all societies (*moral universalism*). Either way, the result of moral development is that we acquire a conscience through incorporating ideas of right and wrong into our personality: a process known as *internalization.*

Just because we have internalized a conscience does not necessarily imply that we always, or even often, live by it. We may have desires to do something that is against the 'rules' and beliefs that form our conscience. The consequence may be guilt or shame, pride or vanity. This *affective* component of moral development was studied by Sigmund Freud. We may do something that contradicts our ideals. This behavioural component was studied by B.F. Skinner and Albert Bandura and others. Our ideas about what constitutes right and wrong, and how we should react, will change with age and experience. This cognitive component was studied by Jean Piaget and Lawrence Kohlberg.

## Freud's psychodynamic theory of moral development

Freud (1935) claimed that one of the hardest tasks of parenthood was the moral development of the children. By the age of about three children are mastering their motor skills, they can communicate quite well, and they can understand much more than they may choose to say. The irrational source of their psychic energy, the id, is still making demands for which their logical ego must find satisfaction. For males during the phallic stage the main demand will be to experience and enjoy the erotic stimulation felt by the 'all important' phallus. Since this stimulation will be provided (inadvertently but naturally) by the mother (at bath time, when dressing, etc.), the id will drive the male to want to be near to his mother. His mother becomes a sexual object of the child's love. His father is seen as a threat since he shares the mother's time and affections, and since he already 'possesses' the mother. The id will energize the death instincts to make the boy feel hostile and jealous towards his father.

At least three major sources of unconscious anxiety combine in the phallic stage. First, negative feelings of hostility and jealousy towards someone who is bigger and more powerful than you lead to frustration. Second, wanting your rival out of the way while loving him at the same time will add further anxiety. Third, anxiety comes from the fear the male child has that his father will find out about his desires, and punish him for them. The ultimate punishment will be to have the source of his erotic pleasure, his penis, cut off. This fear of castration would provide a further source of anxiety. These unconscious anxieties combine into what has been called the Oedipus complex. They can only be overcome by the

---

► A conscience is a set of ethical and moral principles that allows us to evaluate actions and events, which are either real or contemplated.

► To *internalize* means to take in some set of principles or standards of behaviour and thought, which then become a part of our own motives.

► *Affective* refers to human emotions, moods or feelings.

■ Define 'moral development'.

► For a fuller discussion of Freud's psychoanalytic theory see Chapter 1, pages 3–9.

► The id and the ego are the first two parts of personality development in traditional Freudian theory. The third part, the superego, emerges during the phallic stage (3–7). The death instincts and libido are the two instinctive urges that prompt particular behaviour.

child repressing his feelings about his mother, which he does by *identifying* with his father. The process of identification is crucial in Freudian theory. By identification Freud means the way we (mostly unconsciously) transfer ideas we have about someone else to ourselves. The boy adopts his father's attitudes, sex roles, moral values, etc., and so develops his own superego by identifying with his father.

Apart from his own children, Freud really studied only one other child, and that was mostly by correspondence. 'Little Hans' was the son of an admirer of Freud. Hans' father told Freud of his five-year-old son's phobia about horses. The family lived opposite a coaching inn during the first decade of the twentieth century, and the streets were full of horses. One day Hans had seen a large horse fall down in the street, and thought it was dead. His father said that ever since then the boy had been afraid of horses. The child imagined they might fall over, make a frightening noise, or bite him. Freud, and Hans' father, interpreted the horse phobia quite differently, claiming that the boy was suffering the anxieties of the Oedipus complex. Freud told Hans' father to explain to his son what was happening, that he wouldn't be angry with his son for the boy's feelings about him and his mother, and that he was not going to punish Hans. The phobia would then disappear. Hans' father did explain, and the phobia did eventually disappear.

Freud claimed that the case of little Hans supported the truth of Oedipal conflict. Clearly it does no such thing. There are several explanations for why Hans developed his phobia, the most obvious one being that he had seen a large horse fall over and he was afraid that another might fall and hurt him. He had a younger sister and the phobia may also have served to attract his mother's attention away from his sister and back to himself. It may even have been an expression of resentment at having to share his mother's affections with his sister. Most children develop phobias towards something or other during childhood. Surely they can't all be related to unconscious anxieties about parents?

There are also reasons for the disappearance of Hans' phobia that have nothing to do with his father promising not to castrate him. (In fact, his mother, not his father, had actually threatened to castrate him if he played with his 'widdler'.) One explanation for the phobia disappearing is habituation. If you were forced to be exposed to something to which you had a phobic reaction for several hours, the fear would eventually subside. This is called *habituation*. Hans could not have avoided seeing or hearing horses every day of his life. (See Chapter 7 for a discussion of habituation.)

Freud's explanation for how girls acquire their personalities has always seemed bizarre, and hardly anyone takes it at all seriously now. It's called the Electra complex. Little girls are supposed to imagine that their penis has already been cut off by their mothers. They become afraid that their mothers may mutilate them further. They are supposed to suffer 'penis envy' (since the male phallus is supposed to be all important during the

▶ Phobias are defined as irrational fears about people, objects or events. Children usually grow out of their fear of the dark, fear of strangers, fear of open spaces or closed-in spaces.

▶ One of the major criticisms of Freudian theory of personality development during childhood is that it was not derived from studying many children, but rather from the dreams and spoken memories of some 'hysterical' patients. Freud wasn't studying Little Hans 'first-hand' either.

■ What 'evidence' from the case of Little Hans could Freud claim supported his theory? What are the shortcomings of this evidence?

phallic stage). This unconsciously draws the girl to her father, who has a penis. By associating with her father the girl is supposed to imagine that her penis will grow again. This causes conflict with her mother, and anxiety follows. In order to overcome this anxiety the girl represses her sexual feelings towards her father by identifying with her mother. The girl also fears that her mother will lose even more affection towards her, and this increases the need for identification.

Girls would have less strong a reason to identify with their mothers than boys with their fathers, and so supposedly develop weaker superegos. There is no evidence for any of this at all. The concept of the Electra complex has been severely criticized, not least by female psychoanalysts, who point out that it's not a penis that girls envy, but the power that men exert over women, and over everything else in society!

### Summary – The Oedipus complex

Perhaps Freud's most controversial ideas are expressed in his early writings and concern the relationship between childhood sexual feelings and personality growth. The id is demanding that pre-genital sexual feelings must be satisfied. The ego provides the only way to achieve this, which is for the boy to replace his father as the object of his mother's love. He must possess his mother and eliminate his father. At the same time as boys are feeling sexually drawn towards their mothers they feel guilty and fearful of their fathers. Ultimately, they fear their father might castrate them for their desires. Freud described this mass of love, desire, guilt, worry and fear as Oedipal conflict. It was derived largely from interpreting the spoken memories of disturbed adult patients.

■ Explain what Freud meant by the Oedipus and Electra complexes.

The consequence of all this identification is that the child learns to think, act and feel like its same-sex parent. Each child will internalize the values that this parent holds into what Freud called *superego*. The superego embodies our ethical and moral standards, our conscience. Conscience is a set of moral principles held by each of us which will punish us with feelings of guilt, shame and remorse for our wrongdoings. Conscience refers to those things we should not do.

The superego is concerned with ideal behaviour. At first the parents are mainly responsible for showing the child what is ideal and what is not. Other important people such as teachers become involved later, until eventually the child has self-discipline and can control its own behaviour, regardless of what its parents would think. The superego monitors the behaviour of the ego, and orders it to pursue certain behaviour and avoid other kinds. It behaves rather like the parent, whose job it has taken over.

## Summary – Identification

Identification is at the heart of Freud's theory of personality development. It explains how children acquire one of the most important parts of their personalities, their superego. The child experiences (pre-genital) sexual feelings towards its opposite-sex parent and feels angry about the power its father/mother holds over its life. The ego 'reasons' that if the child becomes more like its same-sex parent its same-sex parent will want to be with it. Partly to overcome the feelings of guilt about its feelings towards its father/mother, and partly to appear more desirable to its opposite-sex parent, the child will want to become like its same-sex parent. The child identifies with its father/mother, internalizing the same-sex parent's ideas, beliefs and attitudes, i.e. their personality. One aspect of its same-sex parent's personality will be that parent's ideas about moral conduct. The child acquires its superego from its same-sex parent.

Children do develop consciences, but whether they do so as a result of identification used for repressing sexual feelings is far from accepted. Children do learn by identification (among a number of other strategies), but probably not through any association with their genitals

## Evaluation of psychoanalytic theory

| Theory | Comment |
| --- | --- |
| Freud's evidence is entirely subjective, involving his interpretations of the reported symptoms and case histories of few children and many disturbed adults, mostly living in Vienna in the first three decades of the twentieth century. | Such evidence would be useful starting points for gathering data from which more scientific testing could develop. Attempts at such testing have not proved successful (e.g. Yarrow 1954, Daston 1956, Skodel 1957, Kline 1968). |
| Freud's prediction about what will happen are very deterministic. | Children's psychological development is influenced by many factors affecting the individual. |
| Fear of punishment is the single most motivating factor in acquiring a conscience. | Studies of childrearing styles (Baumrind 1967, Hoffman 1970, Brody and Shaffer 1982, Kochanska 1991, 1993) found that the opposite occurred. |
| Boys have stronger superegos than girls and can resist temptation longer since they have more to fear. | Studies have found no evidence whatsoever for this, or the opposite has been found (Hoffman 1975). |
| The superego is responsible for children's guilt reactions when ideals are transgressed. | Children's feelings of guilt are determined by the situation (and likelihood of getting caught) – there are different types of guilt (Hartshorne and May 1928, Miller and Swanson 1958). |
| Moral development is complete around seven when Oedipal and Electra conflicts have been resolved. | Throughout our lives we are learning more about events, personalities, intentions, motives, and other things that modify and extend our moral sense. |
| Loving, caring, nurturant parenting is desirable, but not particularly important to the development of moral feelings. | Modern psychoanalytic theory (after Bowlby) recognizes the importance of parenting to all aspects of personality development. |

■ **(a) What is the superego and how does it come into existence according to Freud?**
**(b) What is the role of the superego in psychoanalytic explanations of moral development?**

### The behaviourist explanation of moral development

Freud emphasized the role of the threat of punishment in moral development. Generally, behaviourists are sceptical about the usefulness of punishment in childrearing since it only tells children what not to do. They stress the central importance of reinforcement. Reinforcing a child's desirable behaviour will lead to an increase in it. Ignoring undesired behaviour should ensure that it extinguishes on its own, since it hasn't been reinforced. Any number of studies of childrearing styles (Baumrind 1967, Sears, Maccoby and Levin 1957) have shown how children who are reinforced for behaving in a compassionate, generous way are more likely to behave in that way again. If children are reinforced for behaving in an anti-social way, they are probably more likely to behave in that way again too.

---

### Reinforcement and punishment

Reinforcement increases some behaviour.

Consistent reinforcement for good behaviour contributes to well-being and a positive self-image.

Reinforcement for good behaviour provides positive ideas about how to behave in the future.

Punishment decreases some behaviour.

Punishment contributes to misery and a lowered self-image.

Punishment for undesired behaviour provides a system of discipline which should deter repetition of undesired behaviour in the future.

---

► According to Eysenck, CERs are the reflexive, emotional parts of moral behaviour.

► A reinforcer is anything the actor finds beneficial in some way, which then increases the chances of that behaviour recurring when the opportunity for it occurs again.

Hans Eysenck believes that conscience can be explained as a series of classically conditioned emotional responses (CERs). If a child is punished for some wicked act on a few occasions (trials), the pain or discomfort received from the punishment will become associated with the wicked act that elicited the punishment. The next time the child thinks about performing the wicked act it will also remember the pain and discomfort that the punishment provoked. This should be sufficient to stop the wicked behaviour. The best time to punish would be just before the child performs the undesirable act, since the anxiety elicited then will be remembered just before the act could occur the next time. Also, any pleasure or reinforcement the child could have gained from its wickedness will be denied, so cannot become associated with the act and encourage the child to repeat it. In an ideal world we might know when a child is about to commit a wicked act. Unfortunately, we often find out only after the act has occurred, if we ever find out at all!

## Evaluation of behaviourist explanations

| Theory | Comment |
| --- | --- |
| Evidence for 'scientific' behaviourist explanations of all learning comes from animal studies. | The behaviour of lower-order animals is largely instinctive or learned through relatively simple associations. Since animals don't have moral codes of behaviour. |
| The application of behaviourist principles to explain moral development in humans is an abstraction from behaviourist theory. | |
| Humans have higher cognitive centres that allow them to manage their behaviour in many ways. | Behaviourists discount the importance of of 'mental events' since they can't be measured. |
| The roles of modelling and punishment in teaching desired and undesired behaviour are largely ignored. | Both have important roles in shaping moral understanding and behaviour. |

■ **How do behaviourists explain the development of moral behaviour?**

# The social learning theory of Albert Bandura

In Chapter 1 we noted how Albert Bandura and others attempted to reinterpret Freud's concept of identification in behaviourist terms. Identification relies on observational learning, which consists essentially of observation, imitation and modelling. Children learn appropriate behaviour from the important people they see around them. This is moral relativism since individual parents, teachers and 'significant others' place different emphases on different aspects of behaviour. In addition, reinforcement by others both teaches the child what to do, and what not to do, and serves as a reminder to the child of what it should do in any new situation. To this extent learning about right and wrong behaviour is the same as learning about anything else and occurs in no particular order.

■ **Why is observational learning important in socialization?**

■ **What is the relationship between observational learning, modelling, identification and reinforcement in social learning theory's explanation of the development of moral behaviour in the child?**

## Evaluation of social learning theory

| Theory | Comment |
| --- | --- |
| Children learn appropriate behaviour by modelling important adults such as caregivers and teachers. | Some of the influences of siblings and peers will be as important as children grow. |
| These models reinforce their ideas about good and bad behaviour. | Direct reinforcement isn't always necessary to shape behaviour. Media models, for example, can't offer direct reinforcement. |
| Children's knowledge of 'desired behaviour' shapes their moral behaviour. | And often doesn't. Some children have behaved in appalling ways, knowing them to be wrong. |
| Bandura's evidence comes from experimental studies of children imitating aggressive and pro-social behaviour. | At best they demonstrate imitation, not necessarily modelling and identification, and some of the studies are ethically unacceptable. |

# Cognitive theories of moral development

## Piaget's theory of moral development

According to Piaget (1932, 1965), for the first seven to ten years of its life the child's state of maturation does not permit it to use abstract rules and principles to guide its behaviour. He described this type of thinking as pre-operational. The child's thinking is

▶ For a fuller discussion of Piaget's theory of cognitive development, see Chapter 15.

► Below the age of seven Piaget described children's thinking as pre-operational, i.e. illogical (at least according to adult rules of logic!).

dominated by what things look like, and by externally imposed instructions (from adults). Children of this age can't really 'think for themselves'.

Piaget investigated children's responses to moral issues in several ways. He told them stories which involved an issue that could be interpreted in several ways. For example:

> Story A: 'A little boy who is called John is in his room. He is called to dinner. He goes into the dining room. But behind the door there was a chair and on the chair there was a tray with 15 cups on it. John couldn't have known that there was all this behind the door. He goes in, the door knocks against the tray, bang go the 15 cups, and they all get broken.'

> Story B: 'Once there was a little boy whose name was Henry. One day when his mother was out he tried to reach some jam out of the cupboard. He climbed into a chair and stretched out his arm. But the jam was too high up and he couldn't reach it … While he was trying to get it he knocked over a cup. The cup fell down and broke.' (Piaget 1932 , page 122)

Piaget asked children questions such as 'Which is the naughtier child?', 'Are they equally naughty?', 'Why was one naughtier than the other?', 'What punishment should John/Henry be given?' Piaget also played games such as marbles, which had rules that everyone knew, and asked about where the rules came from, and what would happen if we tried to change them. Generally, pre-operational children are egocentric and will obey rules without question. Children in the concrete operations stage are more willing to invent new rules and negotiate changes in existing ones.

► *Heteronomous* means from outside. *Autonomous* means controlled from within.

Piaget identified two stages in the development of moral reasoning. The stage of *heteronomous* morality (or the stage of moral realism) coincides with the pre-operational and concrete operations stage (two to 11 years). The child accepts that all rules are fixed by some external authority such as parents, or even God, and that breaking them will lead to immediate and severe punishment. For the first five years children believe that rules cannot be changed, and have always been the same as they are now. All behaviour will be judged by its consequences, regardless of the intentions or reasons for that behaviour. The children in this stage judged John to be naughtier than Henry, since he broke more cups. From seven to ten years children start to learn that rules can be changed by agreement, or by trial and error. Punishment for wickedness is not automatic, since a child who can decentre can take other intentions and circumstances into account when making moral judgements. The stage of *autonomous* morality (or moral independence) coinciding with the formal operations stage is reached when they have achieved this understanding.

► Telling stories, asking questions and playing games are invaluable tools for investigating children's ideas. But children may become shy, or say things that aren't necessarily what they really mean.

### Evaluation of Piaget's theory of moral development

| Theory | Comment |
| --- | --- |
| Children's moral thinking appears to change with age. | Piaget's methods for investigating moral thinking involved telling stories and asking questions. Children don't always have the |

Distinct stages correspond to a wider theory of cognitive development.

A link is made between cognitive growth and the adherence to moral rules.
A link is made between cognitive development and the ability to make other judgements.

same understanding of the question (or answer) as adults.
The wider cognitive theory has been criticized for underestimating the ages at which the stages occur.
There are different kinds of rules and children respond to them differently at different ages and in different situations. Other research shows that children as young as three can take motives into account if the motives are explained to them.

■ **Outline Piaget's explanation for moral development.**

## Kohlberg's theory of moral development

**Lawrence Kohlberg** (1963, 1969, 1981) set out to retest, refine and extend Piaget's ideas. Kohlberg told children and adults stories involving moral dilemmas. In each story there is a choice to be made between some authority and some 'deserving' individual who is being unfairly treated. Possibly the best known example concerns a man whose wife was very close to death from a particular type of cancer. A new kind of radium had been discovered by a local chemist and the husband tried desperately to buy some, but the chemist was charging much more than the husband could afford and asked if he could pay the rest of the money later. The chemist refused, replying 'I discovered the drug, and I'm going to make money from it'. The man was desperate to save his wife, so later that night he broke into the chemist's laboratory and stole the drug.

▶ A dilemma is a problem that has two or more possible solutions, neither of which is totally satisfactory.

▶ In this story there is a clear dilemma between not doing something illegal and possibly letting someone die, and doing something illegal and saving a loved one's life.

Kohlberg then asked a series of questions such as 'Should the husband have stolen the drug?', 'Why?', 'What should happen to him?', 'Would it have been different if the woman had been a very important person?', 'Should the chemist have refused to sell the drug?', 'Should the police arrest the chemist for murder if the woman died?' Some of the children and adults said that theft is wrong, and that the husband should be punished severely. Others said that theft is wrong, but that the man should receive a moderate punishment since he was trying to care for his wife.

After asking many subjects questions from a series of similar moral dilemmas such as that just described, Kohlberg identified three distinct levels in the development of moral reasoning, with each level comprising two stages. People generally progress through these levels in the order in which they are presented here. However, the stage or level each person reaches can vary greatly according to when they reach it or whether they reach it at all.

## Kohlberg's levels of moral development

### Level One
The level of preconventional morality (up to teens approximately):

Stage 1   Younger children are only concerned with the outcome of behaviour and are unable to take motives into account. Their main preoccupation is avoiding physical discomfort, i.e. punishment.

Stage 2  Older children make judgements according to what gives them, or their favourite people, pleasure.

*Level Two*

The level of conventional morality (13–16 years approximately):

Stage 3  Young teenagers are keen to win approval from others (some kind of 'psychological reward'), so their judgements take into account what they think will make them popular.

Stage 4  Many rules exist that must not be disobeyed, or punishment will certainly follow. Others can be negotiated. The young person will often be 'good' in order to avoid psychological discomfort such as guilt.

*Level Three*

The level of post-conventional morality (16–20 years approximately):

Stage 5  The interests of the wider community are becoming recognized, and sometimes may have to be put before the interests of the individual. The principle of 'the greatest good for the greatest number' may be employed in reasoning moral issues. Ideas about justice and fairness, democracy and what should happen become more usual.

Stage 6  The deepest religious and philosophical reasoning occurs here, and few people ever reach this stage. The individual conscience develops from a conviction that one must be true to oneself and one's own standards.

It is quite likely that some people will be reasoning at the third level by the time they are 20 years old. Some 60-year-olds may never progress beyond level two.

Further researches into moral reasoning, including some by Kohlberg himself, have found little evidence for stage 6 among the general population. It may not be a general stage at all, but accessible only to certain great thinkers. There may even be special stages beyond stage 6.

### Evaluation of Kohlberg's view

| Theory | Comment |
| --- | --- |
| Asking for responses to dilemma stories is supposed to illustrate the stage of moral reasoning. | Kohlberg told rather unrealistic dilemma stories which have little to do with his subjects' real lives and have no personal consequences for them. Perhaps if the children could actually be involved in the stories their reasoning might be quite different (Yussen 1977). |
| Observation of others is unnecessary since the stages are determined by biological maturation. | It is quite likely that being exposed to people who reason at higher levels might contribute to cognitive structures needed to reason at that level oneself. |
| Kohlberg assumes that people in all cultures use the same principles of right and wrong behaviour. | The definition and style of moral reasoning is relative to time and place, and more cognitively advanced children use more advanced forms of moral reasoning. |
| Kohlberg's sample comprised 50 Americans under 17 years of age. | Hardly sufficient to claim that his theory is universally true. |
| The sample were all male. | **Carol Gilligan** (1977, 1982) maintains that females |

■ How does Kohlberg's explanation of moral development differ from Piaget's?

■ How convincing is Kohlberg's explanation in view of the evidence on which it is based?

reason differently from males, emphasizing care and nurturance as being equally as important as the post-conventional abstract modes of thought, which may be more typically male.

Kohlberg assumes that the stage of moral reasoning people exhibit in response to his dilemma stories reflects their actual moral behaviour in real life.

There is no direct evidence for this assumption, since moral conduct is influenced by environmental (such as opportunities to do right or wrong), social (e.g. who else is involved), psychological (for instance the chances of being detected) and other factors.

The order in which cognitive skills are learned is invariant.

Other studies (Rest 1986, Walker 1989) confirm this. However, it depends on which stories are being told. People may appear to miss a stage (Holstein 1976) or regress to an earlier one (Kohlberg and Kramer 1969).

## Summary – Moral development

Freud sees moral feelings resulting from identification with our same-sex parent as a part of the resolution of Oedipal or Electra conflicts. Eysenck believes moral behaviour is conditioned in much the same way as all other kinds of behaviour, through the process of reinforcement. In an attempt to synthesize Freudian identification and reinforcement, Bandura sees a role for observational learning from influential models in explaining children's moral behaviour. Piaget identified heteronomous morality coinciding with the pre-operational stage, and autonomous morality emerging from the formal operational stage of thought. Kohlberg identified six stages in three levels of reasoning, which develop throughout life.

## THE SELF-CONCEPT

Humans are the only animals to have much idea about their selves, about what and who they are, as individuals. Self, or *self concept*, refers to what we know about ourselves. Our sex, age, height, personality, and our likes and dislikes are all part of our self-concept. Self-concept comprises three major forces: self-image, self-esteem and ideal self. Self-image is one's knowledge of the kind of person one is. Self-esteem refers to how one values oneself. One source of information for you to judge your self-esteem is how other people respond to you, as we shall see shortly. Ideal self refers to what one would really like to be like. Maladjustment occurs when one's ideal self differs very sharply from one's actual self-image.

► *Self concept* is the general idea that we each have about the kind of person we are. Write down ten statements answering the question 'Who am I?', and you'll have described your self-concept.

■ Outline the components of the self-concept.

## The development of self-concept

During the first couple of years babies have to learn that they are separate from all the other people and objects around them. By about two years of age children can refer to themselves by name, and soon start using 'my', 'mine', 'yours', etc. They learn about their bodies, and what they look and feel like. They are learning their *existential self*. They will also learn to talk about their *categorical*

► *Existential self* and *categorical self* are two aspects of the self-concept which develop during the first few years.

*self*, describing themselves as 'a girl', or 'a child'. **Michael Lewis** and **Jeanne Brooks-Gunn** (1979) distinguish the existential self – the sense of knowing about being different and separate from others – from the categorical self – knowing our age, sex, height, personality, likes and dislikes, etc. Young babies have no idea about either of these 'selves'. By three years most children have some ideas of categorical and existential self and can identify themselves in photographs, will refer to themselves and their possessions accurately, and will know what other familiar people are called, and something about them.

▶ We have noted some of the problems involved in studying children before. Ingenious experiments have to be constructed, such as those of Tom Bower and Martin Hughes. This simple experiment by Lewis and Brooks-Gunn shows that procedures needn't be complicated with sophisticated apparatus. A mirror and some make-up are easy enough to arrange.

One ingenious technique for investigating the emergence of existential self involves letting a baby watch its own image in a mirror. At first the baby will try to touch, smile at, and generally interact with the image. After a while the investigator distracts the child long enough to place a dab of cosmetic make-up such as lipstick on its nose. The image the baby sees now is clearly different from the previous one. If the child does not show surprise at the new mirror image then it can't know that either of the images was itself. It hasn't developed existential self. If the child looks surprised, and perhaps reaches to touch its own nose, then it must recognize itself as the image in the mirror, and must have some idea of existential self. Up to about 15 months of age very few babies show surprise at the changed image or attempt to touch their nose. By 20 months about 25 per cent do. Between 20 and 24 months this rises to 75 per cent. Lewis and Brooks-Gunn found that during the last few months before their second birthday children pay more attention to any sources of information about themselves, such as video tapes and photographs, and are generally more interested in themselves!

During their third year, and as language skills develop, children begin comparing themselves to others, and enjoy talking about the categorical differences they observe. Sex and size are two easy points of comparison. Big people are seen as having power over small people. Age is also used, although as Piaget has shown, children judge age by appearances, so mistakes occasionally occur. The earliest distinctions are between 'children' and 'adults'.

▶ Self-esteem refers to our judgement of our own worth. Are we truthful, honest, trustworthy, reliable, etc.? Self-esteem appears to be the result of socialization.

Apart from their existential and categorical selves, we also know that children develop evaluations of their own worth – self-esteem – which they at times prefer to keep private. Parents sometimes refer to their children positively (as 'clever girl' or 'kind boy'), and sometimes negatively (as 'wicked boy' or 'stupid girl'). These evaluations will influence the child's self-esteem. High self-esteem (a positive self-concept) will increase a child's confidence and desire to interact socially, to become inquisitive and develop its cognitive skills, and to become independent. Low self-esteem can inhibit the child's confidence and willingness to participate socially. Between the ages of three and five children develop a private as well as a public sense of themselves that other people do not see. Freudians see a potential source for anxiety and repression here that could seriously inhibit personality growth.

As children grow their ability to categorize themselves by what they do, as well as what they are, increases. Asking a four-year-old 'Who is the little girl who goes to playgroup?' may elicit the answer 'Me'. Asking the same child 'Who is the little girl who goes to school?' may confuse the child. Since she does not go to school she can't be 'the little girl' referred to in the question. She is unlikely to be able to say, 'It can't be me because I don't go to school'. As the child passes through school a third system of categories, what we like and dislike, is added. 'Who is the girl who goes to school and likes Alex Wood, but dislikes apples?' could be answered differently by two ten-year-olds, depending on their feelings about Alex and apples!

| Summary – Emergence of self | |
|---|---|
| *Age (years)* | *Sense of self* |
| 0–1 | None |
| 1–2 | Existential |
| 2–3 | Existential and categorical |
| 3–5 | Existential, categorical and private |

Our knowledge of who and what we are like changes throughout our lives. **Charles Cooley** (1902) offers one of the first theories of self known as the 'looking glass theory', in which the self-concept is rather like a mirror reflecting what we are like. Essentially, we use the information other people give us through their responses to us to discover what they think we are like. Cooley says: 'The self that is most important is a reflection, largely from the minds of others.' There are two dimensions to this reflection. First, the illustrative part, that is, guessing what others see when they look at us. Do they see someone who is organized, intelligent, capable, hard-working and good-looking? The second dimension is evaluative: what value do they put on each of those aspects of us that they see? Are we worthy, deserving, honourable, fair-minded, decent, fancyable etc.? So we form our opinions about ourselves from how other people treat us.

**George Herbert Mead** broadened Cooley's looking glass to include many more social experiences than just the reactions of individuals. Mead claims that as we develop psychologically we take on norms and values appropriate to our culture or group. These are internalized into our personality and form part of our conscience. This knowledge about the social context of our behaviour is important in knowing who we are, regardless of how other people regard us. Since our situations (what Skinner calls antecedents – see Chapter 1) are constantly changing because different people are involved, different experiences have occurred, and we have changed from the last time we were in that situation, so our sense of self is also constantly changing. Mead sees self as a reflexive process, constantly modifying itself in line with changing experiences.

Also, we need to see ourselves as other people see us. We are capable of responding to ourselves and changing our attitudes and behaviour as well as we might when responding to other people. This self-interaction develops through the early and middle parts of

► Cooley says: 'We live on, cheerful and self-confident ... until in some rude hour we learn that we do not stand as well as we thought we did, that the image of us is tarnished. Perhaps we do something ... that we find the social order is set against, or perhaps it is the ordinary course of our life that is not so well regarded as we supposed. At any rate we find, with a chill of terror, that the world is cold and strange, and our self-esteem, self-confidence, and hope, being chiefly founded upon the opinions [of] others, go down in the crash.'

► Don't confuse Mead's idea of self with Freud's conception of superego. Once formed, superego remains as an 'overseer' monitoring our behaviour and triggering our emotions. Mead believes self is a constantly changing process that tells us far more than when we are right or wrong.

our lives, as our self-concept is forming. As we grow older and become less concerned with other people's approval, it is of less importance. Mead (1935) says we use role taking to try to 'get outside' ourselves in order to 'become an object' to ourselves. Forming an impression of what we look like to others when we look at ourselves is the key way to understand what other people see when they look at us.

**Erving Goffman** emphasizes the uniqueness of each individual, which we have gained through the countless social roles that we play throughout our lives. You learn more about you from the way your family interacts with you, the way your peers and friends do, your lecturers and tutors, your workmates, and the way acquaintances you come into contact with every day react towards you. Each interaction has us playing a social role. Goffman (1959) says that the collection of social roles each person plays forms that individual's self-concept. In some interactions you may play 'intelligent and appearing to be hard-working' roles. In another you may emphasize 'competitive and determined' sides. This idea links to what John Rowan describes as sub-personalities, as we shall note shortly.

Like Cooley and Mead, **Carl Rogers** (1961), a humanist psychiatrist, thought that the 'self' develops from interactions with others and can change in accordance with those interactions. We do not like to think of ourselves as constantly changing and aim for consistency. Problems can arise when consistency is denied. If you think you are likeable and popular, but you don't think that anyone seems to like you, then a gap develops between your self-concept and reality. This could result in a personality problem, which may need discussing with a friend, relation, or even a therapist.

The problem of consistency is taken up by **John Rowan**. Rowan (1991) has been gathering information from psychological experimental research, from clinical treatments and therapies, and from philosophy to contradict the view that we have a single personality. He says:

> It is an extraordinary thing that all personality theories assume that there is just one personality. The questions they then ask are – what is the structure of this personality, what are the functions of this personality, what are the origins of this personality, what can we predict about this personality?
>
> But these assumptions are just assumptions, and they are made largely because it is convenient to do so … Personologists are lazy people, like the rest of us, and do not want the bother of considering that people might be multiple. And other psychologists studying questions like the self, identity and so forth, are only too pleased to fall in with this for their own particular purposes.

Instead, Rowan (and others) claims that humans have several sub-personalities. The exact nature and function of these sub-personalities is yet to be revealed, but Rowan calls for a radical rethink of our current understanding of the concept of personality.

► Do we have one personality, or many? Is your self-concept consistent and unchanging? Or do you act in quite different ways in different situations? Who do you think you are? And would your best friend agree?

During the 1950s and 1960s **Stanley Coopersmith** (1968) conducted a longitudinal study of children from ten years to early adult life to investigate self-esteem in children. He tested them several times, using questionnaires about how they felt about themselves, about their family, their schoolwork, etc. He found some who had high levels of self-esteem, and others with less liking for themselves and their relationships. Those with lots of friends who were doing well at school were more likely to describe themselves as having high self-esteem.

He also found a positive relationship between children who had high self-esteem and children whose parents also felt good about themselves. The parents were warm and supportive towards their children and treated them as responsible individuals who were rewarded for their successes and encouraged not to fail. The parents with high self-esteem were genuinely interested in their children and encouraged them to have opinions and share them with others. The moral is, if you want to have children with high self-esteem, start improving how you feel about yourself!

▶ Outline some theories of 'self', showing how each explains what self is, how it emerges and how it is maintained.

## Summary – Self

Our ideas about our 'self' start with a knowledge of our own existence, develop into a knowledge of who and what we are publicly, and finally include a knowledge of what we are like. This knowledge may be essentially private, although it is greatly influenced by how our parents have socialized us and how we think others treat us. The level of self-esteem can affect children's performance in many things.

## GENDER IDENTITY AND GENDER ROLES

Knowledge about one's sex is an important part of one's self-concept. One's *gender* is a product of socialization. Gender refers to the knowledge that we acquire about the kinds of behaviour appropriate to our sex. In Britain during the last two hundred years boys have been seen as the future 'breadwinners' who should behave in an authoritative, logical and emotionless way. Girls have been seen as weak, indecisive and dependent upon others. These gender roles have changed.

Young children are not cognitively mature enough to realize that their sex has certain biological implications for their future behaviour, or that their sex won't change as they grow. Learning the appropriate gender role will take a few years. Studies of males and females from several cultures have emphasized the impact of biology on sex role behaviour, whilst others show the importance of social experience. Inevitably, these are characterized as part of the nature–nurture debate. We review evidence for the two claims below.

▶ Sex is a biological fact, a consequence of the mix of X and Y chromosomes received from each parent at the moment of conception.

## The biological contribution

There are differences between male and female infants which can only be explained by their biology. On average boys are heavier, more active, more irritable, more demanding, less hardy, sleep less well and are less easy to comfort than girls. On average girls are walking and talking before boys. However, over the next few years these differences largely disappear and there's no evidence that these early differences explain future gender role behaviour. Those who claim that biology also controls personality, self-concept, gender role behaviour and so on are called reductionists.

There are wide individual differences within averages for those aspects of development that might be explained by biology. Some boys will be smaller, lighter, more intellectually and socially advanced and easier to raise than some girls. Those who believe that environmental influences are important are called interactionists. For further evidence for the influence of biology on sex-linked behaviour we look to theoretical claims for maternal instinct, and the influence of hormones on human and animal bodies and behaviour.

**John Bowlby** (1958) claimed that females have a *maternal instinct* to have and care for their young. In most societies childcare roles are assumed to be mainly performed by females. However, the situation is far more complex and the term 'maternal instinct' is misleading. 'Maternal' implies that only mothers have it, which ignores the fact that fathers also show care and concern for their children. 'Instinct' implies that it is innate and universal. Yet under certain conditions mothers have neglected and even harmed their children. Also, if we list the activities involved in childcare and which partner performs each, we do not find that mothers consistently perform them. On the whole, Bowlby's claim for the existence of a maternal instinct should be dismissed.

### Kohlberg's stages of gender role development

Kohlberg claims that children acquire their gender roles in the same way as they acquire other cognitive skills. He identifies three stages of development.

*1 The stage of basic gender identity*
Children have learned their *basic gender identity* by three years of age and can categorize themselves as a girl or a boy, but have little idea about what that means, or that their sex won't change during their lives. Knowing what sex you are called will encourage you to play with others of the same sex, which reinforces your definition of your sex. You will know that there are other humans called by a different description, but they won't mean much to you.

*2 The stage of gender stability*
During the next few years children ask questions about what they (as members of their sex) do. Parents will say 'boys don't cry' and 'girls are pretty', and the child slowly realizes that little boys and little girls do some things, and those things are different from the

► Hormones are chemical messengers that are released into the bloodstream by some of our glands to instruct various body organs to function in some way. Hormones are concerned in sex-linked behaviour.

things the others do. They gradually realize that their sex is fixed for life and will not change. When they know this they have *gender stability*. However, knowing that one's own sex is fixed for life doesn't mean that a child knows that other people's sex won't change. At four and five years old children are still largely making their judgements of what things are like from what they look like. So, if a child knows that girls have long hair, then they may well describe someone they knew to be a man as a girl if he grew his hair long.

*3 The stage of gender consistency*
By the time children reach six or seven years old they will have developed gender consistency. They no longer use appearance as the main feature in making judgements about people's sex and will have realized that gender can't change.

### Summary of Kohlberg's views

Kohlberg suggests that children learn their sex and gender roles through the same cognitive process by which they learn other things. As their understanding of the world and their cognitive skills develop, so their knowledge of the expectations of their sex increases.

### Influence of sex hormones
The influence of sex hormones on animal behaviour is considerable, and has been demonstrated several times. **W.C.Young** (1964) injected a pregnant monkey carrying a female foetus with the male hormone testosterone every day from the 42nd to the 122nd day of the pregnancy. After birth and during its life the female looked and acted more like a male monkey. It was bigger and heavier, more assertive, challenging others for a place in the group, and it was more independent than typical females. When mature it even tried to mount another female for mating. Numerous experiments with lower-order animals have shown that altering the androgen and oestrogen levels affects the extent of sex-linked behaviour. Increasing oestrogen levels in males produces behaviour more typical of females, while increasing testosterone in females produces more 'male-like' behaviour.

► Testosterone is one of the main androgens. Altering the amounts of the opposite sex's hormones will cause changes in an animal's behaviour.

Evidence links sex hormones to certain kinds of aggression, and aggression is a predominantly male phenomenon. (The androgenous females in the experiments mentioned above usually started fights with their non-androgenous sisters.) This is not to say that females aren't capable of acts of aggression too, for example in defence of their young. However, the environment also influences the amount of hormones released. Monkeys who won their battles against challengers seemed to produce more testosterone than they had before, while the levels of hormones in those who lost their fights went down.

► The level of hormones can affect an animal's behaviour, but the consequences of its behaviour can also affect its hormone levels.

There are many problems in predicting human behaviour from studies of animals. Principally, we have highly developed cognitive

▶ Most lower-order animals rely on instinct and simple association learning. Humans may also have instincts and learn by association, but rely much more on their perceptions, cognition, prediction of outcome, etc.

■ **Summarize the nativist explanation for gender role behaviour.**

▶ As societies change, the roles expected of its male and female members will also change. Changes in the role of women during the twentieth century in the West, for example, have been dramatic.

▶ Fagot's study is a naturalistic observation study, since it took place in the children's home environment.

skills including thinking, reasoning, predicting and imagining. We use our knowledge and understanding, intelligence and communication skills to control our behaviour, including gender-related behaviour.

Hormones are important in human sex-linked development. During pregnancy and at various times in one's life, hormones such as androgens and oestrogens are released, which affect male and female body and brain structures. The androgens affect males by controlling the onset of puberty, the growth spurt, biological fertility and so on. The oestrogens are important female hormones that control the timing of biological maturity and menstruation. It could be that these, and other hormones, also affect psychological development. Both sexes have androgens and oestrogens, males usually having more androgens and females more oestrogens.

Some studies by **John Money** and his colleagues (Money and Erhardt 1972) have been made of girls whose mothers received excessive amounts of androgens during pregnancy (to reduce the likelihood of miscarriage). Some of their babies developed andro-genital syndrome (AGS). As they grew they tended to be more aggressive and 'tomboyish', and less feminine. They preferred male activities with male company, and expressed more interest in a career than in having a family.

## The nurture claim: socialization

According to Bandura's social learning theory children learn their roles from the influential models they observe around them, particularly parents. If the two sexes are treated differently, and have different expectations made of their behaviour, then they will learn to behave differently. Parents have been observed treating their daughters differently from their sons from a very young age, and differences in the children's behaviour has been noted. Boys may be regarded by parents in Western countries as more robust than girls, and so are more likely to be offered rough and tumble-type play. Girls are more likely to receive cuddles and gentle treatment. The evidence for the influence of nurture comes from observations of parenting styles and their effects on children's gender behaviour, cross-cultural studies, and the influence of socialization on hormones.

### Differences in parenting styles

**Beverley Fagot** (1978) studied 24 American families, each with a child between 20 and 24 months old. She visited each family five times, observing parents interacting with their child for an hour on each visit. She was looking for examples of the kind of behaviour parents encouraged and discouraged in their sons and daughters.

Girls were encouraged to ask for help when it was needed, to follow and stay near to a parent, to dance, to take an interest in girls' clothes, and to play with dolls. They were usually discouraged from running around, jumping, climbing, being too active, being aggressive, playing 'rough' games, and generally manipulating and exploring objects. Boys were encouraged to play with and explore toys such as trucks and building blocks in an active, manipulative way which would help build strong muscles. They were firmly discouraged from playing with dolls, from asking for assistance and from anything the parents considered 'feminine'.

The two sexes were not treated equally in what they were discouraged from doing. Boys who started any 'female' activities were more severely criticized than girls who played in a 'masculine' way. It seems that parents will tolerate their daughters being independent and assertive occasionally. They will not tolerate their sons being passive and dependent.

**Smith** and **Lloyd** (1978) conducted an interesting, ecologically valid experiment. They had a baby dressed in either blue or pink and asked mothers who didn't know the child to play with it. When handling the 'boy' the mothers provided more verbal stimulation, more bouncing and jiggling activity, and offered it more assertive toys (such as a rubber hammer) to play with. The 'girl' was offered more soothing, reassuring activity, soft words and smooth caresses, and they chose cuddly toys for 'her' to play with. It seems that mothers' expectations lead to quite different experiences for the child.

► Fagot observed clear differences in the expectations parents have of their boys and girls. Boys were encouraged to be independent and assertive. Girls were encouraged to be passive and dependent.

### Cross-cultural evidence

If gender roles were biological in origin then we would expect that males and females everywhere would have similar roles and expectations. In the 1920s and 1930s **Margaret Mead** conducted some anthropological research among various peoples living in the Pacific region. She found dramatic differences in the ways boys and girls were treated, and in the personalities and behaviour of the adults which appeared to result. In one society there were no gender differences in the behaviour of the two sexes, in another the usual sex roles were reversed, with women being dominant. Although Mead's research has been criticized for sometimes relying on second-hand reports which may have been exaggerated, she does provide some evidence that gender roles result from childhood social experiences. Here is a brief summary of some of her observations.

► Anthropologists study the behaviour and cultures of groups of people who form different societies.

► NB Don't confuse Margaret Mead with George Herbert Mead mentioned earlier!

### Margaret Mead's anthropological studies for gender roles

The Arapesh were a poor, gentle, co-operative people. All jobs, including childcare, were shared equally by husband and wife. The children, too, were treated with respect. Aggression was virtually unknown in either sex. They were a humble, caring, loving people.

Among the Tchambuli, women socialized their male children to be artistic, creative and sentimental. The adult males would sit around the village gossiping, making themselves look pretty, and arranging entertainment for the women. The women took the lead in all matters. They were competitive, efficient and conducted all the group's trade and commerce. The men's lives revolved around the women except in times of war.

Among the Mundugumor people, males and females (both adults and youngsters) were aggressive, argumentative and suspicious of everyone else. They were forever spying on each other, making alliances and truces, and fighting. Children were not welcomed since they might form alliances against one of their parents. Both parents gave as little attention as possible to their children, and the children learned that they had to fight for everything they wanted.

### Influence of peers

It's not just adults who provide their children with models for appropriate gender role behaviour. Other children do, too. **Michael Lamb** studied three- to five-year-old boys and girls playing with a variety of toys. When the children played with their toys in a 'sex-appropriate way' the games were inventive and enjoyable. If a child picked up a toy which its same-sex peers thought was a 'cross-sex' toy (e.g. if a boy started to play with a doll), then they would be very critical and the doll would soon be rejected as the child rejoined its same-sex peers.

▶ Lamb's observational study shows that same-sex peers are a source of approval and disapproval for children as young as three and four.

### Androgenital syndrome

One final item of evidence to support the view that gender roles are learned comes from studies of a small number of androgenital syndrome (AGS) females who were mistakenly identified as boys when they were born, and the mistake went undiscovered for some time. (The infant female's genital organs looked like those of an infant male.) John Money (1972) found that if the error was realized before the child was about 18 months old, then appropriate surgery and changing the way the child was being socialized produced no major problems for the girl. If the error wasn't discovered until the child was three years or over, then there could be serious problems in changing the child's understanding of its sex and gender.

▶ AGS (androgenital syndrome), in very rare circumstances, can result in the wrong decision about the girl's sex being made. A very few girls have been raised as boys for the first few years of life before the error is realized.

Money reported the case of one girl who was thought to be a boy until she was three and a half years old. The parents decided that the risk to the child's personality of changing its sex and gender back to female was simply too great, and the decision was taken to continue to raise the child as a boy. With appropriate surgery and hormone treatment the 'boy' continued to behave like a boy, joining in with the other boys' active play, and taking a sexual interest in girls, etc.

Money also reports the case of a seven-month-old identical twin boy whose penis was damaged by faulty equipment during circumcision. Since he wouldn't be able to function as a male it was decided to make him into a girl. At 17 months he had surgery, and a course of hormone treatment began. With 'female' socialization the child soon started behaving as his parents thought a girl should. By the age of five the differences between the twins were considerable. The 'daughter' enjoyed feminine things such as playing with dolls, having her hair brushed and her face washed. She disliked being dirty, moved carefully and gently, and spoke softly. If gender roles were determined by innate forces then such a change in behaviour would not have been possible since this child was genetically male.

> ▶ Gender roles are the roles that people in society expect of us. Money's study suggests that these roles are largely determined by socialization. However, the children studied were having hormone treatments as well as changed socialization.

## Summary – Gender roles

Nativists claim that hormones and instincts are largely responsible for gender role behaviour. Maturation leads to sex differences in the way children behave, appearing by about two years. However, we have higher cognitive centres which influence our voluntary behaviour.

According to nurturists socialization is vital to acquiring gender behaviour. In our own society parents tend to treat their sons and daughters differently, and have different expectations of them, from a very early age. Cross-cultural studies give evidence of gender role behaviour being very different from Western norms. Studies of children whose sex has been changed after a few years also show that a new personality can develop as a result of changed socialization and hormone treatment.

■ **What evidence is there that gender roles are socially acquired?**

## Exam questions    60 minutes each

1 Compare and contrast explanations that take a relativist and a universalist view of moral development. (*25 marks*)
2 Identify some of the main factors in the self-concept and describe their origins. (*25 marks*)
3 'Boys and girls are made, not born.' Discuss. (*25 marks*)

# Part 6
*Psychological enquiry*

**17** # *The nature of psychological enquiry*

## Introduction

Psychology isn't a unified science with all psychologists agreeing on what they should study and how they should study it. Contrast the grand theories of Freud and Skinner, for example. Humanists and cognitive scientists disagree with both about what psychology should be, and how it should be conducted. Psychoanalytic theory and humanism might be regarded more as philosophy than psychology.

Skinner, Bandura and cognitive scientists see psychology as an applied science, and are called *positivists*. Positivists believe that all things can be studied by the tools of science and they reject any other explanation such as religion or philosophy. Positivists invent and conduct *empirical* research to investigate psychological issues. Empirical means real, actual investigations such as experiments and observations designed to gather some facts. We will review the major methods.

► See Chapter 1 for a discussion of the grand theories, and their alternatives, mentioned here.

## RESEARCH IN PSYCHOLOGY

## *Types of research*

Psychological research can be of three broad types, although some research may well combine them. First, *cross-sectional studies* look at

▶ A *sample* is simply that group that we have identified and are using in our study. Hopefully we have their informed consent.

one aspect of psychological functioning, such as childrearing style, or attitude to abnormal behaviour, in a large *sample* of participants who are, hopefully, typical of the whole group. The group is studied at the same time, so cross-sectional research provides a 'snapshot' of the population being studied. A 'cross-section' could include people of different ages, both sexes, different races, different cultures, and so on.

The main advantage to using cross-sectional research is that it is fairly fast and relatively easy to do. Its main limitation is that we can never be sure that the sample studied really is representative of the larger group.

*Longitudinal studies* take one group of people and study them at several points during their lives. They are useful for seeing the effects of age, or changing environments, on people's attitudes and behaviour, and are used particularly in developmental and social psychology. For example, longitudinal studies measure the extent to which people with similar previous experience (for example, having been orphaned), change after something intervenes in their lives, for example adoption. People from different social backgrounds could be studied at, say, 7, 14, 21 and 28 years of age. Their other advantage is that, since the same individuals are studied, they do not need to be matched in any way with any other group. The major drawbacks are that longitudinal research takes a long time to conduct, and we may lose some of our participants.

Third, we can study a particular group, for example babies below 12 months, or teenagers, in one society or culture and compare them with a similar group in another culture. This is *cross-cultural research*. Its major benefit is that it can show which aspects of development are the result of genetic inheritance (nature), and which are the result of social learning. If all babies start to walk at around ten months we might conclude that this is when they are (genetically) mature enough for walking. If children start walking at different ages in different cultures we might think it was because they were taught to walk at that age. A major problem with comparing people from different cultures is that the people doing the observations, testing and so on may be biased towards their own culture, believing it to be somehow superior to the others they are studying. This *cultural bias* will influence the integrity of cross-cultural findings.

▶ We use the word bias in at least two different ways in psychology. In this sense it is a form of prejudice. *Cultural bias* refers to any ways in which the person conducting or interpreting the research interprets the data in ways which make sense to them, as members of their own culture, but were not necessarily what the people studied intended.

■ What is meant by cross-sectional, longitudinal and cross-cultural research? Identify TWO topics in which psychologists might be (or have been) interested which could be studied by each, and explain why it is the most appropriate type of research for that topic.

## Ethics and research

Ethics is that branch of knowledge concerned with what is acceptable and unacceptable to members of society. It involves moral questions of right and wrong, good and bad, and is socially defined (i.e. it varies over time and place). Psychologists are interested in how and why people behave in the ways they do, and this involves collecting information from them. There is a danger that this might infringe people's civil liberties, and become ethically unacceptable.

The British Psychological Society (1985, 1990, 1995) publishes codes of practice and guidelines for conducting research which intend to ensure the highest possible standards. Its major concerns are to avoid exposing participants to psychological stress or physical danger. Participants should be informed about the nature of the research wherever possible, deception is to be avoided, and researchers must obtain the informed consent of their participants, and fully debrief them afterwards. Participants must be informed of their rights to withdraw from the research without feeling that they must justify their action. Participants' privacy and confidentiality must also be respected. The researchers must be competent in what they are doing, and the highest standards of personal conduct will be expected of them.

Some early research in psychology had been conducted before such guidelines were considered necessary. With the growth of civil liberties and other (including animal) welfare organizations, and the widespread access to information through the media, so people, including psychological researchers, have become more aware of the importance of ethical issues in research using people and animals. However, taking some of the concerns above, Asch's and Milgram's research did cause psychological stress to their participants (see Chapter 3, pages 48–52, 56–62), as did Zimbardo's prison simulation (see Chapter 3, pages 63–7), and Harlow's privated monkey research (Chapter 14, pages 319–20) caused physical harm. None of the participants in the bystander effect research (Chapter 4, pages 77–8) was informed as to the nature of the research, and the students in the computer dance experiments (Chapter 2, pages 26–7) were deliberately misled.

Ethical concerns have been expressed over some of the ways in which children's behaviour has been studied. Exposing children to models behaving in unacceptable ways was central to Bandura's research on aggression (Chapter 4, pages 87–9). Enriching institutionalized children's experiences is desirable, allowing others to continue to be deprived is not (Chapter 14, pages 321–3).

It seems that the only areas of psychology to have escaped major criticism on ethical grounds are the skills-testing approach of cognitive psychologists, and the area of psychopathology. Even here some procedures, such as plunging hands into icy water or administering mild electric shocks to test meaningfulness in memory, or treating depressed patients with ECT, are hardly acceptable to some people.

Most research organizations have ethics committees who consider such issues before any research can go ahead. They estimate the potential harm and weigh it against the potential benefit. They insist that parents are fully informed of the points above where children are involved, and where animals may suffer, the fewest possible may be used, and the knowledge gained has to be of considerable importance and value. For these (and other) reasons psychological research proceeds more cautiously now.

You may have noticed that most of the research criticized here took the form of an experiment. However, this isn't the only

► During the last thirty years the ethical acceptability of procedures used to gather psychological data involving human adults, children and animals has emerged as a serious concern for psychologists, and some of the research described in this book would not be permitted today.

■ **What is meant by ethics and why are ethical concerns important in psychology?**

► It seems that early psychology is littered with examples of research that infringed some people's civil liberties by today's standards. How would you have felt if you had been one of Milgram's or Zimbardo's participants? Would you have learned anything about yourself?

► ECT is a controversial treatment involving deliberately administering an electric shock to someone. It does work with some patients, whilst for others it causes traumatic side effects.

■ **What are some of the main ethical concerns in the way that researchers deal with their participants?**

▶ The most obvious method which may be considered unacceptable is the observation of people without their knowledge. However, such observations have contributed a great deal to our knowledge of behaviour in its natural setting.

▶ We are surrounded and bombarded by figures of one sort or another which are being quoted to support the claims of the people quoting them. All statistics are capable of interpretation.

▶ *Qualitative research* may become quantified later. After conducting countless hours of interviewing patients a psychiatrist might say that 60 per cent of his clients had schizophrenic tendencies, whilst 40 per cent suffered some form of depression.

▶ Positivism is the belief that all phenomena can be studied scientifically, and that this is the only legitimate approach to take to explaining things. Humanists insist that human feelings, thoughts and actions can't be studied scientifically since they arise in response to a complex interaction of biological, social, environmental and cognitive forces which cannot be quantified.

■  What is the difference between quantitative and qualitative research? Name some topics that could only usefully be studied by each, and explain why it must be studied that way.

method that psychologists employ to gather their data, and some others may be just as likely to have ethical implications. The choice of which method to use is the result of the researcher's personal preference, the aims of the research, the use to which the results are to be put, the issue being studied, what previous work has been conducted in this area, the type of participants being studied, the funds available, and potential ethical implications of using that method.

## Quantitative and qualitative research

*Quantitative research* gathers information in the form of numbers, or responses that can easily be converted into numbers, e.g. 80 per cent of thumb suckers do so for the same reason; the average IQ is 100; the average age at which babies say their first word is ten months; 10 per cent of all people in Britain will suffer serious mental health problems; 30 per cent of experimental participants switched their attention when their name preceded the instruction in the unattended ear experiments. We might choose to present the result of our analysis without giving the reason. So anorexia and bulimia sufferers are typically female, and nicotine suppresses bone regeneration.

*Qualitative research* asks for opinions, feelings, attitudes, motivations and so on. It can involve observations, discussions, case studies, interviews and other forms of information gathering. It provides detailed information, often about deeply personal or sensitive issues that could not be easily investigated using quantitative measures. Information about people's perceptions of themselves and their understanding about how other people see them is gathered by counsellors and therapists. It couldn't be gathered by experiments.

Those who believe that psychology should be an applied science that deals with gathering facts prefer quantitative methods. They are said to take a positivist view. Those who think psychology should be about finding out how people think and feel, and how best to help them understand and control their feelings and behaviour, prefer qualitative methods. They are more humanist in outlook. Others simply choose the approach most likely to discover what they need to know from the participants they are researching.

We can divide psychological methods into non-experimental and experimental. Non-experimental methods are favoured by humanist psychologists. Experimental (and quasi-experimental) methods are often preferred by positivists.

## NON-EXPERIMENTAL METHODS

## The observation method

There are several ways of conducting observations, and several reasons for doing so. We could conduct *naturalistic observations*, where the participants, i.e. the people (or animals) we are studying, are all visited in their own familiar environments, such as their own home, a busy street, a playground and so on. The participants may not know that their behaviour is being noted or recorded (possibly by hidden cameras). Alternatively, the researcher becomes familiar to the participants so that they continue to behave normally, despite knowing that they are being recorded. This method first became popular with ethologists from Konrad Lorenz in the 1930s. Child developmental psychologists study all forms of children's behaviour using naturalistic observation.

The advantage to psychologists of naturalistic observations is the very naturalness of the behaviour. This is real life and we can observe things that couldn't be studied by any other method. Naturalistic observation is said to have high *ecological validity* and can be used when it would be impossible or unethical to use any other method. The problems include the limited range of behaviour that can be studied in this way. People only show a small range of all their behaviour in streets, shops, classrooms etc. If someone knows they are being observed they may well behave differently. Observers may be influenced by their own opinions about what ought to happen. Another problem involves ethical questions concerning the right anyone has to spy on someone else without their knowledge. The guidelines say that only behaviour that could be observed by any stranger may be observed in psychological research.

Apart from naturalistic observations there are *controlled observations*. These are conducted by researchers who have deliberately set up a situation to see how someone will react. Mary Ainsworth's strange situation experiments (see Chapter 14, page 309) had cameras record babies' reactions to a stranger or their mother, and Zimbardo hid cameras to record his role players (Chapter 3, page 65). The advantages are that researchers can control exactly those aspects of the situation that they wish to investigate, and therefore need only record the behaviour that they are interested in. However, the more controlled a situation is, the less ecological validity the behaviour may have. People often respond to circumstances in the particular situation and this, too, may reduce the ecological validity of their behaviour.

Both naturalistic and controlled observations are *non-participant*, i.e. the researcher doesn't become involved with the participants. Non-participant observation allows the researcher to stay on the outside and remain detached and able to gather objective data. For example, watching the behaviour of the homeless from the security of a car will give some insights into their lifestyle. The advantage of this method is that it remains objective and allows for some measurement. However, it can never have the qualitative feel for the participants which participant observation can have.

In *participant observation* the observer becomes a part of the *target* group and observes them from the inside. One valuable way in which a psychologist can find out how it feels to be unemployed and homeless in a major city is to live on the streets for a few weeks.

► We all conduct observations. The only differences between our observations and those of psychologists is that we tend to make a relatively small number of observations on any one topic, and we may be rather quicker to give our opinions and judgements as to what caused the behaviour we saw. Psychologists try to be objective, describing precisely exactly what they see. They also try to make a large number of observations so they have more data on which to base their conclusions.

► *Ecological validity* refers to behaviour which occurs in everyday life.

► A *target* group or target population is the people at whom research is aimed. Hopefully we can study at least some of them.

The advantage of this method is that we get very detailed, ecologically valid, highly qualitative data, including quite personal information which reveals such things as attitudes, motivations, feelings, and so on. The disadvantages are that the researcher's own sympathies might be aroused and objectivity might be lost. The data lacks scientific measurement as well. It can also be ethically suspect, and if the people who are being studied find out, it can even be dangerous!

Finally there is *indirect observation*. A researcher might only observe secondary sources of data such as texts or transcripts of conversations, i.e. those sources which someone else has already gathered. The advantage here is that using existing data saves a great deal of time, since we don't have to gather it ourselves, but the data might not be exactly what the researcher wanted. Different questions might have been asked, different aspects of the topic might have been investigated, and so on.

## Surveys

Surveys consist of asking questions to find out people's attitudes, opinions, habits, interests, memories and so on. Surveys comprise interviews and questionnaires.

### Interviews

There are many forms of interview, ranging from the informal, casual chat to the formal clinical interview. They are useful for gathering sensitive data, and confidentiality is therefore most important. Questions should be asked sensitively, one at a time, and the *respondent* (interviewee) must be given time to understand and answer the question.

Interviews may be *structured* and *directive,* where the questions must be taken in the set order. These are used for market research and public opinion surveys rather than psychology. The answers can be quantified and predictions about other people's behaviour may be possible. The clinical interview, on the other hand, is used by psychiatrists and psychologists to gather personal data, and the questions are not usually planned beforehand. The next question asked usually depends on the answer to the previous question. Freud used clinical interviews to discover his patients' symptoms. Piaget used them to investigate children's reasoning.

The main advantages to informal, non-directive interviews is that people tend to answer more naturally, more spontaneously, and often more truthfully than they might in a more formal setting. Clinical interviews provide useful insights into people's mental states. There are problems, though. The main one concerns sampling (finding some respondents to answer the questions). Since most people don't give interviews to psychologists, those that are willing to be interviewed must be untypical. Also, it is not possible to make *generalizations* about anyone else's behaviour from clinical interviews. Whatever we understand about what's going on in your

► Outline the main types of observation and explain the usefulness to psychologists of each.

► *Respondents* are people who respond to questions posed by researchers.

► *Structured* interviews have the pre-set questions presented in a fixed order, and there is no room for clarification or further information. They are useful for gathering relatively simple information.

► To *generalize* means to make statements that apply to other similar people based on studies of some representatives of them.

head will not help us to understand someone else's mental state. Interviews are also expensive. One skilled interviewer may spend quite some time gathering information from just one respondent.

### Questionnaires

Questionnaires are almost written structured interviews. Questions are usually pre-set. They may require multiple choice or open-ended answers. A large sample is needed to make their conclusions useful. Questionnaires are useful for gathering factual information about people's behaviour, or for gathering opinions. If the sample is large enough then the conclusions may well apply to other, similar people. Questionnaires can be relatively cheap if many respondents answer them. There are some disadvantages, though. The wording of questions is quite a difficult task. An ambiguous word can make the whole question mean something different to different respondents. Constructing a reliable questionnaire can be difficult, time-consuming, and therefore expensive, particularly if only a few people are going to answer it.

Questionnaires aren't widely used by psychologists since people probably wouldn't give answers to the kind of questions psychologists might want to ask, although personality inventories are forms of questionnaire that have been used to investigate people's personalities. We can never be sure that respondents are telling the truth anyway.

## Case studies

Case studies are detailed studies of one individual or a small group. They often employ clinical interviews. They allow us to see the effects of one event on another, e.g. severe deprivation during one's early life and later personality, intelligence, social and emotional state (NB Chapter 14, studies by Harlow, Koluchova, Freud and Dann, Skeels and Dye, Dennis and Dennis), or the effects on personality that follow a stroke, heart attack etc. Freud's case studies (e.g. Little Hans, Anna O, the wolf man) are particularly well known.

Detailed case studies are essential in several types of therapy, and may reveal what is causing people's problems. Another advantage is that they allow us to study situations that we couldn't study using any other method. We couldn't deliberately deprive a child of love or stimulation in order to study their effects, yet we can study children who have been so deprived. The disadvantages are that we cannot generalize from one individual to anyone else, so have no way of knowing whether the same effects would follow the same events in other people's lives. Experiences that shape one individual's behaviour may not have been generally shared, or reacted to in the same way. Case studies also involve people trying to remember past events and how they felt at the time. We really cannot rely on people's memories at the best of times, even less so if those people have suffered some mental impairment.

■ Name some items that psychologists would use interviews to investigate. What are the benefits and drawbacks of the interview method for psychologists?

► It isn't usually possible to study everyone who possesses the characteristics we are interested in. We usually need to take a sample of them, and hope that the sample is typical of the rest.

■ Make a list of the uses and limitations of the case study as a method of gathering generally useful psychological data.

## Discourse analysis

Sometimes we need to say something to make a particular point. The point may be sympathetic and intended to be comforting, it may be funny, controversial, or trying to make others realize that our opinion is important or correct. We may choose our words carefully, or we may become confused. We may try to impress, or sound sincere. Discourse analysis has been developing during the last twenty years as a way of discovering what people's conversations actually reveal about how they truly think and feel about what they are saying. The way people construct their arguments, the order and manner in which they say things, the vocabulary they use, and the mannerisms they employ, can reveal much about their attitudes and understanding. For example, Stratton (1986) analysed the things family members said during family therapy sessions which enabled the therapist to be more effective.

The advantage of this method is that it can reveal insights into the way people who are being counselled regard the issues involved, or the way in which language can be used to attack, appease, negotiate or plead with others. The disadvantage is that some people have less-developed language skills than others; better-educated people may have more opportunity to develop language styles. A skilful talker might obscure his or her meaning through careful language use. Discourse analysis can contribute to an understanding of individual perceptions and might have a useful role in case studies.

## Psychometric tests

Psychologists have been trying to devise tests which accurately measure such mental attributes as intelligence, personality, motivation, social and political views as well as potential skills such as mechanical or musical aptitude. To devise a test to measure something assumes that it can be measured. Do we all have a certain amount of intelligence that can be measured? Do we all have a single personality that can be exposed by answering some questions in a psychological inventory? The answer is probably not. However, countless such tests are used throughout industry, commerce and the military to assess people's potentials (e.g. Crutchfield in Chapter 3). Presumably the people who use them imagine that they are measuring something useful.

Devising a test that is likely to be of any use at all is extremely difficult. It may be fun to do the 20-question tests in popular magazines which are supposed to show you who your ideal partner is, or whether you make a good friend or not, but they probably have no scientific truth at all.

## EXPERIMENTAL INVESTIGATIONS OF BEHAVIOUR

The main problem with methods such as case studies and naturalistic observations is that they only allow us to see what is happening, they do not allow for any control over any of the other *variables* in the research situation. A variable is anything that can vary in amount, frequency, or extent. The musical tone of a bell, a piece of food, the number of others present, or the behaviour of someone who is present, are examples of situational variables. Subject (participant) variables include extent of salivation, the likelihood of pushing a lever, giving a conformist response, or administering an electric shock. Experiments measure whether changing one of these variables could cause some change to occur in another.

► Research is often used to discover whether variables are related in any way.

## Controlled experiments

Control is the key to scientific research. To really see how one variable affects another we need to set up a situation in which the variables we are interested in can be present. We alter the state of one variable, called the *independent variable* (IV), and record any changes in the participant's responses, the *dependent variable* (DV), to it. Manipulating variables in various ways allows us to discover any consistent variations occurring between IVs and DVs such that we might be able to claim that the IV is causing a change in the DV.

► The state of independent variables is altered by the experimenter to measure if any corresponding change occurs in the dependent variable.

Let's imagine that we have noticed that we lose more money at arcade games after 9 p.m. than we do in the early afternoon. Our reaction time seems to get longer as we get more tired. This could form a *hypothesis*. A hypothesis is a statement of a relationship between two variables which researchers may wish to test. If this test takes the form of an experiment, we have an experimental hypothesis which investigates the likelihood that changes in one variable are causing changes to occur in another variable. Non-experimental methods may also investigate hypotheses, but are generally less likely to be able to show how changes in one variable cause changes in another. We could conduct a controlled experiment to discover if there is a relationship between the IV 'extent of fatigue' and the DV 'speed of reaction'.

First we must define precisely what we mean by each variable. So 'speed of reaction' becomes 'the time delay between the presentation of a light stimulus on a screen and pressing a computer key'. 'Extent of fatigue' becomes 'the level of arousal after 15 hours' wakefulness'. These are *operational definitions*. For the purposes of this research they are what we mean by extent of fatigue and speed of reaction.

► *Operational definitions* are the meanings we give to every variable we are hoping to control and measure in scientific research.

Let's take a sample of people, and divide them into two *experimental groups*. We'll test both groups' reaction times by getting them to hit the space bar on a computer keyboard as soon as they see a light appear on the screen, and we'll measure how long it takes. We'll wake them all up at 7 a.m. Group 1 can take the test at 2 p.m., seven hours after they woke. Group 2 can take their test eight hours later at 10 p.m. If all the members of Group 2 are quite a bit slower than the members of Group 1 we can claim that the DV reaction time is influenced by the IV, fatigue. We can also predict the direction of the influence – reaction time increases with fatigue.

► An *experimental group* is the group of participants who will be experimented upon. There may be several experimental groups in one experiment.

► A *hypothesis* is a statement of a relationship, usually between two variables, which researchers investigate. It may say that a relationship exists, or it might state the direction of the relationship.

■ **Explain why control is so important in designing and conducting experiments.**

► *Extraneous* means unwanted interference from the outside. *Confounding* means a failure to identify a second variable so that their joint effects cannot be separated.

■ **In view of your answer to the previous question, comment on the role of confounding in experiments.**

► A *control group* contains participants who are similar to the experimental group. Their behaviour is not manipulated by controlling any IVs. They are used for comparison purposes since any change in the experimental group's behaviour (DV) which is not matched by a change in the control group's behaviour may well be caused by the IV. Statistical tests will measure this likelihood.

The advantage of controlled experiments is that we can control and measure the variables we have identified and operationalized. If they do represent what the hypothesis claims for them, then we may well be able to say that we have supported our hypothesis. So if reaction time really can be measured by the speed with which someone can respond to a visual signal on a computer, and if fatigue is induced by having been awake for 15 hours, then we may claim that reaction time increases with fatigue. Of course, some of our sample won't behave according to our hypothesis! Some will be faster at night than others were earlier. We'll have to choose a statistical test that will allow us to decide the probability that the results we did obtain support our hypothesis.

Of course, there's always the chance that the researcher has overlooked another variable that could also be causing the DV to vary. Any variable that we have overlooked, or failed to appreciate that it could affect our results, is called an *extraneous variable*. Background noise could be an extraneous variable in a test of reaction time. Hopefully it won't have any effect, since our participants are concentrating on responding to a visual signal. If it does have an effect then it becomes a *confounding variable*. Confounding means allowing two variables to operate where we believe there is only one. If some of the changes in the DV which we are measuring are being caused by the confounding variable, not by the IV, then our claim that the slowdown in reaction time is the result of fatigue may be wrong. Our results and our study are confounded.

Another source of possible confounding comes from *constant error variables*. These occur where the situation or procedure that members of one group go through are different from those of another group. If those participants that had their reaction time tested early sat in warm, pleasant surroundings, and the late tested group sat in cold, miserable conditions, then the situational variables become constant error and could lead to confounding. Confounding doesn't just happen, it is usually the result of poor design.

### Participant groupings

Most research needs at least two groups, in which case one will be an experimental group. There might be several of these (experimental groups 1, 2, 3 etc.). The other group will be as similar to the experimental group as possible, and will not undergo any experimental manipulation. This is the *control group*. After the manipulation of the experimental group's IVs any changes in its DVs are measured and compared to the control group's DVs. Any differences in them are explained by the only thing that was different between the two groups, the manipulation of the experimental group's IVs.

### Research design

This refers to how we place our sample into the various experimental groups. It must be accomplished carefully as it is a source for potential confounding. There are four possibilities.

## 1 Repeated measures

In a repeated measures design all the participants are placed in each of the *experimental conditions*, i.e. the 2 p.m. condition and the 10 p.m. condition. The advantage is that we obtain twice the number of scores. The problem here is that some of their performances in the 10 p.m. condition may be caused by boredom or practice, since they have already been tested at 2 p.m. If so we have a boredom or a practice effect. Both are examples of *order effects*, because they result from the order in which the tests are taken.

One way to minimize order effects is simple *counterbalancing*, i.e. have half the participants do the 2 p.m. test followed by the 10 p.m., and the other half to do the 10 p.m. on one day and the 2 p.m. the next. Or leave a few days between each test. An alternative is complex counterbalancing, i.e. 50 per cent do the test in the morning then evening (the AB condition), and 50 per cent do evening then morning (the BA condition); then average all the morning (Condition A) scores and average all the evening (Condition B) scores.

Several problems may occur with repeated measures design. For example, the aim of the research can become obvious and the participants may distort their behaviour to fit in with what they think the researcher wants. This is *participant expectation*. Participants may not always be available to be in each experimental condition. Other commitments might mean they will be absent when the test is conducted. Having extra participants to begin with so that we still end up with an acceptably sized sample will increase the complexity and the expense.

It is not possible to use repeated measures when order effects simply can't be eliminated or when it is necessary to use new participants in each condition. Sometimes research will involve representatives from particular groups within society, such as students, the middle class, housewives, and so on. If we compare students to non-students on certain tests, then we can't use the same people in each condition! On the other hand, co-action and audience effects (Chapter 3) are well demonstrated using repeated measures design.

## 2 Independent groups

In independent groups design participants are simply distributed randomly between the various experimental or control groups. If there is a large sample this is usually the best design. With enough participants the groups should be pretty similar to each other, and fairly typical of the whole population. Or if we have two particular groups to study, e.g. boys and girls, then we would have a boy's group and a girl's group.

An obvious drawback of this method compared to repeated measures concerns the number of scores we obtain from our participants. In repeated measures where each participant is placed in two experimental conditions we have two scores for each participant. If there were three experimental conditions we would have

▶ Earlier we said that experimental groups were the participants in an experiment. An *experimental condition* describes what happens to them, i.e. the particular IVs that they are going to be tested on.

▶ *Counterbalancing* will not eliminate potential order effects. It can only hope to minimize them.

■ **What is the difference between experimental groups and experimental conditions?**

■ **Outline repeated measures research design, mentioning benefits and drawbacks.**

■ **Think of two topics that psychological researchers might be interested in which could usefully be investigated with this design, and two which could not.**

▶ In statistics a population is simply any group that we have identified. If we intend to use some of them in some research they become a target population. From this we draw a sample to use according to our research design.

■ What is the essential difference between repeated measures and independent groups design?

■ Which design would be most appropriate for researching the relationship between the dependent variable 'speed of reaction time' and the independent variable 'degree of fatigue':
(a) repeated measures,
(b) independent groups,
(c) either? Explain your answer.

three scores per participant. In independent groups we have one score per participant, so we'll need twice or three times as many participants. This increases the cost and the risk of complications. However, there are some topics which can only be investigated using this design, for example the conformity experiments of Asch and Crutchfield, and Milgram's and Zimbardo's obedience experiments, could only use their participants once (see Chapter 3).

*3 Matched participants*
Very occasionally we may be able to match the groups for the main independent variables, so that we might be even more confident that the groups are as similar as possible. The drawbacks are obvious. Where would we get a sample that would contain enough participants to find identical groups? We don't even always know what the key variables are. Even if we did, testing for them would take a very long time and would be very expensive. Matched participants design is only ever used really with identical twins.

*4 Single participant design*
Very occasionally it is possible to use a single participant to gather data from which further hypotheses can be drawn. Hermann Ebbinghaus (Chapter 13, page 277) devoted many hours to learning lists of German nonsense syllables in order to investigate human memory capacity. Some scientific researchers have used themselves as guinea pigs to test out a new drug or treatment. Sigmund Freud used cocaine in this way (for ten years!). The obvious drawback is that it isn't possible to generalize from a single participant to anyone else in psychological research.

### Controlled experiments – Conclusion
A great deal of useful information about human functioning has been obtained from controlled laboratory studies, particularly in the areas of cognitive, social and developmental psychology. However, by no means all behaviour can be tested in a laboratory study. For example, we couldn't learn much about the dynamics of family life or the psychopathology of schizophrenia in a laboratory experiment.

## Field experiments

Field experiments are conducted in the participants' own natural environment. Playgrounds for studying children, maternity wards for studying the newborn and their caregivers, the classroom for seeing the effects of teaching styles, a dance for assessing the effects of dating technique, are all useful venues for field experiments. In each the IVs are going to be manipulated by the researcher. All the people at Berscheid and Walster's 'computer dance' were matched for their level of attractiveness (see Chapter 2).

Generalizations can usually be made about the behaviour of others from the findings of field experiments since the participants do not know that they are in an experiment, so their behaviour should be fairly typical or customary. However, because little control over the environment is possible, there is the possibility that extraneous variables could intervene and confound any results.

## Natural experiments

Some topics simply cannot be studied by controlled or field experiments. The effects on the personality (DV) of a prefrontal lobotomy (IV) is one! Would you volunteer to be in the sample? In natural (or naturalistic) experiments the IVs already exist and do not need to be controlled. There are some people who have had prefrontal lobotomies. We may be able to find some and conduct experiments on them (following all ethical guidelines, of course).

The benefit of this method is that quite natural behaviour is observed, but there is even less control over the IVs than in field experiments. Many variables that we might want to investigate may not exist naturally. Even if they do, we may not be able to study them for ethical, legal or practical reasons.

■ Outline what is meant by field and natural experiments, and identify two topics that could be investigated using them.

## Degrees of control

Laboratory experiments attempt to control the independent (and other relevant) variables and precisely measure the dependent variable. If our sample is representative and our design effective then we may be able to claim that we have found support for our hypothesis. The problem is that everything might be so tightly controlled that the situation becomes highly artificial and doesn't reflect real life at all. For example, Asch (Chapter 3) had six or eight students saying that a particular line was the same length as another, when it clearly was not, to see if the naive participants would agree. This was supposed to help explain conformity in our everyday lives.

In order of degree of control in experiments we have:

Controlled experiments
Field experiments
Natural experiments

## THE SCIENTIFIC METHOD

The scientific method is the name of the procedure that all scientists use for their investigations. It has several stages and always starts with observation.

## Observation

Observation may be made quite deliberately, because we want to know more about something. For example, Martin Hughes observed that Piaget claimed that five-year-old children are egocentric, so set up his 'policeman doll' and 'boy doll' experiments (see

► By bias we mean a form of prejudice whereby we take an attitude that favours a particular outcome or conclusion. Any research conclusions drawn will have been influenced by that prejudice and so can't be entirely trusted.

► *One-tailed hypotheses* predict the direction in which the DV will change. *Two-tailed hypotheses* predict that a change will occur.

► A *null hypothesis* states that changes in the dependent variable aren't actually dependent on changes in the independent variable at all. Any changes that do occur happen by chance. We use statistical tests to measure the likelihood that any changes did occur by chance. If they find that such changes are too great to have occurred by chance, we will reject the null hypothesis.

■ **Distinguish between the experimental and the null hypothesis.**

Chapter 15). Or the observation might have been quite accidental, such as noticing that you lose more at arcade games at night than in the afternoon.

According to **James Deese** (1972), all research is partially biased because it is based on observations which the researcher has interpreted in some way. That particular topic must have interested the researcher, otherwise why bother to research it? Presumably Martin Hughes had an interest in children's cognition, which is why he knew about Piaget's research, and why he wanted to test it. Deese would argue that Hughes' research must, therefore, be biased.

## Hypotheses

Having made our observation we state what we expect to find as a hypothesis. We said earlier that a hypothesis is a statement of the relationship that we predict exists between IVs and DVs. Hypotheses can predict exactly what will happen to the DV when changes occur in the IV, for example 'Fatigue lengthens reaction time'. This is called a *one-tailed hypothesis* because it specifies the tail or direction in which the change is predicted. Or hypotheses might say that the DV will change, without specifying how. For example, 'Fatigue affects reaction time'. This is a *two-tailed hypothesis*. It says that there is a relationship between the variables, but does not predict which way it goes.

Scientists use statistical tests to analyse their findings. These are tests of probability, i.e. they test the likelihood that the data could have occurred by chance. When scientists state their hypothesis they also state a *null hypothesis*. This says that no relationship exists between the variables, and any that is found occurs by chance. So the hypothesis 'Reaction time lengthens with fatigue' would also be stated in the null form 'Reaction time is not affected by fatigue, and any change in reaction time that is observed happens by chance'. In reality, therefore, we actually test the null hypothesis rather than the experimental hypothesis. If the null hypothesis is supported, then the experimental hypothesis must be rejected. If the null hypothesis is rejected, then the experimental hypothesis is supported.

## Sampling

Unfortunately, psychologists can't usually afford to study very large groups of people so most researchers choose a sample from their target population to represent the rest. Hopefully, the sample chosen will be representative (typical) of all the other members of the target population, otherwise any conclusions drawn from the research may not apply to the rest of the target population, and the research is confounded. The members of your class wouldn't necessarily be representative of the target population 'all psychology students'.

There are several methods by which psychologists might draw a sample. The one chosen will depend on factors such as the researcher's preferences, the time and resources available, the use to which the data is to be put, the nature of the research, and so on. The primary aim is to have a sample that is typical of the target population it represents. Here are some of the main ones used by psychologists.

### Self-selected samples

Milgram (Chapter 3) and other psychologists have advertised in local newspapers for their participants. Those people who reply are self-selected volunteers. According to **J.P. Ora** (1965), most volunteers for early psychology experiments are far from typical of people generally. He claims they are generally more insecure, dependent on others, introverted, aggressive, neurotic and suggestible.

### Random samples

In a random sample every member of the target population has the same chance of being chosen as everyone else. This is rarely used where the target population is large, or not easily accessible. However, if members of the target population all have key variables in common, then any of them could make a useful random sample. Bickman and Beattie used 'passers by' in their obedience research (Chapter 3). They were randomly chosen.

### Opportunity samples

Those participants the researcher can most easily get hold of and persuade to participate in the research (often their students!) are opportunity samples. According to George Miller, 90 per cent of American psychology experiments have used American college students as their participants, yet the results are still generalized to a wider target population. Are American college students representative of all Americans? Or all people?

### Imposed samples

These have no choice about being included in the sample since they don't actually know they're being studied! Most early social psychological research used covert research (where the true purpose is hidden or disguised). Latané and Darley's respondents are examples (see Chapter 3).

Other methods less favoured by psychologists include:

### Systematic samples

A list is made up of the names of all the members of the target population and every third or eleventh or whatever other number (called *n*th) name is taken. If researcher's can't find such a list (called a *sampling frame*), then they won't be able to draw a systematic sample.

### Stratified samples

If the target population has distinctive groupings within it (e.g. A-level psychology students, undergraduates, post-graduates etc.) then the sample might be similarly stratified, with some A-level, undergraduate and post-graduate students.

### Quota samples

There must be the same ratio of male to female undergraduates, post-graduates etc. in the sample as there are in the target popula-

▶ It's probably impossible to find a sample that is truly representative of many target populations, because we usually can't know what the whole target population is really like anyway. How could we discover the characteristics of all the psychology students in Britain to see if our sample were representative of them? This isn't usually a major problem, however.

tion. The ratio of all other distinguishing features must be similarly distributed. This is extremely difficult, hardly worth it, and is rarely used by psychologists.

*Cluster samples*

These are drawn from particular areas where people (or animals) are most likely to possess whatever characteristics the researcher wants. If we want to study long-term memory and the elderly, we could contact some managers of retirement homes to see if we might gain access.

*Snowball samples*

These largely generate themselves and aren't drawn by the researcher in the same way as the others. For example, a researcher investigating illegal drug use might talk to a few users he knows who might then suggest some others he could talk to, and they might suggest others still.

None of these methods guarantees to provide a sample which is necessarily truly representative of the target population, although any of them might.

It may strike you that the larger the sample is, the more representative it is likely to be. A sample of 20 psychology students couldn't have enough A-levellers, undergraduates and post-graduates to contain representatives from each ethnic minority, age group and gender. A sample of 1,000 psychology students stands a much better chance. The problem that researchers face, however, is that the more participants they study, the more testers, recordings, computer time and so on there has to be, and the more expensive the research is to conduct. On the other hand, the fewer (and therefore cheaper) participants there are, the less representative they are likely to be, and the less useful the results may be. The size of the sample will often be a compromise between what we want and what we can afford!

## Conducting a pilot study

Some of our participants may be used in a pilot study, i.e. a small number may be put through the experiment to check that there is nothing wrong with its procedures. Any snags in the design, materials or procedures should show up and can be ironed out before the proper experiment begins.

## Gathering the data

By now the research has been designed with reference to ethical and practical constraints, the materials and apparatus are in place, and the participants have been found and placed into each experimental group. All participants must now be briefed on the instructions and procedures of the experiment in exactly the same way. This is called giving *standardized instructions and procedures*. If some participants heard different instructions or the same words

■ What sampling and method was used by the following researchers?
(a) Freud and Dann studying the Bulldogs Bank children (Chapter 14)
(b) Bowlby's 44 juvenile thieves (Chapter 14)
(c) Kohlberg on moral development (Chapter 16)
(d) Newcomb and friendships (Chapter 2)
(e) Zimbardo and his 'prison' (Chapter 3)

▶ *Standardization* is essential to scientific research. The only difference that should exist between members of various groups should be the IV. Inadequate standardization could introduce other differences and could confound the research.

presented differently, or underwent the procedures in a different way, then we can't fairly compare their performance.

When the data has been gathered participants must be debriefed, i.e. told exactly what the research was all about, and how their part has contributed to it. They must be thanked for their effort, and encouraged to ask any questions or seek further information, either then or in the future. The key objective is to make sure that the participants leave the research in just the same psychological condition as they were in when they started it. They are told that they must contact the researchers in future if they have any need to discuss what has happened during the research.

## Analysis of the data

The nature of the research will largely determine which statistical test to use, so it can now be employed to see if the data does support the null hypothesis or not. If it does, we have not found support for the experimental hypothesis, and it must be rejected. If it does not support the null hypothesis, we can reject the claim that the data could have occurred by chance. Assuming that we have conducted our research in an absolutely honest and accurate way, then we can claim to have found support for our experimental hypothesis.

## Stating a theory

If the hypothesis has been accepted it can be used in support of a particular theory. Theories are suggestions about how things work (such as selective attention or memory – see Chapters 12 and 13) and can result from experimental hypotheses that have been supported by research. Or theories can be suggested first (such as Freudian psychoanalytic theories – see Chapter 1) and support for them sought from testing hypotheses afterwards.

■ Outline the main stages in the scientific method.

## Correlational research

Unlike the methods described so far, *correlation* is not a device for collecting data. Instead it is a statistical procedure for analysing sets of data that have already been gathered. Correlation measures the relationship between those variables which couldn't be measured in other ways. For example, are heavy smokers more likely to be amongst the groups who are at most risk from cancer? Are people who are most likely to conform in social situations also most likely to be less confident? Are the people who own the most books also likely to be amongst the better-educated groups? Experiments are intended to show the differences between groups of people, correlations are intended to show similarities between them.

Some psychologists claim that they can measure intelligence and personality. We could hypothesize that extraverts (outgoing, sociable people) are more intelligent than introverts (shy, solitary people). One hundred people could be asked to complete personality questionnaires and intelligence tests. Each person therefore provides two scores, a score on the personality scale between introvert and extravert, and an IQ score. Applying a correlational procedure would allow us to measure the extent to which the scores were related or co-varied.

Correlation can be described by a number called a *co-efficient of correlation*. If the two sets of scores are related, as the hypothesis predicts, we have a positive correlation and the co-efficient will be above 0 and up to +1. If the opposite occurs then we have a negative correlation, expressed as a minus number below 0 and down to –1. The nearer to +1 or – 1 the co-efficient is, the more (or less) true the hypothesis has been found to be. The nearer to 0 the co-efficient is, the less likely it is that the relationship we predicted between them, or its opposite, exists. There may be no relationship at all between them, or there may be a relationship that we have not tested.

Correlations can also be displayed as a special form of graph called a *scattergram,* where each individual's scores are plotted. If we have a positive relationship they will rise from the bottom left of the graph towards the top right. If the relationship is negative they start at the top near the vertical axis, and descend to the bottom right, as shown in figure 17.1.

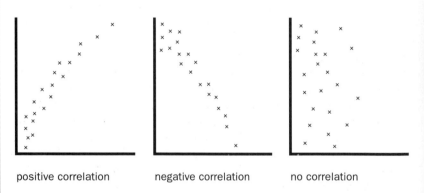

positive correlation        negative correlation        no correlation

*Figure 17.1  Scattergrams*

### Evaluation of correlational research

Correlation can show both the direction and the strength of the relationship between two variables which might not otherwise be measured. The variables may occur naturally, or may need to be measured in some other way. Second, correlations may allow us to make predictions. If we know that there is a positive correlation between heavy smoking and the incidence of lung cancer, we can make a prediction that people who smoke heavily are more likely to suffer from lung cancer in the future. However, there are limitations, the main one being that correlation is only a statistical device for measuring if a relationship does exist, and if so how strong it is, between variables. Correlation makes no suggestion that one variable may be causally related, i.e. that one is causing the change in the other. There are obviously no IVs and DVs in correlation.

## SOME ISSUES IN CONDUCTING SCIENTIFIC RESEARCH

The problems (and the joys) of psychology lie in its subject matter – people. People do and think all sorts of things for all sorts of reasons. For example, someone may not answer some questions truthfully, so conclusions from those methods which rely on asking questions may not be sound. Participants in experiments may try to guess the purpose of the research, and act accordingly. Or an unwary (or unscrupulous) researcher may interpret some responses to fit in with what he or she wants to find. These are participant and experimenter effects.

## Participant and experimenter effects

Humans are social creatures. We seek out the company of other humans and can work co-operatively as well as individually. In any social situation there are group dynamics. That is, we behave in different ways according to who's watching us (audience effects), who's with us (co-action effects), who we're working for (leadership characteristics), who's paying us, what we think people expect of us, and so on. A psychology experiment is a social situation too.

### Participant expectations

No one likes being in a situation where they don't know what's going on or what they should do. It could be embarrassing or even dangerous. So we try to find out. If we know what's going on we're less likely to get caught out and appear foolish or inexperienced. Participants who take part in psychology experiments are also active in the way they interpret the situation. They look for clues about what it's about and what they should do. **Martin Orne** (1962) calls them *demand characteristics*. Participants derive their expectations from such sources as:

- The verbal or written instructions and any other verbal communication with the researchers during the experiment.
- The researcher's tone of voice and non-verbal signals such as facial expressions, body posture, hand movements etc.
- What the participant may have heard about the experiment from others who have taken part in it, or in any other research.
- How the participant was approached to take part in the experiment in the first place.
- The participant's characteristic responses, for example someone who is shy might wonder why a shy person would be asked to take part in this experiment.
- Where the experiment is conducted. The setting may give clues about what sort of behaviour is appropriate.

### Experimenter effects

It is very important that the experimenter does not hint to participants how they should behave. Non-verbal as well as verbal clues must be guarded against. The experimenter must try to be absolutely impartial. Where the experimenter does, even unconsciously, provide clues as to what to expect, we have experimenter effects.

Experimenter effects were demonstrated by **Robert Rosenthal** (1966). He noticed that male experimenters are far more likely to smile at female participants than at male participants. Since a smile often elicits another in return, any study on sex differences conducted by men would be confounded. In a classic demonstration of experimenter effects, Rosenthal told a sample of several hundred students that they would be studying maze learning in rats. Half the participants were told that they would be given some rats who were quick to learn to run a maze and it was up to the students to selectively breed them to see if maze running was biologically transmitted. The other half had slow-learning rats to breed. The students were asked to observe their rats running mazes to confirm that each group had the right rats, which they did. Several generations of rats were bred and the descendants of the 'maze-bright' rats became even better at learning to run mazes, and the slow rats became even slower. Only then did Rosenthal reveal that he had randomly assigned rats to the two conditions in the beginning. Having given the students an expectation of what they would find, they found it. Sherif's autokinetic effect experiment (Chapter 3) demonstrates the experimenter effect as well.

Fortunately, there are ways of reducing experimenter effects in controlled experiments. These are single-blind and double-blind procedures.

### Single-blind and double-blind procedures

In a single-blind procedure the participants do not know whether they are in an experimental or a control condition. For example, in a study to test the effectiveness of a new drug to control schizophrenia 50 per cent of a group of schizophrenics may be given the new drug, the other 50 per cent being given the old drug. None of the participants knows which of the drugs he or she is taking. This way participants' behaviour shouldn't be influenced by their knowledge of their medication. This should reduce participant expectations.

In a double-blind procedure neither the participants nor the researcher know which participants are in which condition. A third party has allocated the participants. This should reduce both participant and experimenter expectations.

## Reliability and validity of psychological research

Two further considerations must be made to ensure that our research is scientifically acceptable. A test is *reliable* if the same sample produces the same results when tested on subsequent occa-

▶ *Reliability* is related to consistency. A reliable test yields consistent results if repeated.

sions. Intelligence tests are claimed to measure intellectual capacities which aren't supposed to change over time. If someone's IQ is measured by a particular test to be 103 on one occasion, it should be about the same when the test is repeated in the future. If so, the test is said to be reliable.

A test is said to have *internal validity* if it can be shown that it actually measures exactly what it claims to measure. If an IQ test can be shown to measure intelligence then it would be internally valid. Since psychologists can't agree as to what exactly intelligence is, they won't generally agree on whether there is any such thing as a valid IQ test. The authors of IQ tests, on the other hand, claim that it isn't necessary to define something in order to measure it and so claim that their tests are valid. A test is said to have *external validity* if we can generalize its conclusions to other members of the target population.

▶ Is the driving test a valid and reliable measure of driving ability? Is a job interview a valid measure of an applicant's suitability?

### What makes good research?

There are three standards which are accepted as good practice in conducting scientific research in psychology. Humanist psychologists would strongly disagree with each of them.

1  It should be possible to generalize from the conclusions of scientific research conducted on a representative sample to the rest of its target population. Positivists claim that there's little value in studying any group if we can't apply our findings from it to other groups.
2  It should be possible to replicate the study, i.e. to follow its procedures exactly, accepting the same definitions of variables, and arrive at the same conclusions.
3  The measures used in the study must be valid. If the research isn't actually testing what it claims to be testing there's not much point in doing it.

■ Note some of the issues involved in conducting scientific research.

## Evaluating the positivist approach

The advantages of the scientific (positivist) approach are that it provides precise operational definitions of all the behaviour that is to be studied and the procedures that will be used. All variables are carefully controlled and all materials and procedures are strictly standardized. All this leads to being able to make scientific predictions about relationships and events.

On the other hand, positivists have to control their variables and procedures so precisely that the test situation can bear little resemblance to real life (e.g. Sherif's autokinetic effect, Asch's target line matching, and Milgram's electric shock research). Further, positivists may assume that their participants are typical or representative of others, but is this ever certain?

But if we are to be cautious about the use of the scientific approach, what might we want to replace it with, or at least use in conjunction with it? The main alternative is advocated by those who support the humanist approach. Humanism tries to study human behaviour in its natural context, with all its meaning. Humanists reject experiments that isolate bits of behaviour from their social context and study them in the laboratory. Instead, they prefer methods that allow qualitative data to be gathered. These include naturalistic observation, open-ended surveys, the diary method and case studies.

No doubt there is room in such a broad subject as psychology for both approaches to co-exist, and each may be useful and appropriate for investigating particular types of behaviour.

## ISSUES IN PSYCHOLOGY

Earlier we mentioned the importance of ethics as an issue in conducting psychological enquiries. Several other issues have been raised concerning the nature of psychology itself. Here are three of the main ones.

### Determinism versus free will

► Positivists believe that human behaviour can be predicted, explained, and largely controlled by the application of scientific principles.

► Behaviourism declined as an explanation for all human behaviour in the 1960s. However, it still offers some useful and effective ways of shaping behaviour.

This issue is essentially a philosophical one concerning the extent to which human behaviour results from external influences determining what we do, or our own free will to choose our actions. It occupied scientific, positivist and behaviourist psychologists, who said that behaviour is shaped, and can be determined by reinforcements, and humanist, intuitive psychologists who favour the role of free will. With the decline of behaviourism, and the emergence of much more interesting areas of psychology, the debate has long since passed its 'sell-by' date.

The actions of parts of machines are determined by the actions of other parts. The actions of plants and trees are determined by the climate, soil conditions, and the actions of some animals. Even much of the behaviour of most lower-order animals is largely determined by instinct and events in their immediate environment. Human actions are determined by many things, especially complex mental events involving thinking. The range of human behaviour is vast, from creating amazing music, art, architecture and fashion to destroying ourselves (through smoking), other animals (through hunting), other people (through war), and even the planet itself (through pollution)!

Since human talents for glory and destruction are so great, philosophers have asked whether we ourselves are controlled by internal and external forces, our genes, our environments, our diet and our daily lives? Do these constraints upon us drive us towards doing certain things that anyone in a similar situation would inevitably do? In which case, much of our behaviour is, at least partly, not under our control.

Or do we have total freedom to choose what to do in most circumstances? Can we refuse to obey when we think the order is wrong, even when everyone else is obeying? Are we independent, intelligent creatures that must go our own way in the world, regardless of others if they strongly disagree with us?

### The determinist case

Determinism is the belief that everything has a cause, and ultimately that cause can be discovered. The aim of science may to be 'to predict, in order to explain, in order to control'. Science seeks cause and effect to discover how one variable changes as another one does. This is fine if we are dealing with physical things such as 'if we apply enough heat to water when it reaches a certain temperature it will boil', or 'if we bend a piece of wood so far it will snap'. But does human behaviour follow similar principles that can be discovered by science?

If we are going to apply scientific principles and procedures to human behaviour then we must be assuming that there are universal laws which govern it. These laws may explain behaviour being caused either by changes in chemical relationships in the brain and body (the molecular, psychophysiological level of analysis). Or behaviour is explained as the consequence of social experiences. Either way, science may be looking for any universal laws by manipulating IVs and measuring DVs. This is a determinist approach.

If any such principles can be found scientists can claim that people are not entirely responsible for their own actions. These actions are caused by changes in body chemistry or social experiences. There is little point in praising someone for doing well, or punishing them when they do badly, if what they do is largely the result of their body state or living conditions. The more we pursue universal causes of behaviour the less it makes sense to hold people responsible for theirs.

### The free will view

The moral/humanistic view is that people have something called 'free will' to choose how to react to everything that happens to them. Each person's experiences have been unique. It isn't possible to generalize from one person to another, and doesn't make much sense to generalize from one group (a sample) to another (a population). However, behaviourists would claim that free will, if any such 'thing' exists at all, is simply another set of chemical states that we call our state of mind, which then determines our behaviour.

### The interactionist view

There is a possible third course. To say that something as vast and complex as human behaviour can be explained by either one thing or another is very limited. Some aspects of human behaviour will be determined by our biology (such as eating). Some will be determined by circumstances (e.g. what and where we eat). Some may well reflect free choice (e.g. whether to have a pizza or a sandwich).

It is quite reasonable to believe that behaviour is the result of free will and still conduct scientific studies of it. Just because we are free to choose does not mean that twenty people will all choose differ-

▶ The determinist view sees aspects of human behaviour being determined by forces beyond our control.

ently. Freedom to choose doesn't mean the choice will be random. Many people might freely choose the same course of action in certain circumstances. In this case we need to make observations and to conduct scientific research.

Rather than trying to solve the 'free will versus determinism' problem we might do better to understand why we might behave in certain ways, and what we are attempting to achieve. This could be achieved partly through scientific study and partly through humanistic interview and interaction.

## *Reductionism versus holism*

Reductionism is the view that complex human behaviour such as cooking a meal or falling in love are best understood when they are broken down into smaller parts and each part analysed in turn. We might gain a better understanding of our meal if we analysed it into mixing the pastry, peeling the onions, washing the lettuce, boiling the rice etc. When it came to enjoying the meal, would such knowledge be of any interest? Can human thinking and feelings be reduced to biochemical reactions to help us understand what we do? No one doubts that ultimately human experience does involve neurological and biochemical reactions. The question is, would studying those reactions help us understand the experience?

William James, one of the founders of academic psychology, tried to reduce human experience to the level of individual sensations (James 1890). Radical behaviourists such as B.F. Skinner (1969) claim that complex learning is only the result of individual S–R associations that have been built up by selective reinforcement. Some psychologists such as Hans Eysenck (1947) continue to argue that human personality is made up of individual traits such as introversion, neuroticism, leadership ability, social responsiveness etc., which can be separated out and studied individually.

However, whilst it may be helpful to a mechanic to reduce a car engine to all its parts in order to learn how they fit together, it doesn't always make sense to try to understand human experiences in this way. For example, a goodnight kiss between boyfriend and girlfriend could be reduced to muscle contractions, co-ordination, controlled breathing and so on. But would this help us to understand why those two people are behaving like that? It would be impossible to learn to drive by learning how to steer first, then learning how to change gear, then how to make the car go forward. Several of these skills have to be learned at the same time.

The alternative to reductionism is holism. This philosophical approach claims that the only way we can understand something is by seeing it as a whole, in its natural context. Freudian psychoanalytic theory takes a holistic view of the personality resulting from the mix of id, ego and superego, driven by libido and death instincts, through the four stages of development using a variety of defence mechanisms to prevent excessive trauma from disrupting the process.

The 'reductionism versus holism' debate centres around the ques-

■ Which side of the free will versus determinism debate would each of the following take?
(a) Freudian psychoanalysts
(b) Skinnerian behaviourists
(c) Humanist psychologists

▶ A reductionist approach would be favoured by determinists.

▶ It makes sense to reduce mechanical devices to their parts. It wouldn't make sense to reduce them any further (by melting them down to their base metal?).

tion of 'what is/are the appropriate levels of analysis on which to base our understanding of human functioning?' **Rose** (1976) says the way to answer this is to see all levels of analysis as a hierarchy, each level having some contribution to make to the final understanding.

holistic

SOCIOLOGICAL

SOCIAL PSYCHOLOGICAL

PSYCHOLOGICAL

PHYSIOLOGICAL

BIOCHEMICAL

CHEMICAL

reductionist          PHYSICAL

*Summary of Rose's hierarchical model*

## The nature–nurture debate in psychology

We have mentioned the nature–nurture debate many times in this book. It concerns the relative contribution to our present state of genetic, biological forces, and environmental, social, learned experiences. The contribution of biology and environment to particular features of human functioning was thought to be important since it would shape society's response to it. For example, if academic performance was determined by intelligence which was genetically inherited, then there wouldn't be much point offering remedial classes and extra help. If it was influenced by social factors then those who are most deprived could have their experiences enriched (Project Headstart – see Chapter 14). Here is a brief summary of the two sides.

► The nature–nurture debate is also called the heredity versus environment debate, since it concerns the influences of inheritance and experience.

### Nature versus nurture

*Nature*

Humans inherit some of their characteristics, such as sex, skin, hair and eye colour, likely height and weight, facial and body shape, through biological transmission. Early psychologists (Binet, Burt, Spearman) and some later ones (Chomsky and Eysenck), believe that psychological features such as intelligence and aspects of personality are also genetically transmitted. Much research has been undertaken to support the claim that aspects of perception such as distance and direction are present soon after birth and so are probably biologically transmitted.

*Nurture*

Humans have tremendous cognitive skills (such as thinking, reasoning, planning, predicting, remembering, interpreting). The capacity for developing these skills is genetically inherited. However, how these skills develop, and what they allow us to do subsequently, is best understood as resulting from social experiences such as socialization, childrearing styles, teaching and learning, identification, observation, imitation and modelling.

■ Name some psychological theories and studies that have emphasized the role of experience in some of these.

A more recent emphasis in this debate concerns how nature and nurture accounts for the differences between people rather than their similarities. From analysis of the results of intelligence test scores Eysenck (1971) claimed that differences in intelligence can be found between the performance of different racial groups (although the many problems with the testing used here means this claim may not be acceptable). There are wide differences in intelligence and personality between people from within any large group. The precise contribution of each cannot be known.

# Further reading

Agras, W.S. et al. (1974) 'Behaviour modification of anorexia nervosa', *Archives of General Psychiatry* 30: 343–52.

Alello, J.R. et al. (1979) 'Psychological, social and behavioural consequences of crowding on children and adolescents', *Child Development* 50: 195–202.

Ainsworth, M. (1978) *Patterns of Attachment*, Hillsdale, NY: Erlbaum.

—(1979) 'Attachment as related to mother–infant interaction', in J.S. Rosenblatt, R.A. Hinde, C. Beer and N. Busnel (eds) *Advances in the Study of Behaviour*, Volume 9, New York: Academic Press.

Allport, D. et al. (1972) 'On the division of attention: a disproof of the single channel hypothesis', *Quarterly Journal of Experimental Psychology* 24: 225–35.

Allport, F. (1920) 'The influences of the group upon association and thought', *Journal of Experimental Psychology* 3: 159–82.

—(1924) *Social Psychology*, Boston: Houghton-Mifflin.

Allport, G.W. (1971) *Pattern and Growth in Personality*, New York: Holt Rinehart & Winston.

Anderson, C. et al. (1987) 'Temperature and aggression: effects on quarterly and yearly city rates of violent and non violent crime', *Journal of Personality and Social Psychology* 52: 1161–73.

—et al. (1989) 'Temperature and aggression: ubiquitous effects of heat on occurrences of human violence', *Psychological Bulletin* 106 (1): 74–96.

Anderson, J.R. (1987) 'Methods of studying human knowledge', *Behavioural and Brain Sciences* 10: 467–505.

—(1989) 'A theory of the origin of human knowledge', *Artificial Intelligence* 40: 313–51.

Andrews, G. (1993) *The Benefits of Psychotherapy in Treatment of Mental Disorders – A Review of Effectiveness*, World Health Organization and American Psychiatric Press.

Ardrey, R. (1966) *The Territorial Imperative*, London: Collins.

Argyle, M. (1967) *The Psychology of Interpersonal Behaviour*, Harmondsworth: Penguin.

—(1982) 'Social behaviour', in D. Fontana (ed.) *Psychology for Teachers*, British Psychological Society and Macmillan Press.

—(1993) British Psychological Society, *Social Psychology Newsletter* no. 30, Winter 1993–4.

Argyle, M. and Henderson, M. (1984) 'The rules of friendship', *Journal of Social and Personal Relationships* 1: 211–37.

Aronson, E. and Linder, D. (1965) 'Gain and loss of esteem as determinants of interpersonal attractiveness', *Journal of Experimental and Social Psychology* 1: 156–71.

Aronson, E. et al. (1966) 'The effect of a pratfall on increasing interpersonal attractiveness', *Psychonomic Science* 4: 227–28.

Asch, S.E. (1951a) *Effects of Group Pressure upon the Modification and Distortion of Judgements: Groups, Leadership and Men*, Pittsburgh: Carnegie Press.

—(1951b) *Social Psychology*, New York: Prentice Hall.

—(1956) 'Studies of independence and submission to group pressure I: A minority of one against a unanimous majority', *Psychological Monograph* 70 (9) (Whole no. 416).

Atkinson, R.C. and Shiffrin, R.M. (1971) 'The control of short-term memory', *Scientific American* 224: 82–90.

Baddeley, A. and Hitch, G. (1974) 'Working memory', *Psychology of Learning and Motivation* 8: 47–90.

Baddeley, A.D. (1976) *The Psychology of Memory*, New York: Harper & Row.

Bailey, C.L. (1979) 'Mental illness – a logical representation', *Nursing Times*, Volume 3, pp. 761–2.

Bailey, K. (1987) *Human Paleopsychology: Applications to Aggression and Pathological Processes*, Hillsdale, NY: Erlbaum.

Bandura, A. (1967) 'Behavioural psychopathology', *Scientific American* 216 (3): 78–86.

—(1973) *Aggression: A Social Learning Analysis*, Englewood Cliffs, NJ: Prentice Hall.

—(1977) *Social Learning Theory*, New Jersey: Prentice Hall.

Bandura, A., Ross, D. and Ross, S.A. (1963) 'Imitation of film mediated aggressive models', *Journal of Abnormal and Social Psychology* 66: 2–11.

Banyard, P. (1989) 'Hillsborough', *Psychology News* 3 (7): 4–9.

Baron, R. and Bell, P. (1975) 'Aggression and heat mediating effects of prior provocation and exposure to an aggressive model', *Journal of Personality and Social Psychology* 31: 825–32.

Bartlett, F.C. (1932) *Remembering*, Cambridge: Cambridge University Press.

Bateson, P.P. (1979) 'How do sensitive periods arise and what are they for?', *Animal Behaviour* 27: 470–86.

Baumrind, D. (1964) 'Some thoughts on the ethics of research after reading Milgram's behavioural study of obedience', *American Psychologists* 19: 421–23.

Baxter, L. (1986) 'Gender differences in the heterosexual relationship: rules embedded in breakup accounts', *Journal of Social and Personal Relationships* 3: 289–306.

Beck, A. (1991) 'Cognitive therapy: a thirty year retrospective', *American Psychologist* 46: 368–75.

Beck, A.T. (1967) *Depression: Clinical Experimental and Theoretical Aspects*, London: Harper & Row.

Bee, H. (1989) *The Developing Child*, London: Harper Collins.

Bell, P.B. and Staines, P.J. (1981) *Reasoning and Argument in Psychology*, London: Routledge & Kegan Paul.

Bentall, R.R. (1991) 'Reconstructing psychopathology', *The Psychologist* 5: 61–3.

Bentall, R. and Day, J. (1995) 'Prescribing skills: skills to do what?', *The Psychologist* 8 (4): 169.

Berne, E. (1968) *Games People Play*, Harmondsworth: Penguin.

Berscheid, E. (1985) 'Interpersonal attraction', in G. Lindzey and E. Aronson (eds) *The Handbook of Social Psychology*, 3rd edn, New York: Random House.

Bickman, L. (1974) 'The social power of a uniform', *Journal of Applied Social Psychology* 1: 47–61.

Blake, R.R. and Moulton, J.S. (1982) 'Theory and research for developing a science of leadership', *Journal of Applied Behavioural Science* 18: 275–92.

Blakemore, C. and Cooper, G. (1970) 'Development of the brain depends on the visual environment', *Nature* 228: 477–8.

Bower, G.H. (ed.) (1977) *Human Memory: Basic Processes*, New York: Academic Press.

Bower, G.H., Clark, M., Lesgold, A. and Winzenz, D. (1969) 'Hierarchical retrieval schemes in recall of categorized word lists', *Journal of Verbal Learning and Verbal Behaviour* 8: 323–43.

Bower, T.G.R. (1971) 'The object in the world of the infant', *Scientific American* 225: 308.

—(1977) *The Perceptual World of the Child*, London: Fontana.

Bowlby, J. (1951) *Child Care and the Growth of Love*, Harmondsworth: Penguin.

—(1958) 'The nature of the child's tie to its mother', *International Journal of Psychoanalyis* 39: 250–373.

—(1971) *Attachment and Loss, Volume 1*, Harmondsworth: Penguin.

—(1975) *Separation: Anxiety and Anger (Attachment and Loss, Volume 2)*, Harmondsworth: Penguin.

Breland, K. and Breland, M. (1961) 'The misbehaviour of organisms', *American Psychologist* 16: 581–684.

Bridges, P. and Williamson, C. (1977) 'Psychosurgery today', *Nursing Times*, 1 September, pp. 1,363–7.

Bright, M. (1984) *Animal Language*, London: BBC Publications.

British Psychological Society (ongoing revisions from 1978) *Ethical Principles for Research with Human Subjects*, Leicester: British Psychological Society.

Broadbent, D. (1958) *Perception and Communication*, Oxford: Pergamon Press.

Brown, G.W. and Harris, T.O. (1978) *Social Origins of Depression*, London: Tavistock.

Brown, H. (1976) *Socialization: The Social Learning Theory Approach*, Milton Keynes: Open University Press.

—(1985) *People, Groups and Society*, Milton Keynes: Open University Press.

Brown, J.A.C. (1961) *Freud and the Post-Freudians*, Harmondsworth: Penguin.

Brown, R. (1973) *A First Language: The Early Stages*, London: Allen & Unwin.

—(1986) *Social Psychology*, 2nd edn, New York: Free Press.

Brown, R. and McNeill, D. (1966) 'The "tip of the

tongue" phenomenon', *Journal of Verbal Learning and Verbal Behaviour* 5: 325–37.

Bruner, J.S. (1966) *Towards a Theory of Instruction*, Cambridge, MA: Harvard University Press.

Bruner, J. and Kenny, H. (1966) 'The development of the concepts of order and proportion in children', in J.S. Bruner et al. (eds) *Studies in Cognitive Growth*, New York: Wiley.

Byrne, D. (1961) 'Interpersonal attraction and attitude similarity', *Journal of Abnormal and Social Psychology* 62: 713–15.

—(1973) 'Interpersonal attraction', *Annual Review of Psychology* 24: 317–36.

Byrne, D. and Buehler, J.A. (1965) 'A note on the influence of propinquity upon acquaintanceships', *Journal of Abnormal and Social Psychology* 51: 147–8.

Campbell, D. (1967) 'Stereotypes and the perception of group differences', *American Psychologist* 22: 817–29.

Campos, J.J. et al. (1983) 'Socio-emotional development', in P.H. Mussen (ed.) *Handbook of Child Psychology*, 4th edn, New York: Wiley.

Charnov, E.L. and Krebs, J.R. (1975) 'The evolution of alarm calls: altruism or manipulation?', *Nature* 109: 107–12.

Cheng, P.W. (1985) 'Restructuring versus automaticity: alternative accounts of skill acquisition', *Psychological Review* 92: 414–23.

Cherry, E.C. (1953) 'Some experiments on the recognition of speech with one or two ears', *Journal of the Acoustical Society of America* 25: 975–9.

Clare, A. (1976) 'What is schizophrenia?', *New Society*, 20 May, pp. 410–12.

Clark, R. and Word, L. (1974) 'Where is the apathetic bystander? Situational characteristics of the emergency', *Journal of Personality and Social Psychology* 29: 279–87.

Clarke, A.M. and Clarke, A.D.B. (1976) *Early Experience: Myth and Evidence*, London: Open Books.

Clarke, P.R.F. (1975) 'The "medical model" defended', *New Society*, 9 January, pp. 64–5.

Clore and Byrne, D. (1970) 'A reinforcement model of evaluative responses', *Personality: An International Journal* 1: 103–8.

Cochrane, R. (1983) *The Social Creation of Mental Illness*, Longman.

—(1995) 'Mental illness in the built environment', *Psychology Review* 1 (4), April.

Coleman, J.C. (ed.) (1979) *The School Years: Current Issues in the Socialization of Young People*, London: Methuen.

Collins, A.M. and Quillian, M. (1969) 'Retrieval time for semantic memory', *Journal of Verbal Learning and Verbal Behaviour* 8: 240–7.

Conrad, R. (1964) 'Acoustic confusion in immediate memory', *British Journal of Psychology* 55: 75–84.

Conway, M. (1992) 'Development and debates in the study of human memory', *The Psychologist* 5 (10), October.

Cooley, C.H. (1902) *Human Nature and the Social Order*, Charles Scribner's Sons.

Cooper, J.E. et al. (1972) *Psychiatric Diagnoses in New York and London*, Maudsley Monograph no. 20, London: Oxford University Press.

Coopersmith, S. (1968) *The Antecedents of Self-Esteem*, San Francisco: Freeman.

Craik, F. and Lockhart, R. (1972) 'Levels of processing', *Journal of Verbal Learning and Verbal Behaviour* 11: 671–94.

Craik, F. and Tulving, E. (1975) 'Depth of processing and retention of words in episodic memory', *Journal of Experimental Psychology* 104: 268–94.

Craik, F. and Watkins, M. (1973) 'The role of rehearsal in short-term memory', *Journal of Verbal Learning and Verbal Behaviour* 12: 599–607.

Crutchfield, R.S. (1954) 'The measurement of individual conformity to group opinion among officer personnel', Institute of Personality Assessment and Research, University of California, Berkeley.

—(1962) 'Conformity and creative thinking', in H. Gruber et al. (eds) *Contemporary Approaches to Creative Thinking*, New York: Atherton, pp. 120–40.

Cumberbatch, G. (1987) *The Portrayal of Violence on British Television*, London: BBC Publications.

Curtiss, S. (1977) *Genie: A Linguistic Study of a Modern Day Wild Child*, New York: Academic Press.

Davenhill, R. and Osborne, J. (1991) 'What relevance psychotherapy?', *Psychologist* 4 (2), February.

Davies, G. and Logie, R.H. (1991) 'Contemporary themes in cognitive psychology', *The Psychologist* 4: 291–3.

Davies, R. (1995) 'Selfish altruism', *Psychology Review* 4 (1), April.

Davison, G.C. and Neale, J.M. (1994) *Abnormal Psychology*, 6th edn, New York: Wiley.

Dawkins, R. (1976) *The Selfish Gene*, Oxford: Oxford University Press.

Deese, J. (1972) *Psychology as Science and Art*, New York: Harcourt Brace Jovanovich.

Delgado, J.M. (1969) *Physical Control of the Mind: Towards a Psychocivilised Society*, New York: Harper & Row.

Dennis, W. and Dennis, M. (1960) 'Causes of retardation amongst institutionally reared children', *Journal of Genetic Psychology* 96: 47–59.

Deutsch, A. and Deutsch, D. (1963) 'Attention: some theoretical considerations', *Psychological Review* 70: 80–90.

Deutsch, M. and Gerard, H.A. (1955) 'Study of normative and social influences upon individual judgements', *Journal of Abnormal and Social Psychology* 51: 629–36.

Dindia, K. and Baxter, L.A. (1987) 'Maintenance and repair strategies in marital relationships', *Journal of Social and Personal Relationships* 4: 143–58.

Dion, K.K. (1972) 'Physical attractiveness and evaluation of children's transgressions', *Journal of Personality and Social Psychology* 74: 707–13.

Dion, K.K., Berscheid, E. and Walster, E. (1972) 'What is beautiful is good', *Journal of Personality and Social Psychology* 24: 285–90.

Donaldson, M. (1984) *Children's Minds*, London: Fontana.

Donnerstein, E. (1979) 'Effects of noise and perceived control on origin of and subsequent aggressive behaviour', *Journal of Personality and Social Psychology* 36: 180–8.

—(1981) 'Victim reaction in aggressive erotic films as a factor in violence against women', *Journal of Personality and Social Psychology* 41: 710–24.

Duck, S. (1973) *Personal Relationships and Personal Constructs: A Study of Friendship Formation*, London: Wiley.

—(1988) *Relating to Others*, Milton Keynes: Open University Press.

—(1995) *Psychology Review* 1 (3).

Ellis, A.W. and Young, A.W. (1988) *Human Cognitive Neuropsychology*, Hove: Lawrence Erlbaum.

Erikson, E. (1963) *Childhood and Society*, 2nd edn, Norton.

Evans, P.J. (1980) 'Thinking of Maslow', *Nursing Times*, 24 January.

Eysenck, H. (1947) *Dimensions of Personality*, London: Routledge.

Eysenck, M. (1993) *Principles of Cognitive Psychology*, Lawrence Erlbaum.

—(1994) 'How many memory stores?', *Psychology Review* 1 (1), September, pp. 8–10.

Eysenck, M.W. (1994) *A Handbook of Cognitive Psychology*, Lawrence Erlbaum.

Eysenck, M.W. and Keane, M.T. (1995) *Cognitive Psychology*, 3rd edn, Lawrence Erlbaum.

Fantz, R.L. (1961) 'The origin of form perception', *Scientific American* 204 (5): 66–72.

Fantz, R.L. and Miranda, S.B. (1975) 'Newborn infant attention to form contour', *Child Development* 46: 224–8.

Felipe, N.J. and Sommer, R. (1966) 'Invasion of personal space', *Social Problems* 14: 206–14.

Festinger, L. and Carlsmith, J.M. (1959) 'Cognitive consequences of forced compliance', *Journal of Abnormal and Social Psychology* 58: 203–10.

Festinger, L., Schacter, S. and Back, K. (1950) *Social Pressures in Informal Groups: A Study of Human Factors in Housing*, New York: Harper & Brothers.

Fiedler, F.E. (1967) *A Theory of Leadership Effectiveness*, New York: McGraw Hill.

—(1968) 'Personality and situational determinants of leadership effectiveness in group dynamics', in D. Cartwright and A. Zander (eds) *Group Dynamics*, New York: Harper & Row.

—(1972) 'Personality, motivational systems, and the behaviour of high and low LPC', *Human Relations* 25: 391–2.

Field, T. (1978) 'Interaction behaviours of primary versus secondary caregiver fathers', *Development Psychology* 14: 183–4.

Fiske, S.T. and Taylor, S.E. (1984) *Social Cognition*, Wokingham: Addison-Wesley.

Flavell, J. (1979) 'Metacognitive development and cognitive monitoring: a new area of cognitive development enquiry', *American Psychologist* 34: 906–11.

Ford, C.S. and Beach, F.A. (1951) *Patterns of Sexual Behaviour*, New York: Harper & Row.

Freud, A. and Dann, S. (1951) 'An experiment in group upbringing', *Psychoanalytic Studies of the Child* 6: 127–68.

Freud, S. (1976a) *The Interpretation of Dreams*, Harmondsworth: Pelican Freud Library.

—(1976b) *The Psychopathology of Everyday Life*, Harmondsworth: Pelican Freud Library.

—(1977a) *Analysis of a Phobia in a Five Year Old Boy*, Harmondsworth: Pelican Freud Library.

—(1977b) *Three Essays on the Theory of Sexuality*, Harmondsworth: Pelican Freud Library.

—(1984) *Beyond the Pleasure Principle*, Harmondsworth: Pelican Freud Library.

Frith, U. (1992) 'Cognitive development and cognitive deficit', *The Psychologist* 5, Presidents' Award Lecture.

Gardner, R.A. and Gardner, B.T. (1969) 'Teaching sign language to a chimpanzee', *Science* 165: 664–72.

Gelder M. et al. (1989) *Oxford Textbook of Psychiatry*, 2nd edn, Oxford: Oxford University Press.

Gelfand M. et al. (1982) *Understanding Child Behaviour Disorders*, New York: Holt Rinehart & Winston.

Gergen, K.J. and Gergen, M.M. (1981) *Social Psychology*, New York: Harcourt Brace Jovanovich.

Gibson, J.J. (1950) *The Perception of the Visual World*, Boston: Houghton Mifflin.

Gibson, E.J. and Walk, P.D. (1960) 'The visual cliff', *Scientific American* 202: 64–71.

Gilligan, C. (1977) 'In a different voice: women's conceptions of self and morality', *Harvard Educational Review* 47: 481–517.

Goffman, E. (1959) *The Presentation of Self in Everyday Life*, New York: Anchor.

—(1968) *Asylums: Essays on the Social Situation of Mental Patients*, Harmondsworth: Penguin.

Goldfarb, W. (1943) 'The effects of early institutional care on an adolescent personality', *Journal of Experimental Education* 12: 106–29.

Gotlib, I.H. and Robinson, L.A. (1982) 'Responses to depressed individuals: discrepancies between self report and observer rated behaviour', *Journal of Abnormal Psychology* 91: 231–40.

Gottesman, I.I. (1991) *Schizophrenia Genesis*, New York: Freeman.

Gray, J. and Wedderburn, A. (1960) 'Grouping strategies with simultaneous stimuli', *Quarterly Journal of Experimental Psychology* 12: 180–4.

Gregory, R.L. (1966) *Eye and Brain*, London: Weidenfeld and Nicolson.

—(1972) 'Visual illusions', in B.M. Foss (ed.) *New Horizons in Psychology*, Harmondsworth: Penguin.

—(1983) 'Visual illusions', in J. Miller (ed.) *States of Mind*, London: BBC Publications.

Hagestad, G.O. and Smyer, M. (1982) 'Dissolving long term relationships: patterns of divorcing in middle age', in S. Duck (ed.) *Personal Relationships 4: Dissolving Personal Relationships*, London and New York: Academic Press.

Haith, N.M. (1980) 'Visual cognition in early infancy', in R.B. Kearsley and I.E. Sigel (eds) *Infant at Risk: Assessment of Cognitive Functioning*, Hillsdale, NY: Erlbaum.

Hamilton, W. (1964) 'The genetical evolution of social behaviour I and II', *Journal of Theoretical Biology* 7: 1–52.

Harlow, H.F. (1949) 'Formation of learning sets', *Psychological Review* 56: 51–65.

—(1958) 'Love in infant monkeys', *Scientific American* 200 (6): 68–74.

Harlow, H.F. and Harlow, M.K. (1962) 'Social deprivation in monkeys', *Scientific American* 207 (5): 136.

Harlow, H.F. and Zimmerman, R.R. (1959) 'Affectional responses in the infant monkey', *Science* 130: 421–32 .

Harlow, H.F., Harlow, M.K. and Suomi, S.J. (1971) 'From thought to therapy: lessons from a primate laboratory', *American Scientist* 59: 74–83.

Hayes, N. (1986) 'The magic of sociobiology', *Psychology Teaching* 2: 2–16.

Hebb, D.O. (1949) *The Organisation of Behaviour*, New York: Wiley.

Heider, F. (1958) *The Psychology of Interpersonal Relations*, New York: Wiley.

Held, R. and Hein, A. (1963) 'Movement-produced stimulation in the development of visually guided behaviour', *Journal of Comparative and Physiological Psychology* 56: 607–13.

Hess, E. (1972) 'Imprinting in a natural laboratory', *Scientific American* 227 (2): 24–31.

Hinde R. and Stevenson-Hinde, J. (eds) (1973) *Constraints on Learning Limitations and Predisposition*, London: Academic Press.

Hinde, R.A. (1982) *Ethology*, London: Fontana.

Hofling et al. (1966) 'An experimental study in the nurse–physician relationship', *Journal of Nervous and Mental Disorders* 143: 171–80.

Hollander, E.P. and Willis, R.H. (1964) 'Conformity independence and anti-conformity as determiners of perceived influence and attraction', in E.P. Hollander (ed.) *Leaders, Groups and Influence*, New York: Oxford University Press.

Homans, G. (1974) *Social Behaviour: Its Elementary Forms*, 2nd edn, New York: Harcourt Brace Jovanovich.

House, R.J. (1971) 'A path–goal theory of leadership effectiveness', *Administrative Science Quarterly* 16: 321–38.

Hovland, C. et al. (1953) *Communication and Persuasion*, New Haven: Yale University Press.

Howarth, C.I. (1989) 'Psychotherapy – who benefits?', *The Psychologist*, April, pp. 150–2.

Howe, M. (1990) *The Origins of Exceptional Abilities*, Oxford: Blackwell.

Hull, C.L. (1943) *Principles of Behaviour*, New York: Appleton Century Crofts.

Jahoda, M. (1958) *Current Concepts of Postive Mental Health*, New York: Basic Books.

Janis, I.L. (1972) *Victims of Groupthink*, Boston, MA: Houghton Mifflin.

Janov, A. (1975) *The Primal Revolution*, London: Sphere Books.

Jarvis, M. (1994) 'Attention and the information processing approach', *Psychology Teaching*, 3 December.

Johnstone, W.A. and Heinz, S.P. (1978) 'Flexibility and capacity demands of attention', *Journal of Experimental Psychology* 107: 420–35.

Jones, E. (1964) *The Life and Work of Sigmund Freud*, Harmondsworth: Penguin.

Jones, M.C. (1924 ) 'The elimination of children's fears', *Journal of Experimental Psychology* 7: 382–90.

Jourard, S.M. (1966) 'An exploratory study of body accessibility', *British Journal of Social and Clinical Psychology* 5: 221–31.

Kadushin, A. (1976) *Adopting Older Children: Summary and Implications*, New York: Columbia University Press.

Kahneman, D. (1973) *Attention and Effort*, Englewood Cliffs, NJ: Prentice Hall.

Kaye, K. (1984) *The Mental and Social Life of Babies*, London: Methuen.

Kellogg, W.N. and Kellogg, L.A. (1933) *The Ape and the Child*, New York: Whiltlesey House.

Kelly, G.A. (1955) *A Theory of Personality: The Psychology of Interpersonal Constructs*, New York: Norton.

Kelman, H.C. (1958) 'Compliance identification and internalization', *Journal of Conflict Resolution* 2: 51–60.

Kelman, H.C. and Hovland, C. (1953) 'Reinstatement of the communication in delayed measurement of opinion change', *Journal of Abnormal and Social Psychology* 48: 327–35.

Kilham, W. and Mann, L. (1974) 'Levels of destructive obedience as a function of transmitter and executant roles in the Milgram obedience paradigm', *Journal of Personality and Social Psychology* 229: 696–702.

Klaus, M. and Kennel, J. (1976) *Maternal Infant Bonding*, St Louis: Mosby.

Kohlberg, L. (1963) 'The development of children's orientation towards the moral order (part I): sequence in the development of moral thought', *Vita Humana* 6: 11–33.

—(1969) 'Stage and sequence: the cognitive developmental approach to socialization', in D.A. Goslin (ed.) *Handbook of Socialization Theory and Research*, Chicago: Rand McNally.

—(1981) *Essays on Moral Development*, New York: Harper & Row.

Krebs, J.R. and Davies, N.B. (1984) *Behavioural Ecology*, Oxford: Blackwell Scientific Publications.

Kuhn, T.S. (1962) *The Structure of Scientific Revolutions*, University of Chicago Press.

Laing, R.D. (1965) *The Divided Self*, Harmondsworth: Penguin.

—(1971a) *Knots*, Harmondsworth: Penguin.

—(1971b) *Self and Others*, Harmondsworth: Penguin.

Laing, R.D. and Esterson, A. (1964) *Sanity, Madness and the Family*, Harmondsworth: Penguin.

Lamb, M.E. and Roopnarine, J.L. (1979) 'Peer influences on sex-role development in preschoolers', *Child Development* 50: 1219–22.

Latané, B. (1981) 'The psychology of social impact', *American Psychologist* 36: 343–56.

—(1990) 'From bystander research to social impact theory', *Journal of the British Psychological Society* 12, February, p. 72.

Latané, B. and Darley, J. (1968) 'Group inhibition of bystander intervention in emergencies', *Journal of Personality and Social Psychology* 10: 215–21.

— and —(1970) *The Unresponsive Bystander: Why*

*Doesn't He Help?*, New York: Appleton Century Crofts.

Latané, B. and Rodin, J. (1969) 'A lady in distress: inhibiting effects of friends and strangers on bystander intervention', *Journal of Experimental Social Psychology* 5: 189–202.

Latané, B. et al. (1979) 'Many hands make light work', *Journal of Personality and Social Psychology* 37: 822–32.

Le Bon, G. (1895) *The Crowd*, New York: Viking.

Levine, M.W. and Shefner, J.M. (1981) *Fundamentals of Sensation and Perception*, London: Addison-Wesley.

Lewin, K., Lippitt, R. and White, R. (1939) 'Patterns of aggressive behaviour in experimentally created "social climates"', *Journal of Social Psychology* 10: 271–99.

Lewis, M. and Brooks-Gunn, J. (1979) *Social Cognition and the Acquisition of Self*, New York: Plenum.

Liebman, R. et al. (1974) 'The use of structural family therapy in the treatment of intractable asthma', *American Journal of Psychiatry* 131: 535–40.

Lilly, J.C. (1965) 'Vocal mimicry in tursiops: ability to match numbers and duration of human vocal bursts', *Science* 147: 520–9.

Lindsay, G. and Colley, A. (1995) 'Ethical dilemmas of members of the Society', *Journal of the British Psychological Society* 8 (10), October, pp 448–51.

Lindsay, P.H. and Norman, D.A. (1972) *Human Information Processing*, New York: Academic Press.

Lippit, R. and White, R. (1947) 'An experimental study of leadership and group life', in *Readings in Social Psychology*, New York: Holt Rinehart and Winston (1957).

Logan, G.D. (1988) 'Towards an instance theory of automatisation', *Psychological Review* 95: 492–527.

Lorenz, K.Z. (1966) *On Aggression*, London: Methuen.

Lott, A. and Lott, B. (1968) 'A learning theory approach to interpersonal attitudes', in A. Greenwold et al. (eds) *Psychologcal Foundations of Attitudes*, New York: Academic Press.

Lovaas, O.I. (1968) 'Learning theory approach to the treatment of childhood schizophrenia', California Mental Health Research Symposium No.

2, Behaviour Theory and Therapy, Sacramento, CA: Department of Mental Hygiene.

McGarrigle, J. and Donaldson, M. (1974) 'Conservation accidents', *Cognition* 3: 341–50.

McKellar, P. (1968) *Experience and Behaviour*, Harmondsworth: Penguin.

Maher, B. (1980) 'Experimental psychopathology', in P.C. Dodwell (ed.) *New Horizons in Psychology 2*, Harmondsworth: Penguin.

Mann, L. (1969) *Social Psychology*, London: John Wiley & Sons.

Marr, D. (1982) *Vision: A Computational Investigation into the Human Representation and Processing of Visual Information*, San Francisco: W.H. Freeman.

Maslow, A. (1962) *Towards a Psychology of Being*, London: Van Nostrand.

—(1970) *Motivation and Personality*, New York: Harper & Row.

—(1972) *The Farther Reaches of Human Nature*, New York: Viking.

Mead, M. (1935) *Sex and Temperament in Three Primitive Societies*, New York: New American Library.

—(1962) *Male and Female*, Harmondsworth: Penguin.

Meadows, S. (1977) *Understanding Child Development*, Hutchinson.

Milgram, S. (1974) *Obedience to Authority*, New York, Harper & Row.

Miller, G.A. (1956) 'The magical number seven plus or minus two: some limits on our capacity for processing information', *Psychological Review* 63: 81–97.

Mishkin, M. and Appenzeller, T. (1987) 'The anatomy of memory', *Scientific American* 256: 80–9.

Mitchell, R. (1982) *Phobias*, Harmondsworth: Penguin.

Money, J. and Erhardt, A. (1972) *Man and Woman, Boy and Girl*, Baltimore: Johns Hopkins University Press.

Moray, N. (1959) 'Attention in dichotic listening: affective cues and influences of instructions', *Quarterly Journal of Experimental Psychology* 11: 56–60.

Moriarty, R. (1975) 'Crime commitment and the responsive bystander: two field experiments', *Journal of Personality and Social Psychology* 31: 370–6.

Morris, P.E. (1979) 'Strategies for learning and recall', in M.M. Gruneberg and P.E. Morrs (eds) *Applied Problems in Memory*, London: Academic Press.

Mundy-Castle, A.C. and Anglin, J. (1974) 'Looking strategies in infancy', in L. Jones et al. (eds) *The Competent Infant*, London: Tavistock.

Murstein, B.I. (1972) 'Physical attractiveness and marital choice', *Journal of Personality and Social Psychology* 22: 8–12.

Navon, D. (1977) 'Forest before trees: the precedence of global features in visual perception', *Cognitive Psychology* 9: 353–83.

Neisser, U. (1976) *Cognitive Psychology*, New York: Appleton Century Crofts.

Newcomb, T.M. (1961) *The Acquaintanceship Process*, New York: Holt Rinehart and Winston.

Nichols, K. (1975) 'Psychodrama', *New Behaviour*, 7 August, pp. 214–17.

Norman, D.A. and Bobrow, D.G. (1975) 'Some priniciples of memory schemata', in M.A. Gernsbacher (ed.) *Handbook of Psycholinguistics*, London: Academic Press.

Oatley, K. (1975) 'New metaphors for mind', *New Behaviour*, 1 May, pp. 68–71.

Ora, J.P. (1965) 'Characteristics of the volunteer', Psychological Investigation Office of Naval Research, Contract 2149, Technical Report 27.

Orne, M.T. (1962) 'On the social psychology of the psychological', *American Psychologist* 17 (11): 776–83.

Packer, C. (1975) 'Male transfer in olive baboon', *Nature* 255: 219–220.

—(1977) 'Reciprocal altruism in *Papio anubis*', *Nature* 265: 441–2.

Palmer, S.E. (1975) 'The effects of contextual scenes on the identification of objects', *Memory and Cognition* 3: 519–26.

Parke, R.D. (1981) *Fathering*, London: Fontana.

Patterson, F.G. (1978) 'The gestures of a gorilla: language acquisition in another pongid', *Brain and Language* 5: 72–97.

Pepperberg, I.M. (1983) 'Cognition in the African grey parrot', *Animal Learning and Behaviour* 11: 179–85.

Perls, F.S., Hefferline, R. and Goodman, P. (1973) *Gestalt Therapy: Excitement and Growth in the Human Personality*, Harmondsworth: Penguin.

Peterson, L.R. and Peterson, M.I. (1959) 'Short term retention of individual items', *Journal of Experimental Psychology* 58: 193–8.

Piaget, J. (1932) *The Moral Judgement of the Child*, London: Routledge & Kegan Paul.

—(1965) *The Moral Judgement of the Child*, trans. M. Gabain, New York: Harcourt.

—(1968) *Six Psychological Studies*, University of London Press.

—(1969) *The Child's Conception of Physical Causality*, Totowa, NJ: Littlefield Adams.

—(1972) *The Child's Conception of the World*, London: Paladin.

Piliavin, I.M., Piliavin, J.A. and Rodin, S. (1975) 'Costs diffusion and the stigmatised victim', *Journal of Personality and Social Psychology* 32: 429–38.

Piliavin, I.M., Rodin, J. and Piliavin, J.A. (1969) 'Good Samaritanism: an underground phenomenon?', *Journal of Personality and Social Psychology* 13: 289–99.

Polivy, J. and Herman, C.P. (1985) 'Dieting and binging', *American Psychologist* 40: 193–201.

Posner, M.I. and Peterson, S.E. (1990) 'The attention system of the human brain', *Annual Review of Neuroscience* 13: 25–42.

Posner, M.I. and Presti, D. (1987) 'Selective attention and cognitive control trends', *Neuroscience* 10: 12–17.

Premack, A.J. and Premack, D. (1972) 'Teaching language to an ape', *Scientific American* 227: 92–9.

Reason, J.T. (1979) 'Actions not as planned: the price of automatisation', in G. Underwood and R. Stevens (eds) *Aspects of Consciousness*, London: Academic Press.

Reisen, A.N. (1947) 'The development of visual perception in man and chimpanzee', *Science* 106: 107–8.

Rice, R.W. et al. (1980) 'Leader sex follower: attitudes towards women and leadership effectiveness: a laboratory experiment', *Organizational Behaviour and Human Performance* 25: 46–78.

Robertson, J. (1953) *Young Children in Hospital*, New York: Basic Books.

Roethlisberger, J.W. and Dickson, W.J. (1939) *Management and the Worker*, Cambridge, MA: Harvard University Press.

Rogers, C.R. (1961) *On Becoming a Person: A Therapist's View of Psychotherapy*, London: Constable.

—(1970) *Encounter Groups*, New York: Harper & Row.

Rose, S. (1976) *The Conscious Brain*, Harmondsworth: Penguin.

Rosenhan, D.L. (1973) 'On being sane in insane places', *Science* 179: 250–8.

Rosenthal, R. (1966) *Experimenter Effects in Behavioural Research*, New York: Appleton Century Crofts.

Rubin, Z. (1973) *Liking and Loving*, New York: Holt Rinehart and Winston.

Rubin, Z. and McNeil. E.B. (1983) *The Psychology of Being Human*, 3rd edn, London: Harper & Row.

Rutter, M. (1979) 'Maternal deprivation 1972–1978: new findings, new concepts, new approaches', *Child Development* 50: 283–305.

—(1981) *Maternal Deprivation Reassessed*, 2nd edn, Harmondsworth: Penguin.

Rycroft, C. (ed.) (1966) *Psychoanalysis Observed*, London: Constable.

Schacter, S. and Singer, J.E. (1962) 'Cognitive, social and physiological determinants of emotional states', *Psychological Review* 69: 379–99.

Schaffer, H.R. (1971) *The Growth of Sociability*, Harmondsworth: Penguin.

—(1987) 'Social development in early childhood', in A.J. Chapman and A. Gale (eds) *Psychology and People: A Tutorial Text*, British Psychological Society and Macmillan Press.

Schaffer, H.R. and Emerson, P.E. (1964a) 'Patterns of response to physical contact in early human development', *Journal of Child Psychology and Psychiatry* 5: 1–13.

— and —(1964b) 'The development of social attachments in infancy', *Monographs of the Society for Research in Child Development* 29 (3), serial no. 94.

Schaffer, Rudolph (1977) *Mothering*, London: Fontana/Open Books.

Schlichte, H.J. and Schmidt-Koenig, K. (1971) 'Zum Heimfindevermogen der Brieftaube bei erschwerte optischer Wahrnehmung', *Naturwissenschaften* 58: 329–30. Discussed in N. Hayes, *Principles of Comparative Psychology*, Lawrence Erlbaum Associates, 1994.

Sears, R.R., Maccoby, E. and Levin, H. (1957) *Patterns of Child-Rearing*, Evanston, IL: Row Petersen and Co.

Secord, P.F. and Beckman, C.W. (1964) *Social Psychology*, McGraw-Hill.

Seligman, M. and Hager (1972) *Biological Boundaries of Learning*, New York: Appleton Century Crofts.

Shaffer, D.R. (1985) *Developmental Psychology: Theory, Research and Applications*, Brooks/Cole Publishing Co.

Shallice T. and Warrington, E.K. (1980) 'Independent functioning of verbal memory stores', *Quarterly Journal of Experimental Psychology* 22: 261–73.

Shapiro, D.A. (1982) 'Psychopathology', in A.J. Chapman and A. Gale (eds) *Psychology and People: A Tutorial Text*, British Psychological Society and Macmillan Press.

Shea, B.C. and Pearson, J.C. (1986) 'The effects of relationship type, partner intent, and gender on the selection of relationship maintenance strategies', *Communication Monographs* 53: 352–64.

Shiffrin, R.M. and Schneider, W. (1977) 'Controlled and automatic human information processing II: perceptual learning, automatic attending and a general theory', *Psychological Review* 84: 127–90.

Shotland, R.L. and Straw, M.K. (1976) 'Bystander response to an assault: when a man attacks a woman', *Journal of Personality and Social Psychology* 34: 990–9.

Sigall, H. and Ostrove, N. (1975) 'Beautiful but dangerous: effects of offender attractiveness and nature of the crime on juridic judgement', *Journal of Personality and Social Psychology* 31: 410–14.

Skeels, H.M. (1966) 'Adult status of children with contrasting early life experiences', *Monographs of the Society for Research in Child Development* 31 (3).

Skeels, H.M. and Dye, H.B. (1939) 'A study of the effects of differential stimulation on mentally retarded children', *Proceedings of the American Association of Mental Deficiency* 44: 114–36.

Skinner, B.F. (1938) *The Behaviour of Organisms*, New York: Appleton Century Crofts.

—(1953) *Science and Human Behaviour*, New York: Macmillan.

—(1957) *Verbal Behaviour*, New York: Appleton Century Crofts.

—(1969) *Contingencies of Reinforcement*, New York: Appleton Century Crofts.

—(1973) *Beyond Freedom and Dignity*, Harmondsworth: Penguin.

—(1974) *About Behaviourism*, London: Jonathan Pope.

Sluckin, W. (1965) *Imprinting and Early Experiences*, London: Methuen.

Sluckin, W. and Salzen, E.A. (1961) 'Imprinting and perceptual learning', *Quarterly Journal of Experimental Psychology* 13: 65–77.

Smith, A.C. (1977) 'The benefits of ECT', *Nursing Times*, 17 March, pp. 368–9.

Smith, C. and Lloyd, B. (1978) 'Maternal behaviour and perceived sex of infant revisited', *Child Development* 49: 1263–5.

Smith, M.L. (1980) *The Benefits of Psychotherapy*, Baltimore: Johns Hopkins University Press.

Smith, M.L. and Glass, G.V. (1977) 'Meta analysis of psychotherapy outcome studies', *American Psychologist*, November, pp. 752–60.

Spearman, C. (1927) 'The doctrine of two factors', in S. Wiseman (ed.) *Intelligence and Ability*, Harmondsworth: Penguin.

Spelke, E. et al. (1976) 'Skills of divided attention', *Cognition* 4: 215–30.

Sperling, G. (1960) 'The information available in brief visual presentation', *Psychological Monographs* 74, no. 498.

Spitz, R.A. (1946) 'Anaclitic depression', *Psychoanalytic Study of the Child* 2: 313–42.

Stern, D. *The First Relationship: Infant and Mother*, Cambridge, MA: Harvard University Press.

Sternberg, R. (1987) 'Intelligence', in R. Gregory (ed.) *The Oxford Companion to the Mind*, Oxford: Oxford University Press.

Stiles, W.B. et al. (1986) 'Are all psychotherapies equivalent?', *American Psychologist* 41: 165–80.

Stodgill, R.M. and Coons, A.E. (1957) *Leader Behaviour: Its Description and Measurement*, Columbus, OH: Ohio State University.

Storr, A. (1966) *Human Aggression*, Harmondsworth: Penguin.

Stratton, G. (1897) 'Some preliminary experiments on vision', *Psychological Review* 3: 611–17.

Szasz, T. (1972) *The Myth of Mental Illness*, London: Paladin.

—(1973) *The Manufacture of Madness*, London: Paladin.

—(1974) *Ideology and Insanity*, Harmondsworth: Penguin.

Terrace, H.S. (1979) 'How Nim Chimpsky changed my mind', *Psychology Today*, November.

Thorpe, W.H. (1961) *Birdsong*, London: Cambridge University Press.

Tinbergen, N. (1951) *The Study of Instinct*, Oxford University Press.

Tizard, B. (1977) *Adoption: A Second Chance*, London: Open Books.

Tizard, B. and Hodges, J. (1978) 'The effect of early institutional rearing on the development of eight-year-old children', *Journal of Child Psychology and Psychiatry* 19: 99–118.

Tizard, B., Rees, J. and Hodges, J. (1975) 'A comparison of three effects of adoption, restoration to the natural mother, and continued institutionalisation on the cognitive development of four year old children', *Child Development* 45: 92–9.

Treisman, A. (1960) 'Contextual cues in selective listening', *Quarterly Journal of Experimental Psychology* 12: 247–80.

—(1964a) 'Verbal cues, language and meaning in selective attention', *American Journal of Psychology* 77: 206–19.

—(1964b) 'Monitoring and storage of irrelevant messages in selective attention', *Journal of Verbal Learning and Verbal Behaviour* 3: 449–59.

Treisman, A. and Riley, J.G. (1969) 'Is selective attention selective perception or selective response: a further test', *Journal of Experimental Psychology* 79: 27–34.

Triplett, N. (1898) 'Dynamogenic factors in pace making and competition', *American Journal of Psychology* 9: 507–33.

Triseliotis, J. (1980) 'Growing up in foster care and after', in J. Triseliotis (ed.) *New Developments in Foster Care and Adoption*, London: Routledge & Kegan Paul.

Trivers, R.L. (1971) 'The evolution of reciprocal altruism', *Quarterly Review of Biology* 46: 25–57.

Tulving, E. (1962) 'Subjective organization in free recall of unrelated words', *Psychological Review* 69: 344–54.

—(1972) 'Episodic and semantic memory', in E. Tulving and W. Donaldson (eds) *Organization of Memory*, New York: Academic Press.

Tulving, E. and Pearlstone, Z. (1966) 'Availability versus accessibility of information in memory for words', *Journal of Verbal Learning and Verbal Behaviour* 5: 381–91.

Vaughan, D. (1986) *Uncoupling*, New York: Vintage Books.

Wadeley, A. (1991) *Ethics in Psychological Research and Practice*, British Psychological Society.

Walster, E. and Berscheid, E. (1974) 'Physical attractiveness', in L. Berkowitz (ed.) *Advances in Experimental Social Psychology* 7, New York: Academic Press.

Walster, G.W., Walster, E. and Berscheid, E. (1978) *Equity Theory and Research*, Boston: Allyn & Bacon.

Watson, J.B. and Rayner, R. (1920) 'Conditioned emotional reactions', *Journal of Experimental Psychology* 3: 1–14.

Willis, R.H. (1963) 'Two dimensions of conformity–non conformity', *Sociometry* 26: 499–513.

Wilson, E.O. (1975) *Sociobiology: The New Synthesis*, Cambridge, MA: Harvard University Press.

—(1978) *On Human Nature*, Cambridge, MA: Harvard University Press.

Wiseman, S. (ed.) (1967) *Intelligence and Ability*, Harmondsworth: Penguin.

Woodman, D.D. (1980) 'What makes a psychopath?', *New Society*, 4 September, pp. 447–9.

Zajonc, R.B. (1965) 'Social facilitation', *Science* 149: 269–71.

—(1968) 'Attitudinal effects of mere exposure', *Journal of Personality and Social Psychology* 9 (2), part 2.

—(1976) 'Family configuration and intelligence', *Science* 192: 227–36.

Zajonc, R.B. and Markus, H.M. (1974) 'Exposure effects and associative learning', *Journal of Experimental Social Psychology* 10: 248–63.

Zimbardo, P.G. (1970) 'The human choice: individuation, reason, and order versus deindividuation, impulse, and chaos', in Arnold and Levine (eds) *Nebraska Symposium on Motivation*, University of Nebraska Press.

—(1972) 'Psychology of imprisonment', *Society*, April, pp. 4–8.

—(1988) *Psychology and Life*, 12th edn.

Zimbardo, P.G., Banks, W.C., Craig, H. and Jaffe, D. (1973) 'A Pirandellian prison: the mind is a formidable jailer', *New York Times Magazine*, 8 April, pp. 38–60.

Zubin, J. and Spring, B. (1977) 'Vulnerability: a new view of schizophrenia', *Journal of Abnormal Psychology* 86: 103–26.

# Index